LAMENESS IN HORSES

O. R. Adams, D.V.M., M.S.

*Professor and Head, Veterinary Clinics and Surgery, College of Veterinary Medicine,
Colorado State University, Fort Collins, Colorado*

Second Edition

362 Illustrations

Lea & Febiger

PHILADELPHIA

Library of Congress Catalog Card Number 66:23238

Printed in the United States of America

Dedicated to

NAN

for her encouragement and patience

and to

GAIL, LYNNE, and ROBERT

for their love of horses

Preface
to the
Second
Edition

THE wide acceptance of the first edition was very gratifying. I am deeply indebted to my colleagues throughout the world for their help in correcting errors and making additions to this text. Many veterinarians have taken the time to give helpful suggestions and constructive criticisms. Illustrations from colleagues were always forthcoming when needed. Thus, the assistance I received has made formulation of the second edition much easier, and it is my hope that the changes will be found useful to the profession.

Sincere appreciation is expressed to Dr. Joe P. Morgan who has written a chapter on radiology. This chapter will be helpful to practitioners attempting to improve their techniques of taking and reading radiographs. Dr. Charles Moritz of Lea & Febiger has continued to give help and encouragement in the revision of the book. Mrs. Pat Dietemann who made the original illustrations and cover, graciously provided the same service for the second edition. Faculty members of the College of Veterinary Medicine at Colorado State University have aided in the procurement of additional photographs and case material. In addition, their helpful suggestions in writing the revision have been most gratifying. Mrs. Jan Post was of special help in typing the manuscript and making grammatical corrections for the revision.

This second edition lists many additional references which will be helpful to those desiring additional information sources. I sincerely hope that readers will continue to help correct errors or omissions, and to suggest ways in which the book may be improved.

O. R. ADAMS

Fort Collins, Colorado

Contents

Contents

Contents

The
relationship between conformation and lameness

Chapter I

THE conformation of a horse is the key to his method of progression. The horse is a working animal, and his value is determined by the condition of his limbs and feet. Poor conformation of limbs contributes to certain lamenesses, and actually may be the cause of lameness in some cases. The proportions of the body conformation, as compared with the limb conformation, may determine whether or not there will be any type of interference of the limbs during progression. Conformation, a major factor in soundness of the limbs, often determines the useful lifetime of a horse. Very few horses have perfect conformation, but in the selection of breeding stock, conformation should be carefully considered and animals with serious weaknesses should be eliminated.

Inheritable conformation predisposing navicular disease, bone spavin, and upward fixation of the patella is prevalent. Conformation of the limb leading to deviation of the foot in flight is also inheritable and should be considered undesirable when either purchasing a horse or when considering a stallion or mare for mating. Whenever possible, the stallion or mare should be mated in the hope of correcting difficulties found in the sire or dam so that the offspring will be improved in conformation.

CONFORMATION OF THE BODY (Fig. 1–1)

Conformation of the body varies among different breeds, and this factor must be considered in the evaluation of the horse. For example, an Arabian has a short back in comparison with a Thoroughbred; a Quarter Horse of certain blood lines has a shorter, heavier body, and shorter legs than a Thoroughbred. In some Quarter Horse blood lines the outcrossing with Thoroughbred breeding has been extensive enough to make the offspring nearly indistinguishable from pure Thoroughbred breeding. Even in the Thoroughbred breed there are conformational differences among American, English

Fig. 1–1 — Normal Horse. The body and limbs should be well proportioned.

and French blood lines.   Therefore, the evaluation of body conformation must be based on individual breed specifications.   Long-
backed horses may develop a swing in the gait which materially
alters the movement of the limbs.   Such horses are prone to speedy-
cutting, and to cross-firing.   Short-backed horses, with legs too long
for the body, may be prone to over-reaching, forging, and scalping.

Certain requirements are essential to all breeds, and the veterinarian must familiarize himself with the ideal body characteristics.
The body should be in pleasing balance with the limbs and should
have good proportion.   Body conformation is not a common cause
of lameness so further discussion in this book will pertain to limb
conformation.

CONFORMATION OF THE LIMBS

To evaluate limb conformation the horse should be observed from
a distance as well as close at hand.   The limbs should be studied at
rest and in motion.   The veterinarian should determine whether
abnormal conformation in the horse develops low in the limb, or
whether it actually begins at the hip and/or shoulder joints.   The
limbs should be well suited to the height, depth, and length of the
body.   The drive of the hindlimbs affects the forelimbs, so over-all
balanced conformation is very important.

Conformation of the limbs also determines the shape of the feet,
the wear of the feet, distribution of weight, and the flight of the
feet.   Faulty limb conformation is not an unsoundness in itself
(curby conformation being the exception); however, it may be considered a warning or sign of weakness, and predisposes the animal
to many lamenesses that would not occur had he been born with
good conformation.

A person can often determine the interference that occurs among
the limbs by observing the walking and trotting gaits.   In the rapid
gaits interference is difficult to perceive because the eye cannot
follow the feet at high speed.   Race horses seldom have limb contact
problems if they have good over-all conformation; however, if slight
conformational abnormalities are present, interference of the limbs
may occur that would not develop if the horse were used less
strenuously (see Chapter 4, page 95).   Contact problems may occur
in a horse with good conformation when he is used for events that
require rapid turning, such as barrel racing, cutting, pole bending,
and reining.

The Forelimbs

The forelimbs bear some 60 to 65 per cent of the weight of the
horse.   This amount can vary according to the conformation of the
horse, whose head, neck, abdomen and croup can present very
diverse proportions.   This means the forelimbs are subjected to more
injuries from concussion and trauma than the rear limbs because the
forelimbs not only bear the weight of the body in movement, but also
aid the hindlimbs in propelling the body.   Ideal or perfect conforma-

tion means proper length of bone as well as proper angulation between these bones. The horse may have good conformation from one view, and poor conformation from another, or may be good in one forelimb and not the other.

Examination for conformation of the forelimbs should be done while the horse is standing with the weight well distributed between the fore and hind feet. When the horse is standing quietly, observe him from a distance, and then examine the limbs from a closer view. Ideal conformation of the forelimb does not put excess strain on any structure of the limb.

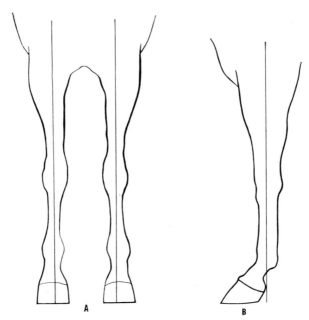

Fig. 1–2.—Anterior and lateral views of normal forelimbs.

A, Line dropped from the point of the shoulder joint bisects the limb.

B, Line from the tuber spinae of the scapula bisects the limb as far as the fetlock and drops at the heel.

Anterior View (Fig. 1–2A).—Both limbs should bear weight equally. The legs should be straight. A line dropped from the point of the shoulder (middle of the scapulo-humeral joint), should equally bisect the leg. The chest should be well developed and well muscled. The toes should point straight forward and the feet should be as wide apart on the ground as the space between the limbs at their origin in the chest. Deviations from a straight limb will cause strain to be placed on the collateral ligaments of the hinge joints in the forelimb. The carpal joints should be balanced and not deviate toward, or away from, one another. The cannon bone should be centered under the carpus and not to the lateral side (Bench Knees) (Fig. 1–16).

Lateral View (Figs. 1–1 and 1–2*B*).—The shoulder should be sloping. A line dropped from the tuber spinae, on the spine of the scapula, should equally bisect the leg to the fetlock joint, then carry to a point just behind the heel. The carpus should not deviate anteriorly or posteriorly. The musculature of the forearm should be well developed and balance the limb. The area just distal to the carpus should not be cut in on the anterior or posterior surface (Cut out under the knees, Tied in knees, Fig. 1–17). The hoof wall should slope at the same angle as the pastern.

The angle of the scapula with the body will vary from 50 to 75 degrees and there is an angle of 85 to 100 degrees between the scapula and the humerus at the point of the shoulder. An angle of about 128 to 132 degrees is present between the humerus and radius at the elbow joint and the angle between the third metacarpal bone and the first phalanx is about 130 to 135 degrees. The angle between the ground surface of the foot and the anterior line of the hoof wall and pastern (foot axis) should be approximately 45 to 50 degrees. These angles vary among different breeds, *i.e.* Arabians ordinarily have more sloping shoulders and pasterns than do Quarter Horses.

Faults of Conformation in the Forelimb

Base Narrow (Fig. 1–3).—In base narrow conformation, the distance between the center lines of the feet at their placement on the

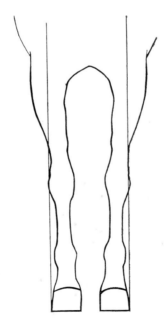

Fig. 1–3.—Base Narrow. Note that the distance between the center lines of the limbs, at their origin, is greater than the distance between the center lines of the feet on the ground.

2

ground is less than the distance between the center lines of the limbs at their origin in the chest when viewed from the front. This is found most often in horses having large chests and well developed pectoral muscles, such as the Quarter Horse. This conformation may be accompanied by a toe-in (pigeon toed) or toe-out (splay footed) conformation.

The outside of the limb takes the most strain in base-narrow conformation, causing the lateral aspect of the limb to be under constant tension. Articular windpuffs of the fetlock joint, lateral ringbone, and lateral sidebone are common pathological conditions resulting from this conformation. In nearly all cases, base-narrow conformation forces the horse to land on the outside wall of the hoof, regardless of whether the feet toe-in or toe-out. This requires that the inside wall be trimmed to level the foot.

Base Wide (Fig. 1–8).—In this conformation, the distance between the center lines of the feet at their placement on the ground is greater than the distance between the center lines of the limbs at their origin in the chest, when viewed from the front. This condition is found most commonly in narrow-chested horses such as the American Saddlebred and the Tennessee Walking horse. In base-wide conformation, the horse often is affected with toe-out (splay-footed) position of the feet. Base-wide, toe-out conformation usually causes "winging" to the inside (Figs. 1–5*B* and 1–9).

The inside of the limb takes the most strain in base-wide con-

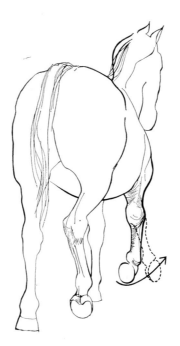

Fig. 1–4.—Paddling. This accompanies toe-in conformation.

formation, causing the medial aspect of the fetlock and pastern joints to be under constant tension. Articular windpuffs of the fetlock joint, medial ringbone, and medial sidebone are common pathological conditions resulting from this conformation. In nearly all cases, base-wide conformation forces the horse to land on the inside wall of the hoof, regardless of whether the feet toe-in or toe-out. This requires that the outside wall be trimmed to level the foot.

Toe-In or Pigeon-Toed (Fig. 1–7).—Toe-in is a position of the feet in which the toes point toward one another when viewed from the front. It is congenital, and the limb may be crooked as high as its origin at the chest, or as low as the fetlock down. It is usually accompanied by a base-narrow conformation but rarely is present when the horse is base wide. In the young foal, the condition may be partially corrected by proper trimming of the feet, and young horses

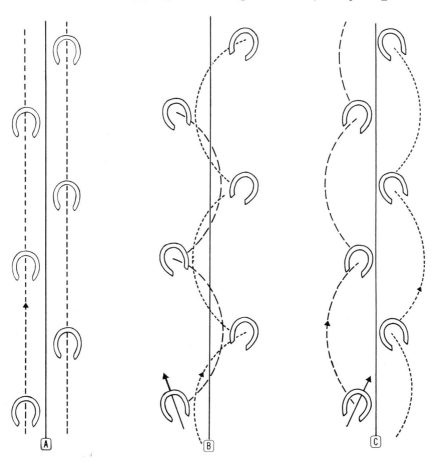

Fig. 1–5.—How toe-in and toe-out affects foot path. *A*, Normal foot path. *B*, Foot path of a horse with toe-out conformation. *C*, Foot path of a horse with toe-in conformation.

may be correctively shod to prevent a worsening of the condition (*see* Chapter 9). When the affected horse moves, there is a tendency to "paddle" with the feet (Figs. 1–4 and 1–5*C*). This is an outward deviation of the foot during flight. The foot breaks over the outside toe and lands on the outside wall. If a horse toes in, he will usually "paddle" whether he is base-narrow or base-wide.

Toe-Out or Splay Footed (Figs. 1–6 and 1–11).—When viewed from the front, the toes point away from one another. The condition is usually congenital and is usually due to crooked legs from their

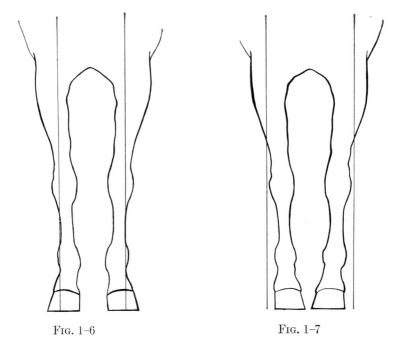

Fig. 1–6   Fig. 1–7

Fig. 1–6.—Base-narrow, toe-out conformation.

Fig. 1–7.—Base-narrow, toe-in conformation.

origin down. In some cases, however, the condition is aggravated by a twisting at the fetlock. It may be accompanied by either base-wide or base-narrow conformation. As with a toe-in conformation, it may be controlled or partially corrected by corrective trimming or corrective shoeing in the young horse (Chapter 9). The flight of the foot goes through an inner arc when advancing, and may cause interference with the opposite forelimb (Figs. 1–5*B* and 1–9). A horse that toes out will usually "wing" to the inside whether it is base narrow or base wide. When toe-out attitude of the feet occurs with base-narrow conformation, there is a greater likelihood of limb interference and plaiting (Fig. 1–12).

Base-Narrow, Toe-In Conformation (Fig. 1–7). — Base-narrow, toe-in conformation causes excessive strain on the lateral collateral ligaments of the fetlock and pastern joints. Articular windpuffs, lateral ringbone, and lateral sidebone are common pathological conditions with this conformation. This is because of the mechanical strains caused by the base-narrow conformation, and results in an excess of body weight on the outside hoof wall. Examination of the foot will show that it is worn low on the outside because the foot lands on the outside wall, causing excessive wear in this area.

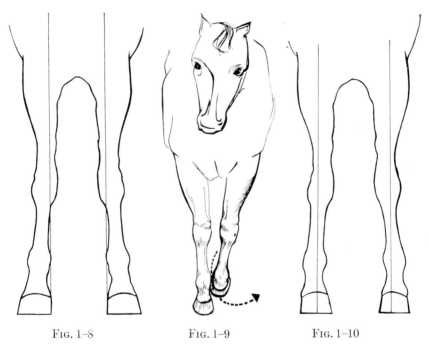

Fɪɢ. 1–8   Fɪɢ. 1–9   Fɪɢ. 1–10

Fɪɢ. 1–8. — Base wide conformation. Note that the distance between the center lines of the feet is wider than the center lines of the limbs at the chest.

Fɪɢ. 1–9. — Winging, which may cause interference, is caused by a toe-out position of the feet.

Fɪɢ. 1–10. — Base-wide toe-in position of the feet.

Trimming the inside wall is required to level the foot. Base-narrow, toe-in conformation usually causes "paddling" (Figs. 1–4 and 1–5C). This is a common type of conformational abnormality and corrective shoeing is discussed in Chapter 9.

Base-Narrow, Toe-Out Conformation (Fig. 1–6). — Base-narrow, toe-out conformation is one of the worst types of conformation in the forelimb. Horses having this conformation seldom can shoulder the strain of heavy work. The closely placed feet, combined with a tendency to "wing" inwardly from the toe-out position commonly causes limb interference. The base-narrow attitude of the limb places the weight on the outside wall as with base-narrow, toe-in conformation. The hoof breaks over the outside toe, swings inwardly and lands on the outside wall. This causes great strain on the limb below the fetlock. Plaiting (Fig. 1–12*A*) may be evident. Corrective shoeing is very similar to base-narrow, toe-in conformation because the foot lands on the outside wall. One should study the foot closely in flight to make sure of the corrections necessary (Fig. 1–12*B*). This usually involves lowering the inside wall and toe to level the foot.

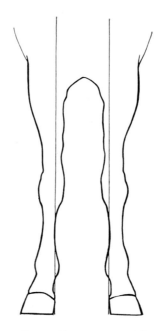

Fig. 1–11.—Base-wide toe-out position of the feet.

Lesions on the medial aspect of the third metacarpal bone, fractures of the second metacarpal bone and an occasional fracture of the medial sesamoid may result from the interference. Diagnosis of interference is discussed on page 95. Corrective shoeing is discussed in Chapter 9.

Base-Wide, Toe-Out Conformation (Fig. 1–11).—When a horse is base wide, the usual attitude of the feet is to toe out. The base-wide conformation places the greatest stress on the inside of the limb. This means that there is greater strain on the medial collateral ligament of the metacarpophalangeal (fetlock) and proximal interphalangeal (pastern) joints. In addition, medial sidebone and ringbone are common. With this conformation, the foot usually breaks over the inside toe, deviates ("wings") to the inside, and lands on the inside hoof wall. This means that the correction is just the opposite from base-narrow, toe-out conformation. When one studies the foot, it will be seen that the outside wall must be lowered to level the foot. Blemishes on the medial aspect of the third metacarpal bone, medial splints, and fracture of the second metacarpal bone occur with this conformation because of interference. Corrective shoeing is discussed in Chapter 9.

Base-Wide, Toe-In Conformation (Fig. 1–10).—This type of conformation is unusual but does occur. The base-wide attitude of the limbs throws the greatest stress on the inside of the limb with the same resulting pathological changes as for base-wide, toe-out conformation. In most cases the horse affected with base-wide, toe-in conformation will "paddle" to the outside even though he breaks over the inside toe and lands on the inside wall.

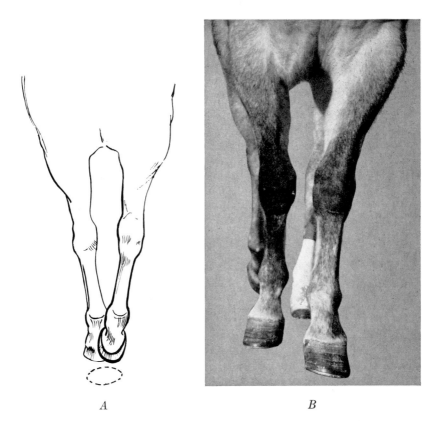

A   B

Fig. 1–12*A*.—Plaiting.

Plaiting is most often found in a horse with base-narrow, toe-out conformation. After the foot travels an inward arc it lands more or less directly in front of the opposite forefoot. In some cases this leads to stumbling as a result of interference.

B, Base-narrow, toe-out conformation. Note left forefoot landing on the outside wall, typical of this type of conformation. There is also a degree of plaiting.

There is always the possibility that other conformational abnormalities of the limb, especially from the fetlock down, may change the path of the foot so it does not correspond to the above descriptions. These abnormalities include twisting of the fetlock so that the base-narrow, toe-in horse actually "wings" to the inside. These variations are rare and since they all cannot be listed, there will be no discussion of them here. The principles of corrective shoeing and trimming can be applied to the variations when accurate observation of the foot flight has been made. In every case, the veterinarian should closely study the progression of the foot to make sure how it lands, so that he can make proper recommendations about correction.

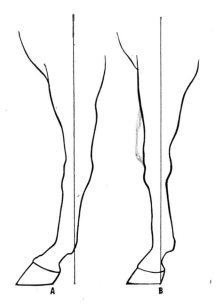

Fig. 1–13.—Examples of poor conformation. Compare with Figure 1–2B.
A, Calf knees—A posterior deviation of the carpus.
B, Bucked knees—An anterior deviation of the carpus.

Plaiting (Fig. 1–12A).—Some horses, especially those with base-narrow, toe-wide conformation, tend to place one forefoot directly in front of the other. This is an undesirable characteristic, since it can produce interference and stumbling resulting from an advancing forelimb hitting the one placed in front of it.

Posterior Deviation of the Carpal Joint (Calf Knees or Sheep Knees) (Fig. 1–13A).—Posterior deviation of the carpal joint is a weak conformation and the legs seldom remain sound under heavy work. This conformation places a strain upon the inferior check ligament, the anterior aspect of the carpal bones, the volar annular ligament of the carpus, and the volar aspect of the carpal joint capsule.

Chip fractures from the third, radial, and intermediate carpal bones are common. Small chip fractures from the radius may also occur (*see* Chapter 6).

Anterior Deviation of the Carpal Joint (*Bucked Knees or Knee Sprung*) (Fig. 1–13*B*).—This condition may also be called "goat knees" or "over in the knees." It is an anterior deviation of the carpus but it causes less trouble than the calf knee condition described above. Anterior deviation of the carpus is caused by contraction of the carpal flexors, *i.e.*, ulnaris lateralis, flexor carpi ulnaris and flexor carpi radialis. Extra strain is placed on the sesamoid bones, the superficial flexor tendon, the extensor capri radialis,

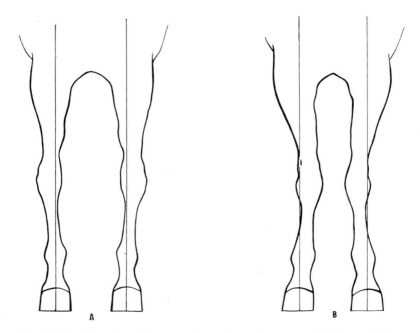

Fig. 1–14.—Examples of poor conformation. Compare with Figure 1–2*A*.
A, Bow legs. *B*, Knock knees.

and the suspensory ligament. The condition often is present at birth, but if it is not severe, usually disappears by six months of age. Congenital forms are nearly always bilateral, and may be accompanied by a knuckling of the fetlocks which results from contraction of the superficial digital flexor tendon (*see* complete discussion, Chapter 6, p. 166). Anterior deviation of the carpal joints may be present in rickets and accompanied by an enlarged epiphysis of the radius (*see* Chapter 5).

Medial Deviation of the Carpal Joints (*Knock Knees or Knee-Narrow Conformation*) (Fig. 1–14*B*).—This is a medial deviation of the carpal joints toward each other. A strain is put upon the inferior check ligament and suspensory apparatus, the capsule of the carpal joint medially, the medial collateral ligaments of the carpus, and the lateral aspect of the carpal bones (*see* complete discussion, Chapter 6, p. 168).

Lateral Deviation of the Carpal Joints (Bow Legs or Bandy-Legged Conformation) (Fig. 1–14*A*).—Bow legs cause an outward deviation of the carpal joints when viewed from the front of the horse. It may be accompanied by a base-narrow, toe-in conformation. This condition causes excessive strain on the lateral collateral ligament of the carpus, the medial side of the carpal bones, and the lateral portion of the carpal joint capsule (*see* complete discussion, Chapter 6, p. 171).

Open Knees.—The term "open knees" refers to an irregular profile of the carpal joint when viewed from the side (Fig. 1–15). This irregularity gives the impression that the carpal joints are not fully closed. This conformation is usually found in young horses (1 to 3 years of age) before full maturity, and often is accompanied by epi-

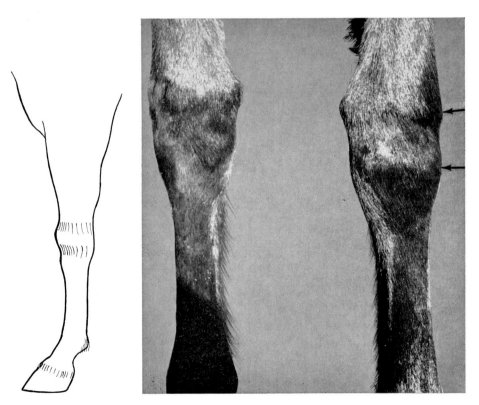

Fig. 1–15.—Open knees. This term refers to the irregular profile of the carpal joint when viewed from the side. It is due to the enlarged epiphysis of the radius and a posterior deviation of the carpal bones. It is usually the result of a mineral imbalance and as the horse grows to maturity becomes less obvious.

physitis (Chapter 5, p. 121) from mineral imbalance. As the horse matures, the joints usually become more pleasing in appearance. Most people regard this as a weak conformation subject to carpal injury. On the basis of experience, this is probably so. Radiographically, this irregularity in the carpal joints does not show outstanding changes.

Lateral Deviation of the Metacarpal Bones (Offset Knees or Bench Knees) (Fig. 1–16). — Offset knee is a conformation in which the

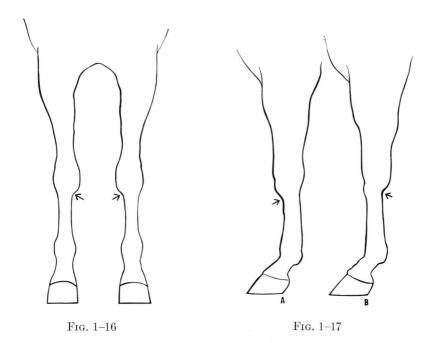

FIG. 1–16   FIG. 1–17

FIG. 1–16. — Bench knees. Note that the metacarpal bones are set too far laterally.

FIG. 1–17. — Examples of poor conformation. Compare with Figure 1–2B.
    A, Cut out under the knees; as indicated by arrow.
    B, Tied-in knees, as indicated by arrow.

cannon bone is offset to the lateral side and does not follow a straight line from the radius. It is evident when the limbs are viewed from the front. It is congenital in origin, and should be considered a weak conformation. The medial splint bone is under greater stress than normal and medial splints are common (Fig. 6–26, p. 203). The medial splint bone normally carries more weight than the lateral splint bone. This is because the medial splint bone has a flat articulation, and the lateral splint bone an oblique articulation. In offset knees there is even more direct weight bearing on the medial splint bone, which in turn carries more weight to the interosseous ligament, increasing the possibility of splints.

Tied-In Knees (Fig. 1–17B). —Viewed from the side, the flexor tendons appear to be too close to the cannon bone just below the carpus. This is poor conformation and inhibits free movement. A heavy fetlock may give the appearance of "tied-in knees" although the condition actually is not present.

Cut Out Under the Knees (Fig. 1–17A). —Viewed from the side, this condition causes a "cut out" appearance just below the carpus on the anterior surface of the cannon bone. It is a fundamentally weak conformation.

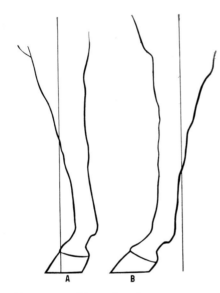

Standing Under in Front (Fig. 1–18A). —This is a deviation in which the entire forelimb, from the elbow down is placed back of the perpendicular and too far under the body when the animal is viewed from the side. This may be brought about by disease and not be caused by conformation.

With this conformation the base of support is shortened, overloading the forelimbs, and limiting the anterior phase of the stride by overburdening the opposite forelimb left on the ground. The limb in motion must come down sooner and therefore has a low arc of foot flight. These steps are faster and combined with low arc of foot flight, the foot is carried too close to the ground, predisposing to stumbling. Overall it causes excessive wear and fatigue of bones, ligaments, and tendons. There is a diminution of speed and the horse is predisposed to falling.

FIG. 1–18. —Examples of poor conformation. Compare with Figure 1–2B.
A, Standing under in front.
B, Camped in front.

Camped in Front (Fig. 1–18B). —This is the opposite condition of that described above. The entire forelimb, from the body to the ground, is too far forward when viewed from the side. This limb attitude may be present in certain pathological conditions, such as bilateral navicular disease.

Short Upright Pastern (Fig. 1–19B). —The short upright pastern increases the effect of concussion on the metacarpophalangeal (fetlock) joint, the proximal interphalangeal (pastern) joint and to the navicular bone (*see* pastern axis, p. 38). A horse with this conformation has increased predisposition to osselets (traumatic arthritis of the metacarpophalangeal joint), ringbone of the proximal interphalangeal joint, and to navicular disease. This type of conformation often is associated with a base-narrow, toe-in conformation, and is most often present in the horse with short legs and powerful body and leg musculature. A straight shoulder usually accompanies this type of conformation.

Long Sloping Pastern (Fig. 1–33*B*).—A long sloping pastern is one characterized by a normal or subnormal angulation of the forefoot (45 degrees or under) with a pastern that is too long for the length of the limb (*see* pastern axis, p. 38). This type of conformation predisposes to injury of the flexor tendons (tendosynovitis), sesamoid bones (sesamoiditis and fractures), and to the suspensory ligament (desmitis).

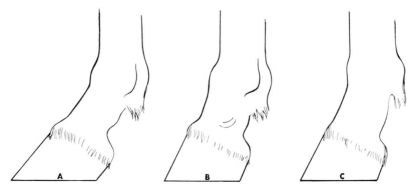

Fig. 1–19.—Examples of pastern conformation. *A*, A normal angulation of hoof and pastern. *B*, A short upright pastern predisposing to injuries of the fetlock joint, ringbone of the pastern joint, and to navicular bursitis. *C*, Long upright pastern predisposes to injuries of the fetlock joint and navicular bursa. This type of conformation does not seem to predispose ringbone as often as does B.

Long Upright Pastern (Fig. 1–19*C*).—A long upright pastern predisposes the metacarpo-phalangeal joint and the navicular bursa to injury. Concussion to these areas is increased, because the normal anti-concussion mechanism of a normally sloping pastern is not present (*see* pastern axis, p. 38). Osselets (traumatic arthritis) and navicular disease are common findings with this type of conformation, and both lamenesses may be present at the same time. The stresses are very similar to those found in the short, upright pastern (Fig. 1–19*B*), but pathology of the proximal interphalangeal (pastern) joint is not so common.

Pressure on the navicular bursa is often increased by efforts of the horseshoer to produce a normal angulation of the hoof wall. This causes a break between the pastern and foot axes at the coronary band (Fig. 1–20). This conformation is most commonly seen in Thoroughbreds and racing Quarter Horses.

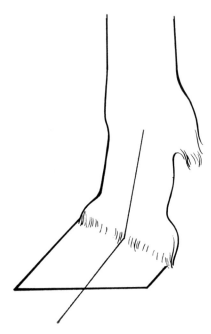

F IG. 1–20.—A long upright pastern with a broken foot and pastern axis caused by lowering of the heels in an attempt to produce normal angulation of the hoof wall. This throws even greater stress on the navicular bursa and is a common example of improper trimming in an attempt to force normal angulation of the pastern.

The Hindlimbs (Figs. 1–1, 1–21 and 1–22)

It is important to understand what constitutes normal conformation of the hind limb, even though there is less lameness there than in the forelimb. Conformation does play an important role in curb, upward fixation of the patella and some forms of spavin.

Rear View.—Viewed from behind, the limb should have a pleasing, well-balanced appearance. The hocks should be large enough to hold the weight of the animal, but smooth. The musculature on the inside of the thigh should carry down into the medial side of the gaskin so that the tibial area does not appear too thin. A line dropped from the point of the tuber ischii should divide the leg into equal parts (Fig. 1–21). This gives equal distribution of weight, equal bone pressure and equal strain on collateral ligaments.

Lateral View.—Viewed from the side, the limb should have a well-balanced appearance. The musculature should not end abruptly at the stifle joint, but should carry down onto the tibia, and taper gradually to the hock. The angle of the stifle and hock should be neither too straight nor too angulated. A stifle and hock which are too straight may cause bog spavin of the hock and upward fixation of the patella. Excessive angulation of the hock (sickle hock) may cause curb and bone or bog spavin. If the stifle is too straight or too angulated, the hock will also be too straight or too angulated because of the reciprocal apparatus. A line dropped from the tuber ischii should hit the point of the hock, go down the posterior aspect of the metatarsal area, and then should strike 3 to 4 inches behind the heel (Fig. 1–22). A line dropped from the hip joint should strike halfway between the heel and toe. These angles cannot be changed by corrective shoeing or other measures.

In judging the hind limbs from the front of the animal, the limbs appear to be in base-narrow position because of the perspective. One must check the horse from behind before evaluating the position of the hind limbs.

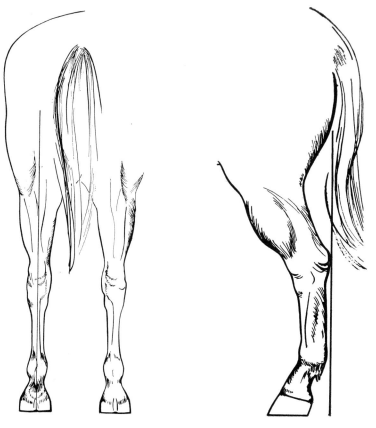

Fig. 1–21   Fig. 1–22

Fig. 1–21.—Normal hind limbs. A line dropped from the point of the tuber ischii bisects the limb.

Fig. 1–22.—Normal hind limbs from side view. A line dropped from the tuber ischii follows the metatarsus.

Faults of Conformation in the Hind Limbs

Base Narrow (Fig. 1–23).—Base-narrow conformation in the hind limbs means that when the animal is viewed from behind, the distance between the center lines of the feet is less than the distance between the center lines of the limbs in the thigh region. This is most commonly evident in heavily muscled horses where there is excessive strain on the lateral aspect of the limb in the bones, ligaments, and joints. The feet may toe-in or have straight toes. Base-narrow conformation is often accompanied by "bow legs" or a condition in which the hocks are too far apart. The legs may appear fairly straight to the hock and then deviate inward. When a horse has good conformation in front, and is base narrow behind, many types of interference can occur between the fore and hind limbs.

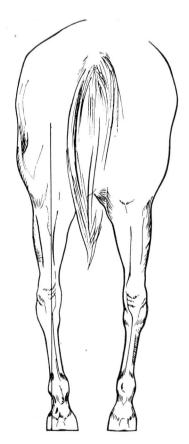

Fig. 1–23.—Base narrow behind. This is often accompanied by bow legs, as shown. Compare with Figure 1–21.

Base Wide (Fig. 1–24).—Base wide means that when viewed from behind, the distance between the center lines of the feet at their placement on the ground is greater than the distance between the center lines of the limbs in the thigh region. Base-wide conformation is infrequent in the hind limb compared with the forelimb. The most common form of base-wde conformation is cow hocks.

Medial Deviation of the Hock Joints (Cow Hocks) (Fig. 1–24).— "Cow hocked" means that the limbs are base narrow to the hock, and base wide from the hock to the feet. Cow hocked conformation is a common defect. The hocks are too close, point toward one another, and the feet are widely separated. Viewed laterally, the horse may be sickle-hocked. Cow hocks is one of the worst hind limb conformations because there is excessive strain on the medial side of the hock joint and this may cause bone spavin.

Excessive Angulation of the Hock Joints (Sickle Hocks) (Fig.

1–25).—When viewed from the side, the angle of the hock joint is decreased so that the horse is standing under from the hock down. The plantar aspect of the hock is under a greater strain, especially the plantar ligament. A horse so affected is predisposed to "curb." This is called "curby conformation" because it predisposes the animal to injury of the plantar ligament.

Base Narrow from Fetlocks Down.—This conformation places stress on the lateral collateral ligaments of the fetlock, pastern, and coffin joints and similar strain on the bones and tendons in this area.

Excessively Straight Legs or "Straight Behind" (Fig. 1–26).—When viewed from the side there is very little angle between the tibia and femur, and the hock joint is correspondingly straight. This predisposes the horse particularly to bog spavin and upward fixation

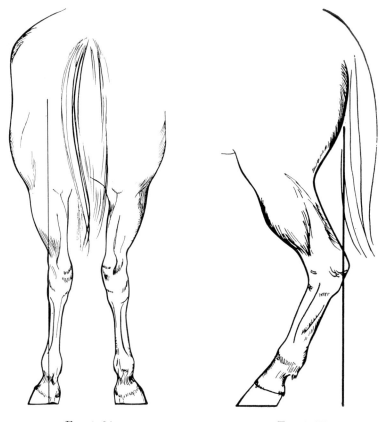

Fig. 1–24   Fig. 1–25

Fig. 1–24.—Cow hocks accompanied by base-wide conformation. Such horses are usually base-narrow as far as the hocks, but base wide from the hocks down. Compare with Figure 1–21.

Fig. 1–25.—Sickle hocks. Note the excessive angle of the hock joints. Compare with Figure 1–22.

3

of the patella. The straight hock places increased tension on the anterior aspect of the joint capsule, causing irritation and chronic distention of the joint capsule with synovia. This type of leg is easily injured by heavy work. It is not uncommon to find upward fixation of the patella accompanying this conformation. The pasterns also will be too straight.

Standing Under Behind (Fig. 1–27).—Viewed from the side, the entire limb is placed too far forward or sickle hocks are present. A perpendicular line from the hip joint would hit the ground at the heel or behind the heel instead of halfway between the heel and toe.

Camped Behind (Fig. 1–28).—Camped behind means that the entire limb is placed too far posteriorly, when viewed from the side. A perpendicular line dropped from the hip joint would hit at the toe, or anterior to it, instead of halfway between the toe and heel. This condition is often associated with upright pasterns behind.

EVALUATION OF LIMB CONFORMATION FOR JUDGING PURPOSES. — In judging horses, one must decide when the good qualities exceed

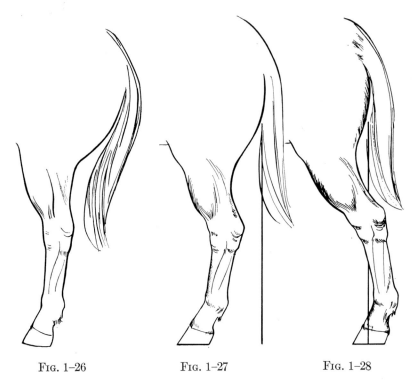

FIG. 1–26   FIG. 1–27   FIG. 1–28

FIG. 1–26.—Too straight behind. There is too little angulation of the hock and stifle joints.

FIG. 1–27.—Standing under behind. Compare with Figure 1–22.

FIG. 1–28.—Camped behind. Compare with Figure 1–22.

the bad or vice versa. Only by understanding the fundamentals of conformation can good judgment be formed in a rapid examination.

When judging one undesirable conformation characteristic of the limbs against another, the following factors should be considered:

Forelimb

1. *Base-Narrow, Toe-Out Conformation.*—Base-narrow, toe-out conformation will consistently cause more locomotion problems than other types of abnormal conformation. The tendency to interfere, resulting in lesions on the medial aspect of the third metacarpal bone, possible fracture of the second metacarpal bone, and occasional fracture of the medial sesamoid bone from trauma by the opposite hoof wall, makes this type of conformation most undesirable.

2. *Base-Wide, Toe-Out Conformation.*—This type of conformation also predisposes interference, but the base-wide foundation keeps the feet further apart and acts as a mechanical separation. However, the foot still travels inward and contact often occurs with the same results as from base-narrow, toe-out conformation. Either of these two types of conformation should be considered more undesirable than base-narrow, toe-in conformation.

3. *Base-Narrow, Toe-In Conformation.*—Although this type of conformation is not good, it is not as undesirable as the above two types. The foot usually travels in an outward arc (paddling) and causes no contact problems. There is greater stress on lateral ligaments, lateral articulations, and the lateral cartilage of the foot.

4. *Anterior Deviation of the Carpal Joint (Buck Knees).*—When slight bilateral anterior deviation of the carpal joints occurs, it is usually the result of contraction of the carpal flexors as a foal. If the condition is slight, it causes only minor stresses on the limbs. If the deviation is marked, it is quite undesirable because of stresses already listed. Unilateral anterior deviation is objectionable because of probable pathologic changes in the limb. Slight bilateral anterior deviation of the carpal joints is not so undesirable as posterior deviation (calf knees) of the carpal joints.

5. *Posterior Deviation of the Carpal Joints (Calf Knees).*—This is a poor type of conformation because of the tendency to produce carpal fractures when the limb is stressed. It is more objectionable than slight anterior deviation of the carpal joints (buck knees).

6. *Lateral Deviation of the Metacarpal Bones (Bench Knees).*—This type of conformation is undesirable in that it tends to increase the possibility of medial splints. Uneven pressures on the carpal bones also are present.

Hind Limb

1. *Straight Hind Leg.*—The straight hind leg predisposes to bog spavin and upward fixation of the patella. Straight hind legs are somewhat less objectionable than sickle hocks.

2. *Sickle Hocks.*—Sickle hocks are thought to predispose to bone spavin. In addition, curb may result from stress on the plantar ligament caused by the excessive angulation of the hock. Sickle hocks are usually accompanied by cow hocks and together constitute the most undesirable conformation of the hind limbs.

3. *Cow Hocks.*—Cow hocks are usually present in most horses in some degree, and alone are not serious when present to a mild degree. When the condition is excessive, it should be considered undesirable. When both cow hocks and sickle hocks are present, the conformation should be considered very undesirable.

CONFORMATION OF THE FOOT

Good conformation of the foot is essential to normal activities of the horse. No matter how good the conformation of other areas, if the foot is weak, that horse is not a useful animal. This fact, perhaps, gives rise to the adage: "No frog, no foot—no foot, no horse." To have good foot conformation, a horse must have reasonably good limb conformation since the foot reflects poor conformation of the limbs.

Much variation in quality of structure exists in the feet of different horses. Ideally, the wall should be thick enough, resistant to drying, pliable, and have normal growth qualities. The sole should be thick enough to resist bruising, and should shed normally. The bars should be well developed and the frog should be large, strong, and should evenly divide the sole, with its apex pointing directly to the toe of the hoof wall. A hoof wall that contains pigment is preferable to a white hoof wall since a white hoof wall is subject to drying and cracking, and is not as resistant to trauma as a pigmented hoof.

In some breeds of horses, the foot is forced into an abnormal conformation. Examples are show stock of the American Saddlebred and Tennessee Walking Horse breeds. Because of the artificial action that these horses are forced to use, the wall is allowed to grow excessively long. This removes frog pressure and contraction of the heel results. These horses are subject to tendon injuries, thrush, and contraction of the hoof wall around the third phalanx or "hoof bound." This artificial foot conformation also aggravates basic conformation weaknesses, such as base-wide-toe-wide position of the feet, and a high incidence of ringbone and sidebone results. It is very difficult to maintain such horses in a sound condition, since fundamental principles of foot health are violated.

Quarter Horses and Thoroughbreds often have feet that are too small to bear the weight of the animal. This is brought about by selective breeding, and, although it gives the horse a pleasing appearance, it subjects the foot to greater concussion, because the shock is distributed over a smaller area. As a result, lamenesses such as navicular disease are more frequent.

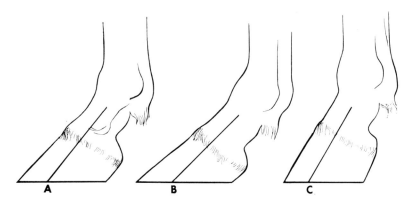

FIG. 1–29.—Side view of foot and pastern axis.

A, Normal front foot and pastern axes; approximately 47 degrees.

B, Foot and pastern axes less than normal. (Less than 45 degrees in front or less than 50 degrees behind.)

C, Foot and pastern axes greater than normal. (Greater than 50 degrees in front or greater than 55 degrees behind.)

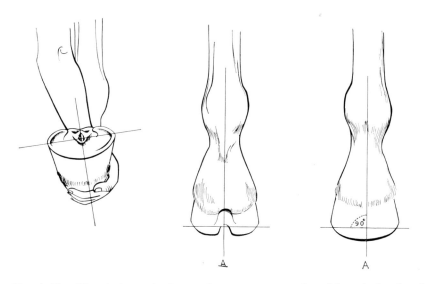

FIG. 1–30.—Line A shows the foot and pastern axes as viewed from in front and from behind. This line should be straight with no deviation of the limb from the fetlock down. The line crossing the foot axis at the gound surface is a line indicating foot level. If the foot is level, these two lines form 90 degree angles, when viewed from in front or from behind the foot (left). When observing the foot after it has been picked up, and imaginary line should be projected down the foot and pastern, and crossing it an imaginary line on the ground surface of the wall at the quarters. If two 90 degree angles are not formed when these lines are projected, the foot is off level and proper correction should be made.

Foot Axis and Pastern Axis.—The pastern axis, as viewed from the front and side, is an imaginary line passing through the center of the pastern. This line should divide the first and second phalanges into equal parts, from both views (Figs. 1–29*A* and 1–30).

The foot axis, as viewed from the side, should be continuous with the pastern axis and should follow the same angle.

The foot axis, as viewed from the front, is an imaginary line passing through the center of the toe of the hoof wall. It extends from the coronary band to the ground surface of the toe, and blends above

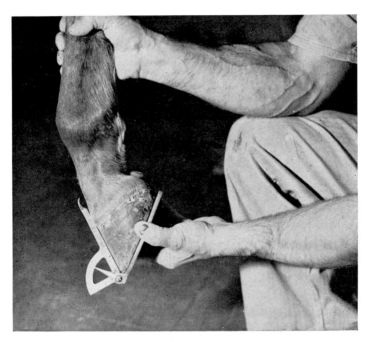

Fig. 1–31.—The use of a foot protractor in determining foot axis.

with the pastern axis. The pastern and foot axes are continuous lines from both front and side views, and ideally should blend at the same angles (Figs. 1–29*A* and 1–30). The angle formed by the ground surface of the hoof wall and dorsal surface of the toe will be the same angle as the foot axis when viewed from the side. When viewing from the side, the normal foot axis in front should be 45 to 50 degrees, and in the hind feet, 50 to 55 degrees. The angle of the hoof can be measured with a foot protractor (Fig. 1–31).

If the foot and pastern axes are too sloping or too steep, pathological changes may occur. Ideally, the slope of the pastern and the slope of the anterior surface of the hoof wall will be identical when viewed from the side (Fig. 1–29). If the foot and pastern axes are too sloping or too steep, but the angles of the pastern axis and of the foot axis are identical, and appear as a smooth continuous line, the foot should not be trimmed or shod to change these angles (Fig. 1–29B and C). Radical changes to bring the foot and pastern to a theoretically normal axis will usually produce pathological changes (Fig. 1–20). However, if the angle of the pastern and the angle of the hoof wall are not identical, then correction by trimming or shoeing is indicated to make the slope of the pastern and the slope of the hoof wall identical (Fig. 1–32).

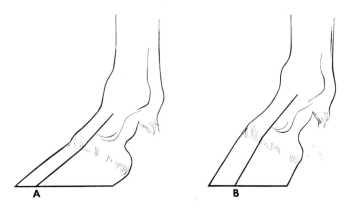

FIG. 1–32.—Examples of broken foot and pastern axis.
A, Broken foot axis with toe too long and heel too low.
B, Broken foot axis with toe too short and heel too high.

The Foot Level

A level foot indicates that the medial and lateral walls are of the same length. To determine foot level, the limb is held so that the ground surface of the foot can be viewed along the longitudinal axis (Fig. 8–1). An imaginary line dividing the longitudinal axis of the cannon bone, fetlock and pastern, crossed by a transverse line that touches the ground surface of each heel should result in two 90 degree angles at the junction of these lines (Fig. 8–1). A level foot indicates that the horse is wearing the foot evenly. A horse that lands on the inside wall will have a low inside wall while the horse that lands on the outside wall will be low on the outside wall. The foot can be flat enough to shoe and yet be off level. Off-level shoeing is a poor method and foot level should be maintained even if one wall has to be shimmed with leather.

Effect of Foot Conformation on Stride and Way of Going

On the lateral view, the foot should break squarely over the toe and the flight of the foot should have a normal, even arc, with the horse landing squarely upon the foot. The heels should land just before the toe and the center of weight should be located at the point of the frog. In the normal foot, the hoof reaches the peak of the flight arc as it passes the opposite supporting limb (Fig. 1–33A).

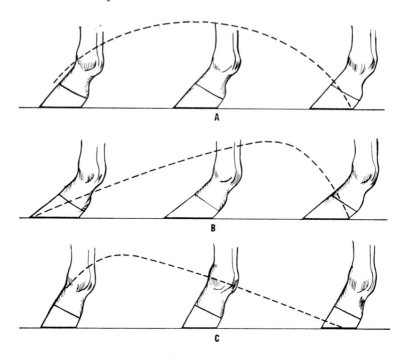

Fig. 1–33.—Examples of foot flight.

A, Flight of a foot with normal foot and pastern axis. The peak of the arc occurs as the foot passes the opposite supporting foot.

B, Flight of a foot with foot and pastern axis less than normal: long toe, low heel. The peak of the arc occurs before the foot reaches the opposite supporting foot.

C, Flight of foot with foot axis greater than normal: short toe and high heel. The peak of the arc occurs after the foot passes the opposite supporting foot.

If the horse has a long toe and low heel, this usually means that there is less than a 45 degree angle to the hoof wall (Fig. 1–29B). A long toe will cause the foot to delay the breakover since it acts as a long leverage point. This delayed breakover causes the foot to reach the peak of the flight arc before the foot passes the opposite supporting limb (Fig. 1–33B). If this conformation is accompanied by identical angulation of the pastern and of the anterior hoof wall, the horse will usually have a sloping shoulder. Sloping shoulders and pastern usually indicate the horse will give a smooth ride.

The center of weight is anterior to the point of the frog with a long toe and low heel. The added effort required to force the foot to break over the long fulcrum causes the horse to have a long sweeping stride, longer than the stride of a horse with a normal foot axis and normal toe length. The toe is sometimes lengthened on trotting and pacing horses for this increased length of stride. Longer toe length increases the strain on the flexor tendons, suspensory ligament, and the promixal sesamoid bones.

When the horse has a short toe and high heel, the foot breaks over quickly and reaches the peak of the flight arc after passing the opposite supporting member (Fig. 1–33C). The foot comes to the ground at a sharp angle and causes a disagreeable ride. A steep foot axis is usually accompanied by a steep angle of the shoulder.

The center of the weight is posterior to the point of the frog with short toe and high heel. There is little strain on the flexor tendons or sesamoid bones in this conformation; however, there is increased concussion, which is a factor conducive to ringbone, navicular disease, and traumatic arthritis of the fetlock. The stride of a horse with a short toe and high heel is shorter than that of a normal horse or one with a long toe and short heel.

The center of weight should not be confused with the center of gravity. The center of gravity lies approximately at a crossing of a horizontal line separating the middle from the ventral (inferior) third of the body and a vertical line through the xyphoid cartilage.

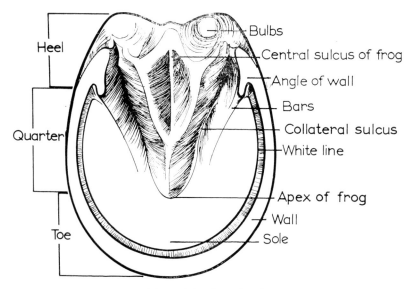

Fig. 1–34.—Normal forefoot showing structures.

The Forefoot (Fig. 1–34)

Ideally, the forefoot should be round and wide in the heels and the shape of the heels should correspond in size to the shape of the toe. The bars should be well developed. The wall should be thickest at the toe and gradually thin toward the heels and the inside wall should be slightly straighter than the outside wall.

The sole should be slightly concave medial to lateral, and anterior to posterior, but an excessive concavity is evidence of a chronic foot disease. There should not be primary contact between the ground and the sole, as it is not a weight-bearing structure.

The foot and pastern axes in the forefoot should be between 45 to 50 degrees. The angle of the heel should correspond to the angle of the toe and there should be no defects in the wall. The foot should show that the animal is breaking squarely over the center of the toe, and not over the medial or lateral portion of the toe. The wall should show that it is wearing evenly.

The frog should be large and well developed with a good cleft, have normal consistency, elasticity, and show no moisture. It should divide the sole into two near-equal halves, and the apex should point to the center of the toe. Unequal size of the two halves may indicate a base-wide or base-narrow conformation of the horse.

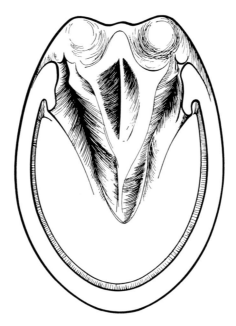

Fig. 1–35.—Normal hind foot. Compare with Figure 1–34. A more pointed toe is present on the hind foot.

The Hindfoot (Fig. 1–35)

The hindfoot should present a more pointed appearance at the toe than does the forefoot. It should show evidence of breaking straight over the toe, and the frog should divide the sole into equal halves. The foot axis should be 50 to 55 degrees and there should be no defects in the wall. The walls should show normal wear on the medial and lateral sides and the sole should be slightly concave medial to lateral, and anterior to posterior. The sole of the hindfoot is normally more concave than the forefoot.

ABNORMAL CONFORMATION OF THE FEET

Flat Feet.—A flat foot lacks the natural concavity in the sole and it is not a normal condition in light horses, but is present in some draft breeds. Flat feet may be inheritable and are much more common in the forefeet than in the hind. The horse will often land on the heels more than normal in order to avoid sole pressure with this condition. Sole bruising, and the lameness that results, are common sequelae of flat feet. No remedy will cure a flat foot but corrective shoeing can be done to prevent aggravation of the condition. Corrective shoeing is discussed in Chapter 9, page 411.

Dropped Sole or "Pumiced Foot." — When the sole has dropped to, or beyond the level of the bearing surface of the hoof wall, this is called dropped sole (Fig. 6–55, page 248). The sole is flat and has no concavity; in extreme cases it may be convex. Dropped sole is a sequel to chronic laminitis. The dropped sole is accompanied by heavy rings in the hoof wall that are characteristic of chronic laminitis (Fig. 1–36).

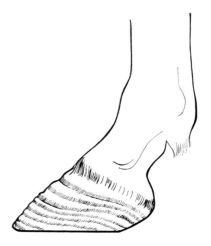

FIG. 1–36.—Rings in the hoof wall produced by chronic laminitis

In addition to being flat, the condition causes the sole to be very thick and composed of heavy flakes. Removal of these flakes will usually bring a pink-colored sole into view. This color is produced by proximity to blood. In some cases the accumulation of this flaky sole will harbor an infection similar to thrush that may actually penetrate into the sensitive laminae.

Dropped sole is usually accompanied by a rotation of the third phalanx (Fig. 1–37). In removing the excess sole it may be found that the tip of the third phalanx is protruding through the sole. If there is a protrusion of the sole below the wall at the toe, this area should be carefully trimmed to prevent exposure of the third phalanx.

Dropped sole is always a serious condition, and, in most cases, the horse is useless for work on hard surfaces. When the third phalanx has protruded through the sole, or there is infection that has penetrated through the sole, treatment is often useless. Corrective shoeing is discussed in Chapter 9, page 412 (*see* Laminitis, Chapter 6).

Contracted Foot or Contracted Heels (Fig. 1–38).—Contracted foot is a condition in which the foot becomes narrower than normal. This is especially true of the posterior half of the foot. This condition is much more common in the front feet than in the hind feet, and

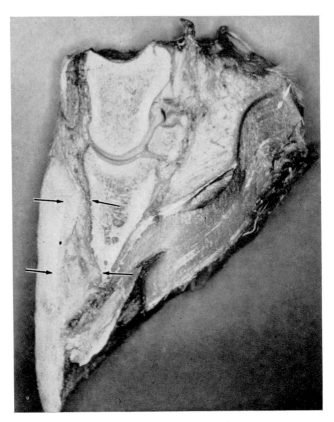

Fig. 1–37.—Rotation of the third phalanx. Note the greater distance between the two lower arrows than between the two top arrows. This represents a discrepancy produced by rotation of the third phalanx as a result of chronic laminitis.

it may be unilateral or bilateral. Local or coronary contraction of the foot is a contraction at the heels confined to the horn immediately below that occupied by the coronary cushion. It is merely an arbitrary subdivision of contracted foot.

A person should bear in mind that certain breeds of horses normally have a foot which more closely approaches an oval than a circle in form. A narrow foot is not necessarily a contracted foot, and donkeys and mules normally have a foot shape that would be called contracted on a horse. Foot contraction is often present in the Tennessee Walking horse and American Saddlebred, when these horses are used for show stock. This is because the hoof wall is allowed to grow excessively long and no frog pressure is present.

Contraction of the foot is always due to lack of frog pressure which may be induced by improper shoeing, and by shoeing a horse unnecessarily, which prevents contact of the frog with the ground. Lameness in the limb from any cause can prevent the horse from

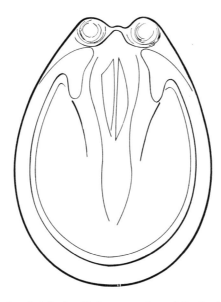

FIG. 1–38.—Contracted foot. Note narrowing of the heels and quarters. Compare with Figure 1–34.

pressing the foot firmly to the ground, and this results in foot contraction from lack of frog pressure. It is also possible that heredity plays a part in some cases of contracted feet, through inherited malconformation. Excessive dryness of the foot, especially in those horses that have been confined in moist pastures and then moved to a dry lot, may predispose the animal to contraction of the foot in hot weather.

True contraction of the foot should be considered pathological in all cases. It may take a year or more to overcome contraction of the foot or heels that may have resulted from one or two months of disuse.

Foot contraction is usually accompanied by a so-called "dished sole" or an increased concavity of the sole, both anterior to posterior and medial to lateral. If the hoof wall contracts sufficiently around the heels, it may press so firmly against the third phalanx that lameness results. This pressure causing lameness is called a "hoof bound" condition.

The diagnosis is based on the appearance of the foot, which shows narrowing, especially at the heel, and the frog is recessed and atrophied. The feet should be compared with one another to determine contraction, but keep in mind that conditions such as bilateral navicular disease or poor shoeing will cause contraction of both forefeet.

The most important factor in diagnosis of this condition is to determine the cause. Contraction can be produced by improper shoeing over a period of time, in which case usually no lameness is present. If lameness is present, though, the cause should be determined and corrected so that frog pressure can be re-established because the frog will be small, and obviously not in contact with the ground. In severe cases the bars may actually touch each other. Thrush may be present in the atrophied frog. Long continued disuse of the foot will cause the wall, sole, and frog to be hard and dry, and trimming is difficult.

In long standing cases of contraction of the foot the os pedis may become deformed and lose its circular shape. The digital cushion will atrophy and become less resilient. This neutralizes the protective action of the digital cushion in the area of the deep flexor tendon and navicular bone, and could conceivably aid in the produc-

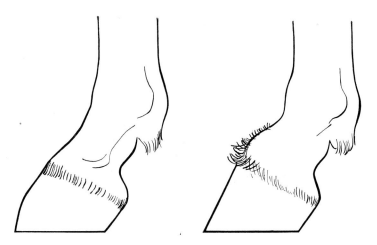

FIG. 1–39. – Bull-nosed foot.   FIG. 1–40. – Buttress foot.

tion of navicular disease. The coronary cushion is affected in the same manner. Corrective shoeing is discussed on page 400.

Brittle Feet.—Brittle feet are usually associated with dryness of the atmosphere and lack of moisture in the soil, and are more apt to occur in unpigmented or white feet. Complications of toe and/or quarter cracks and fractures of the wall resulting from brittleness may occur. Brittleness requires almost daily treatment with a nondrying agent such as lanolin, fish oils, pine tar, olive oil, or a good proprietary hoof dressing. Shoeing may be required to prevent fractures of the hoof wall.

Bull-Nosed Foot (Fig. 1–39).—A foot that has been rasped down in front to fit the shoe is called a bull-nosed foot. If an animal is continually shod in this fashion eventual pathological changes often result.

Buttress Foot (Figs. 1–40, 6–46 and 6–47, page 234).—Buttress foot is an exostosis on the extensor process of the third phalanx. This exostosis may be a low ringbone or the result of a fracture of the extensor process of the third phalanx (Fig. 1–41). A swelling on the anterior surface of the hoof wall at the coronary band results. A squaring of the toe from the coronary band to the ground surface, as a result of deformed hoof growth, is caused by chronic inflammation. Corrective shoeing for this condition is discussed in Chapter 6, page 236.

Rings in the Wall of the Foot (Fig. 1–36). — Some rings are normal and indicate changes of seasons or planes of nutrition. Laminitis is the most common cause of pathological rings. Large, single rings

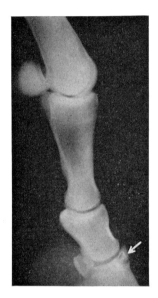

Fig. 1–41. — Fracture of the extensor process of the third phalanx (arrow). This fracture cannot be seen on the anteroposterior view. (Carlson, *Veterinary Radiology,* Lea & Febiger.)

may be the result of a past febrile reaction due to a systemic disease such as pneumonia, but blistering of the coronary band with iodine or other preparations will also produce lines in the foot. Wavy lines on the heels and quarters may indicate a chronic foot disease. Low ringbone may also produce rings in the foot. Dietary changes, inflammatory processes of the foot or coronary band, and systemic rise of temperature over a period of several days may also produce lines in the hoof wall. No treatment is indicated for the lines alone although the hoof is sometimes dressed to eliminate them. This removes the protective outer layer and makes the wall more subject to drying.

Thin Wall and Sole. — Thin walls and sole accompany one another and are inheritable. The conformation of the foot may appear to be normal, but the hoof wall either wears away too rapidly or does not grow fast enough to avoid sole pressure. This condition is especially noticeable at the heels, where the foot axis may be broken by the tendency of the heel to be too low (Fig. 1–32A).

The sole is easily bruised and lameness is common following hoof trimming. On examining the sole with a hoof tester, you may find that it is easily compressible and very thin. Flinching over bruised areas results when the sole is compressed by the hoof tester.

Treatment includes making the hoof wall grow more rapidly and proper shoeing to prevent excessive wear. Mild irritants, such as tincture of iodine, used on the coronary band may stimulate growth of the wall. If the horse is allowed to go barefooted, as much wall as possible should be left. Seldom will the wall ever become too long, since it wears too rapidly. Occasionally, shoe pads of leather or neolite are necessary to prevent lameness resulting from sole bruising. Building up the heels with leather shims under the shoe may be necessary to re-establish proper foot axis.

A horse's foot may be toughened by turning him onto rough ground barefooted. Over a period of time the foot will become more resistant to injury even though it has a thin wall and sole. Six months' time on rough ground will greatly increase the resistance of the foot to lameness from bruising and breaking of the hoof wall.

Club Foot.—A club foot is one that has a foot axis of 60 degrees or more. When club foot is unilateral, it is due to some injury that has prevented proper use of the foot. When it is bilateral, it may be inheritable or due to nutritional deficiency. The condition is accompanied by contraction of the superficial digital flexor tendon, and occasionally the deep flexor and suspensory ligament are shortened. When a horse is immature, nutritional deficiencies can cause club feet. Injury causes club foot by disuse contraction of the tendons.

Horses affected with club feet are usually unfit for saddle use because of an undesirable, rough gait. Stumbling may occur in these cases due to contraction of the superficial digital flexor tendon. Nutritional causes should be corrected, as discussed in nutritional deficiencies of foals (Chapter 5). If the condition is thought to be inheritable, the brood stock should be considered unfit for breeding.

Coon-Footed (Fig. 1–42).—The coon footed horse has a more sloping angle to the pastern than does the anterior surface of the hoof wall. In other words, the foot and pastern axis is broken at the coronary band. It may occur in either the fore or hind feet and causes strain on the flexor tendons, sesamoid bones, and distal sesamoid ligaments. There also may be strain on the common digital extensor tendon. Very little can be done for correction, except to modify the angle of the foot by trimming the heel as much as possible and still have a normal foot axis. The foot axis should not be trimmed to below 45 degrees.

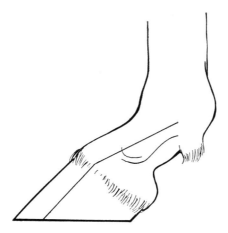

FIG. 1-42—Coon-footed. The foot axis is steeper than the pastern axis.

REFERENCES

1. AXE, J. WORTLEY: *The Horse in Health and* Disease. Vol. *1*, London, Gresham Publishing Co., About 1900.
2. BRITTON, JOHN W.: Conformation and Lameness. California Thoroughbred, *33* (6), 502, 1961.
3. GOLDSCHMIDT, S. G.: *An Eye for a Horse.* New York, Chas. Scribner & Sons, 1933.
4. MCKILLIP, M. H.: Lameness, Consideration of Predisposing Causes As An Aid in Diagnosis. Am. J. Vet. Med., *14*, 270, 1918–1919.
5. RUSSELL, WILLIAM: *Scientific Horseshoeing.* 10th ed., Cincinnati, C. J. Krehbiel & Co., 1907.
6. SMITH, F.: *A Manual of Veterinary Physiology.* 5th ed., Chicago, Alex Eger, Inc., 1921.

Anatomy and Physiology of the foot

Chapter 2

ANATOMY OF THE FOOT*

By definition, the foot of the horse includes the hoof and all structures contained therein, including the sole and frog. The hoof is only the cornified epithelium of the foot (wall, sole and frog), is nonvascular in structure, and has no nerve supply. Nutrition for the hoof is obtained from the combined coriums. The hoof is composed of the following structures.

1. *The Wall* (Fig. 1–34, page 41).—The hoof wall is approximately 25 per cent water, and is a modified cornified epithelium. The wall is composed of keratinized epithelial cells that are solidly cemented with keratin. The keratinized cells are arranged in tubules that result from their formation by the papillae of the coronary corium. These tubules run perpendicularly from the coronary band to the

---

* The term is used here in the popular sense; *i.e.*, to designate the hoof and the structures contained within it.

ground surface of the wall, and parallel one another. The center of the tubule is composed of keratin and dead cells.

The hoof wall is composed of three layers:

A. The first or outer layer is the periople and stratum tectorium. The periople extends about three-fourths of an inch below the coronary band; except at the heels, where it caps the bulbs of the heels. The stratum tectorium is a thin layer of horny scales which gives the glossy appearance to the outside of the wall below the periople. It helps protect the wall from evaporation.

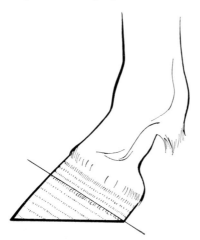

FIG. 2–1.—Diagram illustrating the method of hoof wall growth. This demonstrates that the youngest hoof wall is at the heel.

B. The second, or middle layer, composes the bulk of the hoof wall and is the most dense portion of the wall. This is the layer that contains the pigment in pigmented feet.

C. The third or inner layer is the laminar layer that forms the insensitive laminae of the hoof. This laminar layer is concave from side to side and bears about 600 thin primary laminae. Each of these primary laminae bears 100 or more secondary laminae on its surface. These laminae intermesh with the sensitive laminae covering the dorsum of the third phalanx and firmly attach the hoof wall to the third phalanx. These combined laminae bear much of the weight of the horse.

The ground surface of the hoof wall is divided into areas called the toe, quarters, and heel (see Fig. 1–34). Growth of the wall is quite slow. Roughly, it grows approximately $\frac{1}{4}$ inch per month and it normally takes from nine to twelve months for the toe of the hoof wall to grow out. The hoof wall grows evenly below the coronary band so that the youngest portion of the wall is at the heel (Fig. 2–1). Since this is the youngest wall, it is also the most elastic, which aids in heel expansion during movement. The wall is thickest at the toe and gradually reduces in thickness so that the thinnest portion of the wall is at the heels; however, it thickens slightly at the angles where the bars are formed. This junction of the wall and bar is commonly called the "buttress" of the foot.

2. *The Bars* (Fig. 1–34).—At the heels the wall turns anteriorly to form the bars which converge toward one another, and parallel the collateral sulci of the frog. The sole conforms to the inner curvature of the wall and to the angles formed by the wall and the bar.

3. *The Sole* (Fig. 1–34).—The sole, comprising the majority of the ground surface of the hoof, is approximately 33 per cent water. The

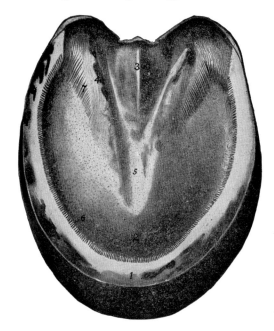

Fig. 2–2.—Section of Hoof of Horse.
The section is cut just above the ridges of the frog and bars parallel with the ground surface. *1*, Wall; *2*, sole; *3*, spine of frog or "frog-stay"; *4*, ridge formed by function of frog and bar; *5*, central furrow over apex of frog; *6*, laminae of wall; *7*, laminae of bar. (Sisson and Grossman, *Anatomy of Animals*, courtesy of W. B. Saunders Company.)

structure is similar to the wall and the tubules run vertically as formed by the papillae of the sole corium. These tubules curl near the ground surface, which accounts for the self-limiting growth of the sole and causes shedding. The sole should not bear weight from the ground surface, but is designed to bear internal weight. If the sole is allowed to contact the ground surface, lameness will often develop from sole bruising. That portion of the sole that conforms to the angle formed by the wall and bars is called the angle of the sole. It is in this area that corns usually develop (Chapter 6, page 277).

4. *The Frog* (Fig. 1–34).—The frog is a wedge-shaped mass that occupies the angles bounded by the bars and the sole. It is quite soft because it contains approximately 50 per cent water. The frog is divided into (1) apex—which is the anterior angle of the frog; (2) base—which is the posterior aspect; and (3) frog stay—which is the central ridge of the internal surface (Fig. 2–2).

WEIGHT BEARING STRUCTURES OF THE FOOT

The wall, bars, and the frog are the weight bearing structures of the foot. The sole should not bear weight except for a strip about $\frac{1}{4}$ inch wide, or less, inside of the white line. The bars should bear weight and in shoeing should not be removed but lowered enough to allow fitting of the shoe. The bearing surface of the wall should be level with the frog to distribute the weight evenly.

OTHER STRUCTURES OF THE FOOT

THE WHITE LINE

This is the junction of the wall and the sole. It is visible as a white line following the circumference of the wall at the junction of the sole and hoof wall (Fig. 1–34).

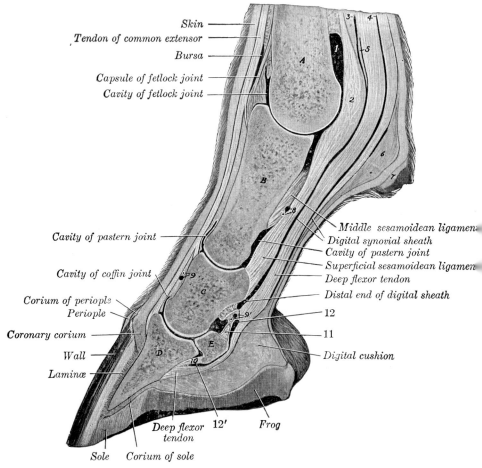

FIG. 2–3.—Sagittal section of digit and distal part of metacarpus of horse.

A, Metacarpal bone; *B*, first phalanx; *C*, second phalanx; *D*, third phalanx; *E*, distal sesamoid bone. *1*, volar pouch of capsule of fetlock joint; *2*, intersesamoidean ligament; *3,4*, proximal end of digital synovial sheath; *5*, ring formed by superficial flexor tendon; *6*, fibrous tissue underlying ergot; *7*, ergot; *8,9,9'*, branches of digital vessels; *10*, distal ligament of distal sesamoid bone; *11*, suspensory ligament of distal sesamoid bone; *12,12'*, proximal and distal ends of navicular bursa. The superficial flexor tendon (behind *4*) is not marked. (Sisson and Grossman, *Anatomy of Animals*, courtesy of W. B. Saunders Company.)

THE CORIUM

The corium is a modified vascular tissue that furnishes nutrition to the hoof. It is divided into five parts and each part nourishes the corresponding part of the hoof.

1. *Perioplic Corium* is a narrow band lying in the perioplic groove above the coronary border of the wall. It is continuous with the corium of the skin, and is marked off below by a groove from the coronary corium. It bears fine short papillae that furnish the perioplic structures around the top of the hoof wall.

2. *Coronary Corium* (Fig. 2–3) occupies the coronary groove and with the perioplic corium forms the "coronary band." It is composed

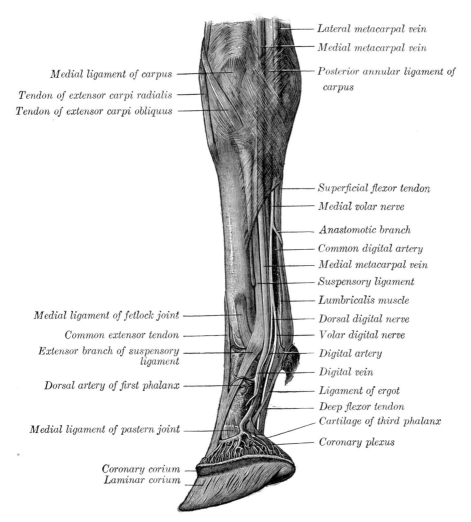

Lateral metacarpal vein
Medial metacarpal vein
Posterior annular ligament of carpus
Medial ligament of carpus
Tendon of extensor carpi radialis
Tendon of extensor carpi obliquus
Superficial flexor tendon
Medial volar nerve
Anastomotic branch
Common digital artery
Medial metacarpal vein
Suspensory ligament
Lumbricalis muscle
Medial ligament of fetlock joint
Common extensor tendon
Extensor branch of suspensory ligament
Dorsal digital nerve
Volar digital nerve
Digital artery
Digital vein
Dorsal artery of first phalanx
Ligament of ergot
Deep flexor tendon
Cartilage of third phalanx
Medial ligament of pastern joint
Coronary plexus
Coronary corium
Laminar corium

FIG. 2–4. — Dissection of Right Carpus, Metacarpus, and Digit of Horse; Medial View. (After Schmaltz, *Atlas d. Anat. d. Pferdes.*)

of villiform papillae on the convex surface. It furnishes the bulk of nutrition to the hoof wall and is responsible for growth of the wall. It is very vascular and lacerations of this structure cause profuse hemorrhage.

3. *Laminar Corium* is attached to the dorsal surface of the third phalanx by a modified periosteum. It bears primary, secondary, and tertiary sensitive laminae that intermesh with the non-sensitive laminae of the hoof wall (Fig. 2–4). The laminar corium nourishes the sensitive laminae, the non-sensitive laminae of the wall, and the interlaminar horn of the white line.

4. *Sole Corium* (Fig. 2–3) is composed of the fine hair-like papillae over the entire inner surface of the sole. The papillae originate from the modified periosteum of the third phalanx that attaches the corium to the third phalanx. These papillae project into cavities in the horny tissues of the sole and furnish nourishment and growth for the sole proper.

5. *Frog Corium* is similar in structure to the sole corium, and furnishes nourishment and growth for the frog. The deep face blends with the digital cushion.

Digital Cushion (Fig. 2–3)

This is a fibro-elastic, fatty, pale yellow, relatively avascular, and yielding pyramidal structure containing islands of cartilage in the posterior one-half of the foot. The primary purpose of this structure is to reduce concussion to the foot. It is bounded laterally and medially by the cartilages of the third phalanx, below by the frog, and above by the second phalanx and the deep digital flexor tendon. Posteriorly it is subcutaneous and forms the bulbs of the heels.

Coronary Cushion

The coronary cushion is the elastic portion of the coronary corium and aids slightly in reducing concussion. It fits into the groove formed at the proximal part of the hoof wall. The cushion is widest at its center and narrows as it joins the heels. At the proximal aspect of the heels, it blends with the digital cushion.

Lateral Cartilages (Fig. 2–5)

These are part fibrous tissue and part hyaline cartilage. They slope upward and backward from the wings of the third phalanx, and reach above the margin of the coronary band, where they may be palpated.

Coronary Band

The coronary band is the combined perioplic corium, coronary corium, and coronary cushion and is the primary growth and nutri-

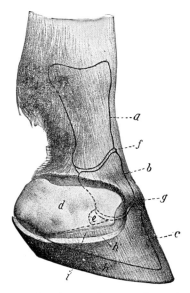

FIG. 2–5.—Digit of horse showing surface relations of bones and joints. The cartilage is largely exposed.

a, First phalanx; *b*, second phalanx; *c*, third phalanx; *d*, cartilage; *e*, distal sesamoid or navicular bone; *f*, pastern joint; *g*, coffin joint; *h'*, cut edge of wall of hoof (*h*); *i*, laminar corium. (After Ellenberger, in *Leisering's Atlas*.)

tional source for the bulk of the hoof wall. Injuries to this structure are serious and usually leave a permanent defect in the growth of the hoof wall.

Bulbs of the Heel

These are located in the posterior aspect of the foot where the perioplic corium covers the angles of the posterior aspect of the hoof wall. They are supported by the digital cushion.

BLOOD SUPPLY TO THE FOOT (Figs. 2–4 and 2–6)

The blood supply to the foot is furnished by the medial and lateral digital arteries which are formed by the bifurcation of the common digital artery in the distal fourth of the metacarpus. The digital arteries diverge and pass over the abaxial surface of the sesamoid bones of the fetlock and descend parallel to the borders of the deep flexor tendon to the volar grooves of the third phalanx. Here the vessels enter the volar foramina of the third phalanx to form the terminal arch (Fig. 2–6). This arch gives off branches through the dorsal surface of the bone that supply the corium of the wall and sole of the hoof. In the area of the pastern, the vein passes anterior to the artery and the posterior digital nerve just behind the artery. So from anterior to posterior they are related vein, artery, and nerve.

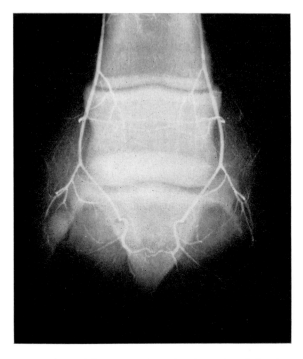

Fig. 2–6.—X-ray of arterial system of equine foot after injection with barium.

NERVE SUPPLY TO THE FOOT (Fig. 2–4)

The nerve supply to the foot is furnished by the medial and lateral volar nerves. These nerves bifurcate at the fetlock joint forming the anterior and posterior digital nerves. Commonly, a third, or middle digital, branch is present.

In almost 50 per cent of the horses examined by me, some variation of the classically described nerve anatomy is present. In many cases, there are small subcutaneous branches arising high on the posterior digital nerve that travel with the ligament of the ergot. If these branches are left following posterior digital neurectomy, sensation is still present to the area of the navicular bursa. This undoubtedly accounts for some of the failures of this operation. Other variations are found such as the anterior digital branch bifurcating and sending a branch posteriorly that will substitute for the posterior digital nerve. These variations are so common that no definite anatomical description can be given.

STAY APPARATUS

A great deal of confusion seems to exist regarding classification of the stay, check, and reciprocal systems. These have not been classified in older literature and therefore there is no standard. Sisson's anatomy text[6] mentions the stay system, but discrepancy exists between the description and the drawings. In consulting several anatomists, I found that the use of these terms is far from standardized. Therefore, I have changed my own classification used in the previous edition of this book and have used suggested changes in an attempt to standardize use of these terms. I realize there will be disagreement, but the descriptions used seem to be the most logical, and combine the thoughts of many authorities.

The stay apparatus of the limbs as interpreted from Sisson, includes the suspensory apparatus of the fetlock joint as well as those structures aiding in supporting the horse while he stands. The stay apparatus supports the limb and fetlock, diminishes concussion, and prevents excessive extension of the fetlock, pastern and coffin joints.

Stay Apparatus of the Forelimb (Figs. 2–7 and 2–8)

Distally

1. *The Intersesamoidean Ligament.*—This ligament fills the space between the two sesamoid bones, forms a groove for the flexor tendons and is more or less molded to their shape.

2. *The Collateral Sesamoidean Ligaments.*—These ligaments, lateral and medial, arise on the abaxial surface of each sesamoid bone and pass forward, attaching to the distal end of the third metacarpal bone and to the proximal end of the first phalanx.

3. *Suspensory Ligament or Interosseous Ligament.*—This ligament attaches proximally to the posterior surface of the third metacarpal/metatarsal bone and to the distal row of carpal/tarsal bones. It lies on the posterior surface of the third metacarpal or third metatarsal bone, and divides in the distal one-third of the metacarpus or metatarsus into two branches. These attach to the abaxial surface of the corresponding sesamoid bone, and a portion passes obliquely downward and forward from each sesamoid bone to the dorsal surface of the first phalanx where they join the common or long digital extensor tendon.

4. *The Distal Sesamoidean Ligaments.*—(A) *The superficial sesamoidean ligament* (straight or "Y" sesamoidean ligament) attaches above to the bases of the sesamoid bones and to the intersesamoidean ligament, and below to the overhanging lip of the proximal end of the volar or plantar surface of the second phalanx. (B) *The middle sesamoidean ligament* (oblique or "V" sesamoidean ligament) attaches to the base of the sesamoid bones and intersesamoidean ligament above and distally on the volar surface of the first phalanx. (C) *The deep sesamoidean ligaments* (cruciate or "X" sesamoidean ligaments) consist of two layers of fibers which arise from the base of the sesamoid bones, cross each other, and end on the opposite proximal eminence of the volar or plantar aspect of the first phalanx.

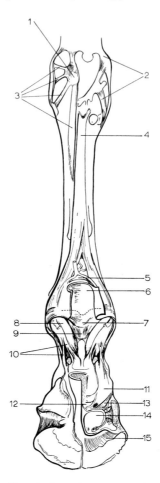

Fig. 2–7.—Diagramatic illustration of some structures in the stay apparatus. Some accessory structures are also shown.

1. Accessory carpal bone
2. Medial collateral ligaments of the carpus
3. Ligaments of the accessory carpal bone
4. Suspensory ligament
5. Diverticulum of metacarpo-phalangeal (fetlock) joint
6. Volar annular ligament of the fetlock (cut and reflected)
7. Intersesamoidean ligament
8. Middle or oblique distal sesamoidean ligament
9. Superficial or straight sesamoidean ligament
10. Volar ligaments of proximal interphalangeal (pastern) joint
11. Medial collateral ligament of the pastern joint
12. Diverticulum of the distal interphalangeal (coffin) joint
13. Suspensory ligament of the navicular bone
14. Flexor surface of navicular bone
15. Insertion of deep digital flexor tendon

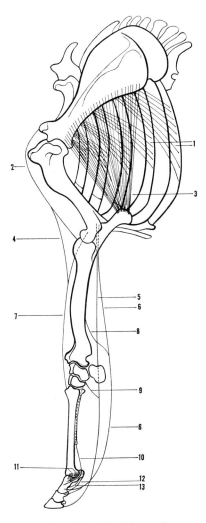

FIG. 2–8.—Stay apparatus of forelimb (not all structures are shown).

1. Fibrous sheet of serratus ventralis
2. Tendon of biceps brachii
3. Long head of triceps
4. Lacertous fibrosus
5. Deep digital flexor
6. Superficial digital flexor
7. Extensor carpi radialis
8. Proximal (superior) check ligament
9. Distal (carpal) check ligament
10. Suspensory ligament
11. Combined collateral sesamoidean ligament and collateral ligament of fetlock joint
12. Superficial (straight) distal sesamoidean ligament
13. Middle (oblique) distal sesamoidean ligament

5. *Short Sesamoidean Ligaments.*—These are short bands which extend from the anterior part of the base of the sesamoid bones and attach to the posterior margin of the articular surface at the proximal end of the first phalanx.

6. *Collateral Ligaments of the Fetlock.*—Although not stated in Sisson, the collateral ligaments of the fetlock are included because of their common attachment with the collateral sesamoidean ligaments.

Proximally

7. *The Serratus Ventralis Muscle.*—This muscle originates on the ribs and attaches to the costal area of the scapula on the facies serrata. The dorso-scapular ligament attaches above from the third to the fifth thoracic spines and its lower fibers intersect the scapular fibers of the serratus ventralis muscle and attach to the scapula.

Anteriorly

8. The *biceps brachii* tendon and the extensor carpi radialis tendon including the lacertus fibrosis tendon from the biceps to the extensor carpi radialis. The *biceps brachii* originates on the tuber scapulii and inserts on (1) the radial tuberosity; (2) the medial ligament of the elbow joint; (3) the fascia of the forearm and the tendon of the extensor carpi radialis. The *extensor carpi radialis* originates on (1) the lateral condyloid crest of the humerus; (2) the coronoid fascia; (3) the deep fascia of the arm and forearm and the intermuscular septum between this muscle and the common extensor. It inserts on the metacarpal tuberosity. It receives a tendon (lacertus fibrosis) from the biceps brachii toward the proximal end of the radius.

Posteriorly

9. (A) *The long head of the triceps muscle.* This is the largest and longest of the three heads of the triceps. It originates on the posterior border of the scapula and inserts in the lateral and posterior part of the summit of the olecranon. (B) *The superior or radial check ligament* which is often termed the radial head of the superficial flexor tendon. It originates on a ridge on the posterior surface of the radius below its middle and near the medial border and fuses with the tendon of the superficial digital flexor near the carpal joint. (C) *The superficial flexor tendon.* This muscle originates on (1) the medial epicondyle of the humerus, (2) a ridge on the posterior surface of the radius below its middle and near the medial border. This latter origination is termed the radial head or the radial or superior check ligament. The muscle inserts on the eminences of the proximal extremity of the second phalanx behind the collateral ligaments of the proximal interphalangeal joint and the distal ex-

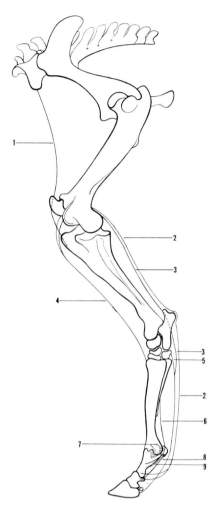

FIG. 2–9.—Stay apparatus of hind limb (not all structures are shown).

1. Tensor fascia lata
2. Superficial digital flexor
3. Deep digital flexor
4. Peroneus tertius
5. Tarsal (inferior) check ligament
6. Suspensory ligament
7. Combined collateral sesamoidean ligament and collateral
   ligament of fetlock joint
8. Superficial (straight) distal sesamoidean ligament
9. Middle (oblique) distal sesamoidean ligament

tremity of the first phalanx also behind the collateral ligaments. (D) *The inferior (carpal) check ligament.* The carpal check ligament originates as a direct continuation of the posterior ligament of the carpus. It joins the deep flexor tendon at approximately the middle of the third metacarpal bone. (E) *Deep digital flexor.* This muscle originates on (1) the medial epicondyle of the humerus, (2) the medial surface of the olecranon, and (3) the middle of the posterior surface of the radius and a small adjacent area of the ulna. It inserts on the semilunar crest of the third phalanx and the adjacent surface of the collateral cartilages of the third phalanx.

Stay Apparatus of the Hind Limb (Figs. 2–7 and 2–9)

In the hind limb, the stay apparatus includes structures 1 through 6 listed for the stay system of the forelimb and the following:

7. *Tensor Fascia Lata.*—This muscle originates at the tubercoxae and inserts on the fascia lata and thus indirectly to the patella, the lateral patellar ligament, and the crest of the tibia.

8. *The Gastrocnemius Muscle.*—This muscle originates by two heads: the lateral head from the lateral supracondyloid crest of the femur and the medial head from the medial supracondyloid crest of the femur. It inserts on the posterior part of the tuber calcis in conjunction with the superficial digital flexor tendon. It is included here because of its close association with the superficial digital flexor.

9. *The Peroneus Tertius Muscle.*—This muscle is primarily tendinous and originates in the extensor fossa of the femur. It inserts on the proximal extremity of the third metatarsal bone, the fibular, third and fourth tarsal bones laterally.

10. *The Deep Digital Flexor.*—The origin of this muscle actually has three heads which unite into a common tendon. It originates (1) the posterior edge of the lateral condyle of the tibia, (2) the border of the lateral condyle of the tibia just behind the facet for the fibula and (3) the middle third of the posterior surface and upper part of the lateral border of the tibia, the posterior border of the fibula and the interosseous ligament. It inserts on the semilunar crest of the third phalanx and the adjacent surface of the collateral cartilages.

11. *The Tarsal Check Ligament.*—Tarsal check ligament originates from the posterior ligamentous tissue of the hock and joins the tendon of the deep digital flexor just below the hock joint.

12. *Superficial Digital Flexor.*—This muscle originates in the supracondyloid fossa of the femur and inserts on (1) the tuber calcis and (2) the eminences on each side of the proximal extremity of the second phalanx and the distal extremity of the first phalanx behind the collateral ligaments of the pastern joint.

CHECK APPARATUS

The check apparatus will be defined in this text as that part of the stay apparatus involving the check (accessory) ligaments. This includes the superior (radial) and inferior (carpal) check ligaments and the superficial and deep flexor tendons in the forelimb. In the hind limb the check apparatus includes the tarsal (inferior) check ligament and the deep digital flexor tendon. These structures aid in supporting the volar surface of the forelimb and the plantar surface of the hind limb. However, in the hind limb, only the tarsal (inferior) ligament is present.

SUSPENSORY APPARATUS OF THE FETLOCK (Fig. 2–7)

The suspensory apparatus of the fetlock joint is that portion of the stay apparatus that supports the fetlock (metacarpophalangeal) joint and prevents it from dropping to the ground. The support extends from the carpus distally in the forelimb and from the hock distally in the hind limb. The following structures are included in the suspensory apparatus.

1. The suspensory ligament (interosseous ligament)
2. Proximal sesamoid bones
3. The intersesamoidean ligament
4. The distal sesamoidean ligaments (superficial, middle, deep)
5. Short sesamoidean ligaments
6. The superficial and deep flexor tendons. These must be included because of their support to the fetlock joint.

RECIPROCAL APPARATUS OF THE HINDLIMB

The reciprocal apparatus is that portion of the stay apparatus in the hind limb which causes reciprocal movement of the hock and stifle joints. The reciprocal apparatus causes the hock to flex whenever the stifle joint flexes, and the stifle to extend when the hock extends, provided all structures are normal. The action is strictly mechanical and can be changed only if one of the reciprocal structures is ruptured. This apparatus also aids in preventing fatigue in the standing position. Structures that compose the reciprocal apparatus of the hind limb are as follows:

1. *Anteriorly*

A. *Peroneus Tertius Muscle.*—This muscle is entirely tendinous in structure. It originates in the extensor fossa of the femur, and inserts on the anterior surface of the proximal extremity of the third metatarsal bone, the third tarsal bone, and on the fibular and fourth tarsal bones. Occasionally this muscle is ruptured following exertion. This results in inability of the hock to flex normally when the stifle joint is flexed (*see* Rupture of the Peroneus Tertius, Chapter 6, page 306).

2. *Posteriorly*

A. *Superficial Digital Flexor Tendon.*—This muscle lies between and under cover of the two heads of the gastrocnemius in its proximal part. It consists almost entirely of a strong tendon. It inserts on

5

the tuber calcis as well as the distal extremity of the first phalanx and proximal extremity of the second phalanx. The fact that it inserts at the tuber calcis causes a reciprocal action with the peroneus tertius muscle. At its origin, and again near its tarsal insertion, the muscle is intimately associated with the gastrocnemius muscle.

B. *Gastrocnemius Tendon.* — Although this muscle is not ordinarily classified as a portion of the reciprocal apparatus, it must be considered because of its close attachment to the superficial flexor. Rupture of the gastrocnemius causes the hock to drop. If both are cut the hock joint will drop to the ground. The combined tendons above the hock are known as the Achilles tendon.

PHYSIOLOGY OF MOTION

Concussion

In a fast gait there is tremendous concussion exerted upon the limbs of the horse. The forelimbs of the horse bear 60 to 65 per cent of the body weight and, therefore, are subjected to greater concussion

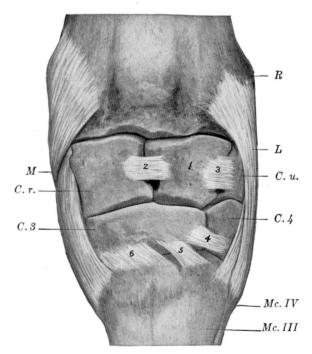

FIG. 2–10. — Left carpal joints of horse; dorsal view. The joint capsule is removed.

R, Lateral distal tuberosity of radius; M, medial ligament; L, lateral ligament; C.r., radial carpal bone; C.u., ulnar carpal bone; C.3., third carpal bone; C.4., fourth carpal bone; McIII, McIV, metacarpal bones; 1, intermediate carpal bone; 2–6, dorsal ligaments. (Site for Injection of the carpus is between radial and intermediate carpal bones.) (Sisson and Grossman, *Anatomy of Animals*, courtesy of W. B. Saunders Company.)

and to a greater incidence of lameness. Concussion to the foot and limb is produced by the weight of the horse and the counter pressure of the earth. A second strain occurs when the limbs leave the ground. This is the compression of propulsion.

The construction of the limbs and feet are such that concussion is countered in numerous ways.

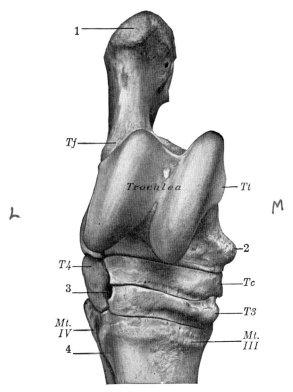

Fig. 2–11.—Right tarsus and proximal part of metatarsus of horse; anterior or dorsal view.

Tt, tibial tarsal bone; *Tf*, fibrular tarsal; *Cc*, central tarsal; *T3*, third tarsal; *T4*, fourth tarsal; *1*, tuber calcis; *2*, distal tuberosity of tibial tarsal; *3*, vascular canal; *4*, groove for great metatarsal artery; *Mt, III, IV*, metatarsal bones. (Sisson and Grossman, *Anatomy of Animals*, courtesy of W. B. Saunders Company.)

1. *The Carpal Joint* (Fig. 2–10).—The carpal joint is composed of three main joints and numerous ligaments. The radio-carpal and intercarpal joints have the greatest range of movement while the carpo-metacarpal joint has very little motion. There is more movement of the seven to eight carpal bones during motion than there is in the tarsal bones. The carpal bones can move in three planes and this greatly aids in diminishing concussion. The carpal bones themselves are bound together by a complex series of liga-

ments. Injury to this ligamentous structure is common and occurs
predominantly over the radial, intermediate, and third carpal bones.

   2. *The Tarsal (Hock) Joint* (Figs. 2–11, 2–12 and 2–13).—The
hock joint, as the carpus, is composed of numerous bones; however,
there is not the degree of motion in these six bones that there is in
the carpal bones. Since there is a partial flexion of the hock joint
at all times this aids in diminishing concussion.

   The oblique ridges in the tibial tarsal bone of the horse cause some
differences in the action of the hock when compared with other
animals in which the ridges are usually straight. As the body weight
passes over the hind limb it is not uncommon to observe a considerable outward twist of the hock joint in some horses. At the same
time the stifle joint and the toe turn in. This effect is due to the
ascent of the lower end of the tibia on the oblique ridges of the

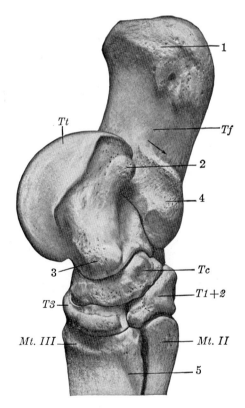

Fig. 2–12.—Right tarsus and proximal part of metatarsus of horse; medial view.

   Tt, Tibial tarsal (trochlea); *Tf*, fibular tarsal; *Tc*, central tarsal; *T1 + 2*, fused first
and second tarsals (dotted line indicates division between two elements); *T3*, third
tarsal; 1, tuber calcis; 2,3, proximal and distal tuberosities of tibial tarsal; 4, sustentaculum; 5, groove for great metatarsal vein; *Mt. II, III*, metatarsal bones.
Arrow indicates course of flexor tendon in tarsal groove. (Sisson and Grossman,
Anatomy of Animals, courtesy of W. B. Saunders Company.)

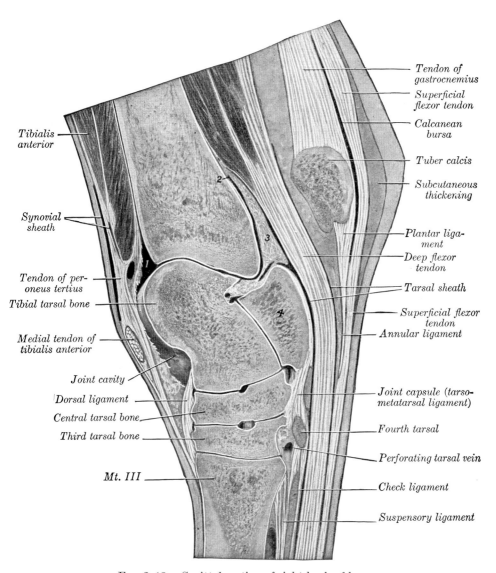

Tibialis anterior

Synovial sheath

Tendon of per- oneus tertius

Tibial tarsal bone

Medial tendon of tibialis anterior

Joint cavity

Dorsal ligament

Central tarsal bone

Third tarsal bone

Mt. III

Tendon of gastrocnemius

Superficial flexor tendon

Calcanean bursa

Tuber calcis

Subcutaneous thickening

Plantar liga- ment

Deep flexor tendon

Tarsal sheath

Superficial flexor tendon

Annular ligament

Joint capsule (tarso- metatarsal ligament)

Fourth tarsal

Perforating tarsal vein

Check ligament

Suspensory ligament

Fig. 2–13.—Sagittal section of right hock of horse.

The section passes through the middle of the groove of the trochlea of the tibial tarsal bone. 1,2, Proximal ends of cavity of hock joint; 3, thick part of joint capsule over which deep flexor tendon plays; 4, fibular tarsal bone (sustentaculum). A large vein crosses the upper part of the joint capsule (in front of 1). (Sisson and Grossman, *Anatomy of Animals*, courtesy of W. B. Saunders Company.)

tibial tarsal bone. During flexion, the oblique setting of the ridges on the tibial tarsal bone apparently aid in turning the stifle joint outward which aids clearance past the posterior ribs.

3. *The Femorotibial (Stifle) Joint* (Figs. 2–14 and 2–15).—The stifle joint is the largest in the body. One function of this joint is to cause the limb to become rigid when the foot is on the ground. This is done by the contraction of the muscles inserted into the patella. The first joints flexed in advancing the hind limb are the coffin,

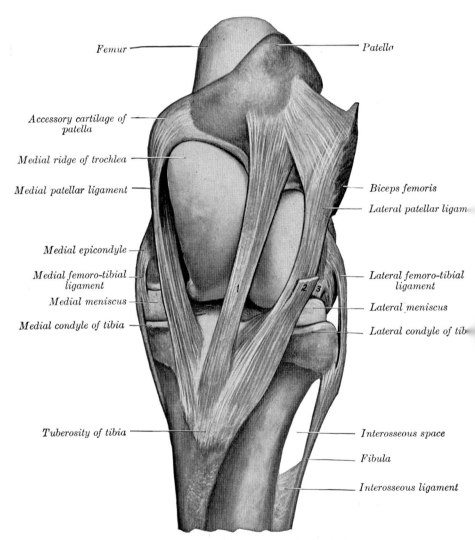

Fig. 2–14.—Left stifle joint of horse; front view. The capsules are removed.

1, Middle patellar ligament; 2, stump of fascia lata; 3, stump of common tendon of extensor longus and peroneus tertius. (Sisson and Grossman, *Anatomy of Animals*, courtesy of W. B. Saunders Company.)

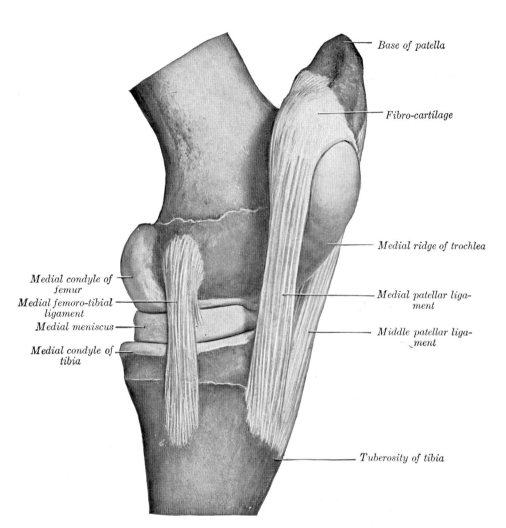

FIG. 2–15.—Left stifle joint of horse; medial view. The capsules are removed. (Sisson and Grossman, *Anatomy of Animals,* courtesy of W. B. Saunders Company.)

pastern and fetlock joints. In upward fixation of the patella where no flexion of the stifle and hock can occur these lower joints can still be flexed (Fig. 6–79). The semiflexed position of the stifle joint aids in decreasing concussion.

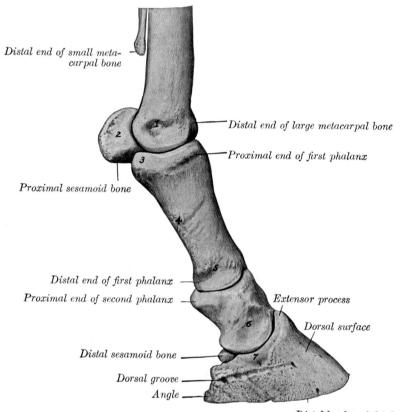

Distal end of small meta-carpal bone

Distal end of large metacarpal bone

Proximal end of first phalanx

Proximal sesamoid bone

Distal end of first phalanx

Proximal end of second phalanx

Extensor process

Dorsal surface

Distal sesamoid bone

Dorsal groove

Angle

Distal border of third phalanx

Fig. 2–16.—Skeleton of digit and distal part of metacarpus of horse; lateral view.

1–7, Eminences and depressions for attachment of ligaments. Cartilage of third phalanx is removed. (Sisson and Grossman, *Anatomy of Animals*, courtesy of W. B. Saunders Company.)

4. *The Metacarpophalangeal (Fetlock) Joint* (Figs. 2–3 and 2–16).— The fetlock joint has a great degree of anticoncussive action. The stay apparatus changes the direction of concussion and weight distribution. In other words, weight is partially directed anteriorly from the distal end of the cannon bone instead of entirely straight down. In addition to the stay apparatus the joint is supported by the tendons of the superficial and deep flexors.

The posterior cul-de-sac of the fetlock joint capsule is so constructed as to allow a great degree of motion. The fetlock joint is subjected to the greatest stress of all joints, and at times the entire body weight may be pressed upon one fetlock joint.

The suspensory ligament has slight elastic properties. The suspensory ligament, sesamoid bones, and the posterior half of the metacarpal phalangeal articulation carry most of the weight of the horse. That portion of the suspensory ligament that joins the common extensor tendon has very little stress on it and is rarely, if ever, injured. If the suspensory ligament is divided, the fetlock sinks but does not come to the ground. If the superficial flexor tendon is cut, a slight sinking of the fetlock occurs. To bring the fetlock completely to the ground, both flexors must be divided, as well as the suspensory ligament. This shows that all three structures support the fetlock joint.

5. *The Proximal Interphalangeal (Pastern) Joint* (Figs. 2–3 and 2–16). — This is the least movable of the phalangeal joints. There is a minimum amount of anti-concussion activity at this joint, and it is possible that this renders it more subject to pathological conditions such as ringbone. Because the foot exerts upward and forward propulsion to the body when the foot is leaving the ground, much of the resulting shock is distributed on the pastern joint.

6. *The Distal Interphalangeal (Coffin) Joint* (Figs. 2–3 and 2–16). — The coffin joint is composed of the second and third phalanges, and the navicular bone (distal sesamoid bone). This joint has a great degree of elasticity and motion, because of the placement of the navicular bone, and considerable anticoncussive action. Direct concussion to the coffin joint is averted by the partial distribution of weight from the second phalanx to the navicular bone. From the navicular bone the weight is then transferred to the third phalanx, which descends slightly because of a yielding of the sensitive and insensitive laminae. The sole also descends slightly from pressure by the third phalanx.

The navicular bone could not withstand great pressures but for the deep flexor tendon supporting it from behind and below. The navicular bursa has a smooth lubricating surface to avoid friction, and the surface of the deep flexor tendon is closely fitted to the surface of the navicular bone.

There is no "pulley" action at the coffin joint because no leverage is gained. There is merely a change in direction of the weight distribution. The greatest pressure between the navicular bone and the deep flexor tendon does not occur when the foot hits the ground, but rather as the body weight passes over the foot. The central ridge of the navicular bone is subjected to the greatest pressure of any portion of the bone.

7. *The Laminae* (Figs. 2–2 and 2–3). — The laminae help absorb shock, as does blood in the vessels of the foot which in normal horses is retained as a hydraulic cushion by the outward movement of the cartilages compressing the venous plexus lateral to the cartilages.

8. *The Digital Cushion* (Fig. 2–3).—This structure decreases concussion in the foot proper as described below.

9. *The Frog* (Figs. 1–34 and 2–2).—The normal resilient qualities of the frog aid in diminishing concussion and, in addition, the frog distributes concussion to the digital cushion.

PHYSIOLOGY OF THE FOOT

In the process of evolution the horse has developed from a multiple digit to a single digit animal. This subjects the single digit to great stress. The frog is the foot pad of the horse, and is the most elastic structure of the foot. When the foot strikes the ground, the heels expand and this aids in distribution of concussion. The heel normally lands slightly before the toe, and this results in immediate heel expansion due to the action of the frog. As the frog is forced upward, the frog stay (Fig. 2–2) acts as a wedge in the digital cushion. This forces the digital cushion to expand, primarily in an outward direction, because it is confined by structures of the foot in the dorsal, volar, and proximal directions. The frog stay coming up from below naturally limits distal expansion of the digital cushion.

The digital cushion expands outward and exerts pressure against the lateral cartilages of the third phalanx. These cartilages are normally elastic and expand outward and backward, and thus compress the veins of the coronary plexus; at the same time the cartilages act as a pump to force venous blood up the limb. The compression against the veins of the coronary plexus acts similarily to valves which are absent in this area. As the foot hits the ground, the blood in the vascular bed of the foot is partially held by the pressure of the lateral cartilages against the coronary plexus. This forms an efficient hydraulic cushion of blood for the third phalanx which further aids in reduction of concussion.

When the lateral cartilages are affected by disease, *i.e.* sidebones, and lose elasticity, their function is lost. As a result, a foot affected with sidebones is subjected to greater concussion and to inefficient venous return of blood which may account for a chronic swelling of the lower limb (stocking) with edema.

If no frog pressure is present, the movement of the digital cushion is downward and outward. Because it can move in a distal direction, it does not expand sufficiently in an outward direction to compress the lateral cartilages and aid in expansion of the foot. This usually causes foot contraction and atrophy of the digital cushion.

GLOSSARY OF TERMS

When reading old texts a person encounters many names of anatomical structures which are different from those cited in modern anatomy books such as Sisson's *Anatomy of Domestic Animals*.[6] Some of these terms are offered as an aid to the reader.

Modern Name	*Old Name*

BONES OF THE HINDLIMB:

Hock

Tibial tarsal bone	Astragalus—talus
Fibular tarsal bone	Calcaneus—os calcis
Central tarsal bone	Cuneiform magnum—scaphoid—navicular
First tarsal bone	Internal cuneiform
Second tarsal bone	Cuneiform parvum—middle cuneiform
Third tarsal bone	Cuneiform medium—external cuneiform
Fourth tarsal bone	Cuboid
Third metatarsal	Great metatarsal—cannon bone

MUSCLES OF THE HINDLIMB:

Long digital extensor	Extensor pedis—anterior digital extensor
Peroneus tertius	Tendinous part of flexor metatarsi
Tibialis anterior	Tibialis anticus—flexor metatarsi
Deep digital flexor	Flexor perforans
Superficial digital flexor	Flexor perforatus

BONES OF THE CARPUS:

Radial carpal	Scaphoid
Intermediate carpal	Semilunar—lunar
Ulnar carpal	Cuneiform
First carpal	Trapezium
Second carpal	Trapezoid
Third carpal	Os magnum
Fourth carpal	Unciform
Accessory carpal	Pisiform
Splint bones or second and fourth metacarpals	Inner and outer small metacarpal bones

MUSCLES OF THE FORELIMB:

Biceps brachii	Flexor brachii
Extensor carpi radialis	Extensor carpi magnus
Deep digital flexor	Flexor perforans
Superficial digital flexor	Flexor perforatus

FOOT:

First phalanx	Os saffragenous—long pastern bone
Second phalanx	Os coronae—short pastern bone
Third phalanx	Os pedis—pedal bone—coffin bone
Navicular bone	Shuttle bone

REFERENCES

1. AXE, J. WORTLEY: *The Horse in Health and Disease. Vols. I and II.* London, Gresham Publishing Co., About 1900.
2. FRANK, E. R.: *Veterinary Surgery*, 6th ed., Minneapolis, Burgess Publishing Co., 1959.
3. KOCH, T.: Termination of the Volar Nerve in the Horse. Vet. Record, *52* (2), 26, 1940.
4. KOVAK, GY.: *The Equine Tarsus—Topographic and Radiographic Anatomy.* Publication House of the Hungarian Acad. of Sciences, Budapest, 1963.
5. RUSSELL, WILLIAM: *Scientific Horseshoeing.* 10th ed., Cincinnati, C. J. Krehbiel and Co., 1907.
6. SISSON, SEPTIMUS and GROSSMAN, J. D.: *The Anatomy of Domestic Animals*, 4th ed. Philadelphia, W. B. Saunders Co., 1960.
7. SMITH, F.: *A Manual of Veterinary Physiology*, 5th ed., Chicago, Alex Eger and Co., 1921.
8. SMITHCORS, J. F.: The Equine Leg. Pt. 1. Mod. Vet. Practice, *42*, 24, 1961.
9. Ibid: Pt. II, *42*, 31, 1961.
10. Ibid.: Pt. III, *42*, 33, 1961.
11. STILLMAN, A. M.: *The Horse in Motion*, Boston, J. R. Osgood and Co., 1882.

Examination for soundness

Chapter 3

THE object of a soundness examination is to determine by examination of the horse his relative commercial value for the service in which he is to be employed. Soundness of the horse might be defined as that state in which there are no deviations from the normal that have resulted in, or that will predispose the animal to, pathological changes that interfere with intended use. Although this is a vague definition, it necessarily must be to encompass all the purposes for which the horse may be used. Soundness might be classified as working soundness and breeding soundness, since a horse that is sound for breeding purposes is not necessarily sound for working, or vice versa. For this reason, all abnormal findings must be recorded in the original examination. Then, if the horse is resold, the veterinarian who made the soundness examination cannot be blamed for not identifying abnormalities that might interfere with a new use of the horse. For example, some minor unsoundnesses would not disqualify a horse for a child's use, but would disqualify him for more strenuous work.

To certify that a horse was sound would imply that he passed both working and breeding soundness examinations. A statement as to soundness of the animal should be preceded by: "At the time of my examination," so that subsequent unsoundness cannot be construed as being present at the original examination.

A working horse must be checked closely for working soundness, and special emphasis must be placed on those qualities needed for the particular use to which the animal will be put. In addition, if there is a possibility that a stallion or mare may be used for breeding purposes, a breeding soundness examination must also be done. However, a stallion or mare may be purchased for breeding purposes and be unsound for work. In such a case, the weaknesses should not be of an inheritable nature, or result from a conformation that might be inheritable.

A person should also consider qualities that do not necessarily bear directly on the examination: *i.e.* the temperament of a horse being purchased for a child should be well suited for that purpose. A bad tempered horse, even though sound in all other ways, might not pass such an examination. The size of the horse as compared with the size of the rider should also be considered.

Insurance examinations should be complete and follow the company's regulations. Stallions, insured as such, should always be checked for descent of both testes. The internal genital health of a mare should be checked if she is insured as a brood animal. The external genitalia of both sexes are routinely examined if the animals are insured as breeding stock. Routine insurance examination includes a check of the locomotor, circulatory, respiratory, digestive, and nervous systems. The circulatory and respiratory systems should be examined before, during and after exercise and a stethoscope should be used as indicated in these examinations. Vision of the horse must be checked routinely, and conformational abnormalities predisposing to lameness should be noted on the insurance papers.

In some cases the soundness examination is limited by age. For example, the examination of yearlings will usually be confined to determining if infectious diseases are present and whether the horse has congenital or inheritable weaknesses. However, the heart should always be closely checked for abnormalities by a stethoscopic examination. Regardless of the type of horse being examined, careful and thorough examination is essential.

The increased incidence of Equine Infectious Anemia (swamp fever), with the various syndromes that it may assume, plus the introduction of Equine Piroplasmosis into the United States, make it important to examine the horse closely for signs of icterus, anemia, edematous swellings of the limbs and abdomen, and temperature rise. The history of the horse should be checked to see if it could have originated from an area where these diseases are prevalent. At the present time, most states have potential Equine Infectious Anemia sources, and Piroplasmosis is known to exist in Florida.

Whenever there is some reason to suspect the presence of Equine infectious Anemia, a precipitin test should be considered on the suspected horse as well as others on the premises. In addition, CBC, hemoglobin and packed cell volume determinations should be done. If Piroplasmosis is suspected, peripheral blood from the ear vein may be drawn for staining purposes. However, in the carrier state, Piroplasmosis is difficult to diagnose, and a carrier of Equine Infectious Anemia may have a negative precipitin test. Whenever possible, injection of blood from a suspected infectious anemia horse should be inoculated intravenously into a nonexposed horse. If the disease is reproduced, a positive diagnosis can be made.

With the increased frequency of use of corticosteroids and phenyl-butazone, there is always a possibility that a horse being sold is under the influence of one or both of these drugs to mask a lameness. In addition, a local nerve block may have been employed, or a neurectomy to produce temporary soundness to promote sale of the horse. Atropine is sometimes used to mask the symptoms of pulmonary interstitial emphysema (heaves). Careful digital examination and needle prick check for neurectomy and local anesthesia should be used. When in doubt, one should obtain a written guarantee that no masking drugs have been used, and a week's period on the new owner's premises allowed for the effects of any such drugs to disappear.

DISCUSSION OF UNSOUNDNESS

In some states the registration of stallions is required by law. In those states that do require an examination, certain unsoundnesses will exclude a stallion from a breeding license. Below is a list of conditions considered to be unsoundnesses in some states. These disqualify the stallion for breeding license.

1. splints (when accompanied by lameness)
2. ringbone
3. sidebone
4. hernias (scrotal or umbilical)
5. curb (when accompanied by curby conformation)
6. bone spavin
7. bog spavin
8. thoroughpin
9. stringhalt
10. cryptorchid
11. contagious disease
12. blindness
13. heaves
14. periodic ophthalmia
15. cataract
16. roaring (laryngeal hemiplegia)
17. parrot mouth
18. shivering
19. any form of venereal disease

In addition to this list many people regard the following as unsoundnesses. These must be understood to be only partial lists, and not to include wounds or other conditions that might make the horse unsound. The combined lists should be used.

1. sand crack
2. thrush
3. corns
4. quittor
5. bowed tendon
6. knee sprung
7. dropped sole
8. navicular disease
9. laminitis
10. leg interference of any type, *e.g.* scalping, forging, over-reaching, cross-firing, interfering, speedy cutting.
11. malignant neoplasms
12. sweeny
13. wind puffs (when due to arthritis)
14. broken and decayed teeth
15. poor apposition of teeth

Some of these conditions may be congenital or acquired. If congenital, the horse is not suited for breeding but if acquired, the horse may in some cases be considered sound for breeding purposes.

The following conditions are considered blemishes and sometimes unsoundnesses:

1. capped hock
2. capped elbow (also known as olecranon bursitis, hygroma of the elbow, or shoe boil).
3. windgalls (wind puffs)
4. thoroughpin
5. scars (especially when accompanied by extensive fibrous tissue)
6. corneal scars associated with previous trauma
7. firing marks
8. saddle sores
9. sit fast
10. crooked tail
11. new bone growth (especially of large size in the lower leg).
12. splints (when not accompanied by lameness).
13. hygroma of the carpus

A blemish is a defect, pathological or otherwise, which is localized in a tissue such as skin or bone, and which diminishes more or less the value of the horse, but does not diminish function.

Good judgment must be used to determine the importance of some of the above conditions. For example, a splint is a minor condition when not accompanied by poor conformation or lameness, and when the splint does not involve any adjacent structure. It will be noted that there are some repeats here from the unsoundness list, such as thoroughpin and wind puffs. A person must be able to decide whether or not these have been produced by sprains and are healed, or whether they are due to poor conformation and consequently the result of a trauma. If they are due to trauma but the animal has good conformation, they are considered a blemish, provided there is no lameness. If they are due to poor conformation, they are considered unsoundness. It is obvious that no hard and fast rule can be made to apply to all cases.

When acting as an advisor in the purchase of a horse, conformational defects not listed above should be noted and the prospective buyer advised of their seriousness. Minor abnormalities should be noted when there is a possibility they might cause pathological changes. The veterinarian must decide for himself when very minor blemishes are to be reported.

Below is a list of conditions considered vices which possibly would render some horses unsound for certain purposes:

1. biting
2. bucking
3. cribbing—wind sucking—stump sucking—swallowing air.
4. kicking (either in the stall or at handlers)
5. running away
6. shying
7. viciousness
8. weaving
9. stall walking
10. tail wringing
11. tail rubbing

PROCEDURE FOR A SOUNDNESS EXAMINATION

A soundness examination should always be done in routine fashion so that the same qualities are checked and the possibility of overlooking defects is minimized.

The horse should always be observed in the box stall before being removed because at this time some conditions are obvious which will not be noticeable after the horse has warmed up. Careful observation on how the horse supports his weight on the limbs is important. Stringhalt or upward fixation of the patella may be evident.

General Appearance

Visual Examination at a Distance.—A definite system of visual examination should be developed as a consistent routine. A person should visualize the horse from the front, from each side, and from behind to determine any gross defects. If this is done in a routine fashion, for every area of the horse, embarrassing mistakes can be avoided. Facial fractures, scars, torn ears, crooked tails, and other defects that might otherwise be overlooked will be detected.

6

Locomotor System

Signs of lameness can best be detected while the horse is in motion. The way of going should also be observed to determine whether or not interference occurs, or is likely to occur. Any conformational defects should be detected. The horse should be turned several times in a tight circle to check for the wobbler syndrome, or other causes of incoordination.

Close-Up Examination. — A spavin test should be administered to both rear limbs, and the tuber-coxae should be checked for knocked down hip. If there is any suspicion that a neurectomy has been performed in any area, a needle puncture test of the skin should be made and the skin checked for scars. The limbs should be observed to see if one fetlock drops farther than the other, indicating injury to the suspensory ligament or to the flexor tendons. Any swelling should be examined closely to determine its importance. The lateral cartilages should be examined and the feet observed for cracks in the hoof. Any atrophy of musculature or bony swellings should be noted and the importance determined.

General Considerations

At the time of the close-up examination, any sign of infectious disease should be recorded. The lymph glands should be checked for enlargement that might indicate a developing respiratory disease complex. Any lacrimal discharge should be examined to see if it accompanies a disease of the eye, tearduct, or a systemic disease. The mucous membranes should be examined for normal color. If icteric or anemic membranes are present, diseases such as Leptospirosis, Piroplasmosis or Equine Infectious Anemia could be involved, so laboratory tests should be made. The temperature should be taken routinely and be within normal limits.

Respiratory System

The lungs should be checked at rest, and following exercise, by a stethoscopic examination. Any signs of alveolar emphysema, indicating the presence of heaves, or any other lung pathology should be noted.

Dilation of the pupils and dryness of the mouth may indicate that atropine or belladonna has been administered to mask the symptoms of heaves.

Following exercise, an examination for roaring should be made. This is done by placing the stethoscope over the larynx and palpating the larynx for muscular atrophy. If there is a suspicion that roaring is present, a rhino-laryngoscope* can be used to observe the laryngeal cartilages.

The trachea and larynx should be palpated to determine if previous tracheotomy or roaring operations have been done. The trachea

* Borescope, American Cystoscope Co.

should be examined for broken rings. During the time the horse is working one can determine if normal wind is present. The nostrils should be observed closely to determine if there is a nasal discharge.

Circulatory System

The heart should be checked with a stethoscope from both the right and left sides. This examination should be conducted both at rest and following exercise, and any abnormalities noted. Common defects found in such an examination are valvular leaks, pericardial friction rub, tachycardia, and partial heart block. If doubt is present concerning a cardiac ailment, an EKG can be used.

Both jugular veins should be checked for excessive jugular pulse which usually indicates a right atrioventricular valvular leak. The jugular veins should also be checked for thrombosis resulting from subcutaneous injection of an irritant drug. The characteristics of the pulse should be noted in either the femoral artery or in the maxillary artery at the angle of the jaw.

Genital System and Inheritable Defects

Under this system the second classification of soundness examination, or the breeding soundness examination, is given. In addition to unsoundnesses listed below, any inheritable abnormalities in the mare or stallion should classify the breeding animal as unsound. Any limb unsoundness present may become worse with the increased body weight caused by pregnancy.

Conditions Considered to be Breeding Unsoundnesses in Mares.

1. Tipped vulva—this may cause sucking of air into the vaginal vault during movement. A mare with this condition, that makes an audible sound when air is sucked into the vagina, is often called a "gilflirt." A person should also check to see if the vulva has been previously sutured to prevent this condition, because special breeding precautions are necessary in such a case.

2. Recto-vaginal fistula or perineal lacerations—the usual problem is a third degree perineal laceration whereby the entire shelf between the rectum and the vagina has been torn out to varying depths in the vagina. Occasionally a single perforating fistula will be found. Mares rarely settle when afflicted with either condition and often abort if they do. Chronic vaginitis will be present with endometritis in some.

3. Abnormalities considered to be unsoundnesses when found on rectal examination—

(a) Ovaries that are hard, fibrous, or excessively large, or that show evidence of adhesions in the fallopian tubes, should be considered abnormal. A single hard ovary is not usually abnormal if the other is normal. It may be inactive and subsequent examination will usually show it to be normal. If both ovaries are hard, small, and fibrous, the mare may be a nymphomaniac. A breeding history and heat cycle chart is helpful in determining the seriousness of the above, since ovaries of the mare show many normal variations. In some cases, no ovaries are found, due to some congenital defect or because the mare has been spayed.

(b) Abnormal uterus and/or cervix—Enlargement of the uterus due to pyometra or to thickened walls resulting from previous infection are unfavorable findings. A uterus that lacks proper tone and is flabby to palpation should be considered indicative of reduced breeding efficiency. Adhesions of the uterus to pelvic structures, and hemotomas present on the wall of the uterus or in the region of the fallopian tubes due to rupture of uterine vessels during foaling, reduce breeding efficiency. Occasionally a person will find an abnormally small uterus or that the uterus is completely absent. This is due to an inheritable factor and the mare is permanently infertile.

A thickened cervix resulting from foaling lacerations or infection reduces breeding efficiency.

4. Abnormalities found on vaginal examination and considered unsoundnesses—

(a) Adhesions of the vaginal wall or cervix indicating previous tears.

(b) Vaginal or cervical inflammation indicating infection and/or windsucking reducing breeding efficiency.

(c) Abnormal exudate indicating presence of infection.

5. Umbilical hernia—this condition is inheritable. The navel should be palpated to detect whether or not repair has been made.

6. The mammary gland should be checked for scar tissue from previous mastitis.

Some of the above unsoundnesses can be corrected, but all should be regarded as potential causes of unsoundness and the purchaser should understand that the mare may not conceive, or that congenital conditions may be passed on to the offspring.

Conditions Considered to be Breeding Unsoundnesses in Stallions.

1. Poor semen quality—A semen evaluation should be done, whenever possible, to determine the quality of semen and the reproductive potential of the stallion.

2. Undescended testicles—Testicles should be descended at birth, and any deviation from this is abnormal. Undescended testes may be unilateral or bilateral and are an inheritable characteristic.

3. Epididymitis—This is a comparatively rare finding in a stallion.

4. Penile pathology—The penis should be examined closely for any signs of pathological changes. Edema of the prepuce may indicate carcinoma, screw worm infestation, or other pathology in the penis and prepuce. A tranquilizer such as promazine* may be given intravenously to facilitate this examination.

*Sparine, Wyeth Laboratories.—Promazine, Fort Dodge Laboratories.

5. Lack of libido — This may be accompanied by underdeveloped testes, or testes of poor consistency. In young stallions it can be due to shyness and may be overcome as the horse matures. Masturbation is a common cause of decreased libido, and a stallion ring should be used to check for improved libido following its use.

6. Umbilical and scrotal hernia — If there is any suspicion of scrotal hernia, a rectal examination should be done. If there is an enlargement of the internal inguinal rings, a hernia may occur so this condition can be considered the same as a scrotal hernia. The umbilical area should be palpated for the presence of a hernia and for signs of previous repair.

7. Any unsoundness of the fore or hind limbs that will prevent the stallion from performing natural breeding service.

Digestive System

The teeth should be checked for dental caries. The age, as indicated by the teeth, should be determined to see if it coincides with that given by the seller. The incisors should also be checked for presence of parrot mouth which is considered inheritable and an unsoundness (Fig. 3-1).

A wearing of the outside edges of the incisors indicates that the horse is a cribber (Fig. 3-2). The molars should be checked for

Fig. 3-1. — Parrot Mouth. Note upper incisors overlap the lower incisors.

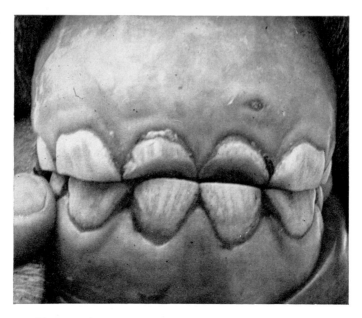

FIG. 3–2.—Photograph of teeth on a two-year-old horse that cribs. Note that the outside portion of the upper central incisors is worn off. This change indicates an unsound horse.

irregularities and missing teeth. Any sign of a split tooth or receding of the gum indicates a defective molar. Caps on the premolars in young horses should also be noted. Both upper and lower jaws should be checked for bony swelling that indicates previous fractures or dental caries.

The tongue should be examined for bit lacerations that may limit its action. The breath should be checked for odors indicating dental problems or necrosis of tissue. It is desirable to do a fecal examination for parasite eggs and a rectal examination to determine the extent of aneurysms at the anterior mesenteric artery or in the iliacs.

Nervous System

The horse should be appraised to determine if his mental attitude is normal. Examination of the locomotor system should have been done previously, and incoordination detected, if present. Incoordination problems include wobbling and shivering syndromes, and the after-effects of encephalomyelitis, or injury to the head or back.

The head should be raised reasonably high with the hand and then released quickly to determine the horse's balance. If he has pathological changes in the area of the semicircular canals, vertigo will usually be shown following this test.

The eyes should be examined, along with the nervous system, for the following conditions:

1. Corneal opacities and lacerations. Ulcers can be detected by the use of fluorescein.
2. Blindness—this examination should include the use of an ophthalmoscope.
3. Hypopyon—this is the presence of a purulent exudate or blood in the anterior chamber of the eye.
4. Adhesions of the iris—these may be detected when determining the reaction of the pupil to light. An anterior synechia is an adhesion of the iris to the cornea. A posterior synechia is an adhesion of the iris to the lens.
5. Cataracts—which may be due to senility, injury or to periodic ophthalmia.
6. Reaction of the pupil to light.
7. Evidence of carcinoma, especially on unpigmented eyelids and on the third eyelid.
8. Follicular lymphoma is not an unsoundness but a blemish on the sclera. Corneal scars in the line of vision are an unsoundness because they interfere with light transmission and cause astigmatism which is especially troublesome for jumpers. Congenital cysts may occur in the iris and be nonpigmented.

Hearing should be tested by observing the reaction of the horse to various sounds.

Common Integument

The skin should be checked for evidence of external parasites and fungous infection. The bursae at the withers, poll, tendon of the biceps brachii, point of the hock, and point of the elbow, should be examined for abnormalities. Examination also should be made for melanoma and squamous cell carcinoma or other tumors. The area of the anus, vulva, penis, and eye are the most common sites for squamous cell carcinoma. Melanomas are most commonly found around the anus (Fig. 3–3). The back should be checked for scar tissue and other lesions that would interfere with a saddle. These lesions are often due to subcutaneous larva similar to *Hypoderma bovis*.

Excessive white (unpigmented areas) although not unsoundness, should be considered undesirable when found on the feet, eye, eyelids, vulva, anus or the penis. The eyelids, vulva, anus and penis are more subject to squamous cell carcinoma under such circumstances. Also, white feet tend to wear faster and crack more easily than pigmented feet. Nonpigmented eyes (glass eyes) are considered undesirable and seem to be more subject to internal eye disease.

All types of unsoundnesses have not been discussed in the above examinations; therefore, other conditions that occur should be evaluated for their seriousness after careful consideration by the veterinarian.

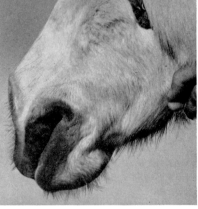

Fig. 3–3.—Melanoma formation on the tail, anal sphincter, vulva and mouth of a mare. When these are in an early stage they can be overlooked in a superficial examination.

REFERENCES

1. AXE, J. WORTLEY: *The Horse in Health and Disease. Vol. 3*, London, Gresham Publishing Co., About 1900.
2. BODDIE, G. F.: *Diagnostic Methods in Veterinary Medicine*, 4th ed., Philadelphia, J. B. Lippincott Co., 1956.
3. *Equine Medicine and Surgery*: 68 Authors, Santa Barbara, Calif. American Vet. Pub. 1963.
4. FRANK, E. R.: *Veterinary Surgery*, 7th ed., Minneapolis, Burgess Publishing Co., 1964.
5. GENDREAU, L. A.: Warranty, Soundness, Unsoundness, Vice and Blemish, Canad. J. Comp. Med., *11*, 17, 1947.
6. JONES, W. A.: Soundness in Horses. Austral. Vet. J., *12*, 115, 1936.
7. MALKMUS, B., OPPERMAN, T.: *Clinical Diagnositics*. 11th ed., Chicago, Alex Eger, Inc., 1944.
8. O'ROURKE, M. J.: Examination of Thoroughbreds. Vet. Med. *38*, 404, 1943.
9. PETERS, J. E.: Physical Examination of the Horse for Soundness. Proceedings A.A.E.P. 109, Dec. 1961.
10. PROCTOR, D. L.: What is a Sound Horse. Western Livestock Jour., *39* (51) 59, 1961.
11. RUBIN, L. F.: Some Aspects of Soundness Examination Relative to the Eye. Proceedings A.A.E.P. 121, Dec. 1963.
12. RUSSELL, WILLIAM: *Scientific Horseshoeing*. 10th ed., Cincinnati, C. J. Krehbiel and Co., 1907.
13. SMYTHE, R. H.: *The Examination of Animals for Soundness*. Springfield, Charles C Thomas, 1959.
14. USDA Farmers Bulletin. No. 779, Revised (August, 1925). Washington D. C.

Diagnosis of lameness

Chapter 4

DEFINITION OF LAMENESS

LAMENESS is an indication of a structural or functional disorder, in one or more limbs, which may be manifested in progression and/or the standing position; it is sometimes called Claudication. Lameness can be caused by trauma, congenital or acquired anomalies, infection, metabolic disturbances (rickets), circulatory and nervous disorders, or any combination of these. The diagnosis of lameness requires a detailed knowledge of anatomy and physiology of the limbs and there are cases of lameness where even the most experienced veterinarians differ in opinion. To the young veterinarian this fact is apt to cause uneasy moments, since a mistake in diagnosis may interfere materially with a successful start in practice. To him it should be said: Never express a decided opinion until you are thoroughly satisfied as to its correctness.

Whenever possible, the horse should be observed in a box stall before being removed. At this time some conditions are obvious which will not be noticeable after the horse has warmed up. Careful observation on how the horse supports his weight on the limbs is important. Stringhalt or upward fixation of the patella may be evident at this time and not after the horse has been moved.

Lameness Has Been Classified by Dollar as Follows

1. *Supporting Leg Lameness.*—This is evidenced when the horse is supporting weight, or lands on the foot. Injury to bones, joints, collateral ligaments, motor nerves, and to the foot are considered causes of this type of lameness.

2. *Swinging Leg Lameness.*—This lameness is evident when the limb is in motion. Pathological changes involving joint capsules, muscles, and/or tendons are considered to be the cause.

3. *Mixed Lameness.*—This is evident when the leg is moving and is supporting weight. Mixed lameness can involve any combination of the structures affected in swinging or in supporting leg lameness.

By observing the gait from a distance a person can determine whether it is supporting leg, swinging leg, or mixed lameness. A veterinarian may use this classification as an aid to diagnosis, but he cannot rely on it completely. Some conditions that cause supporting leg lameness may cause the horse to alter the movement of the limb to protect the foot when it lands. This could lead to a mistaken diagnosis of swinging leg lameness.

The character of the stride of a limb is also important to diagnosis of lameness. When observing the stride, the following characteristics are noted:

1. *The Phases of the Stride* (Fig. 4–1).—The stride consists of an anterior phase and a posterior phase. The anterior phase of the stride is in front of the footprint of the opposite limb and the posterior phase is in back of the footprint of the opposite limb. In lameness, the anterior or posterior phases may be shortened, although the length of the stride must be the same as the opposite limb if the horse is to travel in a straight line. If the anterior phase is shortened,

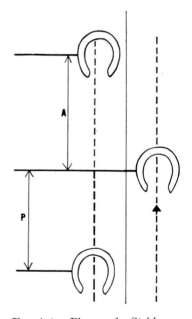

Fig. 4–1.—Phases of a Stride

A, Anterior phase of stride, which is that half of the stride in front of the print of the opposite foot.

P, Posterior phase of the stride, which is that half of the stride in back of the print of the opposite foot.

then there must be a compensatory lengthening of the posterior phase or vice versa. If there is not a compensatory lengthening of the anterior or posterior portion of the stride, the horse will travel with the body at an angle instead of in a straight line.

2. *The Arc of Foot Flight* (Fig. 4–2). — The arc of foot flight is changed when there is pain anywhere in the limb. The arc of one foot is compared to the opposite member. In some cases the arc is changed in both forefeet (bilateral navicular disease, laminitis) or in both hindfeet (bilateral bone spavin). In the hindlimb, the arc may be changed enough to cause the toe to drag when the limb is advanced (bone spavin or gonitis) because of reduced flexion of the hock or stifle joints. Navicular disease, laminitis, nail punctures, etc. cause a lowering of arc because of an effort to reduce pain when the foot lands. Painful conditions of the carpus cause a lowering of arc because of reduced flexion of the carpus.

3. *The Path of the Foot in Flight.* — If the foot travels inward, there may be an interference problem causing medial fracture of a splint bone or painful lesions of the carpus. When the foot travels in an outward path (paddling) no special problem usually results.

4. *How the Foot Lands.* — When a painful lesion is present in the foot, the horse will usually indicate the pain by placing his weight opposite to the pain. For example, in navicular disease the greatest pain is near the heel, so the foot is placed down toe-first. In a nail puncture of the toe, the weight is placed on the heel. If the lesion is on the lateral portion of the sole, the weight is carried on the medial side of the foot and vice-versa.

Close observation of the above stride characteristics will aid in diagnosis of the lameness.

The majority of lamenesses take place in the forelimb, and of those in this region, 99 per cent are in the carpus or below. Approximately three lamenesses will be seen in the forelimb to every lameness in the hindlimb. However, in the Standardbred, hindlimb lameness is involved in approximately 40 per cent of the lameness diagnoses. This is due to his balanced gait. The greatest number of lamenesses occur in the forelimb because they carry 60 to 65 per cent of the weight of the horse, and are subject to much greater concussion than the hindlimbs. The hindlimbs act as propelling limbs, while the forelimbs receive the shock of landing. In the hindlimb, most lamenesses occur in the hock and stifle. A person must remember that the horse may be lame in more than one limb, or may have more than one pathological condition in the limb showing lameness. The veterinarian must also realize that *lameness in one area of the limb may cause the horse to injure a second area in the same limb, or to injure the opposite limb in an effort to protect the original injury.*

Lamenesses in horses will also vary according to the type of work performed. Although there is considerable overlapping, the common lamenesses associated with the type of work should be suspected first; *i.e.* the Thoroughbred is commonly afflicted with carpitis (popped knee), injury to the metacarpophalangeal joint (osselets) tendon and suspensory ligament injury, and sesamoid injury. The Quarter Horse used for barrel racing, calf roping, reining, and cutting, is more commonly afflicted with ringbone, fractures of the phalanges (first, second, and third), sidebone, and bone spavin. Navicular disease is common in both groups. A veterinarian should keep these facts in mind in diagnosis of lameness and be sure to eliminate the common sites of lameness and the common lamenesses first. In all cases the foot should be suspected and eliminated as a cause of lameness.

ANAMNESIS

A person should attempt to obtain an accurate history of every lameness case. In some instances the anamnesis is invalid because the owner has recently purchased the animal, because he deliberately attempts to falsify the history (especially as to duration of the lameness), or he actually believes that the animal is lame in one of the other limbs. In most cases falsification of the history is not malicious, but the owner hesitates to admit that he has not called for professional services more quickly. The successful veterinarian soon acquires the ability of obtaining information in a manner suited to the particular client. This may be done by direct questions or by subtle suggestion to obtain facts essential to the diagnosis.

Questions Important in the Anamnesis

1. *How Long Has the Horse Been Lame?* If lameness has been present for a month or more, it can be considered a chronic condition, since permanent structural changes may have taken place that render complete recovery impossible. The prognosis should always be guarded in this case. A veterinarian should keep in mind that a young horse has a better chance for recovery from a chronic condition than does a mature one.

2. *Does the Owner Know What Caused the Lameness?* The owner may be able to say that he removed a nail from the foot or actually saw the injury occur. This description should include the character of the lameness at the time first noticed. If the lameness was acute initially, this might indicate a condition such as a fractured third phalanx, or if it developed insidiously, an arthritic type of disease might be present.

3. *Does the Horse Warm Out of the Lameness?* If so, muscular structures or arthritic joints (such as bone spavin) may be involved.

4. *Does He Stumble?* Stumbling may be the result of some interference with the synergistic action of the flexor and extensor muscles. It also may indicate that the animal has pain on heel pressure, as in navicular disease or heel puncture wounds, and thereby attempts to land on the toe, which causes stumbling. Painful conditions of the carpus and rupture of the extensor carpi radialis may interfere with flexion enough to cause stumbling and should be ruled out.

5. *What Treatment Has Been Done, and Was It Helpful?* This type of history may influence the prognosis of the case. If the owner has attempted to pass a needle into a synovial structure, suppurative arthritis or tenosynovitis may result. If the horse has received certain types of recommended therapy with no results, the prognosis is guarded because results from further treatment may be unsatisfactory. It is very important to find out if the horse has been on parenteral corticoids or phenylbutazone derivatives. These will mask symptoms of lameness and give a false impression of recovery. Joint injection with corticoids may have been done, and in some cases, it may lead to infectious arthritis when improperly done. If a joint is painful and swollen, careful inquiry must be made about this possible complication.

6. *When Was the Horse Shod?* Sometimes a nail may be driven into sensitive tissue and then pulled out. In this case, evidence of infection may not manifest itself for several days. In other cases the nail remains in the sensitive tissue, and the shoe must always be removed to discover these potential causes of lameness. If the nails do not enter sensitive tissue, but are close to it, they may cause lameness from pressure on the sensitive tissue. This is commonly called "nail bound" and it will not be relieved until the nails are pulled.

PROCEDURE FOR EXAMINATION

Visual Examination

The horse should be observed first following confinement. At this time one may determine any swellings, enlargements, or defects in conformation that would be helpful in diagnosis. The horse is more apt to show lameness following confinement than if he has had exercise. Allow the horse to stand for a short time and observe the efforts he may make to compensate for pain in supporting leg lameness. These compensating efforts will often be a clue to the location of the lameness and to the structures which are involved. For example, if the animal stands with the carpus forward and the heel raised, the carpal, posterior fetlock and heel areas should be examined closely. If the animal points with the affected foot, navicular disease or fracture of the extensor process of the third phalanx may be present. If a forelimb is held posteriorly and the carpus flexed with the toe resting on the ground, the shoulder on that side should be considered in the diagnosis. Elbow joint lameness will often result in the forearm being extended, the knee being flexed and the foot being on a level with or posterior to its opposite member. In addition, the elbow will have a "dropped" appearance. When the limb is carried, fractures, nail punctures, severe sprains and septic phlegmon are considered.

A veterinarian can compare the above findings with the normal attitude of the limbs. In the normal attitude, the forelimbs bear an equal amount of weight and are exactly opposite each other. In bilateral involvement of the forelimbs, the weight may be shifted frequently from one foot to the other, or both limbs may be placed too far out in front, called "camped in front" (Fig. 1–18B). In the hindlimbs it is normal for the horse frequently to shift the weight from one limb to the other. If the horse consistently rests one hind-limb and refuses to bear weight on it for a length of time, or cannot be forced to bear weight on it at all, a veterinarian should consider the possibility of lameness in that particular hindlimb.

Next, the characteristics of the gait of all limbs should be observed from a distance. In most cases it is advantageous to first observe the forelimbs and follow this with observation of the hindlimbs. Once a person is able to accommodate his eye to observing all limbs at once, diagnosis of lameness is simplified. Coordination of all limbs can be checked at this time to rule out diseases such as "wob-bler" syndrome. The horse also should be backed to determine any lameness in this motion. The shoe, if present, should be removed prior to examination.

Proper examination includes watching the horse coming toward the examiner, from the side view and going away from the examiner. In general, forelimb lamenesses are best observed from the front and side views, while hindlimb lameness is best diagnosed watching the horse from the rear and side views.

The Forelimbs.—As a result of lameness in a forelimb, the head will drop when the sound foot lands. When weight is placed on the unsound foot or limb the head will raise. If acute lameness is not present, the trot should be used for diagnostic purposes because any lameness evident in the walk will be increased in the trot because there is only one other supporting foot on the ground. One must be cautious not to confuse a left fore lameness with a right hind lameness, or a right fore lameness with a left hind lameness, in the trotting gait. This could happen, because in the hindlimb the head will raise when weight is put on the sound foot, and drop when it is placed on the unsound foot. The head drops when a lame hind foot hits the ground because of the mechanical effect of taking weight from the affected hind limb when the head is down, whereas in the forelimbs, the head drops when the sound foot hits to allow the majority of the body weight to be taken by the sound limb. No head movement is present in bilateral involvement of the limbs, or in mild lameness.

In the normal gait the heel is lifted first when advancing the limb. When the foot lands, the heel should hit just before the toe. If there is pain on concussion to the heel, the horse will attempt to land on the toe, as in navicular disease, or a nail puncture in the heel area. If there is diffuse pain in the foot, such as with laminitis, the horse will make an exaggerated effort to land on the heel and thereby avoid concussion to the bottom of the foot. This is also the case when pain is present in the area of the toe. If pain is present in the lateral portion of the foot, the weight will be carried medially and

vice versa. In general, involvement in the toe of the foot will cause
a shortened posterior phase of the stride, and involvement of the heel
area of the foot will cause a short anterior phase of the stride. The
arc that the foot makes in flight should be observed (Fig. 4–2). If
it is too low, there is interference with flexion of the shoulder or
carpal joints due to pain or mechanical injury. Fixation of these
joints will reduce the arc of the foot flight, limit the anterior phase
of the stride, and lengthen the posterior phase. In shoulder involvement, the scapulo-humeral joint usually remains semifixed during
progression and the head shows marked lifting and may be pulled
toward the affected side. When involvement of both forefeet is
present, the limbs show a stilted action that causes a false impression
of shoulder involvement.

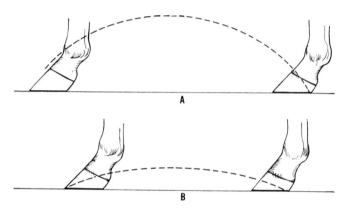

Fig. 4–2.—Normal and Abnormal Arc of Foot Flight.

A, Normal arc of foot flight.

B, Low foot flight caused by lack of flexion in either the fore- or hindlimbs.

If interference of the limbs is suspected, but cannot be seen, the
hoof walls can be coated with chalk and the contact will leave a
mark of chalk on the limb. This can be done for both the fore and
hindlimbs.

Various forms of limb contact are defined as follows:

1. Brushing: This is a general term for light striking, especially
as in forging or interfering.

2. Cross-firing: This is generally confined to pacers and consists
of a "scuffing" on the inside of the diagonal fore and hind feet. It
usually consists of the inside of the hind foot hitting the inside
quarter of the diagonal forefoot.

3. Elbow hitting: This is when the horse hits the elbow with the
shoe of the same limb. It rarely occurs except in those horses with
weighted shoes.

4. Forging: The toe of the hind foot hits the sole area of the
forefoot on the same side.

5. Knee hitting: This is a case of high interference.

6. Interfering: This occurs both in the front and hind feet. It is a striking, anywhere between the coronary band and the cannon, by the opposite foot which is in motion (Fig. 1–9, page 21).

7. Over-reaching: The toe of the hind foot catches the forefoot on the same side, usually on the heel. The hind foot advances more quickly than in forging, stepping on the heels of the forefoot. The toe of the hind foot may step on the heel of the shoe of the forefoot on the same side and cause shoe pulling.

8. Scalping: Here the toe of the front foot hits the hairline at the coronary band or above on the hind foot of the same side. It may hit the anterior face of the pastern or cannon bone.

9. Speedy cutting: Speedy cutting is difficult to determine since it apparently has no positive definition. It may be the same as cross-firing, or it may mean that the outside wall of the hind foot comes up and strikes the medial aspect of the front leg on the same side. Since there is no positive definition, it can literally be defined as any type of limb interference in the fast gait.

Contact problems can occur in horses with good conformation as a result of the type of work; *i.e.*, barrel racing, cutting, pole bending, and reining where the weight is suddenly shifted and the horse may be off balance.

The Hindlimbs.—In observing the movement of the hindlimbs, the arc of the foot flight should be determined (Fig. 4–2). Involvements of the hock and stifle joints reduce the arc of the foot flight and thereby shorten the anterior phase of the stride with a compensating lengthening of the posterior phase. Because of the reciprocal apparatus, incomplete flexion is characteristic of involvement of both the hock and stifle joints. The hock joint is the most common site of lameness and should be inspected first. The toe is worn excessively (dubbed off) in involvement of the hock or stifle, and the horse may kick up dirt or small stones when advancing the limb due to reduced arc of foot flight.

In the hindlimbs when the sound limb strikes the ground, the hip drops on the sound side and the head raises at the same time. The hip on the affected side raises and the head drops when weight is put on the unsound limb. It is best to observe the horse from behind in checking for hip movement.

In involvements of either the fore or hindlimb, the horse should be checked on both rough and smooth surfaces to determine the effect of concussion, and of uneven pressures on the sole.

Examination by Palpation

Following observation of the animal from a distance, close examination of the limbs by palpation and, of course, by visual examination, is in order. A systematic method of palpation should be used so nothing will be overlooked. In palpating, start at the bottom of the foot and make a complete examination of the entire limb.

The Forelimbs.—1. Examination of the bottom of the foot. Determine whether or not there is contraction of the heels. Observe the condition of the frog and determine if the sole appears normal. At this time the sole and frog should be examined with a hoof tester to determine any areas of sensitivity. If the entire sole shows pain upon pressure of a hoof tester, you should consider laminitis, fracture of the third phalanx, and a diffuse pododermatitis from a puncture wound. If the area of sensitivity is localized, you should check for sole bruising, puncture wounds, and separation of the white line (gravel) causing infection. Any separation at the white line, or discoloration of the sole, should be thoroughly explored with a hoof knife until the discoloration disappears or the bottom of the discoloration is found. If a sensitive area is localized in the center third of the frog, navicular disease should be considered, after puncture wounds of the frog have been ruled out. Pain in other areas of the frog may be caused by puncture wounds.

2. Examination of the hoof wall. The hoof wall should be checked for excessive dryness, contraction, cracks, and evenness of wear. Cracks may lead to sensitive laminae, thereby causing lameness. These are most common in the toe and quarter areas of the wall. The shape of the wall should be examined to determine if the hoof is wearing abnormally.

3. Examination of the coronary band. The coronary band should be palpated for increase in heat. This is done by using the back of the hand to compare the coronary region on the affected limb with a sound limb. Increased heat, and a roughening of the hair at the anterior portion of the coronary band, might indicate a developing low ringbone. Drainage at the heel area of the coronary band would indicate a puncture wound in the foot. Drainage in the area of the quarters might indicate quittor.

4. Examination of the lateral cartilages. The cartilages should be examined both with the foot on the ground and with the foot off the ground to determine if calcification has occurred (sidebones).

5. Examination of the pastern area. This area should be examined for change in temperature and swellings that might indicate ringbone. The posterior digital arteries should be palpated, where they lie on the abaxial surfaces of the sesamoid bones, to determine if increased pulsation is present.

6. Examination of the fetlock joint. This joint should be examined for areas of pain on pressure, especially over the sesamoid bones. Distention of the posterior cul-de-sac of the fetlock joint capsule may indicate the presence of a joint disease. This distention occurs between the posterior aspect of the distal end of the cannon bone and the suspensory ligament, and is termed articular windpuffs. This swelling may or may not be indicative of pathology. The joints should be moved with the weight off the limb to check for crepitation and pain on movement. Swelling on the anterior surface of the fetlock joint may indicate osselets.

7

7. Examination of the cannon bone area. This area should be checked on the lateral and medial side for the presence of splints; most commonly found on the medial side. The anterior surface of the cannon bone should be examined for the presence of periostitis (bucked shins). Other abnormalities easily found are usually in the form of traumatic exostoses.

8. Examination of the suspensory ligament. This ligament should be carefully examined by palpation both in the standing position and with the limb flexed. This ligament lies just posterior to the cannon bone. Damage to this structure is most often in the distal one third of the cannon bone where the ligament bifurcates to attach to the sesamoid bones. Pain on pressure, or scar tissue in this structure would indicate pathology.

9. Examination of the inferior check ligament. This joins the tendon of the deep flexor tendon at about the middle of the cannon bone. Damage to this structure can be determined by evidence of pain on pressure over the deep flexor tendon about half way between the carpal and fetlock joints.

10. Examination of the flexor tendons, both superficial and deep. These tendons should be closely examined for tendosynovitis, pain on pressure, and fibrosis. Swelling of the tendon sheath and fibrosis indicate bowed tendon. Swelling of the tendon sheath is most common just above the fetlock joint. This swelling lies between the suspensory ligament and the deep flexor tendon, which differentiates it from articular windpuffs.

11. Examination of the carpus. The carpus should be carefully examined for swellings on the posterior or anterior aspect. Posterior swelling medial to the accessory carpal bone indicates distention of the carpal sheath carrying the flexor tendons. Synovial swellings on the anterior face of the carpus include distention of the joint capsule, swelling of the tendon sheath of the extensor carpi radialis and/or the common extensor tendon, and swelling of the carpal bursa. Swellings of the tendon sheaths and bursa in this area commonly are called hygroma. Firm swellings over the anterior face of the carpus indicates fibrosis and/or exostosis that might be caused by carpitis (popped knee) and/or fracture of one of the carpal bones. The carpal joint should be flexed to determine if movement causes pain or if there is any mechanical limitation to movement. The radial, intermediate and third carpal bones should be palpated while the carpal joint is flexed to determine if swelling indicating fracture is present. The cavities of the radio-carpal and intercarpal joints are usually separated, and careful palpation will determine in which one excess synovial fluid is present (Fig. 4–3).

12. Examination of the soft tissues between the carpus and the elbow. These tissues should be examined carefully for swelling, pain, and puncture wounds.

13. Examination of the elbow and shoulder joints. These joints should be carefully palpated for the presence of pain and crepitation

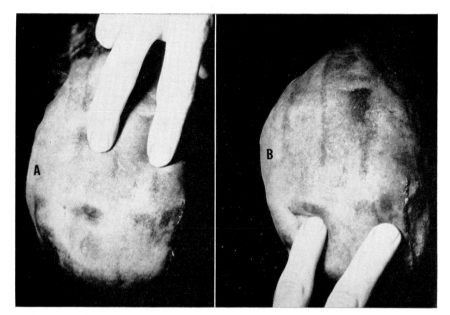

Fig. 4–3.—Palpation of the carpal joints.
A, Palpation of flexed carpal joint with the fingers in the radio-carpal joint space.
B, Palpation of flexed carpus with fingers in the intercarpal joint space.

on movement. The bursa at the point of the shoulder should be checked for bicipital bursitis.

14. The forearm and shoulder and scapular areas should be examined for muscular atrophy indicating a long-standing lameness.

The Hindlimbs.—The hindlimbs are checked in a manner identical to that of the forelimbs, up to the hock joint.

1. The hock joint should be examined carefully for the presence of bog spavin, bone spavin, occult spavin, curb, thoroughpin, and capped hock. Bog spavin swelling is found at the antero-medial aspect of the tarsal joint, or occasionally at the posterior aspect of the joint where the capsule is not limited by surrounding tissues on the medial and lateral side. Thoroughpin is found anterior to the proximal end of the os calcis and is a bilateral distention of the tarsal sheath enclosing the deep flexor tendon of that limb. Bone spavin occurs at the medial aspect of the hock joint and involves the medial aspect of the proximal end of the third metatarsal and the medial side of the third and central tarsal bones. A routine spavin test should be done, in hindlimb lameness, by holding the hindlimb in flexion for one or two minutes (Fig. 6–93, page 318). Immediately following this flexion the animal should be moved; if the lameness is exaggerated, the test is considered to be indicative of occult or bone spavin.

2. The stifle joint should be examined carefully for the presence of upward fixation of the patella and for gonitis. Force the patella

upward and outward with the hand. If the limb can be locked in extension while the patella is held in this manner, the horse is subject to upward fixation of the patella. If soft tissue crepitation can be palpated while forcing the patella over the trochlea of the femur, the possibility of chondromalacia of the patella must be considered.

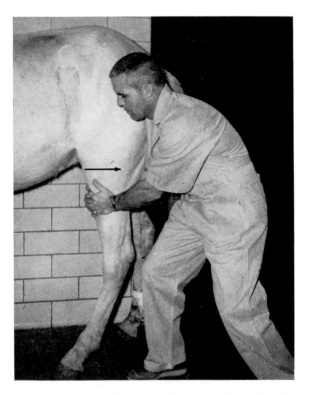

FIG. 4–4. — A test for rupture of a cruciate ligament of the stifle joint. The hands should be locked around the anterior face of the tibia, and exerting quick pressure, the tibia should be pulled backwards, as indicated by arrow.

Inflammation of the stifle joint (gonitis) can be detected by a pouching and thickening of the joint capsule between the patellar ligaments. Rupture of the collateral or cruciate ligaments of this joint should be checked by manipulation of the limb. This is done by abduction and adduction of the limb, and by locking the hands around the anterior aspect of the proximal end of the tibia and producing a sudden movement of the tibia by jerking the hands posteriorly (Fig. 4–4). If any movement is present at all between the femur and tibia, one of the ligaments of the joint is torn.

3. All soft tissue over the stifle and hip areas should be examined for pathological changes, including atrophy.

4. The hip joint should be examined by palpation and by observation of the gait. Involvements of this joint produce a supporting leg lameness and many times an accompanying swinging leg lameness. When the round ligament of the hip joint has ruptured, the stifle joint and toe will point outward, while the hock goes inward. This same appearance will also be present in complete luxation of the joint. This typical attitude cannot be assumed unless the round ligament is ruptured. The femoral head may still be in the acetabulum, but due to the increased range of motion, severe osteoarthritis will be produced.

5. The pelvis should be examined by rectal examination for the presence of fractures. Manipulate the tuber coxae and tuber ischii, while one hand is in the rectum, to determine if any movement is produced at the symphysis pubis or at other potential fracture sites (Fig. 4–5). The sacro-iliac and lumbo-sacral junctions

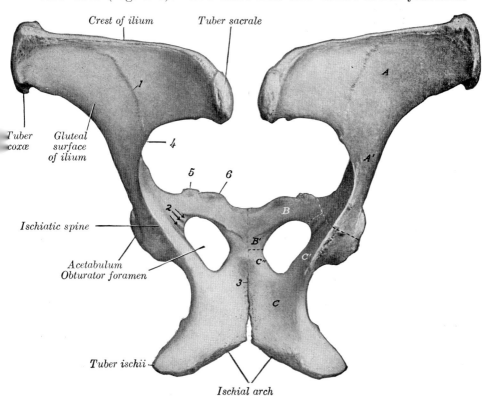

FIG. 4–5.—Ossa Coxarum of horse; dorsal view.

A, Wing; A', shaft of ilium; B, acetabular, B', symphyseal branch of pubis; C, body, C', acetabular branch (or shaft), C", symphyseal branch, of ischium; 1, gluteal line; 2, grooves for obturator nerve and vessels; 3, symphysis pelvis; 4, greater sciatic notch; 5, iliopectineal eminence; 6, pubic tubercle. Dotted lines indicate primitive separation of three bones, which are potential fracture sites. (Sisson and Grossman, *Anatomy of Animals*, courtesy of W. B. Saunders Company.)

also should be examined rectally at this time. Pain produced by rectal pressure over these areas or the ilio-psoas muscles may indicate damage in these areas. If necessary, the horse should be walked a few steps while the hand is in the rectum to see if motion indicates a possible fracture or other pathological changes. Fractures are often accompanied by hematomas that are palpable. Separation of the symphysis pubis may not be accompanied by hematoma. If there is separation of the sacro-iliac junction, no hematoma, only crepitation, will be present.

Special Considerations

Hyperthermia is best checked by testing the area with the back of the hand and by comparing this with the opposite limb. One should bear in mind that an area that has been clipped will feel warmer than an unclipped area, and the sun's rays on one limb will make it feel warmer.

Crepitation may be produced in normal joints, and also there is more movement in the pastern and coffin joints of some horses than in others. One should always compare the lame limb with the opposite limb to determine if abnormalities are present.

Areas of both limbs may appear to show pain on pressure so it must be determined whether the animal is actually exhibiting pain or, through nervousness, is pulling away. Young animals are more difficult to examine than horses that are well disciplined. Some mature horses, though, have nervous temperaments which hamper examination procedures, so some allowances should be made for nervousness or fear. Tranquilization may be necessary, or at least helpful, in conducting a thorough examination.

A person cannot judge the seriousness of enlargements in the limbs by palpation alone, but one must be able to evaluate carefully the importance of these swellings and their proximity to articular, or other structures.

Special Methods of Examination

Hoof Tester.—The use of the hoof tester has been discussed in the examination of the sole. This is not necessarily a special method of examination but is certainly one that always should be used. One cannot begin to diagnose lameness without using a good hoof tester of sufficient size and construction that considerable force can be exerted (Fig. 4–6).

Local Nerve Blocks.—These are of considerable aid in determining the site of some types of lamenesses. They are also valuable in proving a diagnosis to an owner who is not convinced. There are times when a positive diagnosis of a lameness cannot be made. In this case, local anesthesia can be used in a systematic manner to pinpoint the site of lameness. Once the site is located, a detailed examination of the suspected area can be made clinically and radiographically. It is helpful to know the area of pathologic change

Fig. 4-6.—Hoof tester made from plow steel. A hoof tester must be well constructed, and of large enough size to meet the standards necessary.

so that excessive expenditure for radiographs is avoided. In the long run, there is a considerable saving of time to the practitioner when local anesthesia is used because the lameness can be pinpointed more quickly.

In all cases, local anesthesia should be done with a minimal amount of local anesthetic because of residual tissue irritation. In addition, local anesthesia should always be done as an aseptic procedure. To prevent possibility of infection resulting from injection, the area should be clipped closely, shaved when practical, scrubbed with soap and water, and skin antiseptics applied. When joints are injected, the skin should be shaved.

RECOMMENDED ANESTHETIC SOLUTIONS.—In most cases the best agents for local anesthesia are 2 per cent Lidocaine Hcl*, 1 per cent Hexylcaine Hcl†, or 2 per cent Mepivacaine Hcl‡. These solutions are very potent and have rapid effect. They are also quite irritating and minimal amounts should be used. Two per cent procaine hydrochloride can be used but is not as effective as the above drugs. Procaine has no topical effect and is of no value in intra-articular injection for diagnosis of lameness.

* Xylocaine, Astra Laboratories
† Cyclaine, Sharpe & Dohme Laboratories
‡ Carbocaine, Winthrop Laboratories

Sterile needles, sterile syringes and sterile anesthetic solutions should always be used. In no case should the same needle be used on more than one horse without sterilization between usages.

DIAGNOSTIC LOCAL ANESTHESIA TECHNIQUES IN THE FORELIMB. — Once the veterinarian has satisfied himself that he has not been able to determine the lameness in the limb by either clinical examination or by hoof tester examination, the following methods of local anesthesia can be used to aid in localizing the lameness.

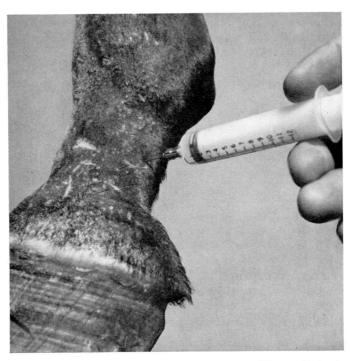

FIG. 4–7.—Blocking the lateral posterior digital nerve. The needle is placed just anterior to the tendon of the superficial digital flexor tendon. The medial nerve is blocked in an identical way. The needle is a 25-gauge, ⅝ inch needle. (Courtesy Norden Laboratories.)

1. The medial and lateral posterior digital nerves are anesthetized (Fig. 4–7) with 2 to 3 cc. of anesthetic solution and a 25-gauge, ⅝-inch needle. These nerves are located just anterior to the superficial flexor tendon. The anesthesia is done about one-half way between the fetlock and the coronary band. The needle is inserted just in front of the superficial flexor tendon. This block desensitizes the posterior one-third of the foot. If the horse is sound after anesthesia of these two nerves, such things as navicular disease, fracture of a wing of the third phalanx, puncture wounds of the heel, corns, and other involvements of the posterior one-third of the foot can be considered.

2. If, following the posterior digital nerve blocks, the horse is still unsound, a ring block can be done just above the proximal interphalangeal (pastern) joint as shown in Figure 4–8. In this case, following anesthesia of the medial and lateral posterior digital nerves, additional anesthetic solution is injected subcutaneously around the anterior surface of the first phalanx above the proximal interphalangeal joint, and over the flexor tendon area posteriorly. This ring block desensitizes the foot below this line. This desensitiza-

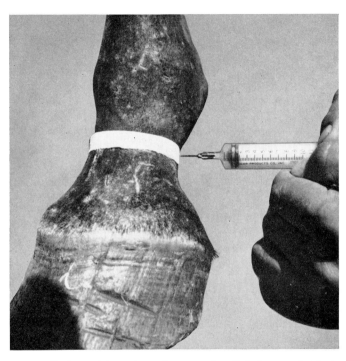

Fig. 4–8.—Needle in position where the posterior digital nerve is blocked. The line of white tape indicates the area injected to complete the ring block above the pastern joint. (Courtesy Norden Laboratories.)

tion will include the distal interphalangeal (coffin) joint and proximal interphalangeal (pastern) joint, provided the block is done above the latter joint. If the horse is sound following this procedure, the lameness has been localized to a point below the ring block. Attention can then be given to defining the type of lameness, using radiography if necessary.

3. The next step in localizing a lameness that has not responded to either blocking the posterior digital nerves or to a ring block in the pastern area, is anesthesia of the medial and lateral volar nerves 2 to 3 inches above the metacarpophalangeal (fetlock) joint (Fig. 4–9). Two to three cc. of anesthetic solution is deposited over each of the

medial and lateral volar nerves. These nerves lie between the suspensory ligament and deep digital flexor tendon, just anterior to the deep digital flexor tendon. The nerves are relatively deep but can be reached by a $\frac{1}{2}$ inch, 25-gauge needle. If the horse is sound after this block, but not sound after the ring block in the pastern area as described above, the area of the fetlock joint can be examined for lameness. However, it is a common experience to find that intra-articular lesions of the metacarpophalangeal (fetlock) joint do not respond to a simple volar nerve block.[1]

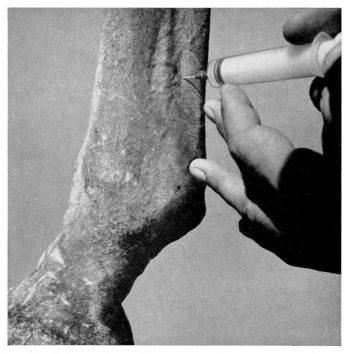

Fig. 4-9.—Needle in position to block the lateral volar nerve just in front of the tendon of the deep digital flexor. The medial nerve is blocked in the same fashion on the medial side of the leg. (Courtesy Norden Laboratories.)

4. If the horse is unsound after blocking the two volar nerves, a ring block is done as shown in Figure 4–10. Approximately 10 cc. of a local anesthetic is necessary to complete the ring block. The area between the two blocked volar nerves and over the flexor tendons is injected subcutaneously. Special attention is given to blocking the area where the second and fourth metacarpal bones join the third metacarpal bone. At this point, there is often a small nerve present that must be anesthetized to obtain a complete ring block. If, following this ring block, the horse is sound but did not respond to the pastern ring block, a detailed examination for articular lesions of the metacarpo-phalangeal (fetlock) joint should be

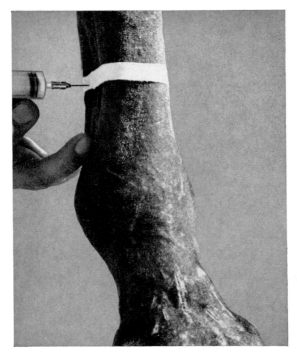

FIG. 4–10. — Needle in position over the medial volar nerve. The white tape indicates the line blocked to complete a ring block above the fetlock joint. (Courtesy Norden Laboratories.)

done. These lesions include small chip fractures of the first phalanx (Fig 4–11) and osselets. Other lesions include longitudinal fractures of the third metacarpal bone and first phalanx (Fig. 4–12). These fractures can be present with minimal swelling and very little lameness. Lesions of the sesamoid bones are also considered. Further proof of an intra-articular lesion can be obtained by injecting the distended volar pouch of the metacarpo-phalangeal joint capsule. Injection of this pouch is done on the lateral side of the joint between the suspensory ligament and the bone at the level of the sesamoid bones (Fig. 11–3). A mixture of 4 cc. of local anesthetic solution and 2 cc. of a corticoid solution are used.

5. If, following the ring block above the fetlock joint, the horse is still unsound, the carpal joints can be anesthetized. There are three joints in the carpus composed of the radio-carpal joint, the intercarpal joint, and the carpo-metacarpal joint. In most cases the joint fluid that is present in the radio-carpal joint is separate from that enclosed by the intercarpal and carpo-metacarpal joints.[20] This means that to effectively block the carpal joints a local anesthetic will have to be injected into both the radio-carpal and intercarpal joints as shown in Figures 4–13 and 4–14. Detailed examina-

tion will quite often reveal distention of a joint capsule or thickening of soft tissues over these joints when pathological changes are present.

After proper preparation of the skin area, the carpal joint is flexed and a small skin bleb is made with a local anesthetic using a 25 gauge, $\frac{1}{2}$ inch needle. An 18 or 20 gauge, 2 inch needle is then placed into the intercarpal joint (Fig. 4–13). Five cc. of 2 per cent Xylocaine or other suitable topical anesthetic is placed in the joint. The author includes a corticoid solution in the injection. If there

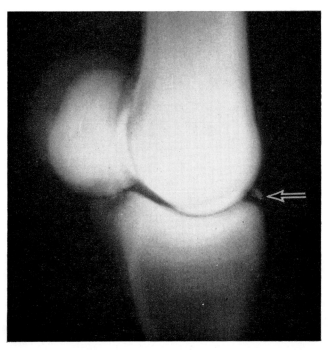

Fig. 4–11.—Radiograph of a small chip fracture from the first phalanx (arrow) This type of lesion is not usually desensitized by an ordinary medial and lateral volar block. A ring block above the fetlock joint must be completed to effectively desensitize this lesion. It can also be desensitized by an intra-articular injection of the metacarpo-phalangeal joint (Fig. 11–3). (Courtesy J.A.V.M.A.)

is no response to blocking the intercarpal joint, the radio-carpal joint is blocked in a similar manner (Fig. 4–14). Flexing the carpus greatly aids passage of the needle directly into the joint.

One should allow fifteen minutes for the local anesthetic to have a topical effect in the joint, whereas blocking a nerve locally, the effect should be noticed within five to ten minutes. One of the local anesthetics mentioned above is recommended to be used in a joint since procaine has no topical anesthetic qualities. Some inflammatory effects may be noted following injection of a joint but they are minimal and if the injection has been done under aseptic conditions, no problems

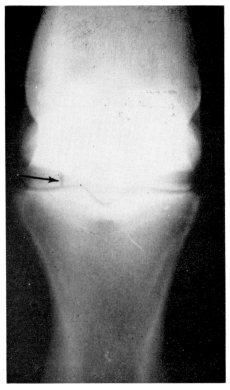

Fig. 4–12.—An example of a fracture of the third metacarpal bone into the articulation of the metacarpo-phalangeal (fetlock) joint. This type of lesion may show minimal swelling and the pain may not disappear following an ordinary volar nerve block. A ring block above the fetlock joint may be required to localize the pain to this area.

will result. A corticoid included in the injection will minimize inflammatory effects. Most horses show no effect at all or actually an improvement of the lameness because of the steroid, provided the site of lameness is localized to this area.

If soundness results following one or both of these injections, osteoarthritis and carpal bone fractures are considered as possibilities and radiographs of the carpus are taken.

6. The entire carpal area and lower leg can be anesthetized by blocking the median, ulnar, and musculocutaneous nerves. This procedure can be used to localize the lameness to the shoulder and elbow when other blocks have failed. These blocks eliminate the lower limb as the site of lameness and one would then consider the elbow and shoulder areas as the cause of lameness.

7. For other lesions that may be causing lameness such as bony enlargements on the metacarpal bones (splints) or swellings that are suspected of causing lameness, an infusion of local anesthetic around

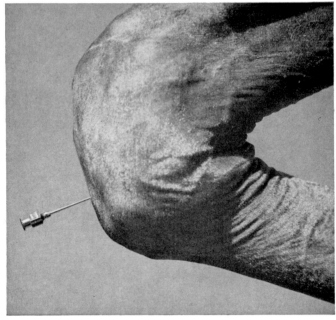

needle in just
medial to mid-line
clip or shave hair
in scalpel
surgical scrub
alcohol
iodine

Fig. 4-13.—Flexed left carpus showing 18 gauge, 2 inch needle in position in the intercarpal joint. (Courtesy Norden Laboratories.)

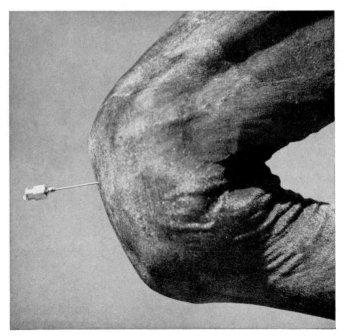

Fig. 4-14.—Flexed left carpus showing 18-gauge, 2 inch needle in position in the radio-carpal joint. (Courtesy Norden Laboratories.)

the lesion down to the periosteum will produce soundness if the lesion is the cause of lameness. In this way, a specific lesion such as a possible fractured splint or metacarpal bone lesions can be anesthetized, and if the lesion is causing lameness, the horse will be sound provided the local anesthetic is carried down to the periosteum.

DIAGNOSTIC LOCAL ANESTHESIA TECHNIQUES IN THE HINDLIMB. —In the hindlimb, the posterior digital block, pastern ring block, volar (plantar) nerve block and the fetlock ring block are the same. When the tarsal (hock) joint is reached, other techniques are employed. If a bone spavin is suspected, local injection of the spavin area with a local anesthetic and a 20 gauge, 2 inch needle will often alleviate the signs. The needle is pushed directly into the spavin area until it reaches bone and approximately 8 cc. of anesthetic solution are used to block this area. If a bone spavin is obviously present and if the block relieves it, one can be certain that the spavin is the cause of lameness. Another block that may anesthetize the hock joint sufficiently to be of diagnostic value is anesthesia of the tibial and deep peroneal nerves as described by Frank.[11] The joint cavity of the hock can also be anesthetized in the tibio-tarsal joint for suspected lesions. The injection site used is medial or lateral to the saphenous vein, directly over the joint capsule (Fig. 11–12). This is not a good block to diagnose bone spavin because the distal intertarsal and tarso-metatarsal joints do not communicate with the tibio-tarsal joint.

The stifle joint may be anesthetized by infusing a local anesthetic, but is somewhat complicated by the separation of the capsule of the femorotibial joint and the femoropatellar pouch. The stifle joint of the horse is composed of two principal joints: the femoropatellar and femorotibial joints. The femorotibial joint is divided into medial and lateral joint cavities. The femoropatellar joint cavity communicates with the medial femorotibial joint cavity by a slit-like opening. A similar but smaller opening may exist between the femoropatellar pouch and the lateral femorotibial joint cavity,[21] but is not consistent. The femoropatellar pouch can be injected and one can expect anesthesia of the medial femorotibial joint capsule but not the lateral femorotibial joint capsule.

The femoropatellar pouch is usually most easily infused between the middle and lateral patellar ligaments (Fig. 11–11) but may be infused between the middle and medial patellar ligaments at the ventral margin of the patella. Ten cc. of 2 per cent Xylocaine or other suitable local anesthetic are infused into the femoropatellar pouch for diagnostic purposes. A corticosteroid is included with the local anesthetic to minimize any inflammatory effects of the local anesthetic. If the lesion in the joint is subpatellar, this block will usually relieve signs of lameness. If the lesion is in the medial femorotibial articulation, the femoropatellar block will usually anesthetize this area. Since lesions of this joint are most commonly located in the medial side, this is an important block. If desired, the medial femorotibial joint may be injected between the medial patellar ligament and the medial collateral ligament of the stifle joint.

The lateral femorotibial joint can be injected between the lateral patellar ligament and the lateral collateral ligament of the stifle joint. Since the femoropatellar joint cavity communicates with the lateral femorotibial joint cavity in only 18 to 25 per cent of the stifle joints, it will be necessary to inject this joint cavity directly.[21] An 18 gauge, 2 inch needle is used to inject the cavities of the stifle joint after anesthetizing the skin with a 25 gauge, $\frac{1}{2}$ inch needle.

Radiography.—Radiographs of suspected pathological areas are invaluable in diagnosis and prognosis. It is sometimes impossible to determine if some hard swellings are bony or fibrous in nature without the use of radiographs. Radiographs are also extremely helpful in determining the proximity of new bone growth to a joint surface. Some fractures of the carpus and the third phalanx are nearly impossible to detect without the use of radiographs, however, radiographs can never replace careful examination and palpation for disease of the soft tissues. See Chapter 12 for a complete discussion of radiological technique.

Thermography as a Diagnostic Aid

A thermograph has been described as a heat camera[27] because it records an image—a thermogram of the skin temperature distribution pattern. The camera scans the area at which it is directed collecting infrared radiation and converting it into visible light which exposes a polaroid film. The relative darkness or lightness of a given region of film negative is proportional to temperature of the corresponding region of skin so that temperature distribution of an area of skin can easily be visualized. Delahanty[28] described experiences with this machine in horses. His conclusions indicated that there are possible indications for use of thermography as a diagnostic aid for lameness. However, the cost of the unit, the difficulties with restraint and the length of time (6 min.) required for examination make improvements necessary before it will receive wide acceptance. It is obvious that an aid of this nature could be very helpful in obscure lamenesses. The use of thermography would show inflammed areas in the limb which might go unnoticed by usual examination procedures. Thermography can also be used on other areas of the body besides the limbs. At the present time, it could probably be safely stated that it is somewhat impractical but with further improvements in the instrument, making possible a more rapid examination, plus possible cost reduction, might make its use more widespread.

REFERENCES

1. ADAMS, O. R.: Chip Fractures of the First Phalanx and the Metacarpophalangeal (Fetlock) Joint. J.A.V.M.A., *148*, No. 4, p. 360, Feb. 15, 1966.
2. ————: Local Anesthesia as an Aid in Lameness Diagnosis. Norden News, January 1966.

3. BLAKELY, R. F.: Radiographic Diagnosis of Injury to the Foot of a Horse. Illinois, Vet., 2 (3), 69, Dec. 1959.

4. BRENNAN, B. F.: Symptoms of Hind Limb Lameness in Standardbreds. Proc. A.A.E.P. Convention, 194–96, 1962.

5. CARLSON, WM. D.: Veterinary Radiology, Philadelphia, Lea & Febiger, 1961.

6. CHENOT, ALGER: Clinical Study of Lameness. Amer. Vet. Rev., 28, 806, 1904–05.

7. CRAWFORD, H. C.: Radiography—Its Limitations as an Aid to the Diagnostician of Lameness. No. Amer. Vet., 13, 39, 1932.

8. DAUBIGNY, F. T.: Halting or Lameness in the Horse. J.A.V.M.A., 49, 648, 1916.

9. FOWLER, W. J. R.: Diagnosis and Treatment of Lameness. Canad. J. Comp. Med., 3, 91, 1939.

10. Ibid, 4, 249, 1940.

11. FRANK, E. R.: Veterinary Surgery, 7th ed., Minneapolis, Burgess Publishing Co., 1964.

12. GIBSON, S. J.: Lameness in Horses. Canad. J. Comp. Med., 9, 103, 1945.

13. KIERNAN, JOHN: Hints on Horseshoeing. Office of Library of Congress, Washington, D. C.

14. LA CROIX, J. V.: Lameness of the Horse. Vet. Practitioners, Series No. 1, Am. J. Vet. Med., 1916.

15. LIAUTARD, A. F. A.: Lameness of Horses, New York, Wm. R. Jacobs Co., 1888.

16. McKILLIP, M. H.: Lameness, Some Basic Principles of Diagnosis. Am. J. Vet. Med., 13, 387, 1918.

17. Merck Veterinary Manual, 2nd ed. Rahway, N. J., Merck & Co., 1961.

18. O'CONNOR, J. J.: Dollar's Veterinary Surgery, 4th ed., London, Bailliere, Tindall & Cox, 1952.

19. VAN PELT, R. W.: Arthrocentesis and Injection of the Equine Tarsus. J.A.V.M.A., 148, No. 4, p. 367, Feb. 15, 1966.

20. VAN PELT, R. W.: Intra-articular Injection of the Equine Carpus and Fetlock. J.A.V.M.A., 140, 1181, 1962.

21. ————: Intra-articular Injection of the Equine Stifle for Therapeutic and Diagnostic Purposes. J.A.V.M.A., 147, 490, No. 5, Sept. 1, 1965.

22. WAY, CASSIUS: Lameness and Arthritis in Horses. No. Am. Vet. 16, 19, 1935.

23. WHEAT, J. D.: Detection of the Site of Lameness. Proc. 8th Annual A.A.E.P. Convention, 198–202, 1962.

24. WILLIAMS, W.: Veterinary Surgery, New York, Wm. R. Jenkins, 1891.

25. WYMAN, W. E. A.: Diagnosis of Lameness in the Horse. New York, W. R. Jenkins Co., 1898.

26. GAUBAUX, A. and BARRIER, G.: The Exterior of the Horse, 2nd ed. Philadelphia, J. B. Lippincott Co., 1892.

27. BARNES, R. BOWLING: Thermography of the Human Body. Science, 140, 870, May 24, 1963.

28. DELAHANTY, D. D.: Thermography in Equine Medicine. J.A.V.M.A., 147 (3), 235, Aug. 1, 1965.

29. GERSHON-COHEN, J. et al.: Medical Thermography: A Summary of Current Status. Radiologic Clinics of No. Am. 3 (3), Dec. 1965.

Diseases of bones, joints and related structures

Chapter 5

ARTHRITIS

ARTHRITIS can be simply defined as inflammation of a joint. This inflammation may involve any or all of the components of a joint, which include the bones forming the joint, the articular cartilages, the joint capsule, and the associated ligaments. The ligaments of a joint consist of the periarticular or collateral ligaments, and, when present, the intra-articular ligaments. The shoulder joint of the horse is the only joint without collateral or intra-articular ligaments.

The joint capsule is composed of an outer fibrous layer, and an inner, or synovial, layer which secretes the synovial fluid. The synovial fluid, which acts as lubricant to the joint, increases in the presence of inflammation. The capsule's fibrous outer portion is strong, and when pulled from its bony attachment, periostitis and new bone growth may result.

Articular cartilage consists of three layers: a narrow calcified base layer bound to the subchondral bone, a broad intermediate layer of great shock-absorbing capacity due to its high content of water, and a very narrow superficial layer of tangential collagen which resists shear and joint motion.[26]

Cartilage nutrition is by diffusion through and across the cartilage from two capillary beds; i.e., the capillary bed of the synovium and the capillary bed of the two bone ends. The rate of diffusion varies in a cycle controlled by use and rest. There is an associated variation in thickness of articular cartilage with activity.

Destruction of the majority of articular cartilage in a joint usually results in ankylosis of that joint. Articular cartilage is usually described as being unable to regenerate. However, if the irritant causing cartilage degeneration is removed, the cartilage has remarkable healing qualities. For example, a chip fracture in the carpal joint may cause considerable damage to the articular surface of the third or radial carpal bones. Removal of the chip fracture allows healing to occur, and in many cases, the horse returns to complete soundness. Subsequent examination of the joint several years later reveals a well-healed articular surface.

In horses, the progression of pathological events leading to total destruction of the joint begins with microscopic changes in the cartilage of the bearing surface.[37] Race horses generate many millions of foot pounds of force per mile and the wear and tear produced both in support and propulsion contributes to the production of osteoarthritis.

According to Sippel[65] the cartilage loses its translucence, becomes more or less discolored, and with use is worn away in fragments of microscopic to several millimeters in size. Scoring or grooving of the cartilage is often observable before the bone is exposed. As subchondral surfaces are laid bare, eburnation becomes marked. Periarticular proliferation of bone commonly accompanies this phase. As more bone is uncovered the periarticular reaction accelerates. In joints which retain motion, the bare bone may become scored with wear. In an immobilized joint, peri- and intraarticular ankylosis progresses until the joint is solidified. Capsular changes vary directly with the speed of progression and with the stage of the disease. Fibrosis may be very extensive in the late stages.

Arthritis may be either primary or secondary. Examples of primary arthritis are trauma to a joint, or direct penetration into a joint cavity by a foreign body. Examples of secondary arthritis are disease of the bone, such as rickets, or localization of a systemic infection in a joint. In other words, primary arthritis is a disease of the joint itself, while secondary arthritis results from localization of a metabolic disease or systemic infection in a joint, or joints, or secondary to poor conformation which causes trauma to a joint, or joints.

Enlargement of a joint can be the result of several causes. An effort should be made to determine the structures involved in the swelling and this determination usually can be made by careful clinical and radiological examinations. The following are causes of joint enlargement, either singularly, or in any combination:

1. Enlargement of the bones forming the joint.
2. Thickening of the joint capsule.
3. Distention of the joint capsule with synovia or other fluid.
4. Swelling of the periarticular tissues.

METHODS OF CLASSIFYING ARTHRITIS

Arthritis Can Be Classified According to Activity as Follows

Acute.—Acute forms of arthritis cause severe inflammation of the joint and thus are self-evident. They may resolve leaving a normal joint or develop into a chronic arthritis.

Chronic.—Chronic forms of arthritis consist of a low-grade joint inflammation which may exhibit acute flareups. Chronic arthritis seldom leaves a horse without permanently damaging the joint.

Classification by Type

Following are the main classifications of arthritis, by *type,* which are applicable to horses: (It should be remembered that one type may progress or regress into another type and that then it must be reclassified. For example, a suppurative arthritis may lead to ankylosis of the joint, at which time it must be reclassified as ankylosing or adhesive arthritis.)

1. *Serous Arthritis.*—Serous arthritis, commonly of traumatic origin, is characterized by an inflammation of the synovial membrane with increased synovia, which causes increased capsular pressure and swelling. Initially, the cartilages and ligaments usually are not seriously involved. If prolonged, though, it can lead to erosion of the joint cartilage and to osteoarthritis.

2. *Suppurative or Infectious Arthritis* (Fig. 5–1).—This is an infection of the joint characterized by distention of the joint capsule with pus. The infecting organisms enter the joint through a wound of the joint capsule, or by means of the blood and/or lymph streams. The joint cartilages and underlying bone may be destroyed, leading to ankylosis of the joint or if the infection is overcome, osteoarthritis will result. Some organisms do not form pus, although the arthritis is still of an infectious type. Radiographs usually reveal the presence of new bone growth in the joint, caused by the periostitis produced by the infection. In addition, radiographs show a widened joint space from destruction of cartilage and bone after the disease has been present for some time.

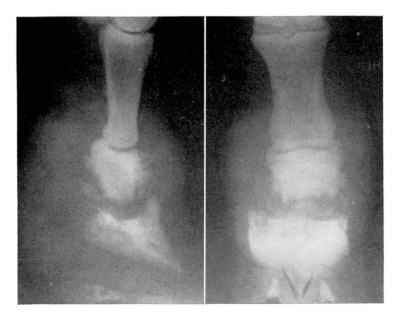

Fɪɢ. 5–1.—Infectious arthritis and osteomyelitis in a horse. The animal was deeply cut by a barbed wire. It was treated with antibiotics, but infectious arthritis developed. There is extensive destruction of the cartilage and adjacent bone. The joint space appears much widened which is typical of infectious arthritis and osteomyelitis. There is secondary new bone proliferation involving the second phalanx. (Carlson, *Veterinary Radiology*, Lea & Febiger.)

3. *Osteoarthrits (Hypertrophic and/or Degenerative Arthritis)* (Fig. 5–2).—Osteoarthritis, which results from a "wearing" of the joint cartilages, is characterized by degeneration and hypertrophy of the bone and cartilage, with a thickening of the synovial membrane. Radiographically, osteoarthritis is characterized by uneven joint spaces (Fig. 5–2). Variable amounts of "lipping" and hypertrophic new bone growth around the joint are present. Sclerosis of adjacent bone may be evident. In severe cases there will be varying degrees of ankylosis because of the hypertrophic bone growth. A joint space usually can be identified, even though there may be much new bone growth around the joint. Ringbone of the pastern joint and bone spavin of the hock may be exceptions, since joint spaces may be obliterated in osteoarthritis in these areas (Figs. 5–3 and 5–10). Osteoarthritis mainly occurs in older horses, and usually is a manifestation of chronic arthritis, especially if caused by some form of trauma. "Wearing" of the joints occurs with age, so older horses often show "lipping" of the joints, which is a form of osteoarthritis. Osteoarthritis can be the result of other types of arthritis, *i.e.* serous arthritis.

4. *Ankylosing or Adhesive Arthritis* (Figs. 5–3 and 5–4).—Ankylosing arthritis is characterized by degeneration and ulceration of the

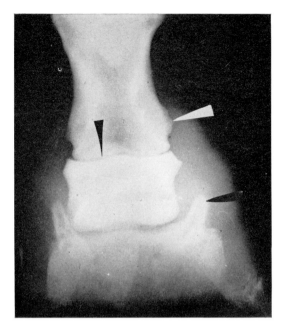

FIG. 5-2.—Osteoarthritis. Note decreased joint space of the pastern as indicated by the upper dark arrow. Careful observation will also reveal "lipping" on the medial and lateral edges of the proximal end of the second phalanx as the result of wearing of the joint. The light arrow shows an area of new bone growth resulting from injury to a collateral ligament of the pastern (High ringbone). The lower, dark arrow indicates sidebone.

articular cartilages, and erosion and flattening of the underlying bone. Around the periphery of the joint usually there is extensive osseous proliferation which leads to ankylosis of the joint. This may be the result of a suppurative arthritis or severe osteoarthritis. Eventually, no radiographic evidence of a joint space will be visible.

5. *Villous Arthritis.*—This is characterized by finger-like growths from the synovial layer of the joint capsule. These villae can result from chronic inflammation in serous or other forms of arthritis. (Villous arthritis is not a satisfactory classification because villae are a *result* of, and not a *cause* or *type* of, arthritis.)

Classification by Etiology

The types of arthritis listed above are often used to describe the following etiological classification:

1. *Infectious Arthritis of Proven Etiology* (Fig. 5-4).—Navel ill (joint ill) is the primary consideration in this classification. The joint involvement is secondary to a septicemia that usually enters through the navel of the newborn foal. The joints may or may not develop suppurative exudate, depending upon the organism in-

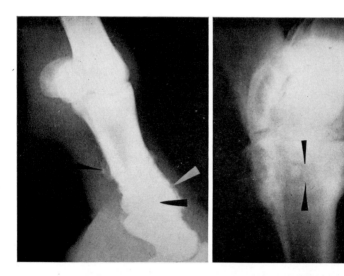

FIG. 5–3   FIG. 5–4

FIG. 5–3.—Ankylosing arthritis of the pastern joint as the result of articular high ring-bone. The upper dark arrow indicates new bone growth on the volar aspect of the first phalanx. The light arrow in front indicates new bone growth at the joint space of the pastern on the anterior surface of the first and second phalanges. The lower dark arrow indicates the area of the former joint space, now obliterated.

FIG. 5–4.—Ankylosing arthritis of the hock joint resulting from infectious arthritis. The dark arrows indicate ankylosis of the intertarsal and tarso-metatarsal joints. The top, light arrow, indicates new bone growth on the tibial tarsal bone; the lower, light arrow, indicates new bone growth on the anterior surface of the central and third tarsal bones.

volved. *Shigella equirulis, Streptococci,* and *Escherichia coli* seem to be the organisms most commonly incriminated in this disease. In some cases foals develop purulent arthritis after they have recovered from an acute intestinal Salmonella infection.[60] *Streptococcus equi* will cause suppuration, while *Escherichia coli* will not. Multiple joints are involved in this form of arthritis.

If the infection is overcome, the joints are predisposed to osteo-arthritis and/or recurrence of infection. Infection can enter a joint by way of the blood stream, through a penetrating wound or by extension of infection from a local septic process.

2. *Probable Infectious Arthritis, Etiology Unproven.*—This is a problematical situation in some cases. Arthritis occasionally appears during an infectious disease, localizing in one or more joints. In such a case, the arthritis would be suspected of being infectious in origin, but often it is difficult to prove the etiological factor, or factors.

Periarticular arthritis of suspected infectious origin is not un-common (Fig. 5–5). This type of arthritis most often involves the

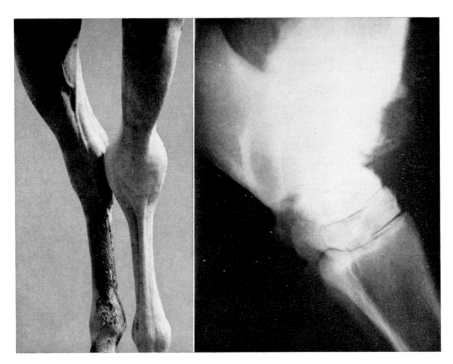

FIG. 5–5.—Periarticular arthritis of infectious origin. The picture of the clinical case on the left shows involvement of the left hock. The disease starts with diffuse swelling of the periarticular structures and eventually works its way into the joint leaving either a severe osteoarthritis or ankylosis of the joint. The radiograph on the right shows the same hock. Note the extensive bone changes on the distal end of the tibia and tibial tarsal bone. There are also periosteal changes on the anterior aspect of the central and third tarsal bones.

hock joint and often it is a year before the final evaluation can be made. The joint enlarges and lameness is present. Initially the swelling appears to involve only the periarticular structures, but progressively the joint itself becomes enlarged. The final result is a joint that shows typical bony changes of infectious arthritis, and ankylosis may occur. In others, the joint may be functional as long as the horse is not used heavily, but permanent swelling of the periarticular tissues and radiographic changes in the bone persist. The source of infection appears to be hematogenous, and may follow an injury such as a sprain of the joint.

3. *Rickets.* (*Metabolic Bone Disease*).—Signs of rickets occur in horses up to three years of age; however, foals between six months and one year most commonly are affected (Figs. 5–6 and 5–7). In older horses, osteoporosis can occur, which is the result of calcium or phosphorus deficiency in mature horses.

Rickets of horses is primarily a disease of the epiphyses rather than the joint itself. However, arthritis of the carpal, pastern, fet-

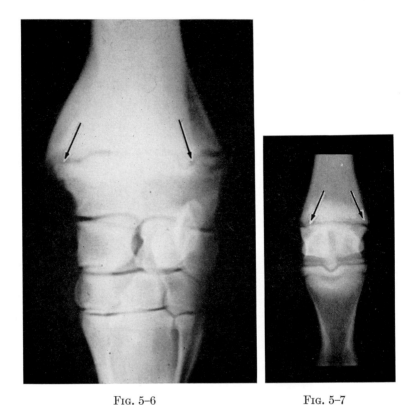

FIG. 5–6   FIG. 5–7

FIG. 5–6.—Anterior-posterior radiograph of the carpus of a foal which has rickets. The arrow indicates a ragged and widened epiphyseal line. Also note the enlarged epiphysis of the radius.

FIG. 5–7.—Anterior-posterior view of the fetlock joint of a foal which has rickets. Arrows point to a ragged and enlarged epiphyseal line at the distal end of the third metacarpal bone.

lock and hock joints may occur. The arthritis of these joints is usually due to stresses caused by conformational changes resulting from epiphyseal changes in the bone. Rickets is a metabolic bone disease resulting from a deficiency of calcium, phosphorus, vitamin D, vitamin C and/or vitamin A deficiencies. A deficiency of any one, or combination of these elements can apparently cause the condition. Clinical study has led this author to believe that adequate levels of vitamin A and/or carotene are essential for proper metabolism of calcium and/or phosphorus. An adequate level of phosphorus is also essential for the proper absorption of vitamin A and carotene.[20] Many rations for horses that are high in protein and composed primarily of grain may contain practically no vitamin A. Also, vitamin A deficiency causes a rough and lusterless hair coat. It is not uncommon for both young and adult horses to have pica appetite—chewing on fences, gates or other wood objects when a deficiency of one or more of the above elements exists.

Some contend that this disease is primarily an epiphysitis and not related to mineral deficiency.[58] However, although there is an epiphysitis present, it is the contention of this author that the disease is initiated by a mineral and/or vitamin imbalance. The deviation of limbs must be initiated by some process and not merely by exercise. Radiographs reveal that the greatest area of epiphysitis is on the medial aspect of the epiphysis in medial deviation of the carpal joints. This is where the least stress is occurring after deviation begins. The compression of the lateral portion of the epiphyses

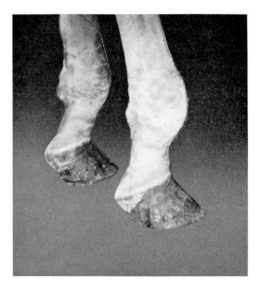

Fig. 5–8.—"Cocked" ankles caused by contraction of the superficial flexor tendon. Note that the heel is still flat with the ground which indicates that the deep flexor is not involved as much as the superficial flexor tendon.

retards growth of the epiphysis laterally. In many cases correction of the mineral or vitamin levels will stop the deviation, and correct it before casts are necessary, when treated before severe deviation is present.

In early phases, rickets causes a knuckling forward of the fetlocks of the front and/or hindlimbs, due to contraction of the flexor tendons (Figs. 5–8 and 9). "Rachitic ringbone" (page 345) may develop in the pastern areas, and enlargement of the carpal, fetlock, and hock areas may occur. New bone growth, "lipping" of the joints and destruction of cartilage, *do not* occur in rachitic arthritis. Characteristic findings in joints affected with rickets are: enlargement of the epiphyses of the bones forming the joint, irregular and widened epiphyseal lines (Figs. 5–6 and 5–7), and, in severe cases demineralization of bone. The bones may become deformed due to the epiphyseal damage, or may fracture easily if demineralized (osteoporosis). Bog spavins may occur in rickets, and, if so, are usually bilateral (*see* Chapter 6). Windpuffs in the fetlock area and the joint capsule and flexor tendon sheath and in the carpal area may occur as a result of the rachitic syndrome. The deficient mineral(s) or vitamin(s) must be determined by a study of the diet and laboratory analysis of the blood.

Excessive feeding of grain can apparently cause the syndrome in horses under three years of age. In such a case, the disease may

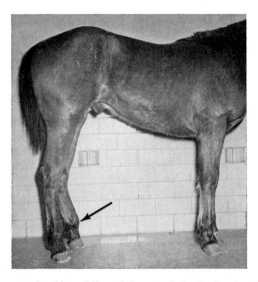

Fig. 5–9.—An example of knuckling of the rear fetlocks due to mineral imbalance (rickets). Note that both rear fetlocks are displaced anteriorly. Also note a very upright positioning of front fetlocks. Contraction of the superficial digital flexor tendons is obvious.

partly be due to increased growth rate stimulated by the concentrate diet. The high rate of concentrate intake must be reduced, and minerals and vitamins balanced before clinical improvement can be seen. Phytic acid, found in oats and wheat, may interfere with the metabolism of calcium and aid in causing rickets when horses are fed greater quantities of grain than are necessary for normal growth.

Krook and Lowe[34] produced nutritional secondary hyperparathyroidism by decreasing the calcium intake and increasing the phosphorus intake. The horses so treated developed typical osteoporosis described in "Bran Disease" or "Miller's Head." Enlargement of the jaw bones and osteoporosis of the mandible were produced. Histologic examination of the bone showed generalized osteitis fibrosa. They maintain that the terms osteomalacia, osteoporosis, and osteitis fibrosa are all the same disease. The horses showed progressive radiolucency in the mandibles and maxillae. The characteristic changes in the metacarpal bones were endosteal roughening and radiolucent linear striations of the cortex.

4. *Arthritis Due to Neoplasia of Joints.*—This seldom occurs in horses, but synovioma and other neoplastic growths may occur.

5. *Arthritis Due to a Structural Derangement of the Joint.*—(*a*) Trauma: Trauma, a common cause of arthritis in horses, usually results in a serous arthritis, and may cause an osteo-arthritis, or an ankylosis if the joint cartilage is severely damaged. Luxation and fracture can occur also. Infectious arthritis of hematogenous origin may follow some joint injuries.

(*b*) Poor conformation: Poor conformation, which also causes trauma, is one of the most common causes of secondary arthritis in horses. Poor conformation can induce stress to joints, because of improper angulation of bone, thereby causing traumatic arthritis, and ringbone. New bone growth may be produced by stress due to poor conformation, where collateral or intra-articular ligaments or the joint capsule have been injured (*see* Chapter 1).

It must be noted that classification as to *type* and *etiology* of arthritis overlap, to the extent that the *types* of arthritis might well be listed as examples of the various *etiological* causes, and the reverse also is somewhat possible.

TREATMENT OF ARTHRITIS

Serous Arthritis

In the acute phase, local anesthesia and sedation can be used to reduce pain. The affected joint or joints should have absolute rest; in some cases it is necessary to use a plaster cast over the joint to enforce this rest. If a cast is not used, the joint should be bandaged heavily so that it will receive support and counter pressure. The joint can be injected with a corticoid (page 447) to relieve inflammation. These injections are valuable, even though theoretically they delay healing. Following two weeks of complete immobilization or supportive wraps, hot Epsom Salt packs and application of liniments should be used to aid mobility. If the joint has been severely injured, immobilization of the joint, by wrapping, should be continued for four to six weeks. Antiphlogistic packs such as Denver Mud* aid in relieving inflammation. Phenylbutazone and oxyphenylbutazone will give temporary relief of pain (page 446). Corticoids, given intramuscularly, will also reduce pain and inflammation, and may be continued one or two weeks as indicated. Giving full doses of both Phenylbutazone and corticoids systemically is contraindicated.

*Demco, Inc., Denver, Colorado

In the chronic phase of serous arthritis, corticoids may be used intra-articularly to reduce inflammation (page 442). Once inflammation is controlled, heat, liniments, and exercise should be used to promote motion. In some chronic cases, the joint may be blistered, or fired, or radiation therapy may be used in the form of X-radiation or gamma-radiation with cobalt or radium. When X-radiation therapy is used, about 1000 to 1200 roentgens is the usual dose; this dose is usually divided into two to three treatments of 500 to 600 roentgens each. Gamma radiation is applied with Cobalt-60 needles or radium, and the material is strapped directly to the affected part. The dosage is calibrated so that it is distributed over several days. The usual total dosage is approximately 1000 to 1200 roentgens. Blistering, firing, and radiation therapy promote an acute inflammation of the joint and when the acute inflammation subsides, the arthritis may heal and a sound joint result (see Chapter 11 for complete discussion of radiation therapy).

Ultrasonic therapy is of doubtful value for joint injury. Although it produces a deep heat, the effect is transitory. Such therapy can be dangerous to use, for if used in overdoses, it may cause bone necrosis. Ultrasound is of most value in relieving the pain of muscle spasms. Diathermy is helpful in producing deep heat in the joint, and by this means aids in mobility (see Chapter 11).

Adrenocorticotrophic hormone (ACTH) parenterally may be of some use in prolonged cases of arthritis if used to follow up corticoid therapy. The administration of ACTH stimulates the adrenal cortex to secrete hydrocortisone (page 446).

An adequate rest period of one to six months, depending on severity, must be enforced if proper healing is to occur. Working a horse prematurely will cause the arthritis to fail to respond to treatment, or may cause a recurrence of the injury.

PROGNOSIS. — The prognosis is usually favorable if bony changes have not occurred. Bone changes and chronicity make the prognosis unfavorable.

Infectious Arthritis (Suppurative Arthritis)

This includes arthritic conditions of infectious origin, either of proven or unproven etiology.

If the joint is open and draining, an effort should be made to establish drainage as low on the joint capsule as possible. If the joint capsule is distended with suppurative material or with infected synovia, it should be drained by needle and the joint rinsed out with sterile saline solution. This saline solution may contain an enzyme, such as trypsin. A culture from the joint contents should be obtained, when possible, and a sensitivity test done to determine the most effective antibiotic. Once the most effective antibiotic has been found, a corticoid should be injected intra-articularly in combination with the antibiotics found to be effective by sensitivity tests (*see* page 447). High levels of this same antibiotic also should be used parenterally until the infection is controlled. The joint should be bandaged so that if drainage is taking place, the opening will not be exposed to air. Repeated injections of corticoids and antibiotics into the joint should be used until the infection is definitely overcome, and signs of inflammation cease. After the infection has been controlled, heat therapy and exercise should be used to maintain mobility of the joint.

PROGNOSIS.—The prognosis of infectious arthritis always should be guarded. Bone changes within the joint capsule, especially on the articular surfaces. Unless the infection is soon controlled, osteoarthritis or ankylosing arthritis often results and causes chronic lameness. Ankylosis is the result of destruction of the cartilage and hypertrophic bone growth.

Osteoarthritis (Hypertrophic or Degenerative Arthritis)

This type of arthritis usually is chronic and may result from arthritis of other types. This arthritis sometimes is treated by counter-inflammation, such as firing, blistering, or radiation therapy. These forms of therapy cause acute inflammation of the joint, and the resulting healing process may cause a remission of symptoms to a degree that the horse may be used.

Firing has sometimes been acclaimed for its ability to remove osseous growth. This is not true, and in some cases it actually promotes additional bone growth. The inflammation it produces rarely causes any demineralization and the only reduction of swelling that occurs is in the soft tissues that are involved. The same also is true of radiation therapy. Healing of the inflammation causes a smoothing of bone, as in fractures, but not destruction of new bone growth.

The true effects of x-ray therapy, and other forms of radiation therapy, are not precisely known at present. Various claims have been made for the pain-relieving effect of radiation therapy, but these claims are difficult to rationalize because of the obvious inflammation radiation causes. The effect of radiation therapy, as claimed by some, is the destruction of leukocytes which may later stimulate phagocytosis. It also has been claimed that decalcification of tissue can be accomplished through radiation therapy by increasing the blood supply to aid in demineralization. However, there has been experimentation in humans, on a controlled basis, showing that the results of treatment of calcified bursitis of the shoulder showed no difference when radiation was actually used, or when the machine was turned on but the lead shutter was closed. At present, a great deal of experimental research remains to be done to determine the full effect and value of radiation therapy in horses.

In some cases arthrodesis (surgical fusion of the affected joints) is the only answer to relief of pain. This operation is most successful in the proximal interphalangeal (pastern) joint (*see* Ringbone, Chapter 6).

Itnra-articular injections of corticoids are often of temporary value in treatment of osteoarthritis, since they reduce inflammation and pain (*see* page 442). Parenteral use of corticoids or phenylbutazone also may cause temporary amelioration of lameness signs, as long as the therapy is continued; signs usually recur once corticoid or phenylbutazone therapy is stopped. Too often, corticoid or phenylbutazone therapy allows the horse to be used, causing further injury before healing has taken place.

PROGNOSIS.—The prognosis is guarded to unfavorable. If new bone growth occurs on the articular surfaces, the lameness is chronic due to mechanical causes. Under proper therapy, some cases become asymptomatic. In bone spavin, soundness may result after ankylosis of the distal tarsal joints.

Ankylosing or Adhesive Arthritis

In this type of arthritis immobility and ankylosis usually results so there is but little chance that the horse would be useful for purposes other than breeding. In some joints, such as the proximal interphalangeal (pastern) joint, afflicted with hypertrophic arthritis in the form of ringbone, ankylosis may occur, but the horse still may be functional. This is more often true when the hindlimb is affected rather than the forelimb.

Some discussion has occurred over whether or not ankylosis of the proximal interphalangeal joint should be stimulated once ringbone has involved the articular surface. This is of value in some cases. When the articulation of the proximal interphalangeal joint is involved, lameness will be present until ankylosis has occurred. As long as a joint space is visible on a radiograph, lameness persists, regardless of how much hypertrophic bone has built up around the joint. This joint must be stripped surgically of its articular cartilage and then cast for several weeks to enable the joint to ankylose (*see* Ringbone, Chapter 6). Once movement of this joint is suspended, pain usually disappears. Since this joint is only slightly movable in the normal state anyway, the treated horse may be able to perform normal functions.

Ankylosis also occurs in joints, such as the distal intertarsal and tarso-metatarsal joints in the hock of the hindlimb (Fig. 5–10), resulting from bone spavin. Once ankylosis has occurred in the above joints, the horse may be completely functional following tenectomy of the cunean tendon. Both articular ringbone and bone spavin usually begin as an osteoarthritis. The main articulation of the hock joint may ankylose as the result of trauma, suppurative arthritis, or periarticular involvement. This type of involvement makes the horse useless. Ankylosis may result from luxation of a joint if the articular cartilage is badly damaged (Fig. 6–107).

PROGNOSIS.—The prognosis is unfavorable. In the case of ringone and bone spavin the prognosis is guarded to unfavorable.

Fig. 5–10.—Lateral radiograph of a tarsal joint affected by ankylosis of the inter-tarsal joint (top dark arrow) and the tarso-metatarsal joint (lower dark arrow) as a result of bone spavin.

Villous Arthritis

Villi form in types of arthritis, such as serous arthritis and hyper-trophic arthritis. There is no specific treatment, as such, for villi. Surgical removal of a bone fragment from a joint often reveals the presence of villi in the synovial layer of the capsule. When villi are present, it is usually best to remove them so that they will not cause persistent pain and joint effusion as a result of their impinge-ment by the joint during motion of the limb.

Rickets (Metabolic Bone Disease)

The normal calcium to phosphorus ratio of the horse should be approximately 2:1 in the blood stream. Although there is some variation, blood should contain about 10 mg. per cent of calcium

9

and 5 mg. per cent of phosphorus. In foals these levels may be slightly higher, while in adults the phosphorus level may be slightly lower. Blood levels of minerals are not always accurate because the blood uses minerals from the bone to maintain near-normal levels as long as possible. For the most accurate interpretation of calcium-phosphorus blood levels in the blood, samples should be taken from several horses on the premises. Establishing a definite trend in a calcium-phosphorus imbalance is very helpful in compounding a therapeutic diet. A reduced blood level of either calcium or phosphorus means that the deficiency has been present for some time. Sippel[65] claims that hair analysis is a good method of determining mineral imbalance. It also represents the condition of the animal for the past six to eight weeks or whatever interval is required to grow out the full length of hair. Methods of handling the hair must be standardized to give accurate results. He used hair analysis to check for minerals other than calcium and phosphorus and found definite correlations between several of these ions. Further testing of this method may provide a more accurate method of determining the true state of mineral levels in the horse. The horse's daily ration should contain a ratio of 2:1 or 1:1 calcium to phosphorus. In areas deficient in phosphorus, this mineral must be artificially supplied to maintain the proper balance with calcium. Mono-sodium phosphate may be used for this purpose. Most authorities agree that horses require 25 to 45 grams daily of calcium and 15 to 28 grams daily of phosphorus.

Show horses fed high grain rations but little hay tend to be lacking in calcium; thus, this mineral must be supplied in the ration. If a horse is deficient in both minerals, it is possible to feed products, such as dicalcium phosphate, that balance both in the proper ratio. However, if a horse is deficient in only one of the minerals, then only that mineral, and not a combination, should be fed. If a combination is fed, the calcium-phosphorus ratio tends to become more unbalanced, if the supplement is a standard product containing more calcium than phosphorus.

Horses that are fed large amounts of grain to increase their growth rate also may show signs of rickets. In some cases this can be attributed to the increased demand for vitamins and minerals because of increased growth, but in other cases it appears that the excessive protein, or at least certain types of protein, when in excess, interfere with mineral metabolism. High protein diets also acceler-ate growth rate to the point that it is nearly impossible to furnish an adequate mineral intake. In addition, phytic acid, present in grains, tends to prevent absorption of calcium; causing further discrepancy in the Ca:P ratio. Such cases improve only upon withdrawal of the heavy ration and protein. The increased demand for minerals and/or vitamins, under these circumstances, is appar-ently greater than the proportionate amount of growth rate increase. Four to six weeks are required for favorable changes in the rickets, after the diet is corrected.

There are several sources of calcium and phosphorus available as feed for horses. Steamed bone meal, dicalcium phosphate, mono-calcium phosphate and spent bone black, supply both calcium and phosphorus, while calcium gluconate, ground limestone, and oyster shell flour, supply calcium only. Monosodium phosphate and disodium phosphate supply phosphorus only. Mineralized salt blocks are not an adequate supply of minerals for horses because not enough of the minerals can be obtained from licking a block. Minerals may be supplemented by mixing monosodium phosphate, for example, half and half with *crushed* salt (fine rock salt), and using this as the only source of salt. When minerals are supplemented in this way, the mixture should be weatherproofed or the minerals harden. One of the most effective ways of supplementing minerals is to combine the desired minerals with alfalfa meal and bind this with molasses. When supplementing minerals one must recognize the fact that feeding one ounce of a particular mineral does not mean that the horse utilizes the whole amount. Depending on the product, absorption of the mineral in a supplement is usually 50 per cent or less. In all cases it is necessary to analyze the diet on the basis of

Table 5-1.—Minimum Daily Requirements of the Weanling Foal* (4–12 Months)

Projected Mature Weight of 1000–1400 Pounds

4 months—Body weight = approximately 300 pounds
Total digestible nutrients (pounds)		6.4
Digestible protein (pounds)		1.16
Carotene (milligrams)		22.5
Calcium (grams)	30	–40
Phosphorus (grams)	18	–24

6 months—Body weight = approximately 400–500 pounds
Total digestible nutrients (pounds)		9.0 – 9.3
Digestible protein (pounds)		1.17
Carotene (milligrams)		30.7 –37.5
Calcium (grams)	33	–45
Phosphorus (grams)	21	–28

8 months—Body weight = approximately 450–600 pounds
Total digestible nutrients (pounds)		9.5 – 9.7
Digestible protein (pounds)		1.19– 1.30
Carotene (milligrams)		33.8 –45.0
Calcium (grams)	33	–45
Phosphorus (grams)	21	–28

12 months—Body weight = approximately 550–800 pounds
Total digestible nutrients (pounds)		9.9 –11.0
Digestible protein (pounds)		1.22– 1.30
Carotene (milligrams)		41.3 –60.0
Calcium (grams)	33	–45
Phosphorus (grams)	21	–28

The above table will give at least a foundation for supplementing the diet of the foal. These figures can be used as a basis for estimating a balanced ration.

*Tables 1, 2 and 3 from Nelson, A. W.: *Nutrient Requirements of the Light Horse*, Courtesy of Am. Quarter Horse Assoc.

known mineral content of its ingredients. Only in this fashion can one arrive at an accurate interpretation of the total intake of minerals and/or vitamins. Mineral supplementation must be done in an intelligent manner and not on a promiscuous basis.

According to A. W. Nelson[50] in his *Nutrient Requirements of the Light Horse*: "Vitamin A and Carotene have been explored as much, if not more than, other vitamins; however, no work was encountered

Table 5–2.—*Minimum Daily Requirements of the Yearling (12–24 Months)*

Projected Mature Weight of 1000–1400 Pounds

12 months—Body weight = approximately 700–800 pounds
    Total digestible nutrients (pounds) 10   –11.2
    Digestible protein (pounds) 1.30– 1.35
    Carotene (milligrams) . . . . 52.5 –60.0
    Calcium (grams) . . . . 16.9 –45
    Phosphorus (grams) . . . . 16.3 –28
24 months—Body weight = approximately 900–1100 pounds
    Total digestible nutrients (pounds) . . . . 11.4 –11.9
    Digestible protein (pounds) 1.40– 1.50
    Carotene (milligrams) . . . . 67.5 –82.5
    Calcium (grams) 15   –40
    Phosphorus (grams) 15   –27

Table 5–3.—*Examples of Mineral Supplements*

Mix No. 1
    1# Monosodium Phosphate
    1# Monocalcium Phosphate
    each ounce contains 2.25 grams of calcium* and 6.6 grams phosphorus*
Mix No. 2
    1# Monocalcium Phosphate
    2# Monosodium Phosphate
    each ounce contains 1.5 grams calcium* and 6.5 grams phosphorus*
Mix No. 3
    1# Monosodium Phosphate
    each ounce contains 6.4 grams phosphorus*
Mix No. 4
    1# Dicalcium Phosphate
    1# Ground Limestone (calcium carbonate)
    2# Monosodium Phosphate
    each ounce contains 6.1 grams calcium* and 6.2 grams phosphorus*
Mix No. 5
    1# Dicalcium Phosphate
    each ounce contains 7.5 grams of calcium* and 5.8 grams phosphorus*
Mix No. 6
    1# Monocalcium Phosphate
    1# Ground Limestone (calcium carbonate)
    each ounce contains 7.7 grams calcium* and 3.4 grams phosphorus*
Mix No. 7
    1# Dicalcium Phosphate
    1# Ground Limestone (calcium carbonate)
    each ounce contains 9.8 grams calcium* and 2.9 grams phosphorus*

*Available mineral in each ounce
One ounce is equal to 30 grams

that established the actual daily requirements for either vitamin A or Carotene. The estimated daily requirements per 100 pounds of body weight for vitamin A ranges from 773 to 1,000 I.U.[18] to 667 to 800 I.U.[14] The estimated daily maintenance requirements per 100 pounds body weight for Carotene ranges from 0.91 to 1.36 milligrams,[18] 0.9 to 1.4 milligrams,[14] and 0.9 to 1.14 milligrams."[10]

Vitamin A palmitate appears to be one of the better supplements of vitamin A, as this product is gelatin-coated to prevent oxidation. Natural sources of vitamin A, such as fish liver oils, oxidize rapidly so their value is quickly diminished. Carotene can be supplemented by feeding fresh alfalfa meal or alfalfa leaf meal. Alfalfa pellets also are valuable as a source of carotene, providing they are fresh and have not lost the carotene content as a result of oxidation. These pellets preferably should be fresh or they may not contain sufficient carotene to prevent vitamin A deficiency. Whenever possible, the carotene intake should be increased because carotene apparently is more efficient in raising the blood levels of vitamin A than any type of vitamin A supplement, including intramuscular injections. The horse may convert carotene to vitamin A more readily than he utilizes a vitamin A supplement. Adequate phosphorus is necessary in the diet for optimum vitamin A and carotene utilization. Excessive nitrates in the diet may depress conversion of carotene to vitamin A. The role of the nitrate is not clear.[20]

When treating a vitamin A deficiency, vitamin A palmitate (30,000 units per gram) should be added to the grain at the rate of 50,000 to 100,000 units a day. Once signs of rickets have disappeared, 1 gram daily (30,000 units) of vitamin A palmitate should be adequate.

A. W. Nelson[50] says: "Vitamin D requirements for the horse are not known. From information obtained in other species, 300 I.U. of vitamin D per 100 pounds of body weight is adequate to meet the daily needs of the adult horse.[49] Way[81] indicated that 700 to 1,000 USP units of vitamin D per 100 pounds body weight would be adequate for training and racing Thoroughbred horses. A provitamin or precursor of vitamin D has been found in the stomach wall and the wall of the first part of the small intestine of the horse and other species.[52] Therefore, the horse may be able to produce at least small quantities of vitamin D." Show horses that are confined indoors the majority of the time to preserve hair coat luster, will be deficient in vitamin D if this vitamin is not supplemented in the diet. Vitamin D can be supplemented in the form of irradiated yeast, giving approximately 5,000 units daily in the grain.

In cases that do not respond to treatment, injections of parathyroid extract are indicated for those deficient in calcium metabolism. The feeding of iodinated casein to stimulate the thyroid gland, and the subcutaneous implantation of thyroid pellets are occasionally helpful in cases that may be hypothyroid.

Deviations of the tarsal joints, carpal joints and the metacarpophalangeal joints are treated by means of casts and epiphyseal stapling. In general, casts are of the most value starting at about three weeks of age. If the foal is presented for treatment after it is approximately four months of age, epiphyseal stapling is more satisfactory because a cast cannot be left on long enough to correct the deviation (*see* Chapter 6).

JOINT MICE

Joint mice, or bodies within the joint cavity, may be formed by a splitting off of a piece of the joint cartilage, by a fracture of an arthritic osteophyte at the joint margin, or a chip fracture of one of the bones forming the joint (Figs. 5–11 and 5–12).

When joint mice occur as free osseous bodies in a joint, such as the carpal or fetlock joints, they may be surgically removed with success. Most of the common chip fractures remain attached to the joint capsule, facilitating their removal (*see* Chapter 6, Carpal Chip Fractures and Chip Fractures of the First Phalanx). Radiographic studies should be made of the joint to determine if erosion of the articular surfaces has occurred. If extensive erosion of these surfaces has occurred, little improvement will be obtained by removing the

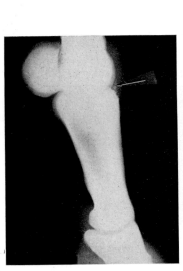
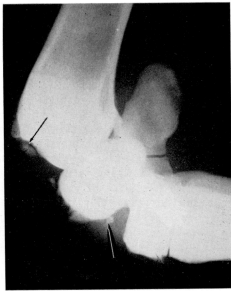

Fig. 5–11   Fig. 5–12

Fig. 5–11.—Joint mouse in the fetlock joint as viewed on a lateral radiograph. The joint mouse is indicated by the dark pointer.

Fig. 5–12.—Severe carpitis on a lateral flexed joint radiograph. The upper arrow indicates the loose joint mouse in the radio-carpal joint and the lower, dark pointer indicates the joint mouse in the intercarpal joint.

joint mouse. Lameness caused by joint mice often is characterized by a sudden onset and a sudden disappearance. Sometimes the horse will be sound, until the joint mouse is caught between the articular surfaces; then he becomes acutely lame. The signs often disappear just as rapidly. Villi resulting from arthritis can cause similar symptoms if they become caught between the bones of the joint. Careful radiographic studies must be made prior to surgery since, in some instances, the calcified objects may be difficult to find.

Large bone chips have been removed from the femorotibial joint and from the scapulohumeral joint by the author. In general, removal of a bone chip is successful if it is removed soon after the injury occurred, and if it does not involve much of the articular surface. The lateral tuberosity of the humerus and portions of the lateral aspect of the femoral condyles are subject to trauma from kicking and may chip off into the joint. These chips must be removed before soundness can occur.

INFLAMMATION OF SYNOVIAL STRUCTURES

1. Bursitis*

Bursitis may be defined as an inflammatory reaction within a bursa. This may vary from a very mild irritative synovitis to suppurative bursitis with abscess formation. A bursa is specifically designed to facilitate motion between contiguous layers of the body. Bursitis can be classified as true or acquired. An acquired bursitis results when a bursa develops as the result of trauma where a natural bursa is not normally present; i.e., carpal hygroma. A true bursitis results when a bursa that is normally present becomes inflamed; i.e., trochanteric bursitis.

TREATMENT.—Treatment is directed toward prevention of repeated injury and reduction of the irritation within the bursa. Aspiration of fluid, local injection with corticoids, protection against direct trauma, and application of pressure bandage to oppose the walls of the sac are used. If the condition becomes chronic and the synovitis is persistent, surgical removal of the bursa may become necessary.

Cosgrove[1] has suggested that *Brucella abortus* may be responsible for bursitis in the stifle, withers, and navicular bursa. He suggests the use of strain 19 vaccine when this etiology is suspected.

Bursitis of Specific Areas

Bursitis of the Point of the Elbow (Olecranon Bursitis, Shoe Boil, Capped Elbow).—Bursitis over the olecranon is caused by trauma at the point of the olecranon. It is usually an acquired bursitis and is due to trauma caused by the shoe on the foot of the affected limb

---

* Definitions for the conditions marked with an asterisk have been taken from O'Donoghue's text, *Treatment of Injuries to Athletes*, courtesy of W. B. Saunders Co.

hitting the point of the olecranon during motion or while the horse is lying down. A false subcutaneous bursa forms and the bursa under the triceps is not usually involved. Most trauma probably occurs while the horse is down with the foot under the point of the elbow. The disease is characterized by a prominent swelling over the point of the elbow, which may contain fluid, or in the chronic stages, may be composed primarily of fibrous tissue. Lameness is usually mild, if present at all.

TREATMENT.—In the acute stages, bursitis of the elbow can be treated with injection of corticoids (see Chapter 11). The swelling should be shaved and prepared for aseptic injection over its lateral aspect. After aspiration of the contents, part of the corticoid solution should be injected into the bursa and part into the surrounding connective tissue. The corticoid injections can be repeated two or three times weekly, if necessary. If the cause is removed, and the case is treated before extensive fibrosis has occurred, results are often reasonably good. Most cases of this type will cause some blemish as the result of scar tissue formation.

Surgical removal is sometimes successful when the bursa is large and composed primarily of fibrous tissue. It is difficult to keep sutures in place because of stress, and an open wound may result that heals with extensive fibrous tissue. If surgical correction is used, the incision should be curved over the lateral portion of the bursa and not be made on the posterior aspect of the elbow. This will reduce stress on the incision during flexion and extension of the elbow joint. Mattress sutures should be used in the skin and a reinforcing quill suture is helpful.

Cross-tying the horse for 10 days postsurgically to prevent lying down will aid healing. Booting the foot or protecting the elbow with donut padding below the elbow joint can be used to protect this area from injury when the horse is getting up and down. This protection should be used when using corticoid injections or following surgical correction.

Capped elbow is sometimes treated by blistering or firing. These methods are usually ineffective and the additional inflammation produced may result in even greater deposition of fibrous tissue.

Bursitis of the Hock (Capped Hock) (Fig. 5–13).—Bursitis of the hock is caused by trauma to the point of |the hock. This is an acquired bursitis caused by trauma induced when the horse kicks a wall or trailer gate. Some horses develop a vice of wall kicking and may only do it at night when they are not seen. The condition is characterized by a firm swelling at the point of the hock and it may be accompanied by curb (Chapter 6, p. 329). Lameness is mild, if present, but the blemish is usually permanent. Swelling may be extensive and accompanied by edema when the injury has been severe.

TREATMENT.—In the acute stage, bursitis of the hock can be treated with injection of corticoids. The area should be shaved and prepared for aseptic injection. After withdrawal of the synovial

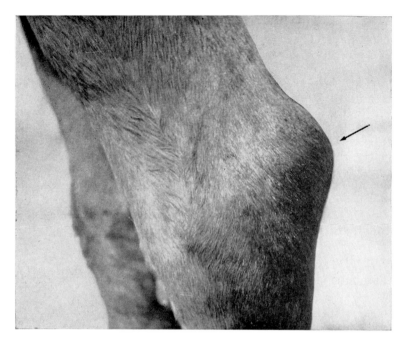

FIG. 5–13.—Capped hock.   Arrow indicates distention of the bursa
over the point of the hock.

content of the bursa, a portion of the corticoid solution should be
injected into the cavity and part into the surrounding tissue.
Corticoid injections can be repeated several times weekly, if necessary.   Whenever possible, a pressure bandage should be used at the
point of the hock.   The hock is difficult to bandage and care must
be used so that a skin slough over the Achilles tendon does not result.
If the injury to the hock occurs only once and the case is treated
before extensive fibrosis has occurred, results are reasonably good.
However, if the injury is repeated several times and extensive fibrous
tissue results, little can be done to correct it.   Surgical intervention
may be used, but if the wound opens, a larger blemish than was
present originally may occur.   When the blemish is very disfiguring,
surgery may be done, dissecting out the fibrous tissue portion of the
mass.   The incision should be made lateral to the bursa and not on
the posterior aspect of the hock.   This will ease the stress on the
incision.   Mattress sutures should be used in the skin with a reinforcing quill suture to prevent tearing of the incision line.   The
horse should be kept tied following surgery to minimize motion.
Counter pressure bandage should be used for ten to fourteen days.

   *Trochanteric Bursitis—Trochanteric Lameness, Whorlbone Lame-
ness.*—This type of bursitis is apparently most common in Standardbred horses and can be classified as a true bursitis (*see* Chapter 6,

Whorlbone Lameness). Trochanteric bursitis is difficult to treat and usually requires repeated injections of Corticoids. Results are inconsistent and accurate diagnosis is necessary. Treatment is under description of the lameness in Chapter 6.

Hygroma.—Hygroma is an acquired bursitis of the anterior surface of the carpus. It is the result of trauma which produces a bursa and the bursitis causes a diffuse swelling over the anterior surface of the carpus (Fig. 6–11) (*see* Chapter 6). If the swelling over the anterior surface of the carpus is not uniform and shows an irregular distribution, it may be the result of a synovial hernia from either the radiocarpal joint or the intercarpal joint. Treatment of hygroma is discussed in Chapter 6.

Bicipital Bursitis.—Bicipital bursitis is found between the biceps brachii tendon and the bicipital groove of the humerus. It is classified as a true bursitis. Description of the lameness and its treatment can be found in Chapter 6.

2. Synovitis

Inflammation of any synovial lining: joint, tendon sheath or bursa.

3. Tendinitis

Tendinitis implies inflammation of the tendon only. This occurs where the tendons have no sheath.

4. Tenosynovitis (Tenovaginitis)

Tenosynovitis may be defined as inflammation of the synovium surrounding the tendons. This inflammation is usually due to strain from unaccustomed overuse or may be due to a direct blow or to infection. The result is a reaction of the relatively avascular synovium with increased blood supply, invasion by inflammatory cells, over-secretion of synovial fluid and development of fibrin causing adhesions between the tendon and its surrounding synovium. The exact manifestations vary greatly depending upon the tendon involved. Pain and distention of the sheath are the first signs which are evident in tenosynovitis. This is usually manifested during motion. As the condition progresses the adherence between the tendon and synovium becomes more firm and finally results in complete loss of the gliding capacity of the tendon within its sheath.

TREATMENT.—Treatment is directed toward pathological changes and the principles of treatment are rest, local heat and local injection of corticoids. Specific treatment will vary according to the site of the condition.

SPECIFIC EXAMPLES OF TENOSYNOVITIS

Thoroughpin.—Thoroughpin is tenosynovitis of the tarsal sheath which encloses the deep digital flexor tendon of the hind limb. The

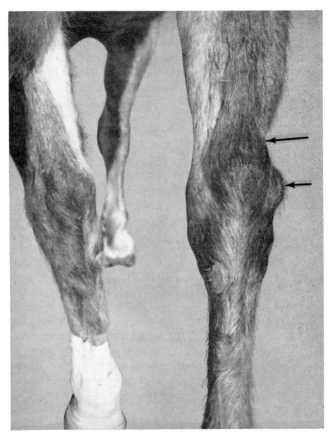

FIG. 5–14.—Upper arrow indicates approximate position of thoroughpin. This example used because it shows the distention of the tarsal joint capsule (lower arrow) that can be confused with thoroughpin. This case shows no clinical evidence of thoroughpin but a good comparison of their locations can be seen.

swelling occurs in the area of the hock at a level approximately the same as that of the point of the hock (Fig. 5–14). This swelling can be confused with bog spavin when bog spavin causes swellings on the medial and lateral sides of the hock joint. Thoroughpin swelling is located approximately 2 inches higher than the swelling that occurs in bog spavin in the posterior part of the joint capsule. Thoroughpin swelling can vary from a small swelling to a large swelling involving most of the tarsal sheath. Thoroughpin is usually unilateral and due to trauma. Mild swellings of both tarsal sheaths may occur when the horse is worked hard. In this case thoroughpin would be classified as "wind puff." When treatment is indicated, the lateral aspect of the thoroughpin is shaved, and under aseptic precautions the fluid is drained as best as possible. The cavity is then injected with a corticoid. It is usually best to infuse the skin with a small amount of local anesthetic, using a 25 gauge, $\frac{1}{2}$ inch needle. Then an 18 gauge, 1 or 2 inch needle is inserted into the tendon sheath, the fluid withdrawn, and the corticoid injected. A tranquilizer and twitch can be used as restraint if necessary. These injections may be repeated two or three times weekly until the swelling does not recur. Results are usually good. Firing and blistering of the area are contraindicated and will not achieve good results.

Tenosynovitis of the Digital Flexor Tendons.—The common tendon sheath of the deep and superficial flexor tendons of the forelimb and occasionally of the hind limb is frequently injured in the fetlock area. This injury produces a swelling that lies between the suspensory ligament and the deep digital flexor tendon. It must be differentiated from the swelling that occurs in the volar pouch of the metacarpophalangeal joint capsule between the suspensory ligament and the cannon bone. When treatment of these swellings is indicated, the lateral portion of the swelling at a distal point is shaved and prepared for aseptic injection. The horse is twitched and a small amount of local anesthetic is infused in the skin with a $\frac{1}{2}$ inch, 25 gauge needle. A 1 inch, 18 or 20 gauge needle is then put into the tendon sheath, the contents withdrawn, and the corticoid infused into the cavity. These injections may be repeated two or three times weekly if necessary. Counter pressure should be applied. The horse must be rested until healing of the injury has occurred.

Treatment of Open Tenosynovitis.—Occasionally a tendon sheath is opened by a lacerated wound. These wounds are always slow to heal and can result in adhesions that will impair the action of the tendon and cause permanent unsoundness. Whenever possible, it is best to treat the wound soon after it occurs by irrigating the tendon sheath with antibiotics and corticoids. The wound should be sutured if it is believed that first intention healing can be attained. It is then best to immobilize the area in a plaster cast. This cast is removed in approximately one week, the wound checked and treated locally, and recast. After approximately three weeks in a cast the wound is usually healed and the limb should then be kept in supportive wrap for thirty days. Systemic antibiotics should be used for at least one week. If the wound does not heal by first intention, it must be treated locally by the infusion of antibiotics, enzymes and corticoids into the sheath. The wound is kept clean, and hair is kept away from the site. The area is wrapped in pressure bandages, which are readjusted daily. Second intention healing invariably results in a prolonged convalescence and the formation of some adhesions.

5. Tendosynovitis (Bowed Tendon, Tendovaginitis) (Fig. 6–25)

A tendosynovitis is the term used when both tendon and sheath are involved. The deep and superficial flexors are most commonly involved above the metacarpophalangeal (fetlock) joint (Chapter 6). Actual pathology occurs within the tendon and hemorrhage within the tendon fibers is present. In some cases, portions of the tendon fibers are torn and it is possible to have actual lengthening of the tendon as a result of the tearing or stretching of these fibers. The tendon sheath is involved and usually there are adhesions between it and the tendon. Adhesions may also develop between the deep and superficial flexor tendons. Tearing of these adhesions cause recurrence of lameness.

6. Desmitis

Inflammation of a ligament; i.e., suspensory ligament injury or ligamentous injury from a sprain.

7. Wind Puff (Wind Gall)

These are synovial swellings of joints or tendon sheaths that result from trauma, but they do not cause lameness. They are a form of synovitis and are classified as articular or tendinous wind puffs depending on their location. The common sites of location are the metacarpophalangeal (fetlock) joint, the flexor tendon sheath above the proximal sesamoid bones, the lateral and common digital extensor sheaths as they cross the carpus, the carpal sheath, and the tarsal sheath (thoroughpin) in the hock. When swellings such as these are present, but are not accompanied by heat, pain, or lameness, they are called wind puffs or wind galls. When these swellings are present and are accompanied by inflammation, they are considered signs of pathology in the structure. Most hard-working horses have some wind puffs, especially in the metacarpophalangeal area. Wind puffs tend to reduce in size if work is decreased, and treatment is usually ineffectual. When lameness and signs of inflammation are present with these swellings, pathological changes in the joint or tendon sheath are present.
Synovial swellings of the common digital and lateral digital extensor tendons may also occur as a congenital defect in newborn foals. Nutritional deficiencies may also produce wind puffs.

8. Ganglion*

Synovial hernia or ganglion is another condition involving a tendon sheath or sometimes a joint capsule. This condition usually results from a defect in the fibrous sheath of the joint capsule or tendon sheath that permits a segment of underlying synovium to herniate through it. The irritation accompanying this herniation results in continued secretion of fluid so that the sac gradually fills up and enlarges. As a rule the synovial hernia will appear as a small discrete, sometimes extremely hard, nodule lying directly over or under the tendon. It may be impossible to tell whether the primary involvement is tendon sheath or joint capsule. It is uncommon in horses, but does occur.

I have observed ganglion underneath the long extensor tendon in the vicinity of the pastern joint in the hindlimb. The same lesion has been observed under the common extensor tendon in the fore-limb. These were diagnosed by the swelling that occurred when the horse was worked. When the horses were rested, swelling dis-appeared. The area was painful to touch and caused lameness. When a local anesthetic was injected the lameness disappeared.

TREATMENT.—Treatment consists of incising directly into the area of swelling in the vicinity of the pastern joint on the anterior surface. The skin is prepared for aseptic surgery and a ring block is used above the fetlock joint to produce anesthesia. The skin and tendon are both incised longitudinally before the ganglion is exposed when it lies beneath the tendon. Only the skin is incised when the ganglion is superficial to the tendon. The tissue and ganglion appear a dark blue color and are obviously thickened synovium. The dis-eased tissue is completely excised. The tendon and skin are then sutured, and the wound kept under bandage for ten to fourteen days. If all tissue in the ganglion is not removed, it will recur.

SPRAIN AND STRAIN

The terms sprain and strain are often loosely used. O'Donoghue[3] classifies these in a logical manner and his classification is used here.

Sprain

Sprain can be defined as an injury to a ligament resulting from overstress. This causes some degree of damage to the ligamentous fibers or their attachment. Certain ligaments may bind two bones firmly together with relatively little motion such as the ligamentous attachment between the second and third metacarpal bones or between the tibia and fibula. Other ligaments serve to reinforce the joint and permit a rather wide range of motion but prevent motion in an abnormal direction. Abnormal motion to a degree beyond the power of a ligament to hold it will cause a sprain. As abnormal force is applied the ligament becomes tense and then gives way at one or another of its attachments or at some point in the substance of the ligament. If the attachment pulls loose with a fragment of bone, it is called a "sprain fracture" but the mechanism is the same. The location of the damage will depend upon the weakest link in the chain of the ligament which may be within the ligament itself or one of its attachments, possibly at the site of an area of previous damage. The extent of the damage depends upon the amount and duration of the force. If the abnormal force is terminated promptly, there may be little actual functional loss to the ligament and only a few of its fibers may be involved. In this instance there is localized hematoma formation with prompt deposit of fibrin in the hematoma. The fibrin is invaded by fibroblasts and they repair the ligament. If the damage is more severe so that there is disruption of numerous

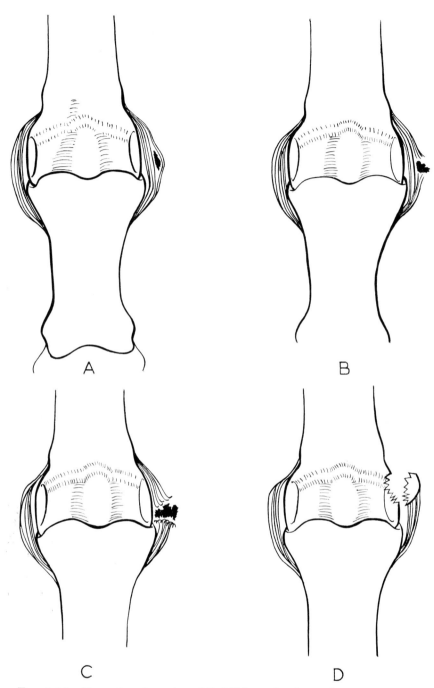

Fig. 5–15.—Examples of sprain. (*A*) Mild sprain—hemorrhage occurs in the fibers of the ligament. (*B*) Moderate sprain—hemorrhage in the fibers of the liga-ments and some of the fibers are torn. (*C*) Severe sprain—complete tearing of the ligament and loss of function. (*D*) Sprain fracture—the function of the ligament is lost in the same fashion as in *C*, but in this case the portion of bone to which the ligament was attached is fractured. (Redrawn from O'Donoghue, *Treatment of Injuries to Athletes*, courtesy of W. B. Saunders Co.)

ligamentous fibers, there may be a considerable functional loss. When the ligament is completely torn, all function is lost. In this case the findings will depend on the location of the tear. Ordinarily, there will be relatively extensive hematoma formation with swelling and edema. The process of repair will be much slower and much less complete and will result in scar formation rather than restoration of normal ligament.

CLASSIFICATION OF SPRAIN.—*Mild Sprain* (Fig. 5–15).—This is a sprain in which a few fibers of a ligament have been torn with some resultant hemorrhage into the ligament but with no actual functional loss.

Moderate Sprain (Fig. 5–15).—A moderate sprain is one in which some portion of the ligament is torn and some degree of functional loss is present. The amount of damage may vary from a tear of a relatively small portion of the ligament to almost complete avulsion. One would not expect wide retraction of torn ligament ends in a moderate sprain. Union can, therefore, proceed in an orderly manner with replacement of fibrous scar by ligament during the process of repair. If the damage is relatively severe, however, there may be considerable permanent scar formation with resultant weakness in this segment of the ligament.

Severe Sprain (Fig. 5–15).—In severe sprain there is complete loss of function of the ligament. The stress tears it completely away from one of its attachments or pulls it apart along its length. There is usually a separation of the ends of the ligament. Efficient repair is dependent upon apposition of the torn ends of the ligament, and it is important to obtain apposition of the ends of the ligament. Ligaments which heal across a gap by scar formation never assume the characteristics of a normal ligament.

Sprain Fracture (Fig. 5–15).—In this case, the portion of bone to which the ligament is attached becomes avulsed.

TREATMENT. —In mild sprain, treatment is relatively unimportant and is designed mostly toward prevention of pain. In moderate sprain the critical factor in treatment is protection in order to permit repair. In severe sprain and sprain fracture where the ligament is ruptured or a portion of bone is avulsed, emphasis must be placed on reapposition of the ends of the ligament in order to assure a ligament of normal length and strength. It is very important that accurate diagnosis is made in the management of ligamentous injuries. Adequate rest is mandatory to obtain healing of ligamentous damage.

Strain

Strain may be defined as damage to a tendon or muscle caused by overuse or overstress. It is important to distinguish between strain and sprain, applying the former term to muscle and tendon and the latter to ligaments. Strain of the tendon could consist of anything from minor irritation to near complete avulsion of the tendon from its attachment or within its substance. Strain of the muscle includes those cases of overuse and overstretching short of actual muscular rupture. Strain can be classified as (1) *Simple Strain* — In this type of strain there is no appreciable hemorrhage and the pathological changes are confined to a low-grade inflammatory reaction with swelling and edema and some disruption of adjacent fibers. Simple strain may completely incapacitate a horse for work until healing has occurred. To continue the work when the strain is present will lead to additional pathological changes. (2) *Violent Strain; Musculo-tendinous Injury* — Those injuries to the musculotendinous unit caused by a single violent injury may be of any degree. Tendinitis, tenosynovitis or tendosynovitis may occur. A tendon may be torn from the bone or pulled apart. The musculotendinous junction may be ruptured or the muscle itself may tear. These injuries result from either violent contraction of the muscle against resistance or from violent overstretching of the muscle while it is forcibly contracted. In the horse one of the most common locations for this type of injury is the attachment of the common digital extensor to the extensor process of the third phalanx. The extensor tendon may be torn from its attachment or avulsion of the extensor process may occur. The peroneus tertius is commonly ruptured, in its length and not at its bony attachment.

TREATMENT. — Treatment of simple strain consists of relieving the acute condition by injection of a local anesthetic and corticoids. Ultrasound therapy is often of value. Local heat and protection against movement which causes pain are additional methods of therapy. The amount of protection applied must vary with the degree of damage so that in some cases all that is necessary is to limit the patient's activity, while in others it may be sensible to prevent motion by immobilization of the part. Criterion for the amount of protection is pain. Function should be resumed as soon as possible but it must be pain free. One must be careful that in a desire to rehabilitate the muscle by active use that overuse will not cause recurrence.

Treatment of violent strain should be preceded by accurate diagnosis. If at all possible, one should determine if there has been a complete disruption of the musculotendinous unit. If disruption has occurred and it is recognized early, immediate surgical repair is the best therapy when possible. Surgical repair may be impossible in horses because of an inability to immobilize the part. Immobilization by means of a plaster cast or other device must be used whether or not surgical apposition is accomplished. If the injury is less than a complete rupture, an attempt should be made to evaluate the degree of tearing and treat it accordingly. Immobilization of the part with plaster cast is one of the best methods of therapy. When tendons have been divided by lacerated wounds, a common lesion in the metatarsal/metacarpal area, a plaster cast with the foot in a flexed position is used. When the extensor tendon is cut, the foot is cast in an extended position. It is not uncommon to find that sutures

10

will not hold in equine tendons and good results may be accomplished with plaster immobilization using frequent cast changing over a period of eight weeks. Changing a cast two or three times over a period of approximately eight weeks followed by the use of a trailer shoe and fetlock support (*see* Chapter 6) will often give gratifying results.

SPECIFIC REFERENCES

1. COSGROVE, J. S. M.: Proceedings 9th Annual A.A.E.P., p. 161, 1963.
2. CRENSHAW, A. H.: *Campbell's Operative Orthopaedics*, 4th ed., St. Louis, C. V. Mosby Co., 1963.
3. O'DONOGHUE, D. H.: *Treatment of Injuries to Athletes*. Philadelphia, W. B. Saunders Co., 1962.

DISEASES OF BONE

1. Aseptic Necrosis (Osteochondritis, Avascular Bone Necrosis, Ischemic Bone Necrosis)

DEFINITION. — Aseptic necrosis of bone is a disease that is not well understood. It seems to affect young horses while the bone is in the growing stages. The bone lesion involves an articular surface in all cases. I have observed it in the carpal bones, tarsal bones, femur and distal end of the metacarpal bone.

ETIOLOGY. — The process is one of degeneration and eventual replacement of the affected portion of bone. It is probable that this disease results from a change in vascularity and blood supply to the affected bone area. Ischemia results in death and demineralization of the affected portion of bone. Essentially it is assumed to be an infarct within the bony epiphysis. Rare cases in man have yielded positive bacterial cultures but in horses this has not been described. However, a high white cell count (above 20,000) may be present.[4] In some cases, this disease has been attributed to hypothyroidism.[5]

During the course of this disease, unless interrupted by surgery or other treatment, the necrotic bone and the cartilage overlying it may gradually separate from adjacent bone and cartilage and together become a loose body. Trauma may play a very prominent part in the cause of this disease.

SIGNS. — The earliest radiographic changes consist of irregularity in the outline of the bone, followed by demineralization. Density of the bone in the early stages is irregular with areas of lysis present. Joint capsule distention may be noted early in some cases. Fragmentation can occur in the tarsal or carpal bones. This fragmentation is probably due to pressures that force the affected pieces in an anterior direction. Cartilage is not affected early in the disease and the normal joint space remains preserved. However, complete destruction of the articular cartilage may occur later. Regeneration produces a bone of normal hardness, and irregularity varies with the degree of compression in the early stages. Later, bony ankylosis may bridge the intertarsal joints and the tarsometatarsal joint may become fused. This is not the case when the metacarpophalangeal joint is affected. It is important that involvement of the tarsal bones does not later become confused with typical osteoarthritic (bone spavin) changes of the tarsal joints.

Signs of lameness are vague, but usually the swelling of the joint plus selective nerve blocking will localize the site. Pain in the joint is one of the most obvious clinical signs.

DIAGNOSIS. — Horses with avascular necrosis seldom show a marked swelling of the joint area involved. Many times the lameness has to be localized by use of nerve blocks (see Chapter 4). On radiographs the avascular bone area will appear as an area of decreased density on the articular surface (Fig. 5–16). Good quality radiographs are necessary for diagnosis. The area of decreased density may not be visible on one view but obvious on another. When avascular necrosis is suspected, oblique views of the joint are helpful in outlining the defect (Fig. 5–16).

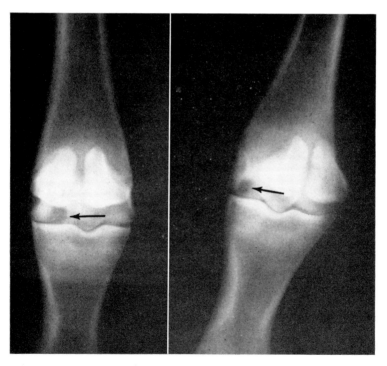

FIG. 5–16.—An example of avascular necrosis in the distal end of the third meta-carpal bone. The figure on the left shows an AP radiograph with arrow pointing at the area of decreased density on the articular surface of the distal end of the third metacarpal bone. The figure on the right shows an oblique radiograph of the same area. Notice that the oblique radiograph confirms the findings on the AP radiograph. The lateral radiograph of this condition would not show the condition nearly so well.

TREATMENT. — A conservative attitude toward the treatment of avascular necrosis seems best. Surgery is usually unnecessary and if the cartilage overlying the avascular bone is well preserved and if the joint is protected as much as possible from weight bearing, the avascular bone will remain in place and become revascularized in three to seven months. Radiation therapy has been a successful treatment in the hands of the author in a small number of cases. However, it is difficult to say whether or not the condition would have healed without the therapy. When the condition becomes an osteochondritis desiccans, where a portion of bone separates, the treatment is not favorable (Fig. 5–17). In this case the tarsal joint or carpal joint may become permanently deformed as a result of bone separation (Fig. 5–17). Surgical removal of a loose body would be indicated if the economic value of the horse warranted it. A large loose body could be fixed in place by use of a bone screw.

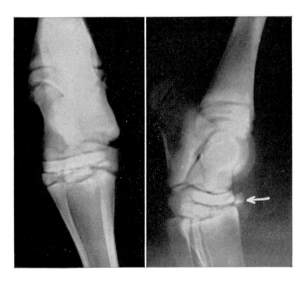

FIG. 5–17. — Aseptic necrosis of the tarsal joint. Notice the crushing effect on the tarsal bones causing avulsion of a portion of the third tarsal bone. When aseptic necrosis involves the tarsal or carpal bones, the horse seldom recovers to full soundness (Carlson, *Veterinary Radiology*, Lea & Febiger).

SPECIFIC REFERENCES

1. American Jockey Club, Conference on Unsoundness of Thoroughbreds, AFIP, Washington, D. C., 1965.
2. CARLSON, WILLIAM D.: *Veterinary Radiology*. Philadelphia, Lea & Febiger, 1961.
3. CRENSHAW, A. H.: *Campbell's Operative Orthopaedics*. St. Louis, C. V. Mosby Co., Vol. 1, 4th ed., 1963.
4. MORGAN, JOE P.: Personal communication.
5. ROONEY, J. R.: *Equine Medicine and Surgery*. Santa Barbara, California, Veterinary Publications Inc.

2. Osteomyelitis and Osteitis

DEFINITION. — By Dorland's[2] definition, osteomyelitis is an inflammation of the bone and medullary cavity. Osteitis is an inflammation of bone including the haversian spaces, canals and their branches. In some cases it also includes inflammation of the medullary cavity. For the purposes of this discussion, the term osteomyelitis will be used and the inflammatory reaction present infectious in nature. These infections may occur with comminuted or compound fractures and can involve long bones, carpal or tarsal bones, and bones of the head and jaw.

ETIOLOGY. — Osteomyelitis most commonly occurs following a compound fracture. In this case the fractured ends of the bone have penetrated the skin and infection enters through the wound. This is always serious and it is not common for an adult horse to

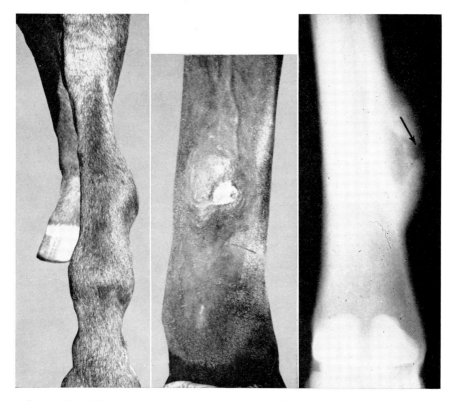

FIG. 5–18. — Three views of a case of osteomyelitis on the lateral aspect of the left third metatarsal bone. *Left* — appearance of the clinical case with fibrous tissue and bony swelling. *Center* — closeup view of the draining tract after surgical preparation. *Right* — radiograph of the same limb with arrow pointing at so-called "cloaca" that is typical of osteomyelitis in this area. A dead piece of bone was found inside the cloacal opening. The fibrous tissue and periosteal new bone growth were removed and full clinical soundness resulted.

recover from this type of injury and infection. Young horses may recover following careful and diligent care.

Osteomyelitis may occur following a comminuted fracture whereby one of the bone fragments is separated from its blood supply. In this case a fragment of bone dies and infection develops by hematogenous source.

Osteosis (necrosis) may occur in a small fracture fragment when a horse has been kicked on one of the metacarpal or metatarsal bones (Fig. 5–18). In this case an abscess develops within the cortex of the bone and the infection does not break into the medullary cavity. This bone fragment acts as a sequestrum and must be removed before healing will occur. Osteomyelitis may also occur in the carpal bones following carpal surgery. It is rare to encounter this difficulty following removal of chip fractures of the carpus, but when exostoses are removed from the carpal bones, osteomyelitis will occasionally occur. In this case the bone inflammation and infection usually appear two to three weeks following surgery, after the incision has healed by first intention. The source of infection is apparently hematogenous, acting on an area of low resistance. Why removal of bony periosteal new bone growth is more apt to result in osteomyelitis than is removal of chip fractures is not known.

Osteomyelitis is not uncommon when a 2nd or 4th metacarpal/metatarsal bone has been fractured, leaving a portion separated from its blood supply (Fig. 6–29).

SIGNS.—Osteomyelitis is characterized by chronic drainage from the wound. In most cases this has occurred as a result of a compound fracture and the wound shows persistent drainage and the bone does not heal at a normal rate. Many weeks are required for a bone callous to form and union may never occur. This type of drainage will also eventually occur when a piece of bone has become necrotic in a comminuted fracture. Drainage will occur as long as the dead piece of bone is present in the fracture site.

In osteomyelitis where a portion of the cortex has fractured, the wound will apparently heal only to break open repeatedly (Fig. 5–18). Drainage will be persistent until the bone fragment is removed. When a portion of a 2nd or 4th metacarpal/metatarsal bone has been fractured and separated from its blood supply, it will also drain intermittently until the fragment is surgically removed. It is usually best to remove the entire distal fragment of the metacarpal/metatarsal bone (see Fractured Splint Bone, Chapter 6).

TREATMENT.—When a compound fracture is present, complete debridement of the wound must be done. The fracture is set and a cast put on over the fracture site. After eight to fourteen days the original cast is removed and if healing is not progressing normally by first intention a new cast is put on and a window is cut into it over the wound site. The wound is then irrigated daily with antibiotics and enzymes until granulation has occurred. It is important to cover the bone with granulation tissue. Whenever possible, pull tissue over the bone by means of sutures. If osteomyelitis develops after a comminuted fracture and it is obvious that an abscess is developing, the fracture site should be opened and the piece of bone that is separated from its blood supply should be removed. A cast with a window cut into it can be used for local treatment of the wound. In all cases parenteral antibiotics are used for a prolonged period (seven to fourteen days).

Whenever a window is used in a cast, it is extremely important that pressure be maintained against the wound to prevent bulging of the soft tissues through the window. When healing of the wound has occurred, a new cast should be applied so that the window can be eliminated.

When a fractured piece of bone has become a sequestrum in a cortex (Fig. 5–18), simple surgical removal of the bone fragment will allow the lesion to heal. Bony proliferation and fibrous tissue over the bone fragment should be removed. The bone should be trimmed to as nearly normal in shape as possible. The cavity where the bone fragment was removed should be curetted thoroughly and the subcutaneous tissues and skin sutured. A counterpressure bandage should be maintained for approximately two weeks over the incision.

SPECIFIC REFERENCES

1. CRENSHAW, A. H.: *Campbell's Operative Orthopaedics*, 4th ed. St. Louis, C. V. Mosby Co., 1963.
2. DORLAND'S *Medical Dictionary*, 24th ed. Philadelphia, W. B. Saunders Co.
3. JUBB, K. V. F. and KENNEDY, P. C.: *Pathology of Domestic Animals*. Vol. 1. New York, Academic Press, 1963.

3. Hypertrophic Pulmonary Osteoarthropathy

DEFINITION.—In the horse, this disease is characterized by a marked change in the limbs with a distinct thickening and deformity by new bone growth. New bone growth is formed beneath the periosteum which is pushed outward. The osteophytic growths are very irregular so that the bone is very rough. In conjunction with this, there is lung pathology in some form; *i.e.*, lung tumor. In the horse it has been described with a granular cell myoblastoma.[1] The bones usually affected are those of all four limbs from the femoro-tibial and scapulohumeral joints to the phalanges. The joint surfaces are not involved although there may be periarticular proliferation and enlargement. Occasionally a bone may attain twice its normal diameter. In later stages there may be considerable pain on movement and palpation. Usually the disease results in death but the course is usually prolonged.

SIGNS.—The disease has been described in man, dogs, sheep, deer and lions[3,4] as a primary respiratory disease. In these species, it usually is preceded by cough, dyspnea or other pulmonary disturbances. In the horse, however, the most marked change is in the limbs where there is a marked thickening and deformity of the limbs by new bone growth (Fig. 5–19). Alexander *et al.*[1] described a case

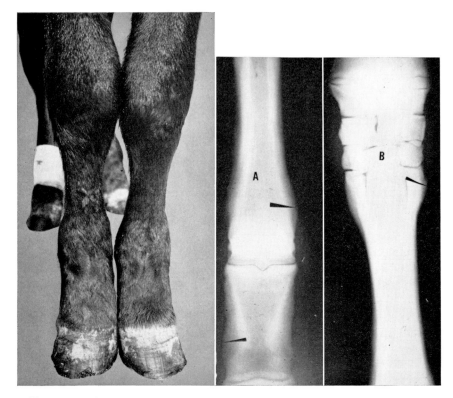

Fig. 5–19.—Hypertrophic pulmonary osteoarthropathy. *Left*—appearance of the limbs of the clinical case. Note enlargement of the distal end of the radius, proximal end of the third metacarpal bone, distal end of metacarpal bones and pastern areas. The rear limbs showed similar enlargement. *Right*—radiographs of the same horse. *A* shows the thickening of the distal end of the third metacarpal bone and of the first phalanx. *B* shows the thickening of the proximal end of the second, third and fourth metacarpal bones.

in which the fetlock, carpal and tarsal joints were grossly enlarged and symmetrical. Passive movement revealed a decreased motion in the carpal and tarsal joints as a result of the bone growth. The horse was obviously lame when it walked. Auscultation of the lungs indicated areas of consolidation. Radiographs revealed extensive subperiosteal hypertrophic osteogenesis of the phalanges, and the metacarpal and metatarsal bones. In the carpal and tarsal joints there was intracapsular involvement but in no case was the articular surface involved. None of the joints were actually fused. A lateral radiograph of the thorax revealed a discrete circular area of increased density approximately 6 inches in diameter. Subsequent necropsy revealed this to be a granular cell myoblastoma.

ETIOLOGY.—The cause of hypertrophic pulmonary osteoarthropathy is unknown. It is very difficult to explain and most believe that lung pathology is primary, with a possible toxin or chronic anoxia causing the bone reaction.

DIAGNOSIS.—A positive diagnosis is rather difficult without necropsy, since radiographs of the lung of a horse are difficult to obtain without powerful equipment. The best diagnostic feature is bilateral bony enlargement of the limbs as shown in Figure 5–19. It should not be confused with hereditary multiple exostosis in which the lesions are more localized. Necropsy findings consisting of lung tumor plus the typical bone enlargements constitute strong evidence of the disease. There is general agreement that the bone is not neoplastic. Metastatic neoplasms in the lung do not appear to be invariably associated with pulmonary osteo-arthropathy.

TREATMENT.—There is no known treatment.

SPECIFIC REFERENCES

1. ALEXANDER, J. E., KEOWN, G. H., and PALOTAY, J. L.: Granular Cell Myoblastoma with Hypertrophic Pulmonary Osteoarthropathy in a Mare. J.A.V.M.A., *146*, No. 7, p. 703, April 1, 1965.
2. CARLSON, W. D.: *Veterinary Radiology*. Philadelphia, Lea & Febiger, 1961.
3. JUBB, K. V. F. and KENNEDY, P. C.: *Pathology of Domestic Animals*, Vol. 1. New York, Academic Press, 1963.
4. SMITH, H. A. and JONES, T. C.: *Veterinary Pathology*. Philadelphia, Lea & Febiger, 1957.

4. Hereditary Multiple Exostosis

DEFINITION.—Hereditary multiple exostosis is a bone disease in which numerous abnormal projections of bone extend out from the normal contour of the affected bones. The new bone growths have a cortex and medulla which are continuous with that of the bones from which they arise. Such exostoses may occur on most of the long bones, as well as the ribs and pelvis. This condition is a developmental anomaly of a proven hereditary cause.

ETIOLOGY.—The disease has been reported in dogs, man, and horses.[1,4] In dogs and man the disease is regarded as being inheritable by nature; this also has been assumed to be the case with horses. In man the disease is presumed to be passed by the male. Two fillies from one affected stallion have been known to have the condition.

SIGNS.—I have observed six cases of this disease. In none of these were signs of lameness severe. A typical case showed enlargement of the carpal and/or hock joints; in one case the carpus had been drained of fluid several times and corticoids had been used intra-articularly. Clinical examination revealed the presence of firm swellings in the region of the dista ends of both radii (Fig. 5–20). Gross nodular swellings at the junction of the middle and ventral thirds of the ribs may be present. The lesions, which may occur on any rib, have been observed as far back as the twelfth rib. They often are unilateral. In addition, lesions may affect the distal

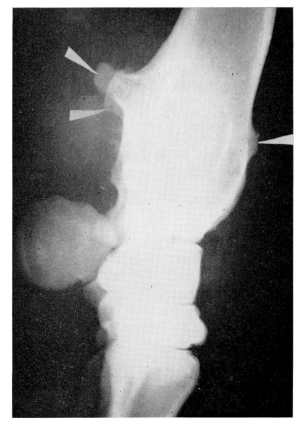

Fig. 5–20.—Hereditary Multiple Exostosis. Pointers indicate the areas of exostosis on the distal end of the radius. Similar growths may occur at the distal end of the tibia; exostosis over the ribs also occurs.

end of the tibia on one, or both, hind limbs. The tarsal joint capsule may be distended. The tuber calcis also may be involved.

DIAGNOSIS.—A horse that shows enlargements of the posterior aspect of the carpal joints, swelling of the hock joints, and bony swelling over the ribs should be suspected of having this condition. Radiographs should be taken of the joints mentioned to determine if these swellings are bone (Fig. 5–20).

Histopathological reports usually will show that there is no neoplasia present in the new bone growth. The medullary cavity of the bone will tend to follow the exostosis; the ends usually will be radiographically smooth on the surface.

TREATMENT.—No known treatment is of value at present.

PROGNOSIS.—The prognosis is unfavorable because there is no known method of removing the exostoses. Some horses, however, may not show lameness and may be functional. The prognosis is unfavorable for a breeding animal.

SPECIFIC REFERENCES

1. AEGERTER, ERNEST and KIRKPATRICK, J. A., JR.: *Orthopedic Diseases.* Philadelphia, W. B. Saunders Co., 1958.
2. CARLSON, W. D.: *Veterinary Radiology.* Philadelphia, Lea & Febiger, 1961.
3. LUCK, J. V.: *Bone and Joint Disease.* Springfield, Ill., Charles C Thomas, 1950.
4. MORGAN, J. P., CARLSON, W. D., ADAMS, O. R.: Hereditary Multiple Exostosis in the Horse. J.A.V.M.A., *140*, 1320, 1962.

REFERENCES

1. ADAMS, O. R.: Nutritional Deficiencies of Foals. Am. Quarterhorse J., *73* (7), 142, April 1961.
2. ANDREYEV, P. P.: On the Structure of the Joints of Horses, J.A.V.M.A., *113*, 483, 1948. (Trans. summary by R. E. Habel from the Veterinarya Feb., *25*, 20, 1948.)
3. AXE, J. WORTLEY: *The Horse in Health and Disease.* Vol. II, London, Gresham Publishing Co., about 1900.
4. BAIN, A. M. and JOHNSTON, K. G.: Bacteroids Arthritis in a Foal, Australian Vet. J., *31*, 210, 1955.
5. BORDEAUX, E. F. J.: Bone Disease in the Horse: A Clinical Study. J. Comp. Path. & Therapy, *37*, 27, 1924.
6. BUNN, C. E. E. and BURCH, J. E.: Hydrocortisone in the Treatment of Traumatic Arthritis in Thoroughbreds. North Am. Vet., *36*, 458, 1955.
7. CAMPBELL, D. M.: Shifting Lameness in the Horse. Vet. Med., *29*, 29, 1934.
8. CARLSON, WM. D.: *Veterinary Radiology.* Philadelphia, Lea & Febiger, 1961.
9. CRAIGE, A. H., JR., and GADD, J. D.: The Determination and Clinical Correlation of Variations in the Calcium, Inorganic Phosphorus and Serum Proteins of Horse Blood. Am. J. Vet. Res., *2*, 227, 1941.
10. CRASEMANN, E.: Landwirtsch. Jahrb. Schweiz., *59*, 504, 1945.
11. DILLON, R.: Corticosteroids in the Treatment of Certain Equine Lamenesses. Vet. Med., *51*, 191, 1956.
12. DIMOCK, W. W. and ERRINGTON, B. J.: Nutritional Diseases of the Equine. No. Amer. Vet., *23*, 152, 1942.
13. EARLE, I. P.: *Grassland Crops as Feed for Horses.* Yearbook of Agriculture, 86–90, 1948.
14. ERRINGTON, B. J.: Variations in Inorganic Phosphorus and Calcium Content in Blood of Horses. Cornell Vet., *27*, 1, 1937.
15. FRANK, E. R.: *Veterinary Surgery.* Minneapolis, Burgess Publishing Co., 1964.
16. GARDNER, ERNEST: Structure and Function of Joints. J.A.V.M.A., *141* (10), 1234, Nov. 15, 1962.
17. GREENLEE, C. W.: Skeletal Diseases of Horses and Their Relation to Nutrition. Cornell Vet., *29*, 115, 1939.
18. GUILBERT, H. R., *et al.*: Minimum Vitamin A and Carotene Requirements of Mammalian Species. J. Nutrition, *19*, 91, 1940.
19. HAYES, I. E.: Treatment of Equine Coxitis with Intra-articular Hydrocortisone. North Amer. Vet., *35*, 673, 1954.
20. HICKMAN, J.: *Veterinary Orthopaedics.* Philadelphia, J. B. Lippincott Co., 1964.
21. HOFFMAN-LAROCHE INC.: *A Primer on Vitamin A for Farm Animals.* Agricultural Division, Nutley, New Jersey, 1965.
22. HOWELL, C. E., HART, G. H., and ITTNER, N. R.: Vitamin A Deficiency in Horses. Am. J. Vet. Res., *2*, 60, 1941.
23. HUTYRA, MAREK and MANNINGER: *Diseases of Domestic Animals,* 5th ed. Chicago, Alexander Eger, *Vol. 3*, 1949.
24. INGLE, H.: The Etiology and Prophylaxis of Equine Osteoporosis. J. Comp. Path. & Therap., *20*, 35, 1907.
25. JENNY, JACQUES: Clinical Diagnosis of Osteoarthritis. J.A.V.M.A., *141* (10), 1253, Nov. 15, 1962.
26. JOHNSON, L. E., THOM, M. A., CHASSELS, J. B., PROCTOR, D. L., and REID, C. F.: *Equine Radiology.* Proceedings 6th Annual Amer. Assoc. Equine Practitioners, Dec., 1960.

27. JOHNSON, LENT C.: Joint Remodelling as the Basis for Osteoarthritis. J.A.V.M.A., *141* (10), 1237, Nov. 15, 1962.
28. JONES, V. B.: Arthritis (A Case of Multiple Arthritis in Thoroughbreds). Vet. J., *102*, 93, 1946.
29. JUBB, K. V. F. and KENNEDY, P. C.: *Pathology of Domestic Animals.* New York, Academic Press, *Vol. 1*, 1963.
30. KATTMAN, J. and KRUL, J.: Intra-articular Injection of Penicillin and Streptomycin Veterinarni Medicina, *5*, 55, 1960.
31. KELSER, R. A. and CALLENDER, G. R.: Equine Degenerative Arthritis. Vet. Med., *33*, 307, 1938.
32. KINTNER, J. H.: The Calcium Phosphorus Ratio in the Ration of Horses, Vet. Med., *35*, 640, 1940.
33. KRIEGER, C. H., BUNKFELDT, R. and STEENBOCK, H.: Cereals and Rickets. J. Nutr., *20*, 7, 1940.
34. KROOK, L. and LOWE, J. E.: *Nutritional Secondary Hyperparathyroidism in the Horse.* New York, S. Karger Basel, 1964.
35. LA CROIX, J. V.: Lameness of the Horse. Veterinary Practice Series, No. 1, Amer. J. Vet. Med., 1916.
36. LIAUTARD, A.: *Lameness of Horses.* New York, Wm. R. Jacobs & Co., 1888.
37. MACKAY-SMITH, MATTHEW P.: Pathogenesis and Pathology of Equine Osteoarthritis. J.A.V.M.A., *141* (10), 1246, Nov. 15, 1962.
38. MANNING, J. P.: Equine Hip Dysplasia—Osteoarthritis. Mod. Vet. Prac., *44* (5), 44, 1963.
39. MANNING, J. P.: Equine Rickets. Proceedings 8th Annual Amer. Assoc. Equine Practitioners, p. 78, 1962.
40. MELLANBY, E.: The Rickets Producing and Anti-Calcifying Action of Phytate (Phytic Acid). J. Physiol., *109*, 488, 1949.
41. MERCK AND COMPANY: *The Merck Veterinary Manual.* Rahway, N. J., Merck & Co., Inc., 557–559, Vol. 2, 1961.
42. MERCK, SHARPE AND DOHME RESEARCH LABORATORIES: *The Adrenocortical Steroids in Veterinary Medicine. An Annotated Bibliography*, Rahway, N. J., Merck & Co., Inc., 1956.
43. M'FADYEAN, J. and EDWARDS, J. F.: Observations with Regards to the Etiology of Joint Ill in Foals. J. Comp. Path. & Therap., *32*, 42, 1919.
44. MILCH, ROBERT A., BURKE, GEORGE J. and FROCK, IRVIN W.: Surgical Management of Degenerative Joint Disease. J.A.V.M.A., *141* (10), 1276, 1962.
45. MILLER, WILLIAM C.: Bone Dystrophy. Irish Vet. J., *15* (8), 156, 1961.
46. MILNE, F. J.: Medical Treatment of Osteoarthritis and Tenosynovitis. J.A.V.M.A. *141* (10), 1269, 1962.
47. MILNE, F. J.: *Subcutaneously Induced Counter-Irritation.* Proceedings 6th Annual Amer. Assoc. Equine Practitioners, p. 25, Dec., 1960.
48. MITCHELL, W. M.: Rheumatic Diseases in the Horse (Osteo-arthritis and Allied Conditions). J. Comp. Path. & Therap., *50*, 282, 1937.
49. National Research Council (Wash., D. C.) Committee on Animal Nutrition: *Recommended Nutrient Allowances for Domestic Animals.* No. VI, 1949.
50. NELSON, A. W.: *Nutrient Requirements for the Light Horse.* Amarillo, Texas, Am. Quarter Horse Assoc., 1961.
51. NICHOLAYSEN, R., et al.: Physiology of Calcium Metabolism. Physiol. Rev., *33*, 424, 1953.
52. Nutritional Review, *16*, 16, 1958.
53. O'DONOGHUE, D. H.: *Treatment of Injuries to Athletes.* Philadelphia, W. B. Saunders Co., 1962.
54. PROCTOR, D. L.: *Meticorten in Equine Practice.* Abstracts of First Veterinary Symposium on Uses of Meticorten and Meticortelone. Schering Laboratories, 1956.
55. RAKER, C. W.: Surgical Treatment of Osteoarthritis and Tenosynovitis. J.A.V. M.A., *141*, 1273, 1962.
56. REID, R. L., FRANKLIN, M. C. and HALLSWORTH, E. G.: The Utilization of Phytate Phosphorus by Sheep. Austral. Vet. J., *23*, 136, 1947.

57. RHODES, W. R.: Radiographic Manifestation of Degenerative Joint Disease. J.A.V.M.A., *141* (10), 1256, Nov. 15, 1962.
58. RILEY, W. F., JR.: Corticosteroids in the Treatment of Certain Equine Lamenesses. Vet. Med., *51*, 191, 1956.
59. ROONEY, J. R.: Epiphyseal Compression in Young Horses. Cornell Vet., *53* (4), 567, Oct. 1963.
60. ROONEY, J. R.: *Equine Medicine and Surgery*, p. 414. Santa Barbara, Calif., Vet. Pub. Inc., 1963.
61. ROONEY, J. R.: Joint Ill. J.A.V.M.A., *141* (10), 1259, Nov. 15, 1962.
62. SCHMIDT, H.: Calcium and Phosphorus Deficiencies in Cattle and Horses, Clinical Picture, Treatment and Prevention. J.A.V.M.A., *96*, 441, 1940.
63. SHARPE AND DOHME: *Arthritis Pt. 1*. Seminar 13, No. 3 (Aug., 1951), 3–19.
64. Ibid.: *Pt. 2*. Seminar 13, No. 4 (Nov., 1951), 3–17.
65. SIPPEL, WILLIAM L.: Equine Degenerative Arthritis. Master of Science Thesis, Cornell University, Ithaca, New York, 1942.
66. SIPPELL, W. L., *et al.*: Nutrition Consultation in Horses by Aid of Feed, Blood and Hair Analysis. Proc. 10th Annual Amer. Assoc. Equine Practitioners, p. 139, 1964.
67. SISSON, S. and GROSSMAN, J. D.: *The Anatomy of Domestic Animals*. 4th ed., Philadelphia, W. B. Saunders Co., 1960.
68. SOKOLOFF, L.: Comparative Pathology of Arthritis. Advances of Vet. Sci. *6*. C. A. Brandly and E. L. Jungher, editors. Academic Press, New York, 193–250, 1960.
69. SOKOLOFF, L., MICKELSEN, O., SILVERSTEIN, E., JAY, G. E., JR. and YAMAMOTO, R. S.: Experimental Obesity in Osteoarthritis. Am. J. Physiol., *198*, 765, 1960.
70. STECHER, ROBERT M.: Discussion of Osteoarthritis. J.A.V.M.A., *141* (10), Nov. 15, 1962.
71. SWENSON, MELVIN J.: Therapeutic Nutrition of Animals. J.A.V.M.A., *141* (11), 1353, Dec. 1, 1962.
72. TEIGLAND, M. B., JENNY, J., WHEAT, J. D., and PROCTOR, D. L.: *Panel on Orthopedic Surgery*. Proceedings 6th Annual Amer. Assoc. Equine Practitioners. Dec., 1960.
73. TEMPLE, J. I.: Fluoprednisolone in Race Horse Practice. J.A.V.M.A., *137*, 136, 1960.
74. TRUM, BERNARD F.: Pathogenesis of Osteoarthritis in the Horse. Laboratory Invest., *8*, 1959.
75. VAN PELT, R. W.: Anatomy and Physiology of Articular Structures. Vet. Med., *57*, 135, 1962.
76. ————: Arthritides of the Diarthrodial Articulation. Mich. State Univ. Vet., *22* (2), 71, Winter 1962.
77. ————: Therapeutic Management of Capped Hocks. Mich. State Univ. Vet., *23* (1), 28, 1962.
78. VIGUE, R. F.: Clinical Evaluation of Prednisolone Trimethylacetate in Arthritis and General Inflammatory Conditions of Horses. Southwestern Vet., *13*, 103, 1960.
79. WATT, L.: Discussion on the X-ray Diagnosis and Treatment of Osteoarthritis. Proceedings Royal Society of Medicine, *26* (1), 337, 1933.
80. WAY, C.: Arthritis and Its Relation to Common Lameness in the Horse. Cornell Vet., *26*, 34, 1936.
81. WAY, C.: The Importance of Vitamin-Mineral Supplements in Equine Nutrition. J.A.V.M.A., *99*, 121, 1941.
82. WAY, C. and HOFFMAN, G. L.: Chronic Equine Arthritis. J.A.V.M.A., *86*, 508, 1935.
83. WAY, CASSIUS: Lameness and Arthritis of Horses. North Am. Vet., *16*, 19, 1935.
84. WHEAT, J. D.: The Use of Hydrocortisone in the Treatment of Joint and Tendon Disorders in Large Animals. J.A.V.M.A., *127*, 64, 1955.
85. WILLIAMS, W.: *The Principles and Practices of Vet. Surgery*. New York, Wm. R. Jenkins Co., 1891.

Lameness

Chapter 6

LAMENESSES IN THE FORELIMB*

1. Sweeny

DEFINITION.—The term "sweeny" can apply to any group of atrophied muscles regardless of location. In popular usage the term more or less applies to atrophy of the supraspinatus and infraspinatus muscles caused by paralysis of the suprascapular nerve.

ETIOLOGY.—Atrophy of muscles results from disuse or loss of nerve supply. In the case of injury to the suprascapular nerve, the etiology is usually trauma from a direct blow to the point of the shoulder.

*For descriptive purposes, lamenesses have been divided into those affecting the forelimb, those affecting the hind limb, and those that are common to both fore and hind limbs. Lamenesses which occur in both fore and hind limbs, but are most common in front, appear in the discussion on lamenesses of the forelimb. Those lamenesses that can occur in both the fore and hind limbs, but are more common in the hind limbs, appear in the discussion of lamenesses of the hind limb. Where it was difficult to make a decision as to whether it was most common in the fore or hind limb, the discussion has been placed in the section dealing with lamenesses common to both fore and hind limbs.

SIGNS.—Atrophy of the supraspinatus and infraspinatus muscles is obvious for it causes the shoulder joint to appear more prominent (Fig. 6–1). The shoulder area appears flattened and the spine of the scapula is prominent. Sometimes the pectoral nerve is involved causing outward bowing of the carpus of the forelimb on the affected side.

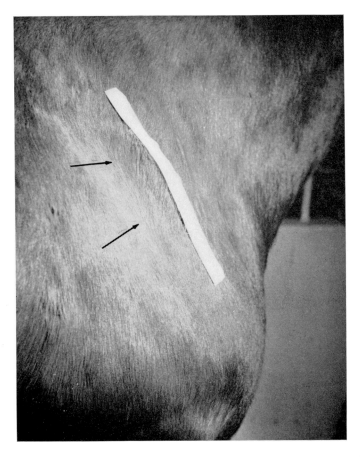

FIG. 6–1.—Sweeny. Arrows indicate atrophy of the infraspinatus muscle. The tape is on the spine of the scapula.

DIAGNOSIS.—Diagnosis of muscular atrophy is easy, but determining the etiology is another matter. A veterinarian should remember that atrophy may result from disuse of the limb as a result of lameness and is not necessarily due to paralysis of a nerve. The attitude of the limb during motion usually reveals whether lameness is present or whether the condition actually is due to paralysis. Muscular dystrophy can occur, and must be differentiated (see page 336).

TREATMENT. —No known treatment is of any value for atrophy due to nerve injury. Antiphlogistic packs and heat applications are probably beneficial to circulation, but they are of no value for nerve damage. Commonly the areas are blistered or fired, but with poor results. Sometimes the atrophied area is injected with subcutaneous irritants to fill the area with scar tissue to cause a normal-appearing shoulder. This is of cosmetic value only.

PROGNOSIS. —Prognosis is guarded to unfavorable. Judgment on the degree of nerve function return should not be made for at least six months, as a long period is required for regeneration of nerves.

2. Inflammation of the Bicipital Bursa (Bursa Intertubercularis) (Bicipital Bursitis)

DEFINITION. —The bicipital bursa, which is quite extensive, is found between the biceps brachii tendon and bicipital groove of the humerus. Movement of the biceps brachii tendon over the groove in the humerus is cushioned by this bursa. The bursa, along with the biceps tendon, is sometimes affected by acute or chronic inflammation, which often is diagnosed as "shoulder lameness." The shoulder, though often blamed for the lameness, seldom is at fault. Race horse trainers often inject the skin over the shoulder with air because of a belief that it is "too tight." This is a ridiculous procedure for the true cause of the lameness often is navicular disease.

ETIOLOGY. —The most common cause of inflammation of this bursa is severe trauma at the point of the shoulder. Other structures also may be injured and fractures involving the scapula or humerus may even be incurred. The same blow may cause "sweeny" as a result of damage to the suprascapular nerve. The bursa may become infected if it is opened, or if an infection causing a septicemia in a disease like navel ill, which results in a suppurative bursitis, localizes here.

SIGNS. —Signs of shoulder lameness include:

1. Marked lifting of the head when the limb is being advanced. This results when the horse tries to advance the limb with a minimum of flexion.

2. Imperfect flexion of the limb causing the foot to be lifted only slightly above ground.

3. Shortened anterior phase of the stride.

4. Stumbling due to insufficient foot clearance and to the short anterior phase of the stride which causes the toe of the foot to land too soon.

5. Fixation of the scapulo-humeral joint, evidenced by restricted movement of the shoulder joint during progression. This is one of the more important signs of shoulder lameness.

6. Indifference to the hardness of the ground. Lameness signs will be approximately the same on hard or soft ground if it is level. Soft ground is more likely to impede movement because of the irregular surface.

11

7. Circumduction of the limb in an effort to overcome the difficulty of advancing it.

8. Dropped elbow if the inflammation is severe, or if the radial nerve also is injured.

When the horse is in motion, he does not flex the limb properly because of the pain. In acute cases, the limb usually is carried while the horse makes a short jump on the sound limb; he usually will not make any attempt to lift the foot of the affected limb when going forward, but he may use the limb in backing. In less acute cases, observation of the horse during movement shows the fixation of the shoulder joint. When the horse is standing, the foot of the affected limb is back of normal position, and usually rests on the toe. Pain usually can be produced by pulling the limb upward and backward. In mild cases, signs similar to navicular disease may occur (page 255).

DIAGNOSIS. —Diagnosis is based on the signs listed above. Swelling of the bursa at the point of the shoulder nearly always is present, but atrophy of the supraspinatus, and other associated muscles, should not be confused with bursitis; atrophy of these muscles causes the shoulder joint to appear to be more prominent. A fixation of the scapulo-humeral joint is one of the most diagnostic signs of shoulder lameness. This is evident when the horse is in motion. If there is doubt about the presence of navicular disease, a diagnostic block of the posterior digital nerves can be done to determine if it is present (page 103). This lameness must be differentiated from fractures of the lateral tuberosity of the humerus, the deltoid process of the humerus, and fracture of the tuber scapulae of the scapula.

TREATMENT. —Injection of the bursa with corticoids, repeated at intervals of approximately one week for four to five injections, plus parenteral corticoid therapy, is one of the most effective methods of treatment. Counter irritation caused by blisters and firing commonly have been employed, but results have not been good. X-radiation might be helpful. The horse must be rested until signs of lameness disappear.

PROGNOSIS. —The prognosis is guarded to unfavorable. If the condition is chronic when the veterinarian first is called, the prognosis is unfavorable because permanent changes may already have occurred.

3. Arthritis of the Shoulder Joint (Omarthritis)

DEFINITION. —Arthritis of the shoulder joint can be due to multiple causes. Most of these causes are due to traumatic bone changes such as fractures. Fracture of the tuber scapulae of the scapula and fracture of the lateral tuberosity of the humerus are the most common of these. In these cases the fractures do not involve large portions of the bone so that the stability of the joint remains. The irritation caused by these fractures produces an arthritis that causes persistent lameness.

ETIOLOGY.—Trauma is the etiology in all cases. Kicks, running into solid objects and other forms of trauma are nearly always involved.

SIGNS.—The signs are highly variable and are not consistent. In some cases they are severe in the early stages, becoming chronic at a later date. In general the signs that are typical of shoulder lameness are present; i.e., holding the head to the affected side when advancing the limb, circumduction of the limb when advancing it to avoid flexion of the shoulder, and standing with the affected limb so that the foot is behind the opposite forefoot. In some cases obvious swelling of the shoulder is present. However, in most cases it is very difficult to distinguish any difference between the normal and abnormal side.

DIAGNOSIS.—Because in many cases there is no obvious swelling of the affected side, differential nerve blocks are helpful. Blocking the median, musculocutaneous, and ulnar nerves will eliminate lamenesses of the lower portion of the limb. When unsoundness still exists after blocking these nerves, the shoulder and elbow joints should receive close scrutiny. Whenever possible, a radiograph should be taken of the shoulder. This requires a good x-ray machine, but if the picture is taken obliquely through the shoulder joint, an adequate radiograph can be obtained. Arthritic changes visible on the radiograph are diagnostic of the condition. Injection of the scapulohumeral joint with 10 cc. of Xylocaine and a corticoid are helpful in diagnosis (see Chapter 11).

TREATMENT.—If osteoarthritis from trauma is in the joint, no treatment will be helpful. However, small chip fractures of the lateral tuberosity of the humerus can be removed successfully. Injection of the shoulder joint with a corticoid may give temporary relief.

4. Paralysis of the Radial Nerve

DEFINITION.—The radial nerve, often the largest branch of the brachial plexus, derives its origin chiefly from the first thoracic root of the plexus. The radial nerve intervates the extensors of the elbow, carpal, and digital joints, and also supplies the lateral flexor of the carpus (ulnaris lateralis). Paralysis of the radial nerve causes inactivity of these muscles.

ETIOLOGY.—In most cases paralysis of the radial nerve is due to trauma of the nerve as it crosses the musculo-spiral groove of the humerus, often accompanying fracture of the humerus. The nerve is traumatized by the fracture, and in some cases is completely severed by a bone fragment. A kick or a fall on the lateral surface of the humerus may produce enough trauma to cause paralysis of the nerve. Prolonged lateral recumbency on an operating table or on the ground may produce radial paralysis in the forelimb next to a hard surface. Whenever a horse is to be cast for a long period of time, it is wise to pad the shoulder if it is next to a hard surface.

Rubber padding, or an inflated tire inner-tube are helpful in preventing injury to the shoulder.

SIGNS.—The signs vary somewhat depending upon the extent or
degree of paralysis. When that portion of the radial nerve supplying the extensors of the digit is affected, the signs are characteristic.
The horse cannot advance the limb to place weight on the foot. If
the foot is placed under the horse, he can bear weight with no diffi-

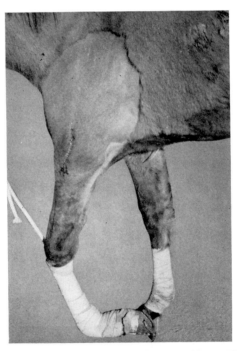

FIG. 6–2.—Paralysis of the radial nerve. Note the "dropped" appearance of the
elbow and the foal's inability to extend the leg and digits. This filly was later
returned to a nearly normal condition by operation to free the nerve from adhesions
and to correct trauma resulting from a fragment of the fractured humerus.

culty. In most cases the branch of the nerve to the triceps muscle
also is involved, so the elbow is dropped and extended while the
digits are flexed (Fig. 6–2). The muscles of the elbow are relaxed,
as are the extensors of the digit, and the limb appears longer than
normal. In severe paralysis, the skin may be worn off the anterior
surface of the fetlock joint, and over the coronary band, from dragging
of the limb. If the injury occurs at the point of the shoulder when
the humerus fractures, the suprascapular nerve may be paralyzed
causing sweeny (page 159).

Occasionally, radial nerve paralysis is accompanied by paralysis
of the entire brachial plexus. In this case the limb shows paralysis

of the flexor and extensor muscles and is unable to bear weight. The elbow is dropped and the affected limb appears to be longer than the opposite limb. The ulna must be carefully examined for fracture when radial paralysis is present. Many cases of radial paralysis are due to external trauma from kicks and the ulna or humerus may be fractured. Examination for crepitation is done by palpating the olecranon and humerus while moving the limb. These areas are also checked for abnormal motion.

Milder cases of radial nerve paralysis may cause little lameness in a slow walk. Then, as the foot encounters an obstacle, the horse may stumble if the toe catches and the foot does not land flat. More difficulty is experienced on uneven ground.

TREATMENT.—Treatment in most cases is of no value and the horse should be stalled to prevent further injury. The limb may be placed in a light plaster cast to prevent contraction of the flexors of the carpus and digits or protected with heavy bandages so that the skin will not wear off the anterior surface of the limb. Manual massage of the muscles of the limb is probably beneficial if this can be accomplished. While waiting for the nerve paralysis to recover, it is usually wise to place the forelimb in a light plaster cast to prevent contraction of the flexor tendons. If recovery does occur, contraction of the flexors is not advanced to the point that no correction can be made. This cast can be changed every two to three weeks.

Limited experience shows that in cases of humeral fracture, surgical correction may be beneficial in repairing the nerve as it crosses the fracture site. The nerve is freed from adhesions and all prominent bone chips are removed so that the nerve is no longer traumatized. If end to end anastamosis can be made it should be done. In other cases, the nerve is stretched, torn and traumatized by the bone fragments. Freeing the nerve, removing the bone fragments, and dissecting out scar tissue will produce a partial or complete recovery in some cases. This procedure should be done between eight and ten weeks following fracture of the humerus so that every possible opportunity is given the nerve to recover before surgical correction is undertaken. Unfortunately, most cases of radial nerve paralysis accompanying fracture of the humerus are permanent and operation is the only alternative for recovery.

PROGNOSIS.—The prognosis is guarded in mild cases, and unfavorable in severe ones. Six months should be allowed for recovery after injury or corrective surgery before any final decision is made. If surgery is used in an attempt to correct the paralysis, it should be done not later than twelve weeks after injury, whenever possible.

SPECIFIC REFERENCE

ROONEY, J. R.: Radial Paralysis in a Horse. Cornell Vet., *53*, 328, 1963.

5. Capped Elbow (see Chapter 5, page 135)

6. Anterior Deviation of the Carpal Joints (Bucked Knees, Knee Sprung, Goat Knees)

DEFINITION.—Bucked knees is a deformity of the carpal joint, consisting of an anterior deviation of the carpus, which causes an alteration in the articulations of the bones forming the joint, and results in constant partial flexion of the carpus (Fig. 1–13B, page 24).

ETIOLOGY.—Several factors are involved in the etiology of bucked knees. Many horses exhibit a mild anterior deviation of both carpal joints, but this may not be serious as it often is the result of a congenital condition from foalhood. Congenital types may be the result of positioning of the limbs in the uterus, or of a mineral and/or vitamin deficiency in the mare. The rickets syndrome of growing foals can produce the condition as a result of a calcium, phosphorus, vitamin A and/or vitamin D imbalance or deficiency (Chapter 5).

Some cases of bucked knees are due to trauma, when certain lamenesses cause inactivity of the flexor group of muscles, allowing them to contract. The muscles most involved are the ulnaris lateralis, flexor carpi-ulnaris, and the deep and/or superficial flexor tendons. Injury to the suspensory ligament, to the deep and/or superficial flexor tendons, or to the heel of the foot, often causes a horse to rest the carpus in an anterior direction. If this is consistent, as the result of pain, the tendons contract to such a degree that they cannot be straightened. In some cases carpal injury, such as carpitis, also may cause anterior deviation of the joint to relieve pain, and thereby cause contraction of the muscles and tendons. Bucked knee due to trauma is usually unilateral.

SIGNS.—Severity of bucked knees varies considerably; in some cases the condition is very mild, while in others it is extreme. When the affected horse is in the normal standing position, one or both carpal joints will be flexed forward at varying degrees. This inhibits normal movement and gait as there is a shortening of the anterior phase of the stride. The condition may be so pronounced that the horse falls to his carpal joints while standing or walking. The carpal joint, or joints, may be unable to support their share of weight, so damage may occur to other areas of the limb. Knuckling of the fetlock also may be present in this condition (Fig. 5–8, page 123) as a result of digital flexor tendon contraction.

TREATMENT.—*Bucked Knees in the Foal.*—If the condition is not severe, meaning that the foal can put its feet flat on the ground without knuckling over to the carpus, and if his nutrition has been good, treatment often is not necessary. Many foals straighten up remarkably well by the time they are six months old. However, if lateral or medial deviation of the carpal joints is present, in addition to bucked knees, corrective procedures may be necessary (*see* Knock Knees, page 168). If medial or lateral deviations are present, or if the condition is considered severe, the limbs may be put into plaster casts.

To correct bucked knees, the following method of casting should be used. The foal should be anesthetized with pentobarbital sodium* and the limb padded with cotton, or other suitable material. A light layer of 4-inch plaster of paris bandage should be applied to the limb from hoof wall to elbow joint using 3 rolls of plaster. As the plaster dries, one or two pieces of moist yucca board, or other suitable material (25 inches long, $\frac{1}{8}$ inch thick, $5\frac{3}{4}$ inches wide) should be placed on the volar aspect of the limb, and two or three more rolls of 4-inch plaster of paris bandage used to pull the carpus toward the rigid support. Considerable tension may be applied to this second layer over the yucca board if proper padding has been placed over the pressure points of the limb. The pressure points are the anterior surface of the carpal joint, and two points on the volar aspect of the limb at the proximal and distal ends of the yucca board or other rigid support.

The foal should be left in the cast for approximately ten days to two weeks. In many cases it will not be necessary to reapply the cast, but if a new cast is necessary, it should not be applied for ten to fourteen days after the first cast is removed. This time interval will allow the foal to partially overcome the effects of disuse atrophy in the musculature. A second cast should be applied in the same manner as the first, and removed following a ten or fourteen day period. (Correction of medial deviation of the carpal joints is discussed on page 169.)

A complete check of the horse's diet should be made, and the diet fortified, if necessary, with those elements considered deficient. Foals that develop bucked knees after birth should be considered rickets suspects and treated accordingly.

Bucked Knees Due to Injury.—When a bucked knee condition is due to injury to the carpus or other structures, it is necessary to direct treatment at correction of the original pathological changes. The bucked knee condition will usually take care of itself. Pathological changes in the flexor tendons, suspensory ligament, the foot, or the carpus, are most often responsible for this type of bucked knee. If the condition is not of long duration, and is corrected promptly, the tendons will gradually stretch and the carpus will again assume a normal position.

Surgical Correction.—When bucked knees are so severe in a foal that the condition cannot be properly corrected with plaster casts, or when the condition persists in a mature horse after injury to some structure, so that there is little hope of natural correction, a tenotomy of the ulnaris lateralis and the flexor carpi-ulnaris tendons should be undertaken. This operation is most successful for bucked knees which result from trauma, and is less successful for those that are congenital. The cause of this is that often times the carpal bones are deformed in congenital bucked knees, whereas in an acquired

*Nembutal, Abbott Laboratories.

condition the carpal bones are relatively normal. In addition, bucked knees which are congenital show contraction of the deep and superficial flexor tendons, the suspensory ligament, as well as the ulnaris lateralis and flexor carpi-ulnaris tendons.

Surgical correction can be performed with the horse in standing position if he is tractable, but the horse should be thrown and tied if unmanageable. Tranquilization with promazine,* $\frac{1}{2}$ mg. per pound of body weight, intravenously, may be necessary if the operation is to be done while the horse is standing. The operative area is 1 to $1\frac{1}{2}$ inches above the accessory carpal bone on the volar aspect of the limb.

The area should be clipped, shaved, and prepared for aseptic operation. Anesthesia should be accomplished by injecting a local anesthetic, such as lidocaine hydrochloride.† If the horse is placed in recumbency, the tendons should be tensed by extending the carpus. The depression between the two tendons is located on the volar surface of the limb about 1 inch above the accessory carpal bone. An incision $\frac{1}{4}$ inch long should be made through the skin and subcutaneous tissue, and a blunt-pointed bistoury inserted through the wound at the side of the tendon of the ulnaris lateralis muscle. The tendon then should be severed by cutting outward with the bistoury until the knife edge can be felt beneath the skin. The limb should be extended during the cutting procedure. The bistoury then should be turned and the tendon of the flexor carpi-ulnaris severed. Care must be exercised not to cut too deeply, or structures underlying the muscles may be injured. One suture should then be placed in the incision and the area kept bandaged for at least ten days. The patient should not be worked for six to eight weeks. If the limb cannot be fully straightened following tenotomy, it is beneficial to place the limb in a cast from elbow to fetlock joint. This cast should be left in place ten to fourteen days before being removed.

PROGNOSIS.—The prognosis is guarded in all acquired cases of bucked knees, and it is to be expected that some horses will never be returned to full use. However, most such conditions can be improved so that the horse can serve as a useful brood animal. The prognosis is favorable in mild, congenital types if the nutrition of the foal has been good or is corrected. Severe congenital types result in an unfavorable prognosis.

7. Medial Deviation of the Carpal Joints in Foals (Knock Knees)

DEFINITION.—Knock knees in foals usually are a congenital condition. The foal may be born with varying degrees of medial deviation of one or both carpal joints, and as he grows older the condition either improves or becomes so severe that permanent

*Sparine, Wyeth Laboratories or Promazine, Fort Dodge Laboratories.
†Xylocaine, Astra Laboratories.

deformity results. A few foals are born with reasonably straight limbs but the deviation occurs as they grow older. A condition similar to knock knees occurs in the hock joints of rear limbs. This will not be discussed as a separate condition because the etiology and treatment are similar to deviation of the carpal joints. Some cases of carpal or tarsal deviations may be due to an inheritable factor.

ETIOLOGY. — If the foal is born with medial deviation of the carpal joints, the condition may be inheritable or due to nutritional deficiency. In cases that develop after birth, it is believed that nutrition, in the form of rickets, plays a role (Chapter 5). The importance of nutrition in those cases present at birth is not fully understood. All cases at birth should be closely checked for nutrition, and, if necessary, blood samples of several horses of the herd analyzed to determine if any deficiencies in calcium, phosphorus, vitamin A, carotene or vitamin D are present.

SIGNS. — The signs are obvious, but determination of the etiology can cause difficulty (Fig. 1–14B, page 25 and Fig. 6–3). An analysis of blood, as mentioned above, should be used if nutrition is suspected as a cause. Some mares repeatedly have foals of this type when bred to the same stallion. In this case, an inheritable characteristic should be suspected.

TREATMENT. — In most cases plaster casts are the best treatment for deviation of the carpal or hock joints (Fig. 6–4). Treatment should begin at an early age, preferably at about three weeks. The foal should be anesthetized with pentobarbital sodium,* and the area to be in the cast covered with 2-inch stockinette. The limb should be padded by placing cotton between the fetlock and coronary band, and by covering the limb with combine pads of $\frac{1}{2}$ inch thick cotton-gauze. The combine pads should be covered with 3-inch gauze and a small amount of tape used to hold the padding in place. This type of padding should be used from coronary band to elbow joint. The pressure points should be given additional padding. These are the outside of the limb below the elbow joint, the outside of the coronary band, and the inside of the carpal joint. Following padding of these points with cotton, the limb should be wrapped with three rolls of blue label, Johnson and Johnson 4-inch plaster of paris bandage. Just as the plaster starts to dry, two pieces of moistened yucca board or other suitable material such as bass wood or aspen wood,† (25 inches long, $\frac{1}{8}$ inch thick, $5\frac{3}{4}$ inches wide) should be placed over the outside of the limb. The moist condition of the wood enables a person to form it to the shape of the limb. Strips of 2-inch tape are used to hold these in position, and then an additional two rolls of blue label, Johnson and Johnson 4-inch plaster of paris bandages should be placed on the limb, pinning the carpus as tightly as possible to the rigid support. Pressure should

*Nembutal, Abbott Laboratories.
†Berbert Surgical Supply, Denver, Colorado.

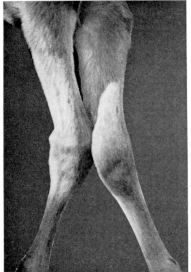

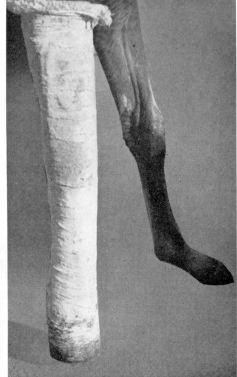

FIG. 6–3   FIG. 6–4

FIG. 6–3.—Knock knees in a foal.

FIG. 6–4.—Cast on forelimb of a foal suffering from medial deviation of the carpus. This cast was applied as described. Both forelegs may be cast at the same time, if necessary.

be especially heavy over the medial aspect of the carpus to straighten the limb. With larger foals, four rolls of 4-inch plaster bandage may be necessary.

The original rolls of plaster of paris, plus the padding, greatly aid in preventing any complications as the result of the plaster cast. The foot should be bandaged so that the hoof wall is incorporated in the cast. The foal and dam should be placed in a box stall so the foal gets little, if any, exercise. After ten to fourteen days, the cast should be removed and the foal left in the stall for another ten to fourteen days. At the time of removal of the cast it will be noted that there has been considerable atrophy of the muscles of the forearm, and that the flexor tendons have been weakened. These conditions will correct themselves. After ten to fourteen days a new cast should be applied in the same fashion as the original, if it is deemed necessary. If the foal shows marked straightening of the limb, a second cast is not necessary because the limb will tend to continue to grow straight. In some cases the condition is bilateral, so casts should be placed on both limbs at the same time.

If the foal shows pain when using the limb, or limbs, during the interval that the cast is in place, the cast should be removed immediately. This may signify excessive pressure and necrosis. The first signs that the cast is causing trouble are disuse of the limb, and an increase of temperature. Decreased use of the limb should be heeded immediately.

Most affected foals can be almost perfectly straightened by the use of one or more casts. However, in some cases the epiphyseal growth centers are damaged so the bone grows more rapidly on the medial side, and permanent deformity results. This is especially true if the condition is unilateral. Epiphyseal staples are of value in this case.

If the carpal joints have a lateral deviation (bowed knees), the casts should be applied in the same fashion, but the rigid support should be placed on the inside of the leg. The pressure points, under the top and bottom of the wood and over the outside of the carpal joint, should receive extra padding. The same type of therapy should be used when the hocks show a medial deviation. The cast should be applied in the same way, with the rigid support on the outside.

When the casts are removed, the flexor tendons will have weakened, and the fetlock will drop further than normal. Until the flexor tendons have strengthened so that the fetlocks are raised to a normal position the foal should be confined to a box stall. After the fetlock assumes a normal position, normal exercise can begin. Normally, confinement should continue ten to fourteen days following cast removal.

Braces with hinge joints have been developed for knock knees and are successful if anterior rotation of the brace can be prevented. Braces require daily attention and resetting. The advantage of braces is that muscular atrophy will not be as great.

After the foal is approximately four months of age, epiphyseal stapling to limit growth of one side of the epiphysis is more effective than casts for straightening the limbs. One must keep in mind that the staples must have several months in which to exert their effect. The various epiphyseal areas close at different times making it mandatory that some areas be stapled sooner than others; i.e., the distal epiphysis of the third metacarpal or metatarsal bone closes between nine and twelve months. This means that any stapling of the fetlock joint must be done at least by six months of age and preferably sooner. In the case of the carpus and tibia, these epiphyses close at approximately twenty-four months of age. There is considerable variation but twenty-four months is the standard age limit used. This means that whenever possible, the staples should be put in at least by fifteen months of age, and preferably sooner.

The fundamentals of stapling an epiphysis are that the staples be put on the convex side of the curvature, thereby limiting growth on that side. This allows the concave side to grow and eventually straighten the bone. The concave side of the epiphysis carries more weight load as a result of the deformity, thus the growth rate on this side is slower than normal. Compression of an epiphysis limits growth, while reduction of weight load allows it to grow faster.

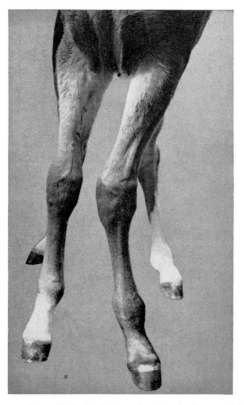

Fig. 6–5.—An example of limb deviation due to uterine positioning. The right forelimb has slight lateral deviation of the carpus and the left forelimb has severe medial deviation of the carpus. Both limbs are bowed toward the same direction. These would require opposite pressures with casts to straighten the limbs.

The stapling technique is relatively simple. The following description can be used for medial or lateral deviation of either the tarsus or carpus. In general, stapling the carpus is more successful than stapling of the tarsus. The foal is anesthetized by a standard method. The convex side of the distal end of the tibia or distal end of the radius is clipped and shaved and prepared for aseptic surgery. A skin incision is made longitudinally over the convex surface of the bone. The epiphysis is identified by its prominence or by radiographs and three staples are placed so that one leg of the staple is below the epiphyseal line and one above it (Fig. 6–7). The legs on the staples are approximately 1 inch long and the body of the staple is approximately 1 inch long. Three staples are ordinarily used in the tibia or a radius. The staples can easily be made from Steinman intermedullary pins. They are approximately $\frac{5}{64}$ inch in

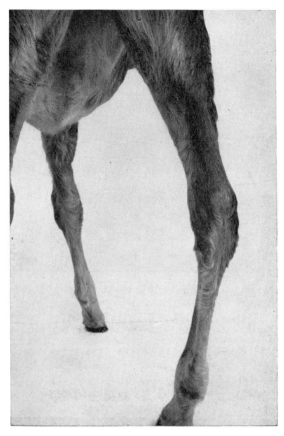

Fig. 6–6.—An example of looseness of the lateral-collateral ligament of the tarsal joint. In this case the limb bows outward when weight is placed on it. At other times it can be pushed to a normal position by hand. This should not be confused with deviation of the limbs from nutritional causes. This type of condition is treated by placing the limb in a cast for approximately four weeks.

diameter, and the ends are sharpened with a file (Fig. 6–9). They are driven into the bone by use of a bone hammer. Special apparatus for holding the pins while driving them is available.[1,2] Ready-made staples are also available. The subcutaneous tissue is closed over the pins with a 00 catgut suture. The skin is then closed with a non-capillary type suture with simple interrupted pattern. A pressure bandage is kept in place over the incisions for approximately two weeks. Exercise should be limited for sixty days.

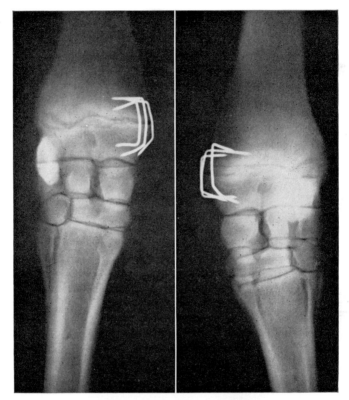

FIG. 6–7.—Radiograph of an example of correcting medial deviation of the carpal joints with three staples on the medial aspect of the distal epiphysis of each radius.

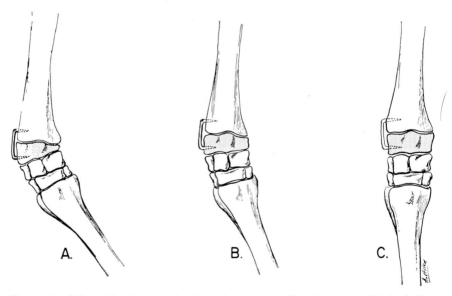

A. B. C.

FIG. 6–8.—Schematic drawing showing placement of the pins in medial deviation of the carpal joints (courtesy of Dr. C. D. Heinze and A.A.E.P.).

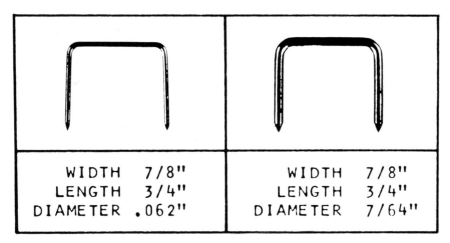

WIDTH 7/8"	WIDTH 7/8"
LENGTH 3/4"	LENGTH 3/4"
DIAMETER .062"	DIAMETER 7/64"

Fig. 6–9.—Examples of epiphyseal staples. On the left, a staple made from .062 Kershner wire. The staple on the right is made from a $\frac{7}{64}$ inch Steinman pin. (Courtesy Dr. C. D. Heinze and A.A.E.P.)

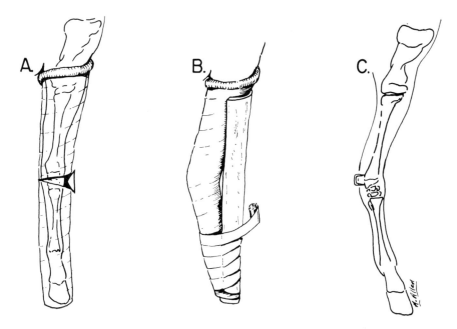

Fig. 6–10.—Examples of various ways of correcting deviation of the forelimb. A, Wedging the dry cast. B, Yucca board applied over green cast. C, Stapling. (Courtesy Dr. C. D. Heinze and A.A.E.P.)

One of the complications of epiphyseal stapling is the production of a large amount of fibrous tissue over the staples. This usually is minimal when the pins are placed in the bone, but is a much greater factor when the staples are removed.

Removal of the staples often proves to be more difficult than placing them in the bone. They are difficult to find because fibrous tissue covers them completely. One should have a special staple remover, or a screwdriver, to drive under the staples for removal. The staples are removed under the same type of anesthetic used to put them in place. The skin, subcutaneous tissue and fibrous tissue over the staples are incised, and the staples located. Some fibrous tissue has to be removed before the staples can be found. A screwdriver type blade is driven under the ends of the staple and they are lifted out with pliers. Once the staple is located they are usually quite easy to remove. Subcutaneous tissue is closed with 00 catgut and the skin with a nonabsorbable skin suture. A pressure bandage should be kept in place at least three weeks to aid in preventing excessive fibrous tissue formation. Fibrous tissue often develops in spite of the best possible technique.

The staples are not removed until the limb is completely straight. It is possible that in some cases it would be best to leave the staples, provided they were causing no irritation and provided the epiphysis was mature and closed. In a growing eiphysis, staples left too long can overcompensate and cause a deviation opposite to the one corrected.

Corrective hoof trimming is indicated for all limb deviations. An attempt is made to keep the hoof wall level. When the carpal joints are bowed inward, excessive wear usually occurs on the inside wall. When they are bowed outward, excessive wear usually occurs on the outside wall. In all cases check to see which wall the foal is landing on and trim the opposite wall. In deviation of the fetlock joints where the foot is deviated medially, excessive wear usually occurs on the outside wall. Corrective trimming must be done every two weeks to prevent the foot from wearing off-level.

PROGNOSIS. —The prognosis is guarded in all cases, but improvement can be expected. However, one must be exceedingly cautious in application of the cast to be sure that all areas are sufficiently padded to prevent complications.

SPECIFIC REFERENCES

1. HEINZE, C. B.: Proceedings 9th Annual A.A.E.P., p. 203, Dec. 1963.
2. ————: Proceedings 11th Annual A.A.E.P., Dec. 1965.
3. MAY, V. R. and CLEMENTS, E. L.: Epiphyseal Stapling; With Special Reference to Complications. Southern Medical J., *58*, 1203, 1965.

8. Hygroma of the Carpus (see Chapter 5, page 138)

DEFINITION. —A hygroma is a synovial swelling over the anterior surface of the carpal joint. Most commonly it is an acquired bursitis as a result of trauma. Normally there is not a subcutaneous bursa in this area but through trauma a bursa may form (see Chapter 5). The tendon sheath of the extensor carpi radialis and/or the common digital extensor, may also be involved. A synovial hernia of the radiocarpal or intercarpal joint capsule can occur. This causes a hygroma-like swelling that is almost indistinguishable from those caused by an acquired bursitis. However, careful examination will reveal that the swelling on the anterior surface of the carpus is irregular in outline and does not uniformly cover the carpus when a synovial hernia has occurred. Acquired bursitis shows an evenly distributed swelling over the anterior surface of the carpus.

ETIOLOGY.—Trauma is the etiology in all cases. Horses that get up and down on hard ground most commonly are involved. Hygroma also can be produced as a result of a horse pawing and hitting the carpus on a hard surface such as a wall.

SIGNS.—Signs are swellings of varying shapes over the anterior surface of the carpus. The swellings vary with the structure or structures involved (Fig. 6–11).

TREATMENT.—Injection of corticoids, followed by counterpressure with elastic bandage, appears to be the most effective method of treatment. Injections should be repeated 3 to 5 times one week apart (page 442). Continued pressure of the elastic bandage is used to promote adhesions between the distended skin

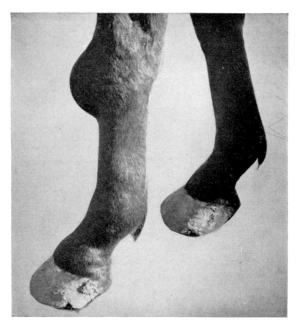

FIG. 6–11.—Hygroma of the carpus. In this case the bursa over the carpal joint is the structure most involved.

and underlying tissues. The distended skin will thicken producing a permanent blemish. A second treatment is to open and drain the hygroma and swab the cavity daily with tincture of iodine. This causes a long continued drainage of the lesion. You must be absolutely certain that the carpal joint capsule is not opened, because it can enlarge in conjunction with a hygroma. Opening of the joint capsule can be disastrous. Injections of the bursal sac with Lugol's iodine also have been used, as have blistering and firing of the area, but these methods are less helpful. If the lesion responds to corticoid therapy, the healing time can be shortened.

A hygroma of long standing with a thickened synovial lining can be surgically removed under general anesthesia. The hygroma is carefully dissected out after preparing the area for aseptic surgery. An elliptical incision is made over the front of the swelling and the mass dissected out by using curved Mayo scissors to separate the tissues. In most cases the bursa can be dissected completely free without puncture. However, if the bursa is punctured, it can be dissected out by staying outside the thickened wall. If the joint capsule is involved, *i.e.*, a synovial hernia resembling a hygroma, the opening to it is closed with catgut. This opening is usually very small. Subcutaneous tissue is closed with 00 catgut, and the skin is sutured with a non-capillary suture using simple interrupted or vertical mattress suture pattern. The operative area is kept under pressure bandage for thirty days following surgery and activity is limited to a box stall during this period.

PROGNOSIS.—Prognosis is guarded to favorable. Old cases will retain considerable swelling because of fibrous tissue that has been laid down in the inflamed area. Such cases usually are of unfavorable prognosis because adhesions may not form following corticoid therapy, and may require surgical drainage or removal.

9. Carpitis (Popped Knee)

DEFINITION.—Carpitis is an acute or chronic inflammation of the carpal joint often involving joint capsule, the associated ligaments of the carpus, and the bones of the carpus. In early stages, carpitis may consist of a serous arthritis due to trauma. Later, the joint may become severely involved with osteoarthritis if the condition is not treated properly, if the original injury is severe, or if the joint is subjected to repeated trauma.

ETIOLOGY.—Concussion and trauma are primary causes of carpitis. The condition is especially common in race horses, as a result of hard training. Horses that are not in condition or are worked too hard, are prone to develop carpitis. Also, poor conformation of the carpus may be an important factor in development of the condition. Bad conformation, such as calf-knees or bench knees, shows poor bone alignment on radiographic examination, and poor bone alignment is probably a predisposing cause of the condition (Chapter 1). Infrequently, new bone growth occurs in these same areas as the result of direct trauma to the anterior surface of the carpal joint as a result of the horse pawing and hitting a wall with the carpus.

SIGNS. — Pathological changes occur predominantly on the anterior surface of the bones forming the carpus; the distal end of the radius, the proximal row of carpal bones, the distal row of carpal bones, and upon occasion, on the proximal end of the third metacarpal bone. The radial and intermediate carpal bones in the proximal row, and the third carpal bone in the distal row are the bones most commonly involved (Figs. 6–12 and 13). The damage usually is in the form of new bone growth in these areas. If the injury is severe in the beginning or if the joint is injured repeatedly, new bone growth will result (Fig. 5–12, page 132, and Fig. 6–13). In most cases, new bone growth is the result of periostitis, probably due to a pulling of the attachments of the joint capsule through the periosteum on the involved carpal bones. In some cases it is possible that a pulling of the intercarpal ligaments, between the carpal bones, aids in production of new bone growth by disturbing the periosteum and causing a periostitis.

Osteoarthritis is present in those cases which show bone changes (Fig. 5–12, page 134, and Fig. 6–13). Mild cases which show no bone change are affected with a serous arthritis of the carpal joint.

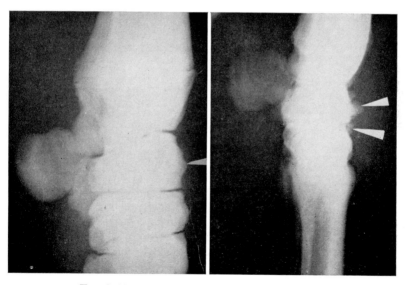

FIG. 6–12   FIG. 6–13

FIG. 6–12. — Carpitis as viewed on a lateral radiograph of the carpal joint. The pointer indicates a healed area of new bone growth on the anterior surface of the intermediate carpal bone.

FIG. 6–13. — Severe carpitis as viewed on a lateral radiograph of the carpus. Pointers indicate extensive new bone growth involving the radial, intermediate, and third carpal bones.

In acute carpitis, lameness is very evident as a supporting and swinging leg lameness. A shortening of the anterior phase of the stride, due to decreased flexion of the carpus, is evident and there is a tendency for the horse to hold the carpus slightly flexed in the standing position. Swelling is present, resulting from a distention of the joint capsule and associated periarticular structures also may be enlarged (Fig. 6–14).

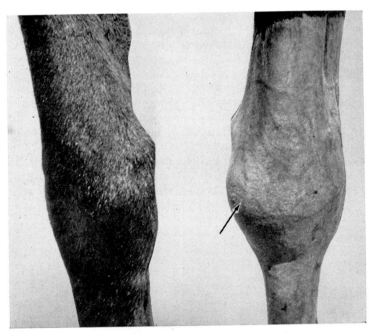

FIG. 6–14.—The arrow indicates swelling commonly observed with carpitis. Without radiographs this condition is difficult to distinguish from the swelling observed as a result of fracture of the radial and third carpal bones.

In a chronic case, lameness may not be evident until the horse is used at a fast gait. Examination will reveal an enlargement on the anterior surface of the intermediate, radial, and third carpal bones and a fibrous inflammatory tissue over the area of the injury. It is sometimes difficult to tell if the fibrous tissue is bony enlargement or soft tissue swelling, unless a radiographic examination is made. Soft tissue crepitation will be evident under pressure on the anterior surface of the carpal joint. Chronic cases may have well developed exostosis present, the extent of which can be determined by radiographic examination.

DIAGNOSIS.—Carpitis, as such, usually is not difficult to diagnose on the basis of the symptoms described above. However, it is always important to bear in mind the possibility of a fracture of one of the carpal bones; the intermediate, radial and third carpal bones are most commonly fractured. Such a fracture can best be determined by taking radiographs of the lateral view, anterior-posterior view, oblique views, and lateral flexed joint view of the carpus. It is important that the carpus be flexed during palpation for diagnosis. Flexing the carpus aids in determining the exact location of the pathological changes (Fig. 4–3, page 99).

TREATMENT.—Cases for treatment should be selected on the basis of radiographic examination. If new bone growth is present on the articular surfaces of the radio-carpal joint, the intercarpal joint, or the carpal-metacarpal joint, treatment often is not successful. The owner should be advised of this fact and treatment undertaken only with proper understanding of the unfavorable prognosis.

If carpitis is in the acute stage, in the form of a serous arthritis, corticoids should be injected into the carpal joint (Chapter 11). Three injections of corticoids, approximately one week apart, are the most satisfactory. The carpus should then be bandaged and the horse rested for a minimum of four months. If new bone growth is present, corticoids will give temporary relief, but symptoms will recur as soon as the horse is put back in training, unless the proper healing time is allowed. The greatest difficulty in treating this condition with corticoids is that the relief afforded by the injections allows the owner to use the horse too soon; thus, reinjury occurs and more new bone growth can be expected. Casting the joint to immobilize it, following injection of corticoids, is also beneficial. The cast should be left in place approximately two weeks.

Blistering is common for this condition, but in general is not satisfactory treatment. If a person wishes to apply a counter-irritant, it should be in the form of firing, or radiation therapy. Carpitis is one condition in which point firing appears to be beneficial. If the joint shows signs of new bone growth, which is not encroaching on the articular surfaces, firing can be done after acute inflammation has disappeared. A leg paint should be applied for a span of twenty-one days following the firing, and the horse should be rested approximately six months before being put back into training. Many horses treated in this fashion can be returned to racing.

Radiation therapy has proved satisfactory in some cases of carpitis. Both x-radiation, (approximately 1000 roentgens) and cobalt-60 therapy, with gamma rays (1000 to 1200 roentgens) have been used. These are also methods of applying counterirritation (see Chapter 11).

In summary, one might say that if carpitis is acute, and in the form of a serous traumatic arthritis, corticoid injections, intra-articularly, are indicated followed by prolonged rest. If new bone growth is present, but is not encroaching on the articular surfaces, firing or radiation therapy is indicated and will aid recovery in most instances. In those severe cases where new bone growth is encroaching on the articular surfaces of the bones, firing or radiation therapy may be used, but with an unfavorable prognosis.

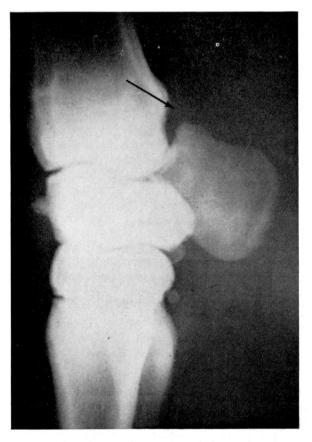

Fig. 6-15.—Radiograph of a carpus showing carpitis with periosteal new bone growth on the radial carpal bone and rupture of the proximal ligament of the accessory carpal bone (arrow). Normally the proximal portion of the accessory carpal bone lies close to the radius. Note how the accessory carpal bone is tilted downward. The prognosis would be unfavorable. Note the presence of the first carpal bone on the radiograph.

Most cases that show new bone growth encroaching on the articular surfaces can be made sound only by surgical removal of the bony growths. The surgical approach is very similar to that for fracture of the carpal bones. The new bone proliferations are removed by means of rongeurs and the surfaces curetted smooth. A cast is used for approximately eight days following surgery and then a pressure wrap for at least thirty days. The horse is confined to a box stall for thirty to forty-five days and no training begun for at least six months. Although the prognosis is more unfavorable than in chip fractures, this type of therapy sometimes yields a sound horse that could be cured in no other way.

PROGNOSIS. — The prognosis is guarded to favorable in early stages, if conformation is good. If new bone growth is present, but is not encroaching on the articular surfaces, prognosis is guarded. If new bone growth is present and is encroaching on the articular surface, the prognosis is unfavorable. When poor conformation is a factor the prognosis is always unfavorable, regardless of type, because of the likelihood of recurrence.

10. Fracture of the Carpal Bones

DEFINITION. — The radial and third carpal bones are most commonly fractured in the carpal joint. The intermediate carpal bone is fractured more rarely. The radial and intermediate carpal bones usually fracture with small chips from the proximal or distal portions of the bone on the anterior surface. The third carpal bone may fracture with a small chip or with a large slab fracture (Fig. 6–16). Chip fractures from the radius and from the third metacarpal bone can occur (Figs. 6–18 and 6–19). Fractures can occur from more than one carpal bone and can include any combination of those listed above.

ETIOLOGY. — Trauma is the etiology of fracture of the carpal bones. From the appearance of the fractures it would seem that overextension of the limb is the probable cause in many cases. This puts great stress on the anterior face of the carpal bones and radius, and portions may fracture off under the circumstances.

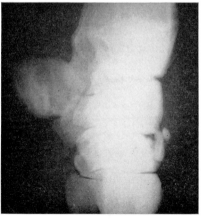
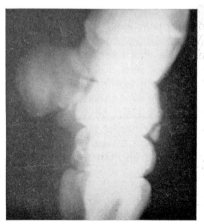

 FIG. 6–16   FIG. 6–17

FIG. 6–16. — Fracture of the third carpal bone. Note that two pieces of the third carpal bone have broken off. The large piece is a typical "slab" fracture.

FIG. 6–17. — Fracture of the radial carpal bone, viewed on lateral radiograph of the carpus. In this case, oblique views were necessary to determine whether the intermediate or the radial carpal bone was fractured.

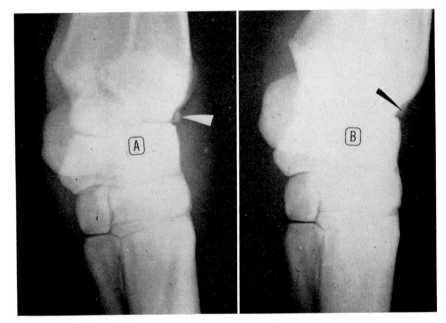

FIG. 6–18.—Chip fracture of the radius.

A, Pointer indicates chip fracture of the radius near the center of the anterior edge of the articular surface of the bone, as viewed on a lateral radiograph.

B, Pointer indicates same area after chip fracture had been removed surgically.

SIGNS.—Signs of fracture of the carpal bones are similar to those of carpitis: heat, pain and swelling of the carpal joint, and lameness. Many times such fractures are fired for what is believed to be carpitis when radiographs have not been used for diagnosis. When no response is noted after firing of a carpitis, radiographs may reveal fracture of one of the above mentioned bones. In most cases, it is advisable to take radiographs of all cases of carpitis prior to treatment to eliminate a possible fracture; oblique views should be taken of the carpus to eliminate the possibility of overlooking a fracture. A hard, prominent swelling is usually noted at the antero-medial surface of the carpal joint after the fracture has been present some time.

DIAGNOSIS.—The radial, intermediate and third carpal bones are fractured most commonly, but chip fractures of the radius may occur. A positive diagnosis can be made only by means of radiographs. These radiographs should include an antero-posterior view, a lateral view, a flexed joint lateral view, and, if necessary, oblique views of the carpus. Oblique views are necessary because these fractures are not evident unless the angle of the radiograph is so that the line of fracture will show up. Persistent lameness with hard swelling at the antero-medial aspect of the carpal joint should cause one to suspect a fracture until this possibility is eliminated by com-

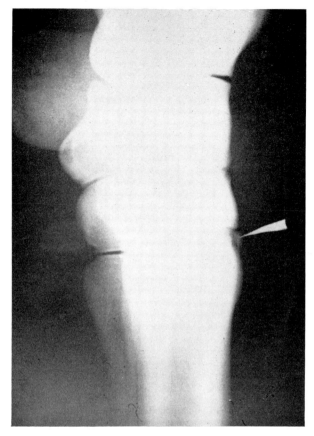

Fig. 6–19.—Chip fracture proximal end third metacarpal bone. This type of fracture in the carpus is quite rare. It can be removed in a similar fashion to that described for other fractures making incision directly over the fractured portion, after determining by oblique radiographs on which side of the tendon it lies.

plete radiographic examination. Careful palpation of the flexed carpal joint enables a person to locate the fracture site with considerable accuracy once radiographs have shown that one is present.

If the synovial lining should form villi from a persistent traumatic arthritis in the joint, similar signs to those of fractured carpus may occur. If the villi become impinged in the joint as it closes, they cause persistent joint effusion and intermittent lameness. When lameness of this nature occurs, and no fracture is present, villi should be suspected. Surgical removal is done when possible.

TREATMENT. — The only effective treatment is surgical removal of the fragments or surgical fixation of the fragments by means of bone screws. Although carpal fractures will sometimes heal without surgical intervention, this is rare and takes many months, during which time considerable periosteal reaction results which often

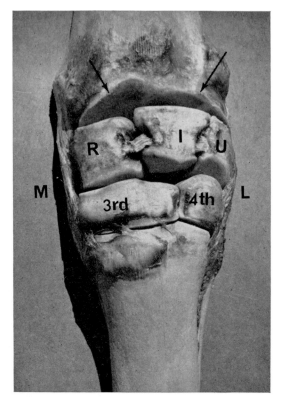

FIG. 6–20.—Normal left bony carpus. U—ulnar carpal bone. I—intermediate carpal bone. R—radial carpal bone. $3rd$—third carpal bone. $4th$—fourth carpal bone. Arrows indicate areas where chip fractures may occur on radius. L—lateral side. M—medial side.

involves the articular surfaces of the joints, causing permanent lameness. The surgical approach to the fracture fragments should be carefully determined by radiographs and palpation. One must positively identify the radiocarpal and intercarpal joints so that the exact joint required may be exposed for fracture removal. Chip fractures of the radial and intermediate carpal bones may be removed either from the radiocarpal or intercarpal joints. Fractures may come only from the top or bottom of these bones and the joint closest to the fracture should be selected. Fractures of the third carpal bone are removed by exposing the intercarpal joint. Fractures of the radius are removed by incision directly over the fracture site in the radiocarpal joint.

The surgical procedure is as follows: The horse is tranquilized, given 250 to 350 cc. of 6 per cent chloral hydrate intravenously and 1 gram of thiamylal sodium intravenously. The thiamylal sodium*

* Surital, Parke, Davis Co.

is given rapidly and the horse will collapse, making the casting and tying more easily done. Thiamylal sodium is then administered to effect intravenously by the use of a polyethylene catheter placed in the jugular vein. It is preferable not to exceed 4 to 5 grams of thiamylal sodium during the surgical procedure. If the leg is clipped and shaved before the horse is cast, this will shorten the time required in recumbency. If desired, the surgical area may be infiltrated with local anesthetic. If the surgeon has the equipment for closed circuit intratracheal gas anesthesia, Halothane* makes an excellent general anesthetic.

A tourniquet above the carpus is used to control hemorrhage. Preferably this is a pneumatic type which does not cause any arterial spasm, but broad rubber elastic bands may be used.

The surgical site is prepared for aseptic surgery and protected with a sterile plastic drape† and shrouds. The joint is flexed so that the radiocarpal and intercarpal joints can be positively identified, and the incision is then made over the affected area. Most fractures will occur medial to the tendon of the extensor carpi radialis muscle on the radial carpal and third carpal bones. The incision is made so that the bursa protecting the tendon is not opened. The extensor carpi obliquus tendon usually lies far enough medially so that it is easily avoided during surgery. Some fractures of the intermediate carpal bone require an incision more lateral, between the tendons of the extensor carpi radialis and the common digital extensor. This is also the approach to those chip fractures of the radius that occur in the center of the anterior surface.

The structures incised are the skin, subcutaneous tissue, dorsal annular ligament of the carpus, fibrous portion of the joint capsule, and the synovial layer of the joint capsule. The surgeon will find that following incision of the synovial lining of the joint capsule, joint fluid will run from the incision. Small bleeders encountered in the dorsal annular ligament and joint capsule can be controlled with cautery, or by torsion and ligation. Visualization of the fracture is aided by flexing the joint so that the articular surfaces of the carpal bones can be observed. At this time one can also appraise the amount of damage done to the joint surfaces, which will aid in prognosis (Fig. 6–22). Some irritation of the articular surfaces is always present as the result of the fracture, but many times this will repair sufficiently to allow the horse to race again. Once the fracture is exposed, one is usually impressed with the proximity of the fragment to its normal position in spite of the wide separation that is apparently present on the radiographs. One will also find that there are often considerable fibrous adhesions present which make the fragment relatively immobile. Some fragments will have broken away completely and are attached to the joint capsule, making removal quite simple.

* Fluothane, Ayerst Laboratories
† Band Aid Adhesive Drape, Johnson & Johnson

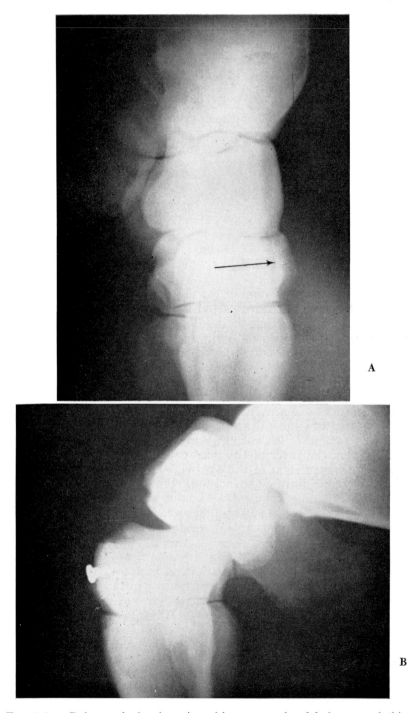

A

B

Fig. 6–21.—Before and after insertion of bone screw for slab fracture of third carpal bone. A—fracture prior to insertion of screw. B—appearance of bone sixty days after bone screw inserted.

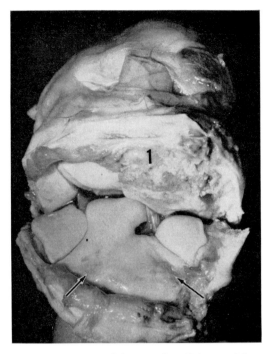

Fig. 6–22.—Necropsy specimen of fractured radial carpal bone. The denuded area (1) shows where the fracture occurred on the radial carpal bone. Arrows indicate erosions in the articular surface of the third carpal bone. Areas such as this have regeneration capability when the fracture is removed.

A periosteal elevator is used to gently work the fragment away from the adjoining carpal bone. The attachments of the carpal bone to the joint capsule on the anterior surface are freed by scalpel and the fragment removed. The fracture area is then palpated for excessive roughness, and if present, the roughened areas are gently curetted till they feel smooth to palpation. The ragged edges of articular cartilage damage are also curetted smooth. Over a period of time the cartilage is replaced by fibrous tissue which eventually modifies and regenerates to articular cartilage. When villi have formed in the synovial layer of the capsule, they should be surgically removed. If they are not removed, they can be impinged in the joint during its closure, causing persistent joint effusion and pain. They are dissected out using scissors and thumb forceps. This constitutes a partial synovectomy.

The joint cavity is then checked carefully to be sure that all fragments are removed, and swabbed to remove hemorrhage. The cavity can be flushed with sterile saline solution if desired. The dorsal annular ligament and fibrous portion of the joint capsule are sutured with 00 medium chromic catgut or collagen* with swaged-

* Ethicon Inc., Somerville, N. J.

on—taper point needle. One should be certain that the needle does not penetrate the synovial lining of the joint capsule since this will sometimes cause rejection of the catgut at a later date. The sutures are placed closely together, and when this suture line is closed, it is optional whether or not corticoids and antibiotics are placed into the joint at this time. The initial application of corticoids is apparently harmless and seems to aid in keeping inflammation minimal for a short time following the surgery. The subcutaneous tissue is closed in the same fashion and the skin is sutured with a monofilament nylon suture with swaged-on cutting edge needle.

Occasionally it is found that the fractured piece of bone is so large that it would definitely harm the joint to remove it. When this is the case, and the fracture is of a suitable type (one piece), a bone screw is used to fix it into position (Fig. 6–21). This is done by making the incision described and drilling a hole in the anterior surface of the fragment and on into the affected carpal bone. A screw of slightly larger diameter is put in place and firmly fixes the fragment in position. A slab fracture that requires a bone screw may slip upwards (Figs. 6–16 and 6–23). This fragment is difficult to replace unless the carpus is flexed during surgery. Flexion of the joint causes the fragment to be pulled downwards because of the fibrous joint capsular attachment. This will greatly facilitate accurate positioning prior to placement of a bone screw.

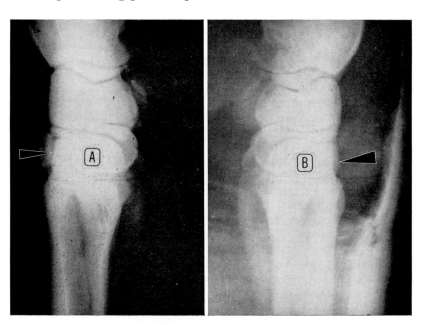

Fig. 6–23.—Fracture of the third carpal bone.

A, Dark pointer indicates line of slab fracture on third carpal bone.

B, Dark pointer indicates the line of fracture after removal of the fragment from the same carpus. The areas of density around the limb are caused by the plaster of paris cast.

Following suturing of the skin, sterile gauze sponges are placed over the wound, and the limb is cast from the fetlock to above the middle of the forearm. The limb must be padded to the same size as the medial and lateral tuberosities of the radius and the accessory carpal bone, or pressure necrosis will occur at these points. The limb should be padded so that it is filled out to the level of these prominences. The cast is intended to protect the joint while the animal recovers from anesthesia, and for the first five to seven days following the surgery it will aid in keeping swelling to a minimum. The cast is removed in five to seven days and one often finds that the joint is the same size it was prior to surgery. At this time the joint is usually cared for by applying snug elastic bandages, and the horse is confined to a box stall for at least thirty days. Counter pressure is maintained by use of an elastic bandage and elastic tape for at least three weeks following surgery. Parenteral antibiotics are given for five to seven days following surgery. Phenylbutazone derivatives are helpful in minimizing pain and swelling for the first ten days after surgery. Their use should be covered by antibiotic therapy.

If any inflammation develops in the carpus following removal of the cast, an antiphlogistic poultice* is recommended till the inflammation disappears. Some authors recommend the use of radiation therapy following surgery. This is contraindicated in the experience of this author.

When exercise is first begun following surgery, the owner must be instructed to hand lead the horse, since the horse often feels so good that he wants to run and play, and may reinjure the joint. For this reason, exercise following thirty days of confinement to a box stall is done at halter and cantering is not permitted until the animal has been cared for in this way for at least an additional thirty days. The horse should not have any hard work for at least six months following surgery.

PROGNOSIS. —The prognosis for those cases that are carefully selected is good. About 75 per cent of the selected cases will campaign successfully again. Large fractures, multiple fractures and those cases that have excessive periosteal new bone growth, especially when near the articular surfaces, should be considered unfavorable surgical risks.

* Denver Mud, Demco Corporation, Denver, Colo.

SPECIFIC REFERENCES

1. ADAMS, O. R.: Surgical Repair of Equine Carpal Fractures. Norden News, p. 20, June 1963.
2. CHURCHILL, E. A., JENNY, J., WHEAT, J. D., RAKER, C. W., REED, W. and PROCTOR, D.L.: Panel on Orthopedic Surgery. Proc. 5th Annual Amer. Assoc. Equine Practitioners, 1959.
3. DELAHANTY, D. D., JENNY, J., REED, W. and WHEAT, J. D.: Panel on Orthopedic Surgery. Proc. 4th Annual Amer. Assoc. of Equine Practitioners, 1958.
4. MANNING, J. P. and ST. CLAIR, L. E.: Surgical Repair of the Third Carpal Bone. Ill. Vet., 3, 106, 1960.

5. Procter, D. L.: *Equine Medicine and Surgery*. p. 725. Santa Barbara, Calif. Vet. Publications, Inc., 1963.
6. Teigland, M.B., Jenny, J., Wheat, J.D., Proctor, D. L. and Reed, W.: Panel on Orthopedic Surgery. Proc. 6th Annual Amer. Assoc. Equine Practitioners, 1960.

11. Fracture of the Accessory Carpal Bone

Definition.—The accessory carpal bone is in a prominent position in the carpus and may fracture from external trauma or from unknown causes. It often fractures in the groove that is formed for passage of the flexor tendons. The fragments usually separate due to the pull of the attachments of the flexor carpi ulnaris and ulnaris lateralis (Fig. 6–24). The articular portion of the bone is firmly attached by the accessory carpal ligaments.

Etiology.—It is assumed that trauma is the etiology in most cases. However, most show no sign of external trauma on the skin and hair, and it may be that the bone can fracture as the result of stress from the tendinous attachments to it.

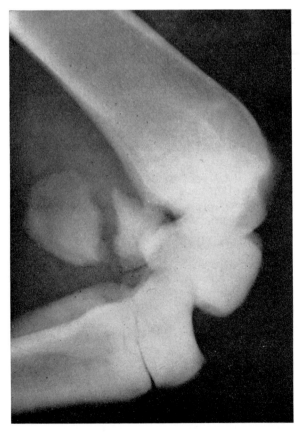

Fig. 6–24.—Fracture of the accessory carpal bone. Notice the separation of the fragments caused by the pull of the carpal flexor tendons.

SIGNS.—Signs of lameness are usually not acute. The horse may not put full weight on the limb soon after the injury, and if extensive swelling is not present, crepitation may be found in the early stages. Soon after the fracture, however, the ends are separated so that it is almost impossible to produce crepitation. The most prominent signs of the lameness are distention of the carpal sheath, and pain on manual flexion of the carpus. Whenever the carpal sheath is distended, accompanied by pain on flexion, diagnostic radiographs should be taken to eliminate the possibility of accessory carpal bone fracture.

DIAGNOSIS.—Whenever a carpal sheath is distended and pain on flexion is evident, radiographs should be taken. The fracture will be evident on the lateral radiograph (Fig. 6–24).

TREATMENT.—It is extremely difficult to immobilize the fragments of accessory carpal bone because of the pull of the carpal flexors. Rarely, a bone screw fixation can be used. If a bone screw is to be used, a close study of the fracture must be made radiographically because of the curve in the bone. It may be impossible to transfix the bone with a straight screw because of this curve. Wire sutures can be used in some cases. In most cases, the fracture is best left alone and eventual fibrous union of the fragments will take place. The horse may be able to return to light work after three to six months and a few are successful at harder work. The carpal sheath may be injected with corticoids to alleviate the distention and relieve the inflammation. A rest of three to six months should be enforced before attempting any work at all with the horse. Immobilization of the carpus by plaster cast may be helpful if the fracture is diagnosed soon after it occurs.

PROGNOSIS.—Guarded to unfavorable.

12. Rupture of the Extensor Carpi Radialis

DEFINITION.—Rupture of the extensor carpi radialis tendon is comparatively rare. The signs of lameness are distinctive, making it easy to diagnose.

ETIOLOGY.—The etiology is trauma. The logical conclusion would be that overflexion of the limb would be most apt to cause rupture of this tendon. In most cases the actual etiology is not known.

SIGNS.—With the resistance of the extensor carpi radialis tendon gone, the flexor tendons are able to overflex the limb. Careful observation of the gait will show that in the affected limb the carpus flexes considerably more than the carpus of the normal limb. Extension is accomplished by means of the common digital extensor and the lateral digital extensor. After the rupture has been present for a short time, atrophy of the muscular portion of the extensor carpi radialis begins. Palpation over the carpus will reveal the absence of the tendon on the anterior surface of the carpus.

TREATMENT.—If the rupture is found soon after it occurs, it may be possible to bring the tendinous ends together surgically. In this

13

case the limb would be kept in a cast for approximately six weeks. In cases of longer duration, it is impossible to bring the tendinous ends together. One may be able to substitute the tendon of the extensor carpi obliquus by using tendon anastomosis.

PROGNOSIS.—Prognosis is unfavorable. In those cases that have enough economic value to attempt surgery either tendon anastomosis or substitution with extensor carpi obliquus may be used.

SPECIFIC REFERENCE

CATLIN, J. E.: Rupture of the Extensor Carpi Radialis Tendon. V.M./S.A.C., *59*, 1178, 1964.

13. Contraction of the Digital Flexor Tendons

DEFINITION.—Contraction of the flexor tendons may either be congenital or acquired and may involve the deep and/or superficial digital flexor tendons. The degree of contraction is highly variable.

ETIOLOGY.—Congenital types of flexor contraction result from inheritable characteristics, malposition of the fetus in the uterus, or nutritional deficiency of calcium, phosphorus, vitamin A and/or vitamin D.

Acquired contraction of the flexor tendons may result from an injury that causes decreased use of the limb, or from nutritional deficiency of the above mentioned minerals after birth. Contraction of the flexor tendons due to injury are unilateral, while contraction resulting from nutrition, heredity, or malposition of the fetus in the uterus, are bilateral.

SIGNS.—The signs vary with each individual case. If only the superficial digital flexor tendon contracts, the fetlock and pastern area knuckle forward causing "knuckling" of the fetlocks (Fig. 5–8, page 123). This may occur in either the fore or hind limbs. When the deep digital flexor contracts, the heel tends to lift from the ground. Contraction of the deep flexor alone seldom occurs; however, contraction of the superficial flexor can occur without the deep flexor showing comparable contraction. In some cases the contraction of the deep digital flexor is so severe that the horse walks on the dorsal surface of the fetlock joint causing lesions that eventually open the joint capsule.

TREATMENT.—If contraction in the newborn foal is not too severe, the tendons may stretch as he grows and treatment may not be required. If the foot can be placed flat on the ground, correction usually is not advisable, providing progressive improvement is shown. If the fetlock and pastern areas knuckle over severely, and the horse has difficulty maintaining the foot flat on the ground, the affected limb should be placed in a plaster cast.

The foal should be anesthetized with pentobarbital* and the affected limbs covered with stockinette. The area between the fet-

*Nembutal, Abbott Laboratories.

lock and coronary band should be padded heavily with cotton. The limbs should be padded from just below the carpus or tarsus to the coronary band with heavy gauze and cotton pads. The limb then should be stretched under anesthesia to see if a normal position can be obtained. If the deformity still is severe, tenotomy of the deep and/or superficial flexor tendons may be advisable. If the heel of the foot remains on the ground when the horse is standing, only the superficial tendon should be cut. Two rolls of blue label, Johnson and Johnson 4-inch plaster of paris bandage should be placed over the padding, and as it starts to dry, two pieces of yucca board, bass wood or aspen wood ($5\frac{3}{4}$ inches wide, $\frac{1}{8}$ inch thick, and long enough to reach from the carpus to the hoof wall) should be placed on the back of the limb. Extra padding should be placed on the top and bottom areas of the wood and over the anterior surface of the fetlock and pastern joints. Two additional rolls of blue label, 4-inch plaster of paris bandage should be used to pull the fetlock and pastern area against the wood. The hoof wall should be incorporated in this cast. The yucca board will more or less conform to the shape of the limb if it is moistened before application. This cast should be left on ten to fourteen days and then removed. The foal should be stalled during this procedure. After observing the results for an additional ten to fourteen days of stall confinement after the cast has been removed, it should be decided to reapply the cast or to give no further treatment. Flexor tendons tend to weaken when cast; this is helpful in the contraction syndrome.

If tenotomy is required, it should be done as follows: the foal should be anesthetized, and a small area over the lateral surface of the flexor tendons should be shaved and prepared for operation. Using sterile gloves and instruments, a small Udall teat bistoury should be pushed through a $\frac{1}{4}$ inch incision in the skin between the two flexor tendons. If only the superficial tendon is to be cut, the edge of the knife should be turned out, the tendon cut, and one nylon suture should be put into the skin. If both tendons are to be cut, the blade should be inserted under the deep flexor tendon through a $\frac{1}{4}$ inch incision and, avoiding the large vessels in the area, both tendons then should be severed by turning the blade and cutting outward. The limb should be held in extension to tighten the flexor tendons while they are being severed. It is not necessary to cut both flexor tendons in the same spot. Some surgeons prefer to cut one of the tendons high and one low. This separates the tenotomies so that not as many adhesions occur. In addition, it is not necessary to cut the tendon through a small opening. An inch and a half incision to properly expose the tendon and vessels can be used without detrimental effects. The skin is sutured with a nonabsorbable type suture using a simple interrupted pattern. The limb should then be cast in plaster with padding under the cast.

PROGNOSIS.—The prognosis is favorable in cases that do not require tenotomy. It is guarded for those cases that require tenotomy. It is unfavorable in those cases that cannot be pulled into a normal position after tenotomy is done. Such a condition indicates that the suspensory ligament also is contracted, but it should not be severed. If tenotomy of a flexor tendon is done, tetanus antitoxin should be administered; antibiotics usually are not necessary if aseptic procedures have been followed. Prognosis is unfavorable in cases where the fetlock joint capsule has been injured by trauma and suppurative arthritis is present.

SPECIFIC REFERENCE

BEDAME, G. F.: A Corrective Appliance for Contracted Tendons in Foals. Proc. 9th Ann. A.A.E.P., 91, 1963.

14. Tendosynovitis (Bowed Tendon) (Tendinitis) (Tendo-vaginitis)

DEFINITION.—Tendosynovitis results from an injury to the deep and/or superficial flexor tendons and their associated tendon sheath. The pathology has been described as a telescoping of the tendon sheath surrounding the deep and superficial digital flexors. The attachments of the sheath are torn from their respective positions on the tendons causing hemorrhage and inflammation to take place. In the middle one third of the metacarpal area there is no sheath present around the tendons. In this case, adhesions develop between the tendons and the surrounding subcutaneous tissues. Adhesions result which bind the tendons to the sheath, and, in addition, adhesions form between the deep and superficial flexor tendons. Fibrous scar tissue also occurs between the tendon sheath and surrounding connective tissue. Hemorrhage occurs within the tendon, and varying degrees of tearing of tendon fibers also occurs. Necrosis may occur within the tendon as a result of torn fibers. In some cases many fibers are torn, causing lengthening of the tendon. The volar annular ligament of the fetlock often is involved, causing adhesions to form between this ligament and the superficial flexor tendon. The "bowed" appearance, from which the disease gets its name, results from the fibrous adhesions on the volar aspect of the metacarpal area. Tendosynovitis is one of the more common causes of retirement of horses from racing.

Tendosynovitis occurs in the following areas:

1. High—just below the carpus
2. Middle—in the middle one-third of the cannon bone. In this area the tendons lack a definite sheath so the condition primarily is tendinitis.
3. Low—in the distal one-third of the cannon bone area, including the volar annular ligament.

Tendosynovitis may occur in the high or low areas alone, but usually not in the middle area alone, in most cases. A severe case may involve all areas.

ETIOLOGY.—Tendosynovitis occurs as a result of a severe strain to the flexor tendon area and is relatively common in the foreleg, but not so common in the hindleg. When it does occur in the hindleg, it usually involves only the low area. Predisposing causes include: long, weak pasterns; forced training procedures; speed and exertion; muscular fatigue at the end of long races; improper shoeing; toes which are too long; muddy tracks; and horses that are too heavy for their tendon structure. The superficial flexor tendon is more commonly involved than is the deep flexor tendon. The time when tendosynovitis is most likely to occur is when the lead forefoot has all body weight on it while it is landing, and again just as it pushes off.

SIGNS.—Signs of acute tendosynovitis lameness occur soon after injury, often toward the end of a long race, causing the horse to pull up lame, or to go lame shortly after the injury. In the acute phase, there is diffuse swelling over the involved area, and heat and pain are evident upon palpation. The condition, which is characterized by severe lameness, will cause the horse to stand with the heel elevated to ease pressure on the flexor tendon area. The carpus usually will be pushed forward while the horse is at rest, and in motion the animal will not allow the fetlock to drop because of the pain. Tendosynovitis also may occur in conjunction with suspensory ligament injury; a careful examination should be made to determine if this is true. The condition is considered more serious and the prognosis less favorable if the suspensory ligament is involved. In some cases the trauma is so severe that the fibers of the tendon actually are torn and stretched. This type of injury can be identified by an abnormal dropping of the fetlock. Stretching of the tendons occurs only in a small percentage of cases. Histological examination of the tendon will reveal various degrees of tendon tearing, necrosis and hemorrhage in the tendon itself.[8] This means that there is injury within the tendon in all cases and that pathological changes are not limited to the peritendinum. Signs of acute inflammation remain for several months, supporting the belief that at least a year's rest is necessary for complete healing.

A sign of chronic tendosynovitis is fibrosis in the area of the original injury (Fig. 6–25). Heat, pain and lameness vary according to the degree of healing. A firm, prominent swelling usually is indicative of the condition. With chronic tendosynovitis the patient often will be sound while walking or trotting, but will go lame under hard training.

Careful palpation should be used to determine whether the inferior check ligament is also involved. The more structures involved, the more serious the condition. The structures should be palpated both with the foot on the ground and with the foot in a raised position when the structures are relaxed. There may be more lameness when the deep flexor and/or inferior check ligament are involved than when the superficial flexor tendon alone is involved.

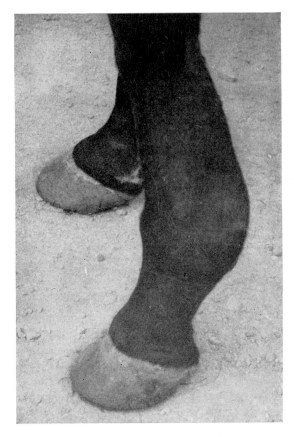

F<small>IG</small>. 6–25.—Tendosynovitis (bowed tendon). Note the extensive swelling on the volar aspect of the limb above the sesamoid bones in the area of the flexors. This involvement includes all of the classification of high, middle, and low bowed tendon.

D<small>IFFERENTIAL</small> D<small>IAGNOSIS</small>.—Suspensory ligament injury and fracture of the proximal sesamoid bones can occur with bowed tendon; such a possibility should be considered. Tendosynovitis has a reasonably characteristic appearance, but only by careful palpation can suspensory ligament injury be determined. Radiographs can be used to determine if fracture of the proximal sesamoids has occurred.

T<small>REATMENT</small>.—In early acute stages, the best treatment appears to be local injection of a corticoid (Chapter 11, page 458) subcutaneously and into the tendon and tendon sheath. This should be done by clipping the hair from the limb and thoroughly disinfecting the skin. A high volar nerve block should then be used and the selected corticoid injected locally into the affected tissues. These drugs should be deposited into the tissues with a 1-inch 20-gauge needle, putting $\frac{1}{2}$ to 1 cc. of solution in each injection area. Injections should be about ½ to 1 inch apart and be made on both sides of the tendon. Similar results may be obtained by a follow-up with parenteral corticoids for ten days following application of the cast. Parenteral corticoids may be used in conjunction with initial local injection or separately without local injection. The limb then should be placed in a light cast from coronary band to just below the carpus for approximately two weeks. At the end of two weeks the cast should be removed, and if necessary another cast applied. If a marked improvement is evident after removal of the cast, the limb should be placed in supporting bandages for another thirty days. The horse should be rested for one year.

This method of treatment gives most consistent results and is most apt to make it possible for the horse to return to racing. Additional corticoids may be given parenterally for seven to ten days to prolong the effect. The use of local and parenteral corticoids plus a cast have given beneficial results even when the case is not acute. Those cases of approximately thirty days' duration that still have heat and swelling in the tendons responded favorably. This method of therapy is at least worth a try if signs of inflammation are still present. Some authorities have recommended the use of multiple skin punctures with a needle in the involved area following corticoid injection. This is termed "cold firing," but should be discouraged because it is not logical to inject an anti-inflammatory agent and then attempt to produce inflammation. "Cold firing" is a poor therapeutic technique since recovery occurs just as rapidly, or even more rapidly, without it. Antiphlogistic packs are sometimes used under bandage after the cast is removed.

If the case is no longer acute when the horse is examined, and he has developed fibrous tissue scarring in the tendon sheath area, little can be done except an attempt to correct the condition surgically. Firing, blistering, and sometimes X-radiation, are utilized, but usually none of these methods of therapy will return the animal to soundness.

Shoeing with a raised heel will give some support to the damaged tendon. This can be used for approximately ten weeks and then should be discontinued to prevent contraction of the tendons.

Surgical Correction.—Surgical correction has been used for tendo-synovitis in recent years in an attempt to return a higher percentage of affected horses to racing. Such operations were successful in returning approximately one of five animals to racing; this probably is no higher percentage than would ordinarily return to soundness if other methods of treatment were used.

Asheim[1] has described an operation for chronic bowed tendon and for suspensory ligament injuries. This operation is most successful when only the superficial digital flexor tendon is involved. Under general anesthesia and after surgical preparation of the skin, subcutaneous tissue and superficial flexor tendon are incised longitudinally in the center of the tendon on the volar aspect of the limb. The incision goes through the depth of the tendon, extending the full length of the damage and into normal tendon above and below. The tendon subcutaneous tissue and skin are sutured in separate layers. An alternate incision can be made over the lateral aspect of the tendon, splitting the tendon through its width over the length of the damage. The limb is then put in a plaster cast for two weeks following surgery. This cast is then removed and replaced with another, which is allowed to disintegrate during a six-week box stall convalescence. The horse is rested eight months but gentle exercise begun in two months.

Asheim claims that this operation increases the circulation to the tendon thereby increasing its ability to heal. He supports this contention with histological studies. When the deep flexor tendon is involved, the incision is recommended to be made laterally into the tendon. Again the incision extends the full length of the damaged tendon. This same technique is also used in a damaged suspensory ligament by using a longitudinal incision into the branch of the involved suspensory ligament. If the body of the ligament is damaged, the incision is made laterally into the ligament.

Sevelius[7] reports that 28 of 40 horses operated on for superficial flexor tendon and suspensory ligament injuries returned to racing.

In my experience, the cases operated on have not had sufficient time to return to racing, so no conclusions are made. I do differ on the method of suturing, since I do not believe the tendon should be sutured with stainless steel. In my opinion, 00 catgut is preferable.

PROGNOSIS.—Prognosis is unfavorable in most cases since the lesion is easily reinjured. If treated in the early stages with a corticoid and a cast, the prognosis is better. In chronic stages when heavy scar tissue is present, the prognosis is strictly unfavorable. If tendosynovitis is accompanied by tearing of the suspensory ligament or fracture of a sesamoid bone, the prognosis also is unfavorable. Only about 20 per cent of the cases of tendosynovitis race successfully again. Further evaluation of Asheim's technique may modify these figures.

SPECIFIC REFERENCES

1. ASHEIM, AKE: Surgical Treatment of Tendon Injuries in the Horse. J.A.V.M.A., *145*, 447, 1964.
2. FISHER, W. F.: Bowed Tendons in the Horse. Vet. Med., *56*, 251, 1961.
3. Proceedings of the 4th Annual American Association of Equine Practitioners. Surgical Treatment of Tendinitis, a panel discussion, December 1958.
4. PROCTOR, D. L.: Tendinitis. *Equine Medicine and Surgery*. p. 728. Santa Barbara, California. American Veterinary Publications, Inc. 1963.
5. PROCTOR, D. L.: Surgical Treatment of Tendinitis. Proceedings of the American Association of Equine Practitioners, December 1957.
6. REED, W. O.: Ligament and Tendon Injuries. JAVMA, *141*, 1258, 1962.
7. SEVELIUS, F.: Surgical Treatment of Bowed Tendons and Strained Suspensory Ligaments by Asheim's Method. 3rd Annual Congress. British Veterinary Medical Association, p. 28, 1964.
8. WHEAT, J. D.: Pathology of Tendon Injuries, Proc. 8th Annual A.A.E.P., p. 27. 1962.

15. Metacarpal Periostitis (Bucked Shins, Sore Shins)

DEFINITION. — This is a periostitis of the dorsal (anterior) surface of the third metacarpal or third metatarsal bone. It is frequent in young Thoroughbreds, during the first few weeks of training. It is common in the forelimb, but is comparatively rare in the hindlimb.

ETIOLOGY. — Concussion is probably the most important etiological factor, especially in young horses. In adult horses, the periosteal attachment to the bone is more mature and periostitis is rarely evident after three years of age. The condition often occurs in both forelimbs at about the same time. The effect of the extensor tendon crossing the area and of the possible pulling of the peritendinous tissues on the periosteum is not fully understood. Injuries to the periosteum, from direct trauma, also may produce periostitis; this possibility should not be overlooked when the condition occurs in only one limb. Direct trauma to the metacarpal or metatarsal areas can produce periostitis in the mature horse, and can produce "saucer" fractures as described by Wheat.[2] All cases should be radiographed to eliminate the possibility of such a fracture.

SIGNS. — A painful swelling on the anterior surface of the third metacarpal or, more rarely, the third metatarsal bone will be present. The condition is easily diagnosed, since this swelling is warm to palpation and painful when pressure is exerted. A variable amount of edema will be in the subcutaneous tissues. Lameness will increase with exercise and the stride will be characterized by a short anterior phase. If only one limb is involved, the horse will tend to rest the affected limb, but if both limbs are involved, he will shift his weight from one limb to the other.

TREATMENT. — Rest is essential if complete recovery is to occur. Nearly all cases will heal if rest alone is used. Many practitioners apply antiphlogistic packs and cold applications during the first twenty-four or forty-eight hours the horse is affected, followed by firing in ten days after the limbs have cooled. The use of counter irritants, firing, x-ray therapy, and cobalt-60 therapy are controversial subjects. All of these methods produce inflammation, but sufficient inflammation is already present in the condition. Subcutaneous injection of corticoids following proper skin preparation (Chapter 11) is a satisfactory treatment, but the rest period must be somewhat prolonged. The leg should be then wrapped and the horse rested for at least thirty days. The anti-inflammatory agent will reduce the swelling rapidly, and recovery will be complete if the rest period is sufficient. Unna's bandage may be helpful (see Chapter 11). The horse should be rested a minimum of one month or the condition may recur. Some trainers purposely work the horse heavily following appearance of the first symptoms of bucked shins in the hope that all pathological changes will occur at once.

PROGNOSIS. — The prognosis is favorable in all cases if the trainer properly rests the horse. If the horse is not rested for a sufficient time, the condition recurs. Permanent new bone growth results if the periostitis is severe or recurs several times, or if a "Saucer" fracture is present.

SPECIFIC REFERENCES

1. GANNON, J. R.: Treatment of Sore Shins with Prednisolone. Austr. Vet. J., *38*, 472, 1962.
2. WHEAT, J. D.: Bilateral Fractures of the Third Metacarpal Bone of a Thoroughbred, J.A.V.M.A., *140*, 815, 1962.

16. Splints

DEFINITION.—Splints, a disease of young horses, most often affect the forelimbs. Splints most commonly are found on the medial aspect of the limb between the second and third metacarpal bones. This is a disease associated with hard training, poor conformation, or malnutrition of a young horse.

ETIOLOGY.—A disturbance of the fibrous interosseous ligament, between the second and third metacarpal bones, or between the third and fourth metacarpal bones, causes splints. This irritation to the periosteum causes periostitis and new bone growth. The condition also may occur, but is less common, between the second and third, or between the third and fourth metatarsal bones. Splints also may be produced by trauma, resulting from blows to the outside of the limb, or from interference to the inside of the limb. Any trauma induced by slipping, running, jumping, or falling, may be enough to disturb the interosseous ligament before it becomes ossified. Faulty conformation may produce splints due to malapposition of bones. Bench knees (Chapter 1, page 27) commonly produces medial splints (Fig. 6–26). Deficiencies of calcium, phosphorus, vitamin A or D also may predispose a horse to splints.

More splints occur on the medial side between the second and third metacarpal bones than on the lateral side between the third and fourth metacarpal bones because of the shape of the proximal ends of these bones. The proximal end of the second metacarpal bone is flat and articulates in a direct weight-bearing fashion with the carpal bones above. The proximal end of the fourth metacarpal bone is slightly oblique thereby sliding the weight toward the inside. This puts the most direct weight bearing on the second metacarpal bone and is why the interosseous ligament between the second and third metacarpal bones is more often disrupted than the one between the third and fourth metacarpal bones. When lateral deviation of the third metacarpal bone (bench knees) is present, there is even more concussion to the second metacarpal bone, and decreased concussion to the fourth metacarpal bone, thereby increasing the possibility of medial splint.

SIGNS.—Lameness is most common in two-year-old horses undergoing heavy training, but occasionally cases occur among three- or four-year-olds. Splints most often are found on the medial aspect of the limb, because the second metacarpal bone normally bears more weight than does the fourth metacarpal bone; therefore, it is more subject to stress. Lameness primarily is due to concussion, and usually is most obvious in the trot. Heat, pain, and swelling over the affected area may occur anywhere along the length of the splint bone. Splints most commonly occur about 3 inches below the carpal joint (Fig. 6–26). One large swelling, or a number of smaller enlargements may occur along the length of the splint bone at its junction with the third metacarpal or third metatarsal bone.

If new bone growth occurs near the carpal joint, it may cause carpal arthritis. Extensive new bone formation on a splint may encroach on the suspensory ligament and cause chronic lameness unless it is removed. Growths of this kind can be determined by palpation and radiographic examination. Splint lameness becomes more marked with exercise |on hard ground. In mild cases no lameness may be evident in the walk, but lameness is exhibited during the trot. After the original inflammation subsides, the enlargement usually become

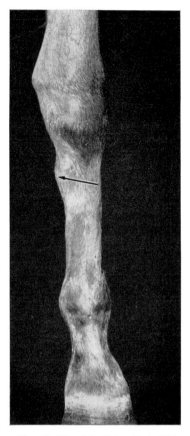

FIG. 6–26.—Medial splint. This horse also was affected by bench knees.

smaller but firmer 'as a result of the ossification of the inflammatory process. The reduction in swelling is usually the result of resolution of fibrous tissue and not from a decrease in size of the actual bone formation. In the early stages the greatest bulk of the swelling is fibrous tissue and this normally resolves to a much smaller size. This often misleads one into thinking that a method of treatment such as blistering or firing has reduced bony swelling. This is not true and in many cases the actual new bone growth is larger than when originally treated. Some cases of splints may never cause lameness.

DIAGNOSIS.—Splints are a lameness of young horses. If the affected limb is examined carefully the obvious signs will lead to a diagnosis. Heat, pain, and swelling over the areas mentioned, plus lameness, are enough for diagnosis. Fracture of the splint bone is commonly confused with splints. In a fractured splint bone, the edema of the limb usually is distributed over a larger area and the animal remains chronically lame for a longer period. Whenever you suspect that one of the splint bones is broken, radiographs should be taken (Figs. 6–27, 6–28 and 6–29). An important part of diagnosis is to determine whether the carpal joint is involved or not, and if the new bone growth has extended posteriorly far enough that the suspensory ligament is involved. New bone growth resulting from trauma occurs on the third metacarpal or third metatarsal bones, and may be mistaken for splints. Palpation and radiographs though will show that these swellings are anterior to the junction with the splint bones. This type of new bone growth is most often caused by interference. Radiographic examination reveals that the splint bone is not involved and the bony growth is almost entirely on the third metacarpal bone. When doubt exists as to whether it is a splint or due to interference, the medial aspect of the hoof wall should be marked with chalk, and the horse worked to see if chalk comes off in the area of the bony swelling.

TREATMENT.—A number of different treatments are used for splints. Some veterinarians prefer to treat the limb with hot and cold applications, and then apply antiphlogistic packs* to reduce inflammation. Resting the horse thirty days, while continuing treatment, often will permit the horse to be returned to training. Other veterinarians prefer to apply a blister or fire the splint area within two weeks of the occurrence of pathological changes. Firing is probably more effective than the application of blisters. In no case does firing or blistering ever reduce the amount of bone swelling. Healing of bone causes the swelling to lessen because it smooths the surface of the bone, but a person should not be misled into believing that the inflammation produced by blistering or firing has done this. The swelling may lessen because of the reduction of swelling in the soft tissues surrounding the splint area. Radiographs taken prior to, and following, the application of blisters or firing of a splint will show that the bony exostosis actually may have become larger, but that the swelling has been lessened because of the reduction in soft tissue swelling.

Another method of treatment is to inject the splint area with a corticoid (Chapter 11, page 458). This treatment reduces inflammation and may help prevent excessive bone growth. Corticoid therapy should be accompanied by counter-pressure bandage. In this case the horse must be rested longer than thirty days and should not be returned to training as rapidly as if counterirritation were used. However, the swelling may be considerably less. It also is true that a case of splints will heal without therapy, provided adequate rest is given. This rest should be a minimum of thirty days without training.

In some cases it is necessary to remove the bony exostosis which interferes with the action of the suspensory ligament, the carpal

*Denver Mud, Demco Corp., Denver, Colorado

joint, or is so large that it is being hit repeatedly by the opposite foot. In other cases, surgical removal of a splint is done because the horse is a halter class horse and the owner feels that the blemish will lessen his chances of winning in the ring. Splints, though, should not be regarded by judges as a serious blemish, provided they are not accompanied by poor conformation (bench knees). Successful removal of the bone growth can be accomplished in about half of the cases; in the other half the bone growth will return to about the size it was before removal. The bone growth should be removed in the same manner that fractured splint bone is removed (*see* page 206).

In every case it is important to analyze the horse's diet and possibly his blood to determine if deficiencies exist that predispose the animal to the condition.

PROGNOSIS.—Prognosis is favorable in all cases except those in which the exostosis is large and encroaches on the suspensory ligament and/or the carpal joint.

SPECIFIC REFERENCE

O'CONNOR, J. P.: Treatment of Functional Splints. Proc. 8th Annual A.A.E.P, Convention, p. 139, 1962.

17. Fracture of a Splint Bone

DEFINITION.—Fracture of a splint bone, commonly confused with splint lameness, may involve either the second or fourth metacarpal or metatarsal bones. Fracture though, is most common on the second metacarpal (inside splint bone) as a result of the opposite foot hitting the bone. Fracture of the external splint bone (fourth metacarpal or fourth metatarsal bone) is less common.

ETIOLOGY.—Trauma is the etiology in all cases. The bone may be broken anywhere along its length, but most commonly in the distal one-third of the bone. Occasionally a fracture may occur just under the carpal joint. When the second metacarpal or metatarsal bone is broken, it is usually because this bone has been hit by the opposite foot during turns, or because of interference (Fig. 6–27). Fracture of the outside splint bone (fourth metacarpal or fourth metatarsal bone) usually results from a kick or other external trauma (Figs. 6–28 and 6–29).

SIGNS.—The horse often displays a typical splint lameness which becomes more marked upon exercise and is most noticeable at a trot. A swelling of the area is commonly present. This swelling is more diffuse than is the swelling with ordinary splints, and may extend the entire length of the splint bone. Chronic passive congestion may result in persistent swelling in the metacarpal area over the affected splint bone.

DIAGNOSIS.—A persistent swelling over the affected splint bone, exhibiting heat and pain when pressure is applied, should lead one to suspect fractured splint bone. Some fractured splint bones closely resemble the disease called splints. Some such fractures heal, but the bony swelling is confused with splints unless radio-

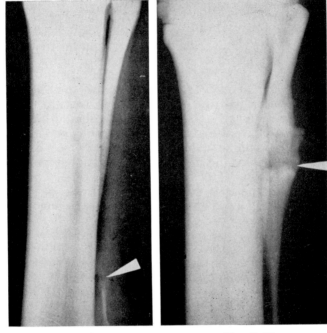

FIG. 6–27   FIG. 6–28

FIG. 6–27.—Fracture of the distal end of the second metacarpal bone, as indicated by the pointer.

FIG. 6–28.—Fracture of the fourth metatarsal bone, as indicated by the pointer.

graphs are taken. Radiographs are necessary in all cases to diagnose positively fractured splint bone and to differentiate fracture of the splint bone from the disease called splints (Fig. 6–26).

Osteomyelitis may be present when a fragment of bone is separated (Chapter 5, page 149, Fig. 5–18).

TREATMENT.—If the splint bone is healed, as shown by radiographic examination, usually it is not advisable to disturb the condition, providing no lameness, swelling, heat, or pain are present. If the fracture has been present some time and shows no signs of healing, it should be removed, since healing often occurs more rapidly following surgical removal. In race horses the fractured splint is sometimes removed soon after fracture rather than waiting for it to heal.

To remove the fractured bone, the operation may be performed with the horse in either the standing or recumbent position. The area over the fractured splint should be clipped, shaved, and prepared for operation. A local anesthetic should be injected in a ring block proximal to the surgical site. An incision then should be made parallel with the anterior border of the affected splint bone, and the periosteum over the splint bone incised and reflected when easily identifiable. The distal fragment of the broken splint should be

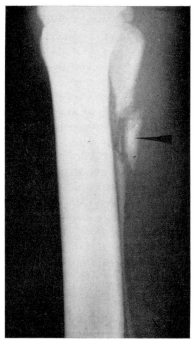

FIG. 6–29.—Fracture of the fourth metatarsal bone with a chip broken from the bone as indicated by the pointer.

removed regardless of its length.   This should be done by teasing the bone away from its attachment to the third metacarpal bone with a chisel. The proximal end of the fracture should be left intact, but the distal end of this proximal segment should be tapered so that it will not cause irritation to the subcutaneous tissues. This also may be done by using a chisel. The periosteum should be closed with No. 00 catgut followed by a layer of No. 00 catgut in the subcutaneous tissues. The skin then should be closed with simple interrupted sutures of a non-capillary, non-absorbable suture.   The line of incision should be covered with a sterile petrolatum gauze bandage, and then an elastic bandage applied to maintain compression on the area for at least two weeks. This bandage can be reapplied every two days to make sure that it maintains constant pressure. Sutures should be removed in two weeks. Recovery usually occurs. Training can begin in thirty days if sufficient recovery has occurred.

PROGNOSIS.—The prognosis usually is favorable, unless the new bone growth is large enough to involve the suspensory ligament behind or the carpal joint above.

SPECIFIC REFERENCES

1. METCALF, J. W.:   Removing Fractured Splint Bones. Proc. A.A.E.P., p. 142, 1962.
2. WINTZER, H. J.:   Fractures of Equine Small Metacarpal or Metatarsal Bones. Berl. u Muench Tieraerztl. Wchschr., *73*, 244, 1960.

18. Sprain (Desmitis) of the Suspensory Ligament

DEFINITION. —The suspensory ligament is the largest structure in the stay apparatus of the limbs (see Chapter 2), and is commonly injured in race horses. It is a rare condition of the hind limb; most cases occur in the front limb.

ETIOLOGY. —Trauma is the etiology in all cases. At its point of bifurcation in the distal one-third of the metacarpal or metatarsal area, the suspensory ligament is most subject to injury resulting from hyperextension of the fetlock joint. This type of injury, which tends to occur toward the end of a long race, is common in Thoroughbreds and Standardbreds. The suspensory ligament also can be injured at its attachment to the sesamoid bones, causing periostitis and sesamoiditis (page 224), with formation of new bone growth on the sesamoid bones (Fig. 6–40, page 224). The ligament tends to tear longitudinally when injured at its bifurcation.

SIGNS. —Injury to the suspensory ligament alone seldom occurs; the lameness often is due both to injury to the flexor tendons and to the suspensory ligament. The lameness, which is similar to that evident in tendosynovitis (page 196) is acute, causing swelling in early stages. The horse tends to hold his carpus forward and rest his heel lightly on the ground. The fetlock joint will be forward. When the horse walks he will not allow the fetlock joint to descend to its proper level but will get off the affected limb as rapidly as possible. In the chronic form of the disease there is considerable fibrosis and swelling of the suspensory ligament either at its bifurcation or at its attachment to the sesamoid bones or both.

DIAGNOSIS. —The diagnosis must be obtained by careful palpation and observation of the limb. The suspensory ligament should be palpated carefully at its bifurcation in the distal one-third of the metacarpus or metatarsus and at its attachment at the sesamoid bones. If scarring or thickening is present at either of these points, injury to the ligament has occurred. When the ligament is torn at its bifurcation, the horse will usually show considerable pain on pressure. Injury at this point must be differentiated from injury to the inferior check ligament, which joins the deep flexor in the middle of the metacarpus. Pain on pressure will identify which structure is damaged if careful palpation is done. In examining a horse with bowed tendon, one should carefully examine the suspensory ligament to be sure that this structure is not also injured. The prognosis of bowed tendon is even more grave if the suspensory ligament is injured. If the suspensory ligament is injured at its point of attachment to the proximal aspect of the sesamoid bones, radiographic changes of these bones will be evident approximately thirty days following the injury, and these changes will be shown in the form of new bone formation on the sesamoid bones (Fig. 6–40, page 224). Radiographs should be taken in the acute stage to be sure that no fracture of the sesamoid bones has occurred. In old injuries of the suspensory ligament at its attachment to the sesamoid

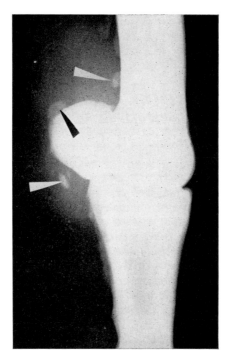

Fig. 6–30. — Sprain of the suspensory and distal sesamoidean ligaments. The top, light arrow indicates calcification in the suspensory ligament. The dark arrow indicates new bone growth on the sesamoid bone or calcification in the attachment of the suspensory ligament; the lower, light arrow, indicates calcification in the distal sesamoidean ligaments.

bones, calcification of the ligament may show radiographically (Fig. 6–30). Desmitis and calcification of the distal sesamoidean ligaments are not uncommon.

TREATMENT. — If the injury is seen in the acute stages, the area should be injected with corticoids (page 458) and immobilized in a cast for two to four weeks. After the cast is removed, the leg should be kept in supporting elastic bandages for a least a month. The horse should be rested for six to twelve months. The cast should extend from the hoof wall to just below the carpal joint. Some cases are treated with antiphlogistic packs on the limb to reduce swelling, and these packs are also valuable after the cast is removed.

In the chronic form of the disease there is little treatment that is effective as the scarred area is subject to reinjury because of decreased elasticity of the ligament. Firing and blistering are often done but are of doubtful value. X and gamma ray therapy are said to be helpful, including those cases with calcification in the ligament. The horse should be rested for a year, and, if put back in training, he should be run in elastic or rubber supporting bandages.

14

A surgical method of correction for desmitis of the suspensory ligament has been described.[1,2] This method consists of a longitudinal incision into the affected branch or branches of the suspensory ligament. Under surgical anesthesia and proper preparation of the skin, the skin and subcutaneous tissues are incised exposing the involved branch(es) over the medial and/or lateral aspect of the ligament. An incision is made into the ligament for the length of the involvement going into normal tissue above and through the depth of the ligament. The incision in the ligament is then closed with simple interrupted sutures of catgut. The subcutaneous tissue is closed with 00 catgut and the skin is closed with a 00 monofilament nylon. The author of this method uses stainless steel for suture, but it is unnecessary, and in many cases detrimental, to bury steel in an area such as this. The horse is then placed in a cast for two weeks. The cast is then removed and a second cast is put on and left for approximately six weeks. The horse then begins mild exercise but no racing for eight months. A similar type incision can be made into the body of the suspensory ligament if it is involved. After the same type of preparation, an incision on the medial or lateral side of the suspensory ligament is made and an incision extending the length of the involvement is made through the body of the ligament. This incision follows the same direction as the fibers of the ligament. The explanation given is that this increases the circulation to the ligament allowing it to establish better healing. Further testing of this method will determine its merit.

PROGNOSIS.—Prognosis is unfavorable in nearly all cases. Some horses will return to racing if they are treated in the acute stages with corticoids and the fetlock immobilized in a plaster cast. Since tendosynovitis of the flexor tendons commonly occurs with injury to the suspensory ligament, only about 20 per cent of the cases can be expected to race successfully again.

SPECIFIC REFERENCES

1. ASHEIM, AKE: Surgical Treatment for Tendon Injuries in the Horse. J.A.V.M.A., 145, 447, 1964.
2. SEVELIUS, F.: Surgical Treatment of Bowed Tendon and Strained Suspensory Ligaments by Asheim's Method. 3rd Annual Congress, British Equine Vet. Assoc., p. 28, 1964.

19. Longitudinal Articular Fractures of the Third Metacarpal Bone into the Metacarpophalangeal Joint

DEFINITION.—Longitudinal fractures that extend into the articulation occur at the distal end of the third metacarpal bone. These fractures show little, if any, crepitation, and signs of lameness are often not severe. The diagnosis of the fracture may be missed entirely unless a radiograph is taken.

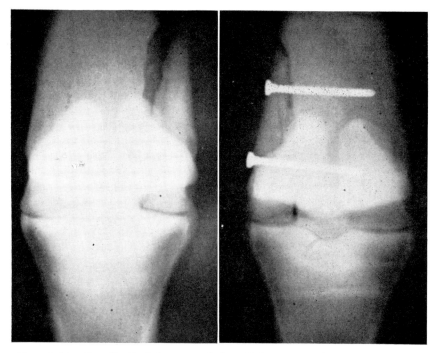

FIG. 6–31.—Longitudinal fracture of the third metacarpal bone. On the left, appearance of the fracture prior to repair. The figure on the right shows the same fracture with two bone screws in place. Note that there is still some defect at the articulation. However, this horse went back into training for racing.

ETIOLOGY.—Trauma is considered to be the etiology of this type of fracture. The great forces exerted on this bone during a full gallop plus possible unevenness of the terrain can produce uneven pressures in the joint. This probably forces a portion of the metacarpal bone to split away.

SIGNS.—Signs of lameness are very similar to those caused by osselets and chip fracture of the first phalanx into the metacarpophalangeal joint. Lameness at the trot, and swelling of the metacarpophalangeal joint and its capsule are present. Swelling of the joint capsule is best found between the suspensory ligament and the third metacarpal bone at the level of the sesamoid bones. Some pain may be exhibited on pressure over the area. Radiographically, varying types of fractures may be found. The type in Figure 6–31 is easily found radiographically, but the type shown in Figure 6–32 may be overlooked if careful examination of the radiograph is not made.

DIAGNOSIS.—Diagnosis can be established only by radiographic examination. A horse that shows considerable swelling of the fetlock and pain on pressure over the bony tissue should always be examined radiographically for the possibility of fracture.

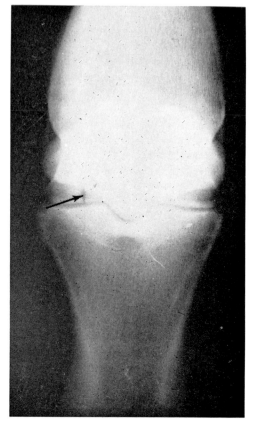

FIG. 6–32.—An example of an articular fracture of the third metacarpal bone that can be repaired by using only a snug cast (arrow). The diagnosis of this fracture could be missed without careful examination of the radiograph.

TREATMENT.—Treatment usually can be done in two ways. If there is no displacement of the fracture, the limb may be placed in a plaster cast for six weeks. This cast should be put on without padding and enclose the hoof wall, extending to just below the carpal joint. When there is displacement, as in Figure 6–31, the fragment must be fixed. Bone screws may be used for this fixation. The horse is anesthetized, the skin prepared for surgery, and a longitudinal incision made over the fracture site. The fragment is identified and forced into proper position. A radiograph may be taken at this point to see whether or not the fragment is properly fitted, but ordinarily this can be determined by digital palpation by dissecting the subcutaneous tissues far enough to feel the fracture edges. A drill only slightly smaller than the bone screw is used to act as a guide hole for the screw. If the hole drilled in the bone is not nearly the same size as the bone screw, the screw may be twisted off while attempting to set it in place. The bone has many of the characteristics of oak wood and will bind the screw very tightly. The subcutaneous tissue is sutured with an interrupted pattern of 00 catgut. The skin is closed with a monofilament non-capillary suture with a simple interrupted pattern. The limb is put in a cast for six weeks. The cast includes the hoof wall and extends to just below the carpus. This author does not remove the bone screws. Some surgeons prefer to put in a larger screw and remove it at a later date.

PROGNOSIS.—The prognosis is guarded, but many cases can be returned to normal function by the above procedures. The prognosis is better when there is practically no separation of the bone fragments. However, there is apparently good regeneration tissue in this area as evidenced by those that return to soundness with as much separation as shown in Figure 6–31.

20. Deviation of the Metacarpophalangeal (Fetlock) Joint

Deviation of this joint occurs from nutritional causes as well as from uterine positioning and possible inheritable factors. When the foal is a few weeks of age, the deviation can usually be corrected by means of a plaster cast. The foal is anesthetized with pentobarbital sodium.* The pastern area is padded with cotton so that it will blend with the prominence of the fetlock joint and coronary band. Stockinette is then placed over the limb and two rolls of 4-inch plaster of paris bandage are applied to include the foot and extend to below the carpus or tarsus. A rigid support of bass wood or aspen wood is then placed on the concave side of the deviation. The proximal and distal portions of the wood are padded with cotton as is the convex side of the metacarpophalangeal area. Then two rolls of 4-inch plaster of paris bandage are wrapped around the wood and the limb so that pressure is exerted against the convex side of the fetlock joint, pulling it toward the rigid support. In most cases it is not possible to produce complete straightening of the limb in the cast, but this is not necessary. It is apparently only necessary to get the limb started growing straight again. The cast is removed in ten to fourteen days and left off an additional ten to fourteen days before making a decision whether or not to cast the limb in a similar fashion again. Corrective trimming of the foot must be done every two weeks to keep the foot level. Ordinarily one or two applications of a cast will produce a straight limb.

If the foal is presented for treatment after it is three to four months of age, it is much more difficult to produce straightening with a cast. At this time, epiphyseal stapling is used (see page 171). Under surgical anesthesia, the skin and subcutaneous tissues are incised over the convex side of the deviation. The epiphyses in these bones are more difficult to identify positively than in the radius or tibia.

* Nembutal, Abbott Laboratories

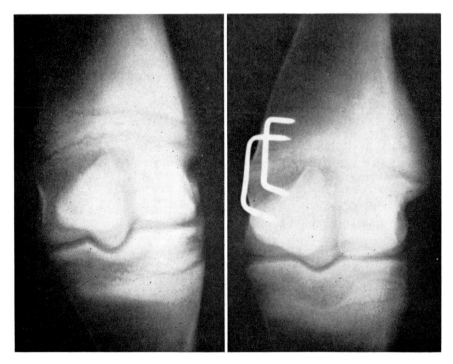

FIG. 6–33.—Radiographs of the metacarpophalangeal (fetlock) joint before and after stapling. The radiograph on the left shows the deviation present in the distal epiphysis of the third metacarpal bone. The radiograph on the right shows the same limb a day after the staples were employed. This limb straightened adequately for normal use and appearance of the horse. The foal was four and one-half months of age when the staples were placed and not removed until after it was one year of age.

It may be best to take a radiograph prior to placing the staples to positively identify the proper positioning. Any metallic object can be used as a landmark to help identify the position of the epiphysis in the radiograph. Two staples are ordinarily sufficient to correct deviation of the metacarpophalangeal (fetlock) area (Fig. 6–33). One must keep in mind that staples must be placed in these bones much sooner than is required for the tibia or radius. Ideally the deviation would be corrected when the foal was just a few weeks old by the means of a cast. However, if too much time has gone by to use a cast, staples are used. Preferably staples are in place by four months of age so that when the epiphysis closes by nine to twelve months of age, the deviation is corrected.

21. Fracture of the Proximal Sesamoid Bone(s)

DEFINITION.—Fracture of the proximal sesamoid(s), most common in Thoroughbreds, results from stress accompanied by fatigue as the result of a long race. Races of a mile to one and one-fourth miles fatigue the limbs so that the fetlock joints actually may touch ground. It is at this point that injury is most apt to take place. Most fractured sesamoids occur in the front limb, but occasionally they are found in the hind limb.

ETIOLOGY. — Trauma is the etiology in all cases. The fatigue and strain of a long race are most apt to produce such injury, but cases have been recorded where a simple injury, such as stepping on a golf ball, produced the fracture. Interference may cause medial sesamoid fracture.

Some radiographs I have viewed showed signs of fractured sesamoids which appeared to be a congenital condition. In this case the proximal portion of the sesamoid bones showed fracture lines through both of the sesamoids on both forelimbs. This was not accompanied by any detectable heat, pain, swelling, or history of lameness. It is possible that occasionally there is congenital imperfection in the bone, and this would be termed *bipartite* sesamoids.

SIGNS. — The medial, lateral, or both, sesamoid bones may be fractured. Lameness is very pronounced in acute stages, the horse is reluctant to bear weight on the limb, and he will not permit the fetlock to descend to normal position. Swelling, heat and pain are prominent in the fetlock area. Tendosynovitis, which also may be present, may confuse the diagnosis if radiographs are not taken. The horse evidences pain when pressure is applied to the affected bone or bones. Descent of the fetlock causes pain. Observation of the gait will reveal that the fetlock is held rigid so that it cannot descend as much as the opposite normal fetlock. The fracture in the bone may occur in any area of the sesamoids, but proximal fractures are more common than distal fractures; proximal fractures also are more favorable to treatment (Figs. 6–34, 6–35 and 6–36). Desmitis of the distal sesamoidean ligaments may occur concurrently with fractured sesamoids.

DIAGNOSIS. — Diagnosis is based on radiological examination of the affected fetlock and the physical changes described above. If a fetlock joint is severely swollen and the horse shows pain when pressure is applied over the sesamoid bone(s), radiographs should be taken to rule out the possibility of fracture. Cases of tendosynovitis also should be radiographed to eliminate the possibility of fractured sesamoid accompanying this disease. Sesamoiditis causes similar signs but radiographs will show no fracture.

TREATMENT. — Treatment is based upon surgical correction and removal of the bone fragment, or upon casting of the leg in an attempt to obtain union of the two fragments.

If the bone fragments are in close apposition and show very little displacement, it often is advisable to attempt a plaster cast. The horse should be tranquilized and the limb cast, in standing position, in as nearly normal position as possible. The cast should be left on twelve to sixteen weeks with periodic changes to make sure that it will remain snug. If after one or two weeks the horse shows

Lameness

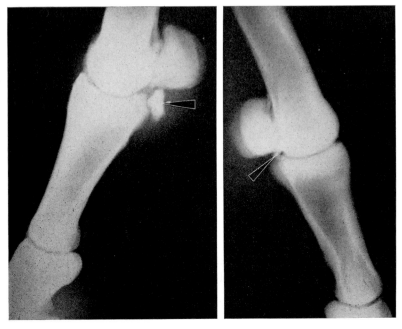

FIG. 6–34   FIG. 6–35

FIG. 6–34.—Fracture from the base of a sesamoid bone is indicated by the dark pointer. With such a large fracture the prognosis would be guarded to unfavorable for removal because the entire base of the sesamoid bone is gone.

FIG. 6–35.—Small distal fracture from the sesamoid bone, as indicated by the dark pointer. Removal of this fracture would be possible.

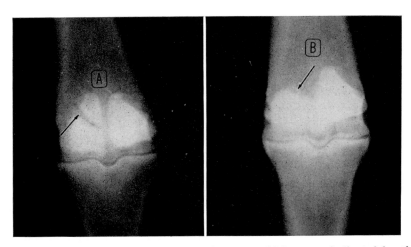

FIG. 6–36.—A, Fracture of the apex of a sesamoid bone, as indicated by the arrow. This fragment is bordering on the largest piece that should surgically be removed from this area. The prognosis would be guarded.

B, Arrow indicates the same sesamoid bone following removal of the fragment.

improvement in walking, confinement is necessary to keep him from breaking down the cast and possibly reinjuring the area. Sesamoid bones are very slow to heal and the fracture line will be evident a long time. The prolonged period in a cast is necessary because of the slow healing process. When casts are applied shortly after the injury, the results often are very gratifying.

If there is separation of the bone fragments, but the horse is not to be used again for racing, it usually is advisable to cast the limb. Surgical removal of the fragment is not necessary if the animal is to be used only for breeding purposes.

If a fractured portion of the bone is displaced, or if the bone was fractured some time before diagnosis and has not healed, it usually is advisable to remove the fragment if possible; however, this procedure is limited to fractures that constitute less than one-third of the total size of the bone. Fractures through the middle of the sesamoid bone should not be removed surgically because of poor results. Removal of a proximal fragment is more successful than removal of those in the distal portion of the bone; small chips, though, may be removed from the distal portion of the bone with satisfactory results (Figs. 6–35 and 6–36).

Operation is most easily performed when the horse is in lateral recumbency. The limb should be prepared for aseptic operation and the horse given a general anesthetic to control struggling. The volar nerves may be blocked with local anesthetic to aid in reducing the amount of general anesthetic. A tourniquet should be used to control hemorrhage. An Esmarch's bandage, used to force blood from the limb before the tourniquet is applied, will give one an almost bloodless field. An Esmarch's bandage may be fashioned from a piece of rubber inner tubing approximately 2 inches wide.

When the fragment is in the apex of the bone, the incision should be made between the suspensory ligament and the posterior surface of the cannon bone (Fig. 6–36). The incision should be made proximal to the sesamoid bone so that the collateral ligament of the sesamoid bone will not be severed. After the incision is made, the fetlock should be flexed slightly to reduce tension on the flexor tendons. This enables one to pull the suspensory ligament posteriorly so that the apex of the sesamoid bone can be seen. The fragment should be gently dissected away from the rest of the bone. Some authorities say sharp instruments cannot be used within the joint cavity, but they may, providing caution is used. The fragment can be grasped with a small pair of rongeurs to permit dissection of the fibrous attachments from the bone. After the fragment is removed, a layer of simple interrupted sutures should be placed in the joint capsule, and adjacent tissues, with 00 catgut with swaged-on taper point needle. The point of the needle should not go through the synovial layer of the capsule. A second layer of simple interrupted sutures should be placed in the subcutaneous tissues and the skin closed with a noncapillary, nonabsorbable, plastic suture. A corticoid plus 2 cc. of penicillin-streptomycin mixture may be injected into the joint capsule after the subcutaneous layer of sutures are finished. The skin incision should be protected with a layer of sterile petrolatum gauze, and the limb heavily wrapped in supporting elastic bandages or placed in a plaster cast approximately ten days. After ten days to two weeks the horse should be walked daily for short periods. Supporting wraps should be kept on for a minimum of thirty days; they are especially important during the two weeks following surgery to prevent as much swelling as possible.

For fragments of the distal portion of the bone the incision can be made directly over the fragment and extend through the distal sesamoidian ligaments. These fragments are somewhat more difficult to remove because of the ligamentous structure attached to the bone. The horse should be confined in the manner described above and the area over the fracture should be prepared for aseptic operation. An incision directly over the fragment should be made after careful radiographic identification of its position. After the fractured bone has been identified, the fibrous adhesions joining it to the large fragment should be disected away, as should the attachment of the sesamoidean ligaments to the bone. After removal of the fragment the ligamentous tissue should be sutured with 00 catgut with swaged-on taper point needle. The skin should be closed with a noncapillary plastic suture, and the incision line protected as mentioned above. A cast, or bandage described above, also should be used. Large ventral fragments should not be removed since this severs the attachment of the distal sesamoidean ligaments to this bone.

Distal fragments can also be removed by extending the incision made to remove proximal fragments; i.e., between the suspensory ligament and cannon bone. If this incision is extended down through the collateral ligament of the sesamoid bone, some distal fragments can be reached. Those fragments that lie entirely on the posterior aspect of the sesamoid bone cannot be reached by this approach.

Another incision that can be used to remove basal sesamoid fractures is made on the posterior aspect of the fetlock on the medial or lateral side of the ergot depending on which side the fracture is located. The incision extends down through the volar annular ligament and the flexor tendons are pushed aside. This exposes the distal sesamoidean ligaments which can then be incised horizontally in order to reach the basal portion of the sesamoid bone. The incision in the distal sesamoidean ligaments is sutured as a separate layer. The volar annular ligament and tendon sheath are sutured as one layer, then subcutaneous tissue and skin separately. It is best to use a plaster cast for approximately one week following surgery if this incision is used.

Severing the branch of the suspensory ligament to the affected sesamoid has been described.[5] However, in a study of a number of cases, it was found that surgical removal of the fractured fragment proved superior to both conservative treatment and to cutting the branch of the suspensory ligament to the affected sesamoid bone.

PROGNOSIS.—The prognosis is unfavorable if more than one-third of the bone has been fractured, as it is for fractures of long standing that have not been cast or surgically treated. Small fragments of long duration may be removed successfully, but the sooner after acute inflammation subsides the better, as far as the outcome of the patient is concerned. Small fragments may be removed with a guarded to favorable prognosis. Those cases that are placed in a plaster cast soon after the fracture occurs often can return to racing if the fragments are in apposition. If both sesamoids are fractured, operation will not be as successful; fragments of both bones can be removed during the same operation.

SPECIFIC REFERENCES

1. CHURCHILL, E. A.: Sesamoid Fractures. Proceedings A.A.E.P. Convention, p. 206, 1962.
2. ————: Surgical Removal of Fracture Fragments of the Proximal Sesamoid Bone. J.A.V.M.A., *128*, 581, 1956.
3. PETERS, J. E.: Fractures of the Third Phalanx and Sesamoids in the Race Horse. J.A.V.M.A., *114*, 405, 1949.
4. PROCTOR, D. L.: *Equine Medicine and Surgery*, p. 694, Santa Barbara, California. American Veterinary Publications, Inc., 1963.
5. SEVELIUS, F. and TUFVESSON, G.: Treatment for Fractures of the Sesamoid Bones. J.A.V.M.A., *142*, 981, 1963.
6. WHEAT, J. D. and RHODE, E. A.: Surgical Treatment of Fractures of the Proximal Sesamoid Bones in the Horse, J.A.V.M.A., *132*, 378, 1958.
7. WIRSTAD, H. F.: Fractures of the Proximal Sesamoid Bones. Vet. Rec., *75*, 509, 1963.
8. WIRSTAD, H. F., TUFVESSON, G. and SEVELIUS, F.: Fractures of the Proximal Sesamoid Bones. Nord. Vet. Med. 14, supplement to p. 33, 1962.

22. Chip Fractures of the First Phalanx in the Metacarpophalangeal (Fetlock) Joint

DEFINITION.—Chip fractures of the proximal end of the first phalanx are relatively common in the forelimb of the horse. Most fractures of this type involve the anterior surface of the proximal end, just medial or lateral to the common digital extensor tendon. The medial side is affected more often than the lateral side. Other areas are not so commonly involved. Concussion and overextension of the joint are factors in the production of these fractures. Chip fractures from the distal end of the third metacarpal bone also occur but are less common.

ETIOLOGY.—Trauma is the cause of these chip fractures of the first phalanx in the horse. From the appearance of the fractures, it would seem that overextension of the joint is probably involved. Overextension places stress on the anterior aspect of the proximal end of the first phalanx as it is pressed against the third metacarpal bone. Limb fatigue is a factor in overextension of the metacarpophalangeal joint. Why the fracture most frequently occurs medial to the midline is not fully understood (Fig. 6–37).

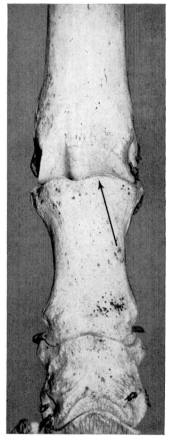

FIG. 6–37.—Skeleton of the equine metacarpophalangeal joint revealing the most common area where fractures of the first phalanx occur (arrow). These fractures occur less commonly on the lateral aspect of the proximal phalanx. (Courtesy J.A.V.M.A.)

SIGNS.—Signs of chip fractures in the metacarpophalangeal joint are similar to those of osselets. There is arthritis in the joint, and permanent damage to the joint may result if the fragment grooves the articular surfaces. Serous arthritis of the fetlock joint indicated by distention of the joint capsule (between the suspensory ligament and the volar surface of the cannon bone) is commonly found.

Lameness is most obvious in the trot. It is primarily a concussion lameness. Some horses have only a small amount of swelling or lameness to indicate that there is a chip fracture. There is often fibrous enlargement on the anterior surface of the fetlock joint which is easily palpated. However, anterior swelling is often seen in osselets. Lameness will usually increase after exercise, and a workout or a race may cause the horse to be markedly lame. It is difficult to produce pain in the affected area by digital pressure, but some heat can usually be detected over the anterior surface of the joint. After prolonged rest, the horse may be sound, only to go lame again when returned to training. Occasionally, there may be acute lameness followed by dramatic relief when a chip, which became caught in the joint, is dislodged.

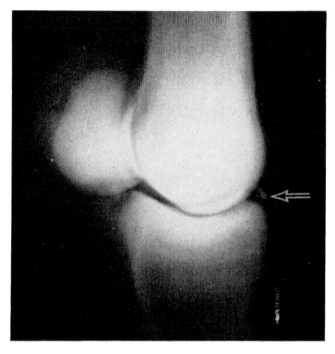

FIG. 6–38.—Lateral radiograph of the metacarpophalangeal joint revealing a chip fracture (arrow) of the first phalanx. (Courtesy J.A.V.M.A.)

DIAGNOSIS.—Diagnosis cannot be made without radiographic examination. The usual clinical case of chip fracture in the metacarpophalangeal joint appears much like a case of osselets. Affected horses are commonly blistered or fired when radiographs have not been taken.

The lateral radiograph is most revealing diagnostically (Fig. 6–38). Oblique radiographs should be taken to determine if the chip is on the medial or lateral side of the midline. This is important, since the surgical approach must be made directly over the chip (Fig. 6–39).

DIFFERENTIAL DIAGNOSIS.—The lameness is most commonly confused with osselets. Radiographs will enable differentiation.

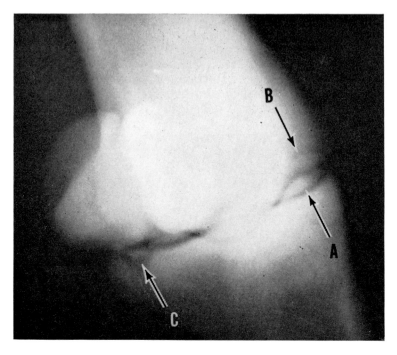

FIG. 6-39.—Oblique radiograph of the medial aspect of the metacarpophalangeal joint showing the fracture fragment from the first phalanx (B). The articular surface of the metacarpophalangeal joint is shown (A). An additional lesion in the first phalanx is on the posterior aspect (C). The old lesion (C) may have been aseptic necrosis or a fracture that did not involve the articulation. (Courtesy J.A.V.M.A.)

The lameness can be alleviated by injecting lidocaine hydrochloride* into the volar pouch of the joint capsule or by using a ring block above the metacarpophalangeal joint (Fig. 4-10). Local anesthesia of the volar nerves above the fetlock may not relieve the lameness without the use of a complete ring block.

TREATMENT.—Surgical removal of the bone fragment is the only successful treatment. Once the exact location of the chip has been established (most chips are located medial to the midline), surgical removal is done if economically feasible. General anesthesia is administered and the area of incision prepared for aseptic surgery. The hair is clipped from the coronary band to the carpus. The area of incision is shaved and scrubbed, and skin antiseptics are applied. A tourniquet is placed in the metacarpal region to reduce hemorrhage. A plastic adhesive drape† is placed over the incision site. This is a self-adhering sterile drape that prevents fluid from

* Xylocaine, Astra Pharmaceutical Products Inc., Worcester, Mass.

† Band-Aid Adhesive Drape, Vetco Division of Johnson & Johnson, New Brunswick, N.J.

soaking through and contaminating the area. The area is then prepared further by placing 4 sterile towels around the area of incision, plus 2 surgical muslin drapes. Using sterile gloves and instruments, a longitudinal incision is made to the side of the common digital extensor tendon. Since most fractures are medial to the tendon, no other structures are involved. However, when the fracture is lateral to the tendon, the incision must be kept between the common and lateral digital extensors.

The incision over the fracture is made through the skin, fascia, annular ligament of the fetlock, and the fibrous and synovial layers of the joint capsule. The knife that is used to cut the skin and fascia is discarded, and a second knife is used to cut into the joint. The joint is flexed slightly to better reveal the chip. If the incision has been properly made, the chip is obvious once the joint is exposed. The incised area should be cleared of synovia and hemorrhage by using sterile sponges so that the fracture line in the first phalanx can be seen. The chip is removed with a small periosteal elevator, and any rough portions on the joint cartilage or bone are curetted smooth. The fibrous portion of the joint capsule is approximated with 00 catgut or collagen* with a taper point, swaged-on needle. A simple interrupted suture pattern is used. Next, the subcutaneous fascia is approximated with a simple interrupted suture pattern of 00 catgut or collagen. At this point, a steroid may be administered into the joint cavity if desired. This is a routine practice followed by the author.

The skin is then closed with 00 monofilament nylon or 00 dacron,† using a simple interrupted pattern. A light bandage is then placed on the wound, and the foot is placed in a cast that includes the hoof and extends to just below the carpal joint. This cast is left in place for six to eight days, then removed and replaced by a pressure bandage. Pressure bandaging is used for at least two weeks, and the horse is confined for thirty days. Six months' rest is recommended before training is resumed. The cast prevents injury to the incision during recovery from anesthesia, acts as an effective pressure bandage, and seemingly prevents postoperative swelling. When a cast is not applied, enlargement of the metacarpophalangeal joint with fibrous tissue is common.

PROGNOSIS.—When the bone chip is removed before damage to the articular cartilage has occurred, excellent results can be expected. Some cases with articular damage of long duration recover following surgery, making the operation worthwhile in valuable horses.

SPECIFIC REFERENCES

1. ADAMS, O. R.: Chip Fractures into the Metacarpophalangeal (Fetlock) Joint. J.A.V.M.A., *148*, 360, 1966.
2. MILNE, F. J., *et al.*: Equine Lameness Panel, Proc. 10th An. A.A.E.P., p. 259, 1964.

* Collagen Suture, Ethicon Inc., Somerville, N.J.

† Mersilene, Ethicon Inc., Somerville, N.J.

23. Sesamoiditis

DEFINITION.—Sesamoiditis, or inflammation of the proximal sesamoid bones, is usually accompanied by a periostitis and osteitis of these bones. The suspensory ligament and the distal sesamoidean ligaments also may be affected and show calcified areas.

ETIOLOGY.—Any unusual strain to the fetlock area may produce sesamoiditis. Most common in race horses, hunters and jumpers, it can affect any type of horse.

SIGNS.—Symptoms are similar to those caused by fracture of the sesamoid bones—pain and swelling of the fetlock joint, especially at the volar aspect. Pressure over the sesamoid bones will cause the horse to flinch. When the horse is in motion the pain is most evident when weight is placed on the limb. The horse will not allow the fetlock to descend to normal level. After the disease becomes chronic, radiographs will show periosteal new bone growth on the convex surface of the sesamoid bones (Fig. 6–40). In addition, calcification of the suspensory ligament above the sesamoid bones, or in the distal sesamoidean ligaments below, may occur (Fig. 6–30, page 209).

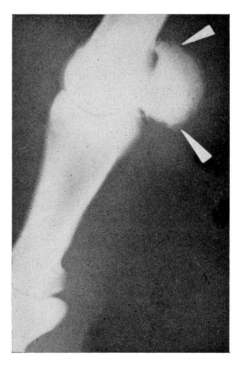

FIG. 6–40.—Arrows indicate new bone growth on the sesamoid bones as a result of sesamoiditis. This bone growth resulted from irritation of the periosteum as a result of injury to the suspensory ligament, at the top, and to the distal sesamoidean ligaments, below.

DIAGNOSIS.—Diagnosis usually can be made by careful examination of the limb. Radiographs should be taken approximately three weeks after onset of the condition to determine if bony changes are occurring on the sesamoid bones. The condition may occur with tendosynovitis, fracture of the sesamoid bones, and injury to the suspensory ligament from which it must be differentiated.

TREATMENT.—Efforts should be made to reduce the inflammation. Alternating cold and hot packs, as well as antiphlogistic packs should be used. One of the best methods of therapy of early acute cases appears to be immobilization of the limb, from the hoof wall to just below the carpus, with a plaster cast. This cast should be left in place two to three weeks and then removed and replaced, if necessary. In chronic stages, volar neurectomy, firing and blistering have been used but only with limited success. Volar neurectomy should not be used on a horse that will be ridden. X-ray and gamma ray radiation are considered to be valuable therapy by some authors, including the treatment of calcification in the suspensory ligament.

PROGNOSIS.—The prognosis is guarded to unfavorable, depending upon the amount of periosteal reaction and new bone growth that occurs on the sesamoid bones.

24. Traumatic Arthritis of the Metacarpophalangeal (Fetlock) Joint (Osselets)

DEFINITION.—Osselets are a traumatic arthritis of the metacarpophalangeal joint. All other changes that occur are secondary to this fact. In addition to the arthritis present, there is an inflammation of the periosteum at the distal end of the third metacarpal bone and/or the proximal end of the first phalanx due to stress on the fibrous portion of the joint capsule. The anterior surfaces of these bones most commonly are involved. In addition, the attachment of the lateral digital extensor, at the antero-lateral surface of the proximal end of the first phalanx, commonly is involved. The term "green osselets" applies to early stages of the condition when it is limited to serous arthritis, and before new bone growth has occurred. A similar condition rarely appears in the hind limb.

Osselets are most common in young Thoroughbreds and Standardbreds in early training; most cases start at two years. Once the condition is established, it commonly affects the horse for several years, eventually causing the horse to be retired from racing.

ETIOLOGY.—Concussion is probably the main factor responsible for osselets. A horse having upright pasterns is more apt to develop the condition than one having sloping pasterns because greater concussion is exerted on the fetlock joint as a result of the upright conformation. New bone growth is caused by the periostitis which results from pulling of the joint capsule attachments, or by pulling of the periosteum at the attachment of the lateral digital extensor tendon. It has also been suggested that pressure from the synovia may elevate the joint capsule attachments when the fetlock is

15

flexed. This pressure would result from increased synovia as a result of serous arthritis caused by concussion.

SIGNS.—The traumatic arthritis causes distention of the volar pouch of the joint capsule between the suspensory ligament and cannon bone. The fact that arthritis is present should always be kept in mind. If work is continued after injection of corticoids, osteoarthritis will probably develop, damaging the articular cartilage.

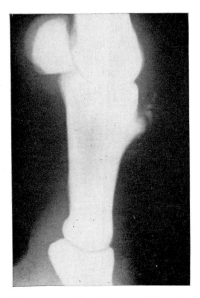

FIG. 6–41.—Osselets resulting from periostitis at the insertion of the lateral digital extensor. Some calcification in the joint capsule also is present. (Carlson, *Veterinary Radiology*, Lea & Febiger.)

Osselets result from concussion and/or a pulling of the attachment of the fibrous portion of the joint capsule at the distal end of the third metacarpal bone, or at the proximal end of the first phalanx, causing a disturbance of the periosteum and periostitis. In addition, or separately, the attachment of the lateral digital extensor may be pulled sufficiently to produce a periostitis in that area. The resulting periostitis in these areas often produces new bone growth which may affect the articular surfaces of the joint, or which may be located in an area that does not involve the articular surfaces (Fig. 6–41). When new bone growth involves the joint, osteoarthritis is present.

There is swelling on the anterior surface of the metacarpophalangeal joint that varies in size, and in most instances extends at least half way around the joint. This is due to thickening in the fibrous portion of the joint capsule. This swelling must be carefully examined because it is firm to palpation and may resemble new bone growth. Very often what is thought to be new bone growth will turn out to be only this type of soft tissue damage.

If both fetlock joints are involved, the horse moves with a short choppy gait. If only one fetlock is involved, the horse obviously shows lameness in that limb. Palpation will reveal pain, heat, and swelling over the anterior surface of the affected fetlock joint, or joints. Pressure over the involved areas will cause the horse to flinch. Fibrous enlargement of the joint capsule on the anterior surface of the fetlock joint is present and is easily palpated. A choppy gait may lead one to believe that the shoulders are involved, but careful clinical examination will disclose the pathological changes at the fetlock joint. Lameness will increase with exercise, and, if only one limb is involved, the horse may point with the affected limb.

Radiographs should be taken to determine if new bone growth is present and if it is encroaching on the joint surfaces. New bone growth is most common on the anterior surface of the proximal end of the first phalanx, but may appear on the anterior surface of the distal end of the third metacarpal bone. Calcification in the joint capsule may be present.

DIAGNOSIS.—Diagnosis is based upon the presence of hot, painful swellings on the anterior surface of the fetlock joint and upon other signs previously mentioned. Radiographs should always be taken to determine if periostitis is causing new bone growth, and if so, where, and how much. Some cases show the presence of a joint mouse (a loose piece of bone within the joint capsule), which can can be determined only by radiographs (Fig. 6–38).

TREATMENT.—Rest is absolutely necessary, so the horse must be removed from training. Antiphlogistic packs, ice packs, or cold water applications commonly are used to reduce acute inflammation. In addition, it is often helpful to inject the inflamed joint capsule with a corticoid (see Chapter 11). Corticoids decrease inflammation of the joint capsule and help prevent some new bone growth if used soon enough. The affected fetlock should be wrapped in supporting wraps for about two weeks. The corticoid therapy can be repeated at weekly intervals for three injections if this is necessary. The injections should be made using strict aseptic techniques. The fetlock may be fired after the inflammation has been reduced.

After acute inflammation recedes, x-ray therapy sometimes is beneficial; x-ray therapy should not be combined with other methods, such as firing or blistering. When x-ray therapy is used, 1000 to 1200 roentgens is the usual dose, given in two or three treatments of 300 to 500 roentgens each. Gamma ray therapy with cobalt-60 (1000 to 1200 roentgens) will produce similar results.

When osselets are in the chronic phase, firing and blistering often are used. Blistering is probably of little value, but firing is helpful in many cases because it creates an acute inflammation. When this process heals, the chronic arthritis may disappear. In all cases, the horse must be rested approximately six months before being put back into training. Horses that receive corticoid therapy often are put into training too quickly because they appear to be normal. This results in a recurrence of the disease.

In horses that are affected with a joint mouse, operation will be necessary to remove the bony tissue so that it will not catch between the articular surfaces of the cannon bone and the first phalanx and cause acute lameness. The lameness will disappear as soon as the body is dislodged from the joint unless damage to the articular cartilage has occurred (page 134). In some cases, bony tissue may be present in the wall of the joint capsule in a fixed position. This calcification of the joint capsule should not be confused with a joint mouse. (See chip fracture of first phalanx, page 219.)

PROGNOSIS.—The prognosis is favorable when the condition is only a serous arthritis and a periostitis has not resulted in new bone growth. When new bone growth is present, the prognosis still may be favorable, providing the bone growth does not encroach on the articular surfaces of the joint. Many horses can run normally even though much new bone tissue is present, providing it does not involve joint surfaces.

If the new bone growth involves the articular surfaces of the joint, the prognosis is unfavorable. The prognosis also is guarded if a joint mouse is present, since major surgery is necessary to remove it, and because permanent damage may have been caused to the articular cartilages as a result of grooving, if the joint mouse has been caught repeatedly in the joint.

If the horse has steep conformation of the pastern, the prognosis is unfavorable, because this type of conformation increases concussion to the fetlock and thus increases the chances of recurrence of the injury.

25. Ringbone (Phalangeal Exostosis)

DEFINITION.—Ringbone is new bone growth which occurs on the first, second or third phalanges. It is the result of a periostitis, and may lead to an osteoarthritis or ankylosis of the pastern or coffin joints. This condition is seldom found in Thoroughbreds, but is relatively common in other breeds.

RINGBONE IS CLASSIFIED IN TWO WAYS

1. *High or Low Ringbone*

A. High ringbone: This is new bone growth occurring on the distal end of the first phalanx and/or the proximal end of the second phalanx (Figs. 6–42 and 44).

B. Low ringbone: This is new bone growth occurring on the distal end of the second phalanx and/or the proximal end of the third phalanx, especially at the extensor process of the third phalanx (Fig. 6–43).

2. *Articular or Periarticular*

A. Articular ringbone: Articular ringbone means that the new bone growth involves the joint surface at the pastern or coffin joints (Fig. 6–47, page 235).

B. Periarticular ringbone: Periarticular ringbone means that the new bone growth is around the joint but does not involve a joint surface. It is most common in high ringbone (Fig. 6–45).

In describing ringbone, the following terminology is used: periarticular, high ringbone; articular, high ringbone; periarticular, low ringbone; or articular, low ringbone.

ETIOLOGY.—Trauma is the usual etiology of ringbone. A periostitis produced by pulling of the collateral ligaments of the joints involved, pulling of the joint capsule attachments to the bone, pulling of the attachment of the common extensor tendon to the first, second or third phalanx, or direct blows to the phalanges are

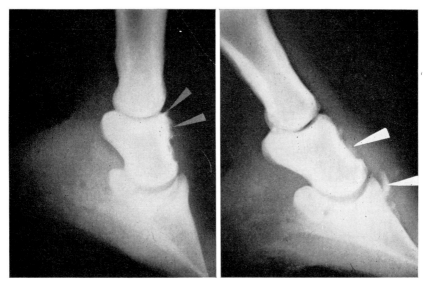

FIG. 6–42   FIG. 6–43

FIG. 6–42.—High ringbone. The top pointer indicates new bone growth at the edge of the pastern joint. The lower arrow indicates new bone growth on the anterior surface of the proximal end of the second phalanx. These growths resulted from a pulling of the fibrous portion of the joint capsule, or from a pulling of the attachment of the common digital extensor.

FIG. 6–43.—Low ringbone. The upper arrow points to new bone growth on the distal end of the second phalanx while the lower arrow shows avulsion of a portion of the extensor process of the third phalanx. These changes are due to tension on the common digital extensor.

the most common causes of ringbone. Pulling of these structures does not cause rupture or tearing, although this can occur, but when these structures are "pulled," the periosteum is disturbed and periostitis and new bone growth result. Wire cuts in the pastern region may cause periostitis, that will cause ringbone, if the cut extends into the periosteum (Fig. 6–45). Ringbone also has been described as resulting from uneven spacing of the articular surfaces of the pastern joint and insufficient height of the ridge dividing the articular surfaces on the proximal surface of the second phalanx.[1]

In some cases, one of the phalanges will fracture in the area of the pastern, and this may lead to an ankylosis of the pastern joint and to severe ringbone. Fracture of the extensor process of the third phalanx results from tension on the common extensor tendon (Fig. 1–41, page 47). In the process of healing, this fracture results in a large, low ringbone. If the insertion of the common digital extensor tendon is strained, but the extensor process of the third phalanx does not break, a periostitis still can result causing new bone growth and low ringbone.

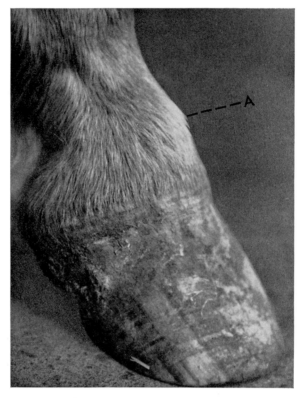

Fig. 6–44.—Clinical appearance of high ringbone on the distal end of the first phalanx and proximal end of the second phalanx. Notice the bulging effect approximately 1 inch above the coronary band (*A*).

Pulling of the collateral ligaments, joint capsule, and tendon insertions may be predisposed by poor conformation. Horses that toe-in are predisposed to ringbone on the lateral side of the joints, while horses that toe-out are predisposed to ringbone on the medial side of the joints. This is because the foot and leg conformation exerts greater stress on these areas. Ringbone is considered to be inheritable by some authors,[2] but it is probably inheritable through poor conformation. Pasterns that are overly upright will result in increased concussion to the pastern joint. Toe-in and toe-out conformations also predispose ringbone (*see* Chapter 1). The inheritability factor would not affect all forms of ringbone, because some result from trauma. Poor conformation increases stress on ligamentous and tendinous attachments to the phalanges.

Signs.—Ringbone may occur in either the front or hind feet, but is more common in the forefeet.

Signs of lameness are not specific. Lameness usually is evident in all gaits and upon turning. Heat and swelling will be present over the involved areas, and the horse will flinch when finger pressure is applied to the area of the active ringbone. In a case of low ringbone, where the distal end of the second phalanx or the extensor process of the third phalanx is involved, the hair on the coronary band will stand erect at the front of the foot. There also will be heat and pain present in this area, and after the condition becomes chronic, there

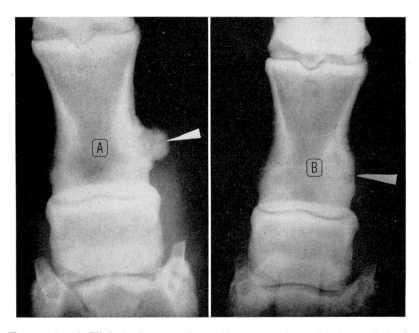

Fig. 6–45.—A, High ringbone on the medial aspect of the distal end of the first phalanx as the result of an old wirecut. Periostitis produced by external trauma will produce ringbone, as shown. This growth was successfully removed surgically as shown in B. Removal was necessitated because the growth caused chronic lameness as the result of interference to the tendon of the superficial digital flexor.

will be a change in shape of the toe of the hoof wall (Fig. 6–46, Buttress foot, Pyramidal disease, page 234). When there is bilateral osteoarthritis of the distal interphalangeal joints the horse may point the feet and shorten the anterior phase of the stride much as in navicular disease.

Some cases of ringbone are relatively asymptomatic, especially if they are periarticular. Those cases of ringbone that are nonarticular may have little if any lameness, and no heat or pain is present after they are healed. Articular ringbone is accompanied by arthritis (usually osteoarthritis) of the affected joint but ankylosis of the pastern joint may occur (Fig. 5–3, page 120). Radiographic examination of ringbone will show minor to extreme bony changes on the first, second, and third phalanges.

Early cases of high ringbone, especially those involving the proximal end of the second phalanx, may show periodic swellings and lameness that will disappear with corticoid injections. This will reappear after the horse is put back to work until the firm swellings of ringbone are recognized. Radiographic changes showing periosteal new bone growth will then be present. The gait in these cases often resembles that of laminitis with the heel landing excessively before the toe. D rupture middle sesamoidean liq /inf. sesam. liq. et

DIAGNOSIS.—A positive diagnosis of ringbone cannot be made without radiographic examination. In early cases, when swelling is not marked, the diagnosis is based on finding heat and pain in the involved areas. Careful comparison with the opposite limb should be made. One must be exceedingly cautious when bilateral swellings that are cold are present. Some horses will demonstrate this, but radiographic examination will reveal normal bones with only an enlarged distal epiphysis on the first phalanx.

TREATMENT.—If a case is diagnosed in the very early stages before new bone growth begins, limiting motion of the joints by placing the limb in a plaster cast from the hoof wall to just below the carpal joint is a good method of treatment. The foot should remain in a cast for a minimum of four weeks and be rested for a minimum of four months. Injection of the area with a corticoid is indicated before application of a plaster cast (Chapter 11, page 458).

When the pastern joint has become ankylosed, signs of lameness may not be present. This is especially true in the hind limb, where fractures of the phalanges may heal by ankylosing the pastern joint (Fig. 5–3, page 120). If the ringbone is articular in nature, the horse will be lame until the pastern joint is ankylosed. Too often the joint refuses to ankylose and this results in massive deposits of new bone growth around the joint with a hairline articular space shown on radiographs.

In chronic cases a plaster cast is of little value, and the area is commonly fired or blistered. Neither of these methods of treatment are of value in articular ringbone, but firing is indicated and will usually help in periarticular ringbone. Ankylosis may be stimulated by surgically stripping the pastern joint of its articular cartilage. Then the limb should be placed in a plaster cast for eight weeks to allow complete ankylosis of the pastern joint to occur. Ankylosis of the proximal interphalangeal joint may be done under general anesthesia by means of a drill bit or an osteotome. The method preferred by me is as follows: After a general anesthetic has been administered and the skin area prepared, an incision is made on the antero-lateral aspect of the proximal interphalangeal joint, between the lateral collateral ligament and the common digital extensor tendon. After identification of the proximal interphalangeal joint, a one-fourth inch drill is introduced between the collateral ligament and common digital extensor tendon, between the first and second phalanges. The drill is introduced from one hole, but is used to strip as much cartilage and cancellous bone as possible. The drill from the one hole is moved anteriorly, posteriorly and medially numerous times to insure as much destruction of the joint as possible. Cancellous bone as well as articular cartilage must be removed to get a good ankylosis. Caution should be used not to allow the drill bit to become hot and cause bone necrosis. Another precaution is to not allow the drill bit to encounter the medial digital artery, vein or nerve. In addition, the tendons behind should not be injured. It is not important to remove bone fragments left by the drill since they will help to fuse the joint.

Similar destruction of the joint can be done using an osteotome. In this case, the articular cartilage and cancellous bone adjacent to the joint are chiseled away. Caution must be used not to destroy the collateral ligaments, tendons or vessels. After destruction of cartilage and cancellous bone is done, the subcutaneous tissues are sutured with 00 catgut with a simple interrupted pattern. The skin is then closed with 00 monofilament nylon with simple interrupted pattern. Dry gauze sponges are placed over the wound prior to application of stockinette for the cast.

The limb is then immobilized to just below the tarsus or carpus in a plaster cast. The foot must be included in the plaster cast. The cast has no padding except stockinette. The first layers of plaster are merely laid on without pressure. After two or three rolls of 6-inch plaster have been put on, plaster splints 4 inches wide and 18 inches long are used to reinforce the front and back of the cast. Then an additional three or four rolls of 6-inch plaster are used to thoroughly immobilize the joint. Some pressure can be put on these latter rolls since the original plaster and splints are beginning to harden somewhat by this time. After the cast is finished, it is well to either paint the cast with a quick-drying enamel, or to enclose the foot of it in a piece of rubber tubing, to prevent moisture from seeping through the bottom part of the cast. The cast is changed if any increased lameness is shown, or if it cracks in any portion. It is usual to have to change the cast once or twice during the ten-week period the foot is immobilized. Each time the cast is changed, the horse should be restrained with general anesthesia. A radiograph can be taken when the cast is removed to check progress of the ankylosis. The foot should be cast in as normal a position as possible. After final removal of the cast, a 3-inch trailer shoe is used to support the fetlock. This shoe is worn approximately four weeks.

If the coffin joint is involved, there is little hope of ever obtaining a sound horse (Fig. 6–47, page 235). A neurectomy is sometimes performed to remove the pain. If a bilateral volar neurectomy is done, the same precautions should be used as described under posterior digital neurectomy for navicular disease. Stumbling and loss of hoof wall are described as complications but are probably due to loss of blood supply rather than nerve supply. This is because connective tissue and nerve regeneration efforts surround and occlude the volar arteries. In some cases the anterior or posterior branch of the digital nerve may be cut to remove pain. X-ray and gamma ray therapy are used for treating ringbone, but without outstanding results. Periarticular ringbone may respond favorably to this therapy.

Horses with ringbone usually are shod with full roller motion shoes (*see* Chapter 9) which aid in removing some of the action from the ankylosed or involved joints.

In some cases of non-articular ringbone it is indicated to remove the new bone growth because it is causing lameness by encroaching on adjacent structures (Fig. 6–45). This is successful in about one-half of the cases.

PROGNOSIS.—The prognosis is always unfavorable if the ringbone is articular. It is guarded if the ringbone is periarticular.

SPECIFIC REFERENCES

1. HAAKENSTAD, L. H.: Investigations on Ringbone. Nordisk Veterinaermedicin Bd., 7, 1, 1954.
2. STECHER, R. M.: Discussion of Osteoarthritis. J.A.V.M.A., *141*, 1249, 1962.

26. Pyramidal Disease (Buttress Foot)

DEFINITION.—Pyramidal disease, due to new bone growth in the area of the extensor process of the third phalanx, is a form of low ringbone. This new bone growth may be due to fracture or periostitis of the extensor process. Healing of the pathological changes produces new bone growth, causing an enlargement at the coronary band at the center of the hoof (Fig. 1–40, page 46; Fig. 6–46). The

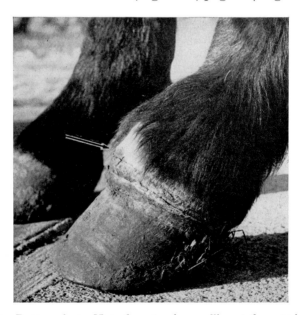

FIG. 6–46.—Buttress foot. Note the extensive swelling at the anterior portion of the coronary band as the result of low ringbone. This is the same foot as shown in Figure 6–47.

same bony enlargement occurs from periostitis of the extensor process, making the clinical picture identical to fracture of this process.

ETIOLOGY. — Pyramidal disease is caused by excessive strain on the long or common digital extensor as it inserts on the extensor process of the third phalanx. This results in a periostitis that causes new bone growth, or in a fracture of the extensor process of the third phalanx which heals with excessive callus (Fig. 1–41, page 47; Fig. 6–47).

SIGNS. — Signs of lameness are not specific, but the horse often will show a tendency to point with the affected foot and the anterior phase of the stride will be shortened. In early stages, heat, pain, and some swelling are evident at the coronary band in the center of the wall and lameness is present in all gaits. The hair shows a tendency to stand upright at the center of the coronary band (Fig.

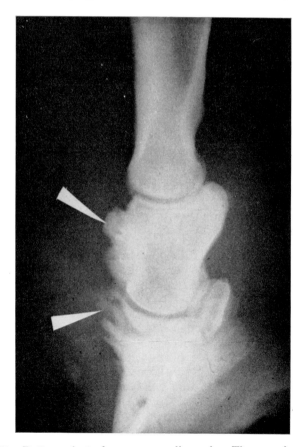

FIG. 6–47. — Buttress foot changes on radiograph. The new bone growth is extensive as shown by the upper pointer on the second phalanx. The lower pointer shows new bone growth on the extensor process of the third phalanx. This is the same foot as shown in Figure 6–46. Since the proximal end of the second phalanx is involved, the horse actually had high and low ringbone.

6–46) and the horse flinches when finger pressure is put on the affected tissues. Arthritis of the coffin joint results and usually becomes chronic in the form of an osteoarthritis (Fig. 6–47). After some time, a change takes place in the shape of the front of the hoof wall, with a bulging from the coronary band to the bearing surface of the wall. Radiographs reveal variable changes in the second and third phalanges and in the coffin joint (Fig. 6–47).

TREATMENT. — No treatment is of particular value in relieving this disease. Firing and blistering have been used, but these are of doubtful value. In early cases, injection of corticoids and immobilization of the part with a plaster cast may be of some help. Anterior digital neurectomy may relieve signs of lameness and allow limited use of the horse. Corrective shoeing consists of using full roller motion shoes on the affected foot to take as much motion as possible from the coffin joint.

PROGNOSIS. — The prognosis is unfavorable in all cases.

SPECIFIC REFERENCE

FRANK, E. R.: Pyramidal Disease. No. Am. Vet., *16*, 34, 1935.

27. Fracture of Extensor Process of the Third Phalanx

DEFINITION. — Fracture of the extensor process may occur unilaterally or bilaterally in the forefeet of horses. More rarely it is seen in the hind feet. It may or may not be accompanied by buttress foot which is produced by periosteal new bone growth (page 234).

ETIOLOGY. — The apparent etiology would be excessive pressure on the common digital extensor tendon. This could produce enough pressure to fracture the process. Bilateral cases could be due to congenital fractures (Fig. 6–48). In this case, it may be that the process has attempted to ossify from a separate ossification center, weakening the process and allowing it to be separated from the rest of the bone. Cases of this type do not have large amounts of periosteal new bone growth and the appearance of buttress foot (Fig. 6–48).

SIGNS. — Lameness signs are relatively obscure. The anterior phase of the stride is shortened and the horse shows a stride similar to navicular disease. However, there is no reaction to the hoof tester over the frog or other parts of the foot. After the condition has been present for some time there is a change in the shape of the hoof wall, with a tendency for V-shaped foot. If the condition has been present a year or longer, this shape will extend the full length of the hoof wall. Lateral radiographs of the foot reveal the fracture or a separated extensor process (Fig. 6–48). If extensive amounts of periosteal new bone growth are present, the foot assumes the typical appearance of buttress foot, which has been discussed as a separate condition (page 234). Pain may be shown when pressure is applied over the center of the coronary band.

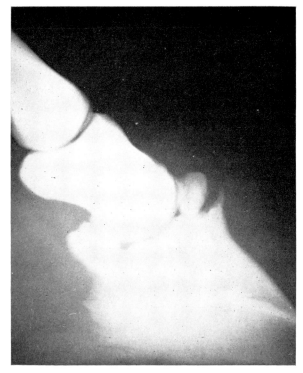

FIG. 6–48.—Bilateral fracture of the extensor process of the third phalanx. This horse was affected with fracture of the extensor process on both forelimbs. It is possible that such a condition has a congenital origin when bilateral and not accompanied by periosteal new bone growth. Such fragments can be surgically removed.

DIAGNOSIS.—Diagnosis is established by the changes in the shape of the hoof wall, pain on pressure over the extensor process (which may or may not be present) and radiographs (Figs. 1–41, 6–48).

TREATMENT.—Fragments of the extensor process can be surgically removed. The surgery is done under general anesthesia and with accepted aseptic technique. A midline incision is made over the center of the common digital extensor tendon, just above the coronary band. The incision need not extend the full depth of the coronary band. The common digital extensor tendon is separated longitudinally and the fragment can be palpated and grasped with a forcep. An alligator-type forcep works very well. Adhesions to the fragment are dissected and the fragment removed. The tendon is sutured with simple interrupted stitches of 00 catgut or collagen. The subcutaneous tissues are closed in a similar fashion and the skin is closed with a 00 monofilament nylon with a simple interrupted suture pattern. The foot is placed in a cast that extends to below the carpus for one week. The cast is removed and the foot kept in supporting bandage for thirty days. The horse should not be worked for at least six months.

PROGNOSIS.—Prognosis is guarded because osteoarthritis of the distal interphalangeal joint is present and may persist. New bone growth involving the joint makes an unfavorable prognosis.

SPECIFIC REFERENCE

NUMANS, S. R. and WINTZER, H. F.: Surgical Treatment of Apophysial and Chip Fractures. Berl. u. Munch. Tierazart, Wschr., *74*, 205, 1961.

28. Quittor

DEFINITION.—Quittor is a chronic, purulent inflammation of a collateral cartilage of the third phalanx characterized by necrosis of the cartilage and sinus drainage through the coronary band. It is most common in the forelimb (Fig. 6–49).

ETIOLOGY.—Injury near the coronary band over the region of the collateral cartilages may cause quittor as a result of production of a subcoronary abscess. Quittor can be secondary to a penetrating wound through the sole where infection has gained access to the collateral cartilage, or to trauma of the cartilage as a result of wire cuts or bruises which damage the cartilage and reduce circulation in the area. Interfering may cause quittor by damaging a medial collateral cartilage.

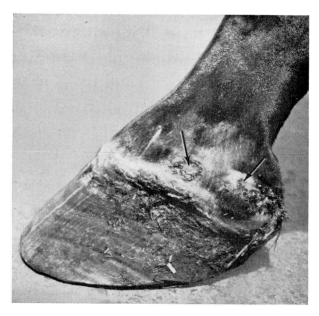

FIG. 6–49.—Clinical appearance of typical quittor. Arrows point to two draining tracts. This case was cured through the surgical procedure described, making an elliptical incision above the coronary band. The anterior tract led posteriorly, and only the posterior tract had to be followed to necrotic cartilage.

SIGNS. — The condition may occur over either the medial or lateral collateral cartilage. Swelling, heat, and pain over the coronary band, in the region of the affected collateral cartilage, and chronic suppurative sinus tracts which tend to heal and then break open at intervals, characterize quittor. Lameness occurs in acute stages but may show remission when the lesion appears to be healing. Some sidebone may occur with the lesion, and permanent swelling usually results over the area of the involved collateral cartilage. Permanent damage and deformity of the foot may result, causing persistent lameness.

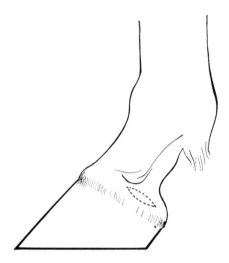

FIG. 6–50. — The dotted lines show the site of a quittor operation for removal of necrotic cartilage.

DIAGNOSIS. — Enlargement over the affected collateral cartilage, characterized by one or more sinus tracts that show chronicity and recurrence, is diagnostic of quittor. It can be differentiated from shallow abscesses by using a probe. Drainage at the coronary band occurs with "gravel" (page 353) and other foot infections; these should be differentiated from quittor.

TREATMENT. — A few early cases of quittor will respond to irrigation of the tract with an escharotic agent, such as 20 per cent silver nitrate, followed in ten minutes by saline injections which neutralize the silver nitrate. These injections may be repeated daily until all necrotic tissue is removed. A follow-up therapy to the above treatment is to apply an enzyme solution or ointment,* which aids in the removal of necrotic tissue. The lesion should be cleaned, shaved and bandaged prior to and following therapy. Surgical removal of the necrotic cartilage may be necessary in older cases;

* 1. Varidase, Lederle Laboratories
  2. Elase Ointment, Parke Davis Co.
  3. Kymar Ointment, ArmourLabs.

some veterinarians prefer surgical correction to routine treatment. A number of surgical procedures, which are quite radical and involve sectioning of the coronary band, are recommended; however, I have found that elliptical incision, over the sinus tract, above the coronary band (Fig. 6–50), approximately 2 to $2\frac{1}{2}$ inches long and $\frac{1}{4}$ to $\frac{1}{2}$ inch above and parallel to the coronary band, facilitates removal of all necrotic tissue and cartilage. The advantages of this incision are shorter healing time and lack of involvement of the coronary band which would result in cracks in the hoof wall. The elliptical portion of skin should be removed, and all necrotic cartilage curetted out. Necrotic cartilage can be recognized by its dark blue color. All tracts should be followed to their end, and all involved tissues removed. The incision should not be sutured but is bandaged with a poultice such as Denver Mud.*

PROGNOSIS. —The prognosis is guarded to unfavorable depending on the duration.

SPECIFIC REFERENCE

PROLIC, I.:   Treatment of Quittor, Veterinaria, Sarajevo, *11*, 27, 1962.

29. Sidebones

DEFINITION. —Sidebones, an ossification of the collateral cartilages, usually are found in the forefeet and are most common in horses having poor conformation. The condition is not common in Thoroughbreds.

ETIOLOGY. —Concussion of the quarters of the foot causing trauma to cartilages is probably the cause of most cases. Some authorities believe that there is a hereditary predisposition, but this is probably through poor conformation. Horses that toe-in are prone to develop lateral sidebone, while horses that are toe-wide are prone to develop medial sidebone. However, in both these conformations, sidebone may eventually develop in both cartilages.

Poor shoeing may cause increased concussion resulting in sidebone. Shoeing with long heel calks for a prolonged period may cause the condition by increasing concussion. Shoeing a horse off level may throw more stress on the inside or outside of the hoof wall, thereby increasing concussion to one of the cartilages. Such trauma can produce sidebone. Some cases of sidebone are produced by traumatic lesions, such as wire cuts that damage the cartilage.

SIGNS. —Lameness may or may not be present. Often lameness is blamed on sidebones, when actually they are not guilty. Lameness resulting from sidebone is rare, usually being present only when the cartilages are in the process of becoming ossified and when inflammation is present. Lameness may be evident when the horse turns, but seldom are the signs acute. Massive bone formation may cause mechanical interference to foot action.

*Demco Company, Denver, Colorado

If sidebones are a cause of lameness, there will be heat and pain over one or both of the cartilages. Careful examination of the cartilages will reveal that hardening is present. Pressure on the area will cause the horse to flinch if the cartilage is in the active stages of bone formation. In some cases there will be a visible bulging of the quarters at the coronary band. Sidebone may accompany other lamenesses, such as navicular disease, and may be mistaken for the cause. Radiographs will reveal that the cartilages have partially or completely ossified (Fig. 6–51). After ossification stops, there usually are no signs of lameness, although the involved cartilages no longer function in the normal physiological processes of the foot (Chapter 2). Occasionally a side bone is fractured, causing a small proximal fracture that can be surgically removed or a fracture through the third phalanx (Fig. 6–69).

DIAGNOSIS.—A diagnosis of sidebone as the cause of lameness should not be made unless pain and heat are present over the involved cartilage or cartilages. Radiological examination will

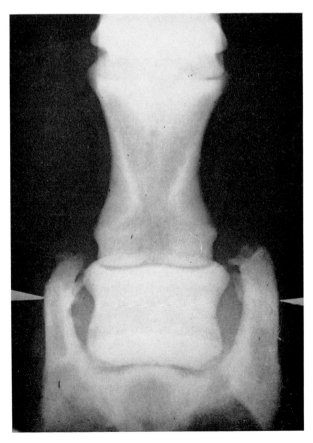

FIG. 6–51.—Ossification of collateral cartilages of the third phalanx (sidebones).

16

reveal bone formation in the cartilages, but this does not necessarily mean that sidebones are the cause of lameness. Most cases of sidebones can be palpated, but again, their presence does not mean they are the cause of lameness.

TREATMENT.—If the sidebones are definitely the cause of lameness, the quarters may be grooved or thinned as prescribed for contracted foot (Fig. 9–18). This permits expansion of the foot and relieves the pain. The horse should be shod with full roller motion shoes (Chapter 9, page 403) to decrease the action in the coffin joint area.

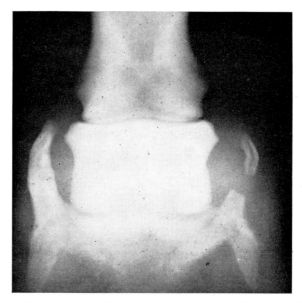

FIG. 6–52.—Sidebones. On the left, notice the large sidebone. On the right, note the separate ossification center in the sidebone. This should not be confused with fracture of a sidebone which is sometimes surgically removed. This type of ossification does not require surgical removal.

When sidebones are fractured causing more acute signs of lameness, small proximal chips can be removed but large fractures should not be surgically removed. If the fragment involves the proximal end of a side bone, it can easily be removed by surgical incision over the area.[1] The incision is made through skin and connective tissue down to the fragmented portion of bone. The fragment is dissected loose and the subcutaneous tissue and skin are closed with sutures. A pressure bandage is kept in place for two weeks. One must not confuse proximal fractures of sidebones with separate ossification centers (Fig. 6–52). No attempt should be made to remove large proximal fragments and the foot should be immobilized in the third phalanx fracture shoe until healing has occurred (see fracture third phalanx, page 269, Fig. 6–69).

Rest should be enforced until the inflammatory process resolves. The area commonly is fired or blistered, but these methods of treatment are probably of little, if any, value. In some cases where it is felt that a sidebone causes chronic and persistent lameness, a posterior digital neurectomy can be done on the affected side or sides.

PROGNOSIS. — The prognosis is guarded to favorable unless exostosis is extensive.

SPECIFIC REFERENCE

1. LUNDVALL, R. L.: Surgical Removal of Fractured Sidebones. Proc. 11th Ann. A.A.E.P. 1965.

30. Laminitis (Founder)

DEFINITION. — Laminitis is an inflammation of the laminae of the foot. It may be caused by either infectious or noninfectious agents and is characterized by passive congestion of the laminae with blood. Severe pain results from the inflammation caused by pressure on the sensitive laminae. Laminitis due to systemic causes may be acute or chronic and may involve two feet or all four; usually it affects both forefeet.

ETIOLOGY. — Laminitis is caused by numerous etiological factors, not all of which are fully understood. Causes commonly recognized include:

1. *Grain Founder.* — Grain founder is caused by ingestion of greater quantities of grain than can be tolerated by the horse. The amount varies, since a certain degree of tolerance develops in those horses accustomed to eating large quantities of grain. Signs of founder may occur suddenly in a horse that is eating considerable quantities of grain as a daily ration, or the founder may be accidental, such as when the horse gains access to open grain bins. This type of founder is associated with gastroenteritis and the grains that most commonly are involved are wheat and barley. Ingestion of oats usually is not as serious, and signs of founder will be mild or may not appear at all. Many other grains are capable of causing the disease including: rabbit feed, chicken feed, and pig feed; if the horse has access to them. The toxin "histidine" known to be formed in grain during digestion is decarboxylated to histamine, which is thought to cause the laminitis. This toxin is not present in cooked grain. The disease can be transmitted through the stomach contents of an affected horse.

2. *Water Founder.* — Ingestion of large amounts of cold water by an overheated horse is considered to be a cause of laminitis. Although the phenomenon is not fully understood, it may be due to gastroenteritis or possibly to histamine formation. Horses that are overheated should be allowed only small amounts of water until they have cooled.

3. *Road Founder.*—Road founder is the result of concussion to the feet from hard work or fast work on a hard surface. Unconditioned animals are especially subject to this type of laminitis, as are those horses having thin walls and soles.

4. *Postparturient Laminitis.*—A mare may develop this type of laminitis shortly after foaling as a result of retaining a portion of the fetal membranes or a uterine infection without retention of fetal membranes. Always a serious form of laminitis, it also may occur as a sequel to severe pneumonia or other systemic infections.

5. *Superpurgation.*—Superpurgation, described as a cause of laminitis, follows administration of purgative drugs; the exact cause is unknown.

6. *Grass Founder.*—Grass founder is common among horses which are grazed on summer grass pastures. Pastures containing clover and alfalfa apparently are more apt to cause the condition than grass pastures. However, cases resulting from grass pastures have been recorded, but these commonly are lush pastures. Horses that develop grass founder usually are overweight. Often affected horses have a heavy crest on the neck caused by fatty tissue. Shetland ponies, Welsh ponies, or fat horses of other breeds are especially subject to the disease. It would appear that geldings are more subject than mares; however, this has not been proven statistically. The cause of this type of laminitis is unexplained. The same type of laminitis is seen occasionally in winter affecting fat horses fed on legume hays. It is not uncommon for horses that previously have been affected with grass founder to show recurrence of laminitis in winter when fed on legume hay. However, laminitis can occur in horses fed on legume hay during the winter with no previous history of grass founder. Hormonal factors may be an etiological factor in some cases, if the grasses or legumes contain estrogens. Such estrogens, if present, especially affect geldings. It could also be due to histamine release.

7. *Miscellaneous Causes.*—Laminitis has been recorded in mares which had absolutely no exposure to any of the above causes. In some cases, these mares did not show estrus; once brought into heat, the laminitis ceased almost immediately. In other cases, mares that were in continuous estrus developed laminitis. It has been noted in a few cases that if this persistent heat was corrected, the laminitis ceased. It is possible that in some cases hormonal influences, other than those in grass founder, are an etiological factor. In these types of laminitis, permanent changes in the feet do not occur as rapidly as from other causes. There are other miscellaneous causes of laminitis, one of which is overeating of beet tops. It is common practice in some areas to turn horses into beet fields following harvest. It is not uncommon for these horses to develop "beet top founder." The pathogenesis is similar to grain founder.

Laminitis may be seen following viral respiratory disease. A similar disease is also seen following administration of some drugs. Neither of these types of etiology has been proven. However, they are suspect and research needs to be done to determine if these causes are factual. In these cases, the overall changes are not as marked as they are in other types of laminitis (Fig. 6–53). The sole shows extensive changes, and rotation of the third phalanx rapidly occurs. In some cases, portions of the sole slough out, exposing the third phalanx. Some horses lose the hoof wall completely, even

FIG. 6–53.—Typical attitude of a horse with laminitis. The rear feet are carried up further forward to help take more weight off the forefeet which are extended anteriorly. This horse had laminitis following a respiratory infection. He was beginning to lose the hoof walls as evidenced by cracking at the coronary band. Hoof wall changes were minimal but the sole had dropped and the third phalanges were protruding through the soles of the forefeet.

though the typical laminitis rings are not present. This begins as a crack at the coronary band, eventually extending completely around the hoof wall and the hoof wall loosens and comes off. Several weeks may elapse before slough of the hoof finally occurs.

Horses showing this type of laminitis may have a history of previous viral respiratory disease two to six weeks prior to onset of the laminitis. Study needs to be done to see if these viruses possibly cause an endarteritis. Others have a history of having been wormed or having received large doses of corticoids or phenylbutazone derivatives. Whether or not these causes are valid is not truly known.

SIGNS.—All signs of laminitis are similar; therefore, they will be described here as acute and chronic. Signs for a specific type of etiology will be described in detail.

Acute Laminitis.—Acute laminitis may affect both front feet or all four feet. If all four feet are affected, the horse tends to lie down for extended periods. When standing, the horse carries his hind feet well up under him and carries the forefeet posteriorly so that there is a very narrow base of support. Most commonly only the two front feet are involved. In this case, the hind feet are carried well up under the body and the front feet are placed forward with the weight on the heel of the foot (Fig. 6–53). The horse shows great reluctance to move.

Heat is present over the sole, the wall, and the coronary band. There is an increased digital pulse as palpated on the digital vessels over the fetlock joint. Many horses show anxiety, trembling of the musculature from severe pain, increased respiration, and variable elevation of temperature. The mucous membranes are injected as the result of toxemia. It is often difficult for the horse to lift one foot from the ground as he throws additional weight on the other affected foot or feet. If a person uses a hoof tester, a uniform tenderness will be noted over the entire area of the sole.

Signs of grain founder usually do not appear for twelve to eighteen hours after ingestion. This often leads the owner to believe that the horse will not be affected. Then laminitis, diarrhea, toxemia, muscular tremors, increased pulse and respiration appear and there is a variable rise in temperature.

In mares suffering from laminitis resulting from metritis, the temperature will often be high—104° to 106° F.; the mucous membranes will be injected, and considerable increase in pulse and respiration will be present. Uterine examination will reveal a dark watery fluid in variable quantities, and portions of the fetal membranes may be found.

Death may result from acute laminitis, but it is not common. In severe laminitis, the hoof may slough as the result of separation of the sensitive and insensitive laminae due to suppuration or edema.

Chronic Laminitis.—In chronic laminitis, rotation of the third phalanx will occur as demonstrated by radiographs (Fig. 1–37, page 44, and Fig. 6–54). This rotation may cause the toe of the third phalanx to push out through the sole of the foot. Rotation of the third phalanx may be caused partially by the inflammation which causes some separation of the sensitive and insensitive laminae. The pull of the deep flexor tendon at its attachment on the semilunar crest of the third phalanx may also aid in displacement of the bone. Once rotation of the phalanx has occurred, it cannot be returned to normal position without trimming the foot to make the distal border of the third phalanx parallel to the ground and using plastics to change the hoof shape.

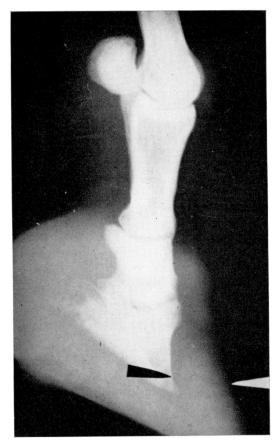

Fig. 6–54.—Rotation of the third phalanx, caused by laminitis. Note the difference, in distance, between the anterior border of the third phalanx and the anterior aspect of the hoof wall, beteeen the arrows, as compared with the proximal areas of these two structures.

Horses suffering from chronic laminitis exhibit a tendency to land on the heel in an exaggerated motion. The sole is dropped and flat, showing excessive quantities of flaky material (Fig. 6–55). The hoof wall grows more rapidly than normal because of chronic inflammation, and the feet may develop a long toe that curls up at the end (Fig. 6–56). Chronic laminitis causes heavy ring formation on the wall; these rings, usually present throughout the life of the horse, are caused by inflammation in the coronary band (Fig. 1–36, page 43).

Once the horse has suffered an attack of laminitis he seems more subject to recurrent attacks regardless of the etiology. Horses that develop grass founder one year may develop it in subsequent years

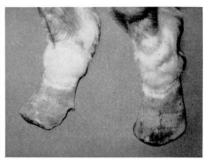

Fig. 6–55   Fig. 6–56

Fig. 6–55.—Dropped sole on a foot affected with chronic laminitis. Note the excessive flaking of the sole, and the area, between the two arrows, which has broken through into the sensitive tissues. The white line is widened and is affected with "seedy toe."

Fig. 6–56.—Long curled feet affected by chronic laminitis. Due to chronic inflammation of the feet, the wall grows at a more rapid rate than normal. This often causes a curling of the toes, as shown.

and often are rendered useless by a second attack if they recover from the first. They are also subject to laminitis if fed on legume hay.

"Seedy Toe," resulting from separation of the sensitive and insensitive laminae, is usually present in chronic laminitis. Enough separation of the white line may occur to allow infection to penetrate the sensitive laminae (see Gravel, page 353). An infection similar to thrush may invade the flaky sole in chronic laminitis and destroy all protection to the third phalanx.

When trimming the feet on a horse that has been affected with laminitis, it is easy to cause reddening and bleeding of the sole because the vascularity of these areas increases with laminitis. This increased tendency toward hemorrhage remains for many months following an attack of laminitis.

DIAGNOSIS.—Diagnosis of laminitis is relatively easy from the signs that are observed. The typical attitude of the animal, the increased pulsation of the digital arteries, the heat in the foot, and the pain evidenced by hoof testers, should furnish adequate proof of laminitis. Chronic laminitis shows characteristic changes in the foot and a typical gait. In some cases, the etiology is difficult to determine; occasionally the cause is never determined.

TREATMENT.—1. *Grain Founder.*—In grain founder the treatment is directed at neutralizing the effects of the ingested grain. Purgation should be used, either with mineral oil or magnesium sulfate.

This should be repeated at approximately four to six hour intervals until all grain has been removed from the intestinal tract. To aid the mineral oil, peristaltic stimulant drugs, such as aloes or carbachol, may be used. It usually is best not to use maximum doses of purgative or peristaltic stimulants, but rather smaller doses repeated at intervals. Antihistamines are useful in counteracting the effect of histamine. Intramuscular blood is sometimes used by injecting approximately 50 to 200 cc. of blood intramuscularly, divided into several doses. The blood can be taken from a donor or from the patient. This apparently has a vaso-constrictor effect upon the vessels of the feet. Parenteral therapy with phenylbutazone or corticoids may be used to reduce the inflammation of the feet. Daily administration may be required (*see* Chapter 11, page 442).

Intravenous dextrose and electrolytes should be used as replacement fluids for the diarrhea which results both from ingestion of grain and purgation. An effort to cool the feet by standing the horse in a stream, in a pit filled with cool water, or by using ice bags, may be helpful. Many times, though, this is not of much value. Standing the horse in warm epsom salts soaks seems to be of as much value as using cold packs. Forced exercise, advocated by some, relieves congestion of the feet. Older literature suggests the use of alum orally, 2 ounces every four hours for an astringent, though this is of doubtful value. Other books suggest draining the feet at the point of the frog to relieve pressure, but this also is of doubtful value in my experience.

Roberts[15] has described the use of intra-arterial steroids in acute laminitis with beneficial results. By applying a tourniquet, following the injection of a corticoid into the digital artery as it passes over the abaxial surface of the sesamoid bone, he feels he can hold the corticoid in the area for better action.

2. *Water Founder.*—Mild purgation at repeated intervals, antihistamines, intramuscular blood, phenylbutazone and corticoids parenterally are used to treat water founder. Cold pack or hot soaking of the feet also may be employed.

3. *Postparturient Laminitis.*—In postparturient laminitis the mare must be treated for metritis as well as for laminitis. If retained membranes are still present in the uterus, they should be removed manually and the uterus packed with antibiotics and/or sulfonamides. A drug, such as purified oxytocic principle (P.O.P.), 5 cc. injected intramuscularly, may be used to constrict the uterus. The infection in the uterus should be treated parenterally with intravenous or intramuscular broad spectrum antibiotics or intravenous sulfonamides. This therapy should be continued for three to five days. Antihistamines, phenylbutazone, or corticoids (Chapter 11) also are useful. Local treatment of the feet, as described for grain founder, should be used.

4. *Grass Founder.*—In grass founder probably there is no gastroenteritis present; however, the horse often is treated with purgation at repeated intervals. Antihistamines, phenylbutazone, or corti-

coids, and intramuscular blood are all used to treat this type of laminitis. The feet may be soaked in either hot or cold packs and the feed restricted to dry grass hay only. In a limited number of cases it appears that perhaps testosterone used intramuscularly in fat geldings is necessary to counteract effects of possible estrogens in the forage in the pastures. A drastic reduction of food intake is necessary to aid in weight loss.

Iodinated casein and thyroid extract have been recommended for grass founder upon the theory that they increase metabolism and aid in reducing the weight of the horse. Obesity accompanies many cases of grass founder, but not all obese horses have laminitis. Iodinated casein does not give spectacular results, but may be worthwhile in reducing weight. Thyroid subcutaneous implants (Cytobin*) can be used to increase the metabolism. In geldings this implant can be combined with the use of repositol testosterone (100 mgs.) at three-week intervals for three injections.

For mares that develop laminitis accompanied by prolonged anestrus, it often is beneficial to infuse the uterus with 500 cc. of sterile saline solution to bring them in estrus. In some cases, laminitis symptoms disappear with the onset of estrus. For mares that are in heat prolonged periods with accompanying laminitis, repositol progesterone (500 mg.), or other appropriate drugs, should be used intramuscularly.

5. *Chronic Laminitis.*—In chronic laminitis the foot should be trimmed as nearly normal as possible and more often than is necessary for a normal horse. Shoes with a wide web may be used as an aid in preventing additional dropping of the sole. The sole can be protected by using rubber or leather pads, or even a sheet metal plate. A rocker or memphis bar shoe is sometimes recommended (Fig. 7–8).

Grooving the hoof wall by various methods, or rasping the quarters to thin the wall and provide expansion of the quarters, as described for contracted heels and laminitis in Chapter 9, page 402, are often of value if combined with corrective shoeing. Neurectomies or alcohol block of the median or volar nerves are sometimes used to alleviate pain, but this should be discouraged because of the potential danger to a rider of the horse. Testosterone injections may be valuable in fat geldings when they are affected with recurring chronic laminitis.

When infection is present in sensitive tissues as a result of a defect in the white line, the defect should be opened to allow drainage. The foot should be treated locally with tincture of iodine and the foot bandaged. Tetanus antitoxin should be administered. If the sole becomes infected with *Spheropherus necrophorus*, the sole should be thoroughly trimmed and treated locally with 10 per cent *sodium* sulfapyridine solution and bandaged. Tetanus antitoxin should be administered.

* Smith, Kline & French Laboratories, Philadelphia.

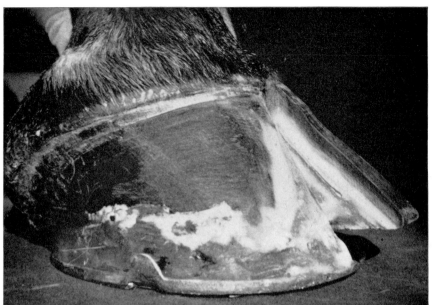

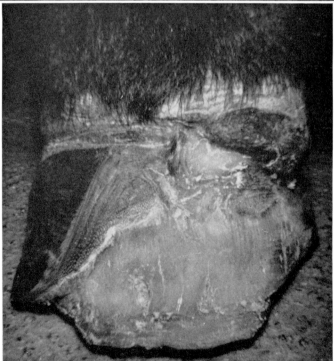

Fig. 6–57. — *Above:* A foot affected with laminitis that has been cut in half, showing how the foot appears after shaping and shoeing, in comparison to the half that is untreated.

Below: A foot affected by laminitis after reshaping and before plastic is applied. (Courtesy Dr. Jacques Jenny, Dr. Loren Evans and A.A.E.P.)

Jenny et al.[8] have described the use of foot trimming and plastics for correction of third phalanx rotation. The fundamental principle of this treatment is to lower the heel so that the distal border of the third phalanx will parallel the surface of the ground when the foot is bearing weight. The changes in the hoof wall caused by chronic laminitis are corrected by trimming and rasping (Fig. 6–57). A shoe is then placed on the foot and held by means of the plastic and clips (Fig. 6–58). The front of the hoof wall is rasped down until, in some cases, one actually encounters blood at the toe. The junction of the normal and abnormal wall is undermined with a motorized burr to give an anchor to the plastic. The foot is changed as much as possible to resemble a normal hoof and the heel is lowered as far as possible to drop the distal border of the third phalanx. Hemorrhage is controlled, if encountered while trimming, by cauterization. The sole is thoroughly cleansed and trimmed. The foot is then painted with some of the plastic catalyst to facilitate adhesion. The plastic is then mixed with its catalyst and applied to the foot. The plastic incorporates a shoe which has toe and quarter clips on it to aid holding it to the foot. Plastic is also applied to the sole to protect the areas where dead sole has been removed. It is important to raise the toe with a layer of plastic to return the third phalanx to a more normal position (Fig. 6–60). The area is then covered with aluminum foil to facilitate shaping the plastic (Fig. 6–59).

This type of treatment is used approximately every six weeks until the foot resumes a more normal appearance and the third phalanx has begun to resume its normal position. In some cases, this type of treatment must be done for as long as a year before the foot assumes a normal shape. Each time the plastic is reapplied, the foot is reshaped and the heel lowered to accomplish the proper results. Several kinds of plastics are available: *Hoof repair material** is available but the cost is prohibitive for most horses. The advantages of this plastic are that it is available in a type that is about the consistency of the frog, a type of about the hardness of the wall and it sets up quite rapidly. Ordinary fiberglass can be used at a much more reasonable cost. Fiberglass is available in a powdered form and by adding extra catalyst it can be forced to harden more rapidly. When using fiberglass, the catalyst should be mixed with the fiberglass prior to the time the hoof wall is being prepared because it takes longer to set. It also dries to a harder consistency, but is satisfactory.

PROGNOSIS.—The prognosis is always guarded in any case of laminitis. If the symptoms continue for more than ten days, the prognosis is unfavorable. However, some cases, such as those that seem to be associated with hormonal imbalances, may continue for prolonged periods without causing excessive changes in the foot, such as rings on the wall and rotation of the third phalanx. Some

* H. D. Justi Co., Philadelphia.

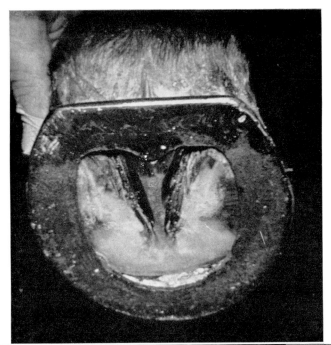

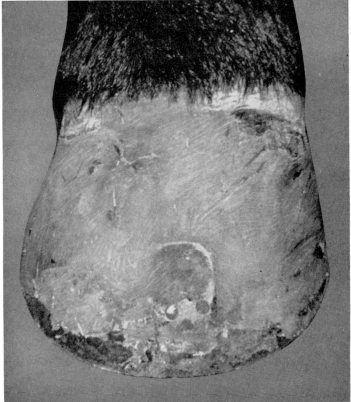

FIG. 6–58.—Foot affected with laminitis after reshaping and application of a shoe with toe and quarter clips and plastic to reshape the foot. The clips on the shoe help the plastic to anchor it to the foot. (Courtesy Dr. Jacques Jenny, Dr. Loren Evans and A.A.E.P.) (253)

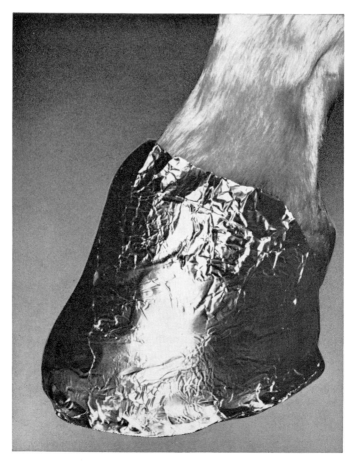

FIG. 6-59.—Hoof wall wrapped in aluminum foil to aid in holding and shaping the plastic while it hardens. (Courtesy Dr. Jacques Jenny, Dr. Loren Evans, and A.A.E.P.)

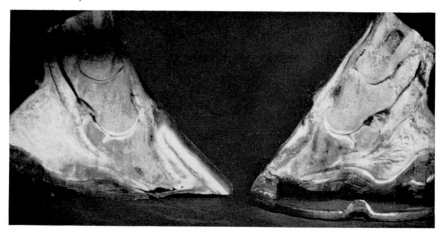

FIG. 6-60.—A foot affected with laminitis cut in half. The left half shows appearance before reshaping and plastic application. The right half shows the same foot after reshaping, plastic and shoe application. Note raised toe and realignment of third phalanx with the hoof wall. (Courtesy Dr. Jacques Jenny.)

cases of laminitis continue for a long period and then become sound but leave the feet distorted. The third phalanx often is rotated when viewed on radiographs (Fig. 6–54). Whenever rotation of the phalanx has occurred, the prognosis is unfavorable. Occasionally infection will enter the pododerm of the foot as the result of separation at the white line (seedy toe) caused by disunion of the sensitive and nonsensitive laminae, or through the sole, making the prognosis unfavorable. If cracks appear in the coronary band, the hoof is likely to slough, making the prognosis unfavorable.

SPECIFIC REFERENCES

1. AKERBLOM, E.: The Etiology of Laminitis. Aust. Vet. J., *13*, 254, 1937.
2. BACKUS, W. O.: Lameness in the Horse with Special Reference to Acute Laminitis. J.A.V.M.A., *91*, 64, 1937.
3. BAIRD, J.: Laminitis. J.A.V.M.A., *83*, 44, 1933.
4. BRITTON, J. W.: Spontaneous Chronic Equine Laminitis. Calif. Vet., *15*, 17, 1959.
5. CHAVANCE, JEAN: Histamine Theory and Treatment of Laminitis. Vet. Med., *41*, 199, 1946.
6. GROSS, D. R.: Treatment of Laminitis. Mod. Vet. Pract., *42*, 58, 1961.
7. HALLET, C. S.: Laminitis in Horses. Vet. Med., *31*, 339, 1936.
8. JENNY, J.: Mechanical Treatment of Laminitis. Proc. 8th Ann. A.A.E.P., p. 212, 1962.
9. KOCHAN, W. F.: Antihistamine Treatment of Laminitis. Vet. Med., *43*, 478, 1948.
10. LAWSON, M. R.: Acute Laminitis in the Horse. Vet. Record, *66*, 615, 1954.
11. MARTIN, W. J.: Equine Laminitis. Am. J. Vet. Med., *11*, 297, 1916.
12. MERILLAT, L. A.: The Treatment of Acute Laminitis. Am. J. Vet. Med., *15*, 535, 1920.
13. MOORE, R. C.: Equine Laminitis or Pododermatitis. Am. J. Vet. Med., *11*, 281, 1916.
14. NILS, OBEL: *Studies on the Histopathology of Acute Laminitis.* Almquist & Wiksells, Boktrycekeri Ab. Uppsala, 1948.
15. ROBERTS, W. D.: The Treatment of Laminitis by Intra-arterial Infusion of Adrenocorticoid Steroids. Proc. 10th Ann. A.A.E.P., p. 241, 1964.
16. RODEBAUGH, H. D.: Surgical Treatment of Chronic Laminitis. Vet. Med., *33*, 288, 1938.
17. SELBY, O. C.: Acute Laminitis. Am. Vet. Rev., *35*, 433, 1909.
18. SULLIVAN, M. W.: A Complicated Case of Acute Laminitis. J.A.V.M.A., *93*, 394, 1938.
19. THOMAS, E. F.: Autogenous Blood Therapy in Laminitis. No. Amer. Vet., *26*, 278, 1945.

31. Navicular Disease (Navicular Bursitis, Bursitis Podotrochlearis)

DEFINITION. — Navicular disease begins as bursitis of the navicular bursa between the deep flexor tendon and the navicular bone (Fig. 2–3, page 54, and Fig. 6–61). As the disease progresses, degenerative and erosive lesions of the fibrocartilage begin on the tendinous surface of the bone. The degenerate fibrocartilage becomes frayed and pitted near the sagittal ridge. The articular surfaces of the joint are not affected. Pathological changes are confined to the tendinous surface of the bone, the bone substance and the adjacent tendon of the deep flexor. Fibrils of the tendon are torn adjacent to the distal edge of the navicular bone. The surface of the tendon is progressively destroyed and may eventually rupture spontaneously, especially after neurectomy, which allows normal action of the foot. As the disease advances, the bone becomes hyperemic and rarification (osteoporosis) occurs. Rarely, fracture of the bone will

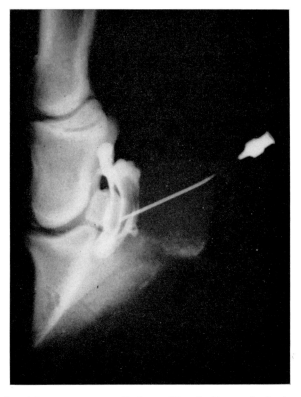

FIG. 6–61.—An eighteen-gauge needle in position in the navicular bursa. A small amount of radio-opaque material has been injected to outline the bursa, as shown.

occur. In advanced cases, calcification of the suspensory ligament of the navicular bone occurs, as well as extensive rarification of the navicular bone.

This is an insidious disease that shows improvement upon rest in the early stages, but reappears when the horse is put back into training. Navicular disease affects only the front feet so no description is available of the disease in the hind feet. It is one of the most important causes of lameness in horses.

ETIOLOGY.—Navicular disease has been described as an inheritable disease resulting from upright conformation and a weak navicular bone. Concussion also is a definite factor in the etiology. Horses that perform hard work, such as racing, cutting, calf roping and barrel racing, are especially subject to the disease. If the work is performed on rough or hard surfaces, concussion is greatly increased, so the likelihood of disease is greater. Upright conformation definitely increases concussion to the navicular area. The navicular bone transmits a portion of the weight, as distributed through the second phalanx, to the third phalanx. In doing this, the bone is forced posteriorly against the deep flexor tendon. An even greater pressure against the tendon occurs as the body weight passes over the foot during motion. The pressure of the navicular bone against the tendon may be an exciting factor in beginning bursitis. The small feet characteristic of some horses, which has been promoted by selective breeding, undoubtedly may be a factor in increasing concussion. The small foot does not have as large an area over which to distribute concussion and weight, and thereby increases pressure per unit area to the foot.

Pressure of the deep flexor tendon against the navicular bone is commonly increased by improper trimming and shoeing (see Chapter 1, Fig. 1–20). It is common to trim the heel too low on a horse that has upright pasterns. This breaks the pastern and foot axes and produces greater pressure of the deep flexor tendon against the navicular bone.

The hind limbs are not involved in navicular disease, unless caused by puncture wounds, because they primarily are the propelling agents and the forelimbs receive most of the shock. Puncture wounds of the navicular bursa can cause the disease, but this usually is a suppurative condition and so will not be considered in this discussion. Senile decay of the bone may occur in some horses that have been used heavily for a period of years. In such a case, demineralization of the bone occurs as the result of chronic bursitis. Defective or irregular blood supply to the navicular bone also has been described as a cause. This could be brought about by hard work followed by prolonged periods of rest, at which time the blood supply to the bone may be reduced, causing gradual necrosis of the bone. The hyperemia that occurs with the bursitis of navicular disease is generally blamed for the decalcification (osteoporosis) of the navicular bone.

SIGNS.—The affected horse often has a history of intermittent lameness which decreases when he is rested. Following heavy work the horse may be noticeably worse the next morning. In the early stages of the disease, rest will produce alleviation of the clinical signs, suggesting that the horse is cured, but as soon as hard work is begun, signs of the disease reappear.

Both front feet usually are involved in navicular disease; however, one foot often shows more lameness than the other, and it may not be until a nerve block has been used on the foot that it is noticeable that lameness also is present in the opposite forefoot. If both feet are involved, the horse often points alternately with one foot and then the other, or stands with both feet too far in front (camped in

17

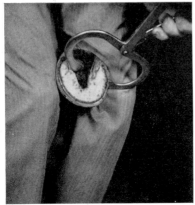

A

B

Fig. 6–62.—*A*, Using hoof testers to check the medial and lateral sides of the center one-third of the frog for navicular disease. Sensitivity in this area should be checked against other feet to help determine the amount of pain that is present.

B, Using hoof testers to check the ends of the navicular bone. This test is less reliable than the test of the center one-third of the frog. Reaction here should be compared with reaction in other feet which are sound.

front). If only one foot is involved, or if one foot is more severely involved than the other, the horse points with the most severely affected foot.

During movement the horse tends to land on the toe of the foot to avoid concussion to the heel area. The navicular bone underlies the middle third of the frog so the horse attempts to prevent pressure to this area. The attempt to protect the heel area hinders a roping horse in stopping and slows a race horse by shortening the anterior phase of the stride. The effort that the horse makes to land on the toe is most noticeable in the walk and trot, and causes a shortened anterior phase of the stride. The toe may show signs of being excessively worn and the horse may stumble in the walk or trot because of the tendency to land on the toe. Increased lameness will be evident if the horse is on irregular ground due to frog pressure caused by irregularities of the ground. Increased lameness also will be noted when the horse is turned in the direction of the affected foot or feet. Examination of the foot with a hoof tester will pinpoint the pain at the center third of the frog and to a lesser extent over the ends of the navicular bone (Figs. 6–62A and B). Normal horses will show some variation in reaction to the hoof tester over the ends of the navicular bone and over the center third of the frog. The lame foot should be compared with the opposite forefoot, if it is sound, and if not, compared with the reaction of the rear feet.

It is not uncommon for a horse with navicular disease to develop bruising of the sole at the toe. This may be misleading in examination, both clinically and with a hoof tester. If the bruising of the sole at the toe is severe enough, the horse will begin to walk back on the heel, causing one to think more of a laminitis type of action. With a hoof tester there is considerable sensitivity in the bruised area. Peeling the sole with a hoof knife will show increased vascularity of the sole. One must be careful not to allow this to confuse the diagnosis. If pain is shown over the center one third of the frog, the horse shows some improvement following blocking of the posterior digital nerve, and if radiographs aid in positive identification of navicular disease, the condition should be treated as navicular disease. Sole bruising will disappear after several months as the horse begins to use a more normal gait. Early cases of bilateral low ringbone may cause signs similar to navicular disease, but typical findings on hoof tester examination and relief of lameness by posterior digital nerve block are not obtained.

The shuffling gait exhibited in navicular disease often causes the owner to believe his horse is lame in the shoulders. The shortened anterior phase of the stride causes a very disagreeable ride, and to the inexperienced the horse appears to be favoring the shoulder areas.

Over a period of time the foot gradually changes shape. The effort to avoid frog pressure causes the heels to contract and to raise. The sole becomes more concave both anterior to posterior and medial to lateral, and the foot narrows across the quarters. If the navicular disease is unilateral, the foot will become smaller due to contraction (Fig. 6–63).

Radiological examination of the navicular bone reveals changes in less than half of the cases. Some authors claim that navicular disease is not present if radiological changes are not evident, but this cannot be true, for such changes are evident only after the condition has become well established. Radiological changes occur in the form of osteoporosis, exostosis, enlarged vascular channels, narrowing of

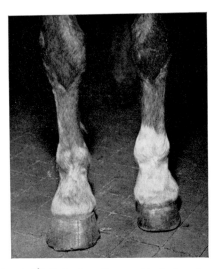

FIG. 6–63.—Contracted left foot as the result of chronic navicular disease.

the articular space, sclerosis, and osteolysis (Figs. 6–64 and 6–65). The above changes indicate a well advanced case. Radiological changes often can be demonstrated in the navicular bone after it has been removed and all extraneous tissues scraped away. This, however, is of no value in diagnosis of the disease. Technically high quality radiographs are necessary for identification of the disease if changes are to be shown.

Changes in the navicular bone and bursa, found at necropsy, are erosions of the cartilage of the bone, discoloration of the tendon and bone, fibrous adhesions between the deep flexor tendon and the bone, osteoporosis, exostosis of the bone, enlargement of the nutrient foramina of the bone, and, in some cases, fracture of the navicular bone.

DIAGNOSIS.—Signs of lameness are reasonably characteristic and one should watch closely to see if the toe lands before the heel and if the anterior phase of the stride is short. Other signs that are very helpful are the reactions of the horse to a hoof tester applied to the center third of the frog. Considerable pressure must be put on this

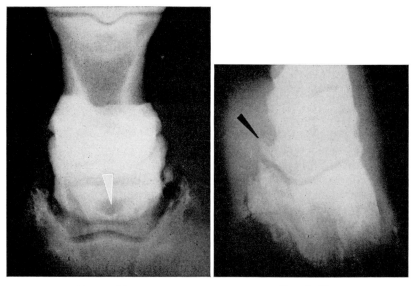

FIG. 6-64   FIG. 6-65

FIG. 6-64.—The pointer shows an area of demineralization in the center of the navicular bone. Changes of this type indicate a long-standing case of navicular disease.

FIG. 6-65.—The pointer shows a spur on the end of the navicular bone, in an oblique view of the bone. This spur indicates a long-standing case of navicular disease.

area since the foot takes great pressure when the foot is put down. A good set of hoof testers will cause the horse to flinch when pressure is applied over the center third of the frog (Fig. 4-6, page 103; Fig. 6-62). However, this reaction should be compared with the reaction of the hind feet or the opposite forefoot, if sound. One should keep in mind that in most cases there is at least some degree of involvement in the opposite forefoot. Sole bruising from constant landing on the toe is a factor that should be kept in mind in using hoof testers. Pain may be shown over the toe area of the sole in chronic navicular disease. As mentioned previously, this pain may be so severe as to force the horse to walk back on the heel. Radiographs, blocking the posterior digital nerve and good judgment will aid in deciding whether sole bruising is primary or secondary.

Blocking of the posterior digital nerves can be an aid in diagnosis. The landmark for blocking these nerves is located between the posterior edge of the first phalanx and the anterior edge of the superficial flexor tendon. The nerve lies closer to the edge of the tendon than to the first phalanx and runs parallel to the edge of the deep flexor tendon. A small amount of 2 per cent lidocaine hydrochloride*

*Xylocaine, Astra Laboratories.

should be placed over the area of the nerve on the medial and lateral sides, about one-third of the way between the fetlock and the coronary band. A 25-gauge, $\frac{1}{2}$-inch needle should be used to deposit the local anesthetic over the nerves and the horse should be twitched to facilitate the nerve block. After allowing five to ten minutes for the block to take effect, the horse should tend to show improvement if affected by navicular disease. This nerve block also is an indication of the amount of relief that can be obtained from posterior digital neurectomy.

Local anesthesia of a navicular bursa can be accomplished by injecting it with 2 per cent lidocaine hydrochloride. A topical anesthetic of some type must be used to produce local anesthesia in this area. Only 5 cc. should be used since the fluid of the bursa may be diffused to other areas by osmosis. The procedure for injecting the navicular bursa is as follows:

The fossa of the heel should be shaved and prepared with skin antiseptics for passage of an 18-gauge, 2-inch needle into the navicular bursa. A small area of skin $\frac{1}{2}$ inch in diameter should be blocked with 2 per cent lidocaine hydrochloride using a 25-gauge, $\frac{1}{2}$-inch needle between the heels (Fig. 11–5, page 448). The foot should be placed on a wooden block and an 18-gauge, 2-inch needle passed through the skin at the anesthetized fossa of the heel in a line paralleling the angle of the coronary band (Fig. 11–6, page 448). When the needle encounters bony tissue, it is in the navicular bursa (Figs. 11–7 and 11–8, page 448). The digital cushion seems to be relatively insensitive, so usually the horse offers no resistance to passage of the needle, even without deep injection of a local anesthetic. Once the needle is in the bursa, 5 cc. of 2 per cent lidocaine hydrochloride should be injected. If the needle is not in the bursa, difficulty will be encountered in trying to inject the fluid. One can feel the bursa fill with fluid; when it is tense, injection should be stopped. The suspected area of foot pathology must be well localized before this type of block is used, because the spread of the local anesthetic fluid will block some third phalanx fractures or possibly other foot pathology.

Following nerve block of the posterior digital nerves, or injection of the navicular bursa with a local anesthetic, the horse should be checked to see if there is improvement of the gait. Improvement signifies that navicular disease is present, if other lamenesses have been ruled out. This improvement is gradual, so the horse should be worked ten to twenty minutes to achieve the best diagnostic results. Radiographs are helpful in diagnosis of some cases of navicular disease (Figs. 6–64 and 6–65), but since the highest percentage of cases are not advanced enough to show changes, negative findings are not significant.

DIFFERENTIAL DIAGNOSIS. — Differential diagnosis should include puncture wounds of the sole and frog, fractured navicular bone, fractured third phalanx, laminitis, sole bruising, corns, and ringbone. Careful physical examination and radiographs can quickly narrow the considerations. In laminitis, the action of the shoulders looks similar to bilateral navicular disease, but the foot lands on the heel and not the toe. Navicular disease is the most common of this group of lamenesses. Osteoarthritis of the distal interphalangeal joints can cause similar signs to navicular disease but can be differentiated on hoof tester and radiographic examinations.

TREATMENT.—Injection of the navicular bursa with a corticoid can be done in the same manner as an injection of a local anesthetic. Intra-bursal corticoids give temporary relief, but are of little value as a permanent cure. Injection of the navicular bursa with irritants, such as Lugol's iodine, has been described in some of the older literature. This is not now recommended since it causes the horse pain but seldom effects a cure. Treatment with x-ray therapy has not given consistent results. Bilateral posterior digital neurectomy is the only method of achieving any degree of permanent relief. Corrective shoeing may relieve symptoms temporarily but posterior digital neurectomy usually has to be done eventually. Complications of posterior digital neurectomy are as follows:

1. *Neuroma Formation.*—The cause of neuromas is not definitely known. However, irritation of the nerve produced by injection of local anesthetic and trauma during surgery can be contributing causes. In addition, exercising the horse too soon after surgery can be an additional irritant. In the experience of the author, the following are helpful in avoiding some of the causes of neuroma.

a. Inject the posterior digital nerve at the level of the proximal sesamoid bone. This will block both the anterior and posterior digital nerves but will keep the irritation of the local anesthetic away from the surgical site.

b. Incise the tissues cleanly with a knife and avoid trauma to the subcutaneous tissues and deep fascia as much as possible.

c. Stretch the nerve slightly before it is cut and incise it with a clean guillotine cut. This allows the cut end to retract proximally for a short distance.

d. Keep a pressure bandage on the wound until it is completely healed.

e. Postoperative injections of butazolidin and/or corticoids parenterally are probably helpful in preventing inflammation at the surgical site.

f. Wait at least six weeks before putting the horse back to active use. If neuromas appear to be developing following neurectomy, local injection of .5 cc of a corticoid into each surgical site every three days, accompanied by parenteral injections of a corticoid or phenylbutazone and poulticing of the wound area may be helpful in preventing their further development.

2. *Rupture of the Deep Digital Flexor Tendon.*—This occurs when posterior digital neurectomy has been done for a long-standing case of navicular disease. In cases of long duration, the deep flexor tendon becomes adherent to the navicular bone by means of fibrous adhesions. As soon as the horse starts using the foot in a normal

fashion, these adhesions are torn and the weak, necrotic deep digital flexor tendon ruptures. This may not occur for several weeks following the surgery. It is recognized by the fact that the toe of the foot raises from the ground on weight bearing. There is nothing that can be done for treatment.

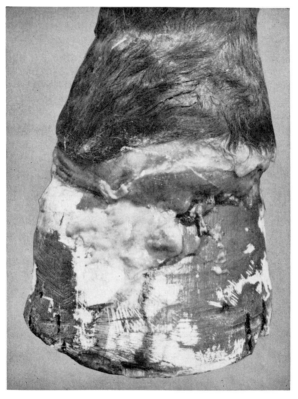

Fig. 6–66.—Appearance of a foot that sloughed following two operations for neurectomy. The first one was for posterior digital neurectomy and the second for removal of neuromas. Several weeks later the foot presented the above appearance. At necropsy the vessels and nerves were dissected out and it was found that neurofibers and scar tissue had completely occluded and even invaded the digital arteries. Water could not be forced through the arteries by syringe.

3. *Loss of the Hoof Wall.*—When a posterior digital neurectomy has been done and follow-up surgery must be done for removal of neuromas, a hoof wall may slough (Fig. 6–66). Dissection of these specimens reveal that it is not due to loss of nerve supply, but due to the fact that the trauma produced by surgery plus the efforts of the nerve to regenerate surrounds the posterior digital artery with tissue that occludes its lumen. This leads to a dry gangrene of the hoof and it sloughs off. Whenever more than one operation must be done in the same site, great care should be taken to avoid tissue injury.

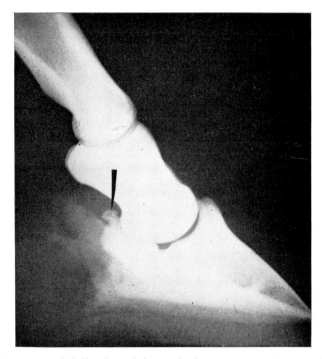

Fig. 6–67.—Calcification of the navicular suspensory ligament in a long-standing case of navicular disease.

4. *Regeneration of the Posterior Digital Nerves.*—Regeneration of the posterior digital nerves may occur any time after six months following posterior digital neurectomy. This is evidenced by recurrence of symptoms. If one-half inch or more of the nerve is removed at time of surgery, this is considered adequate. However, in some cases this gap is bridged by the regenerative efforts of the nerve. Re-operation is the only effective treatment.

5. *Incomplete Desensitization of the Heel.*—Approximately 50 per cent of the horses will show nerve pattern variations. These include small branches coming from the posterior digital nerve high up at its origination. These small branches come down subcutaneously and often follow the ligament of the ergot. Careful examination should be made for these branches during the posterior digital neurectomy. If accessory branches are not found and removed, partial sensation to the heel remains, making the operation only partially successful. In addition, another nerve variation sends a branch from the anterior digital nerve back to the heel area low down in the foot. In this case the only solution would be severance of the anterior digital nerve.

Ordinarily neurectomy of the volar nerves is not recommended. Loss of the hoof wall has been described, blaming loss of nerve supply. In my opinion, the hoof wall is not lost from the loss of nerve supply, but due to the encroachment on the volar arteries by fibrous tissue and nerve tissue resulting from scar formation and nerve regeneration efforts. Once the blood supply is limited or shut off to this area, the hoof wall will slough. This points again to the minimal trauma during surgery, and adequate rest following surgery, to aid in preventing this type of complication. Many horses are perfectly sound following volar neurectomy, but in general its use should probably be discouraged.

Neurectomy of the posterior digital nerves is performed as follows: The horse should be tranquilized with Promazine,* and the area for neurectomy clipped and shaved. The skin should be prepared for operation, about one-half of the distance between the fetlock and coronary band, just in front of the tendon of the superficial digital flexor. Two to 3 cc. of lidocaine hydrochloride or other suitable anesthetic should be injected through a 25-gauge, $\frac{1}{2}$-inch needle over the nerve on the abaxial surface of the medial and lateral sesamoid bones. One can palpate the artery as it crosses this area and the nerve lies just behind it. By infusing the anesthetic around the artery, local anesthesia of both posterior and anterior digital nerves can be accomplished. This aids in keeping the irritating effect of the anesthetic away from the surgical site. However, if neurectomy is to be done soon after a diagnostic block of the posterior digital nerve has been done one-third the distance between the fetlock and the coronary band, this same block can then be utilized for the surgical procedure. A nose twitch should be applied to the horse during these injections. After checking the posterior aspect of the foot with a needle to be sure that the nerves have been anesthetized, an incision $\frac{1}{2}$ to $\frac{3}{4}$ inch long should be made at the anterior border of the superficial flexor tendon. The incision is made through the skin and subcutaneous tissues. At this point the tissues may be separated by the jaws of a hemostat or by careful knife dissection. The important part is to not do any more damage to the tissues than necessary. The ligament of the ergot, which lies subcutaneously, can be removed or pushed aside. The nerve will be found lying just posterior to the artery at about $\frac{1}{2}$ inch depth. One should positively identify the nerve before cutting it. The relationship of the structures are: vein in front, artery in the center and nerve posteriorly. The nerve can be identified by placing a hemostat under it, and then, with the thumb nail, identifying the longitudinal strands of the axons. The nerve should be cut proximally first and then a $\frac{1}{2}$ inch section removed. The incisional area should be sutured with 00 monofilament nylon and the procedure repeated on the opposite nerve, and if necessary, the opposite foot. A pressure bandage should be applied and changed every other day for seven days. The sutures should be removed in ten days; the horse can be put back to work in four to six weeks.

Whenever the nerves do not look the proper size, careful checking should be done for accessory branches. About 50 per cent of horses

*Promazine, Fort Dodge Laboratories; Sparine, Wyeth Laboratories.

operated will show some degree of nerve variation. Commonly there is a subcutaneous branch traversing with the ligament of the ergot. It is found subcutaneously and not so deep as the posterior digital nerve. It is a small branch, but enough to prevent full effect of posterior digital neurectomy (*see* Chapter 2, page 58).

Corrective shoeing consists of aiding the horse in going the way he is trying to use the foot. This consists of raising the heels by building them up, rolling the toe, and using a bar across the heels. In addition, the branches of the shoe are slippered from the quarters through the heels to aid the hoof wall in expansion. The slippering effect is done by tapering the branches of the shoe so that the wall will slide outwards (Chapter 9, Fig. 9–16). The rolled toe and raised heel aid quick breakover. The raised heel and bar across the frog protects the frog from ground pressure. The slippered quarters and heels of the shoe aid expansion of the hoof wall to help counteract the effect of the bar on the shoe. Rasping the quarters of the hoof wall or putting in vertical or parallel grooves on the quarters, also aid foot expansion, and help overcome foot contraction (Chapter 9, Fig. 9–18). In most cases, corrective shoeing is not necessary if neurectomy is done, but can be tried first to see if it will preclude the need of neurectomy.

PROGNOSIS.—The prognosis is unfavorable in all cases, but neurectomy can aid in providing several years of useful service from the horse. Posterior digital neurectomy is not legal in all states on race horses so the veterinarian should check with his state racing commission before performing the operation. As long as only the posterior digital nerve is neurectomized, one need not expect complications. Although the heel area is desensitized, nail punctures in this area will cause the inflammation to spread to sensitive areas in a very short time. Complications of neurectomy have already been described and include neuroma formation, rupture of the deep digital flexor tendon, regrowth of the nerve, accessory branches of nerve supply to the heel and loss of the hoof wall. For neuroma formation and regeneration of the nerve the neurectomy is redone and if a neuroma is present it is dissected out. If it is suspected that accessory nerve supply is present, surgery should be done with a careful check for the small branches that lie subcutaneously near the ligament of the ergot. Methods of attempting to prevent neuroma have already been discussed.

SPECIFIC REFERENCES

1. BRYDEN, W.: Navicular Disease. Am. Vet. Rev., *16*, 19, 1892.
2. DONAHUE, M.: Navicular Disease in Horses. Vet. Med., *30*, 244, 1935.
3. DRAKE, H. S.: Navicular Arthritis. Am. Vet. Rev., *20*, 476, 1897.
4. GORMAN, T. N., NOLD, M. M. and KING, J. M.: Use of Radioactivity in Neurectomy of the Horse. Cornell Vet., *52*, 542, Oct. 1962.
5. HICKMAN, J.: Navicular Disease. Third Ann. Congress. British Eq. Vet. Assoc., p. 13, 1964.
6. HOLLINGSWORTH, J. B.: Navicular Disease. Am. Vet. Rev., *28*, 263, 1904.
7. HUME, W.: Neurectomy in Foot Lameness. J.A.V.M.A., *8*, 115, 1913.

8. JUBB, K. V. F. and KENNEDY, P. C.: *Pathology of Domestic Animals*, Vol. 2, New York, Academic Press, 1963.

9. KOCH, T.: Termination of the Volar Nerve in the Horse. Vet. Record, *52*(2), 26, Jan. 13, 1940.

10. LIAUTARD, ALEXANDER: What is Navicular Disease? Am. Vet. Rev., *30*, 1, 1906.

11. OLSSON, STEN ERIK: On Navicular Disease in the Horse, A Roentgenological and Patho-anatomical Study. Nordisk Veterinaemedicin, *6*, 547, 1954.

12. OXSPRING, G. E.: The Radiology of Navicular Disease, with Observations on Its Pathology. Vet. Rec., *15*, 1433, 1935.

13. ROBB, A. H.: Navicular Disease in the Horse. Vet. Rec., *70*, 962, 1958.

14. SCHEBITZ, H.: Podotrochleosis in the Horse. Proc. 10th Ann. A.A.E.P., p. 49, 1964.

15. ————: Zur Podotrochlase, Spotergluis nach Neurektomic der Rami Volares. Berliner und Munchener Tierarztliche Wochenschrift 78, Jahrgang, Heft 2, S21-26, 1965.

16. VAN HOOSEN, N. W.: Corrective Shoeing for Navicular Disease. A.A.E.P. Program for A.V.M.A. meeting, Portland, 1965.

17. WILKINSON, G. T.: Pathology of Navicular Disease. Brit. Vet. J., *109*, 55, 1953.

32. Fracture of the Navicular Bone

DEFINITION.—Fracture of the navicular bone is rare, but may follow navicular disease or result from trauma to the foot.

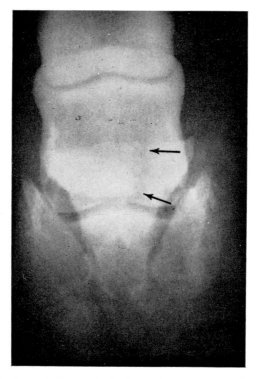

FIG. 6–68.—Fracture of the navicular bone (arrows). Caution should be used not to confuse the lines of the lateral sulci of the frog that sometimes appear to be navicular fractures (see Chapter 12).

ETIOLOGY.—Violent concussion to the foot may cause fracture of the navicular bone or the condition may follow a chronic case of navicular disease. When a navicular bone has been demineralized by chronic inflammation, adhesions between the deep flexor tendon and the navicular bone may fracture the bone after posterior digital neurectomy, when the horse starts to use the foot normally. The demineralized bone breaks because of pressure from the adhesions.

SIGNS.—The signs are identical to those caused by navicular disease, but they may be more acute. Radiographs will reveal the fracture (Fig. 6-68).

DIFFERENTIAL DIAGNOSIS.—Great care must be used in diagnosing fracture of the navicular bone. This is because lines from the lateral sulci of the frog cross the area, and commonly appear as fractures in the navicular bone or second phalanx. If these lines extend above or below the navicular bone, it is not a fracture line. When in doubt, retake the radiograph at a slightly different angle, and if what appears to be the fracture line extends above or below the bone in this new view, it is not a fracture (see Chapter 12).

TREATMENT.—Posterior digital neurectomy is the only treatment that will permit the horse to be used or to travel without pain.

PROGNOSIS.—The prognosis is unfavorable, but posterior digital neurectomy will permit limited use of some horses.

SPECIFIC REFERENCES

1. SMYTHE, R. A.: Fracture of the Navicular Bone. Vet. Rec., 73, 1009, 1961.
2. VAUGHN, L. C.: Fracture of the Navicular Bone. Vet. Rec., 73, 95, 1961.

33. Fracture of the Third Phalanx (Pedal Bone, Os Pedis, Coffin Bone)

DEFINITION.—Fracture of the third phalanx can occur in any class of horses and is not uncommon in either race horses or working Quarter Horses. Fracture of the third phalanx, though, is much more common in the forefeet than in the hind feet.

ETIOLOGY.—Trauma, especially when accompanied by a twisting action as the foot lands, is the predominant cause of fracture of the third phalanx. Occasionally, the third phalanx may be fractured as a result of the penetration of a foreign body through the sole. The third phalanx also may be fractured as the result of trauma to a large sidebone (Fig. 6-69). In such a case, the phalanx usually breaks through one of the lateral wings.

SIGNS.—If the third phalanx is fractured through the center of the bone involving the articular surface, the lameness is an acute supporting leg lameness. In some such cases, the horse may refuse to place the affected foot on the ground for as long as seventy-two hours. The history will often reveal that the lameness occurred suddenly during work and that no known trauma had occurred.

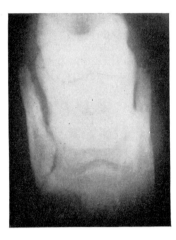

FIG. 6-69.—Fracture of the third phalanx through one of the lateral wings. This horse had large sidebones. A cow stepped on the horse's foot causing fracture of the) third phalanx on the left side. (Carlson, *Veterinary Radiology*, Lea & Febiger.)

There will be increased pulsation and heat in the affected foot, and examination with hoof testers will reveal uniform pain over the entire sole area (Fig. 6-70). Sometimes the bone will be fractured near one of the lateral wings of the phalanx and the lameness will not be so severe (Figs. 6-69 and 6-71). Hoof testers will cause less pain over the entire area of the sole but considerable pain over the affected quarter. If the fracture has been present for some time, signs of lameness will not be as evident, and the history, hoof testers, and radiographs will be necessary to diagnose it.

Fractures of the third phalanx in the hind limb can be overlooked because the attitude of the limb may be similar in appearance to injuries further up the limb. Any acute weight bearing lameness should be examined for the possibility of third phalanx fracture.

DIAGNOSIS.—The diagnosis can be positively confirmed only by use of radiographs. These should be taken to determine not only if the fracture is present, but also where it is. In some cases it may be necessary to take special views of the lateral wings to find the crack in the third phalanx. The defect in the bone may remain for long periods of time and, in some cases, never show clinical union. Horses so affected may be sound even though clinical union is not obvious on the radiographs. Caution must be used so that normal vascular channels are not confused with fractures during interpretation of radiographs.

Examination of the foot with hoof testers, plus the history, is often the most accurate way of establishing a diagnosis before radiographs have been taken.

TREATMENT.—In treatment of this condition the third phalanx should be immobilized as effectively as possible by use of a full bar shoe with quarter clips (Figs. 6-72 and 6-73). The bar should be

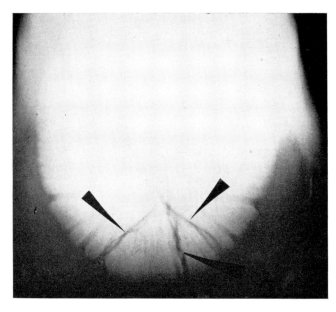

FIG. 6–70.—Fracture of the third phalanx. This fracture occurs in three places, as indicated by the pointers, and extends into the coffin joint.

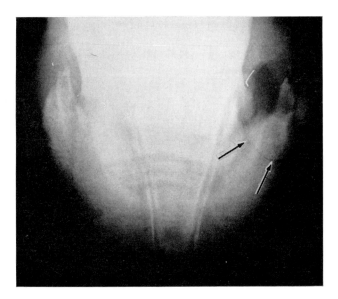

FIG. 6–71.—The arrows show a fracture of the lateral wing of the third phalanx. The fracture line is not distinct so careful radiography must be used. When the hoof tester is used, a horse affected with such a fracture would show the greatest pain over the affected area, rather than diffuse pain evidenced by the foot pictured in Figure 6–70.

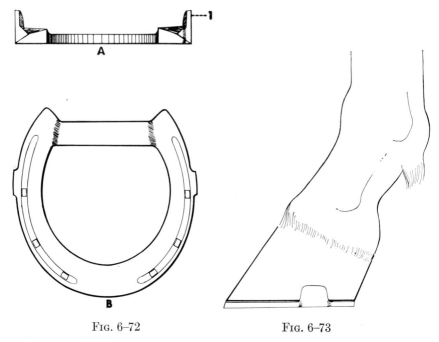

FIG. 6–72   FIG. 6–73

FIG. 6–72.—Full bar shoe used in case of fracture of the third phalanx.

A, Rear view of shoe showing quarter clips (1).

B, Ground surface view of the shoe showing full bar and quarter clips welded to shoe.

FIG. 6–73.—Side view of shoe used for third phalanx fracture showing quarter clip in place.

placed on the shoe so that it is recessed from the frog, and no frog pressure results. The quarter clips should be welded to the outside of the branches of the shoe near the junction of the heel and quarters. This prevents the quarters from expanding, and, when combined with the bar to prevent frog pressure, reduces movement of the phalanx. The foot should be kept in this type of shoe for three to six months, with the shoe reset every four to six weeks. After clinical relief of the symptoms, the horse should be shod with either quarter clips or a bar for a time before both are removed. Some horses require continual use of clips or bar to ensure working soundness. The affected horse should not be worked for approximately six months, and in some cases, one year of rest may be advisable if symptoms do not disappear at the end of six months.

If the fracture has been caused by a puncture wound, the wound must be treated as discussed under puncture wounds of the foot (page 275). In such a case tetanus antitoxin always should be administered. A bone abscess or demineralization of the third phalanx may result from such a fracture (Fig. 6–74). A corrective shoe may be necessary.

In some cases of persistent lameness resulting from fracture of the third phalanx, neurectomy of the posterior digital nerves may afford enough relief that the horse can be returned to full use. The success of this operation can be determined before operation by blocking the posterior digital nerves with a suitable local anesthetic.

PROGNOSIS.—The prognosis is always guarded, but most horses can be returned to working soundness if treatment is instituted soon after the fracture. Fractures through the wings of the third phalanx are most favorable. A greater chance of chronic lameness exists if the fracture is through the center of the bone, involving the articular surface of the coffin joint. If small splinters of bone separate from the third phalanx, a sequestrum may result causing prolonged lameness even after being removed. Radiographic evaluation of the fracture line is difficult because it will be apparent after the bone is clinically healed. Fibrous union occurs long before calcification.

SPECIFIC REFERENCE

PETERS, J. E.: Fracture of the Third Phalanx and Sesamoids in the Race Horse. J.A.V.M.A., *114*, 405, 1949.

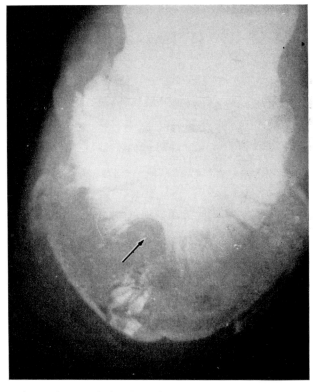

FIG. 6–74.—Area of necrosis in the third phalanx caused by an old puncture wound. Pedal osteitis is present. This should not be confused with the normal notch that occurs at the center of the toe of the third phalanx in some horses.

34. Pedal Osteitis

DEFINITION.—Pedal osteitis is a demineralization of the third phalanx as the result of inflammation. It may also manifest itself as a roughness on the borders of the third phalanx, most commonly on the lateral wings.

ETIOLOGY.—Persistent inflammation of the foot, due to numerous causes, may cause rarification of the third phalanx. Chronic bruising of the sole, persistent corns, laminitis (especially from concussion-road founder), puncture wounds and other inflammations over a long period of time may cause the disease. In some cases of osteitis there is actually an osteomyelitis present. Whenever an infected corn or a puncture wound causes damage to the third phalanx, this is the case. Other causes, such as laminitis or persistent sole bruising, are not infectious causes of pedal osteitis.

In some cases, the osteophytic development may be the result of local periostitis due to detachment of a few sensitive laminae. However, osteophytic outgrowths of this type are not uncommon in horses that show no lameness, and great care must be used in evaluating their significance.

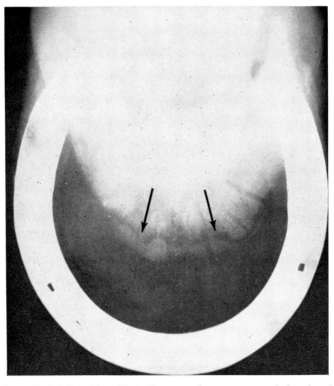

FIG. 6–75.—Pedal Osteitis. Note the ragged appearance of the tip of the third phalanx indicating osteomyelitis and fragmentation. This was caused by a sole abscess at the toe, and osteomyelitis resulted.

SIGNS.—Lameness is obvious in all gaits, and examination with a hoof tester will reveal pain at the bottom of the foot. This pain may be diffuse or localized. Pedal osteitis merely may be a sign of one of the diseases mentioned in etiology. Radiographs indicate demineralization at one or more points in the third phalanx, but a veterinarian must be careful not to confuse the normal notch of the toe of the third phalanx, that occurs in some horses, with rarifying osteitis (Fig. 6–74). Roughened areas along the distal border of the third phalanx may appear anywhere from the toe to the lateral wings. These ridges are not normally smooth because of vascular patterns in the bone and careful evaluation must be made when they are present.

TREATMENT.—Treatment of this disease is dependent upon the cause. The causes can be found elsewhere in this chapter. Shoeing may help by keeping the sole away from the ground and preventing pressure on it. Pads of leather or neolite under the shoe also may be helpful. When pedal osteitis affects the lateral wings of the distal border of the bone, neurectomy of the posterior digital nerves may be helpful, provided soundness occurs after blocking these nerves with a local anesthetic.

PROGNOSIS.—The prognosis is unfavorable because demineralization indicates that the disease is chronic; such a condition is difficult to reverse.

35. Puncture Wounds of the Foot

DEFINITION.—Puncture wounds in the foot are quite common in horses. A variety of objects may produce the wounds. Some puncture wounds are extremely difficult to find, especially if they occur in the frog and the foreign body is missing. Puncture wounds in the middle one-third of the frog are most serious because of the possibility of puncture of the navicular bursa. Puncture wounds of the sole may cause osteomyelitis, fracture, and necrosis of the third phalanx or necrosis of the digital cushion.

SIGNS.—In some cases the foreign body will still be in the foot, making the diagnosis relatively simple. In such a case, the type of foreign object and the damage that has occurred to underlying structures should be determined. The attitude of the gait of the horse often is very helpful in determining the location of the puncture wound, if it is not obvious. If the wound is in the toe area of the sole, the horse tends to land excessively on the heel. If the puncture is in the heel area of the sole, the horse attempts to land on the toe. If the wound is in the medial side of the sole, the horse attempts to put most of his weight on the lateral side of the foot. If the wound is on the lateral side of the sole, the horse attempts to carry most of his weight on the medial side of the foot. Because of variation in this type of lameness, no characteristic signs can be assigned. The foot always should be checked thoroughly with a hoof tester to localize the site of the wound. Cracks in the white line, nail punctures, and shoe nail punctures can be identified as black spots in the sole. These black spots should be probed until their full depth is determined, or until it is determined that they lead into sensitive structures.

Lameness may not be evident until after infection has caused a pododermatitis. If infection is present in the foot and the puncture wound has no drainage, the infection will force drainage at the coronary band near the heel. (Occasionally, drainage will occur slightly forward of the heel, but in most cases it occurs at the heel.) A veterinarian should not make the mistake of believing that drainage at the heel is the entire pathology; the bottom of the foot always should be checked for puncture wound. In all cases supporting leg lameness usually is evident because of the pain in the foot.

It is not uncommon to find that puncture wounds of the foot cause distention of the flexor tendon sheath just above the fetlock joint. Again, a veterinarian should not be confused by this swelling. Careful examination of the tendon sheath usually will reveal that there is no pain on pressure, although heat may be evident. Examination of the foot with the hoof testers will reveal a painful spot; this spot should be investigated to determine the position of the puncture wound.

Some cases of puncture wound in the foot will cause a septicemia and phlegmon of the limb with elevation of temperature and severe systemic manifestations. Other conditions that may occur as the result of puncture wounds include: infectious laminitis, necrosis of the third phalanx (Fig. 6–74), fracture of the third phalanx, infection of the navicular bursa or digital cushion, fracture of the navicular bone, and tetanus.

Puncture wounds of the hind foot may cause a stringhalt attitude to the gait. The horse will move the limb in a hyperflexed manner causing suspicion of lameness involving structures further up the limb. A lameness in any limb warrants full examination of the foot and sole for pathological changes.

DIAGNOSIS.—If a veterinarian is conscientious about examining the bottom of the foot for any lameness, very few puncture wounds will be overlooked. A person should always be sure that a shoe nail or separation of the white line (gravel, page 353) does not cause the lameness. These conditions cause the same pathological changes and signs as direct puncture wounds. A hoof tester is essential for diagnosis of puncture wounds. Radiographs should be taken to determine damage, if any, to bony structures. Puncture wounds of the frog are the most difficult to locate, because once the foreign body has pulled out, the spongy frog closes over the wound making the wound difficult to find.

TREATMENT.—To treat a puncture wound establish drainage of the lesion, keep the area clean until protective healing occurs, and prevent tetanus. The entire sole, frog, and sulci should be cleaned and washed. The area of the puncture wound should be drained so that there is at least a $\frac{1}{4}$ inch opening into the sensitive laminae. The walls of the drainage hole should not be vertical but should widen toward the ground surface of the sole so that it is not apt to become occluded. If the wound is in the frog, the tract should be trimmed away until adequate drainage is established.

Following drainage, the wound should be cleaned with hydrogen peroxide or an enzyme preparation. The opening of the wound should be packed with tincture of iodine or antiphlogistic paste such as Denver Mud, and the foot bandaged thoroughly. The foot should be bandaged to protect it from moisture and filth, and the horse should be kept stalled, if possible, or at least in as dry an area as possible. Tetanus antitoxin always should be administered and antibiotics should be used as indicated.

When the infection causes drainage from a sinus at the heel area, it is advisable to soak the foot daily in a magnesium sulfate solution. The foot should be carefully checked so the original puncture site can be located and drained as described above. Following soaking, tincture of iodine should be applied to the drainage established in the sole and the foot should be bandaged. Once healing begins it is not essential that soaking and bandaging take place daily; every three to four days should be sufficient. It is essential to keep the wound clean until protective healing occurs.

If the puncture wound penetrates the navicular bursa, the bursa may require drainage through the center third of the frog. The foot is thoroughly cleansed and soaked in an antiseptic for twenty-four hours. The volar nerves should be blocked with local anesthetic and the center third of the frog trimmed out. When the plantar aponeurosis of the deep flexor tendon is exposed, a window should be cut in it to provide drainage to the bursa. The foot should be kept bandaged with antiseptics until healing has occurred. The navicular bursa also can be treated by injecting antibiotics and corticoids as described in treatment of navicular disease (pages 262 and 263).

PROGNOSIS.—The prognosis is favorable in early cases when the puncture wound has not damaged underlying structures. If the underlying bone or navicular bursa are damaged, the prognosis is guarded to unfavorable.

36. Corns and Bruised Sole

DEFINITION.—A corn is an involvement of the sensitive and insensitive tissues of the sole at the angle formed by the wall and the bar (Fig. 1–34, page 41). Corns most frequently occur on the inner angle of the front feet and rarely are found in the hind feet. This may be due to the fact that the front feet bear more weight than the hind feet. Flat feet (see Chapter 1) predispose the sole to bruising.

ETIOLOGY.—Corns usually are due to improper shoeing. When shoes are left on the feet too long, the heels of the shoe are forced inside of the wall and cause pressure on the sole at the angle of the wall and the bar. Heel calks will increase this effect. This pressure bruises the sole and causes corns. Improper trimming of the feet, making the heels too low, increases pressure at the angle of the wall and bar and also may cause corns. If a horse is shod too closely at the quarter, corns may result. Lack of frog pressure, causing bruising of the buttresses, and over-reaching, also may cause corns. A long, weak fetlock, and a narrow foot may cause corns to appear at the bars, while in a wide foot, corns are more likely to occur in the sole.

Corns are rare among horses that are used barefooted but sole bruising does occur as a result of trauma to the sole from rocks and other objects. Horses with thin soles are more subject to the disease, as are horses that have been affected previously with laminitis.

SIGNS.—Three types of corn lesions may be evident:

Dry Corn.—In this case hemorrhage on the inner surface of the horn resulting from bruising of sensitive tissue usually causes red stains in the corn area.

Moist Corn.—This is caused by severe injury which results in serum beneath the injured horn.

Suppurating Corn.—The corn becomes infected resulting in necrosis of the sensitive lamina, of the plantar aponeurosis, or of the digital cushion.

Pathological changes due to bruised sole are similar to those caused by corns but occur in the toe or quarter area of the sole rather than at the angle of the wall and bar. Bruised sole also may be of dry, moist, or suppurating types.

The horse will show varying degrees of lameness depending upon the severity of the bruise or corn, while the attitude of the lameness will vary according to the location of the bruise or corn. Hoof testers will reveal the location of the pathology. A cleaning of the flaky sole from the bottom of the foot with a hoof knife will reveal red stains in the sole indicatingra bruised area. In some cases this area may show a bluish discolo ation, especially if a sole abscess is developing.

The horse will tend to favor the heel, especially on the affected side. If the corn is present at the inside heel, the horse will tend to place more weight on the outside of the foot because of the pain. In some cases, the horse will tend to bear most of the weight on the toe and will rest the foot with the knee forward to decrease heel pressure. If the toe area of the sole is bruised, the horse will tend to land on the heel to protect the toe.

TREATMENT.—In cases where shoeing is the cause, removal of the offending shoe may be all that is necessary. To prevent shoes from causing corns, the heels of the shoe always should extend well back on the buttresses and should fit full on the wall at the quarters and heels. Heel calks increase the chance of corns if a horse is shod too short at the heels or if the shoe is left on too long. Removal of some of the tissue over the corn helps relieve pressure, but sensitive tissue should not be exposed. The horse should be rested and should not be reshod until symptoms disappear.

In the case of a suppurating corn, the sole over the area should be removed until drainage into the sensitive tissues is established. The foot should be soaked daily in an antiseptic or in a solution of magnesium sulfate. The foot should be bandaged and protected from contamination and tetanus antitoxin should be administered. Antiphlogistic packs can be used under the bandage for their ability to draw out infected fluids from the area.

If the horse must be used for some reason, the wall and bar in the area of the corn should be removed from pressure on the shoe. Either a half or full bar shoe should be applied, as for quarter crack (Figs. 6–112, page 349; 7–7, page 372). These shoes allow the frog to absorb the concussion that normally would be distributed to the corn area. When the shoe is applied, the half or full bar should exert about $\frac{1}{8}$ inch of pressure against the frog to aid in preventing further contraction of the foot.

In cases of sole bruising the horse should be rested from heavy work, especially if his soles are abnormally thin. When possible, the environment of the horse should be changed so that he is not worked on rough ground.

If the bruised area becomes a sole abscess, it should be drained by cutting away a portion of the diseased sole and exposing the sensitive laminae. The foot then should be soaked daily in magnesium sulfate solution, treated with tincture of iodine, and bandaged with an antiphlogistic paste until a protective healing can occur. Tetanus antitoxin should be administered.

PROGNOSIS.—The prognosis is always guarded since some such cases tend to become chronic, which eventually may cause osteitis of the third phalanx (Pedal osteitis).

LAMENESSES OF THE HINDLIMB

1. Azoturia (Monday Morning Disease)

DEFINITION.—Azoturia is a severe destruction of muscle that occurs in horses kept on full feed when they are not worked. It is characteristically associated with a full diet of grain and a period of rest of one or two days or more while kept on full rations. When the horse is put back to work, signs appear even though the amount of work may be very light, consisting only of the act of a stallion breeding a mare in some cases. It also can occur as a sequel to casting for surgical procedures. This fact supports the contention that a horse should be starved twenty-four hours prior to a surgical procedure that requires casting and anesthesia. The muscles most characteristically affected are the iliopsoas, quadriceps and triceps muscles. The gluteals and biceps femoris may be involved in severe cases.

ETIOLOGY.—During the rest period a large amount of glycogen accumulates in the musculature. Upon exertion, this glycogen is broken down and large amounts of lactic acid accumulate.[5] Lactic acid causes muscular destruction and release of myoglobin with subsequent destruction of muscle cells. As the acid is formed, it cannot be eliminated fast enough, and the accumulation of acid destroys the muscle. As a sequel to the muscular damage, renal lesions caused by the passage of the myoglobin through the kidney and characterized by lower nephron degeneration, may cause death. Other unknown factors may be present other than the acid.

Staron[6,7] claims that studies have shown the causative agent of azoturia to be malonic acid which blocks the enzyme system (succinoxydase). This organic acid behaves mainly as a structural antagonist of the succinic acid system. He claims he has confirmed this hypothesis by demonstrating a direct relationship between the severity of the disease and the high blood level of malonic acid. Experimental injection of this compound into animals (horse, dog) caused symptoms which were typical of myoglobinuria.

SIGNS.—Signs of azoturia usually occur within a few minutes after the horse is put to work. This is as compared to the tying up syndrome which occurs after severe muscular exertion has already been done. Usually within fifteen minutes or less after starting to walk or run, signs of pain, stiffness, incoordination and muscular tremor occur. If exercise is continued, these signs increase until the horse may be unable to stand. It is accompanied by profuse sweating and the eyes show evidence of acute pain. Palpation of the affected muscles causes pain and they are firm to the touch. If the horse goes down and is unable to rise, he may struggle and further aggravate the condition. Urine passage will be dark colored to the point of being almost black in severe cases. The dark color is due to myoglobin in the urine.

DIAGNOSIS.—Diagnosis can usually be established on the basis of the rapidity of the onset and clinical signs following work. Also, the history that the horse has been rested and kept on full feed is helpful. Azoturia must be differentiated from thromboembolism, which decreases circulation to the hindlimbs and causes a very similar syndrome as far as incoordination, pain, sweating, etc. are concerned. In thromboembolism usually some signs of poor circulation can be found, either by palpating the femoral arteries or by rectal examination of the iliac arteries (see page 287). In thromboembolism there is no coffee-colored urine, and rest will relieve symptoms. In azoturia, rest will also usually produce a lessening of signs, but not nearly so rapidly. If a S-GOT level is done on a case of azoturia, it will be found to be extremely high—over 1,000 units. Blood urea nitrogen (BUN) levels may be high if the kidney has been damaged.

TREATMENT.—The horse must be stopped immediately from any work that he is doing. It usually pays to not even walk him back to a stall. The horse should be kept from moving and protected until treatment can be instituted. Treatment consists of reducing acidity by using intravenous and oral sodium bicarbonate. Two ounces of sodium bicarbonate can be administered in 2,000 cc. of sterile saline solution intravenously, plus up to $\frac{1}{2}$ to 1 pound orally. Thiamine injections intravenously appear to hasten recovery. Calcium gluconate can be administered intravenously (250 to 500 cc. of 20 per cent solution) and may be of some help. Intravenous corticoids such as prednisolone sodium succinate* are indicated and very helpful. Tranquilization of the horse will decrease muscular activity and apprehension. Staron[6,7] claims that specific treatment consists of giving .1 to 1 gr. of 4 per cent pentamide† intravenously, but others have not been able to duplicate his results.[3]

Each occurrence of azoturia produces muscular destruction and scarring in the muscles. If at all possible, subsequent attacks must be prevented by being very cautious about overfeeding during rest periods and using regular exercise instead of layoff periods. One attack seems to predispose the horse to further attack.

PREVENTION.—Injections of selenium and vitamin E are given for treatment and prevention of this condition. One cc. of E-Se‡ per 100 pounds body weight is administered intramuscularly, and can be repeated. This product seems helpful in preventing recurrences.

SPECIFIC REFERENCES

1. BAKER, R. H.: Oxygen Therapy. Proceedings A.A.E.P., p. 144, 1962.
2. DODD, D. C.: Equine Med. & Surg., p. 473, Santa Barbara, Calif. Am. Vet. Pub. Inc. 1963.
3. FERRIOT, M.: Treatment of Myoglobinuria. Bull. Soc. Vet. Pratique, 45(6), 214, 1961.
4. Panel Report: Azoturia in the Horse. Mod. Vet. Prac. 41(5), 45, 1960.
5. SMITH, H. A. and JONES, T. C.: Veterinary Pathology, 3rd Ed., Philadelphia, Lea & Febiger, 1966.
6. STARON, T.: Pathogenesis and Treatment of Paroxysmal Myoglobinuria in Horses. Clinica Veterinaria, 82, 169, 1959.
7. STARON, T.: Treatment of Azoturia in the Horse. Vet. Bull., 29, 700, 1959.

2. Tying-Up Syndrome (Cording Up)

DEFINITION.—The tying up syndrome is a myopathy that occurs after active muscular exertion such as in racing. Horses affected are usually on a high grain ration and commonly have been rested one or two days from training. It is a painful condition of the iliopsoas group of muscles that occurs within minutes after the exertion of a race is finished. The true physiological development of the condition is hypothetical at this time.

The condition can be seen following nervous exertion such as during transportation or following a temperamental outburst when breaking the horse to saddle. Nervousness apparently can contribute to development of the disease and this may be why it is

* Solu-delta-cortef, Upjohn Co., Kalamazoo, Mich.

† Diamino-4-4'-diphenoxypentane, Specia Labs., Paris, France.

‡ H. C. Burns, Oakland, Calif.

seemingly more common in mares than in males. Although there is considerable disagreement among authorities, it would appear that this disease is a mild form of azoturia, but relationship to azoturia has not been proven. Horses once affected with the condition seem to be subject to recurrence of the disease. Tying up is not to be confused with complete muscular fatigue that occurs when a horse is overworked at one particular time.

ETIOLOGY.—Etiology of the condition is controversial. However, it would appear that like in Azoturia, lactic acid accumulates in the affected muscles. It does not accumulate in amounts that cause muscular destruction as in Azoturia. In tying-up, the horse is in better condition and builds up lactic acid levels more slowly. There probably is little, if any, actual muscular necrosis in the tying-up syndrome. Briefly, there are two sources of energy: one is anaerobic and the other is aerobic. Our primary interest is in anaerobic energy because it is used in the severe exertion of racing. Through glycolysis, lactic acid is formed after exertion by anaerobic oxidation. If sufficient oxygen is present, lactic acid is quickly converted to pyruvic acid and is broken down to carbon dioxide and water through the Krebs cycle. However, in the tying-up syndrome there apparently is a decreased blood flow in the affected muscles caused by spasm of the arterioles supplying the involved muscles. This results in decreased blood flow at a time when a good supply is needed, and the lactic acid is not broken down as rapidly as it should be. Acid accumulation apparently results in a cramping of the muscles, as they are hard and firm to palpation. Many horses are not properly trained for racing, and this factor is probably also a contributing cause to some cases of the tying-up syndrome. The horse is an athlete, and an athlete cannot train one hour a day and spend twenty-three hours in a 12 × 12 room and expect to do well in athletic competition. Individual differences also probably contribute to resistance to the tying-up syndrome.

In recent years vitamin E and selenium has been used in the treatment and prevention of the tying-up syndrome with some success. This brings to mind the possibility of deficiency of selenium and/or vitamin E as a cause of the tying up syndrome. Deficiency of these has been incriminated in white muscle disease of other species. The selenium-tocopherol mixture is said to be essential in some enzyme systems.[4]

SIGNS.—After severe exertion, such as racing, the horse shows stiffness and the hindlimbs do not flex normally. The back is rigid and the horse walks as though he has back pain. Pain can be produced by hand pressure over the loin region. It can also be produced by palpating the ilio-psoas group of muscles by rectal examination. The muscles feel hard to the touch. In some cases, the muscular involvement may extend to the gluteals and the quadriceps. These also feel hard to the touch, and pain is shown by the horse when these muscles are palpated. More commonly only the muscles in the region of the loin and the ilio-psoas group are involved. The S-GOT (serum glutamic-oxalacetic transaminase) level is usually elevated above 1000 units[6] and there is a mild degree of myoglobinuria. If the horse is walked for a variable period of time, the signs usually disappear.

DIAGNOSIS.—Diagnosis is made on the basis of the clinical signs and history. It occurs within a few minutes after exertion and hand pressure over the longissimus dorsi in the region of the lumbo-sacral junction will produce pain. Rectal examination will also produce pain when the ilio-psoas group of muscles are palpated. There is a rigidity of the back and stiffness of the gait in both hind-limbs. In more severe cases, pain is shown over the gluteals and quadriceps.

TREATMENT.—No specific drug treatment is necessary in the usual case of tying up. Walking the horse for thirty to forty minutes will usually relieve the signs. Treatments that are used to hasten recovery are intravenous corticoids, intravenous calcium gluconate 20 per cent (250 to 500 cc.), intramuscular Calphosan* (20 cc.) and alkalinization of the bloodstream with sodium bicarbonate solution (one ounce in one liter of sterile water). Thiamine and tranquilizers are also used as well as Robaxin† (20 cc.) intravenously for muscular relaxation. For prevention, selenium and vitamin E injections‡ are used at the rate of 1 cc. per 100 pounds body weight. This can be repeated at weekly intervals for as many as four injections. Some horses respond to one injection and others never respond. Oral calcium lactate, magnesium hydroxide and vitamins A and D as a preventative have been recommended for prevention of tying-up syndrome.[7] This type of preventative therapy has been quite inconsistent. Grain ration should be cut in half prior to a race.

PROGNOSIS.—The prognosis for recovery from the syndrome is good. However, it may recur upon subsequent racing or exertion. Apparently there is very little muscular damage with each attack since atrophy and fibrosis of the muscles involved seldom occur. The prognosis is good if the horse stops showing signs of the condition after injection of selenium and vitamin E.

SPECIFIC REFERENCES

1. BLOOD-HORSE: Prevention of Tying Up, *85*(17), 780, 1963.
2. BONE, J. F.: *Equine Medicine and Surgery*, p. 475. Santa Barbara, Calif., Vet. Pub. Inc., 1963.
3. BRENNAN, B. F. *et al.*: Proceedings 5th Annual A.A.E.P. Convention, p. 157, December 1959.
4. BURNS, H. C.: Data Book on Selenium—Tocopherol Mixtures. Oakland, Calif.
5. CARDINET, C. H., III; FOWLER, M. E.; and TYLER, W. S.: Effects of Training, Exercise and Tying Up on Serum Transaminase. Am. J. Vet. Res., *24*(102), 980, 1963.

* Carlton Corp., New York, N.Y.

† Robaxin, A. H. Robbins Co., Richmond, Virg.

‡ E-Se, H. C. Burns Co., Oakland, Calif.

6. Cornelius, C. E., Burnham, L. G., Hill, H. E.: Serum Transaminase Activities of Thoroughbred Horses in Training. J.A.V.M.A., *142*, 639, 1963.

7. Dodd, D. C. *et al.*: New Zealand Vet. J., *8*, 45, 1960.

8. Fries, J. H.: Treatment of the "Tying-Up" Syndrome. Proceedings 7th Annual A.A.E.P., 1961.

9. Hartley, W. J. and Dodd, D. C.: New Zealand Vet. J., *5*, 61, 1957.

10. Hill, H. E.: Selenium-Vitamin E Treatment of Tying Up Horses. Mod. Vet. Prac., *43*, 66, 1962.

11. Miller, W. C.: Atypical Myoglobinuria. Irish Vet. J., *15*, 154, 1961.

12. Steele, J. R.: Tying Up in Mares. Proceedings 9th Annual A.A.E.P., p. 148, 1963.

3. Myositis of the Psoas and Longissimus Dorsi Muscles

DEFINITION. — Following severe muscular exertion such as racing or other work utilizing fast starts, the longissimus dorsi and psoas major and minor muscles may develop myositis. The area of pain in the loin region often causes the owner to think the horse has "kidney trouble."

ETIOLOGY. — Trauma from muscular strain is the etiology. The psoas group of muscles are very important in the driving action of the hind limbs, and are subject to injury when the horse is improperly trained. They are also involved in azoturia and the tying-up syndrome and myositis may be one of the after-effects of one of these diseases.

SIGNS. — The horse carries himself with a stiffened attitude of the back. He will not exert normal propulsion of the hind limbs, and exhibits pain on pressure over the loin, which may cause him to groan and drop the back under hand pressure. Hand pressure on the psoas group of muscles by way of rectal examination will also produce pain. The action of the hindlimb is not normal in that the gait appears to be stiffened in both hindlimbs. The abdomen may be held rigid as though intra-abdominal pain were present. S-GOT levels would probably be elevated in the active stage of the lameness.

DIAGNOSIS. — Diagnosis is made by the response of the horse to digital pressure over the loin and pressure to the psoas group of muscles on rectal examination. It must be differentiated from injury to the sacroiliac and lumbosacral junctions. Disc injuries are rare in the horse, but if suspected must be differentiated. The latter three conditions seldom respond permanently to treatment. The signs are present for several days, or even weeks, differentiating it from the "Tying-Up" syndrome (page 281).

TREATMENT. — Proper rest and training procedures are mandatory. The period of rest will vary with the severity of the injury. In most cases a minimum of thirty days is required. In addition, injections of vitamin E and selenium* at the rate of 1 cc. per 100 pounds are useful. These injections may be repeated at weekly intervals for 3 to 4 injections if necessary. Some cases will not respond immediately and others may require six weeks for evidence of recovery.

---

* E-Se, H. C. Burns Co., Oakland, Calif.

Thiamine and corticoid injections are also useful. The horse should not be put back in training until all signs of pain have disappeared for three weeks after therapy is discontinued.

PROGNOSIS.—The prognosis is guarded because of the possibility of recurrence of injury. However, most horses return to full use.

4. Fractures of the Pelvis

DEFINITION.—Fractures of the pelvis in horses are relatively common. They are most commonly found in the shaft of the ilium, but fractures of the tuber coxae, symphysis pubis and obturator foramen also occur.

ETIOLOGY.—Trauma is the etiology in all cases. Horses that slip and fall on their sides may fracture the pelvis. Horses also can fracture the ilium by fighting a sideline or struggling while the hindlimbs are tied in a casting harness. The coxofemoral articulation of horses rarely is dislocated because of the strong formation of the hip joint; the ilium usually fractures instead.

SIGNS.—Signs of fracture of the pelvis are variable because of the different sites of fractures (Fig. 6–76). If the tuber coxae is fractured, very little lameness will be present, but when the horse is observed from behind, the hip on the fractured side will be flatter than the hip of the sound side (knocked down hip). In some cases these fractured pieces of bone become sequestra and must be removed surgically. In severe cases of fracture of the tuber coxae the skin may be broken and the fractured ilium may protrude through the skin where the tuber coxae was present.

If the shaft of the ilium is broken, it may break above, below, or through the acetabulum. If there is overriding of the fragments, the limb of the affected side will appear shorter than the opposite limb. The horse will be very lame, often refusing to place the foot of the affected limb on the ground. The lameness will closely resemble hip joint lameness when the horse walks, especially if the fracture has occurred through the acetabulum. The anterior phase of the stride will be short and the horse will evidence pain as his weight passes on to the affected limb.

If the fracture occurs through the symphysis pubis or through the obturator foramen, the horse often will appear to be lame in both hindlimbs walking with a hesitating gait that is short in the anterior phase of the stride.

DIAGNOSIS.—Diagnosis is dependent on physical signs and examination by rectal palpation. The most accurate method of diagnosis is to move the horse while you hold one hand in the rectum. Crepitation will be detected as the horse moves, and often the site of fracture can be pinpointed. In some fractures of the ilium, large hematomas that are easily palpable will be present. In other cases, one of the iliac arteries may be severed by the fractured ilium so the horse will die a short time after injury because of internal hemorrhage. Fractures of the symphysis pubis and obturator foramen may have

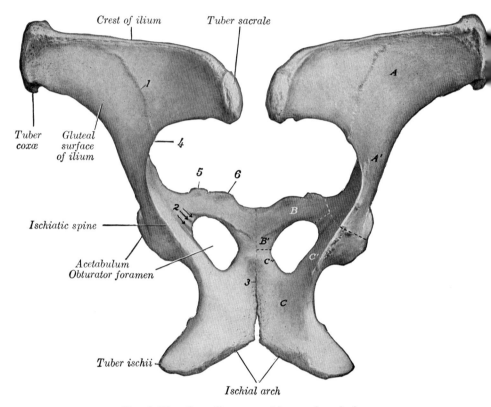

Fig. 6–76.—Ossa Coxarum of horse; dorsal view.

A, Wing; *A'*, shaft of ilium; *B*, acetabular, *B'*, symphyseal branch of pubis; *C*, body, *C'*, acetabular branch (or shaft), *C"*, symphyseal branch, of ischium; *1*, gluteal line; *2*, grooves for obturator nerve and vessels; *3*, symphysis pelvis; *4*, greater sciatic notch; *5*, iliopectineal eminence; *6*, pubic tubercle. Dotted lines indicate primitive separation of three bones, which are potential fracture sites. (Sisson and Grossman, *Anatomy of Animals*, courtesy of W. B. Saunders Company.)

no hematomas so they should be detected by movement of bone fragments on rectal palpation. Grasping the tuber coxae and attempting to move it while keeping one hand in the rectum is helpful in distorting the pelvis and producing crepitation if fracture is present. Crepitation will not be obvious in all cases, so careful and continued examination is necessary for an accurate diagnosis. Separation of the sacro-iliac junction must be included in the differential diagnosis.

TREATMENT.—At present, no surgical methods have been devised for correcting fracture of the pelvis of horses. The best treatment now appears to be to place the horse in a box stall and limit his movement. It is beneficial to sling the horse, whenever possible, for six to eight weeks. Healing of the pelvis though sometimes does not take place until a year after the original injury. So, if the horse is valued highly by the owner, destruction should not be carried out for this length of time, providing the horse is not suffering great pain. Close confinement will be necessary for long periods and maximum space requirement will be a small paddock. Preferably, the horse should be box stalled as long as three months or more. Surgical removal of a bone fragment from a fracture of the tuber coxae will be necessary if the fragments become sequestra.

PROGNOSIS.—The prognosis is guarded in all cases. Death may occur from internal hemorrhage as the result of a severed iliac artery.

SPECIFIC REFERENCE

COCHRAN, DAVID: Lameness of the Hip Joint. Am. Vet. Rev., *43*, 491, 1913.

5. Thrombosis of the Posterior Aorta or Iliac Arteries

DEFINITION.—Thrombus formation in the posterior aorta, iliac arteries, or in the femoral artery, as the result of damage by *Strongylus vulgaris*, occasionally causes lameness in horses. Such thrombi cause lameness of the hindlimb as a result of circulatory interference (Fig. 6-77). Thrombus formation also has been recorded in the brachial artery of the forelimb, causing lameness of that limb.

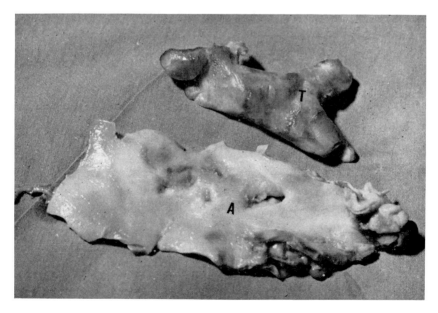

FIG. 6–77.—Portion of aorta (*A*) and its enclosed thrombus (*T*). The bifurcation of the thrombus on the right shows how it had occluded not only the aorta but the iliac division. The horse afflicted with this thrombus was able to move only a few steps before incoordination and pain began. The limbs were cold and the condition was diagnosed by rectal examination, which revealed very weak pulsation in the iliac arteries.

ETIOLOGY. — The thrombi nearly always are caused by larval forms of *Strongylus vulgaris*, causing damage to the intima of the arteries and subsequent thrombus formation.

SIGNS. — Signs vary with the size of the thrombus and the amount of occlusion of the blood vessel. Signs also vary in time of their appearance after exercise. If the thrombus is small, and the occlusion of the vessel is not great, the horse may be exercised vigorously before lameness occurs; however, in most cases the lameness occurs shortly after exercise begins, and so may be confused with azoturia. While at rest the blood supply to the muscles may be adequate to prevent lameness, but some horses will be lame even when walking.

When lameness appears, profuse sweating, pain and anxiety occur if the horse is forced to continue the exercise. The affected limb will be cooler than the opposite member, and pulsation of the femoral artery will be less than that in the opposite limb, unless both limbs are involved. An outstanding characteristic of this lameness is its intermittent character; it appears with exercise and disappears with rest. If the thrombosis is bilateral in the aorta, the horse may have difficulty in supporting his hind quarters.

The veins on the affected limb will be more or less collapsed while the veins on the normal limb will stand out. Another sign that may be present in a unilateral affliction is that the affected limb will not sweat, while the opposite normal limb does.

DIAGNOSIS. — Diagnosis is established by rectal examination; examining the aorta and the iliac arteries. If there is a noticeable decrease of pulsation in the iliacs of the affected side or if there is fremitus in these arteries, thrombosis should be suspected. In some cases the thrombosis actually may be palpated. The femoral artery pulsation on the inside of the thigh may be compared in both limbs; this is helpful in diagnosis. Coldness of the affected limb or limbs is present, while in azoturia, the quadriceps muscles become hard and coffee colored urine is formed. Improvement occurs without treatment in thrombosis.

TREATMENT. — As a general rule, no treatment is of value. With time, the vessels may be able to establish collateral circulation that will overcome the effects of the thrombus. However, some horses become progressively worse, so destruction is necessary.

PROGNOSIS. — The prognosis, always guarded, is unfavorable if it is a bilateral involvement or if the horse seems to be getting progressively worse.

6. Dislocation of the Hip Joint

DEFINITION. — Dislocation of the hip joint of horses is not common. In horses, the ilium tends to fracture before dislocation of the hip occurs; in cattle the opposite is true. However, the disease should be considered if hip lameness is present.

ETIOLOGY. — Trauma is the etiology. Tethered horses that catch their foot in a rope may dislocate the hip in the struggle to free themselves. The hip also may be dislocated if the horse fights a sideline or as a result of some other such trauma. The acetabulum is deep and the head of the femur is large so a great trauma would be necessary to dislocate this joint.

SIGNS.—The horse which has both an accessory and a round ligament of the hip joint must suffer a tear of the round ligament for the hip to dislocate (Fig. 6–78). The femur usually is displaced upward and forward when the hip luxates. Signs that usually accompany dislocation are limited anterior stride, because of a pronounced shortening of the limb, and more prominence of the greater trochanter of the femur. Soft tissue swelling may make this prominence difficult to determine in early stages. Crepitation of the joint, as a result of the femur rubbing on the shaft of the ilium, may cause one to think the pelvis is fractured. A rectal examination should be made to eliminate such a possibility. By placing the hand on the posterior aspect of the greater trochanter and pushing forward one often can move the femur a greater distance than is normal when dislocation has occurred. The limb appears to dangle somewhat because of shortening. The toe and stifle turn outward and the hock inward.

TREATMENT.—Replacing the head of the femur in horses is almost impossible without general anesthesia and a surgical approach. The horse should be anesthetized and the area over the greater trochanter prepared for surgical procedure. An incision 8 inches long should be made anterior to the greater trochanter and the muscles divided by blunt disection. Traction should be placed on the foot, using a block and tackle or a calf puller, and the limb pulled downward until the head of the femur rests in the acetabulum. This can be determined by exploring with the fingers while you are palpating the head of the femur and the acetabulum through the incision. This operation should be done soon after the dislocation occurs, otherwise sufficient contraction of the muscles will be present making it very difficult to reduce the dislocation. In addition, the acetabulum will tend to fill with connective tissue making it difficult to identify. In some cases muscles may be severed to facilitate relocation of the head of the femur.

In cattle there is little possibility of the head of the femur remaining in the acetabulum, once in place. In horses though there is a better chance of it remaining; if it remains in place approximately three months, the muscles will keep it in place. An operation is possible using a toggle pin to hold the hip in place, as is done in cattle.[1]

PROGNOSIS.—The prognosis is guarded to unfavorable. Horses may return to complete soundness after the head of the femur is replaced, but this is the exception and not the rule. Most horses though can be made sound enough for breeding purposes. If the animal is valuable, surgical correction is advisable and should be done for otherwise destruction will be necessary.

19

SPECIFIC REFERENCES

1. ADAMS, O. R.: Preliminary Report on Repair of Coxofemoral Luxation and Coxo-femoral Subluxation in Cattle. J.A.V.M.A., *130*, 515, 1957.
2. JOGI, P. and NARBERG, I.: Malformation in the Hip Joint of a Standardbred Horse. Vet. Rec., *74*, 421, 1962.
3. ROTHENBACHER, H. and HOKANSON, J. F.: Coxofemoral Joint Luxation in a Quarter-horse J.A.V.M.A., *147*, 148, 1965.

7. Rupture of the Round Ligament of the Coxofemoral Joint

DEFINITION.—The hip joint of the horse has several ligaments to help hold it together. The largest and strongest is the round ligament between the head of the femur and the acetabulum. Occasionally stresses occur which cause rupture of the round ligament, but do not produce coxofemoral luxation. In this case, the head of the femur has greater motion than is normal, causing osteoarthritic changes in the joint.

ETIOLOGY.—Trauma is the etiology of round ligament rupture. The same stresses that cause luxation of the coxofemoral joint can cause rupture without the actual luxation occurring.

SIGNS.—Signs of round ligament rupture are very similar to luxation. The notable exception is that the limbs are of the same length. The signs that characterize round ligament rupture are: toe-out, stifle-out and hock-in appearance of the affected hindlimb. This same appearance is also present in luxation of the coxofemoral joint, but the limbs are uneven in length (Fig. 6–78). Crepitation over the joint may be present from the excessive motion of the femur allowed by rupture of the ligament, or from osteoarthritic changes that occur. Crepitation from these sources may be palpated either externally or per rectum. Comparison of the length of the limbs will show that they are equal in length when the ligament is ruptured and luxation has not occurred.

DIAGNOSIS.—Diagnosis is based on the signs of stifle-out, toe-out and hock-in appearance with equal length of both limbs. If the horse is anesthetized and laid on his back, a radiograph of the joint can be taken. If the condition is of long standing, it will show severe degenerative osteoarthritic changes radiographically. Otherwise, the abnormal position of the femoral head in the acetabulum can be identified.

TREATMENT.—No effective treatment can be used except to use a toggle pin apparatus in the joint. However, in horses this is not practical because the joint is never sound enough to permit galloping. This procedure is done in cattle successfully but in cattle the gait seldom exceeds a walk.

PROGNOSIS.—Prognosis is unfavorable since the increased range of motion of the femoral head causes severe osteoarthritis before regeneration can occur.

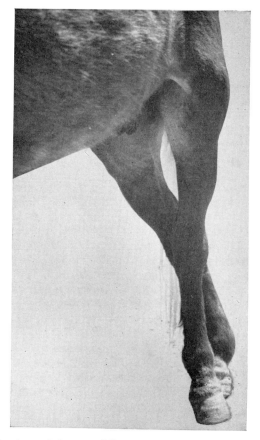

FIG. 6–78.—Rupture of the round ligament of the coxofemoral joint. The stifle-out, toe-out, hock-in attitude of the limb typifies rupture of the round ligament. This same limb attitude is also present when the joint has luxated. When the round ligament ruptures, but the joint does not luxate, the limbs are the same length.

8. Trochanteric Bursitis—Trochanteric Lameness (Whorl-bone Lameness)

DEFINITION.—This lameness, most common in Standardbreds, is an inflammation of the bursa beneath the tendon of the middle gluteus muscle as it passes over the great trochanter of the femur. The tendon of the middle gluteus muscle also may be involved, as well as the cartilage over the trochanter major. The deep portion of the gluteus medius muscle has a strong, flat tendon which passes over the convexity of the trochanter before it inserts into the crest. The trochanter is covered with cartilage and the trochanteric bursa is interposed between it and the tendon.

ETIOLOGY.—Lameness is caused by bruising as a result of the horse falling on the affected side or straining the tendon during racing or training. It also has been found following an attack of distemper. In some cases bone spavin also exists in the affected hind limb and hock lameness may produce the bursitis.

SIGNS.—Pain may be evident when pressure is applied over the great trochanter. Careful examination should be made for pain because some horses naturally tend to shy away when pressure is applied over the hip joint. At rest the limb may remain flexed; as the horse moves, weight is placed on the inside of the foot so that the inside wall of the foot wears to a greater extent than the outside wall. This can be best seen when observing the horse from behind. From this observation it can be seen that the foot is carried inward and the horse sets the foot down on a line between the forelimbs. The horse tends to travel "dog fashion" since the hind quarters move toward the sound side because the stride of the affected limb is shorter than that of the sound side. After the condition has been present for some time, atrophy of the gluteal muscles occurs.

DIAGNOSIS.—The foregoing symptoms should be used in diagnosis. The condition is difficult to differentiate from inflammation of the coxo-femoral joint, or from a fracture through the acetabulum, if the fracture shows no crepitation. The lameness, which is not common, may be confused with spavin lameness. In some cases diagnosis is made when the true cause of lameness is not known.

TREATMENT.—Injection of the bursa with corticoids apparently is the most effective method of treatment (see Chapter 11). Other treatments consist of injections of Lugol's solution of iodine into or around the bursa as a counter-irritant. Hot packs applied to the affected area in the acute stages will relieve some pain. Phenylbutazone given orally also may relieve pain (page 446).

PROGNOSIS.—The prognosis is guarded to unfavorable. If the horse responds to therapy within four to six weeks, he may again become sound. However, if the injury is more severe, the lameness may remain indefinitely, or recur when the horse is put back into training.

9. Femoral Nerve Paralysis (Crural Paralysis)

DEFINITION.—Paralysis of the femoral nerve affects the quadriceps femoris group of muscles. This muscle group is composed of the rectus femoris muscle, the vastus lateralis muscle, the vastus medialis muscle, and the vastus intermedius muscle. This large muscular mass covers the front and sides of the femur and inserts into the patella.

ETIOLOGY.—Femoral nerve paralysis may arise from trauma, from azoturia, or from unknown causes. Injury to the nerve may occur from overstretching of the limb during exertion, kicking, slipping, or while the horse is tied in a recumbent position.

SIGNS.—The horse will not be able to bear weight on the affected limb. In standing position all joints of the affected limb will be flexed as a result of this condition. The horse will have difficulty advancing the limb, but can do so because the hock can be suffi-ciently flexed to pull the limb forward. During movement, the horse will not be able to bear weight on the limb, so compensation must be made in the gait. After the condition has been present some time, atrophy of the quadriceps muscles occurs causing these muscles to lose their normal softness and become more like tendinous structures.

DIAGNOSIS.—The signs listed above are characteristic and are used for diagnosis. The condition should be differentiated from lateral (true) luxation of the patella, rupture of the quadriceps femoris muscles, and avulsion of the tibial crest. Any of these conditions could cause a similar syndrome; however, all of these are rare. Lateral luxation of the patella can be diagnosed by palpation of the displaced patella; rupture of the quadriceps femoris muscle can also be palpated. Radiological examination can determine avulsion of the tibial crest where the patellar ligaments insert.

TREATMENT.—No treatment is known. If the condition is due to injury of the femoral nerve, the animal should be stalled for a long time. Massage of the muscles should be done whenever possible, and, if some function returns, exercise should be used to prevent atrophy from occurring. If the cause is due to azoturia, exercise is a most important part of the treatment.

PROGNOSIS.—Prognosis is guarded to unfavorable. Prognosis should be withheld until sufficient time has elapsed to determine if any function will return. Thirty days is required, at a minimum, for function to return completely.

10. Upward Fixation of the Patella

DEFINITION.—Upward fixation of the patella occurs on the medial trochlea of the femur between the middle and medial patellar liga-ments (Fig. 6–80, page 295). The fixation of the patella on the medial trochlea of the femur prevents flexion of the affected hindlimb. It is sometimes called a luxation, although this is a misnomer. The terms "luxation" or "lateral luxation" of the patella should not be used for this condition; although true luxation may occur, the signs are entirely different from upward fixation.

ETIOLOGY.—It is generally considered that upward fixation of the patella may have hereditary predisposition. This predisposition is brought about by conformation. A horse having a steep angle between femur and tibia, or so-called "straight hind leg" (Fig. 1–26, page 34), with what appears to be a long tibia is more predisposed to the condition than is a horse of normal conformation. Some cases of upward fixation can be the result of trauma when the limb was overextended. Long straight legs predispose the horse to upward fixation of the patella due to traumatic causes. Debility and poor conditioning also can be predisposing factors. Once upward fixation occurs, the ligaments may be stretched so recurrence is common. The condition may be visible in only one hindlimb, but careful examination often will reveal a susceptibility of both hindlimbs. Shetland ponies probably are most often affected in this manner.

SIGNS.—In acute upward fixation of the patella, the hindlimb is locked in extension (Fig. 6–79). The stifle and hock cannot flex, but the fetlock can. The condition may temporarily relieve itself only to lock again in a few steps, or it may remain locked for several

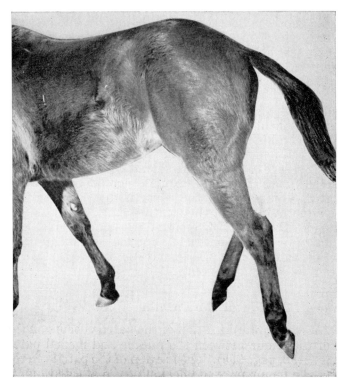

FIG. 6–79.—Upward fixation of the patella. The limb is locked in extension as the horse attempts to pull the limb forward. Note that the left fetlock, pastern, and coffin joints are flexed while the stifle and hock joints are locked in extension.

hours or even days. In some cases there is only a "catching" of the patella as the horse walks and the leg never truly locks in extension. This "catching" of the patella is most noticeable when the horse is turned in a short circle toward the affected hindlimb.

Upon palpation, when the limb is locked in extension, the ligaments of the patella are tense and the patella is locked above the medial portion of the trochlea of the femur (Fig. 6–80). When the horse is forced to move forward with the limb locked, he drags the front of the hoof on the ground. In some cases a snapping sound may be heard when the patella is released from the trochlea.

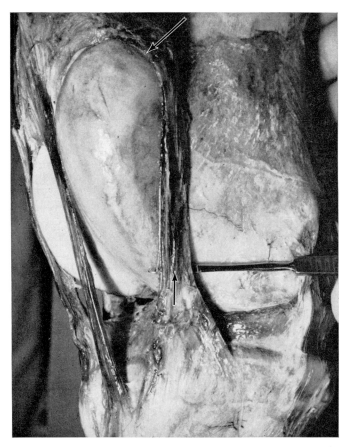

Fig. 6–80. — Upward fixation of the patella. The lower arrow shows the approximate site for cutting the medial patellar ligament. The arrow above shows how the
medial patellar ligament locks over the medial trochlea of the femur. The view
is of the medial aspect of the limb, and to reproduce locking, the patella must be
pushed upward and laterally.

DIAGNOSIS. — The signs are typical and, if the limb is locked, diagnosis is simple. In cases where the owner describes a partial locking,
or complete locking, the limb should be checked by forcing the
patella upward and outward with the hand. If the limb can be
locked in extension for one or more steps, it is predisposed to upward
fixation of the patella. In some cases, this condition is chronic
causing an inflammation of the stifle joint (gonitis) or chondromalacia
of the patella. The arthritis or chondromalacia in the joint may
remain even though upward fixation is corrected. The joint capsule
should be checked for distention by palpating between the lateral
and middle patellar ligaments, and between the middle and medial
patellar ligaments. Excess fluid or thickening of the joint capsule
indicates that gonitis is present.

The condition is commonly bilateral even though it may be worse in one limb. In some vague cases it will be noted that the horse tends to drag the toe when advancing the limb. The flight of the foot has a low arc, and there is a short anterior phase to the stride. In such a case, the patella usually can be locked in upward fixation with the hand; if so, surgical treatment should be instituted.

TREATMENT.—In acute upward fixation of the patella, a sideline may be applied to the affected limb so that as the limb is drawn forward, the patella is pushed medially and downward, which often disengages the fixed patella. Some authorities have advocated startling the horse with a whip so that the sudden jump will release the patella. In other cases, backing the horse while at the same time pushing inward and downward on the patella will release it. Blistering and firing the stifle also have been recommended, but only as temporary measures for preventing extension of the stifle joint, through pain.

Surgical intervention (medial patellar desmotomy) is the best treatment for all cases. The area over the middle and medial patellar ligaments should be shaved and prepared for surgery by using skin antiseptics. The horse should be tranquilized with promazine,* and the tail wrapped to keep it from switching into the surgical sites. Two cubic centimeters of lidocaine hydrochloride† should be injected subcutaneously over the middle patellar ligament with a 25-gauge, $\frac{1}{2}$-inch needle. Then a 2-inch, 20-gauge needle should be inserted through this skin bleb to infiltrate the subcutaneous area over the medial patellar ligament, and to infiltrate the medial patellar ligament itself at its tibial attachment. Five to 8 cc. of lidocaine hydrochloride should be adequate for this injection.

The operator should wear sterile gloves and use sterile instruments. A $\frac{1}{4}$- to $\frac{1}{2}$-inch incision should be made over the middle patellar ligament near the tibial attachment of the ligament. A blunt Udall's teat bistoury, or other suitable bistoury, then should be pushed underneath the *medial* patellar ligament close to its tibial attachment (Fig. 2–14 and 2–15, pages 70 and 71; Fig. 6–80). The blade should be turned outward so that the cutting edge is against the ligament (Fig. 6–80). Then, using a sawing action, and pushing with the forefinger on the ligament, from the skin surface, the medial patellar ligament should be severed. All fibers of the ligament must be cut, but the operator should not go too far posteliorly. A definite cavity will be felt with the forefinger when the rigament is cut. One suture then should be placed in the skin incision and the area covered with collodion and cotton. The horse should be given tetanus antitoxin and given box stall rest for one week. No riding or training should be permitted for approximately six weeks so that full accommodation to the loss of the ligament can occur before stress is imposed on the joint. Both limbs may be done at the same time, if necessary. If surgical correction is carried out

*Promazine, Fort Dodge Laboratories; Sparine, Wyeth Laboratories
†Xylocaine, Astra Laboratories

before gonitis or chondromalacia become evident, the method of treatment affords a high rate of recovery.

When upward fixation occurs in yearlings, it may be advisable to delay surgery to determine if the horse will grow out of the condition. However, if the limb, or limbs, locks in extension, surgery should be performed at once. Delaying surgery is advisable only for those young horses that show intermittent "catching" of the patella because fixation may cease before they are two years of age.

PROGNOSIS.—The prognosis is favorable, provided surgery is done before gonitis becomes evident. Rarely the ligament will regenerate and will require another desmotomy.

SPECIFIC REFERENCES

1. COCHRAN, DAVID: Stifle Lameness. Am. Vet. Rev., *42*, 308, 1912–13.
2. DELAHANTY, D. D.: Medial Patellar Desmotomy in a Pony. Sci. Proc. A.V.M.A., *81*, 1963.

11. Chondromalacia of the Patella

DEFINITION.—Chondromalacia of the patella is a degeneration of the articular cartilage of the patella (Fig. 6–81). It may occur from an inflammatory disease of the stifle joint or from a combination of inflammation and pressure exerted upon it from a partial or complete upward fixation of the patella.

ETIOLOGY.—In most cases the etiology is pressure produced between the patella and medial trochlea of the femur. This pressure is usually induced by a partial fixation of the patella between the

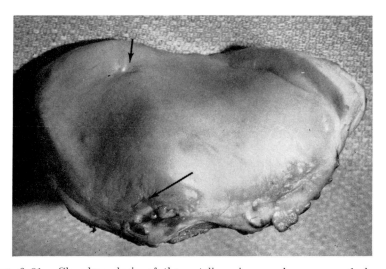

FIG. 6–81.—Chondromalacia of the patella. Arrows show areas of chondromalacia on the articular surface and on the distal border of the patella. This type of injury to the patella takes several months to regenerate, after the medial patellar ligament is cut.

medial and middle patellar ligaments (Fig. 6–80). Erosions in the surface of the cartilage are produced from the pressures and consequent inflammation results in distention of the femoropatellar pouch, with excess synovia, and in the more chronic phases, a thickening of the capsule of the femoropatellar pouch. Traumatic injuries to the stifle joint will also produce chondromalacia. Ligamentous tears such as rupture of the anterior cruciate or medial collateral ligaments of the joint can produce inflammation that will result in accompanying chondromalacia of the patella.

SIGNS.—Gonitis and stifle lameness are the primary signs of chondromalacia of the patella. The lameness is usually mild and may be difficult to diagnose. In the trot the hip will be elevated as it is with a hock or stifle lameness. Using the spavin test may cause the horse to show a mild reaction because of the arthritis that is present. This should not be confused with true bone spavin in which the reaction is usually much more pronounced. Reduced flexion of the stifle and hock, shortening of the anterior phase of the stride, and possible dragging of the toe are the most common signs during movement. Careful palpation of the femoropatellar pouch will reveal distention of this pouch with synovial fluid between the patellar ligaments. In addition there may be thickening of the femoropatellar pouch and careful comparison between the unsound joint and the sound joint must be made. However, chondromalacia can be bilateral. Pressing the patella upward and outward with the limb in an extended position may produce a partial locking of the joint or a soft tissue crepitation between the patella and the medial femoral condyle. This crepitation is indicative of an inflammatory reaction and thickening of the synovium. It is regarded as a sign that chondromalacia of the patella is probably present.

TREATMENT.—Treatment is directed at removing the cause and reducing inflammation. Injection of the femoropatellar pouch with a corticoid will temporarily alleviate the inflammatory reaction (see Chapter 11). However, in most cases it is best to sever the medial patellar ligament as described for upward fixation of the patella. This relieves tension of the patella against the medial trochlea of the femur and aids in removing the cause of the chondromalacia. Following cutting of the medial patellar ligament, at least six months must be allowed for regeneration of the articular cartilage and relief of symptoms. In some cases the disease is advanced to the point that no cure can be accomplished.

DIAGNOSIS.—Diagnosis is based on the signs of lameness, palpation of the femoropatellar pouch for distention and thickening, palpation of the patella over the trochlea and diagnostic anesthesia of the femoropatellar pouch. The femoropatellar pouch can be injected with 10 cc. of Xylocaine plus a steroid (see Chapter 11), and if lameness is relieved, this is good evidence that the site of lameness is in this joint.

PROGNOSIS.—The prognosis is guarded, but if relief of symptoms occurs within six months following medial patellar desmotomy, the horse may remain sound.

12. Gonitis

DEFINITION.—Gonitis, or inflammation of the stifle joint, includes a number of inflammatory conditions. Arthritic changes in the joint are caused by injury to bones forming the joint, the cartilages of the joint, and to the collateral and cruciate ligaments of the joint. Gonitis, a serious disease even in its mild forms, often results in permanent disability of the affected horse.

ETIOLOGY.—Gonitis may result from many causes and all are due to trauma. The following are conditions of the joint that may cause gonitis:

1. *Partial or Complete Upward Fixation of the Patella.*—This is one of the most common causes of gonitis, and in addition, may produce chondromalacia of the patella. Irritation causes thickening of the synovium, and roughening of the patella and medial trochlea of the femur may occur.

2. *Sprain of the Medial or Lateral Collateral Ligaments.*—Sprain may occur to these ligaments in any of the categories listed in Chapter 5. Any form of sprain from mild to sprain fracture will produce gonitis. The medial collateral ligament is the one most commonly ruptured. Rupture causes complete incapacitation because of resulting osteoarthritic changes.

3. *Injury to the Anterior or Posterior Cruciate Ligaments.*—Sprain of these ligaments may occur to any degree described in Chapter 5. Sprain fracture also occurs (Fig. 6–82). If the ligament is sprained but not ruptured or a partial sprain fracture occurs, diagnosis is difficult. Radiographs may reveal separation of the tibial spine (Fig. 6–82). The anterior cruciate ligament is the one most commonly ruptured and may be damaged along with the medial collateral ligament.

4. *Injury to the Menisci.*—Miniscal injuries occur in the horse but are difficult to diagnose. The medial meniscus is the one most commonly damaged. Persistent effusion of the joint and chronic lameness can be the result.

5. *Injuries to the Joint Capsule.*—The joint capsule may be injured and the fibrous portion partially torn from its attachment. This type of injury is rare.

6. *Severe trauma to the joint* may produce an injury such as a fractured trochlea of the femur or fracture of the patella (*see* Fig. 6–83). This is also a rare type of injury.

7. *Chondromalacia of the Patella* (see page 297).—Chondromalacia of the patella is produced from partial or complete upward fixation of the patella. Even when the patella does not lock, there is tension of the patella against the trochlea of the femur and chondromalacia occurs, causing persistent effusion of the joint and chronic lameness.

From the above, it can be seen that gonitis can be a complex thing. Any one, or any combination of the above structures, may be injured. Sometimes small fractures of the joint are confused with inflammation from other causes, and go undiagnosed. Several types

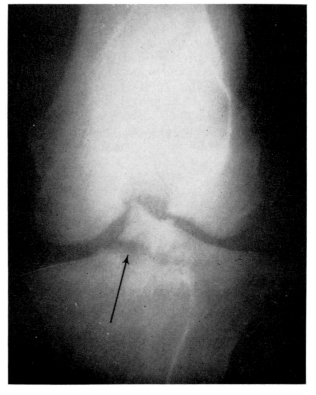

Fig. 6-82.—Fracture of the tibial spine associated with rupture of the anterior cruciate ligament (sprain-fracture) in a horse. Fracture of this spine usually does not accompany rupture of the cruciate ligaments.

of arthritis may affect the stifle joint including serous arthritis, osteoarthritis, and suppurative arthritis. Navel ill of foals is the most common cause of suppurative arthritis (*see* Chapter 5).

SIGNS.—The degree of lameness in gonitis varies according to severity of the injury. Involvements of the menisci and the cruciate or collateral ligaments usually produce severe lameness. Complete or incomplete upward fixation of the patella also can produce gonitis, but cause less acute signs of lameness. If the patella partially or completely locks, irritation of the synovial structures occurs, and eventually chronic distention of the joint capsule and persistent lameness result. Thickening of the joint capsule can occur in conjunction with distention. The capsule should be carefully examined by palpation between the patellar ligaments to determine if either of these signs are present. In chondromalacia of the patella, soft tissue crepitation can be palpated with the hand as the patella is forced upward and outward over the medial trochlea of the femur. This crepitation means that there is thickening of the synovium

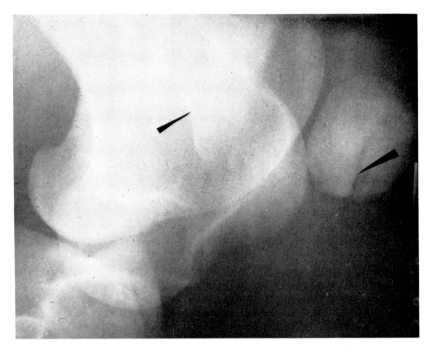

FIG. 6-83.—Fracture of the patella. Severe trauma to the stifle joint accompanied by fractures can cause gonitis. In this case there was a fracture of the patella as shown by pointer and a fracture of one of the femoral trochlea indicated by the second pointer. Trauma to the anterior portion of the stifle causes this type of lesion.

between the patella and the trochlea of the femur and is quite indicative of chondromalacia resulting from partial or complete upward fixation of the patella. If upward fixation of the patella is corrected by medial patellar desmotomy, lameness may persist as a result of chronic gonitis and chondromalacia of the patella. Involvement of the stifle joint with suppurative arthritis, as the result of joint ill in foals, usually affects both stifle joints. Aspiration of the contents of the swollen capsule will reveal suppurative material. Some organisms, such as *E. coli*, may not produce pus but will produce infectious arthritis. A markedly swollen joint and temperature accompany this disease.

Signs of gonitis, from whatever cause, include distention and thickening of the joint capsule between the middle and lateral patellar ligaments and between the middle and medial patellar ligaments. In severe cases the capsule also is distended over the lateral surface of the joint. The horse will experience pain when moving the leg forward, causing him to shorten the anterior phase of his stride. The stifle joint often will be kept flexed as much as possible as the horse strives to keep the foot of the affected limb off the ground; at the very least the heel will be raised with the fetlock joint pushed forward. The horse does this to prevent contact of the affected joint surfaces. The horse will put as little weight as possible on the limb, when moving or standing; therefore, the lameness is classified as supporting leg lameness, although it is swinging leg lameness in the sense that the horse attempts to protect the limb from concussion and thereby alters the stride of the limb.

If one or more of the collateral or cruciate ligaments are destroyed, movement can be produced between the femur and tibia, and crepitation may be present when moving the joint. This may be checked if you lock your hands around the anterior face of the tibia and pull the tibia backward with a quick motion (Fig. 4–4, page 100). If any movement is produced between the femur and tibia in an anterior-posterior direction, you know definitely that a ligament, usually a cruciate ligament, is torn. The anterior cruciate ligament most commonly is involved. The limb should be abducted and adducted to check for rupture of the medial and lateral collateral ligaments. Lameness will be persistent and severe if any of these ligaments are ruptured.

DIAGNOSIS. — Diagnosis of gonitis can be made by careful observation of the gait, palpation of the joint, and by elimination of other types of lameness. If no swelling of the joint capsule of the stifle joint is present, there probably is no gonitis. A person must acquaint himself with the normal tension of fluid in the joint capsule, as palpated between the patellar ligaments, and carefully compare the two stifle joints. Determination of the structures involved can be difficult, but every effort should be made to do so. Ligamentous injury usually can be detected where one or more of the ligaments are torn. Any movement between the femur and tibia in an anterior-posterior direction or upon movement of the limb in abduction or adduction is indicative of ligamentous injury. This should be considered a serious injury. Sprain of a collateral or patellar ligament, that does not cause its rupture, can usually be diagnosed by the pain over the ligament produced by digital pressure.

Gonitis that results from upward fixation of the patella can be diagnosed, if the patella can be locked by hand as described under upward fixation of the patella (see page 293). Radiographs should be taken of the stifle joint to determine if fractures are present and if any osteoarthritic changes are evident. Injuries to the joint capsule, or the medial or lateral menisci, can only be estimated and can not be diagnosed positively.

Horses affected with gonitis may react to the spavin test. The reaction is usually not as severe as when the horse is truly affected with bone spavin. Any mild reaction to the spavin test should be viewed suspiciously and the stifle joint given a complete examination for the signs mentioned above. Stifle and hock lameness can be difficult to differentiate because of the similarity of signs when the horse is in motion. When considering any lameness of the hindlimb, puncture wounds of the foot and fractured third phalanx should always be ruled out. One tends to get careless about examination of these areas since the majority of lamenesses in the hindlimb occur in the hock and stifle.

TREATMENT.—If there is a rupture of one of the collateral or cruciate ligaments of the joint, treatment is unfavorable and chronic lameness will result. If radiological examination indicates that there are osteoarthritic changes or fractures within the joint, treatment also is unfavorable. If you believe that the gonitis is due to sprain and injury to the joint capsule or to ligamentous attachments without rupture, absolute rest should be enforced for a long period. Confinement should consist of a minimum of thirty days in the box stall and then a minimum of two months in a small paddock, or, in some cases, three months in a box stall may be necessary. Injection of the stifle joint with a corticoid is recommended, if no infection is present. These injections should be repeated at least three times at one-week intervals (Chapter 11, page 443). Injections can be made between the middle and lateral patellar ligaments, or between the middle and medial patellar ligaments. Firing, blistering and subcutaneous injection of irritants have been employed. Of these, firing probably is most beneficial with chronic gonitis, but only when it is a serous arthritis. Results of firing are inconsistent and corticoids are of greater value. Corticoid therapy should *not* be combined with a treatment that produces inflammation. In suppurative arthritis of the stifle joint, the joints should be treated with intra-articular antibiotics after antibiotic sensitivity of the organism has been determined. Parenteral antibiotics also should be given. After infection is controlled, corticoid in conjunction with the antibiotics used intra-articularly are recommended (*see* Chapter 11, page 442).

SPECIFIC REFERENCE

COCHRAN, DAVID: Stifle Lameness. Am. Vet. Rev., *42*, 308, 1912–13.

13. Osteochondrosis of the Tibial Tuberosity

DEFINITION.—Reportedly this condition affects horses. It is definitely known to occur in dogs and man; in man the disease is known as Osgood-Schlatter disease. To me it appears that the diagnosis has been abused as has "fracture of the fibula." Many of the so-called pathological changes of the tibial crest, which appear on radiographs, are normal for young horses. The tibial crest has an epiphyseal line of its own which often is irregular in outline.

ETIOLOGY.—Trauma to the tibial crest resulting from tension on the patellar ligaments inserting into the tibial crest, due to training of the young horse, has been blamed for the condition. However, it is also possible that so-called "avulsion" of the tibial crest can occur from partial upward fixation of the patella. It is very possible that some mild cases of upward fixation of the patella are called osteochondrosis, without the careful examination necessary to determine partial upward fixation. Osteochondrosis is found in horses one to three years old; this is the time that the tibial crest shows a normal epiphyseal line making it appear to be separated from the tibia.

SIGNS.—Signs of this condition are vague. They include swelling, tenderness and pain in the tibial crest following strenuous exercise. The horse will trot in "dog fashion" because of the short stride of the affected hind leg. If the lesion is bilateral, the stride will be shorter in both hind legs and the toe may be "dubbed off" as a result of the low arc of the foot in flight. Radiographic examination may show a partial avulsion of the tibial crest, and islets of bone in the cartilage which appear to suggest incomplete separation. These changes are difficult to differentiate from a normal epiphyseal line of the tibial crest (Fig. 6–84).

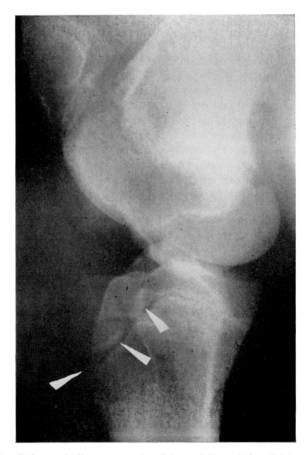

FIG. 6–84.—Pointers indicate normal epiphyseal line of the tibial crest which is often irregular; osteochondritis may be diagnosed, erroneously, if caution is not used. Variations from normal will appear in different horses.

DIAGNOSIS.—Diagnosis is based mainly on radiographic examination. Radiographs should be taken of both hind limbs for comparison purposes. Although osteochondrosis can occur, a careful examination should be made to eliminate other causes of lameness. A practitioner who has not examined numerous radiographs of young horses could easily be confused by the appearance of the epiphyseal line of the tibial crest. Tension on the patellar ligaments that attach to the tibial crest can occur as the result of intermittent upward fixation of the patella and can cause signs similar to those described for osteochondrosis.

TREATMENT.—Subcutaneous injection of Lugol's iodine over the affected area has been used to hasten recovery. A treatment suggested as a result of work with humans is drilling of the tibial crest to produce inflammation. Corticoid therapy is not effective, and such cases are only mildly responsive to analgesics such as phenylbutazone. Stall rest or confinement in a small paddock for three months is essential. Rest is important because exertion may cause complete avulsion of the tibial crest; however, this is unlikely since it is extremely rare to find avulsion of this process, even in cases of severe trauma.

PROGNOSIS.—The prognosis is guarded. The horse should be returned to work or not on the basis of the findings on the radiographs.

SPECIFIC REFERENCE

BAKER, H.: Osteochondrosis of the Tibial Tuberosity of the Horse. J.A.V.M.A., *137*, 354, 1960.

14. Fracture of the Fibula

In recent years it has become popular to diagnose obscure lameness of the hindlimb as fracture of the fibula. This is a common diagnosis in Standardbreds and Thoroughbreds, but this diagnosis has been misused greatly. Extensive radiological studies have revealed that what often appears to be a fracture of the fibula is merely a defect in the union of the proximal and distal segments of the bone (Fig. 6–85). No definite clinical symptoms have been propounded, and anything from sore back to undiagnosed ailments of the hindlimb has been termed fracture of the fibula. This defect in union of the bone can be demonstrated in a high percentage of horses. When radiographs are taken of the opposite fibula, it usually is found that the defect is present here too. Although fracture of the fibula undoubtedly can occur as a result of a direct trauma, it probably does not cause the lameness, and in most cases careful examination will reveal the true cause.

20

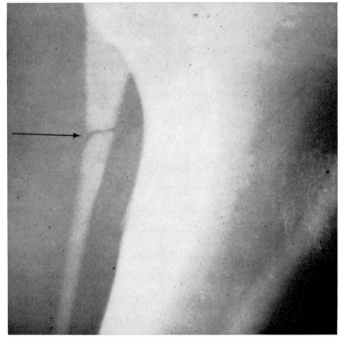

Fig. 6–85. — "Fracture" of the fibula in the horse. The arrow indicates a normal epiphyseal line, a fibrous junction in the bone found in many normal horses.

SPECIFIC REFERENCES

1. Banks, W. C. and Schultz, C. W.:   Additional Studies of Fibular Defects in Horses. J.A.V.M.A., *133*, 422, 1958.
2. Delahanty, D. D.:   Defects—Not Fractures—of the Fibulae in Horses. J.A.V.M.A., *133*, 258, 1958.
3. Editorial: A Phenomenon in Equine Lameness.   J.A.V.M.A., *130*, 51, 1957.
4. Lundvall, R. L.:   Fracture of the Fibula in the Horse.   J.A.V.M.A., *129*, 10, 1956.
5. Lusk, N. D. and Rosborough, J. P.:   Fibular Fracture in a Filly. J.A.V.M.A., *130*, 4, 1957.
6. Zeskov, F.:   A Study of Discontinuity of the Fibula in the Horse. Am. J. Vet. Res., *78*, 852, 1959.
7. Zeskov, Mardt, Vukelic, and Dolinar: Fracture or Congenital Discontinuity of the Fibula in the Horse.   Brit. Vet. J., *144*, 145, 1958.

15. Rupture of the Peroneus Tertius

Definition. — The peroneus tertius is a strong tendon which lies between the long digital extensor and the tibialis anterior muscle of the rear limb.   It originates in common with the long digital extensor from the extensor fossa of the femur, and inserts on the anterior surface of the proximal extremity of the third metatarsal bone and on the fibular and fourth tarsal bones.   It is an important part of the reciprocal apparatus, mechanically flexing the hock when the stifle joint is flexed.   When this muscle is ruptured, the stifle flexes but the hock does not.

ETIOLOGY.—Rupture of the peroneus tertius is usually due to overextension of the hock joint. This may occur if the leg is entrapped and the horse struggles violently to free his limb. Rupture also may occur during the exertion of a fast start, when tremendous power is transferred to the limb causing overextension.

SIGNS.—Signs of rupture of the peroneus tertius are well defined. The stifle joint flexes as the limb advances and the hock joint is carried forward with very little flexion. That portion of the limb below the hock tends to hang limp, giving the appearance of being fractured as it is carried forward. When the foot is put down the horse has no trouble bearing weight and shows little pain. As the horse walks though, it will be noted that there is a dimpling in the tendon of Achilles. If the limb is lifted from the ground, one can easily produce a dimpling in the tendon of Achilles by extending the hock (Fig. 6–86). It will be noted that the hock can be extended without extending the stifle; this cannot be done in the normal limb.

DIAGNOSIS.—Diagnosis is easily made by the symptoms described above.

TREATMENT.—Complete rest is the only known treatment. The horse should be placed in a box stall and kept quiet for at least four to six weeks. Then limited exercise should be given for the next

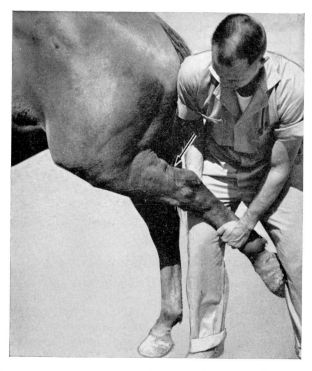

FIG. 6–86.—Rupture of the peroneus tertius. The arrow indicates a dimpling in the tendon of Achilles when the limb is extended. Note that the hock is extended but the stifle is flexed; this cannot be done by a normal limb.

two months. Most cases will heal and show normal limb action, and, if properly conditioned most horses can return to normal work. Surgical intervention is not advisable.

PROGNOSIS.—Prognosis is guarded to favorable. When the horse is properly rested by box stall confinement, healing usually occurs. If healing is not evident at the end of four to six weeks, the prognosis is unfavorable meaning the tendon may not unite. Final appraisal should not be made for at least three months following the injury.

16. Rupture of the Gastrocnemius Muscle

DEFINITION.—Rupture of the gastrocnemius muscle may occur in one or both hindlimbs. It is rare for both the superficial flexor tendon and the gastrocnemius muscle (Achilles tendon) to be ruptured at the same time. The gastrocnemius muscle apparently ruptures before the superficial flexor tendon.

ETIOLOGY.—Trauma is the etiology in all cases. In some cases the horse is found with the condition in one or both limbs, but the cause is not known. Rupture of this muscle can result from strenuous efforts at stopping or from any other exertion where great stress is applied to the hock in an attempt to extend it.

SIGNS.—Signs of gastrocnemius muscle rupture are characteristic. The hock or hocks of the affected limb(s) is dropped so that there is an excessive angle to the hock joint. If the condition is bilateral, the horse appears to be squatting and he cannot straighten his hindlimbs. The limb, or limbs, can be advanced and the horse can walk, but at no time do the hock joints assume a normal angle. If the entire tendon of Achilles is ruptured, the limb cannot support weight.

TREATMENT.—No treatment is known at present. Because of the persistent flexion of the hocks, the muscle ends are unable to make contact making recovery difficult. Placement of the horse in a sling so that tension on the gastrocnemius muscle and superficial flexor tendon is eased may be beneficial if used for prolonged periods. A modified Thomas splint made from $\frac{3}{4}$ inch electrical conduit may be helpful if the horse will tolerate it.

PROGNOSIS.—Prognosis is unfavorable because healing of this muscle seldom occurs.

17. Fibrotic Myopathy and Ossifying Myopathy

DEFINITION.—Fibrotic and ossifying myopathy most commonly occur in the hind legs of horses. It results from an old injury to the semitendinosus, semimembranosus and biceps femoris muscles. The fibrotic lesion in the semitendinosus muscle is most important because adhesions form between this muscle and the semimembranosus and biceps femoris muscles. These adhesions limit the action of the semitendinosus muscle causing an abnormal gait. This lameness most often occurs in Quarter Horses because of the type of work they perform. Ossifying myopathy in the hind limb, which also results from previous injury to these muscles, is assumed to be an ossification of a fibrotic myopathy lesion. The signs of lameness are the same as with fibrotic myopathy because the adhesions extending from the bony lesion to the adjacent muscles cause a similar restriction of the limb. Ossifying myopathy has been observed in the foreleg.[4]

ETIOLOGY.—Trauma is thought to be the cause of fibrotic myopathy and ossifying myopathy. Ossifying myopathy is a complication of the fibrotic lesion that also results from trauma. Involved muscles may be injured during sliding stops in rodeo work, or in other ways such as resisting a sideline or catching a foot in a halter. The lesions usually are unilateral, but a case of bilateral fibrotic myopathy resulting from a trailer accident has been recorded. In some cases the exact cause of the injury is not known since clinical signs are not present during the myositis stage. When the injury heals and adhesions form between the involved muscles, these adhesions cause lameness.

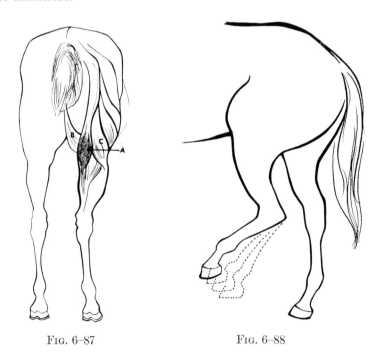

FIG. 6–87   FIG. 6–88

FIG. 6–87.—Muscles involved in fibrotic myopathy.
A. Fibrotic myopathy area in semitendinosus muscle.
B. Semimembranosus muscle.
C. Biceps femoris muscle.

FIG. 6–88.—Typical action of a hindlimb affected by fibrotic, or ossifying, myopathy of the semitendinosus muscle. The foot jerks backward three to five inches just prior to the time it is put on the ground.

When ossification of the fibrotic myopathy lesion occurs, it is presumed to be caused by osteoblasts that have developed from fibroblasts by metaplasia.

SIGNS. — The signs are due to adhesions between the semitendinosus muscle and the semimembranosus muscle medially, and between the semitendinosus and the biceps femoris muscle laterally (Fig. 6–87). These adhesions partially inhibit normal action of the muscles. In the anterior phase of the stride, the foot of the affected hindleg is suddenly pulled posteriorly for 3 to 5 inches, just prior to contacting the ground (Fig. 6–88). Usually the lameness is most noticeable when the horse walks. The anterior phase of the stride is shortened, so consequently the posterior phase is lengthened. This abnormal gait, which is easily identified, may result either from fibrotic or ossifying myopathy. An area of firmness can be palpated over the affected muscles on the posterior surface of the affected limb at the level of the stifle joint and immediately above (Fig. 6–89).

Microscopic lesions of fibrotic myopathy consist of hyalinization of the muscle cell cytoplasm with loss of striations, and moderately pyknotic nuclei. No evidence of inflammation or neoplasia will be present. Bone tissue removed from an ossifying myopathy lesion will have normal structure.

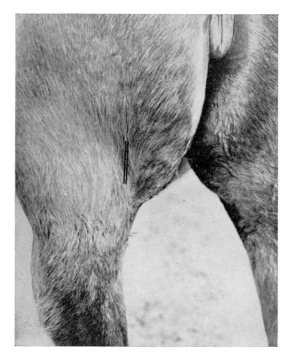

FIG. 6–89.—The double lines indicate the area most commonly involved with fibrotic or ossifying myopathy. They also indicate the site of incision for surgical correction of the condition.

DIAGNOSIS.—Diagnosis is based upon the altered gait and by palpation of a hardened area on the posterior surface of the leg at the level of the stifle joint. In making diagnosis stringhalt also should be considered. In stringhalt the limb is pulled toward the abdomen, while in fibrotic myopathy the foot is pulled toward the ground in a posterior direction just before the foot contacts the ground. In fibrotic myopathy the limb is limited in the anterior phase of the stride by adhesions, and by lack of elasticity in the affected area of the muscle belly, causing the limb to be pulled posteriorly before the full length of stride is reached.

TREATMENT.—The most effective therapy is surgical section or removal of a portion of the semitendinosus tendon at the level of the stifle joint. This may be done as a simple section of the tendon with a bistoury, or by a more extensive operation in which approximately 3 inches of the involved semitendinosus tendon are removed at its junction with the muscle belly before the tendon divides. The latter operation includes separation of adhesions between the semitendinosus muscle and the semimembranosus and biceps femoris muscles.

For simple section of the tendon, the operative area over the semitendinosus tendon at the level of the proximal end of the tibia should be clipped, shaved, and prepared for operation. Local infiltration of the affected tissues with 2 per cent lidocaine hydrochloride* should be used. The horse may be tranquilized if necessary. The operation may be done with the horse in either a recumbent or standing position. A small vertical incision should be made over the semitendinosus tendon on the posterior side of the leg where it is easily palpated (Fig. 6–89). A bistoury then should be inserted under the semitendinosus tendon, and the tendon cut near the junction with its muscle belly and before the tendon divides. This tendon is thick so digital palpation of the wound must be used to make sure that the entire tendon is cut. In some horses new adhesions form following transection of the tendon, so 3 to 4 inches of the affected muscle tendon must be removed.

When a portion of the tendon is to be removed, the horse should be tranquilized, cast with the affected side up, and given enough chloral hydrate to produce deep narcosis. The posterior aspect of the leg, over the involved muscles at the level of the stifle joint and above, should be prepared for operation and locally infiltrated with lidocaine hydrochloride as described previously. The affected limb should be extended to facilitate surgical procedure. A vertical incision 6 inches long should be made on the posterior aspect of the semitendinosus tendon (Fig. 6–89). The tendon should be identified and the adhesions from the semimembranosus and the biceps femoris muscles removed. The muscle belly of the semitendinosus muscle should be isolated and a 3-inch portion removed. The part removed should comprise $1\frac{1}{2}$ inches of tendon and $1\frac{1}{2}$ inches of muscle belly.

*Xylocaine, Astra Laboratories, Worcester, Mass.

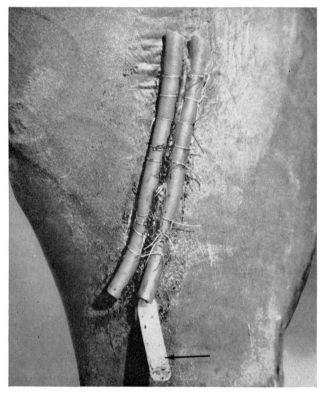

FIG. 6–90.—Method of suturing used for operation on fibrotic myopathy. A quill-type suture (vertical mattress), using rubber tubing as the quill portion, reinforces the incision line so that it will not break open. A plastic drain (arrow) is placed into the wound and sutured to the skin. This plastic drain will allow serum and blood to drain from the wound so that it will not accumulate. Even though this is second intention healing, it is much faster than trying to obtain first intention healing and have the sutures tear open from internal pressure. The tube is removed in seven days and the quill sutures removed in approximately two weeks. The wound is rinsed daily through the plastic drain tube with sterile saline solution and an antibiotic solution of choice.

Following removal, the remaining muscle will contract immediately and a large cavity will result. The fascia should be closed over the cavity with No. 2 catgut. The skin should then be sutured with simple interrupted stitches of 0.6 mm. synthetic suture.* A quill suture (vertical mattress) of the same suture material is then placed to reinforce the suture line. Rubber intravenous tubing is used for the quill sutures (Fig. 6–90). A plastic drain is placed in the bottom of the incision line to allow drainage (Fig. 6–90). The wound can be flushed daily through the drain which is removed in approximately seven days. The wound should be protected with

*Vetafil, Norden Laboratories, Lincoln, Nebraska.

collodion and cotton and tetanus antitoxin should be administered. Antibiotics usually are not necessary, provided asepsis has been maintained during the operation.

If ossifying myopathy is present, presurgical treatment is the same, but after the incision is made, the skin should be reflected and the bony cover over the semitendinosus muscle dissected away. The adhesions on the medial and lateral sides of this muscle should be cut and the skin closed as described above.

PROGNOSIS.—Some relief will be evident in all cases. In most cases, removal of a 3-inch section of muscle gives better results than does simple section of the tendon. After healing, some cases develop characteristic, but less pronounced, signs, although limb function will be nearly normal and signs will not be noticeable except in the walk. Occasionally, it takes three to seven days for maximum benefits of surgical correction to become evident.

SPECIFIC REFERENCES

1. ADAMS, O. R.: Fibrotic Myopathy and Ossifying Myopathy in the Hindlegs of Horses. J.A.V.M.A., *139*, 1089, 1961.
2. ADAMS, O. R.: Lamenesses of Rodeo Horses. Veterinary Scope, Upjohn Co., Spring 1962.
3. ADAMS, RAYMOND D., BROWN, D. D. and PEARSON, C. M.: *Diseases of Muscle*, New York, Harper and Brothers, 1953.
4. RILEY, W. F.: Personal Communication, Michigan State University, 1957.

18. Stringhalt

DEFINITION.—Stringhalt is an involuntary flexion of the hock during progression and may affect one or both hindlimbs.

ETIOLOGY.—The true etiology is unknown although the condition has been blamed on nervous diseases, degeneration of the sciatic and/or peroneal nerves, and on affections of the spinal cord.

In most cases the condition is considered to be an involvement of the lateral digital extensor. Some cases are observed following trauma to this tendon, and adhesions of the tendon may form as it crosses the lateral surface of the hock joint. Most cases show at least partial relief of signs following removal of the tendon of the lateral digital extensor, so it must be assumed that involvement of this tendon is at least partially responsible for the condition.

SIGNS.—Signs of the disease are quite variable and some horses show a very mild flexion of the hock during walking, while others show a marked jerking of the foot toward the abdomen. The anterior surface of the fetlock joint may actually hit the abdominal wall in severe cases. Some horses show these signs at each step, while in others it is spasmodic. In nearly all cases the signs are exaggerated when the horse is turning. It usually is most noticeable after the horse has rested, but the signs may be intermittent and disappear for variable periods of time. Any breed may be affected, and mild cases may not hinder the horse in use. Cold weather may cause an increase in signs, and usually there is a tendency toward decreased intensity of signs during warm weather. Most horses affected have a nervous disposition, which may play a part in the etiology.

DIAGNOSIS.—The lameness is easily diagnosed, but in some cases signs may be absent at the time of examination. The condition must be differentiated from fibrotic myopathy in which the foot is jerked suddenly downward and backwards before being put to the ground (page 308).

TREATMENT.—The treatment is surgical and consists of removal of that portion of the tendon of the lateral digital extensor that crosses the lateral surface of the hock joint. Surgical correction can be performed in a standing position, with the horse cast on the ground, or on a surgical table. If the horse is to be operated on in the standing position, he should be tranquilized prior to preparation of the area for operation. If the horse is cast, the affected leg should be uppermost. The area should be prepared for surgical procedure by shaving the hair and application of skin antiseptics. A local anesthetic should be injected into the muscle of the lateral digital extensor about 1 inch above the lateral malleolus of the tibia. A second injection of local anesthetic should be made over the tendon below the hock joint just before it joins the long digital extensor tendon. Lidocaine hydrochloride* is recommended as a local anesthetic.

An incision approximately $1\frac{1}{2}$ inches long is made over the muscle of the lateral digital extensor just above the level of the point of the hock (Fig. 6–91). The muscle belly cannot be identified until several layers of fascia have been severed. Just overlying the tendon is a heavy layer of strong fascia. This is incised and the muscle belly can be identified. An instrument is passed under the muscle belly so that it can be properly identified and tension put on it. Pulling on the muscular portion will reveal movement in the distal portion just before it attaches to the long extensor. An incision approximately $\frac{1}{2}$ inch long is then made over this distal portion before it joins the long extensor. The skin and subcutaneous tissues are cut with a scalpel making an incision one-half inch long. A blunt bistoury such as Udall teat knife is slipped under the tendon and it is severed. Pressure is then exerted on the proximal portion, pulling out the tendon. Considerable tension is sometimes required to break adhesions that are formed around the tendon where it crosses the hock joint. If it seems as though undue pressures are required to pull it out, further dissection of the proximal portion of the tendon should be done to free it from adhesions. When the complete tendon is exposed, about 7 inches of it has been pulled through the upper incision (Fig. 6–91). The tendon should be cut off, removing a $1\frac{1}{2}$ inch portion of the muscle belly with it. Following removal of the tendon, the subcutaneous fascia should be

*Xylocaine, Astra Laboratories.

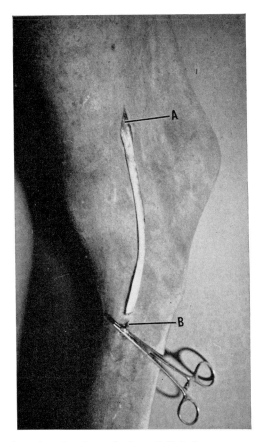

FIG. 6–91.—Section of tendon from the lateral digital extensor removed to correct stringhalt.

A. Site of the proximal incision just above the lateral malleolus of the tibia.

B. Site of distal incision just before the lateral digital extensor joins the long extensor.

sutured with 0 catgut sutures using a simple interrupted pattern. The skin incisions are closed with simple interrupted sutures of a noncapillary, nonabsorbable plastic suture. The wounds are kept bandaged for ten days. Opening of the upper wound sometimes occurs because of the stringhalt action of the limb. In this case the skin sutures are replaced. Tetanus antitoxin should be used, but antibiotics are usually unnecessary. The incisions should be covered with collodion and cotton. Most cases show an almost immediate improvement and will be nearly recovered within two to three weeks. Other cases may take several months for any great improvement to occur or may never show complete recovery. On those cases that recur after several months or a year, an additional portion of the lateral digital extensor muscle is removed. An incision is made at the previous proximal incision site, extending 2 inches above the previous scar. The lateral digital extensor muscle is isolated and an additional 3 to 4 inches of the muscle removed. This will stop signs of stringhalt in some cases.

PROGNOSIS.—Prognosis is guarded to favorable. Nearly all cases show some improvement following surgery, but the degree of improvement is not predictable prior to operation.

SPECIFIC REFERENCE

SEDDON, H. O.: Sudden Case of Stringhalt in a Horse. Vet. Rec., *75*, 35, 1963.

19. Shivering

DEFINITION.—Shivering is characterized by involuntary muscular movements of the limbs and tail. Both hind limbs and the tail are usually affected, but sometimes the forelimbs may be involved.

ETIOLOGY.—The etiology of shivering is unknown. Apparently it is a nervous or neuromuscular disease.

SIGNS.—In mild cases the signs may be difficult to detect, since they occur at irregular intervals, but in most cases the signs are characteristic. They usually are evident when an attempt is made to back the affected horse. As the horse attempts to back, he jerks a hind foot from the ground and holds it in a flexed position abducted from the body. The limb shakes violently, while the tail is elevated and quivers. After a short time the quivering ceases and the limb and tail return to a normal position. The symptoms usually recur if attempts are again made to force the horse to back. In some horses, the signs are most evident when the horse is turned, forced to step over an object, or when his foot is raised from the ground by hand. The eyelids and ears may flicker, and the lips may be drawn backward.

If a forelimb is involved, the limb will be raised and abducted with the carpus flexed. The muscles above the elbow joint will quiver until signs disappear.

TREATMENT.—No efficient method of treatment is known, but treatment with mephenesin* intravenously may be tried.

PROGNOSIS.—The prognosis is unfavorable since the signs usually tend to increase in severity over a period of time. Cases that are affected with mild symptoms may be used for work in some cases.

20. Spavin

DEFINITIONS.—*Bone Spavin.*—A periostitis, or osteitis, usually affecting the medial aspect of the proximal end of the third metatarsal bone and the medial aspect of the third and central tarsal bones. The condition usually results in an ankylosis of the distal intertarsal and the tarso-metatarsal joints (Fig. 5–10, page 129). It

---

*Tolserol, Squibb Laboratories.

causes an osteoarthritis of the tarsal joint, and, in most cases, ankylosing arthritis of the distal intertarsal and/or tarso-metatarsal joints.

Jack Spavin.—A bone spavin of large proportions.

High Spavin.—A bone spavin located higher on the hock joint than ordinary bone spavin.

Bog Spavin.—A chronic distention of the joint capsule of the hock, causing a swelling of the antero-medial aspect of the hock joint.

Blood Spavin.—Blood spavin has no true definition. It usually applies only to an enlarged saphenous vein crossing a bog spavin. It will not be discussed here.

Occult or Blind Spavin.—A typical spavin lameness without any visible radiographic or clinical changes.

BONE SPAVIN.—*Etiology.*—Bone spavin commonly is due to poor conformation. Sickle hocks and cow hocks predispose a horse to bone spavin (Figs. 1–24 and 1–25, page 33). These two malconformations which often accompany each other, make some cases of bone spavin inheritable. Sickle and cow hocks tend to cause stress to the medial aspect of the hock joint. Bone spavin also may be caused by trauma, especially that trauma produced by quick stops during roping. Mineral imbalances or deficiencies, *i.e.* rickets, may predispose some horses to bone spavin. Horses with narrow, thin hocks are more subject to the disease than those with full, well-developed hocks.

SIGNS.—Pain when the horse flexes the hock joint causes a reduction in the height of the foot flight arc (Fig. 4–2, page 95), and a shortening of the anterior phase of the stride. The foot lands on the toe, and over a period, the toe becomes too short and the heel too high. Because of the lower arc of the foot flight, the horse tends to drag the toe, causing it to wear on its anterior edge.

Bone spavin lameness tends to be worse when the horse is first used. Horses with mild cases tend to warm out of the lameness after working a short time; in severe cases exercise may increase the lameness. Bone spavin causes an enlargement of variable size on the inner aspect of the hock (Fig. 6–92). This enlargement sometimes can be difficult to determine, especially if bilateral spavin is present or if a horse normally has large boxy hocks. When standing, the horse may flex the hock periodically in a spasmodic manner. Most cases of bone spavin react positively to the spavin test. The spavin test consists of flexing the hock for one to two minutes and then putting the horse into a trot (Fig. 6–93). A positive reaction to the test is for the horse to take several steps that show more lameness than before the test. Other conditions though may cause this same reaction, especially arthritis in older horses, but in general, the spavin test is considered accurate. It often is advisable to conduct the test on both limbs for comparison or for diagnosis of bilateral bone spavin. Gonitis from any cause can produce a mild reaction to the spavin test. Mild reaction to the spavin test should be viewed with suspicion and the stifle joint should be carefully examined for

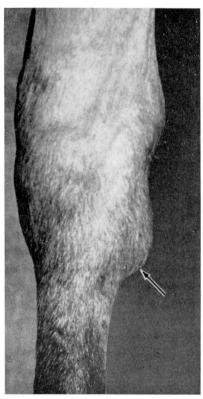
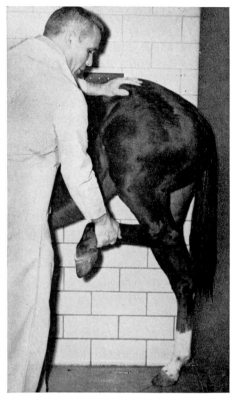

FIG. 6–92   FIG. 6–93

FIG. 6–92.—Site of bone spavin on the right hindlimb. The arrow indicates the
prominence of new bone growth. (Reprinted from *Veterinary Scope*, courtesy
Upjohn Company.)

FIG. 6–93.—Spavin test. The hindlimb should be held in this position one to two
minutes and the horse observed for increased lameness in the first few steps he takes.
Increased lameness is considered to be a positive reaction to the spavin test.

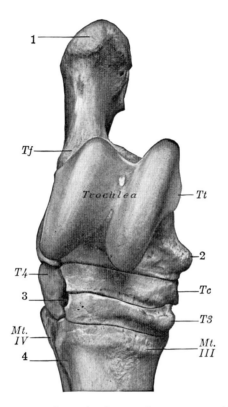

Fig. 6–94.—Right tarsus and proximal part of metatarsus of horse, anterior or dorsal view.

Tt, tibial tarsal bone; *Tf*, fibular tarsal; *Cc*, central tarsal; *T3*, third tarsal; *T4*, fourth tarsal; *1*, tuber calcis; *2*, distal tuberosity of tibial tarsal; *3*, vascular canal; *4*, groove for great metatarsal artery; *Mt*, *III*, *IV*, metatarsal bones.

The joints most commonly involved with bone spavin are the distal intertarsal joint between the central and third tarsal bones and the tarsometatarsal joint between the third tarsal and third metatarsal bones. Any spavin that involves the proximal intertarsal joint between the tibial tarsal bone and the central tarsal bone has a more unfavorable prognosis. (Sisson, *Anatomy of Domestic Animals*, courtesy W. B. Saunders Co.)

pathological changes. The average bone spavin will cause a marked change in the gait, while stifle pathology usually causes milder reaction to the test.

The reduced flexion of the hock results in an exaggerated hip action. As the affected limb is advanced the hip on that side raises. The hip raises because the horse does not allow the hip on the affected side to drop as weight passes over the unsound limb. This means the horse advances the affected limb with imperfect flexion. The foot or shoe may show more wear on the outside because the horse attempts to place most of his weight on the outside of the foot to relieve the pain of the spavin.

DIAGNOSIS.—The reduced arc of the foot flight, reduced flexion of the hock, wearing of the toe, and the spavin test are used in diagnosis. Blocking of the posterior tibial and deep peroneal nerves with a local anesthetic is a reasonably accurate diagnostic method for spavin. However, you must remember that other structures are

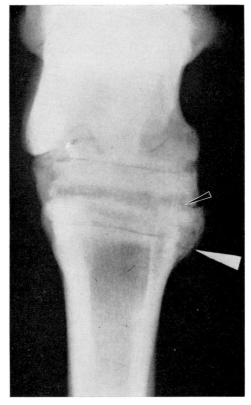

FIG. 6–95.—Bone spavin. Dark pointer indicates ankylosis of the distal intertarsal joint. The white arrow indicates new bone growth on the medial aspects of the third and central tarsal bones. These are typical changes in bone spavin, but the tarso-metatarsal joint is not ankylosed.

blocked in addition to the spavin area. Lamenesses of the hock and stifle cause practically identical symptoms. Therefore, careful examination must be given to the stifle as well as to the hock. An enlarged head of the second metatarsal bone may produce a swelling that looks similar to bone spavin. This can be differentiated by palpation, its location, and by radiographs. The hocks must be examined carefully both from in front of the horse, comparing the two hocks by observing between the front legs, and from behind by observing the hocks straight-on and from oblique views. Uneven enlargements are easily detected (Fig. 6–92), but if the hocks are bilaterally involved it may be difficult without radiographs to determine if the swelling is normal or not. In most cases, radiographs show that the involvement is on the medial aspect of the proximal end of the third metatarsal bone and on the medial aspect

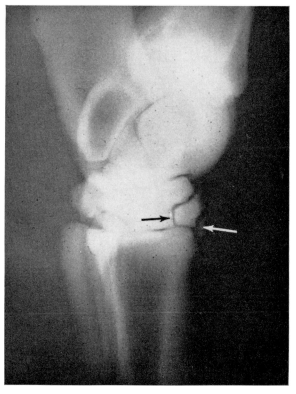

Fig. 6–96.—Fracture of the third tarsal bone. Third tarsal bone is fractured (black arrow) and there is a small chip from this bone anteriorly (white arrow). Notice the abnormal shape of the third tarsal bone proximally. This horse showed signs of bone spavin clinically. The periosteal new bone growth on the proximal aspect of the third tarsal bone probably caused the fracture from downward pressure on it by the central tarsal bone. The horse recovered after ankylosis of the distal intertarsal and tarsometatarsal joints. Surgical intervention should not be used when there is a good possibility of this type of repair.

21

of the third and central tarsal bones with ankylosis of the distal intertarsal and/or tarso-metatarsal joints (Fig. 5–10, page 129; Fig. 6–95); more involvement is present in some cases. Radiographs are essential to accurate diagnosis and prognosis. Radiographs also aid in determining tarsal bone fractures (Fig. 6–96).

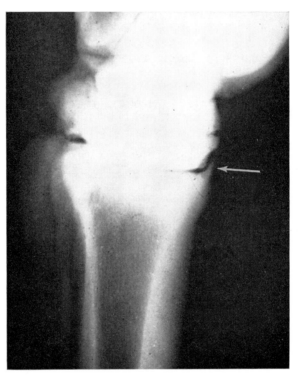

Fig. 6–97.—A type of bone spavin in which most of the lesions are located anteriorly. Clinically the typical bone spavin swelling still occurs antero-medially. Arrow points at new bone growth extending from the third metacarpal bone. This new bone growth may later fracture. This type of fracture could then be treated by waiting for ankylosis of the tarsometatarsal joint to occur, or by surgical removal of the fracture fragment.

TREATMENT.—The treatment that gives most consistent results is the removal of a portion of the cunean tendon from the tibialis anterior muscle. The surgery can be performed with the horse in the standing or recumbent position. The area over the tendon should be clipped, shaved and prepared with skin antiseptics. A local anesthetic then should be injected over the tendon and an incision 1½ inches long made over the center of the longitudinal axis of the cunean tendon where it crosses the medial aspect of the hock (Figs. 6–98 and 6–100). The incision can be made vertically if desired. The tendon should be isolated and 1 to 1½ inch section removed

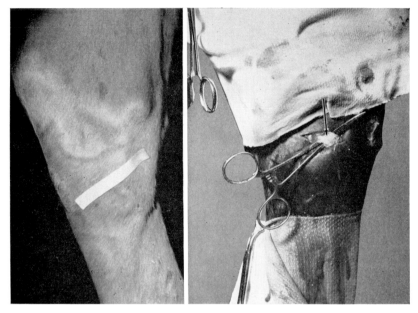

Fig. 6–98   Fig. 6–99

Fig. 6–98.—The white tape indicates the course of the cunean tendon where it crosses the medial aspect of the tarsal joint. This is the site of incision for cunean tenectomy.

Fig. 6–99.—The cunean tendon is seen over the hemostat which has been placed underneath it. One to one and one-half inches of this tendon is removed in cunean tenectomy.

(Fig. 6–99 and 6–100). The skin then should be sutured with a noncapillary, nonabsorbable suture which should be removed in ten to fourteen days. Tetanus antitoxin should be administered, but antibiotics are unnecessary if aseptic techniques are used. The horse should be rested at least two months.

Cunean tenectomy removes the source of pain where the tendon crosses the spavin area, and the results of such an operation are better than with other methods of treatment.

Wamberg[7,8] uses a modified operation that he claims is superior to others. He states that the majority of pain comes from the tissues around the bone and not from the bone itself. Under general anesthesia, he makes a rhomboid-type incision around the spavin exostoses. The skin is loosened from the subcutaneous tissue with dressing forceps, and with a guarded knife, he cuts through all tissues in a more or less diamond-shaped pattern around the spavin. This blade goes through all tissues down to bone regardless of the structures it encounters. It is his theory that the nerve supply to the spavin area is thus cut and the pain relieved. The horse is

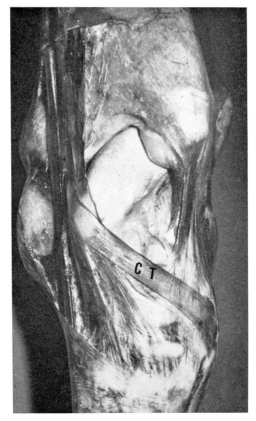

FIG. 6–100.—Antero-medial view of the cunean tendon (*CT*). Approximately 1 inch of this tendon is removed to treat bone spavin.

exercised daily for thirty days after the operation, and to adapt the scar tissue to movement, he recommends 50 to 100 yard dashes for the horse. The knife is forced underneath the saphenous vein at the forepart of the exostosis. Subcutaneous tissues and skin are sutured, the blood forced out through the incision, and then bandage is applied. He states he can get full working capacity from the horse as early as eighteen days after surgery.

In my hands, this type of operation has been no more successful than the type of surgery described above. As long as there is no ankylosis of the distal intertarsal and/or tarsometatarsal joints, pain will be present. Regardless of the type of surgery done, one must wait until ankylosis of these areas is complete before best results can be obtained.

Peter's spavin operation consists of cutting through the cunean tendon into the periosteum of the involved bones. Some persons modified this process by cutting the tendon and periosteum in two places. Neither of these methods is as effective as removal of a portion of the tendon. Cutting of the periosteum stimulates ankylosis of the intertarsal and/or the tarso-metatarsal joints, but this usually occurs naturally in spavin without stimulation. Favorable results can be expected in 60 to 75 per cent of all spavin cases which do not have involvement above the distal intertarsal joint.

Firing and blistering of the area often is performed, though blistering is useless since the inflammation produced is only superficial. Firing stimulates ankylosis of the above joints; the firing point is driven directly into the affected bones of the spavin area. The operator attempts to puncture the cunean tendon with the needle point in an effort to sever it. Firing is not as effective, though, as cunean tenectomy, although it sometimes is used following a cunean tenectomy in an effort to produce healing of an unsuccessful case. Neurectomy of the posterior tibial and deep peroneal nerves also is sometimes used as a last ditch effort to cure the lameness. This procedure, though effective in some cases, is not recommended.

If corrective shoeing is used, an effort should be made to force the foot of the affected limb to break over the medial aspect of the toe. This can be done by using two heel calks and two additional calks, one near the center of the outside toe, and one between the first and second nail holes on the inside. Another method of shoeing is to weld a $\frac{1}{4}$ inch round steel rod on the inside edge of the ground surface of the branches of the shoe. On the inside branch the rod should extend from the heel to midway between the first and second nail holes. On the outside branch, the rod should extend from the heel nearly to the center of the toe, leaving the inside toe open to stimulate break over in that area (Fig. 9–20, page 405). Another method of corrective shoeing is to raise the heels of the shoe and roll the toe. This simply aids the horse in his way of going. In Standardbreds the heel is commonly raised by turning the heels of the shoe back to form calks, but the heels are turned completely back and blended with the shoe so they will not catch and stop the foot (Fig. 9–19, page 403). A memphis bar (Fig. 7–8, page 373) is also used or an oval bar across the heels.

PROGNOSIS.—The prognosis of spavin is always guarded. Those cases that show bony changes in the tibio-tibial tarsal articulation are unfavorable. A prognosis usually should be withheld until operation or other methods of therapy are used, especially in those cases showing ankylosis of the intertarsal and/or the tarso-metatarsal joints. Complete recovery should not be expected but a useable horse is often the result. The horse commonly will be slightly lame until warmed up, especially in cold weather.

BOG SPAVIN.—*Etiology.*—Bog spavin usually is caused by one of three etiological factors:

1. Faulty conformation.

   A horse that is too straight in the hock joint is predisposed to bog spavin (Chapter 1). If a horse with straight legs is not affected by bogs as a young horse, he may develop them after training begins.

    2. Trauma.

        Injury to the hock joint as a result of quick stops, quick turning or other traumas, will cause bog spavin.

    3. Rickets.

        Nutritional deficiencies in calcium, phosphorus, vitamin A and/or vitamin D, alone, or in any combination, apparently can produce bog spavin.

Bog spavin causes a blemish that is serious when due to conformational or nutritional causes; these causes should be considered strong possibilities in a bilateral condition.

SIGNS. — Bog spavin has three characteristic, fluctuating swellings; the largest of which is located at the anterior-medial aspect of the hock joint (Fig. 6–101). Two smaller swellings occasionally occur on either side of the posterior surface of the hock joint at the junction of the tibial tarsal and fibular tarsal bones. These swellings are lower

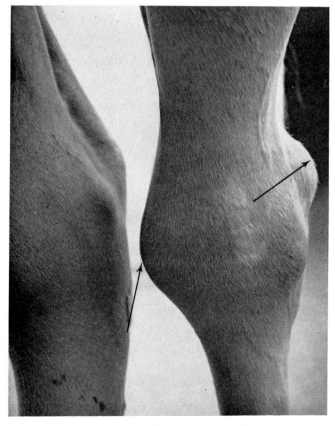

FIG. 6–101.—Bog spavin. Arrows illustrate the swellings that occur in typical bog spavin. The antero-medial swelling is the largest. The swellings at the posterior aspect of the hock on the medial and lateral sides will vary in size.

than the swellings of thoroughpin. When pressure is exerted on any one of these swellings, the other enlargements will show an increase in size and an increase of tension of the joint capsule if held. Lameness, which usually accompanies only traumatic bog spavin, results in heat, pain, and swelling over the hock joint. No bone changes will be evident in uncomplicated bog spavin either upon palpation or on radiographs.

DIAGNOSIS.—Signs of bog spavin are diagnostic; the only variation is in the size of the three swellings. In most cases the antero-medial swelling is the largest, but in some cases the two posterior swellings are more prominent. These three areas are spots where the joint capsule is least inhibited by surrounding tissues. They must be differentiated from thoroughpin which occurs posteriorly at the level of the point of the hock (see Chapter 5, page 139). The most important factor in diagnosis is to determine the etiology. One should attempt immediately to establish if the condition is due to conformation, trauma, or nutritional deficiency.

TREATMENT.—Treatment is limited to bog spavins caused by trauma and nutritional deficiencies. Those bog spavins due to conformational conditions are exceedingly difficult to treat since this is a recurring cause. When trauma is the cause of bog spavin, injection of a corticoid into the joint capsule at weekly intervals for two to three injections is recommended (see Chapter 11, page 443). Corticoids decrease inflammation of the synovial lining and help to prevent formation of excess fluid. Corticoids should be injected into the antero-medial swelling at the most prominent portion of the swelling (Chapter 11, page 450). The horse should be twitched and the skin shaved and prepared with antiseptics. A 20-gauge, 2-inch needle should be inserted into the capsule, after a skin block (Figs. 11–12 and 11–13, page 451), all fluid drained that will come out easily, and the corticoid injected. Counter pressure by bandaging, following injection of the capsule, is also recommended. Best results with counter pressure are obtained if elastic bandages or elastic braces are used. The horse should be rested approximately three weeks after all signs of lameness, if present, have disappeared.

Chronic cases of bog spavin often are fired or blistered or injected subcutaneously with irritant drugs. These methods are unsuccessful, in general, though a few cases seem to respond. Injection of irritants increases the risk of suppurative arthritis. Irritation is already present in the joint capsule and producing more irritation usually is not of therapeutic value. At no time should blistering and firing be used in conjunction with corticoid therapy. These two treatments have opposite effects and complications may result. Ligation of the saphenous vein, above and below the tarsal joint, has been used with success in some cases. This is most helpful for bog spavins that occur quickly, from undetermined causes, and which are not accompanied by lameness. This treatment also may be helpful in bog spavin resulting from conformational causes.

Treatment of bog spavin caused by nutritional deficiencies usually is of no avail unless proper corrections of diet are made. If the deficient mineral(s) and/or vitamin(s) are added to the diet, the overall nutrition is regulated, and the horse freed from internal parasites, bog spavins usually disappear in four to six weeks. Bog spavin resulting from nutritional causes is most common in horses six months to two years of age.

PROGNOSIS.—Prognosis is guarded if the cause is traumatic or nutritional; it is unfavorable if due to conformation.

OCCULT SPAVIN (BLIND SPAVIN).—*Definition.*—Occult spavin is a a disease which originates within the hock joint causing typical spavin lameness but showing no palpable or radiological changes. Occult spavin is least common of the spavins. It is probable that the majority of those conditions diagnosed as occult spavin are truly in the stifle joint. Pathological changes in the stifle joint will cause a mild reaction to the spavin test. Careful examination of the stifle joint must always be done to determine if there is excessive fluid and/or thickening in the joint capsule prior to making a diagnosis of occult spavin.

Etiology.—It is presumed that trauma is the etiology in nearly all cases of occult spavin. Most cases of this type of spavin lameness are assumed to be due to intra-articular lesions. This damage is usually in the form of ulceration of the articular cartilages. Other pathological changes may occur, however, such as injury to the small interosseous ligaments that bind the tarsal bones. These changes are not sufficient to be evident on radiological examination.

SIGNS.—Signs of this disease are those of typical bone spavin lameness, with the exception of physical changes. The anterior phase of the stride is shortened because of the lowered arc of the foot flight resulting from incomplete flexion of the hock (Fig. 4–2, page 95). The same type of rolling action of the hips occurs as in bone spavin. The horse tends to drag the toe of the hoof wall, or of the shoe, and it will wear excessively. The horse responds positively to the spavin test and shows all of the symptoms of spavin lameness, but no evident physical changes. The lameness usually continues throughout the life of the animal, though detectable physical changes are never found other than lameness and reaction to the spavin test.

DIAGNOSIS.—Bone spavin and gonitis must be differentiated from occult spavin.

TREATMENT.—Since pathological changes are difficult to determine, treatment is difficult. One can only assume that some damage has taken place in the joint, since it is not evident on clinical or radiological examination. Treatment is unfavorable for these reasons. Some horses respond temporarily to intra-articular injections of a corticoid. A minimum of three injections, a week apart, should be attempted before evaluating this type of therapy. Blistering and firing of the joint, or cunean tenotomy are of no value in most cases.

PROGNOSIS.—The prognosis is unfavorable.

SPECIFIC REFERENCES

1. DYKSTRA, R. R.: Bone Spavin. Am. J. Vet. Med., *8*, 143, 1913.
2. GOLDBERG, S. A.: Historical Facts Concerning Pathology of Spavin. J.A.V.M.A., *53*, 745, 1918.
3. MANNING, J. P.: Diagnosis of Occult Spavin. Ill. Vet., *7*, 26, 1964.
4. MARTIN, W. J.: Spavin: Etiology and Treatment. Am. Vet. Rev., *24*, 464, 1900.
5. McDONOUGH, JAMES: Hock Joint Lameness. Am. Vet. Rev., *43*, 629, 1913.
6. SCHEBITZ, H.: Spavin; Radiographic Diagnosis and Treatment. Proc. 11th Ann. A.A.E.P. 1965.
7. WAMBERG, K.: A New Treatment for Spavin in Horses. Proc. 15th Int. Vet. Congress, Pt. 1, Vol. 2, p. 957, 1953.
8. ————: A New Treatment for Spavin in Horses. Proc. 15th Int. Vet. Congress, Pt. 2, Vol. 2, p. 371, 1953.
9. WATTLES, J. H.: Injection of Iodine in Bone Disease. Am. Vet. Rev., *19*, 51, 1895–96.
10. ZUILL, W. L.: Surgical Treatment of Diseases of the Hock. Am. Vet. Rev., *18*, 247, 1894.

21. Thoroughpin (*see* Chapter 5, page 138).

22. Curb

DEFINITION.—Curb is an enlargement at the plantar (posterior) aspect of the fibular tarsal bone due to inflammation and thickening of the plantar ligament.

ETIOLOGY.—Predisposing causes include sickle hocks (curby hocks) and cow hocks. Such abnormal conformation causes additional stress to the plantar ligament and thus tends to produce curb. Occasionally a foal is born in which curb appears soon after birth, as a result of faulty conformation of the hocks. Exciting causes include violent exertion, trauma from kicking walls or tailgates in trailers and violent attempts to extend the hock. These causes can produce curb in hocks of normal conformation.

SIGNS.—Curb is indicated by an enlargement present on the plantar surface of the fibular tarsal bone (Fig. 6–102). If the condition is in the acute phase, there will be signs of inflammation and lameness. The horse will stand with the heel elevated and the leg at rest, and heat and swelling can be palpated in the area. Swelling usually does not diminish with exercise, and exercise may only increase lameness in acute curb. In a severe case, where trauma has been the exciting cause, periostitis on the plantar aspect of the fibular tarsal bone may result in new bone growth. In chronic cases, tissues surrounding the area often become infiltrated with scar tissue and a permanent blemish results. Lameness may not be present even though a considerable blemish is evident. Occasionally the proximal end of the fourth metatarsal bone is large and causes false curb. Careful examination will reveal that the swelling in this area is lateral to the plantar ligament and not on the ligament itself. This enlargement can be confirmed by radiological examination if necessary.

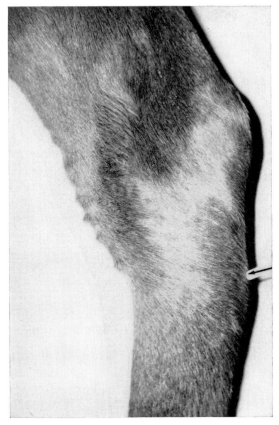

FIG. 6–102. — The arrow indicates the swelling caused by inflammation of the plantar ligament, typical of curb.

TREATMENT. — In the early stages of curb, in which acute inflammation is still present, the hair should be clipped from the area and the skin scrubbed with soap and water and prepared with suitable antiseptics. Following tranquilization and local anesthesia, the area of the curb should be injected subcutaneously with a corticoid (Chapter 11, page 442). This usually is followed by a marked reduction of swelling. In spite of this reduction, some scar tissue may remain after healing has taken place. The affected horse should be rested and cold packs applied, in addition to the anti-inflammatory agents. Chronic cases often are fired or blistered, but the efficiency of these methods of therapy is doubtful.

PROGNOSIS. — If the horse has good conformation, the prognosis is favorable providing the initial acute inflammation is controlled with corticoids. If the horse has poor conformation, this serves as a continuing cause and the prognosis is unfavorable. In most cases, some permanent blemish will remain following recovery, even though most horses will be serviceably sound, if conformation is good.

23. Capped Hock (*see* Chapter 5, page 136).

24. Weak Flexor Tendons in the Foal

DEFINITION.—Some foals are afflicted with very weak flexor tendons at birth. Weak flexors may allow the fetlock to hit the ground, and the toe of the foot will be off the ground (Fig. 6–103). These will usually strengthen in a few days without help, but some do require support (Fig. 6–103).

ETIOLOGY.—This is a congenital condition and the true etiology is not known.

SIGNS.—All gradations of the condition will be seen from mild to severe. When it afflicts the rear legs, the hock conformation also is usually bad (sickle hocks). It is more common for the rear flexors to show weakness than the fore. In some cases, all legs show it.

TREATMENT.—Supporting the foot with a trailer shoe is usually all that is necessary. Since the foal is too small to apply a horse shoe, ordinary hinges 5 inches long and triangular in shape are used. One is placed on the medial side of the foot and one on the lateral side

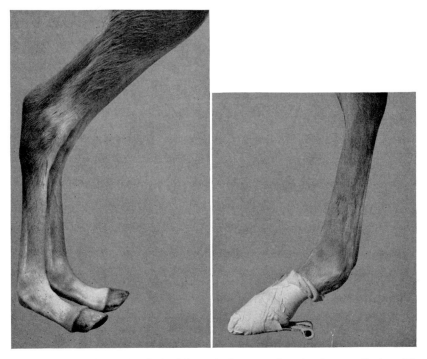

FIG. 6–103.—Views of a foal with weak flexor tendons in the rear limbs. The view on the left shows the attitude of the limbs prior to treatment. The view on the right shows the limbs immediately after placing two 5-inch door hinges on the bottom of the foot and taping them to the foot. A piece of iron $\frac{3}{16}$ inch thick, 2 inches wide and 5 inches long can substitute for this type of device. Support is only necessary for seven to ten days.

of the foot and they are either taped or fixed with 2-inch plaster of paris bandage to the hoof wall. In just a matter of days, the support can usually be removed. The supports are most satisfactory in the hindfoot, because when used on a forefoot the trailer may be stepped on by the hindfoot. An ordinary piece of flat steel 2 inches wide, 5 inches long and $\frac{3}{16}$ inches thick can be substituted for the hinges. The hinges are particularly effective because the area where the pin goes through constitutes a raised heel (Fig. 6–103). The example in Figure 6–103 is shown before and immediately after corrective therapy was used. This shows the amount of correction that can be done by this method.

PROGNOSIS.—Prognosis is usually favorable provided injury of the fetlock joint has not been done prior to correction.

25. Canker

DEFINITION.—Canker is a chronic hypertrophy of the horn producing tissues of the foot, which may involve any one or all of the feet; it most often is found in the hind feet. It is a rare condition in modern horse practice.

ETIOLOGY.—The chief etiological agent is presumed to be unhygienic stabling, but exceptions to this may occur. The disease develops in horses that stand in bedding that is soaked with urine and feces, or mud and whose feet do not receive regular attention. The specific cause is believed to be an unidentified infection. Lack of proper frog pressure also may be an etiological factor.

SIGNS.—Lameness usually is not present in early stages of the disease; since neglect of the feet is a contributing cause, the disease may not be detected until well advanced. When the foot is examined it usually has a fetid odor and the frog, which may appear intact, has a ragged appearance. The horn tissue of the frog loosens easily and when removed reveals a foul smelling, swollen corium covered with a caseous white exudate. The corium shows chronic vegetative growth. The disease may extend to the sole or even to the wall of the foot. It has little, if any, tendency to heal and the tissues bleed easily.

DIAGNOSIS.—Diagnosis can be made by the appearance of the foot and by the offensive odor. It must be differentiated though from ordinary thrush.

TREATMENT.—Treatment often is ineffective and improvement, if it occurs, is slow. All loose horn and affected tissues should be removed and an antiseptic, astringent dressing applied. A 5 per cent picric acid solution should be applied under the bandage. Caustic agents, such as a mixture of copper sulfate and zinc sulfate crystals, sometimes are used. Successful treatment of canker with penicillin has been described.[2] Penicillin was used at the rate of 3 million units intramuscularly daily until improvement was shown. Then a similar dose was given every second day until the condition was nearly cured and then treatment was administered every third day.

Penicillin ointment was used locally with a foot bandage. Duration of treatment varied from ten days to six weeks. After improvement is noted, an antiseptic powder, such as sulfapyridine powder, or 10 per cent sodium sulfapyridine solution, can be used. Dressings should be kept on the foot to protect it from further infection and the horse should be stabled in clean surroundings, preferably dry, rocky pastures.

PROGNOSIS.—Prognosis is guarded to unfavorable.

SPECIFIC REFERENCES

1. BARRIS, J. and SKUSEK: Experiences in the Treatment of Canker of the Foot. Berl. u. Muench. Tieraerztlt. Wochnschr., 73, 186, 1960.
2. MASON, J. H.: Penicillin Treatment of Foot Canker. J. So. Afr. Vet. Med. Assoc., 23, 223, 1962.

LAMENESSES COMMON TO BOTH LIMBS

1. Wobbler Syndrome (Ataxia of Foals, Wobbles of Foals, Equine Incoordination)

DEFINITION.—The wobbler syndrome of horses is a more or less specific incoordination appearing in horses. The syndrome is recognized universally, but authorities differ as to cause. Probably there are several causes. They will be discussed here. The condition has occurred in Thoroughbreds, Standardbreds, Arabians, American Saddlebreds, Tennessee Walking Horses, and Quarter Horses. Other breeds undoubtedly are involved.

ETIOLOGY.—The etiology of wobbler syndrome is complex. Some authors blame it upon protrusions of the intervertebral discs and malformation of the articular processes of the cervical vertebrae. They say changes cause a constriction of the related spinal foramina and of the spinal canal itself. The lesions, if present, are believed to be primarily located in the cervical spinal canal since both the front and hindlimbs are involved. However, cerebellar hypoplasia should also be considered. Parasitism of the spinal cord and ingestion of toxins from an unknown origin have been blamed by some as an etiological agent of this condition. Nutritional deficiency also has been considered as an etiological agent, as well as trauma resulting in injury to the spinal canal and cord.

Dimock[3] considers wobbler syndrome to be an inheritable disease of horses. In a study of 191 cases of the syndrome of which 164 were Thoroughbreds, 121 cases had been sired by closely related stallions. Forty-three per cent of these cases occurred in one line of Thoroughbreds from one of the foundation lines of the breed. One to 14 per cent occurred in other Thoroughbred lines. Dimock believes it is not a simple recessive characteristic since it was found in more than three times as many males as females. He was unsuccessful in transmitting the disease to healthy horses by blood transfusion, injection of spinal fluid or macerated spinal cord. He does not believe infectious agents are a factor in the condition. Some 85 per cent of his cases showed no gross lesions at necropsy. Dimock says that autopsy findings on recently developed cases with typical symptoms reveal cord and bone lesions which could not have developed in a short time. He reports that there is only one case on record of a wobbler sired by a wobbler, so apparently the condition is transmitted by non-wobblers.

Many horse owners associate injury with the production of wobbler syndrome, but in most such cases the syndrome had been present in a mild degree before the injury and had gone unnoticed. At some time, due to incoordination, the horse falls, or in some other way becomes injured, because of awkwardness produced by the wobbler syndrome. Following the injury the horse may appear to become worse due to the actual injury that has occurred or due to the normal course of the disease. In most cases where trauma is blamed for production of the disease, the disease was present before the injury.

The etiology probably is best summarized this way: There is a definite possibility that the wobbler syndrome is inheritable. While cases actually may occur as a result of traumatic injury to the cervical region, this is not the likely cause of all cases since it is extremely rare for a horse to show improvement from the wobbler syndrome; if trauma was the cause, more horses should recover. Still other cases may be due to nutritional deficiencies of calcium, phosphorus, vitamin D and/or vitamin A; this has not been proven and requires research to establish a basis in fact. Nematode invasion of the cord should be included among traumatic forms. This rarely would be considered a cause of the disease. Disc protrusion and osteoarthritis of the cervical articular processes may be a cause in some cases, but more likely are a result of the disease. Toxins are not a probable cause of wobbler syndrome. Cerebellar hypoplasia may be involved in a low percentage of cases.

SIGNS.—Signs of the condition may appear any time from birth to three years, but a majority of cases become evident before two years.

The disease, which begins as an incoordination of the hind limbs, is always bilateral and almost always strikes first in the hind limbs. In most cases the forelimbs become involved, to a greater or lesser extent, as the disease progresses. Change is gradual and any change, whether it be an improvement or worsening of the condition, occurs within the first few weeks. It is rare for any horse to show improvement once the syndrome is evident, but some will improve slightly. Some horses become involved to such a degree that on turning they fall and may require destruction. Early cases cause dragging of the toes of the hind feet and errors in rate, range, force, and direction of movement. The horse appears healthy in every other way and has normal temperature, appetite and metabolic functions. Most affected horses tend to reach a certain level of incoordination and remain indefinitely at this point.

At necropsy a few cases show no lesions at all. Some cases show constrictions in the cervical canal or inflammation at the articular processes that may impinge the spinal nerves. Rooney[7] found significant lesions between C3 and C4 in about 60 per cent of the cases, between C2 and C3, C4 and C5 in about 14 per cent each, and least frequently between C5 and C6, C6 and C7 (5 per cent for each). Three variations of malformation were observed: (1) misdirection of articular processes resulting in fixation, flexion, and anatomical narrowing of the spinal canal. (2) An overgrowth of the ventral medial lip or edge of the articular process encroaching upon the lumen of the spinal canal. This type causes anatomical narrowing of the spinal canal which is exaggerated by flexion. (3) Asymmetrical formation of the articular processes, causing them to be of different shapes or size on the right or left articulations. In this form there is no anatomical narrowing but rather functional narrowing during flexion. In his experience this is the most common type of deformity. Other authorities consistently have reported finding pathological changes in the cord from compression by protrusions of cervical discs, and from osteoarthritis and enlargement of the articular processes of the cervical vertebrae.

DIAGNOSIS.—The diagnosis is well defined by the syndrome described above. If recovery from incoordination is shown, you can be reasonably certain that the wobbler syndrome was not present. Few other diseases will cause a similar syndrome without producing other signs of disease, e.g. encephalomyelitis. A horse with incoordination of the hind limbs, or of the fore and hind limbs, but having good health in other respects, should be suspected of having wobbler syndrome.

Fractures, tumors, abscesses, intervertebral disc protrusion and other pathological processes involving the brain and spinal cord can cause incoordination. These can usually be differentiated by signs peculiar to the particular condition.

TREATMENT.—There is no known treatment for this condition although injection of corticoids has been reported to effect a cure in a few cases. In others, such injections have caused improvement but the animals suffered a relapse when injections were stopped. Other cases reportedly have responded to some degree to supplemental feeding of minerals and vitamins. In general, it can be stated that no treatment is effective and that after six to eight weeks the horse probably will remain at whatever state of incoordination he is in at that time. Some affected horses can be used for breeding purposes if incoordination is not serious. However, such use has two disadvantages: the likelihood of injury during breeding and the possibility of transmission of the syndrome to the offspring, with the possibility that they may either carry the factor or be affected with the disease.

PROGNOSIS.—The prognosis is unfavorable. It would be rare for a horse to recover from this disease. In the past, insurance companies have recognized this disease as a legitimate cause for euthanasia.

SPECIFIC REFERENCES

1. BARDWELL, R. E.: Osteomalacia in Horses. J.A.V.M.A., *138*, 158, 1961.
2. DIMOCK, W. W. and ERRINGTON, B. J.: Incoordination of Equidae: "Wobblers." J.A.V.M.A., *95*, 261, 1939.
3. DIMOCK, W. W.: "Wobbles."—An Hereditary Disease of Horses. J. Heredity *41*, 319, 1950.
4. ————: Wobblers in Horses. Ky. Ag. Expt. Sta. Bull. #553 (1950).
5. JONES, T. C., DOLL, E. R., and BROWN, ROSS: *The Pathology of Equine Incoordination.* Proc. Book A.V.M.A., 139–149, 1954.
6. OLAFSON, PETER: Wobblers Compared to Ataxic Lambs. Cornell Vet., *32*, 301, 1942.
7. ROONEY, J. R.: Equine Incoordination. I. Gross Morphology, Cornell Vet., *53*, 411, July 1963.
8. STEEL, J. D., *et al.*: Equine Sensory Ataxia (Wobbles). Australian Vet., J., *35*, 442, 1959.

2. Muscular Dystrophy

DEFINITION. — Muscular dystrophy has been observed by the author in two cases. In one case only the semitendinosis muscle was affected, and in the other, the right masseter muscle and the left semitendinosis muscle were affected. Muscular dystrophy differs from simple atrophy in that the muscle completely disappears.

ETIOLOGY. — The etiology of muscular dystrophy is unknown.

SIGNS. — Complete loss of the muscular tissue is obvious. Signs of lameness have not been observed. In the cases observed by me, the horse affected with dystrophy of the right masseter showed only bone to palpation on the affected side. The semitendinosis on the left hindlimb was completely absent. In the other case the semitendinosis on the right hindlimb was completely absent. Dystrophy leaves a deformity in the limb and a deep grooving where the muscle was previously present.

TREATMENT. — No treatment is known for muscular dystrophy.

PROGNOSIS. — Unfavorable. The prognosis is unfavorable and if dystrophy should involve muscles in other areas it could cause lameness and permanent disability.

SPECIFIC REFERENCE

CECIL, R. L. and LOEB, R. F.: *A Textbook of Medicine,* 11th Ed., Philadelphia, p. 1451, W. B. Saunders, 1963.

3. Traumatic Division of the Digital Extensor Tendons of the Fore and Hindlimb

DEFINITION. — Division of the common and/or lateral extensors of the forelimb, and the long and/or lateral extensor in the hindlimb, is relatively common. In the hindlimb the tendon or tendons usually are severed just below the hock joint as a result of wire lacerations. In the forelimb the common digital extensor or lateral digital extensor often is severed between the fetlock and the carpus, again as a result of wire lacerations. If the laceration is below the middle of the metatarsus in the hind limb, where the lateral and long extensor are combined, only one tendon is cut.

ETIOLOGY. — Trauma is the etiology in all cases. Wire cuts account for most cases.

SIGNS. — The horse will be unable to extend the toe of the foot. When his foot is put down, the toe may catch and his weight may force the anterior surface of the fetlock to the ground. When the limb is set under the horse properly though, he can bear his weight normally. The lateral digital extensor may be cut without any accompanying signs in either the fore or the hind limb because division of the common digital extensor and of the long digital extensor cause most signs. Other signs are contingent upon the extent of the laceration that caused division of the tendons.

TREATMENT. — If the wound is fresh it should be cleansed, shaved and sutured. Usually, no attempt is made to bring the tendon edges together with tendon sutures; the extensor tendons have a better chance to rejoin than the flexor tendons, and with time, most horses will regain normal function of the limb. Following suturing of the wound, the limb should be placed in a cast, from hoof wall to above the carpus, with the foot in normal position. Antibiotics can be used locally and/or parenterally, depending upon the severity and contamination of the wound.

The tarsus is difficult to enclose in a cast because of the reciprocal apparatus. The cast should end just below the tarsus in the hind limb. The cast keeps the foot in normal position at all times. The foot and leg should be kept in this cast four to six weeks. The cast should be changed, if necessary, because of breaking of the cast or decreased usage in the limb, which might indicate skin necrosis. If a limb is properly padded, though, no necrosis will be encountered.

The foot should be placed in a corrective shoe if the division of the tendon(s) has been present some time when first examined, or when the cast has been removed. This shoe has an extended toe of approximately 3 inches. A metal bar is welded to the toe extension so that it conforms to the shape of the anterior surface of the metatarsus or metacarpus. The front of the limb should be padded and the bar at the front of the limb bound to the leg by adhesive tape, plaster, or elastic bandages. This helps keep the toe in extension. With further improvement, the bar on the anterior surface of the limb may be discontinued, and only the toe extension left on the shoe, until the limb appears to assume nearly normal function. Complete healing usually occurs in about four months, and the horse will again use the extensor tendons normally.

PROGNOSIS. — Prognosis is guarded to favorable depending upon the duration and extent of the wound. The seriousness of the wound itself may be enough to indicate euthanasia. In some cases wire may cut into the hock joint making euthanasia advisable, if suppurative arthritis is present. In other cases, the bone may be badly damaged so the prognosis must be withheld until the case has been evaluated.

4. Traumatic Division of the Digital Flexor Tendons of the Fore and Hindlimb

DEFINITION. — Traumatic division of the digital flexor tendons usually occurs between the carpus and the fetlock, or between the tarsus and the fetlock.

ETIOLOGY. — Trauma is the cause in all cases. Numerous types of accidents may be the cause; they are not all listed here. Injury may occur as a result of backing into or kicking a sharp object or being cut down in a race by a horse coming from behind. In such a case the hind limb would be involved. A horse may cut his own flexor tendons by overreaching and cutting the tendon area of the forelimb with a toe grab of the shoe on the hind foot of the same side.

SIGNS. — All degrees of laceration have been found. The superficial digital flexor tendon alone may be severed, while in other cases the deep digital flexor also may be severed. In some cases, both flexor tendons and the suspensory ligament may be cut. If the flexors are cut above the middle of the metatarsus or metacarpus, the inferior check ligament also may be severed. If only the superficial flexor tendon is cut, the fetlock joint will drop, but it will not touch the ground. If the superficial and deep flexor tendons are cut, the fetlock will drop and the toe will come up in the air when weight is applied to the affected limb. If both flexors and the suspensory ligament are cut, the fetlock will rest on the ground.

If the wound has been present some time, there may be infection of the tendon sheath, and suppurative tendosynovitis may be present, and varying amounts of swelling in the limb may result. Lameness, which is severe, will vary according to severity and duration of the wound. In some cases the wounds are greatly lacerated, while in other cases the wound may look as if it were cut with a knife.

DIAGNOSIS. — The dignosis is obvious, but one should determine what structures have been severed by observing the clinical attitude of the foot and by probing of the wound.

TREATMENT. — If the laceration extends through both tendons and the suspensory ligament, treatment is inadvisable and euthanasia is recommended. If the wound is fresh and only the superficial flexor tendon is severed, the wound should be cleaned, shaved, prepared for surgical correction and the tendon sheath should be injected with corticoids in combination with antibiotics. The skin edges should be brought into apposition by sutures and the limb placed in a plaster cast from hoof wall to the tarsus, or from hoof wall to the carpus, depending upon the limb. This cast should be left in place approximately four to six weeks and changed as indicated. The cast should be put on with the fetlock flexed so that the tendon will have a better chance to heal. If effort is made to suture the tendon by surgical procedure, the horse should be confined in lateral recumbency, by using general anesthetic, and the wound extended longitudinally over the posterior aspect of the tendon. The tendon should be sutured with a recommended tendon

suture.[1] The skin and subcutaneous tissues should be closed and
the limb, to the carpus or tarsus, placed in a cast so that the fetlock
and phalangeal joints are in a flexed position. This should be done
to relieve tension on the flexor tendons. If the foot is permitted to
assume normal position, the sutures almost invariably will tear out.
The foot should be kept cast, in this position, for four to six weeks.
Change the cast as often as necessary to prevent loosening or skin
necrosis. The opposite limb should be kept in a supporting bandage
to prevent it from breaking down.

  If both flexors are cut, or if both flexors and the inferior check
ligament are cut, the horse should be given a general anesthetic,
and the wound prepared by shaving and cleansing. The wound
should be extended so that the tendons can be seen. They should
be sutured with a recommended tendon suture.[1] One of the most
valuable types of tendon sutures is one that can be removed after
the wound heals by pulling the sutures out by means of guy wires
placed under the sutures during surgery. Following repair of the
tendons and closure of the skin, the wound should be protected
with sterile petrolatum gauze, and the leg well padded and cast
from hoof wall to the tarsus or hoof wall to the carpus, so that the
fetlock and phalangeal joints are flexed. This reduces the amount
of tension on the flexor tendons, since all sutures will tear out if the
foot is allowed to assume a normal position.

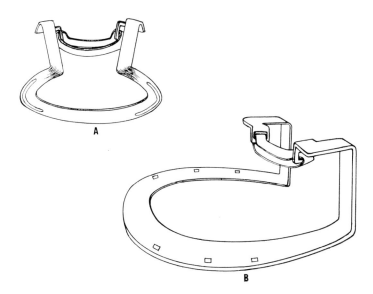

Fig. 6–104.—Corrective shoe for traumatic division of the flexor tendons.
  A. Posterior view of the shoe which has a leather strap to hold up the fetlock
joint.
  B. Side view of the shoe showing how the leather strap is inserted to support the
fetlock joint. Also note that the heels are about three inches longer than normal
to help support the limb.

After four to six weeks in a cast, the limb should be placed in supporting bandage and the foot shod with a fetlock supporting shoe (Fig. 6–104). This enables the fetlock to rest in a leather strap so it will not drop below normal position. This shoe also can be used for division of the superficial flexor tendon only. The shoe should be used for three to six months, depending upon the horse's improvement, and should be reset every four to six weeks. After this, a shoe with 2 to 3 inch trailers on the heels should be used for support until the fetlock regains normal strength. Trailers on front shoes must be shorter to prevent pulling of the shoe by the hind foot.

Antibiotics and corticoid therapy should be given as indicated with any type of laceration. Whenever an attempt is made to bring the flexor tendons into position by surgical correction, parenteral antibiotic therapy should be continued at least seven days following the operation. Corticoid therapy should be given as indicated.

PROGNOSIS. — The prognosis is guarded to unfavorable, depending upon the number of structures that are severed. If both flexors and the suspensory ligament are cut, the prognosis is unfavorable. The presence of suppurative tendonitis makes the prognosis more unfavorable. If the vascular supply is cut, gangrene may result.

SPECIFIC REFERENCE

BOYES, J. H.: *Bunnell's Surgery of the Hand.* 4th ed., Philadelphia, J. B. Lippincott Co., 1964.

5. Windpuffs—Windgalls (*see* Chapter 5, page 141)

DEFINITION. — This is distention of a joint capsule, tendon sheath, or bursa, with excess synovia, not accompanied by lameness.

ETIOLOGY. — Young horses under a heavy training schedule nearly always will develop windpuffs of the fetlock joint capsules. Race horses, rodeo horses, and even gaited horses, subjected to heavy work, will develop windpuffs to some degree as a result of trauma. Once windpuff has started in any area, it usually remains for life. Nutritional deficiency, a possible cause of windpuffs among young horses should not be overlooked as a possible etiology among those horses not under heavy training. The diet should be closely checked in any young horse to make sure that nutrition is not a factor.

SIGNS. — Firm, fluid swelling just above, and anterior to, the sesamoid bones between the suspensory ligament and the cannon bone, indicate articular windpuffs of the fetlock joint capsule. Windpuffs of the flexor tendons occur between the suspensory ligament and the flexor tendons, just above the sesamoid bones. Bursae may swell, and mild distentions of other joint capsules or the tarsal sheath may occur. These sometimes are called windpuffs or windgalls but the name is usually reserved for conditions below the carpus and tarsus. Longstanding cases may harden as a result of fibrosis of the area. Windpuffs themselves are not a cause of lameness, but when accompanied by arthritis, bursitis or tendonitis they should be treated and regarded as a sign of the disease involved.

TREATMENT. — In general, treatment is not effective, nor required, if windpuffs or windgalls are not accompanied by lameness. Treatment for serous arthritis and tenosynovitis, described in other sections of this book, should be used when windpuffs are a sign of these diseases. If no lameness is evident, the horse usually is not rested, but the work is decreased for a few days when they first occur. Windpuffs or windgalls usually will remain for the life of the horse. No treatment is recommended providing lameness does not occur. If lameness does occur, enforced rest and treatment, as described under arthritis and tenosynovitis, should be employed. Intrasynovial injections of a corticoid usually are the most effective treatment if lameness is present. Injections should be accompanied by adequate rest. Swelling will usually reduce if elastic wraps are applied following the injection.

PROGNOSIS. — Prognosis is favorable if no lameness is present and guarded if lameness is present. The pathological changes causing the windpuff or windgall should be determined.

6. Fracture of the First and Second Phalanges

DEFINITION. — Fracture of the first and second phalanges is most common among cutting and barrel racing horses because such horses often make very sharp turns on one hind leg in their work. These fractures also may occur in the fore legs, but are slightly more common in the hind leg.

ETIOLOGY. — Trauma is the cause, especially if accompanied by a twisting action. Shoeing with heelcalks predisposes phalangeal fractures. The calks anchor while the weight is on the foot, and the twisting action of a cutting horse or barrel racing horse causes fracture.

SIGNS. — The bone, or bones, usually are badly comminuted so crepitation is obvious. The lameness is severe and the horse hesitates to put any weight on the affected limb. Swelling will be observable over the pastern area, and, in old cases, bony swelling resembling ringbone will be present. In some cases, only the second phalanx will be fractured, while in others only the first phalanx will be involved (Figs. 6–105 and 106). Occasionally, both the first and second phalanges will be fractured. Some horses are affected with small chip fractures of these bones, or with single longitudinal fractures, especially of the first phalanx.

DIAGNOSIS. — A history of sudden lameness while working, plus crepitation and signs of inflammation over the phalanges usually are diagnostic. Radiographs are necessary to confirm the damage and to determine the bones which actually are broken. Occasionally, luxation of the pastern joint occurs between the first and second phalanx; this causes crepitation which is similar to fracture. Luxation can be determined by radiographic examination (Fig. 6–107). Crepitation is difficult to produce when there is only one fracture line.

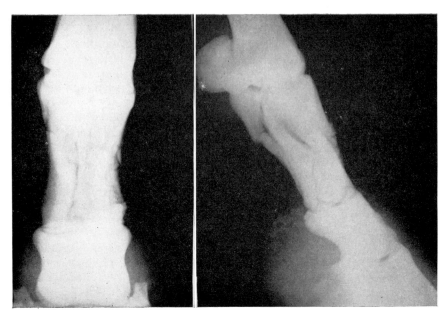

Fig. 6–105.—Comminuted fracture of the first phalanx involving both metacarpophalangeal (fetlock) and proximal interphalangeal (pastern) joints. (Carlson, *Veterinary Radiology*, Lea & Febiger.)

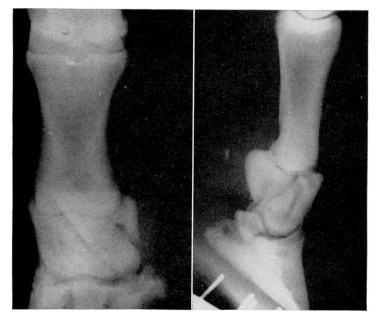

Fig. 6–106.—Comminuted fracture of the second phalanx. The prognosis would be guarded to unfavorable in this case because it has fractured into the coffin joint. The pastern joint can ankylose with some chance of soundness. (Carlson, *Veterinary Radiology*, Lea & Febiger.)

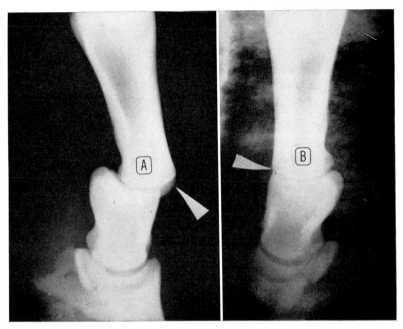

Fig. 6-107.—Luxation of the pastern joint on lateral radiograph.

A. Pointer shows over-riding distal end of first phalanx.

B. The same joint in a plaster cast with the luxation reduced. The pointer shows the decreased joint space, indicating beginning ankylosis as the result of destruction of the articular cartilage.

TREATMENT.—Casting the affected limb in plaster is the usual method of therapy. The cast should be applied to the limb with the horse in recumbency. The horse should be surgically anesthetized for repair of first or second phalangeal fracture. To a 1000 lb. horse give 0.5 mg. of Promazine per pound body weight followed by enough 6 per cent chloral hydrate I.V. to make the horse unsteady on his feet. The amount of chloral hydrate will vary from 250 to 500 cc. of a 6 per cent solution, depending on the tolerance of the individual horse. Following administration of chloral hydrate, 2 grams of 10 per cent Surital sodium* are administered rapidly I.V. The horse will go down following administration of the Surital and anesthesia will often last till the cast is dry enough to bear weight and the anesthetic procedure seldom requires more Surital sodium to keep the horse anesthetized for the casting procedure. Pentobarbital may be substituted for Surital if desired. Following anesthesia, the foot is thoroughly cleaned and any shoes present are removed on either the front or hind feet. If trimming of the hoof wall is required, it is done at this time. The leg is powdered with talcum or boric acid and 3-inch stockinette is applied to the limb

* Parke Davis Co.

from the hoof wall to the carpus or from the hoof wall to the tarsus, depending on which limb is involved. Orthopedic felt is applied where the top of the cast will fit.

The limb is positioned so that the fracture ends are in as near normal apposition as possible, and the foot is cast in a slightly flexed position. Start with 4- or 6-inch blue label Johnson & Johnson plaster of paris and put on 3 rolls before reinforcement is applied. These first layers are not pulled tight, but merely pulled up so that there is no looseness. One should be very careful to fold the plaster in behind the pastern joint so that it fits snugly for support against the back of the pastern joint. Otherwise, there will be no support in this area for the phalanges. The 6-inch wide plaster tends not to support this area sufficiently unless careful attention is paid to this. The plaster of paris goes over the sole and hoof and up to just below the carpus or tarsus. There should be no motion at all in the phalangeal area.

After three rolls of 4- or 6-inch plaster have been rolled on, apply plaster splints $\frac{1}{4}$ inch thick, 15 inches long and 4 inches wide to the anterior and posterior surface of the limb. These splints adequately support the cast in the fetlock area. Splints can also be formed from a roll of plaster by merely folding it back and forth to the proper length. These splints should be carefully folded in behind the pastern for support and then an additional 3 or 4 rolls of 4- or 6-inch blue label Johnson & Johnson plaster are rolled on to finish the cast. Green label plaster of paris can be used if faster-setting plaster is required.

Try to plan the anesthesia so that the horse will stay quiet until the plaster is dry. By the time he tries to get up, a solid cast should be formed so he can put weight on it without damaging it.

The cast may have to be changed every two to three weeks depending on the individual case. The whole procedure has to be repeated as discussed if the cast must be replaced. Repair of a phalangeal fracture may be a long, tedious and costly affair, but it must be done properly. If the cast shows looseness, it must be changed. It is also changed if ulceration develops at the proximal portion of the cast. It is best to change the cast and be wrong, than to leave it and have irrepairable damage. At the time the cast is changed, the area can be examined and a corticoid ointment applied to any lesions present. Radiographs could be taken at this time, if necessary. Eight to ten weeks are required for a phalangeal fracture to heal. The horse is confined to a stall for at least thirty days following removal of the cast, while strength in the tendons returns. A 3-inch trailer shoe is applied to support the tendons for four to six weeks after cast removal.

The pastern joint of the hind leg may become completely ankylosed as described on page 232 and the horse may still be functional. Ankylosis of the pastern joint in the foreleg causes greater interference with action. The affected horse should not be used for at least six months, and once healing occurs the foot should be kept properly trimmed and should be shod with a full roller motion shoe. A polo shoe can be substituted for a full roller motion shoe.

When only a small chip is broken from the first or second phalanx, (Fig. 6–108) or one of these bones is split in a longitudinal direction, it sometimes is beneficial to correct the fracture surgically by applying one or more bone screws transversely through the fragments. The limb then should be cast as described above. Bone screws are beneficial only with minimal fragments. The opposite normal fetlock should be supported by elastic wraps to prevent injury from excess weight-bearing.

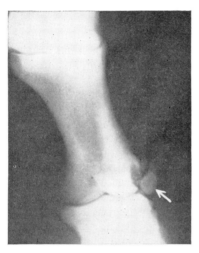

Fig. 6–108.—Chip fracture of the first phalanx. Fractures of this type may be repaired, if treated in the early stages, by use of a bone screw. (Carlson, *Veterinary Radiology*, Lea & Febiger.)

Clients should be advised not to shoe cutting horses and barrel racing horses with calks. Only flat plate shoes should be used in order to prevent the anchoring effect of calks.

PROGNOSIS.—If the first phalanx is fractured into the fetlock joint, the prognosis is unfavorable. If the second phalanx is fractured into the coffin joint, the prognosis also is unfavorable. If the pastern joint only is involved, the prognosis is guarded. Some horses can be returned to active use, while others can only be used as brood animals. The normal limb must be protected against excess weight-bearing.

7. Rachitic Ringbone (*see* Chapter 5, page 123)

DEFINITION.—Rachitic ringbone is a fibrous tissue enlargement of the pastern area of young horses. The disease usually develops before the horse reaches two years of age and is most common between six and twelve months of age. Clinically, the fibrous tissue swelling resembles new bone growth caused by true ringbone. In rachitic ringbone there are no bone or joint changes, other than fibrous tissue enlargement, around the pastern joint; therefore, this is not true ringbone or arthritis.

ETIOLOGY. — Rachitic ringbone is due to a deficiency of calcium, phosphorus, vitamin A, vitamin D, or possibly vitamin C, either singularly or in combination. Vitamin A, calcium, and phosphorus deficiencies most commonly are involved.

SIGNS. — Usually more than one foot is involved. In some foals both forefeet, both hindfeet, or possibly all four feet, are involved. Some lameness usually is exhibited and joint soreness is evident. Other symptoms, such as enlargement of the carpal joints, bog spavin, and contraction of flexor tendons also may be evident (see Chapter 5). Radiographs of the pastern areas will not reveal bony changes, but will show soft tissue swelling. On palpation, this swelling may be confused with new bone growth because of its firmness.

TREATMENT. — Determination of the deficient elements in the diet must be made by analysis of the ration and by blood chemistry tests. Once the deficiencies are determined, the diet should be corrected by addition of the deficient elements (see Chapter 5, page 129). If the diet correction is made early enough, the signs will regress and as the horse grows older the swellings will not be evident. However, other changes which may accompany rachitic ringbone can permanently disable the horse. Four to six weeks are required after diet correction for favorable changes to be evident.

PROGNOSIS. — Prognosis is guarded, but if the diagnosis is established early enough and the diet is corrected, a sound, mature condition can be obtained. If changes in the limbs are advanced at the time of the original examination, prognosis is guarded to unfavorable until the effect of the dietary correction can be determined.

8. Toe Cracks, Quarter Cracks, Heel Cracks (Sand Cracks)

DEFINITION. — These are cracks in the wall of the hoof, starting at the bearing surface of the wall and extending to a variable distance up the hoof wall, or cracks originating at the coronary band, as the result of a defect in the band, and extending downward. These cracks, identified as toe, quarter, or heel, depending upon their location in the hoof wall, may occur in either the front or hind feet.

ETIOLOGY. — Excessive growth of the hoof wall, causing a splitting of the wall, from lack of trimming of the feet, is a common cause. Injury to the coronary band, producing a weak and deformed hoof wall, will lead to cracks originating at the coronary band. Weakening of the wall due to excessive drying or excessively thin walls also causes hoof cracks.

SIGNS. — The presence of the split in the wall will be obvious. Lameness may not be present, but will become evident if the crack extends into the sensitive tissues, allowing infection to gain access to these structures. An exudate under the cracks or simple inflammation of the laminae may be present, depending upon the size of the opening into the sensitive tissues. The location of the crack will be obvious. Variable lesions will be found above the coronary band in those cases where the crack is due to injury of the band. Lesions may result from lacerated wounds or from other causes, such as over-reaching and interfering.

DIAGNOSIS. — The diagnosis is based on the presence of the crack which is easily identified, and is classified according to its location.

TREATMENT. — Treatment will depend upon the location of the crack.

Toe Crack. — For toe cracks, the hoof wall on the bearing surface should be lowered about 1 inch on either side of the crack. If the crack does not extend into the coronary band, a pattern should be grooved or burned into the crack (as shown in Fig. 6–109) to limit its upward progress. The horse should be shod with a toe clip on either

FIG. 6–109. — Correction for toe crack. Triangle and bar design below the coronary band is burned or cut in, as shown, to limit the extension of the crack. The hoof wall is trimmed away below the crack so that it will not bear weight on the shoe, as shown by *A*; *B* and *C* are the toe clips used on the shoe to support the wall so that the crack cannot expand under pressure.

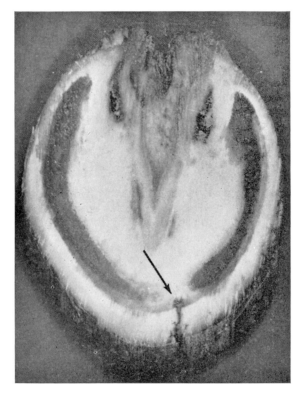

Fig. 6–110.—Section through foot to show depth of toe crack into sensitive tissues. Notice walled-off appearance around the laminae (arrow). This shows the need to fill some hoof cracks with plastics to protect the sensitive laminae and prevent abscess formation (courtesy Dr. K. J. Peterson).

side of the crack to prevent expansion of the wall (Fig. 6–109). Lowering of the wall from the bearing surface of the toe aids in preventing expansion of the crack. The crack should be thoroughly cleaned and tincture of iodine applied if it is determined that infection is present; tetanus antitoxin should be administered. An alternate method of treatment is to strip out the crack with an electric cast cutter, a hoof groover, or a firing iron. When treated in this manner, the crack is enlarged to about ¼ inch in width, and is opened down to, but not into, the sensitive laminae so that it can be filled with epoxy glue or plastic. Corrective shoeing should be applied as described above. If the horse is not shod but is allowed to go barefoot, the bearing surface of the wall on either side of the crack should be lowered and, whenever possible, a pattern or plastic filling to stop the progress of the crack should be used.

Quarter Crack.—For quarter cracks, the bearing surface of the hoof wall should be lowered posteriorly to the crack (as shown in Fig. 6–111). A half bar shoe should be applied with the bar on the heel of the affected side (Fig. 6–112). This bar should press against the frog with ⅛ to ¼ inch of pressure when the shoe is applied. This allows the frog to bear the weight that normally would be taken by the hoof wall which has already been lowered. A pattern should be used at the top of the crack (as shown in Fig. 6–111), if it does not extend into the coronary band. The corrective shoe also may have a quarter clip on either side of the crack to help prevent

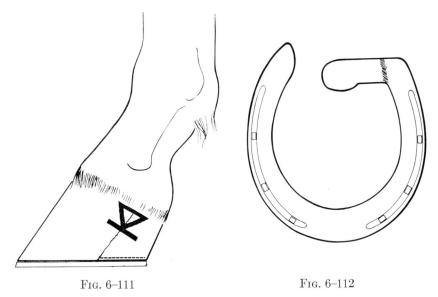

Fig. 6–111   Fig. 6–112

Fig. 6–111.—Quarter crack and correction. A triangle and bar design is burned or cut above the crack, as shown. The dotted line indicates the area of hoof wall which should be cut away so it will not bear weight on the shoe.

Fig. 6–112.—Ground surface view of a half bar shoe used in treating quarter crack and heel cracks. The bar is shaped so that it will apply one-eighth to one-fourth inch of pressure against the frog when the shoe is nailed on.

expansion of the crack (Fig. 6–73, page 272). Quarter cracks may be stripped to ¼ inch width down to the sensitive laminae, as described for toe crack and filled with epoxy glue or plastic. The wall may be thinned with a rasp over the area of the crack to make the wall more flexible. Corrective shoeing should be used with rasping of the wall. If the horse is not to be shod, the wall should be lowered posterior to the crack, and a pattern should be grooved over the crack to check its spread. Tetanus antitoxin should be administered if the crack extends into the sensitive tissues.

Heel Crack.—Heel cracks should be treated like quarter cracks, except it may not be necessary to apply a half bar to the heel of the shoe. The wall posterior to the crack should be lowered so that it does not touch the shoe or ground.

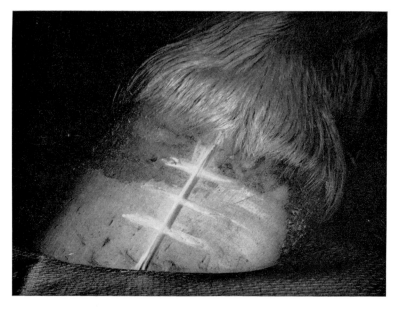

Fig. 6–113.—One method of preparing a quarter crack for filling with plastic. The crack has been widened and undermined so that the widest part is closest to the sensitive laminae. Transverse grooves are put along the crack, with the highest one close to the top of the crack. These grooves are also undermined so that they are wider near the sensitive laminae than they are near to the surface. This work is done with a motorized burr or a Stryker cast cutter.

Whenever the bearing surface of the wall is lowered from the shoe, in any type of crack, the space between the shoe and the wall should be cleaned daily with a hack saw blade to ensure that dirt does not fill the space and cause pressure. In all cases where it is believed that the crack has permitted infection to enter the sensitive tissues, tetanus antitoxin should be administered. When there are lacerations of the coronary band that have caused distorted growth of horn, the horn growth should be rasped every two weeks to keep it as nearly normal in shape as possible. Hard, dry areas on the coronary band should be rubbed daily with olive oil to keep them soft.

Any type of hoof crack or hoof defect can be treated by the use of plastics. Epoxy glues, fiberglass, or special hoof repair material* can be used. The crack must be thoroughly cleaned and undermined to aid holding the plastic in place. There are numerous ways to aid binding of the plastic and one is to enlarge and undermine the crack with a small motor tool burr or Stryker cast cutter, and then traverse the crack with horizontal grooves (Fig. 6–113). Cross drilling and lacing with umbilical tape prior to applying acrylic has been de-

* H. D. Justi Co., Philadelphia.

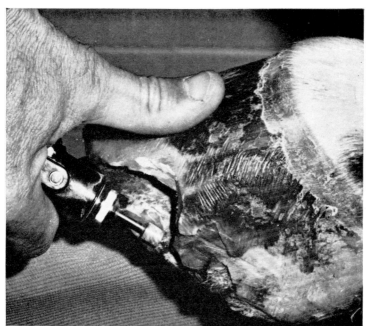

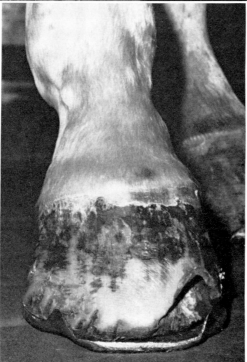

FIG. 6–114.—Top: Hoof defect being undermined with a motorized burr.
Bottom: Appearance of defect after it is prepared for plastic application. Note
shoe is in place with clips to help hold it. (Courtesy Dr. J. Jenny, Dr. L. Evans, and
A.A.E.P.)

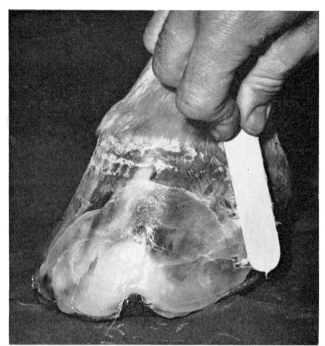

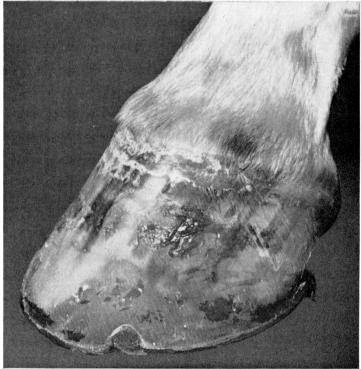

Fig. 6–115.—Top: Applying plastic to foot in Figure 6–114.
Bottom: Appearance of hoof defect after it is filled with plastic and the hoof
rasped to normal shape. (Courtesy Dr. J. Jenny, Dr. L. Evans and A.A.E.P.)

scribed by Evans.[1] The main thing is to give the plastic an anchor to keep it in place. Whatever type of plastic is used, the crack is painted with the catalyst first. The crack is then filled with the glue, fiberglass, or plastic material and allowed to harden. With fiberglass this process can be speeded up by adding more catalyst. After the material is hardened, it can be rasped to conform to the shape of the hoof wall.

Plastics are an excellent way to repair hoof cracks since they seal the crack and prevent infection of the sensitive tissues. Defects in the hoof wall can also be filled with such plastics (Figs. 6–114 and 115).

PROGNOSIS.—The prognosis is favorable if the crack originates at the bearing surface of the wall and if infection has not entered the foot. The prognosis is guarded if infection is present. In cases where the crack originates in defects of the coronary band, the etiology will be persistent so corrective shoeing may be necessary for the life of the horse. This makes the prognosis guarded to unfavorable. A considerable period may be necessary for the crack to grow out, because the wall grows approximately $\frac{1}{4}$ inch a month.

Infection of cracks may cause foot abscesses, which break and drain at the coronary band similar to "gravel."

SPECIFIC REFERENCES

1. EVANS, L. H., JENNY, J. J. and RAKER, C. W.: The Repair of Hoof Cracks with Acrylic. J.A.V.M.A., *148*, 355, 1966.
2. GRAHAM, C. W.: Postoperative Results from Plastic Hoof Repair. Proc. 11th Ann. A.A.E.P., 1965.
3. JENNY, J.: Application of Plaster Cast and Plastic Repair of the Hoof. Proc. 9th Ann. A.A.E.P. 237, 1963.
4. JENNY, J. and EVANS, L. H.: Self-Curing Acrylic Plastics for Hoof Repair. Penn. Vet., *6*, 6, 1964.
5. KEOWN, G.: Quarter Cracks. Proc. 8th Ann. A.A.E.P., 143, 1962.

9. Gravel

DEFINITION.—Gravel is a lay term for what supposedly is a migration of a piece of gravel from the white line to the heel area. This does not occur; what does happen is that a crack in the white line permits infection to invade the sensitive structures. Because there is no drainage, inflammation follows the line of least resistance and drainage occurs at the heel area as it does with puncture wounds that cannot drain through the sole.

ETIOLOGY.—A crack in the white line, or in the sole, may occur in feet that are excessively dry. In addition, chronic laminitis with its associated "seedy toe," causing a poorly defined seal in the toe area of the white line, may cause this condition. The sole and white line should be carefully examined to determine the real cause.

SIGNS.—Lameness usually will appear before drainage at the heel area occurs, but the condition may go undiagnosed until after drainage takes place. Signs of lameness vary according to severity

23

of the infection and location of the entry of infection. The horse will modify his gait, as described in puncture wounds of the foot, according to the location of the entry. Careful examination of the white line and sole will reveal black spots which should be probed to their depth. Examination with a hoof tester will determine the approximate area of penetration. If the black areas are probed to their depth, one will be found that penetrates into the sensitive laminae. After the depth of the crack has been probed, pus often will exude from the wound. When the condition has been present some time, the heel area will drain at the coronary band. Systemic reaction to the infection varies, but in most cases infection remains localized.

The horse will show a supporting leg lameness. If routine examination with a hoof tester is made on all lameness cases, some cases can be diagnosed prior to drainage occurring at the heel.

DIAGNOSIS.—Diagnosis is made by careful examination of the foot with a hoof tester. All cases of lameness should have this examination. Most cases can be diagnosed before the heel area breaks and drains, providing the owner seeks help in time. Careful observation of the way the horse sets his foot on the ground will be helpful in localizing the area of penetration.

TREATMENT.—Treatment consists of establishing proper drainage for the infection, as described in puncture wounds of the foot. Soaking of the foot in epsom salts may be used even if heel drainage has not begun. Applying tincture of iodine to the drainage area in the sole and bandaging the foot until it is healed are necessary. Antiphlogistic pastes can also be used under the bandage. Tetanus antitoxin always should be administered. After the first week of involvement bandaging of the foot may be delayed to once every three or four days providing it stays dry.

PROGNOSIS.—Prognosis is favorable if the condition is diagnosed before drainage at the heel occurs, except in those cases where the foot is subject to recurrence of the condition because of chronic laminitis. The prognosis is guarded if drainage at the heel already has occurred. Careful treatment though will permit many of these horses to be returned to complete soundness. If the condition is of long standing, prognosis is unfavorable because permanent changes already may have occurred.

10. Thrush

DEFINITION.—Thrush, a degenerative condition of the frog involving the central and lateral sulci, is characterized by the presence of a black necrotic material in the affected areas. The infection may penetrate the horny tissues and involve the sensitive structures.

ETIOLOGY.—The predisposing causes of thrush are unhygienic conditions, (especially when horses are kept in poorly managed stalls or filthy surroundings), dirty, uncleaned feet, and lack of frog pressure resulting from poor shoeing or poor foot trimming. Many organisms probably are involved, but *Spherophorus necrophorus* is the most important of these.

SIGNS.—There is an increased amount of moisture and a black discharge in the sulci of the frog. This discharge which varies in quantity has a very offensive odor. When the affected sulci are cleaned, it will be found that they are deeper than normal and may extend into the sensitive tissues of the foot causing the horse to flinch when they are cleaned. The frog will be undermined, and large areas of it may require removal because of the loss of continuity with the underlying frog. In severe cases which have penetrated into the sensitive structure of the foot, the horse may be lame and the foot may show the same signs of infection that would be encountered in puncture wound of the foot.

DIAGNOSIS.—Diagnosis is based on the odor and physical characteristics of the black discharge in the sulci of the frog.

TREATMENT.—Treatment is cleanliness, removal of the cause, and return of the frog and hoof to normal conformation and condition. The foot should be cleaned daily and the cleft of the frog packed with a proper medication. Some medications that may be used include equal parts of phenol and iodine, tincture of iodine, 10 per cent formalin, and others. The best treatment consists of packing the sulci with cotton soaked in 10 to 15 per cent *sodium* sulfapyridine solution. This treatment, which is very effective, should be repeated until the infection is controlled.

The cause can be removed by placing the horse in cleaner surroundings, or by daily cleansing of the frog, after removal of the debris. Degenerated frog tissues should be removed and an effort should be made to return the frog to normal by cleaning up all infection. A bar shoe may be applied to exert pressure to the frog until it returns to normal size.

Some veterinarians recommend blistering of the heel areas to stimulate growth of the frog. In some cases it may be necessary to protect the foot with a leather boot to prevent contamination. This is especially true if the sensitive tissues are involved. The hoof wall should be lowered as far as possible to stimulate frog pressure, but normal foot axis should not be changed.

PROGNOSIS.—The prognosis is favorable if the disease is diagnosed before extensive damage to the foot has occurred. It is guarded if the sensitive structures are involved.

11. Wounds

Wounds are classified as follows:

Open Wounds.—A. *Incised Wounds.*—These are wounds produced by sharp objects, but where tissue damage is at a minimum. Very little bruising to underlying structures has occurred, and hemorrhage is not severe unless a large vessel has been cut. Separation of wound edges usually is at a minimum, unless the wound is deep, or severs the lines of tension. A minimum amount of pain is present, and the chief danger is damage to underlying vital structures.

B. *Lacerated Wounds.*—These wounds are usually produced by irregular objects, such as barbed wire, and by horn gores and bites. This type of wound is characterized by extensive damage to underlying tissues, especially to the skin and subcutaneous connective tissue. It may be accompanied by abrasion or contusion. Hemorrhage usually is not profuse, unless large vessels are opened, because the vessels often are torn, and there is a marked constriction of arteries. Pain usually is marked, and the greatest danger is infection, with pockets of pus, tissue necrosis, and gangrene, if tissues are torn away from the blood supply.

C. *Puncture Wounds.*—These wounds are produced by sharp objects whose length exceeds their diameter, and are characterized by small, superficial punctures with a considerable amount of deep injury. They often are produced by bites, horn gores, nail punctures, and objects such as pitchforks.

Puncture wounds are further classified as:

    1. *Penetrating*—goes into a body cavity.
    2. *Perforating*—goes into a body cavity and back out.
    3. *Stab*—goes into deep tissue only.

D. *Burns.*—(Burns will not be considered in this discussion.)

Closed Wounds.—Closed or subcutaneous wounds are those in which the skin is not broken through all layers. They are caused by external violence which results in tissue damage without loss of continuity of the skin. At a later date, necrosis or sloughing may take place. Closed wounds are classified as:

A. *Wheal.*—This is a bleb in the skin, usually interdermal; no hemorrhagic extravasation is present.

B. *Abrasions.*—These are injuries to the superficial surface of the skin or mucous membrane where the epidermis is damaged, but the damage has not extended through all the skin layers or the mucous membrane. These cause oozing of serum and a small amount of hemorrhage. A scab forms over the area of abrasion and constitutes a form of second intention healing.

C. *Contusions.*—Contusions are caused by a trauma which causes a rupture of subcutaneous or deep blood vessels. The skin is not broken but subcutaneous hemorrhage occurs. Contusions are classified as follows:

    1. *First Degree Contusion.* Here there is some hemorrhage into, and under, the skin producing discoloration, but very little hematoma.

    2. *Second Degree Contusion.* This is a hematoma; if it is small it probably will be absorbed. If it is large, it may lead to formation of scar tissue and possible blemish. It also may lead to a seroma, after blood cells of the clot are absorbed; the serum remains. This type of contusion most commonly results from kicks over the area of the hip and gluteal region and from rubbing on the brisket region. There is some danger of abscess formation from hematogenous origin.

3. *Third Degree Contusion.* These are so severe they damage the tissue beyond repair. The skin is not broken from the original blow but thrombosis of the vessels occurs underneath the skin and sloughing of the superficial areas occurs.

DIAGNOSIS.—Diagnosis of a closed wound usually is relatively simple. However, in some cases it may be confused with hernia or abscess, so the swelling always should be tapped, under aseptic procedure, to determine the contents. This is especially important for those hematomas that occur over the abdominal wall and thus must be differentiated from hernia.

The chief danger of all wounds is injury and/or infection to deep structures, especially joint capsules, sensitive portions of the foot, tendon sheaths, blood vessels, and nerves. Lack of free drainage and spread of infection may enhance this danger. Malignant edema and tetanus may be sequelae to wounds and prophylactic treatment should be used against diseases resulting from wounds that develop anaerobic conditions. Healing of a superficial part of the wound, which traps infection underneath, may lead to an abscess or cellulitis. In other cases, undetected foreign bodies may be left in a wound, later to cause abscessation and sinus tracts.

CONDITIONS INTERFERING WITH HEALING OF WOUNDS.—1. *Interference with Circulation.*—In the vicinity of the wound due to swelling, improper bandaging, laceration, prolonged infection and exuberant granulation tissue.

2. *Invasive Infection.*—Infection causing phlegmon or cellulitis will interfere with healing. Drainage should always be established if infection is present. Failure to use aseptic procedures in dressing wounds may be the cause of this type of infection.

3. *Devitalized Tissue.*—Gapping of wounds leads to drying and will cause tissue to be devitalized. Any tissue that is pulled away from circulation will also be devitalized and undergo necrosis. A triangular skin flap with the apex of the flap pointed toward the incoming blood supply will usually lose the apex portion of the triangle, due to loss of blood supply.

4. *Inadequate Drainage for Collection of Blood and Discharges in the Wound.*—Inadequate drainage interferes with circulation and forms an ideal medium for growth of bacteria. Hemorrhage should be controlled by ligation to prevent this type of accumulation.

5. *Foreign Bodies.*—Any foreign body in the wound will interfere with healing and cause a sinus tract drainage.

6. *Continued Trauma to the Wound.*—This is usually due to lack of restraint allowing the horse to abuse the wound area. Ideally a wound is immobilized to aid healing. In the lower limb this can be done by means of a plaster cast or a corrective shoe.

7. *Subcutaneous Air.*—Subcutaneous air will produce devitalization of tissue by separating the skin from the underlying structures. Wounds of the axillary space are especially prone to development of subcutaneous air. In some cases subcutaneous air is due to the type of organism present; i.e., *Clostridium septicum* (malignant edema). This is an unfavorable development.

8. *The Effect of Wound Medications.*—Wound medications often are more detrimental than helpful in the healing of the wound. Irritant antiseptics and drugs should be avoided in all cases. Such drugs as copper sulfate, antimony trichloride (butter of antimony), and alum are irritant. Although these products will destroy superficial exuberant granulation tissue, they irritate the deep tissues so that the end result is a wound with more subcutaneous fibrous tissue present than would have resulted if the wound had been treated properly. If exuberant granulation tissue is present, it should be surgically removed by scalpel or cautery. It is then kept under a pressure bandage with a corticoid and antibiotic ointment till the wound is healed. Bandages should be changed frequently enough to avoid irritation. Wet bandages containing wound discharges will delay healing. In most cases a bandage should not be allowed to stay in place for longer than three days. Contamination should always be avoided when applying a dressing.

9. *Nutrition.*—Poor nutrition of the horse will delay healing of a wound. Parasitism, bad teeth, and inadequate feeding may contribute to delayed wound healing. All these factors should be considered when poor condition is present.

TREATMENT OF LACERATED AND INCISED WOUNDS.—The horse, more than other species of animal, must have proper care in treatment of wounds. Mistreatment will result in exuberant granulation, excessive scarring, blemishing, and sometimes unsoundness. Wounds below the carpus and tarsus are especially sensitive, so require careful treatment to prevent complications. Tetanus antitoxin should always be administered if the horse is not on a toxoid program. Toxoid should be given as a booster when the horse has been immunized previously with this product.

Hemorrhage should be controlled by ligation and/or torsion of the vessels, and the wound should be thoroughly cleansed. Hair on the edges of the wound should be shaved for at least $\frac{1}{2}$ inch away from the wound edge. Such hair will irritate the wound and may produce enough irritation to cause exuberant granulation tissue. Following shaving, the skin edges should be painted with a skin antiseptic and the wound injected with a local anesthetic such as 2 per cent procaine or 2 per cent lidocaine hydrochloride. The distal fragment of the wound requires very little local anesthesia because it is torn from the nerve supply. The proximal fragment, though, will be most sensitive. In conjunction with local anesthesia, the horse may be tranquilized with promazine $\frac{1}{2}$ mg. per pound body weight, to facilitate treatment.

Debridement of all wounds must be done fully and carefully. All dirt, hair, and tissues obviously torn from the blood supply must be removed from the wound. The tissues of a horse tend to waterlog when cleansed with ordinary water, so it is recommended that normal saline solution be used. Using sterile gauze sponges and saline, the wound should be thoroughly cleaned so that a healthy surface is present. In all cases, care must be used to avoid increasing contamination of the wound, so rubber gloves are called for. Local antibiotics, such as penicillin-streptomycin mixture used for intramuscular injection, can be placed in a wound or injected into the tissues around a wound.

Any fresh incised or lacerated wound that lends itself to suturing should be sutured. This is especially true if the wound is below the carpus and the tarsus. Fresh wounds often will show remarkable healing qualities if properly debrided and sutured. However, this means that the wound must be handled properly. All deep muscular layers should be sutured with catgut, while the skin should be sutured with a nonabsorbable, noncapillary suture. In areas of considerable skin tension, the suture lines should be reinforced with the quill-type suture. Skin often tears with triangular-shaped flaps. If the apex of the triangle points toward the blood supply, the tip of the flap is often lost. However, it is worthwhile suturing to minimize skin loss.

If it is obvious that there is going to be pocketing of the wound permitting the accumulation of discharges, ventral drainage should be established. Some wounds do require this drainage, but the wound still should be sutured and ventral drainage established. If it is not possible to suture a wound because the skin surface has been torn away or because duration or swelling does not permit apposition, debridement and a counter-pressure bandage with proper topical medication is recommended. A counter-pressure bandage helps keep wound edges in apposition; it should be used until the wound is nearly healed, especially for wounds below the carpus and tarsus. If the pressure is removed, exuberant granulation tissue tends to develop. Bandages should be changed often enough so that exudate cannot accumulate and irritate the wound area.

Early medication under the bandage should consist of nonirritating ointments containing antibiotics. Mastitis ointments often are used. After a granulating surface is present, application of an ointment containing a corticoid is recommended. This type of ointment, plus counter-pressure bandaging, prevents exuberant granulation tissue. Bandages should become progressively lighter to permit air to the wound.

Wounds that sometimes are impractical to suture, such as those in the upper forearm where sutures tear out, can be treated very nicely by shaving and cleansing the wound and by daily application of a soothing wound ointment that contains no irritants.

Wounds below the carpus and the tarsus, which are so small that bandaging is not required, should be treated daily with agents that tend to retard granulation tissue, such as 2 per cent picric acid, 2 per cent tannic acid, and triple dye* following shaving and cleansing.

Wounds on the coronary band or the volar aspect of the pastern region, sometimes are treated by applying a plaster cast over the sutured wound area. Since immobilizing a wound is one of the

*A combination of brilliant green, acriflavine and gentian violet in an alcohol base.

fundamentals of wound therapy, a plaster cast does an excellent job of promoting first intention healing. As long as the sutures remain intact, discharges will be minimal, providing the wound has been properly treated. The cast should be removed in seven to ten days to check on results, and if necessary a new one applied.

Wire cuts involving the coronary band require that the wound edges be in close apposition to heal. Otherwise granulating surfaces that have no tendency to unite will develop. These wounds either must be sutured or kept under pressure bandage until healing is nearly complete. Application of an ointment containing antibiotics and a corticoid under the bandage is recommended. A horseshoe nail may be driven into the toe of the wall to help anchor the gauze bandage so considerable pressure can be applied against the lacerated tissues.

When a joint capsule or a tendon sheath is opened, as the result of a wound, corticoids, plus a penicillin-streptomycin mixture, should be injected into the joint or tendon sheath. The capsule or sheath and the overlying tissues should be sutured if it is a fresh wound. The leg then should be kept in a snug bandage and parenteral antibiotics should be given for four to seven days.

Most common mistreatment of open wounds includes permitting wounds below the carpus and the tarsus to heal without counterpressure bandage or sutures, improper cleansing, failing to shave the hair from the wound area, and application of irritant drugs. In no case should caustic or irritant drugs be applied to wounds of horses. Caustic drugs will remove superficial areas of granulation tissue, but at the same time they irritate and stimulate underlying tissues so that this tissue grows back in a short time. Continued irritation may cause a non-healing wound, exuberant granulation tissue, or excessive fibrosis of the healed wound, causing a permanent blemish. Topical application of ointments containing a corticoid are much better for this purpose since they relieve inflammation, and, combined with pressure bandages, are of considerable aid in preventing exuberant granulation tissue. If removal of large amounts of granulation tissue is required, it is best done surgically. Following surgical removal, counter-pressure bandaging, and application of ointments containing antibiotics and a corticoid, are recommended.

TREATMENT OF PUNCTURE WOUNDS.—Puncture wounds are dangerous in horses, since they may lead to malignant edema, cellulitis, or tetanus. Tetanus antitoxin always should be administered unless the horse is on a toxoid program, and parenteral antibiotics usually are recommended. This type of wound may penetrate a tendon sheath or a joint capsule. The wound opening should be properly cleansed and shaved, and the wound flushed daily with antibiotic ointments, such as those used in treating mastitis.

A puncture wound on the forearm, or above the hock, often causes the distal portion of the leg to become enlarged with edema. This edema may be due to the gravitational effects of the inflammation, or to developing cellulitis. Soaking of this type of wound in magnesium sulfate is recommended because of the action of the drug in reducing swelling. The wound opening should be covered with a light bandage, so it is not exposed, and a poultice of Denver Mud* or other satisfactory antiphlogistic paste should be applied under the bandage. Parenteral and local antibiotic medication should be continued until the wound obviously is healing properly. It sometimes is necessary to establish ventral drainage.

A chronic, draining sinus tract in horses in the area of the limbs very often is due to a retained foreign body resulting from a puncture wound. This possibility must be eliminated. Radiographs will not reveal foreign bodies which are composed of wood or other soft materials.

TREATMENT OF CLOSED WOUNDS.—Minor closed wounds, such as wheal, seldom require treatment. They usually are caused by insect bites or stings, and antihistamines are the usual form of therapy. Abrasions are treated by cleansing of the wounds with normal saline, soap and brush. A moist antiseptic dressing should be applied, usually in the form of an ointment. These ointments should be continued to keep the scab soft as the lesion heals. If infection develops under the scab, the scab should be removed and antibiotic ointments applied. Abrasions also may be treated with drugs such as triple dye, and acriflavine 1:1000.

Contusions of the second and third degree are those that usually require therapy. For second degree contusions, cold packs should be applied to stop hemorrhage and limit the extent of the hematoma. After the clot has formed, the serum may be drained in an attempt to obtain union of the skin with the subcutaneous tissue. However, in many cases, union does not occur, so to obtain healing drainage must be established by incision. Daily swabbing of the lesion with tincture of iodine should be used to irritate the two surfaces. It is important that the drainage be ventral and that it remain until the wound heals to prevent continual separation of the skin and subcutaneous tissue by serum accumulation.

Third degree contusions usually will slough a localized area of tissue. All that can be done is to trim out necrotic tissue, keep the wound clean, and prevent infection by local antibiotic ointment.

REFERENCES FOR WOUNDS

1. DAVIS, L.: *Christopher's Textbook of Surgery.* 7th ed., Philadelphia, W. B. Saunders Co., 1960.
2. FORMSTON, C.: Wound Management. 3rd Ann. Cong. B.E.V.A., 3, 1964.
3. FRANK, E. R.: *Veterinary Surgery.* 7th ed., Minneapolis, Burgess Pub. Co., 1964.
4. GUARD, W. F.: *Surgical Principles and Techniques.* Published by the author, 1953.
5. ROBERTS, W. D.: Equine Wound Management. Vet. Med., *57*, 773, 1962.
6. ————: Wound Management in Ranch Horses. Proc. 8th Ann. A.A.E.P. 33, 1962.

*Demco, Inc., Denver, Colorado.

12. Equine Sarcoid

DEFINITION.—Equine sarcoid is a recurring granulation tissue
that affects equines. Sarcoid is most common following wounds of
the lower part of the limb, but may involve the head, neck or prepuce.
It is usually characterized by a raw, granulating surface that is
somewhat mushroomed shaped in that the base of attachment is
usually smaller than the granulating surface, or it may appear as
a wart-like growth.

ETIOLOGY.—Etiology has not been definitely proven but it is very
suspicious that this disease is due to an infectious agent such as a
virus.[4] The lesions have been transmitted from horse to horse, and
Olson[3] has produced similar lesions with bovine wart virus.

SIGNS.—Equine sarcoid is difficult to differentiate from ordinary
exuberant granulation tissue. The tendency to recur following
surgical removal is indicative of the disease. It often has a mush-
room type of growth with a small base of attachment compared to
the large raw granulating surface. Sarcoid is common in wounds
below the carpus and tarsus. Wounds that occur in areas where
motion is present seem especially susceptible to this lesion. It
rarely develops when a wound has been treated properly by means of
proper non-irritating medications, pressure bandages and plaster
cast. Sarcoid can occur spontaneously without previous trauma to
the skin. Histologically it is characterized by irregularly arranged
fibroblasts with larger than normal nuclei and frequent mitotic
figures that tend to form whorls. Proliferation of epithelium with
extension and branching of rete pegs into the tumor mass is present.
The histology is also similar to exuberant granulation tissue of
fibrosarcoma.

TREATMENT.—Equine sarcoid should be surgically removed and
the base cauterized by electrocautery when necessary to control
hemorrhage or to kill cells that were not removed surgically. It is
removed down to skin level and hemorrhage stopped by means of
pressure bandage or thermocautery since hemorrhage is profuse
when removing this type of lesion. If cobalt 60 therapy is available,
it is one of the more successful methods of treatment. Three
thousand to 4,000 roentgens of gamma ray radiation with this are
used after surgical removal. When the lesion is over the carpus, near
a carpal bone, the radiation dosage is reduced to 2000 R because of
possible damage to the carpal bones.[1] Whether or not radiation
therapy is available, the sarcoid area should be kept clean and all
hair kept shaved away from the wound every ten days to two weeks.
A corticoid ointment containing antibiotics is applied to the surface
of the lesion and a pressure bandage applied using conforming gauze*
and elastic tape† until the wound is healed. The bandage is changed at
intervals of two to three days, and must be used until healing is
complete. If the bandage is discontinued prior to complete healing,

* Kling, Johnson & Johnson
† Elastikon, Johnson & Johnson Co.

the sarcoid may recur. Sarcoid on the head and neck are removed by elliptical surgical incision, sutured, and bandaged as effectively as possible. If the lesions begin to recur, a corticoid ointment containing antibiotic is used daily on the wound. If available, cobalt needles can be implanted into these areas for radiation therapy. The use of bovine wart vaccine and a killed vaccine made from the lesions of a horse affected with sarcoid have given variable results. In some cases vaccines of this type may suppress or inhibit growth of sarcoids.

SPECIFIC REFERENCES

1. GILLETTE, E. L.: Clinical Radiologist, Colorado State University. Personal communication, 1966.
2. LEWIS, R. E.: Radon Implant Therapy of Squamous Cell Carcinoma and Equine Sarcoid. Proc. 10th Ann. A.A.E.P., 217, 1964.
3. OLSON, C.: Equine Medicine and Surgery, p. 121. Santa Barbara, Calif., American Veterinary Publications, Inc., 1963.
4. VOSS, J. L.: Transmission of Equine Sarcoid. Thesis, Colorado State University, 1965.
5. VOSS, J. L.: Equine Sarcoid Transmission. Proc. 11th. Ann. A.A.E.P., 1965.

REFERENCES FOR CHAPTER 6

Each of the following references describes several types of lameness, but was not listed in the bibliography following each section because this would have resulted in needless repetition. References for a specific lameness are not listed here, but can be found at the end of each section.

1. ADAMS, O. R.: Local Anesthesia as an Aid to Diagnosis of Lameness. Norden News, Jan. 1966.
2. ————: Veterinary Notes on Lameness and Shoeing of Horses. Published by the author, 1957.
3. ALGER, CHENOT: Clinical Study of Lameness. Am. Vet. Rev., 28, 806, 1904–05.
4. ARANEZ, J. B. et al.: Preliminary Observations on the Incidence of Leg Ailments Among Race Horses in the Philippines. Philippines J. Vet. Med., 1, 1962.
5. AXE, J. WORTLEY: The Horse in Health and Disease. 3 vols., London, Gresham Publishing Co., about 1900.
6. BAIRD, JOHN: Lameness and Its Treatment in the Horse. J.A.V.M.A., 83, 39, 1933.
7. BELL, ROSCOE: Shoulder Lameness in the Horse. Am. Vet. Rev., 23, 477, 1899.
8. BLOOD, D. C. and HENDERSEN, J. A.: Veterinary Medicine, 2nd ed., Baltimore, Williams & Wilkins, 1963.
9. BRENNAN, B. F.: The Veterinarian in Race Track Practice. Vet. Scope 3, summer 1958.
10. CAMPBELL, D. M.: Shifting Lameness in the Horse. Vet. Med., 29, 29, 1934.
11. CARLSON, W. D.: Veterinary Radiology, Philadelphia, Lea & Febiger, 1961.
12. CAWLEY, A. J.: Radiology V. Canad. Vet. J., 1, 554, 1960.
13. CHAPMAN, GEORGE T.: Lameness in the Horse. New York, Wm. R. Jenkins Co., 1901.
14. CHURCHILL, E. A.: The Causes of Lameness. Bloodhorse, 85, 602, 1963.
15. CHURCHILL, E. A. et al.: Panel on Orthopedic Surgery. Proceedings Fifth Annual Am. Assoc. Equine Practitioners, 1959.
16. COCHRAN, DAVID: Lameness of the Hip Joint. Am. Vet. Rev., 44, 491, 1914.
17. ————: Stifle Lameness. Am. Vet. Rev., 42, 308, 1912–13.
18. CRAWFORD, H. C.: Equine Lameness: A Brief Resume. N.A.V., 12, 29, 1932.

19. ———: Radiography: Its Limitations as an Aid to the Diagnostician of Lameness. N.A.V., *13*, 39, 1932.
20. Danks, A. G.: *Williams' Surgical Operations*. Ithaca, N. Y., Published by the author, 1943.
21. Daubigny, F. T.: Halting or Lameness in the Horse. J.A.V.M.A., *19*, 648, 1916.
22. Davidson, A. H.: *Lameness, Firing, Etc.* Third Annual Stud Managers Course, Lexington, Ky., 1953.
23. ———: *Lameness.* Fourth Annual Stud Managers Course, Lexington, Ky., 1954.
24. Delahanty, D. D. *et al.*: *Orthopedic Surgery in the Horse—A Panel Discussion.* Proceedings Fourth Annual Am. Assoc. of Equine Practitioners, 1958.
25. Dixon, R. T.: The Nature of Injuries Causing Foot Lameness in Fast-Gaited Horses. Aust. Vet. J., *39*, 177, 1963.
26. Dykstra, R. R.: Anatomical Changes in Lameness of the Horse. J.A.V.M.A., *71*, 425, 1927.
27. Equine Lameness Review. Vet. Med., *56*, 165, 1961.
28. *Equine Medicine and Surgery*, 68 authors, Santa Barbara, Calif., Amer. Vet. Pub. Inc., 1963.
29. Fowler, G. R.: Diseases of the Foot of the Horse. Vet. Med., *33*, 216, 1938.
30. Fowler, W. J. R.: Diagnosis and Treatment of Lamenesses. Can. J. Comp. Med., *3*, 91, 1939.
31. Ibid: *4*, 249, 1940.
32. Frank, E. R.: Obscure Lameness, N.A.V., *18*, 39, 1937.
33. ———: *Veterinary Surgery.* 7th ed., Minneapolis, Burgess Publishing Co., 1964.
34. Gibson, S. J.: Lameness in Horses. Can. J. Comp. Med., *9*, 103, 1945.
35. Gray, T. E.: Foot Lameness in the Horse. Mod. Vet. Pract., *42*, 38, 1961.
36. Grenside, F. C.: Why Horses are Oftener Lame in Front Than Behind. Am. Vet. Rev., *35*, 43, 1909.
37. Guard, W. F.: *Surgical Principles and Techniques*, Columbus, Ohio. Published by the author, 1953.
38. Hanshew, E., Jr.: Dropped Elbow in the Horse. A.V.R., *21*, 411, 1897–98.
39. Hayes, Isaac E.: Shoulder Lameness in the Horse. Vet. Med., *42*, 249, 1947.
40. Hoare, W. E.: Discussion of Ephemeral (Transient) Lameness. J.A.V.M.A., *9*, 113, 1914.
41. Hume, Wm.: Neurectomy in Foot Lameness. J.A.V.M.A., *8*, 115, 1913.
42. Jenny, J.: Hoof Repair with Plastics. Proc. 9th Ann. A.A.E.P., 137, 1963.
43. ———: Management of Bone and Joint Injuries in the Horse. Vet. Scope VI, 1961.
44. Johnson, L. E. *et al.*: *Equine Radiology; A Panel Discussion.* Sixth Annual Meeting, Am. Assoc. Equine Practitioners, pp. 35–64, 1960.
45. Jubb, K. V. F. and Kennedy, P. C.: Pathology of Domestic Animals, Vols. 1 and 2, New York, Academic Press, 1963.
46. Kiernan, John: *Hints on Horseshoeing.* Office of the Library of Congress, Washington, D. C., 1894.
47. La Croix, J. V.: Lameness of the Horse. Amer. J. Vet. Med., Chicago, 1916.
48. Liautard, A.: *Lameness of Horses.* New York, Wm. R. Jenkins Co., 1888.
49. Lundvall, R. L.: Lameness of the Upper Hind Leg. Iowa Sate Univ. Vet., *29*, 7, 1961–62.
50. ———: *Problems in A Pony Practice.* Proceedings Fifth Annual Association of Equine Practitioners, 1959.
51. Mackay-Smith, M. P. and Raker, C. W.: Mechanical Defects on the Equine Stifle—Diagnosis and Treatment. Scientific Proceedings 100th Annual Meeting, A.V.M.A., 80–85, 1963.
52. Maqsood, M.: Thrombosis of the Iliac Arteries in Race Horses. Indian Vet. J., *20*, 133, 1944.
53. McCunn, James: Lameness in the Horse with Special Reference to Surgical Shoeing. Vet. Record, *63*, 629, 1951.
54. McDonough, J.: Hock Joint Lameness. Am. Vet. Rev., *43*, 629, 1913.
55. ———: Lameness and Its Most Common Cause. J.A.V.M.A., *49*, 653, 1916.

56. McGee, W. R.: *Veterinary Notebook*. Lexington, Ky. The Blood Horse, 1958.
57. ————: *Veterinary Notes for the Standardbred Breeder*. Columbus, Ohio, U.S. Trotting Assoc. No publishing date.
58. McKinney, W. J.: Mechanical Lameness. Am. Vet. Rev., *39*, 288, 1911.
59. Meginnis, Paul: Myostitis in Race Horses. J.A.V.M.A., *130*, 237, 1957.
60. Merck & Co.: *The Merck Veterinary Manual*. 2nd ed. Rahway, N.J., 1961.
61. Milch, R. A., Burke, G. J., Frock, I. W.: Surgical Management of Degenerative Joint Disease in the Race Horse. J.A.V.M.A., *141*, 1276, 1962.
62. Milne, F. J. *et al.*: Panel on Lameness. Proc. A.A.E.P., p. 259, 1964.
63. O'Connor, J. J.: *Dollar's Veterinary Surgery*. 4th ed, London, Bailliere, Tindall & Cox, 1952.
64. O'Connor, J. T.: *Standardbred Lameness*. Proceedings Fourth Annual Am. Assoc. Equine Practitioners, 1958.
65. Pearson *et al.*: *Diseases of the Horse*. USDA, 1942.
66. Peters, J. E.: Lameness Incident to Training and Racing of the Thoroughbred. J.A.V.M.A., *96*, 200, 1940.
67. Pope, G. W.: The Diagnosis and Treatment of Lameness. Am. Vet. Rev., *28*, 952, 1908.
68. Pritchard, G. C.: Mechanical Treatment of Lameness. Am. Vet. Rev., *21*, 25, 1898.
69. Raker, C. W.: Clinico-Pathologic Conference. J.A.V.M.A., *143*, 1115, 1963.
70. Reed, W. O. *et al.*: Panel on Equine Lameness. 8th Ann. A.A.E.P. Proc., 191, 1962.
71. Reeks, H. C.: *The Horse's Foot*. Chicago, Alex. Eger Pub. Co., 1918.
72. Roberts, E. J.: Carpal Lameness. Third Annual Congress. British Eq. Vet. Assoc., 18, 1964.
73. Rooney, J. R.: Pathology of Equine Lameness. Proc. 9th Ann. A.A.E.P., 45, 1963.
74. Smith, H. A. and Jones, T. C.: *Veterinary Pathology*, 3rd ed. Philadelphia, Lea & Febiger, 1966.
75. Smythe, R. H.: *Clinical Veterinary Surgery. Vol. 1*, London, C. Lockwood & Son, 1959.
76. Ibid: *Vol. 2*, Springfield, Charles C Thomas, 1960.
77. Sturge, E.: Penetrant Cauterization in the Treatment of Lameness from Ostitis. Am. Vet. Rev., *18*, 205, 1984.
78. Teigland, M. B. *et al.*: *Orthopedic Surgery*. Sixth Annual Am. Assoc. Equine Practitioners, 1960.
79. Vaughan, J. T.: Analysis of Lameness in the Pelvic Limb and Selected Cases. Proc. 11th Ann. A.A.E.P., 1965.
80. Wheat, J. D.: Hypertrophy of Synovial Membranes. Proc. 8th Ann. A.A.E.P., 208, 1962.
81. ————: Trochlear Fractures of the Tibiotarsal Bone. Proc. 9th Ann. A.V.M.A. Convention, 86–87, 1963.
82. Wheat, J. D. and Rhode, A.: Luxation and Fracture of the Hock of the Horse. J.A.V.M.A., *145*, 341, 1964.
83. White, G. R.: Shifting Lameness. Am. Vet. Rev., *34*, 482, 1908.
84. Williams, W.: *The Principles and Practice of Veterinary Surgery*, New York, Wm. R. Jenkins & Co., 1891.
85. Wright, J. G.: *Veterinary Anesthesia*. 4th ed., Baltimore, The Williams & Wilkins Co., 1957.
86. Wyman, W. E. A.: *Diagnosis of Lameness in the Horse*, New York, Wm. R. Jenkins Co., 1898.

Classification of horseshoes and horseshoe nails

Chapter 7

Horse shoes are classified in several ways, and sizes vary with different types of shoes. Shoes are sometimes classified as iron or aluminum shoes. Iron shoes are any type shoe made of iron, and used on a working horse, including a steel racing shoe which is very light. Aluminum shoes are made primarily for racing horses.

Various iron shoes come in different weights as follows: extra extra light, extra light, and light. The extra extra light shoe is used most commonly. Iron shoes are available in plate shoes, cowboy shoes, pony shoes, keg shoes, mule shoes, and several other types. Iron shoes also can be purchased or made with a variation of heel calks and toe calks or "toe grabs." They can be handmade in any form for corrective shoeing. Cowboy and plate shoes usually are sized from 00 to size 8. A size 00 shoe is the smallest, while size 8 is the largest. Sizes 00, 0, and 1 are the most commonly used sizes for saddle horses. Keg shoes are pre-sized and fitted cold, while most others, with the exception of steel and aluminum racing plates and polo shoes, require heating and cutting of the heels to be fitted. Keg shoes are available in plates, and with toe and heel calks.

Polo shoes are iron shoes and come in a separate size pattern, from 00 to No. 3. A polo shoe (Fig. 7–1) has a high inside rim which makes it a full roller motion shoe. Polo shoes should not be used on roping horses because of the tendency of the inside rim to stop the foot when sliding, possibly causing the horse to injure the fetlock area. Racing aluminum plates, also sized in a different manner, vary from size 2 to size 7 (Fig. 7–11). Steel racing plates are sized in the same way while pony plates range from 00 to No. 4 in pony sizes. In addition to these there are mule shoes, which are shaped to correspond to the shape of the mule's foot. The following table gives the approximate comparative sizes.

Phoenix Plate Shoes	Polo Shoes	Steel and Aluminum Racing Plates
Pony No. 4	00	2
00	0	3 or 4
0	1	5
1	2	6
2	3	7

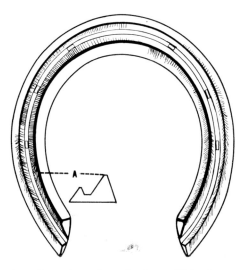

FIG. 7–1.—Ground surface view of a polo shoe. This also serves as a full roller motion shoe because of the high inside rim (A) on the web. Inset shows a cross-section of the web.

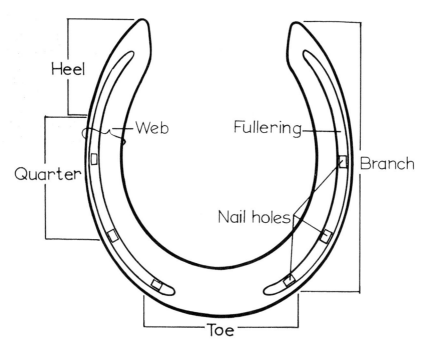

FIG. 7–2.—Ground surface view of a front plate shoe with the parts labeled.

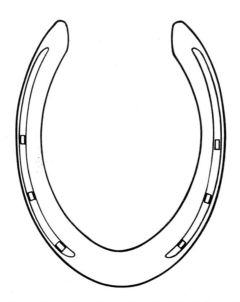

FIG. 7–3.—Ground surface view of a hind plate shoe.
Note the pointed appearance of the hind shoe.

24

A shoe may be made with variable amounts of creasing into which the nail heads fit. In some cases no crease is present at all, while in others the crease encircles the shoe which is called a "full swedged shoe." The crease may also be termed "fullering" or "swedging." The branch of a shoe is divided into toe, quarters and heels, and the width of the branch is called the web (Figs. 7–2 and 7–3).

Horse shoe nails usually are sized from $2\frac{1}{2}$ to 12 (Fig. 7–4). No. $2\frac{1}{2}$ is the smallest and 12 is the largest. No. 3 through No. 6 are used most commonly. Horse shoe nails also have different shaped

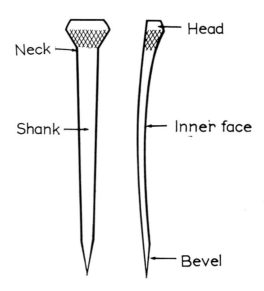

Fig. 7–4.—Horseshoe nail with parts labeled.

heads. A regular head is larger than the city head which is small enough to fit into the fullering of the shoe, for shoes such as racing plates. In addition, there are horse shoe nails with frost heads which are chisel shaped for increased traction. In shoeing race horses, the $3\frac{1}{2}$ to $4\frac{1}{2}$ nails with city heads ordinarily are used. For saddle horses, the Nos. 5 and 6 nails commonly are used, with city or regular heads, depending upon the size of the crease in the shoe. The head of the nail, after it is driven in, should project about one-sixteenth of an inch below the ground surface of the shoe.

Effects of Shoe Weights

Weights added to the foot only change gaits at a high speed. Weights are used mostly for gaited horses and trotters. Toe weights, which cause a horse to reach farther, are usually applied as a roller toe weight. Heel weights cause the horse to lift the foot higher in its action. Some trotters may carry as much as 5 to 10 ounces additional weight on the toe to cause increased reach.

When weights are added to the branches of the shoe for correction, they actually may cause aggravation of the interference which is to be corrected. When weights are added to the sides, even though on the correct side, increased deviation of the limb may occur. Weight reduces speed, decreases agility, and increases fatigue of the limb, so the lightest shoe possible, for the work to be done, should be used.

Corrective Shoes

Corrective shoes have a number of descriptive terms:

1. *Roller Toe.* There is a rolled toe on the shoe to facilitate easy break over at the toe (Fig. 7–5).

2. *Full Roller Motion.* The web of the shoe has a high inside rim all the way around the shoe. This can be accomplished in several ways, such as with a polo shoe which is normally made in this fashion, by welding a quarter inch round rod around the inside of the web of the shoe, or by grinding off the outside edge of the branch of the shoe all the way around to lower the outside edge (Figs. 7–1, 7–5-*3* and 7–6).

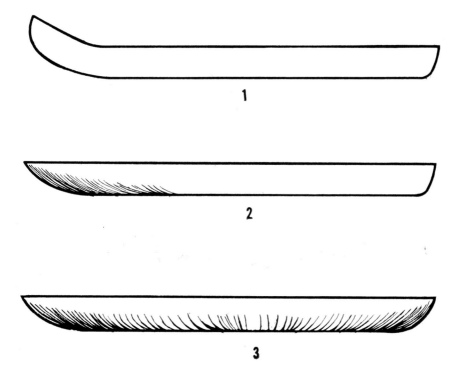

FIG. 7–5.—No. 1. Side view of rocker toe shoe. The wall must be cut away at the toe to fit the shoe. This permits easy breakover at the toe.

No. 2. Side view of roller toe shoe. This shoe also enables the horse to break over more easily at the toe.

No. 3. Front view of a full roller motion shoe in which the outside of the shoe has been ground off around the entire shoe.

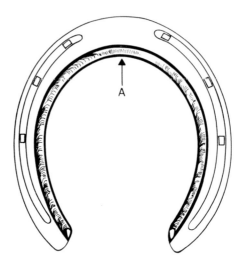

FIG. 7–6.—Full roller motion shoe made by welding a one-fourth inch round rod around the inside of the web on the ground surface.

A, indicates the rod has gone around the toe as well as the branches of the shoe. This type of shoe enables the horse to break over in any direction more easily.

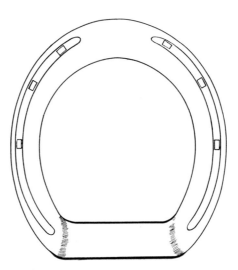

FIG. 7–7.—Ground surface view of a full bar shoe. A full bar shoe can be used to produce or to remove frog pressure.

3. *Bar Shoe.* This may be a full bar across the heels, or a half bar which extends from one of the branches (Figs. 6–112 and 7–7). Bars on the shoe can be used to increase or decrease frog pressure. A full bar can be used to either increase or decrease frog pressure, while a half bar is usually used to increase frog pressure. To increase frog pressure, the full or half bar must press in against the frog about $\frac{1}{4}$ inch when the shoe is nailed on. The full bar is recessed from the frog if frog pressure is to be lessened.

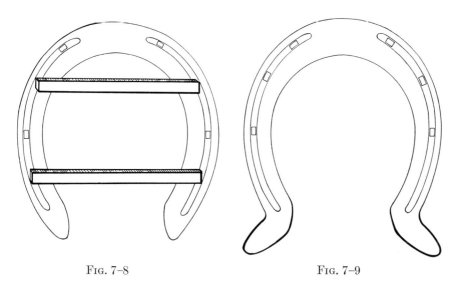

FIG. 7–8   FIG. 7–9

FIG. 7–8.—Memphis bar shoe showing two bars welded to the ground surface of the shoe to produce roller action.

FIG. 7–9.—Plate shoe with trailers on both heels. Trailers, which may be put on one or both heels, may be of varying lengths. In general, they should be turned out at a 30 to 45 degree angle. In addition, calks may be used on one or both heels.

4. *Rocker Toe* (Fig. 7–5-1). This is used to increase the ease of breakover.

5. *Memphis Bar Shoe.* These are two bars across the branches, on the ground surrace, to cause a roller action (Fig. 7–8).

6. *Trailer Shoe.* This shoe has one or both heels extended for corrective purposes (Figs. 7 9, 9–10, page 396). Trailers may be used on one or both heels. They should be turned to the outside rather than being used as a straight projection of the heel of the shoe. Care should be taken when applying inside heel trailers to a horse that tends to interfere, as the trailer may cut the opposite foot. Care also must be taken in applying trailers to the front foot, as the hind foot may strike them and pull the front shoe. The length of a trailer seldom should exceed $\frac{1}{2}$ inch. Trailers sometimes work better when applied contrary to recommended position. Before

nailing the shoes tight, the shoes can be reversed to opposite feet and checked for this effect.

7. *Rim Shoe* (Fig. 7–10). This shoe has a rim on the outside edge of the web. Such a shoe may be used to increase traction or to correct a condition. The rim may be full or half depending on need. A full rim shoe is often used to increase traction of Standardbreds.

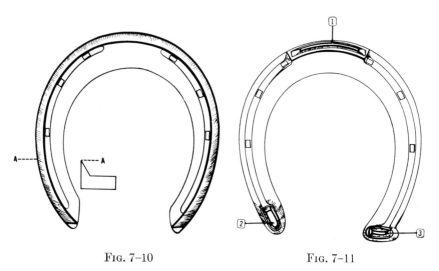

Fig. 7–10   Fig. 7–11

Fig. 7–10.—Full rim shoe. This full rim on the outside edge of the web is used to increase traction, especially among Standardbreds. Inset shows a cross-section of the web with rim (*A*) on the outside.

Fig. 7–11.—Diagram of aluminum racing plate shoe.
1. Toe grab. *2.* Block heel. *3.* Heel sticker.
The same forms are available in steel racing plates. Front shoes usually have toe grab only or possibly a heel sticker. Hind shoes often have a toe grab and block heels, or one block heel and one heel sticker for increased traction.

8. *Toe Grab.* This is a wedge-shaped bar across the toe of the shoe to increase traction. A toe grab commonly is used on racing plates (Fig. 7–11).

9. *Heel Calks.* These are composed of differently shaped projections on the heels and are called jar corks, heel calks, block heels, or heel stickers, depending upon their shape (Figs. 7–11, 9–7, page 394).

10. *Quarter Clips and Toe Clips* (Figs. 6–73, page 272, 6–109 page 347). These are used to reinforce the toe or quarter areas in case of hoof cracks. Quarter clips also are used to prevent foot expansion as a result of fracture of the third phalanx.

Many other forms of shoes are available, but it is impractical to try to describe them here.

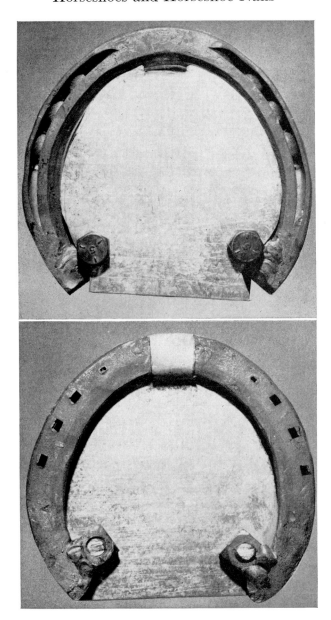

FIG. 7–12.—Two views of a treatment shoe that can be used for nail punctures or for protection of the sole when needed for other reasons. The photo above shows the ground surface with two bolts holding a galvanized steel plate to the shoe. After unscrewing these bolts the plate can be removed for treating the foot. The photo below shows the shoe as it goes next to the hoof wall. The hoof wall must be lowered at the toe to allow the point of the treatment plate to be inserted between the toe and the shoe.

REFERENCES

1. ASMUS, R. A.: *Horseshoes of Interest to Veterinarians.* Plant City, Florida, Ken Kimbel Book Company, 1946.
2. AXE, J. WORTLEY.: *The Horse in Health and Disease. Vol. III.* London, Gresham Publishing Co. About 1900.
3. HOLMES, C. M.: *The Principles and Practice of Horse Shoeing.* Leeds, The Farriers Journal Publishing Co., Ltd., 1949.
4. RICHARDSON, C.: *Practical Farriery.* London, Pitman Publishing Co., 1950.
5. Technical Manual. TM 2-220. *The Horseshoer.* War Dept., Wash., D.C., March 11, 1941.

Trimming
and shoeing
the
normal foot

Chapter 8

TRIMMING should be done every four to six weeks on horses that
are used barefoot, while shoes should be reset every four to six
weeks on horses that are shod. The object of proper trimming is to
make the shape of the foot, the angle of the foot axis, and foot level
(Fig. 8–1) as nearly normal as possible (*see* Chapter 1). However,
trimming should not be too drastic in an effort to make the horse
meet perfect foot axis because each horse has his own axis of the
pastern and hoof, and any radical alterations may produce pathological changes.

The foot should be trimmed so that pastern and hoof axis form
an unbroken line (Figs. 1–29 and 1–32, pages 37 and 39). Even if a
horse does not have a normal foot axis, drastic changes should not
be made if the pastern axis and hoof axis are of the same angle.

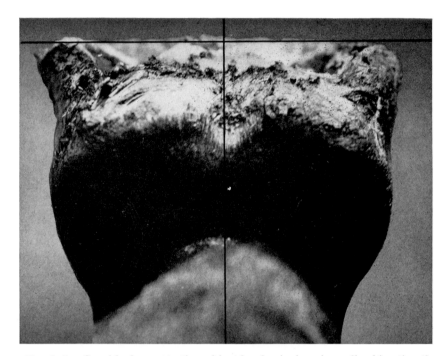

Fig. 8–1.—Graphic demonstration of foot level. An imaginary line bisecting the limb longitudinally and a transverse line across the heels should give two 90 degree angles at their intersection. If the transverse line is tilted either way, the foot is off level.

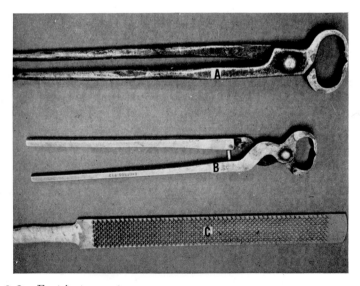

Fig. 8–2.—Foot instruments.

A. Shoe puller. Note the deep throat on this instrument as compared with B.

B. Hoof nipper. The cutting edges of the hoof nipper have a long taper to facilitate cutting of the hoof wall.

C. Tang rasp used to rasp the foot.

The horse should be observed at rest and in motion to better determine the normal angles of the feet. Following observation, the foot should be cleaned of all debris with a hoof pick. Dead portions of the sole and frog should be cut away with a hoof knife. This is done only shallowly because normal frog and protective layers of the sole should not be removed. Keeping in mind the proper angles for this particular horse, the wall should be trimmed with hoof nippers (Fig. 8–2). One usually begins at the heel and trims to the opposite heel, or trims from the heel toward the toe (Fig. 8–3). If the wall

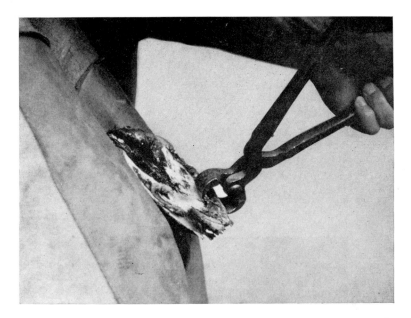

Fig. 8–3.—Trimming the foot. This view shows one side which has been trimmed from heel to toe; this should be followed by trimming of the other side.

is trimmed near the sole, all around, the wall will be concave at the quarters, thus, more wall should be left projecting below the sole at the quarters than at the heel or toe. The wall usually should be trimmed approximately to the level of the frog, but never past the sole. One should watch carefully the angle of the hoof nippers and avoid irregularities in the bearing surface of the wall (Fig. 8–4). The bars should be trimmed to the level of the wall at the heels.

A tang rasp (Fig. 8–2) should be used to smooth the foot and level it following proper trimming. The rasp should be held flat and level so that one wall is not made lower than the other (Fig. 8–5). "Opening the heels" or cutting away the wide part of the frog, between the bar and the frog, should *not* be done as this weakens the heel area causing contraction.

FIG. 8–4.—Note that the hoof nippers are held so that the bearing surface of the hoof wall will be flat following the trimming. A person must be careful not to trim the wall to a taper from inside out.

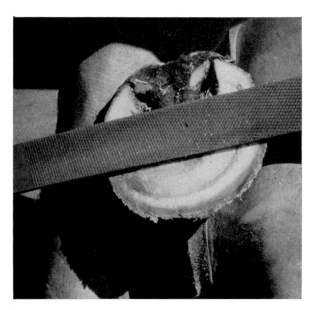

FIG. 8–5.—This shows the final preparation of the foot for shoeing with a tang rasp. The rasp must be held so that one side of the wall is not cut below the other.

If the horse is to go barefoot, about a quarter of an inch of wall should project below the sole at the heel and toe. Sharp outside edges of the wall should be smoothed to reduce the chance of splitting or cracking of the hoof wall. If the horse is to be shod, the wall should be trimmed level with the sole at the toe, and as low as necessary at the quarter and heel to establish the proper foot axis.

Shoeing the Normal Foot

Shoeing, accurately described as a "necessary evil," should only be done when required for traction, or when the use to which the horse is put causes excessive wear of the feet. Normal feet should have shoes reset every four to six weeks when shoes are required. After the foot is properly trimmed and leveled, as described above (Fig. 8–6), the desired shoe of the correct size should be selected. To be the correct size, the shoe should follow the contour of the hoof wall, and the heel of the shoe should be about $\frac{1}{4}$ inch longer than the heel of the hoof. The shoe definitely should be fitted to the foot rather than the foot fitted to the shoe (Fig. 8–7). The branches of the shoe should extend beyond the wall about $\frac{1}{16}$ inch at the heel and quarter to allow for foot expansion. The size of the shoe also is determined by the last nail hole of the shoe. This nail hole should not be past the bend of the quarter of the hoof wall, or two-thirds of the length of the foot measured from the toe. Expansion of the foot is limited if nails extend beyond the bend of the quarter of the wall.

Fig. 8–6.—A foot that has been trimmed and rasped and is ready for application of a shoe.

FIG. 8–7.—A shoe of proper size for the foot. The shoe is centered by using the frog for a pointer, if the foot is normal. The shoe is wider than the wall, by about one-sixteeth of an inch at the quarters.

The shoe should be accurately centered on the foot (Fig. 8–7). For those horses with normal feet, the shoe can be centered by using the point of the frog as a guide. For horses that toe-in or toe-out, the frog usually points off center; thus, the shoe cannot be centered by this method.

Shoes may be applied hot or cold but the hot method is preferred because more accurate shaping can be done to a hot shoe. However, the shoe still must be fitted to the foot, rather than being burned into place to save time. Final shaping of machine-made shoes usually can be done by hammering the cold shoe into form. For most pleasure horses a plate shoe, such as the Phoenix* plate, is preferable to a shoe with heel calks. Heel calk shoes are not recommended for horses used for general purpose riding since they distort the correct foot axis. If heel calks are used, a toe grab of the same height must be used to maintain proper foot axis. Such a combination relieves the frog of necessary pressure, except in very rough terrain. Heel calks should not be used on horses whose work consists of many quick turns. Cutting cattle, barrel racing, pole bending and reining are in this category. In these events, the horse often twists with the entire body weight on one foot, especially a hindfoot. If the heel calks anchor the foot, the first and/or second phalanx may fracture.

If the foot is worn excessively on one side as a result of poor conformation, it may not be possible to level the foot properly by trimming. In this case the branch of the shoe on the low side should be shimmed with leather or neolite so that the foot is level when the shoe is in place.

* Trademark of Phoenix Shoe Company, Joliet, Illinois.

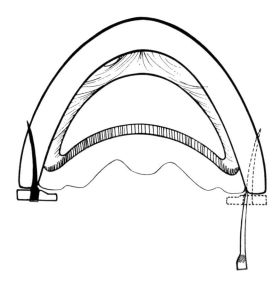

Fig. 8–8.—Diagram of a shoe nail in the proper place. The nail should enter at the white line and come out approximately three-fourths of an inch above the junction of the shoe and hoof wall, or about one-third of the length of the hoof wall from the coronary band to the ground surface.

Once the shoe is fitted to the foot, the nails should be driven in. A nail should be selected with a head that protrudes about $\frac{1}{16}$ inch above the ground surface of the shoe, after it is driven in. If the head is too small, it fits too deeply in the crease, and the shoe becomes loose. The nail holes should be over the wall, starting at the outer aspect of the white line (Fig. 8–8). Authorities differ on which nail should be driven in first; some claim that the right heel nail should be driven in first, while others say that the right toe nail should be first. Location of the nail to be driven in first does not matter greatly, as long as the shoe is balanced so that it does not sit too far to the medial or lateral side, and is not out of position in relation to the toe, following the driving of the first nail. The shoeing hammer should be used to tap the shoe into position after driving the first nail. If the heel nails are driven first, the toe nails should be next; if the toe nails are driven first, the heel nails should be next, and then should come the remaining nails.

The beveled side of the nail point should be toward the inside so that it is directed outward when driven in. The beveled side can be determined by the rough spot on the head since the rough spot and the beveled side of the point are on the inside of the shoe nail (Fig. 7–4). The nail should be held straight and its course appraised for its approximate exit on the hoof wall (Figs. 8–8 and 8–9). In general, the nail should come out approximately $\frac{3}{4}$ inch above the

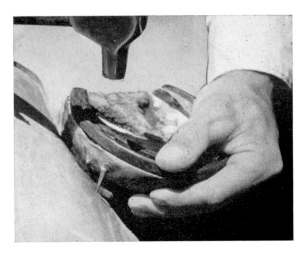

Fig. 8–9.—Exit of nail following driving. As nearly as possible the nails should come out in an even line.

junction of the shoe and hoof wall or at about one-third of the way up the wall. If the nail comes out too low or too high, it should be pulled and redriven.

If the horse flinches obviously during the driving of the nail, the sensitive laminae may have been punctured. In such case tincture of iodine should be applied to the nail opening and the nail should be pulled and left out, or a new nail should be driven in at the proper spot. Tetanus antitoxin should be administered and the horse should be watched closely for signs of foot infection.

The path of a horse shoe nail, upon entering the horn structure of the wall, should be parallel with the horn fibers so that the nail does not cut or sever these fibers. The point of the nail will follow a path parallel with the horn fibers if light blows of the driving hammer are used. To force the nail through the outer surface of the wall at the desired point, the shoer should use light blows until the nail is driven two-thirds of the required height, then he should strike a sharp, hard blow on the head of the nail to force the point through the surface of the wall at the desired height. The bevel on the point of the nail causes the nail to angle outward. The bevel is most effective when the nail is being driven rapidly through the horn. Nails driven to a uniform height add to the good appearance of the work; however, if the nail comes out the wall at a point near the desired position, it is advisable to allow it to remain, providing that the horn is sound. If it is removed to make a better appearance, the second perforation may weaken the wall and cause a loose shoe.

Under ordinary circumstances, three nails on either side are enough, but most machine-made shoes have four nail holes per side. All four holes need not be filled with nails. As quickly as each nail is driven, it should be bent over so the point will not injure the shoer if the horse jerks the foot away (Fig. 8–10). The nail can be bent by using the claw of the hammer. After all nails are driven in and bent over, they should be clinched by placing a small block of steel on the bent edge of the nail and hitting the head of the nail with the hammer (Fig. 8–11). Nails should be clinched firmly, but not so tightly that the horse will be "nail bound." Following clinching, the nails should be cut so about ⅛ inch of nail protrudes (Fig. 8–12). Then, using the rasp, a small groove should be cut under each nail, where it emerges from the wall (Fig. 8–13). Clinching tongs then should

Fig. 8–10.   Fig. 8–11

Fig. 8–10.—Bending of nails with the claws of the shoeing hammer so that they will not injure the shoer if the horse pulls the foot away.

Fig. 8–11.—Clinching the nails by the use of a clinching block and hammer. The clinching block is held under the bent edge of the nail and the head is struck with the hammer to clinch the nail firmly.

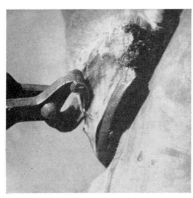

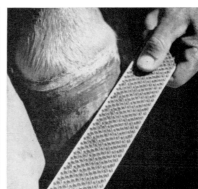

Fig. 8–12.   Fig. 8–13

Fig. 8–12.—The nails are cut so that approximately one-eighth inch of the nail protrudes above the hoof wall.

Fig. 8–13.—The rasp should be used to cut a small groove under each nail so that the nail can be clinched into the groove with a tong.

be used to clinch the nail into the groove. The clinched end should be rasped lightly and the hoof wall smoothed at its junction with the shoe (Fig. 8–14). Only a minimum amount of rasping should be done or the hoof will be deprived of its protective outer covering. The shoe should fit well enough to the wall that no rasping has to be done to fit the toe to the shoe. After shoeing, the horse should be observed at rest and in motion to see if the shoes fit properly.

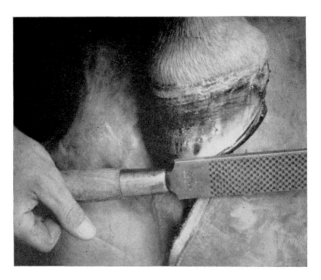

Fig. 8–14.—Final light rasping of the nails and rasping of the line between the shoe and the hoof wall.

Removing Horseshoes

Shoes should be removed by cutting the clinched nail ends on the hoof wall with a clinch cutter, or by filing off the clinches with a tang rasp. The foot then should be picked up and placed between the knees so that pulling pinchers can be used (Fig. 8–15). The pinchers should be placed under the shoe, starting at the heel, the handles closed and pushed away from the person pulling the shoes, and slightly toward the median line of the foot (Fig. 8–16). After one heel is loosened, the opposite heel should be loosened. The pinchers should not be twisted, and the foot of the horse should be braced with one hand under the toe so that no injury will result to the fetlock joint. The procedure should be continued by moving down each of the branches as the shoe is loosened (Fig. 8–17). The pulling should be gentle enough that undue pain is not caused, and no sprain occurs. After the shoe has been removed, any pieces of nail left in the hoof wall should be pulled, and the foot trimmed, as previously described.

 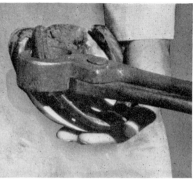

FIG. 8–15   FIG. 8–16

FIG. 8–15.—Application of a shoe puller under the heel of one side of the shoe.

FIG. 8–16.—Pushing the shoe pullers away from the operator and toward the midline.

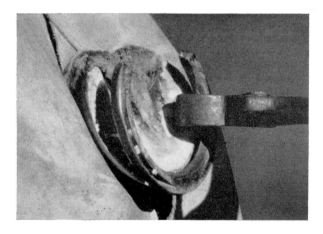

FIG. 8–17.—Final loosening of the inside heel following loosening of the outside heel. The pullers should be reapplied on the shoe until it works free of the foot.

REFERENCES

1. ARMISTEAD, W. W., and PATTERSON, C. M.: *Care of Horses Feet.* Texas Agric. Exper. Sta. Bull. MP-198.
2. AXE, J. WORTLEY.: *The Horse in Health and Disease, Vol. III,* London. Gresham Publishing Co. About 1900.
3. BERNS, GEO. H.: Lameness of Obscure Origin and Some of its Causes. J.A.V.M.A., *54,* 217, 1918–1919.
4. BUTZOW, R. F.: Anatomy and Care of the Equine Foot. Ill. Vet., *4,* (4), 98, Fall 1961.
5. CHAPMAN, G. T.: *Lameness in the Horse,* New York, Wm. R. Jenkins Co., 1901.
6. DOLLAR, JOHN A.: *Handbook of Horse Shoeing,* New York, Jenkins and Company, 1898.
7. FRANK, E. R.: *Veterinary Surgery,* 7th ed. Minneapolis, Burgess Publishing Co., 1964.
8. GRAHAM, C. W.: Care of the Horse's Foot. Vet. Med., *60,* (3), 255, March 1965.
9. HOLMES, CHARLES: *The Principles and Practice of Horse Shoeing.* Leeds, The Farriers Journal Publishing Co., Ltd., 1949.
10. KIERNAN, JOHN: *Hints on Horseshoeing.* Office of Library of Congress, Washington D.C., 1894.
11. LAYTON, E. W.: Care of the Horse's Foot. Vet. Med., *60,* (3), 248, March 1965.
12. LUNGWITZ, A., and ADAMS, JOHN, W.: *A Textbook of Horseshoeing,* 11th ed., Philadelphia, J. B. Lippincott Co., 1897.
13. McDONOUGH, JAMES: Lameness and Its Most Common Cause. J.A.V.M.A., *49,* 653, 1916.
14. Phoenix Manufacturing Co. Bulletin: *How to Care for the Feet of Horses and Mules.* Joliet, Illinois, Phoenix Shoe Co., (1943).
15. PROCTOR, D. L.: *Anatomy, Care and Trimming of Feet.* Third Annual Stud Managers Course, Lexington, Kentucky. (Nov., 1953).
16. RICHARDSON, C.: *Practical Farriery.* London, Pitman Publishing Co., 1950.
17. RUSSELL, WILLIAM: *Scientific Horseshoeing,* Cincinnati, C. J. Krehbiel and Co., 1907.
18. Technical Manual. TM 2-220. *The Horseshoer.* War Dept., Washington, D.C., March 11, 1941.
19. U.S.D.A.: *Diseases of the Horse.* Bureau of Animal Industry. U. S. Govt. Printing Office, Washington, D.C., 1942.

Methods of corrective trimming and shoeing

Chapter 9

FUNDAMENTALS OF CORRECTING FAULTS IN GAITS

If a horse is to maintain a normal gait, his feet must be balanced and in alignment with the body at the moment the feet leave the ground. Faults in the gaits of a horse may occur if the rider is unskilled or the horse's equipment is not properly adjusted. The horseshoer obviously has no control over these matters, but a skillful horseshoer can control the position of the foot in rest and in flight. However, the shoer must understand the structure of the foot and leg of the horse, and the action of leg and foot in flight before he can successfully apply corrective measures. Each horse must be considered individually as to type of shoe to correct a

(389)

faulty gait. Even though two or more horses have the same fault in gait, each may require a separate method of shoeing for correction.

Also, shoeing alone will not always completely correct a faulty gait, though it will often reduce the harmful effects of such a fault. Some horses, though, do not follow the usual pattern when affected by malformations. For example, a horse that toes out may land on the inside toe and wall, or on the outside wall depending on whether he is base wide or base narrow. Therefore it is essential that careful observation be made to determine the animal's way of going so that proper correction can be made. The effect of shoeing should be studied, and if necessary, more than one method of shoeing should be tried to see which is most effective.

The veterinarian, through his knowledge of anatomy and physiology of the limb, is well qualified to recommend corrective shoes, even though he may not be a skilled horseshoer. Study of the basic principles of shoeing, plus the application of physical laws, will usually indicate an effective method of correction of most faulty gaits.

Although the art of making shoes has been lost in most communities for lack of competent horseshoers, corrective shoes can be fashioned from ordinary plate shoes by using some welding and ingenuity. Many types of corrective shoes can be made by simply welding metal to a common shoe. The shoe should be fitted to the horse and then taken to a welder for the proper additions. For example, extension toe shoes can be made of round steel rod welded on the shoe to form a lateral extension. Bars, both half and full, can be welded on and shaped by the welder. Quarter clips and toe clips of $\frac{1}{8}$ inch thick steel can be added (Figs. 6–73 page 272, 6–109 page 347).

Even though all of the methods of correction may be recommended for a particular condition, often several methods of correction are attempted before the best method is found for that individual. *As a general rule it is best to use the least severe corrective measure which will produce a functional gait.* Radical changes may produce pathological changes in the limb. Corrective shoeing follows physical laws, and keen observation of the gait and way of travel of a horse will give the necessary clues to correcting the problem; although some defects are so bad they cannot be corrected. Corrective measures should start with corrective trimming in the young horse, when possible. Faulty gaits in mature animals can not be corrected; they can only be modified and improved.

CORRECTIVE TRIMMING

In corrective trimming it sometimes is not necessary to trim the worn hoof away but is only necessary to pare down those areas that have grown too long as a result of poor conformation. The object of corrective trimming is to trim the foot until it is level and has normal foot and pastern axis for the horse (Figs. 1–29 and 1–30, page 37).

The feet should be observed in flight from both front and rear views to determine where the foot lands. The wall on which the foot lands will be low, and the opposite wall is trimmed to level the foot (Figs. 8–1 and 9–1). The hoof should be trimmed so that there is no break in the foot and pastern axes (*see* Chapter 1).

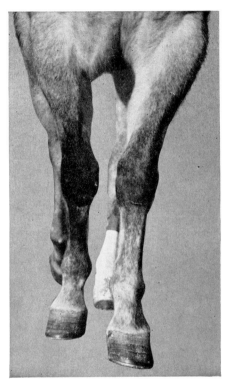

Fig. 9–1.—Base-narrow, toe-wide horse landing on the outside wall. Notice how the right forelimb is in a toe-out position while the left forelimb is landing on the outside wall. With the foot landing in this way the outside wall will be lower than the inside wall if corrective trimming is not used at each shoeing.

If a horse is base narrow and toes in, or is base narrow and toes out, the outside wall and heel are usually worn too low and a compensating portion must be removed from the inside wall from toe to heel to level the foot. If the horse is base wide and toes out, the inside wall and heel may be worn down and the outside wall must be trimmed to bring the foot near a normal foot level. It is important to carefully observe the gait of the horse and watch where the foot lands from both front and rear views before deciding where to correctively trim the foot. Squaring the toe and leveling the foot of young horses helps them break over the center of the toe. If a horse is shown at halter, squaring the toe may cause a judge to mark the horse down. By watching the horse walk you can determine how the foot lands. If the foot is put down unevenly, that area of the wall that takes a majority of the weight when the foot lands will be low, while other areas of the wall will be high and, therefore, must be lowered (Fig. 9–1). Any portion of the wall that has begun to flare outward as the result of poor conformation must be rasped down on the outside of the wall and trimmed to the proper level (Fig. 9–2). Rasping the ground surface of the flared-out wall so that the wall does not bear weight may also aid the hoof wall in growing straight. If the wall is rasped on the outside and ground surface consistently, the hoof wall tends to regain more of a normal shape.

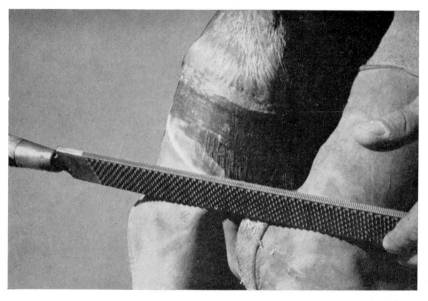

Fig. 9–2. — Rasping the outside of a wall that is flared outward. In time a foot may be changed to a more normal shape by proper trimming and rasping of the flared portions.

CONDITIONS THAT REQUIRE CORRECTIVE SHOEING

All corrective shoes listed here should be applied to a level foot or the foot should be shimmed with leather under one of the shoe branches, so that the foot is level when the shoe is applied.

Base-Wide, Toe-Out in Front (Splay Footed) (Toe-Wide)
(Fig. 1–11, page 22)

In a base wide toe-out conformation, the foot is not level because the horse wears off the inside wall from toe to heel. The foot breaks over the inside toe and lands on the inside toe and wall. This condition should be corrected, if possible, by trimming the outside wall

from toe to heel to level the foot. Even if no shoe is to be used, this
method should be followed. The feet of young foals can be rasped
periodically in this manner, and some correction will take place as
the foals grow. Once the foot is leveled, numerous methods of
correction can be applied. If the foot is excessively off level, a
leather shim can be used under the low wall to raise the branch of
the shoe on that side.

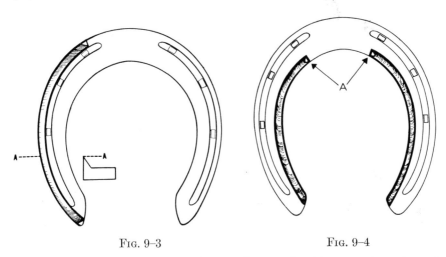

FIG. 9–3   FIG. 9–4

FIG. 9–3.—Half rim shoe. This shoe can be used for either a toe-in or toe-out
condition to help raise that side of the foot which is low and to aid in causing
breakover at the center of the toe. Inset shows cross-section of web with rim (A)
on outside.

FIG. 9–4.—High inside rims with open toe. This shoe aids breakover at the
center of the toe (A) for toe-in or toe-out. Breakover is made easy because of the
high inside rim.

A. *Half Rim Shoe* (Figs. 9–3 and 9–5).—This type of shoe has a
rim on the outside edge of the inside branch from the heel to approximately the first nail hole. This shoe raises the inside of the foot,
when it is placed on the ground, and interferes with breakover,
except at the center of the toe. A $\frac{1}{4}$ inch rod welded to the outside
edge of the inside branch will accomplish the same purpose (Fig. 9–5).

B. *High Inside Rims and Open Toe* (Fig. 9–4).—In this type of
correction, a $\frac{1}{4}$ inch rod is welded to the inside of the branches of the
shoe from the heel to the first nail hole of both branches. This helps
the horse break over the center of the toe. The same thing can be
accomplished by welding the rod on the outside of the branches
and leaving the toe open, but this makes breakover somewhat more
difficult (Fig. 9–6).

C. *Calks* (Fig. 9–7).—A calkin is set at each of the heels, and then
one in the area of the first nail hole on each side. This accomplishes
the same purpose as the quarter inch rod mentioned in B, by forcing
the horse to breakover the center of the toe.

FIG. 9–5.—Half rim shoe using $\frac{1}{4}''$ round steel rod welded on the outside edge of the branch of the shoe from the first nail hole to heel. This type of shoe is used with the rod on the outside branch for base-narrow, toe-out or toe-in and on the inside branch for base-wide, toe-out horses.

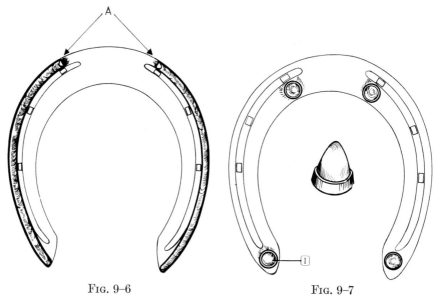

FIG. 9–6   FIG. 9–7

FIG. 9–6.—High outside rims with open toe. The high outside rim is made of one-fourth inch round steel rod welded to the outside of the web. This aids in forcing the foot to breakover the center of the toe (A), but more leverage is applied than when a high inside rim is used.

FIG. 9–7.—The use of calks (1) to force breakover at the center of the toe for toe-in or toe-out condition. These calks are approximately one-half inch high and are pointed at the ground surface. Inset shows close-up view.

D. *Steel Bar Across the Area of Breakover* (Fig. 9–8).—In this case a piece of steel approximately $\frac{1}{4}$ to $\frac{3}{8}$ inch square and $1\frac{1}{2}$ inches long is welded to the toe of the shoe at the area where the foot is breaking over. The bar interferes with breakover at that point and forces the foot to break over the center of the toe.

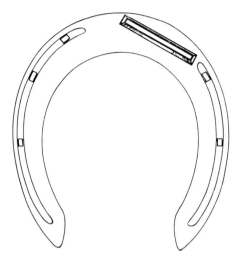

FIG. 9–8.—The use of a small wedged piece of steel across the area of breakover to force the foot over the center of the toe. This bar should be placed over the area where the foot breaks over.

E. *Square Toe Shoe* (Fig. 9–9).—This shoe will aid many mild cases of toe-out. As the foot starts to break over, the square toe forces the foot to breakover the center of the toe. The shoe should be fitted so that the square portion of the toe is even with the toe of the hoof wall. A square toe can be combined with shoes A and F.

F. *A Short Inside Trailer* (Fig. 9–10).—This is of value in forcing the foot to land straight. As the foot lands, the trailer catches the ground and turns the foot in. The trailer should be turned out at a 30 to 45 degree angle, not exceeding $\frac{1}{2}$ inch in length. If a horse wings in badly, caution must be exercised or the trailer may lacerate the opposite limb. A short calk on the trailer may be of additional aid. A trailer can be used with A, B, D, E, G, and I corrective shoes listed here.

G. *A Toe Extension* (Fig. 9–11).—An extension from the shoe, or a welded extension, projects from the inside toe helping to force the horse to break over the center of the toe. A toe extension interferes with breakover on the inside toe. The extension should blend with the shoe and extend to the second nail hole. This can be dangerous on a splay-footed horse since most such animals tend to wing inside, and the extension may cause trauma to the opposite forelimb.

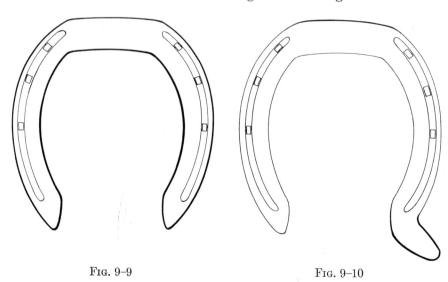

Fig. 9–9   Fig. 9–10

Fig. 9–9.—Ground surface view of a square-toe shoe. The square-toe shoe is a useful shoe for toe-in or toe-out condition of either the front or hind feet. If the square portion of the shoe is fitted flush with the edge of the toe, the squared edges aid in forcing the foot to break over the center of the toe as the foot leaves the ground.

Fig. 9–10.—Ground surface view of a square-toe shoe with trailer. If the square toe shoe, shown in Figure 9–9, is not sufficient a trailer may be added. The trailer is added to the inside heel for base-wide toe-out horses, and to the outside heel for base-narrow toe-in horses.

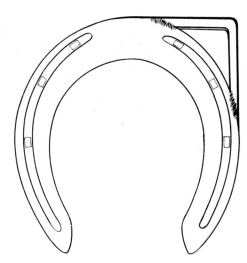

Fig. 9–11.—Ground surface view of toe extension shoe. The toe extension is added to aid in forcing the foot to break over the center of the toe. The toe extension is used on the inside of the toe for base-wide toe-out horses, and on the outside toe for base-narrow toe-in and toe-out horses.

H. *Half Shoe* (Fig. 9–12). — One half of a plate shoe or steel racing plate is used on the inside half of the foot where the wall is wearing excessively. This aids in leveling the foot and delaying wear on the inside wall. The ends are beveled to blend with the wall.

I. *A Plate Shoe with Thinned Outside Branch* (Fig. 9–13). — This shoe is thinned from the first nail hole, on the inside branch, to the heel of the outside branch. The thickness of the inside branch, plus the thinned outside branch, tends to turn the toe forward and cause the foot to break over the center of the toe. This shoe also may work with the thinned branch on the inside wall.

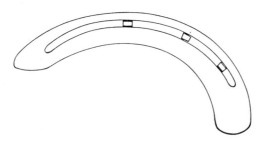

FIG. 9–12. — Ground surface view of a half shoe. A half shoe may be applied to the area of the foot wall which shows the greatest wear in toe-in or toe-out conformation. In base-wide toe-out, conformation, the half shoe should be added to the inside of the hoof; for base-narrow toe-out and base-narrow toe-in conformation it should be added to the outside wall. The toe end is beveled to blend into the wall.

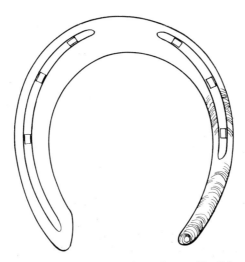

FIG. 9–13. — Ground surface view of plate shoe with thinned branch. The thinned branch is placed on the outside wall of a horse which has toe-wide conformation, and on the inside wall of the horse with toe-in conformation. This type of shoe sometimes works better when applied in reverse to these directions.

Base-Narrow, Toe-Out, Landing on Outside Wall in the Forefeet (Fig. 1–6, page 20)

This is a bad conformation and is aggravated by shoeing methods ordinarily used for base-wide, toe-out conformation. The outside of the wall is low because the weight of the horse falls on this area (Fig. 9–1). The foot breaks over the outside toe, wings to the inside and lands on the outside wall. The feet are leveled by lowering the inside wall and toe. Any of the methods of shoeing for base-wide, toe out conformation can be used by reversing the correction, however, the following methods of shoeing seem to be the most successful.

A. *Half Rim Shoe* (Figs. 9–3 and 9–5). — This type of shoe has a rim on the outside edge of the outside branch of the shoe from the heel to the first nail hole. This shoe raises the outside of the foot, when it is placed on the ground, and interferes with breakover except at the center of the toe. A $\frac{1}{4}$ inch round steel rod welded to the outside edge of the outside branch will accomplish the same purpose (Fig. 9–5). This is one of the most successful methods of shoeing base-narrow, toe-out conformation.

B. *High Outside Rims and Open Toe* (Fig. 9–6). — In this type of correction, a $\frac{1}{4}$ inch steel rod is welded to the outside edge of both branches of the shoe from the heel to the first nail hole. This helps the horse break over the center of the toe.

C. *Square Toe Shoe* (Fig. 9–9). — This shoe will aid many mild cases of toe out. As the foot starts to break over the square toe forces the foot to break over the center of the foot. The shoe should be fitted so that the square portion of the toe is even with the toe of the hoof wall. A square toe shoe can be combined with shoe A or D.

D. *Short Inside Trailer* (Fig. 9–10). — This trailer is of value in forcing the foot to land straight. As the foot lands the trailer catches the ground and turns the foot in. The trailer should be turned out at a 30 to 40 degree angle and not exceed approximately $\frac{1}{2}$ inch length to prevent interference. A short block heel on the trailer may be of value. A trailer of this type can be used with shoes A and C.

E. *Half Shoe* (Fig. 9–12). — One half of a plate shoe or steel racing plate can be used on the outside half of the foot where the wall is wearing excessively. This aids in leveling the foot and delays wear on the outside wall. The end is beveled to blend with the wall.

F. *A Toe Extension* (Fig. 9–11). — Extension from the shoe, or a welded extension, projects from the outside toe helping to force the horse to break over the center of the toe. A toe extension interferes with breakover on the outside toe. Extension should blend with the shoe and extend to the second nail hole. It can be combined with shoe D.

Base-Narrow, Toe-In (Pigeon-Toed) (Toe Narrow)
(Fig. 1–7, page 20).

With toe-in conformation, the feet usually are off-level. In this case the horse tends to wear down the outside toe and wall, since breakover occurs on the outside toe, and the foot lands on the outside wall. Corrective trimming is done by paring down the inside wall until the foot is as level as possible. If the foot is excessively off-level, a leather shim is placed under the outside branch of the shoe to bring the foot to normal level. In correcting toe-in conformation many of the same methods used to correct base-narrow, toe-out can be used.

A. *Half Rim Shoe.* — The half rim can be a $\frac{1}{4}$ inch rod welded on the outside of the branch of the shoe beginning at the heel and ending about the first nail hole on the outside of the branch. This helps to force the foot to break over the center of the toe (Figs. 9–3 and 9–5).

B. *One-Fourth Inch Rod on the Outside of Both Branches.* — The rod, which extends from the heel to the first nail hole, aids the horse in breaking over at the center of the toe (Fig. 9–6).

C. *Calks.* — Two heel calks and a calk at the area of the first nail hole on the outside of each branch of the shoe will help the foot break over at the center of the toe (Fig. 9–7).

D. *A One-Fourth Inch to Three-Eighth Inch Square Steel Bar One and One Half Inches Long.* — If such a bar is welded over the point of breakover on the outside toe, it interferes with breakover at this point and causes the foot to break more nearly toward the center of the toe (Fig. 9–8).

E. *A Short Trailer on the Outside Heel* (Fig. 9–10). — This is sometimes of value in catching the foot as it lands and turning it straight, preventing the horse from landing in a toe-in position. A small block heel may be added to the bottom of this extension. Such a trailer can be used in conjunction with A, B, D, F, G, and I corrective shoes listed here.

F. *A Square Toe Shoe.* — This accomplishes the same purpose as for toe-out; it forces the foot to break over the center of the toe. It is one of the best and mildest methods of correction (Fig. 9–9). The square toe should fit the outside edge of the toe of the wall.

G. *A Toe Extension.* — This is added to the outside of the toe area and should extend as far as the second nail hole. This forces the foot to break over the center of the toe (Fig. 9–11). There is no danger of interfering with toe-in conformation, since the foot tends to break in an outside arc.

H. *Half Shoe* (Fig. 9–12). — One-half of a plate shoe or steel racing plate is added to the outside half of the wall. This aids in leveling the foot and delaying wear to the outside wall. The edges of the shoe should be beveled to blend with the wall.

I. *A Plate Shoe With a Thinned Inside-Branch* (Fig. 9–13).—The shoe is thinned from the first nail hole on the outside branch to the heel of the inside branch. The normal thickness of the outside branch, plus the thinned inside branch, tends to turn the toe forward causing the foot to break over the center of the toe. This shoe also may work with the thinned branch on the outside wall.

Base-Wide, Toe-In, Landing on the Inside Wall of the Forefeet

This is bad conformation and it is aggravated by some shoeing methods ordinarily used for base-narrow toe-in conformation. The inside wall is low because the weight of the horse lands on this area. The feet should be leveled and shod so that the inside toe and wall are slightly raised. To raise the inside wall a piece of $\frac{1}{4}$ inch steel rod should be welded to the outside edge of the inside branch of the shoe from the heel to the first nail hole (Figs. 9–3 and 9–5). This tends to level the action of the foot and to force the foot to break over the center of the toe. It is difficult to correct this type of defect.

Contracted Heels

Treatment of contraction of the foot fundamentally is based on producing frog pressure. This must be accomplished in order to re-establish normal foot function; but above all the primary cause of contraction must be corrected. In other words, an accurate diagnosis must be established prior to treatment.

If the foot does not require shoeing for the work of the horse, proper trimming to allow frog pressure may promote foot expansion, provided the trimming is done often enough. If the horse requires shoeing but does not do heavy work, a tip shoe can be used (Fig. 9–14). Other shoes, such as a half bar shoe, full bar shoe, T shoe, slipper shoe of Broûe, and slipper and bar clip shoe of Einsiedel, may be used (Figs. 6–112, 7–7, 9–15 and 9–16). When a half bar or full bar shoe is used, the half or full bar must press inward about $\frac{1}{4}$ inch against the frog when the shoe is set. More complicated methods of treatment, such as the Smith Expansion shoe, a Chadwick spring (Fig. 9–17), and Deffay's vice can be used, but these are not necessary in most cases. The front of the toe area on the hoof wall can be rasped in conjunction with the use of a Chadwick spring. This will make the toe area more flexible and the action of the spring more effective. Care should be taken not to attempt too rapid expansion of the heels or lameness may result.

In addition to shoeing, other procedures sometimes used to aid expansion of the quarters include thinning the region of the quarters with an ordinary Farriers rasp. Be careful not to rasp a $\frac{1}{2}$ inch wide portion of the wall immediately below the coronary band. The thinning should be to the greatest amount starting $\frac{1}{2}$ inch below the

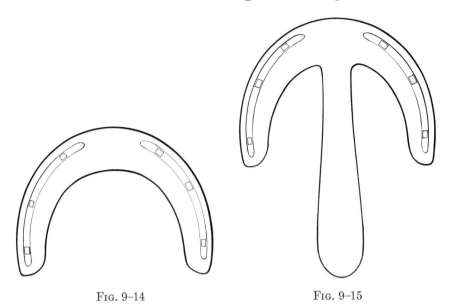

Fig. 9–14 Fig. 9–15

Fig. 9–14.—Ground surface view of a tip shoe. This shoe may be used in contraction of the foot to protect the toe from wear yet leave the heels unshod for frog pressure. The ends of the shoe are tapered to blend into the wall, or the wall of the toe is cut more deeply to receive the shoe.

Fig. 9–15.—Ground surface view of a T shoe. This shoe is used for contraction of the foot so that the center bar causes pressure on the frog to promote foot expansion. The heel areas of the hoof wall are unshod to aid frog pressure. The wall of the toe area may be cut more deeply to receive the tip portion of the shoe.

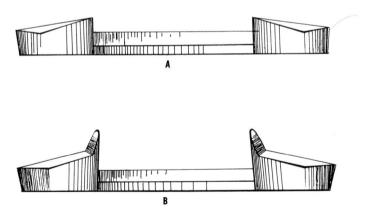

Fig. 9–16.—A. Posterior view of slipper shoe of Broûe. This shoe permits the heels to slide outward when the foot is put down to promote expansion of the heel.

B. Posterior view of a slipper and bar clip shoe of Einsiedel. The inside clips prevent the heels from coming together and the taper of the walls aid in causing the heels to go outward when the foot is set down.

Fig. 9–17.—Chadwick spring in place in a foot. The Chadwick spring is forced outward by a round pin in the center, as shown. The pin can be hammered outward if more pressure is needed against the heels. The heels are under constant pressure from the spring.

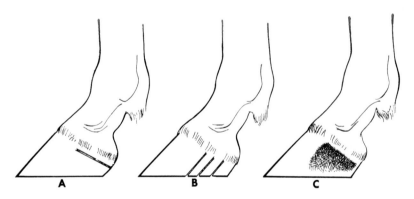

Fig. 9–18.—Methods of increasing hoof wall flexibility and expansion.

A. Groove one-fourth inch wide, one-half to three-fourths inch below the coronary band to aid in heel expansion. The groove penetrates to the sensitive laminae, but not into the blood supply.

B. Three vertical grooves used along the quarters of the hoof wall to promote hoof expansion. These grooves penetrate to the sensitive laminae but not into the blood supply.

C. Rasping away the quarters of the hoof, with the deepest areas of rasping one-half inch below the coronary band and the thinnest at the bearing surface of the hoof wall. The rasping extends from the heel of the wall three inches forward. All these methods aid in expansion of the quarters of the foot. They are used in hoof contraction, sidebones, and sometimes for laminitis. A foot with chronic laminitis may be grooved at the toe and across the sole instead of at the quarters.

coronary band and at the heels. Thinning should decrease gradually for $2\frac{1}{2}$ to 3 inches forward and downward, until at the ground surface of the wall the normal thickness is left (Fig. 9–18-C). The foot should be shod with a pressure bar shoe, and the foot treated daily with a hoof compound to prevent the wall from cracking.

Another method of promoting expansion of the wall is to groove the wall over the quarters and heels with a series of vertical lines, or simply by one groove paralleling the coronary band $\frac{3}{4}$ inch below it (Fig. 9–18-A,B). This groove should extend from the heel forward for 3 to 4 inches. Following either method of grooving the wall, a pressure bar shoe should be applied. The grooves, which aid in expansion of the heel areas of the hoof, may be placed in the hoof wall with a Stryker cast cutter, a hoof groover, or a firing iron. Such grooving methods give the hoof wall a chance to expand. When a single groove parallel to the coronary band is used, the proximal portion of the hoof wall may actually expand and overlap the hoof wall below it in the process of growing out.

Ringbone

This condition is discussed in Chapter 6. Corrective shoeing consists of shortening the toe and applying a full roller motion shoe to transfer the action from the pastern and coffin joints to the shoe area. If the horse has good conformation, the toe alone can be rolled; if not, a full roller motion shoe should be applied.

Sidebones

This is discussed in Chapter 6. Corrective shoeing is usually intended to roll the foot or shoe on the affected side. The affected side of the shoe is given a roller motion by grinding off the outside edge of the branch of the shoe. Full roller motion shoes also may be used (Figs. 7–1, 7–5 and 7–6).

A shoe with swedged up heels and rolled toe may be used on horses that work on soft ground where a full roller motion shoe may lose its effectiveness upon sinking into soft dirt (Fig. 9–19).

FIG. 9–19.—Side view of shoe with swedged up heels and rolled toe. This type of shoe causes a quicker breakover of either the front or hindfoot. It also has been used in navicular disease to protect the frog from pressure. It is also used sometimes for bone spavin in Standardbreds.

Navicular Disease

This condition is discussed in Chapter 6. Corrective shoeing may delay or eliminate the necessity of a posterior digital neurectomy in a horse that is not used in such strenuous work as racing. A roller toe, swedged up heel (Fig. 9–19), full bar and slippered heels are used (Figs. 7–7 and 9–16). The raised heels and rolled toe make it easier for the horse to break over and land in a way that decreases concussion of the deep flexor against the navicular bone. The raised heels also reduce frog pressure and the full bar across the center one third of the frog eliminates trauma to this area and prevents the painful reaction that occurs. The slippered heels tend to cause the wall to slide outward and thereby help to overcome contraction that is already present, and that would be induced by the raised heel and bar. In addition, it is wise to thin or groove the quarters (Fig. 9–18) to aid wall expansion that is stimulated by the slippered heels.

Cow Hocks

Roping horses having this condition slide wide when stopping. This is corrected by use of a small heel calk on the inside heel of the shoes of the hind feet. When the horse slides the calk tends to force the hind feet to slide straight. Cow hocked horses used for other purposes can be shod with a small inside trailer on the hind shoes, and, in some cases, with the addition of a heel calk to the trailer. As the foot lands the heel calk tends to hold the foot inward forcing it to break over straight. If the horse tends to interfere, the trailer may hit the opposite limb. A trailer sometimes is effective on the outside branch, except for use with roping horses. Before the shoes are set completely, this outside trailer can be checked by reversing the shoes. A square toe on the shoe will help the foot break over the center of the toe, and an inside trailer with a calk if necessary (Fig. 9–10).

Bone Spavin

When corrective shoeing is used for bone spavin, the heels should be raised with calks and a short outside trailer should be used. In speed horses, calks may slow the horse and the heels of the shoe can be turned back on themselves to make a smooth calk that will slide (Fig. 9–19). In trotters and pacers, a memphis bar shoe (Fig. 7–8, page 373) or an oval bar across the heels is sometimes used. A second method is to use a $\frac{1}{4}$ inch steel rod on the inside of the branches leaving the inside toe open (Fig. 9–20). This tends to force the horse to break over the inside toe, which is the object of most corrective shoeing for spavin. This action tends to relieve pressure in the spavin area. Shoeing, though, often is not helpful so this condition can best be treated surgically as described in Chapter 6.

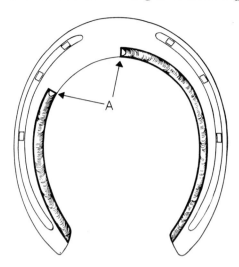

FIG. 9–20.—Ground surface view of a shoe which causes a tendency to break over the inside of the foot (A) in bone spavin. The raised areas are of one-fourth inch round steel rod welded to the inside branches while the inside of the toe is left open. This shoe would be for the left hindfoot.

Cross-firing

Cross-firing is a condition in which the inside of the toe, or inside of the wall of the hind foot, strikes the inner quarter or under surface of the inner branch of the shoe of the opposite forefoot. It is most likely to occur in pacers, especially those that toe out in front and toe in behind. With this conformation the flight of the fore feet is forward and inward during the first half of a stride, and the flight of the hind feet is forward and inward during the last half of the stride. This causes foot contact. Corrective shoeing is used to force the front and hind feet to move forward, in a manner that will approximate a straight line, correcting the deviations in flight. If the foot can be forced to point straight ahead on landing and can be forced to break over near the center of the toe again on take off, straight line flight is more nearly accomplished.

Shoeing the Front Feet.—A. Since most cross-firing horses are toe wide in front, corrective shoeing for toe wide is used. Shoeing methods *A, B, E,* and *G* in the discussion for correcting base wide toe out (page 392) may be used. In addition, the edge of the ground surface of the inside branch of the shoe should be rounded, so that if striking does occur, it will not break the skin.

B. The inside branch can be fitted with a $\frac{1}{4}$ inch to $\frac{3}{8}$ inch trailer on any of the shoes in *A,* above, so that it will strike the ground just before the lateral branch, thereby rotating the toe inward.

C. A cross-firing horse should always wear quarter boots for protection.

D. A square toe shoe is often used on trotters and pacers to straighten breakover.

Shoeing the Hind Feet.—A. Short trailer on outside branch.

B. The inner branch is cut short, and is thinned progressively from the toe to the heel.

C. Bevel or round the ground surface edge of the inside branch. This is used in trotters and pacers, and is called a half round shoe on the inside and a half swedge shoe on the outside.

Other methods of corrective shoeing, discussed under toe-out, may be used in front. Other types of shoeing the hind feet are discussed under toe-in (page 399).

Forging and Overreaching

Forging is a defect of the gait in which the toe of the hindfoot overtakes and strikes the bottom of the front foot, of the same side, at the moment the front foot is starting flight. The front foot is too slow in breaking over and leaving the ground to avoid the forward extension of the advancing hind foot.

Overreaching is similar to forging except the hind foot comes up more quickly than it does in forging. This means that the hindfoot steps on the heel of the front foot on the same side before the forefoot can leave the ground or just as it is leaving the ground. In this case, the shoe of the front foot is often pulled because the toe of the hind foot steps on the heels of the shoe on the front foot.

Forging and overreaching may be due to faulty conformation, leg weariness, improper adjustment of the saddle, and improper riding or improper shoeing. Faults in conformation which tend to cause forging include a short body with relatively long legs; front or hind feet set too far under the body; short front legs and long hind legs. Leg weariness may result from debility or overexertion. Improper preparation of the feet, or improper shoeing, may slow the breakover of the front feet, decreasing the height of their action causing forging. Young horses with good conformation and properly balanced feet often are subject to forging while being trained and developed. In this case, forging is caused by fatigue of underdeveloped muscles.

*Corrective Shoeing for Forging and Overreaching.—*The method of correction should be governed by the cause of the forging and the nature of the work the horse performs. The horse should be ridden at a walk and a trot to determine the rate of speed at which forging and overreaching are most pronounced. You should watch for lack of coordination between the front and hind feet during flight. Look for conditions which would aggravate an unbalanced gait. Determine if the conformation is good or faulty, if the feet are balanced laterally from toe to heel, if the shoes are correctly fitted and are of suitable weight. Three fundamentals are essential in correcting forging:

1. The front foot must leave the ground before being struck by the oncoming hindfoot.

2. The hindfoot must take a slightly shorter stride so it will not hit the front foot.

3. The heel of the front shoe and the toe of the hind shoe must be shortened to avoid contact.

A. Prepare and balance the front feet and shoe with rocker or rolled toe shoes of equal and light weight. Prepare and balance the hind feet but leave the hoof a little longer than normal, and shoe the horse with light weight shoes. Fit the hind shoes fully to the point of the toe, and extend the heels back about $\frac{1}{2}$ to $\frac{3}{4}$ inch beyond the buttresses. The heels of the shoe should be turned slightly outward.

This increases the rapidity of breaking over of the front feet and decreases the rapidity of breaking over of the hind feet. The extended heels tend to stop the hindfoot as it is being put down.

B. Prepare and balance the front feet, and shoe with rocker or rolled toe shoes equal in weight. Prepare and balance the hind feet and shoe with heel calks $\frac{1}{2}$ inch long, $\frac{1}{4}$ inch deep, and $\frac{1}{8}$ inch wide, and a rocker toe.

This method of shoeing induces greater hock action in the elevation of the hind feet in flight, but decreases forward extension. Therefore, there is more clearance between the front and hind feet in action. The calks tend to stop the hindfoot before it hits the front foot.

C. Prepare and balance the front feet and shoe with rocker or rolled toe shoes of equal weight. Prepare and balance the hind feet leaving the hoof a little longer than normal; shoe with a square toe shoe; extend the heels of the shoe back about $\frac{1}{2}$ to $\frac{3}{4}$ inch beyond the buttresses; turn the heels of the shoe out slightly. The straight section of the shoe at the toe should be set back about $\frac{1}{4}$ inch from the outline of the wall at the toe. The wall that projects beyond the shoe at the toe should not be removed.

This method of shoeing increases the rapidity of breaking over the front feet and causes higher action. The preparation of the hind feet, plus the greater length of shoes, delays the break over of the hind feet, thus allowing more time for the front feet to be carried to sufficient elevation to allow clearance. By setting the shoe back from the point of the toe you prevent the clicking noise when the hind foot strikes the front shoe. The extended heels on the rear shoes stop the hind feet more quickly and thereby aid in avoiding contact with the front feet.

D. Prepare and balance the front feet and shoe with rocker or rolled toe shoes of equal weight. Prepare and balance the hind feet, keeping the toe short; shoe with square toe shoe. This allows the hind foot to break over quickly causing it to go higher, and allowing the front foot to get out of the way.

A full roller motion shoe (Chapter 7, Figs. 7–1, 7–5 and 7–6 pages 368 and 371) can be substituted for a rolled toe or rocker toe in corrections of the fore feet. A polo shoe acts as a full roller motion if no other type is available or if such a shoe cannot be made. The high inside rim facilitates breakover in any direction.

If you are unable to stop forging or over-reaching, a spoon on the heels of the front shoes may be applied so the shoe cannot be pulled. A spoon closely fits the heels of the front foot and covers the bulbs of the heel, thereby giving the hind shoe no area in which to pull the front shoe (Fig. 9–21). This type of shoe must be changed often or it may cause corns.

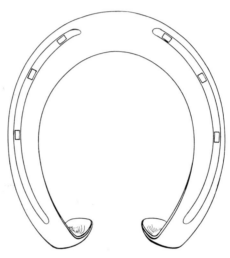

Fig. 9–21.—Ground surface view of spoon shoe. The spoons extend upward and cover the heels of the foot. They must fit closely at the heels; they prevent the horse from pulling a shoe if he overreaches.

Interfering

Interfering is a fault of the gait causing the horse to strike any part of the inside of one leg with the inside of the foot or shoe of the opposite foot. The injury may be at any spot from the coronary band to the carpus of the front legs. In most cases, injuries are more common to the hind legs and the fetlock joint is most commonly injured. Temporary causes of interfering include fatigue, faulty preparation of feet, and improper shoeing. Faulty conformation may be a permanent cause. Such horses are either base wide or base narrow with toe-wide conformation (*see* Chapter 1). They often are narrow chested or, in the case of the hindlimbs, cow-hocked.

Corrective Shoeing for Interfering.—For temporary causes, correct any obvious faults in shoeing or trimming. Be sure that the shoes are of proper weight and proper fit.

For conformational causes, the methods of correction vary depending upon whether the horse is mature or still growing. If correction is begun early with a foal, corrective trimming may prevent interference by gradually straightening the feet (page 390). Before applying corrective shoes, the horse should be observed at the walk and trot to determine the degree of severity of interference. If interference cannot be seen, chalk may be put on the hoof wall and shoe to determine where interference is occurring and whether one or both feet are involved.

In the fore limbs most of the shoeing methods used to correct base-narrow or base-wide toe-out horses also will aid in preventing interference (page 392). In the hindlimbs, most of the shoeing methods used to correct cowhocks will also aid in correcting interference (page 404).

A. If the horse strikes the inside portion of the fetlock of the forelegs, prepare and balance the feet and shoe with a square toe shoe. The straight section of the shoe should come to the point of the toe, level with the outline of the wall, and extend laterally slightly beyond the wall on both sides of the toe of the hoof. The inside branch of the shoe should be rasped and smoothed on the outside edge of the ground surface for the entire length of the branch, so that if it does strike, it will not injure the tissues.

B. The base-wide, toe-out horse can be shod with a medial (inside) extension of the toe of the shoe as described under base-wide toe-out conformation (page 392). This is often a good shoe for those horses that definitely deviate from the fetlock to the foot. These shoes are fitted even with the wall at the point of the toe. The outline of the shoe extends $\frac{1}{4}$ inch beyond the outline of the wall at the junction of the oval and straight sections. Graduate the fullness to zero at a point just to the rear of the second nail hole of the shoe. From this point to, and including the heel, the shoe should be closely fitted to the wall. The outside portion of the toe should be closely fitted, but full from the bend of the outside quarter to the heel (slightly fuller than for normal shoeing). The edge of the ground surface of the inside branch of the shoe should be rasped and smoothed.

The medial toe extension forces the foot to break straight over the toe and this tends to reduce the inward swing during flight. The fullness of the shoe at the natural breaking over point of the foot on the inside toe acts as a lever to turn the foot to a straight forward position while the heels are being raised. Hand-made shoes are preferable to factory shoes.

C. The base-narrow, toe-wide horse can be shod with a half rim shoe on the outside branch from the first nail hole to the heel (Figs. 9–3 and 9–5). A short inside trailer can also be used. The foot should always be leveled prior to applying this type of shoe. In some cases this means that the outside wall must be shimmed with leather prior to applying the shoe. Other methods of corrective shoeing are described under base narrow, toe out conformation, (p. 398).

D. If the horse is striking the inside portion of the hoof at the coronary band, and if the cause is due to a narrow chest, and front legs which are too close together, the feet should be balanced, prepared, and shod with rocker toe shoes made of extra light shoes. The inside branch of the shoe should be closely fitted and the outside edge of this branch should be rasped and smoothed.   It is advisable to use interference boots for this condition if the horse is to be used for long rides; leg weariness tends to aggravate the condition.

E. If the horse is striking the inside portion of the fetlock joints in the hind legs, and the cause is faulty leg conformation because the horse is bow-legged (*see* Chapter 1), such a horse is base-narrow. The feet should be prepared, leveled, and shod with extra light shoes with square toes and a trailer on the outside branch (Fig. 9–10). The trailer should not exceed $\frac{3}{4}$ inch in length, with a turned heel calk about $\frac{3}{8}$ inch in height. If the heel calk is not turned on the shoe it may be welded to the ground surface (Fig. 7–11 page 374). The inside branch of the shoe should be closely fitted, following the outline of the wall from the quarter to the buttress and rasped and finished smoothly.   No heel calk should be put on the inside branch of the shoe. Such a shoe, when properly adjusted, will balance the foot and reduce the inward swing of the foot in flight.

F. If the horse is striking the inside portion of the fetlock joints on the hind legs, and the cause is faulty leg conformation because the horse is cow-hocked and the feet are in toe-out position, the feet should be prepared, leveled, and shod with inside extension toe shoes with trailers on the inside branches, but with no calks (Fig. 9–11).   The trailer should be about $\frac{1}{2}$ inch in length and turned out at a 30 to 45 degree angle.   The inside branch of the shoe should be closely fitted and rasped and smoothed.   This type of shoe tends to force the foot to break over the center of the toe and reduce inward swing of the foot in flight.   A square toe shoe with an inside trailer may be substituted for a shoe with inside toe extension.   The square toe should be fitted to the front edge of the toe wall.

G. Most trotters and pacers interfere in front and usually hit the knee.   Horses that will not hit on a mile track may contact on a one-half mile track. Every effort is made to use a correction that will not slow down the feet.   A shoe with longitudinal corks is sometimes used. These corks are 2 to 3 inches long, $\frac{1}{8}$ inch wide, and $\frac{1}{4}$ inch deep.   They set inside of the nail holes on the branches beginning at the first nail hole.

Corns

These are discussed in the section on corns in Chapter 6.

Toe and Quarter-crack

Corrective shoeing for toe and quarter-cracks is discussed under these conditions in Chapter 6.

Wire Cuts in the Coronary Band

A bar shoe is used to place pressure on the frog. This may be a half bar or a full bar. The hoof wall is shortened on the affected side beneath the wire cut area. The wall is trimmed so it will not bear weight and the weight that would be borne on this portion of the wall is transferred to the frog by use of the bar. This reduces movement in the area of the cut and aids healing (Fig. 9–22).

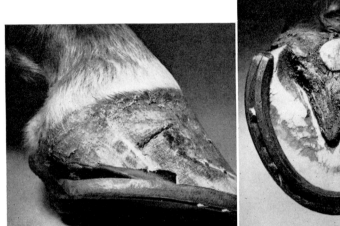

Fig. 9–22.—Use of half bar shoe to correct hoof wall or quarter crack defect. Left—hoof wall lowered to prevent weight bearing from the wall defect to the heel. Right—Ground surface view of half bar shoe shows how the weight is taken on the frog rather than over the hoof defect area.

Flexor Tendonitis or Suspensory Ligament Injury

In this case the heels are raised, with blunt heel calks, to remove some of the pressure from the flexor tendons. Trimming of the toe alone may be of value. Proper levels and angles are observed but the heel is raised by the shoe. You must be careful that the tendons do not contract when the heels are raised for long periods of time.

Flat Feet

In trimming of the foot, the sole should not be trimmed excessively and the frog should not be trimmed at all. The wall should be trimmed, but only enough to smooth it for application of a shoe.

The shoe should be seated moderately on the sole. If seating is excessive and bearing is allowed only on the wall, there is a tendency for the wall to push outward, and the sole to drop still farther. Conversely, if the web of the shoe is too wide and too much bearing is given to the sole, there will be excessive pressure on the sole, and sole bruising, with lameness, will result. The shoe should cover the whole of the wall, and the whole of the white line, but just touch upon the sole. The heels of the shoe should be of full length to avoid causing a corn. In addition, shoe pads of leather or neolite may be necessary.

Dropped Sole or "Pumiced Foot" (Fig. 6–55 page 248)

In less severe forms, corrective shoeing, similar to that discussed for flat feet, may be of value. A broad-webbed shoe that will give wall pressure, plus protection to the white line to prevent further dropping of the sole, is indicated. Avoid creating sole pressure if possible; pads of leather or neolite may be necessary. In many cases, the white line is very wide. In some cases, seedy toe is present as a result of the separation of the sensitive and insensitive laminae. Further corrective measures are discussed under chronic laminitis (Chapter 6).

REFERENCES

1. ADAMS, O. R.: Corrective Shoeing for Common Defects of the Forelimb. Proc. 11th Ann. A.A.E.P., 1965.
2. ARMISTEAD, W. W., PATTERSON, C. M.: *Care of Horses Feet.* Texas Agric. Extension Service Bulletin, MP-198.
3. ASMUS, R. A.: *Horseshoes of Interest to Veterinarians.* Plant City, Florida, Ken Kimbel Book Company, 1946.
4. BRITT, O. K.: Corrective Shoeing. Southeastern Vet., *2*, 49, 1959.
5. DOLLAR, JOHN A.: *Handbook of Horseshoeing*, New York, Jenkins & Company, 1898.
6. HOLMES, C. M.: *The Principles and Practice of Horseshoeing.* Leeds, The Farriers Journal Publishing Co., Ltd., 1949.
7. LA CROIX, J. V.: *Lameness of the Horse.* Am. J. Vet. Med. Chicago, Illinois, 1916.
8. LUNGWITZ, A., and ADAMS, JOHN W.: *A Textbook of Horseshoeing*, 11th ed., Philadelphia, J. B. Lippincott Co., 1897.
9. McCUNN, JAMES: Lameness in the Horse with Special Reference to Surgical Shoeing. Vet. Record, *63*, 629, 1951.
10. REEKS, H. C.: *Diseases of the Horse's Foot.* Chicago, Alexander Eger, 1918.
11. RICHARDSON, C.: *Practical Farriery*, London, Pitman and Sons, 1950.
12. RUSSELL, WILLIAM: *Scientific Horseshoeing*, Cincinnati, C. J. Krehbiel and Co., 1907.
13. Technical Manual. T. M. 2-220: *The Horseshoer.* War Dept., Washington, D.C., March 11, 1941.
14. USDA: *Diseases of the Horse.* Bureau of Animal Industry. U. S. Govt. Printing Office, Washington, D. C. (1942).

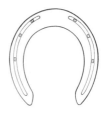

Natural and artificial gaits

Chapter 10

NATURAL gaits of the horse are the walk, trot and gallop. The running walk, amble, rack (broken amble or singlefoot), and the pace may be either natural or artificial gaits. The canter is a restrained or collected gallop.

A three-gaited horse is required to show at walk, trot, and canter. Five-gaited horses, in addition to the three gaits mentioned, must also show a "slow-gait" (fox trot or amble) and a fast rack. Tennessee Walking Horses (Plantation Walkers) must show the flat foot walk, running walk, and the canter.

For descriptive purposes the terms "near" and "off" are used to describe the feet in motion. The "near" side of a horse is the left side, while the "off" side is the right.

The terms "step" and "stride" are used as descriptive terms in determining distance covered by the feet. A step is the distance between the foot prints of the two forelimbs or between the two hindlimbs. It is not a measurement of distance between the forelimb and the hindlimb. The distance between two foot prints of the right and left forelimb would be measured or the distance between the foot prints of right and left hindlimb. The stride is the distance between successive imprints of the same foot or feet. A stride is therefore longer than a step.

The Walk (Fig. 10–1)

This is a four-beat gait. Walking can be of various forms, but regardless of the form, it must be an even four beat gait. When a regular sequence is lost, identified by four hoof beats at precise intervals, the horse is no longer walking. The walking sequence is

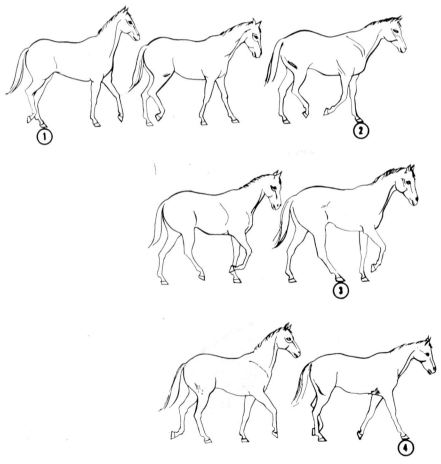

Fig. 10–1.—The walk.
Numbers indicate the foot sequence causing the four-beat gait.

lateral because both feet of one side hit the ground before the two feet of the opposite side strike. Propulsion primarily results from the hindlimbs, and the forelimbs simply follow. The length of stride in the walk will usually vary between $5\frac{1}{2}$ and 6 ft. This distance is measured between successive imprints of the same foot. The step will vary between 33 and 39 inches and is the measurement made between the imprints made by a pair of forefeet or the imprints made by a pair of hind feet. The sequence of hoof beats can be described according to this pattern: (*1*) near-hind, (*2*) near-fore, (*3*) off-hind, (*4*) off-fore (Fig. 10–1). This gait is sometimes described as beginning with a forelimb as: (*1*) off-fore, (*2*) near-hind, (*3*) near-fore, and (*4*) off-hind. This description is not proper according to the way the horse starts, but it is proper after he is in motion.

In the walk there is never a moment at which fewer than two feet are in contact with the ground. There is no period of suspension or no moment when only one foot is in contact with the ground.

The Flat Foot Walk

The flat foot walk is the natural walk of the Tennessee Walker. The feet land in the same sequence as described above, but, due to the normal loose action of the horse, this gait propels the horse forward very rapidly.

The Running Walk

This is the fast walk of the Tennesse Walking Horse. It is a four-beat gait intermediate between a walk and a rack. In this gait the hind foot oversteps the foot print of the front foot from a few inches to as much as 18 inches, giving the horse a gliding motion. The gait is characterized by a bobbing and nodding of the head, a flopping of the ears, and a snapping of the teeth, in rhythm with the movement of the legs. It is easy on both horse and rider. Upon close observance, the gait resembles a pace with the hindlimb hitting ground before the forelimb of the same side.

The Trot (Fig. 10–2)

The trot is a two-beat gait in which opposite fore and hindfeet hit the ground together. The left forelimb and right hindlimb move together, as do the right forelimb and left hindlimb. A trot can be of various forms, but to be a true trot it must be in two-beat time. An "impure" trot is one in which forelimb hits ground before the diagonal hindlimb or vice versa. When the hindlimb is in advance of the correct tempo, forging may be evident. The length of stride in a trot will vary from slightly over 9 ft. in an ordinary horse to 17 ft. or more in a racing trotting horse.

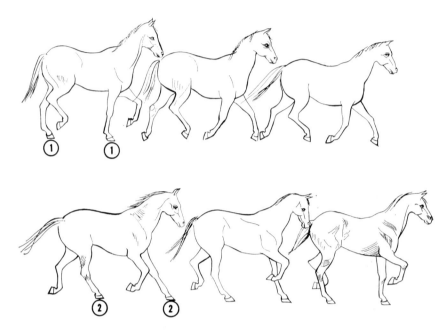

FIG. 10–2. – The trot. Opposite fore and hindlimbs pair to make this a two-beat gait. Numbers 1 and 2 show the pairing of the limbs.

The trot is sometimes classified as ordinary trot, collected trot and extended trot. A Standardbred horse characterizes the extended trot with length and rapidity of individual strides. The Hackney characterizes the collected trot with extreme flexion of knees and hocks. In the trot there is a diagonal base of support, but there may be a moment of suspension during the interval at which one pair of limbs is moving toward the ground and the other pair is leaving the ground.

The Gallop or Run (Fig. 10–3)

In a straight-away gallop, the horse normally changes leads periodically to relieve fatigue. As a horse turns to the left, he should lead with the left forelimb and right hindlimb, and as he turns to the right, he should lead with right forelimb and left hindlimb. When a horse is in the left (near) fore lead, the right (off) hindlimb is said to be the lead hindlimb, but when a horse is in the right (off) forelimb lead, the left (near) hindlimb is said to be the lead hindlimb. A horse should change leads, both in front and in back, at the same time during the period of suspension when the lead forelimb leaves the ground (Fig. 10–4). However, some horses change lead in front without changing in back immediately; this makes the gallop rough and difficult for the rider. When this happens the horse is off lead behind and runs like some dogs, landing on the lateral hind leg on the same side as the leading forefoot instead of the opposite hind foot. The gallop is a fully extended gait in which the head is stretched forward and the strides reach their maximum length. The three-time beat of the canter is not possible at this speed, so the gallop becomes a gait of four beats. The length of stride in a gallop will vary between 15 and 22 ft. Some horses can stride in excess of 22 ft. The difference is essentially in the spring of the leg in the leading forefoot.

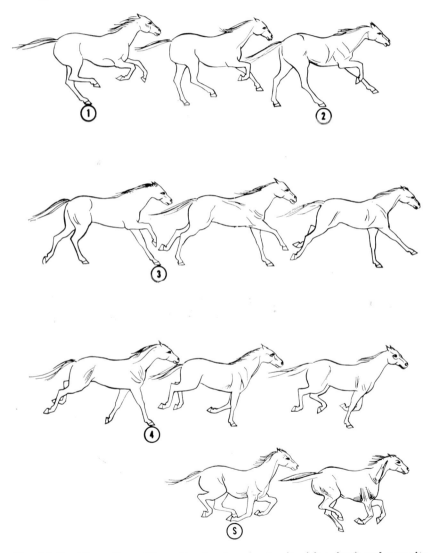

FIG. 10–3.—The gallop. The gallop is a four-beat gait with a front and opposite hind limb leading and the other fore and hind limbs paired. This illustration shows a right forelimb and left hindlimb lead with the sequence of foot beats indicated by numbers. A period of suspension exists, as shown by S, after the lead fore foot leaves the ground.

27

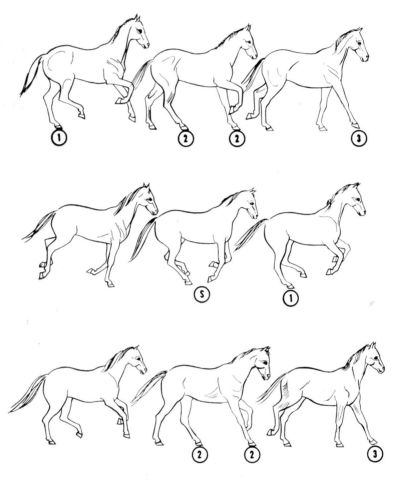

FIG. 10–4.—This shows the correct change of leads in a canter. In the first sequence the horse is in a right (off) fore lead with a left (near) hindlimb lead. At *S* the horse is in a period of suspension and properly changes leads at this time, coming down with right (off) hindlimb lead and a left (near) forelimb lead, as shown by the second sequence of foot beats.

Using as example a horse with the right, or off-fore leading, the gallop sequence is as follows: (*1*) near-hind, (*2*) off-hind, (*3*) near-fore, and (*4*) off-fore (followed by a period of suspension) (Fig. 10–3). The gait is very similar to the canter, with the exception that the paired, non-leading, diagonal limbs do not land together. The non-leading hindlimb lands slightly before the non-leading forelimb. The forelimb, with which the horse leads, and its diagonal hindlimb bear more weight and are subject to more fatigue than are the opposite diagonals. The propulsion is chiefly from the hindlimbs, while the forelimbs are subject to great concussion.

In a left or near-fore lead, the beat is as follows: (*1*) off-hind,

(2) near-hind, (3) off-fore, and (4) near-fore, (followed by a short period of suspension). Another way of describing the same beat, beginning with the lead limb in an off-fore (right) lead would be: (1) off-fore, (suspension) (2) near-hind, (3) off-hind, (4) near-fore. In a near-fore (left) lead, the beat is as follows: (1) near-fore (suspension), (2) off-hind, (3) near-hind, (4) off-fore.

The Canter (Fig. 10–5)

The canter is a restrained gallop, which, like the gallop, imposes greater wear on the leading forefoot and its diagonal leading hind-foot. It is a three-beat gait in which two diagonal legs are paired. The single beat of the paired legs falls between successive beats of the two unpaired legs. The unpaired legs act independently and are the lead limbs. The forelimb with which the horse leads and its

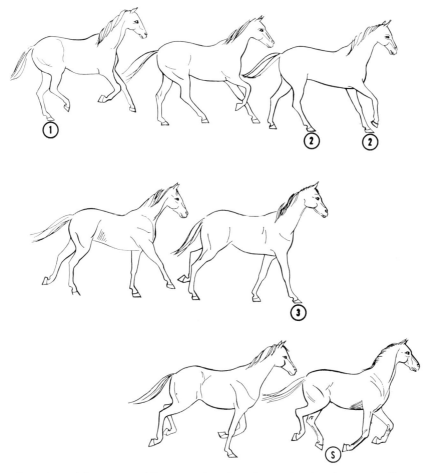

FIG. 10–5.—The canter. The canter is a three-beat gait with the feet landing, as shown by the numbers, followed by a period of suspension (S). The non-leading fore and hindlimbs are paired to cause one beat of the three beats.

diagonal leading hindlimb bear the most weight and are subject to more fatigue than are the paired limbs. This is the reason leads should be changed frequently. The length of stride in the canter will vary between 9'8" and 11'8". The distance between steps will usually vary between 37" and 43". In a right or off forelimb lead, the beat is as follows: (*1*) near-hind, (*2*) diagonal off-hind and near-fore together, (*3*) off-fore (followed by a short period of suspension) (Fig. 10–5). Another way of describing the same beat, beginning with the lead limb in an off-fore (right) lead would be: (*1*) off-fore (suspension) (*2*) near-hind, (*3*) diagonal off-hind and near-fore together. In a near-fore (left) lead, the beat is as follows: (*1*) near-fore (suspension), (*2*) off-hind, (*3*) near-hind and off-fore together.

If the canter is exceptionally animated (collected), a four-beat gait may result, similar to the four-beat gait of the gallop. When the gait becomes a four-beat cadence, the paired fore and opposite hindlimb do not land together; the hindlimb lands just before the forelimb or the forelimb lands shortly before the hindlimb. When the horse changes leads in a canter both the fore and hindlimbs should change leads at the same time, or a disagreeable gait will result. When the horse changes stride in front but not in back the hindlimb on the same side as the leading forefoot lands before the hindlimb opposite the lead forefoot.

The Pace (Fig. 10–6)

The pace is a fast two-beat gait in which the lateral fore and hind-feet strike the ground simultaneously. It is a faster gait than the trot, but is not as rapid as the gallop. Such a gait is not suited to mud or snow. Because the gait causes a rolling motion, the horse is said to be a body or leg pacer, depending upon the amount of

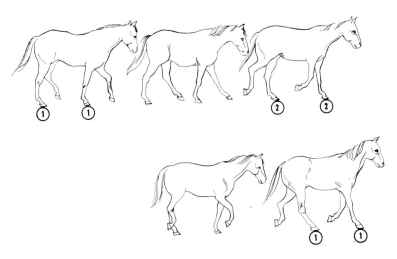

FIG. 10–6.—The pace. The pace is a two-beat gait in which the lateral fore and hindlimbs are paired, with the feet landing as shown.

rolling of the body during movement. The base of support is always on the two lateral limbs and there is a brief moment of suspension as two limbs leave the ground and the other two strike it. The length of stride in the pace is 12 to 14 ft.

The Amble

The amble is a pace at walking speed and is classified as a "slow-gait." Some authorities have said the amble is not a pace because the hindfoot lands slightly before the forefoot. There is no period of suspension, since one foot is always on the ground. The legs work in lateral pairs, but the forefoot of one lateral pair remains on the ground until the hindfoot of the opposite lateral pair touches the ground. Therefore, it is not a true pace.

The "Slow-gaits" (Running Walk, Fox Trot, or Amble)

The five-gaited horse must show one of the slow-gaits plus a rack in addition to the walk, trot, and canter.

The Fox Trot.—This is a slow, short, broken trot in which the head usually nods during movement. The horse brings each hind-foot to the ground an instant before the diagnonal forefoot strikes.

The Rack or Singlefoot (Broken Amble).—This is an artificial gait, in most cases. An exaggerated walk of four beats, it is a fast, flashy gait in which each foot meets the ground separately at equal intervals. Originally known as the singlefoot, the rack is easy on the rider but difficult on the horse. It should not be confused with the pace; although it looks similar because the hindlimb lands just before the forelimb of the same side. The rack differs from the running walk in that there is more up and down motion of the limbs, and the hindfoot does not overreach the forefoot as much as in a running walk.

Backing

This is done at the two-beat diagonal gait of the trot. Both left-hind and right-fore and the right-hind and left-fore move in unison when the horse is backing with any speed.

REFERENCES

1. AXE, J. WORTLEY.: *The Horse*, London, Gresham Publishing Co., *Vols. 1 and 3*, about 1900.
2. HILDEBRAND, M.: How Animals Run. Scientific American, *202* (5), 148, 1960.
3. ————: Symmetrical Gaits of Horses. Science, *150*, 701, Nov. 1965.
4. SELF, MARGARET CABELL: *The Horseman's Encyclopedia*, New York, A. S. Barnes & Co., 1946.
5. SMITH, F.: *A Manual of Veterinary Physiology.* 5th ed., Chicago, Alex Eger, 1921.
6. TAYLOR, B. M., TIPTON, C. M., ADRIAN, M. and KARPOBITH, P. V.: Action of Certain Joints in the Leg of the Horse Recorded Electrogoniometrically. Am. J. Vet. Res., *27*, 85, Jan. 1966.
7. WYNMALEN, HENRY, and LYNE, MICHAEL: *The Horse in Action*, New York, A. S. Barnes & Co., 1954.

Methods of therapy

Chapter 11

1. Physical Therapy

The aim of physical therapy is the restoration of function and promotion of tissue healing by assisting normal physiological processes. Methods of physical therapy are heat, cold, massage, exercise, light, electricity, manipulation and mechanical devices. Not all of these methods are applicable to horses. The physiological response of physical therapy is its effect on the vascular supply; this in turn reflexly reproduces similar changes in deeper tissues.

A. Cold.—The application of cold is used in treatment of acute and hyperacute inflammatory processes. It aids in relief of pain and is used to prevent edema and tissue swelling. There is a decrease of tissue metabolism and the possibility of some anesthesia. Cold is best combined with compression bandage and rest to further limit swelling. Cold can be applied through a bandage and is used the first twenty-four to forty-eight hours after trauma has occurred.

After this time, it is of no value. It is applied for twenty- to forty-minute applications and at least one hour should elapse before it is reapplied.

Cold application can be made by running cold water through a hose on the part or by using a tub or canvas bag to cover the limb. This type of moist therapy should not be used if there is an open wound. Ice bags or ice contained in plastic is very helpful in acute–noninfectious inflammatory processes. This type of therapy limits swelling from the acute injury and will shorten the recovery period. Swelling is limited by causing a vasoconstriction. If cold is applied too long, there may be a reflex vasodilation, and there is also the possibility of vasodilation after the cold is removed. These are additional reasons why compression bandage should be used in conjunction with cold application. Alternating heat and cold are often used on acute–noninfectious inflammatory conditions (such as sprain) after an interval of twenty-four hours following the injury. Cold is used for injury of muscles, tendons, ligaments, joints and burns.

B. Heat (Thermotherapy).—Heat can be applied as radiant heat, conductive heat and conversive heat.[20] Physiological effects of the three methods are basically the same. Radiant heat is applied by infrared light, conductive heat by hot water bottle, electric heating pad, hot fomentations and poultices. Conversive heat is developed in tissues by resistance to high frequency electrical energy (diathermy) or sound waves (ultrasound).

Heat is used in an attempt to cause resorption of swelling caused by blood or serum. Heat causes vasodilation and increases the number of phagocytes in the area, as well as increasing oxygen to the part. There is increased metabolism in local cells, increased lymph flow and a rise in temperature caused by the vasodilation. Vessel permeability is also increased and this must be considered when using heat because increased vessel permeability can lead to increased absorption of toxins or occurrence of tissue edema following its use. Heat is usually not used alone, but is combined with active or passive action, either manually or by exercise. Heat can spread bacteria and toxic products deeper into surrounding tissues and should not be applied following injury if infection is present. Heat should not be used until infection is under control by antibiotics. Heat should not be used on any injury until twenty-four to forty-eight hours have passed.

Superficial Heat.—Some methods of applying heat cause only superficial inflammation that does not extend far beneath the skin. Hot water poultices, heating pads, turbulator (whirlpool) and ultraviolet light are used for this purpose. Hot water poultices and turbulator (whirlpool) are application of moist heat, and drugs may be added to facilitate penetration. For this purpose, magnesium sulfate or mild liniment solutions are commonly used. Magnesium sulfate also acts as an agent to draw swelling from the tissue, because of the higher osmotic tension in the magnesium sulfate solution. Magnesium sulfate should be added at the rate of approximately two cups per gallon of water for this purpose. A turbulator can be used to give passive massage to the part during the application of hot water heat. A turbulator is a motorized device that agitates the water around the part by pump action. These are expensive and carry some risk of electrical shock. An inexpensive turbulator can be made by reversing a vacuum cleaner hose so that the air blows from the machine instead of sucking air. With the vacuum hose deep in the water that is around the limb, the machine blows air through the hose and turbulates water around the part. Superficial heat of this type is often combined with massage and following application of heat with one of the above methods, the part may be massaged using alcohol or other mild rubifacient solutions. These solutions do not have any particular therapeutic value, but they aid the massage and cause a superficial erythema. Many times the liniment may be blamed for improvement of a part when actually the only benefit was the result of the heat and massage.

For deeper penetration, infrared light, both luminous and non-luminous, is used. The luminous type of infrared is used mostly for atmospheric heating for young pigs and calves. It also can be used for frost bite, or to aid in pointing abscesses. There is a danger of a thermal burn caused by infrared light and the source should be at least 18 inches away from the part being treated. There is no pain, and evidence of thermal burn occurs later. It can be applied for twenty- to forty-minute applications and repeated at hourly intervals if necessary. The nonluminous type of infrared light heats a metal coil and this coil radiates the infrared light. This form is usually the best type to use since there is no danger of bulb breakage.

Deep Heat.—1. *Diathermy.*—Diathermy will penetrate to approximately a 2-inch depth. There is a problem of arcing and electrical shorting in treating animals. Ultra short wave diathermy units are available in which the current oscillates several million cycles per second. The tissue heats because of resistance to this energy and it is unable to expel the heat produced. Diathermy treatments can be used twice daily if necessary.

Heating by high frequency electrical energy is obtained by including the tissues in the circuit. The high frequency electrical energy passes from one electrode through the tissues to the other electrode. Resistance in the tissues produces a variable rise in tissue temperature due to a variation in the degree of impedance to the electrical energy. Therefore, all tissues will not be heated to the same degree. The greater the fluid content of the tissue, the higher the temperature recorded. Fatty tissues are the most resistant and may be damaged earlier than other tissues. Bone and tendon have lower water content and do not heat as much as the surrounding moist tissues. Diathermy is a relatively impractical way of treating horses. The difficulty in getting the coils to adapt to the part, the possibility of the horse moving and damaging equipment, plus the danger of possible short circuit shocking of the horse, make this method of therapy cumbersome and it is not commonly used. If bone screws or pins are present in the bone, they may heat to a high enough temperature to cause bone necrosis.

2. *Ultrasound.* — Ultrasound consists of ultra high frequency sound waves produced by conversion of high frequency electrical energy waves to sound waves by the crystal in the head of the instrument. There is a mechanical vibration produced by the sound waves. This crystal converts electricity to sound which is measured in watts of output per square centimeter of head surface. Use of ultrasound involves the passage of these high frequency sound waves (above 20,000 cycles per sec.) through tissues. The resistance of the tissues to these waves produces heat. This heat will penetrate to the bony structures of a joint or limb. Ultrasound is best used for deep heat penetration of muscles (myositis), nerve damage, tendon injury, trauma, bursitis and scars in contracted tissue. In some cases it may be better than corticoids for these conditions, and can be used in combination with them. Ultrasound restores function by relief of pain, which is caused by the production of heat. It is not of value in bone damage, and if enough is used, bone destruction may occur because of the heat produced. It has been said by some that the bone chips from sesamoids and other small bones can be removed by use of this agent. However, this is undesirable since healthy bone may be demineralized as a result of inflammation caused by this treatment.

Ultrasound penetrates deeper (approximately 3 to 5 inches) than does diathermy or other forms of heat application described, and also causes a micromassage of tissue. The chassis of the machine should always be grounded to prevent accidental shock to the horse.

Dosage. — For tendons or superficial tissue: .5 watts per sq. centimeter of head surface is used. For deeper penetration: 1 to 2 watts per square centimeter of head surface is used. Duration of application varies between five and ten minutes and the head should be kept in motion and in contact with the skin. Ultrasound waves do not pass through the air or through hair on the surface of the body. The part should be clipped and shaved, and a coupling agent, such as mineral oil, must be used to establish contact between the head and tissue. High doses of ultrasound will cause a rise in tissue heat to as high as 106°.[6] The high temperature rise can cause bone or tissue damage and care should be taken not to use too high a dosage for too long a period of time. The head should be kept in motion to prevent heat from accumulating in the tissues underneath the head surface.

Ultrasound should not be used for forty-eight to seventy-two hours after injury since it can cause hematoma and seroma if used before this. It can disseminate cancer cells, and should not be used over an area of local anesthesia, because the horse cannot feel it, and would not object to the heat if it was causing discomfort. Ultrasound can be used more safely than diathermy in the presence of pone pins, screws and other metalic objects.

Ultrasound can be used for approximately ten days prior to radiation therapy but is not used for at least two months after radiation therapy has been administered because radiation therapy causes a prolonged inflammatory reaction.[12] Ultrasound is of most use when there are no bone changes and when only soft tissues are damaged.

C. *Massage.*—Massage is used in subacute and chronic swellings and can be combined with the use of liniments, although the main benefit is from massage. The lubrication quality of the liniment usually aids in the massaging. Many liniments receive credit for being good therapeutic agents, when actually the massage causes the reduction of edematous swelling and aids in relieving pain of an injured tendon or joint. The effect is transitory and must be done several times a day to be of most value. Massage aids in reducing tissue edema and also aids in freeing scar tissue adhesions of the skin to underlying tissues.

2. Other Methods of Therapy

A. *Immobilization of the Part.*—Immobilization is one of the most beneficial methods of therapy for acute inflammatory conditions, but it can be difficult to employ in horses because they may resist the restraint. Immobilization of the part will aid in preventing the spread of inflammation and reduce swelling as it reduces movement. It also permits the tissues to heal with minimal scar formation. Immobilization will also support damaged structures to aid their healing, which is especially valuable in healing of tendons. Immobilization is best done by the use of a plaster cast. When this is not possible or feasible, compression bandages such as Ace bandages, cotton bandage, or nylon bandages may be of help. Compression bandages should not be used in acute infectious inflammatory conditions until the infection is under control by the use of antibiotics. Unless the infection is controlled by antibiotics, the compression might tend to force bacteria and associated toxic products deeper into the tissues. In no case should a compression bandage be left on longer than three days without changing. Skin loss from necrosis can occur if this rule is not observed. Strong liniments should not be used under bandages because they can cause blistering.

At this point, it might be well to mention the fact that ordinary gauze is extremely non-elastic, and when left in place for longer than twenty-four hours may cause loss of skin. When gauze is used under a compression bandage, it is usually best to use the type known as "Kling"* or "conforming" gauze which is much more elastic and does not rigidly oppose the tissue. The same is true of ordinary adhesive tape and preferably only elastic adhesive tape is used.†

* Johnson & Johnson Co.
† Elasticon, Johnson & Johnson Co.

Application of a Cast. —A cast is applied to allow healing of bone and tendon, to immobilize a wound, and to offer support to a limb to prevent contraction of tendons or overstress. In this discussion the use of a cast for fracture of long bones is not described.

The following are examples of plaster of paris and plaster-resin products available for use. The products from Vetco Div., Johnson & Johnson Co., New Brunswick, N.J. are used for examples.

1. Blue label "specialist" plaster of paris, fast setting, five to eight minutes. Available in 2- to 6-inch widths. This product is satisfactory for ordinary splinting.

2. Extra fast setting, green label "specialist" bandages. Available in 2- to 6-inch widths. Setting time two to four minutes.

3. Zoroc resin-plaster bandages. Zoroc combines plaster, resin and catalyst in one product. It is applied the same as other plaster bandages but is stronger and shows more resistance to the effects of moisture. It is available in 3- to 6-inch widths. Setting time five to eight minutes. Zoroc bandages are more than twice as expensive than the blue and green label plaster bandages. If care is taken to either paint the bottom of the cast with quick drying enamel or to cover it with rubber inner tubing to prevent moisture from seeping through and destroying the bottom portion of the cast, a water resistant cast material is usually not necessary.

4. Plaster of paris splints. —These are available in the blue and green label products. The blue label with a setting time of five to eight minutes and the green label with a setting time of two to four minutes. The following sizes are available: 3 × 15 inches, 4 × 15 inches, 5 × 30 inches. A splint of this type can also be made by rolling an ordinary plaster bandage back and forth on itself until the proper length and thickness are attained.

5. Orthopedic stockinette. —This is available in 2- to 10-inch widths and can be cut to length.

6. Orthopedic felt. —For protecting the skin at the top of the cast and for padding around prominences.

(1) *Application of Cast for Lacerations in the Lower Limb; i.e., Lower Metacarpal Region to the Coronary Band.* —Lacerations of this region often involve tendon(s) and/or tendon sheath. Application of a cast to lower limb lacerations often proves to be one of the best methods of therapy. It immobilizes the tissues while they heal and causes union of lacerated surfaces where it might not normally occur with just a pressure bandage. This is especially true in lacerations in the region of the coronary band.

Procedure. —The wound is clipped, shaved and cleansed. Debridement of the wound is done and sutures are placed if practical or indicated. The wound is dressed with sterile bandages and the limb covered with stockinette. A cast may be put on in the standing position under tranquilization if the horse is of good disposition. Otherwise, it is best to administer tranquilization, 6 per cent chloral hydrate until incoordination exists and then put the horse down with

1 gram of thiamylal sodium.* An additional gram of surital can be given a 1000 pound horse to keep him immobilized during the casting procedure. After the limb is covered with stockinette, 3 rolls of 4- or 6-inch blue label Johnson & Johnson plaster of paris are applied enclosing the foot wall and extending to just below the carpus or tarsus. Optionally, $\frac{1}{4}$ × 3-inch orthopedic felt can be placed under the top of the cast in a ring formation around the limb. Orthopedic felt can also be placed around the coronary band to prevent chafing, but this is not necessary when the foot is completely immobilized by the cast. After three rolls of plaster have been applied, plaster splints (4 inches wide, 15 inches long or 5 × 30 inches) are used on the dorsal and volar surfaces of the limb. A $\frac{1}{4}$ inch thickness of plaster splints is used on each surface. The splint should go over the bottom of the sole of the foot and conform closely to the pastern and fetlock areas. The first rolls of plaster are put on with very little tension. They are merely laid over the limb and smoothed without pulling them tight. After the plaster splints are applied, an additional three or four rolls of 4- or 6-inch plaster are used to reinforce the cast. More tension can be put on these latter rolls because the first rolls of plaster and the plaster splints are beginning to dry and will resist pressure. This does not mean that one can put great pressures on the plaster but it should be pulled up reasonably snug. The cast is allowed to dry and hopefully the horse will not bear weight on the cast until this occurs.

When the cast is applied while the horse is standing, the limb should be picked up from the floor to apply the plaster splints on the dorsal and volar surfaces and to enclose the foot with the plaster rolls.

When applying a cast over a wound, it is usually necessary to remove the cast in approximately eight days and apply a new one because of discharges that occur. When the cast is removed, strong odors may be present, but these are not necessarily indicative of destructive changes and are usually due to putrefaction of discharges from the wound. The wound is thoroughly cleansed and a new cast applied in a similar fashion to the first one. After removal of the second cast, in another eight days, the wound is usually healed sufficiently so that a cast is no longer necessary if a tendon is not cut, and the wound can be treated by a pressure bandage and topical medication.

(2) *Cast Following Removal of Sesamoid Fractures, for Fractures of the First and Second Phalanges and for Other Orthopedic Procedures in the Lower Limb.* —The horse is ordinarily under surgical anesthesia for an orthopedic procedure and the cast is put on in the recumbent position. If an incisional area is present, it is bandaged with sterile gauze and elastic tape. The limb is then covered with stockinette and the proximal portion of the cast just below the carpus or tarsus

* Surital, Parke Davis Co.

is covered by $\frac{1}{4}$ × 3 inch orthopedic felt. Three rolls of 4- or 6-inch blue label Johnson & Johnson plaster of paris are applied to the limb including the hoof and sole. These rolls are applied without tension. Special emphasis is placed on supporting the posterior aspect of the pastern. After the three rolls of plaster are applied, plaster splints (4 inches wide, 15 inches long) are placed on the dorsal and volar surface of the limb. These splints also cover the bottom of the foot. The splints are molded carefully to the limb and an additional three rolls of 4- or 6-inch plaster are used to reinforce the cast. These latter rolls may be pulled fairly snugly because the original rolls of plaster and splints will act as protection against getting the cast too tight. In addition to uses already mentioned, this cast can be used following surgery to promote ankylosis of the proximal interphalangeal joint, following removal of fractures of the extensor process of the third phalanx, and following removal of chip fractures of the first phalanx into the metacarpophalangeal joint. It also can be used for longitudinal articular fractures of the third metacarpal bone that have no separation of fragments (see Chapter 6). The foot of the cast is protected from moisture by spraying with quick drying enamel or applying a piece of rubber over the bottom of the cast.

(3) *Cast for Protection of the Carpus Following Carpal Surgery.*— The cast is applied with the horse in a recumbent position as soon as the skin incision is closed with sutures. Orthopedic felt is used to pad the limb in the region of the accessory carpal bone and lateral and medial malleoli of the radius. Padding is not placed over these areas but the adjacent limb is padded to the same circumference as these points. This distributes pressure more evenly, and aids in preventing skin necrosis over these prominences. The limb is then covered with stockinette after the incision is bandaged. One-fourth by 3-inch orthopedic felt is placed just above the fetlock joint and at the proximal portion of the cast just below the elbow joint. Four rolls of 6-inch plaster are then placed on the limb between the elbow joint and the proximal aspect of the metacarpophalangeal joint. Following this, plaster splints 4 inches wide, 30 inches long and $\frac{1}{4}$ inch thick are placed over the dorsal and volar surfaces of the limb. The first rolls of plaster are only laid upon the limb and not pulled up snugly. Following the application of the plaster splints three to four more rolls of 6-inch plaster of paris is put on the cast to reinforce it. These latter rolls can be pulled more tightly than the first ones because of the resistance of the original plaster in the drying process. All casts should be rubbed thoroughly to cause blending of the layers. This cast is removed in six to eight days following carpal surgery. The cast acts as protection against injury to the carpus while the horse is recovering from anesthesia, and as an excellent pressure bandage during this period of time. It is followed up with elastic pressure bandages for an additional thirty days.

(4) *Casting Procedure for Immobilization of the Hock.*—Casting of the hock joint must be done carefully or necrosis over the tuber calcis or the malleoli of the tibia may occur. Casting this area is

frequently indicated for wounds on the anterior surface of the tarsal joint. Other indications are fractures, tendon lacerations, luxation of the tarsal joint, and rupture of the gastrocnemius muscle. In most cases, it is best for the cast to include the hoof. The tremendous muscular power of the hind limb is somewhat restrained by including the hoof rather than stopping the cast at the fetlock joint.

A 1000 lb. horse is restrained with $\frac{1}{2}$ mg./lb. promazine,* enough 6 per cent chloral hydrate to make him unsteady on his feet (250 to 500 cc. 6 per cent solution) and 2 gm. of thiamylal sodium† given intravenously. This will ordinarily give enough anesthesia to allow application of a cast and time enough for it to dry before the horse attempts to get up. The wound is cleaned and dressed, if one is present, and the limb is covered with stockinette. One-fourth by 3-inch orthopedic felt is applied in the region of the malleoli of the tibia so that the adjacent limb is built out to the level of these prominences. It is best to do it in this fashion rather than try to pad the prominence itself. The limb is covered with stockinette and several rolls of 6-inch blue label Johnson & Johnson plaster bandage are applied. In most cases four to five rolls are applied prior to applying plaster splints. These initial rolls are not pulled down tightly but laid on to conform to the limb without putting on pressure. At this time blue label Johnson & Johnson plaster splints 5 by 30 inches and $\frac{3}{8}$ inch thick are applied to the plantar and dorsal surfaces of the limb. These splints are centered over the point at the hock. One strip on the plantar surface and one strip on the dorsal surface are used. This will reinforce the cast in the area of greatest stress. An additional four or five rolls of plaster are then applied to the limb. The cast is carried up close to the stifle joint and down to and including the hoof wall. If desired, plaster splints may also be applied in the region of the fetlock joint, including the foot. If tendon injury has occurred, it is best to apply splints in this area as described for the forelimb extending proximally to just below the tarsal joint.

The hock must be restrained so that no motion occurs in order to avoid skin necrosis over the point of the hock. The cast is removed in six to eight days if it is being used for a wound. If being used for a fracture, it is removed and changed as it loosens. Six to eight weeks in a cast are required for severed flexor tendons or ruptured gastrocnemius tendon.

B. *Application of Counterirritation.*—Counterirritation is used to stimulate a subacute or chronic inflammatory process to a more acute process in the hope that resolution will occur when the acute inflammation heals. Counterirritants may be classified by their strength:

(1) Rubefacient Drugs.—These produce redness and mild heat by increasing circulation. They are commonly present in various

* Promazine, Ft. Dodge Labs.
   Sparine, Wyeth Labs.
† Surital, Parke Davis Co.

braces and liniments. Many terms are applied to products used for rubefacient effect. The terms "liniment," "tightener," "brace," and "sweat" are often used. In reality there is very little difference in any of them.

A *liniment* is any combination of drugs used for rubefacient effect and examples are as follows: A preparation of camphor and cottonseed oil, camphor and soap liniment—a preparation of hard soap, camphor, rosemary oil and alcohol; chloroform liniment—a preparation of chloroform with camphor and soap base.

A liniment usually contains one or more of the essential (volatile) oils. Their use on the legs of a horse can result in considerable edema and skin soreness. If the reaction is severe or neglected, scars and denuded areas can result. A horse should not be ridden while skin soreness or edema are present. The blistering effect of a liniment is increased when a bandage is used to cover the area where liniment was applied.

A *tightener* is a term applied to various drug mixtures that appear to aid removal of edema or filling of a joint capsule or tendon sheath. The so-called tightener effect comes about from removal of edema or synovia so that the tendons and suspensory ligament are more palpable. In most cases this effect is not due to the drug but due to the massage when applying the drug and the compression bandage that is applied over the area after the tightener has been rubbed in. An example of a tightener is as follows: tincture of belladonna—4 oz. (not used in preparations prescribed at race tracks); tannic acid powder—2 oz.; menthol crystals—2 oz.; camphor crystals—1 oz.; alcohol—q.s. 1 qt. There should be no skin soreness present when a product of this type is used. It is applied daily and covered with a cotton and roll bandage for five days.

A *sweat* is a product that causes some moisture accumulation on the skin following its use. Most products, including alcohol, will do this. The skin of a horse can actually exude serum from its surface in the presence of inflammation. A plastic wrapping, oiled silk, or waxed paper is usually applied around the limb following the use of this type of drug mixture. These wrappings themselves can cause the skin to "sweat." In addition to alcohol alone, equal parts of alcohol and glycerin are also used for this action. Many other proprietary remedies are available.

A *brace* is a mixture of drugs that is used routinely following workouts. The limbs of the horse are rubbed down prior to putting on leg wraps each night. In most cases the massage used in applying the mixture is of much more benefit than the mixture itself, but the drugs are given credit for action such as prevention of tendon sheath and joint capsule filling. Massage, plus the compression bandage, would accomplish the same purpose in most cases. Alcohol (ethyl or isopropyl) will serve this purpose satisfactorily. A proprietary remedy* made of wormwood (oil of chenopodium), thymol,

---

* Absorbine Jr., W. F. Young Inc., Springfield, Mass.

chloroxylenol, menthol and acetone is also very popular. This latter mix is also sometimes used as a "tightener" and a "sweat."

There is great overlapping of the above compounds, and in many cases, "secret formulas" are only variations of common drugs like camphor, ammonia, alcohol, oil of wintergreen (methyl salicylate), turpentine, glycerin, acetone, menthol, and thymol. Depending on concentrations of various products incorporated in them, they may or may not produce a severe irritation when enclosed under a bandage. Some types of leg paints are used that contain iodine which will produce a blistering effect if applied several days in a row under wraps. A mixture of 120 cc. 7 per cent tincture of iodine, 30 cc. turpentine and 30 cc. glycerin are an example of a type of leg paint that can produce this effect. If this type of product is used, it is better not to apply a bandage over it because a reasonably severe skin irritation can occur.

In summary one would have to say that most of these products are not really effective, but the massage and bandaging that occur with them probably are. As long as the product does not cause pain to the horse and irritation to the skin, no harm is done. The rubefacient effect is very temporary and must be repeated once or twice daily for any beneficial effect at all. An area of muscular soreness or joint soreness that is massaged will show pain relief following application of this type of drug. However, in just a short time the effect is gone.

(2) Blisters or Vesicants.—These agents produce blistering and inflammation of the skin down to the subcutaneous tissue. Red iodide of mercury and cantharides (Spanish Fly) are examples.

  (a) General rules for application of blisters:
    1. Clip area.
    2. Apply blister with a piece of cork or stick. Do not use hand.
    3. Rub in for about five minutes.
    4. Remove according to directions on blister as early as six to eight hours and as late as twenty-four hours.
    5. Apply petroleum jelly on outer ring where blister was applied so that if it runs, it will not disturb adjacent tissues.
  (b) Precautions in applying blisters:
    1. The horse must be cross-tied while the blister is in effect, because if he is able to lick or chew the area, considerable damage to the tongue and mouth may occur. A neck cradle may be necessary after the blister is removed.
    2. Do not use red iodide of mercury on very young horses because of severe irritation that may occur.
    3. When a blistering agent such as red iodide of mercury has been used, it may interfere with interpretation of radiographs because of deposits of iodine on the skin. The limb should be thoroughly scrubbed before x-ray films are taken.

28

    4. Always give tetanus antitoxin or have the horse on a tetanus toxoid program prior to using a blister.

(c) Conditions for which blistering agents are used: (subacute or chronic inflammation):
1. Chronic inflammations of joints (hock, stifle, fetlock, carpus)
2. Chronic bone conditions (ringbone, bog spavin, exostosis, side bones)
3. Tendonitis
4. Tendosynovitis
5. Synovitis
6. Curb
7. Pointing abscesses

(d) Contraindications are:
1. Acute and hyperacute inflammatory conditions
2. Open wounds
3. Flexor surfaces except the fetlock
4. Near mucous membranes
5. Weak or emaciated animals
6. In an area where corticoids have been injected recently (within thirty days)

(e) Results of blistering:
1. Blistering and scurfing of the skin—its effectiveness is questionable, especially in bony conditions. In general it can be said that blistering is an ineffective and painful method of therapy. Results are obtained due to the enforced rest of the horse.

(3) Therapeutic cautery (firing)

Purpose.—To produce an acute inflammatory process in a chronic or subacute inflammation in hope that it will undergo resolution.

Indications.—It is one of the most misused therapeutic agents in veterinary therapy. It is often used on normal tissue and on conditions for which it is contraindicated.

Conditions for Which Therapeutic Cautery is Used:

(a) Soft tissue damage: especially around joints, ligaments and tendons.

(b) Carpitis (popped knee).—In this condition it is of most value when no periosteal new bone growth is present.

(c) Chronic arthritis.

(d) Osselets.—Osselets is one of the conditions for which firing may be of definite value. By creating an acute inflammation, resolution of the chronic arthritis may occur as healing takes place. This also usually makes it easier to obtain the proper rest for the horse. Four to six months' rest should follow firing of osselets. It is of little value after periosteal new bone growth involves the joint.

(e) Tendosynovitis and tendinitis.—Although firing is commonly used on these conditions, there is little indication to do so. There is already too much inflammation and scar tissue present.

(*f*) Sesamoiditis.—Firing is of doubtful value in this condition. It is commonly used but seldom effects a cure.

(*g*) Bone spavin.—Bone spavin is commonly fired in an effort to aid ankylosis of the distal intertarsal and tarsometatarsal joints. These joints will ankylose regardless of whether or not firing is done. Cunean tenectomy is of more value.

(*h*) Splints are commonly fired even though they will heal without any therapy. Rest must be enforced to obtain healing of the splint and firing usually will aid in forcing this rest.

Contraindications for Therapeutic Cautery:

(*a*) Near open wounds.

(*b*) Areas of dermatitis or infection.

(*c*) Acute inflammation.—Any area that is fired should be rested until the acute inflammation has subsided.

(*d*) Flexor surface of a joint, especially the flexor side of the carpus where skin folds upon itself.

(*e*) Healthy tissue.—In some areas it is a common procedure to fire horses prior to training in the mistaken belief that it will strengthen the parts. Scar tissue is not so strong as normal tissue and it is poor practice to fire in this fashion.

(*f*) Very young horses.

(*g*) Weak and emaciated animals.

(*h*) New bone growth in an active stage.—Firing may cause a flare-up of the bone activity and the new bone growth may be greater than it would have been otherwise.

(*i*) In an area where corticoids have been recently used (within thirty days).

Instruments for Firing.—A Number of Instruments are Available for Firing:

(*a*) Ether firing iron.—This instrument makes objectionable noise and when the flame goes out, it makes a loud report that disturbs the horse.

(*b*) Hand-made irons.—Hand-made irons are constructed so that the point is backed up by a large portion of iron. The heat in the iron will keep the point hot so that 4 or 5 points can be made in the skin before it requires reheating. This type of iron is usually heated by a blowtorch.

(*c*) Crude apparatus such as heating nails, etc. have been used in the past.

(*d*) Electric cautery.—This is by far the best instrument for therapeutic cautery. Different-sized points are available as well as instruments for cauterizing and removal of granulation tissues (see Fig. 11–1). These instruments are silent and portable. A variation in points decreases danger of puncturing a joint capsule. A smaller point should be used for firing fetlocks than for carpal joints.

(*e*) Line-firing instruments.—Line firing is not recommended and does not cause any more irritation than blistering. A flat instrument, $\frac{1}{8}$ inch wide, is ordinarily used and the skin must not be penetrated with the instrument. Lines should not be closer than $\frac{1}{2}$ inch apart. Various lines and chevron patterns are made but these are strictly up to the artistic ability of the operator. Point firing is more effective than line firing.

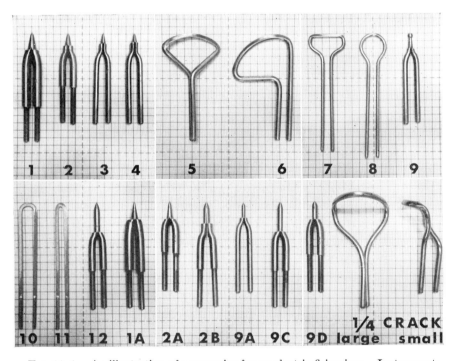

Fig. 11-1.—An illustration of accessories for an electric firing iron. Instruments for point firing, line firing, cautery and removal of granulation tissue are shown. (Courtesy Nicholson Manufacturing Company, Denver, Colorado.)

Point Firing.—If at all possible, the horse should be fired in a standing position. A tranquilizer can be given for sedation of nervous horses. Many horses that are docile become alarmed when they can smell the burning hair. In some cases two or three penetrations of the skin are all that can be made before the horse will move. By making only two or three firing holes and then stopping before the smoke reaches the horse's nostrils, this can be overcome. A horse that is fired in a recumbent position invariably has a poor firing pattern.

Technique:
    (a) The area to be fired is clipped with a #40 clipper blade.
    (b) The skin surface is then scrubbed with soap and water and a skin antiseptic applied. All scurf must be removed.
    (c) Induction of local anesthesia:

1. Carpus.—The carpus can be blocked in two ways. The author prefers to infiltrate the anterior surface of the carpus subcutaneously with 1 per cent procaine. A line block is put across the top of the carpus and then by injecting down the sides of the carpus and under the skin of the dorsal surface, a pad of 1 per cent procaine is formed under the entire skin area. This type of block produces good anesthesia, and protects the joint capsule as well, by cooling the firing point.

   The carpus can be anesthetized by blocking the median, ulnar and musculocutaneous nerves. This block is effective for anesthesia but does not give as much protection to the joint capsule. Protection of the joint capsule is advisable in case a horse jumps suddenly into the firing iron. When a procaine pad has been used, the firing point would rarely penetrate the capsule because of the cooling effect of the procaine. The capsule can be inadvertently punctured if there is no protective pad.

2. Fetlock.—Modern anesthetics make it possible to completely anesthetize the fetlock, using a ring block approximately 3 inches above the metacarpophalangeal joint. The volar nerves are located between the suspensory ligament and the deep flexor tendon (Fig. 4–9). Both medial and lateral volar nerves are blocked at this point and then a subcutaneous block is used to complete a ring block around the limb (see Chapter 4, p. 105). Special attention should be given to blocking a small nerve that runs between the second and third, and third and fourth metacarpal bones. It lies in the groove at the junction of these bones and a 25-gauge needle is used to carry local anesthetic to the bone at these points. At all other points around the limb it is satisfactory to use subcutaneous block. Using a drug like 2 per cent lidocaine hydrochloride* the block can be completed with approximately 12 cc. of the local anesthetic.

3. Other areas such as a bone spavin or splint can be blocked by subcutaneous infiltration of the local anesthetic over the part.

Point-Firing Patterns.—A point-firing pattern can be set up in a block pattern or diagonal pattern (Fig. 11–2). When applying the point, it is better to make the pattern first and then if the points are not deep enough, they can be retraced until the firing point has reached proper depth. Each hole in the pattern should not be closer than $\frac{3}{8}$ to $\frac{1}{2}$ inch from each other.

Factors to Consider in Point-Firing:

1. Heat of firing iron.—A cherry red heat is the correct heat for firing. If it is hotter than this, it will burn tissue excessively.

* Xylocaine, Astra Laboratories

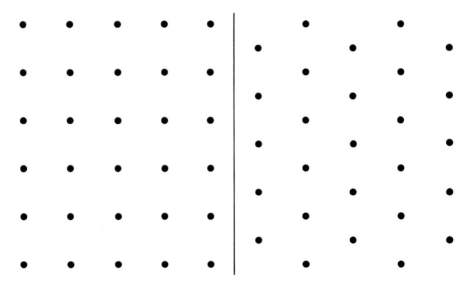

Fig. 11–2.—Rectangular and diagonal pattern used for point-firing. The points of the pattern should not be closer than ⅜ to ½ inch apart.

2. Length of time firing point is in the skin.—It is better to touch a firing hole twice quickly than to hold the iron in place too long. Leaving the firing point too long in the skin or making the holes too close will cause necrotic areas which can coalesce and cause sloughing of skin.
3. Do not use excessive pressure. It may cause penetration of a synovial structure or penetrate bone. Bone penetration causes risk of osteomyelitis or local bone necrosis, and is done only over splints or bone spavin.
4. Watch for sudden movements of the horse. One arm resting on the horse can often give the operator an indication that movement is about to occur.
5. When firing the fetlock joint, care should be taken not to penetrate the digital artery or vein on the abaxial surface of the sesamoid bone. Although this is usually not serious, it is unsightly and can be avoided by not allowing the firing point to penetrate beneath the skin in this area.

Technique for Line Firing.—Line firing is ordinarily used along the volar surface of tendons or over the long axis of the stifle joint. It is done under local anesthetic and the edge of the instrument should not be greater than ⅛ inch wide. I feel that line firing is ineffective enough that it does not deserve consideration. It causes no more inflammation than an ordinary blister.

Aftercare of Firing.—I discourage the use of a blistering agent after firing. Some veterinarians have recommended the use of mercuric iodide blisters following firing. If the firing points are as deep as they should be, the blister may cause severe sloughing of skin by causing subcutaneous tissue necrosis. This sloughing is serious, unsightly, and requires a long healing period. A leg paint, in my opinion, is preferable to a blistering agent. A leg paint that is effective in producing prolonged irritation as well as having some anesthetic qualities is compounded as follows: 2 parts 7 per cent tincture of iodine, 1 part glycerine, 1 part liquid phenol. Although it can be argued that the alcohol in the tincture of iodine will neutralize the phenol, this does not seem to be entirely true. Enough of the phenol is neutralized so that it does not cause necrosis, and the presence of some phenol seems to have an anesthetic effect. It is rare to have a horse that will chew at a bandage when this type of leg paint is used. The leg paint is applied daily for twenty-one days, using a brush to apply the paint into the wounds. The limb is then wrapped for protection with 14 × 16 inch combine pads* and muslin wraps. Leg paint acts as a local anesthetic, a germicidal agent, and prolongs irritation. In approximately ten days, a scaling will occur that shows that the superficial layers of skin are sloughing as a result of the leg paint. This is not serious and does not go deeper than the very superficial layers of the skin. After twenty-one days the leg paint is stopped but the limb is kept in wraps for a variable period of time. The horse should be rested six months following firing.

Unfortunate Sequelae of Firing:

(a) Sloughing of skin
(b) Tetanus
(c) Wound infection and septicemia
(d) Laminitis (from the inflammation produced by firing)
(e) Suppurative arthritis and synovitis (from penetrating these structures with a firing iron)

General Considerations for Firing. —Radiographs are essential for proper evaluation of the bones and whether or not firing should be used. Firing is most favorable for chronic and subacute conditions of soft tissue but it is used where periosteal new bone growth has occurred but is not in the active stages. Firing is of no value if periosteal new bone growth involves the articular surface of a joint.

(4) *Other Methods of Producing Counterirritation.* —Methods of producing irritation using caustic agents have been used but they are not recommended. The application of acid to a perforated piece of plastic to allow the acid to cause necrosis of skin at selected points approximately $\frac{1}{2}$ inch apart has been described but is not so effective as therapeutic cautery.

Injection of irritants to produce counterinflammation has been described.[25] This technique has been shown to be more effective in producing inflammation than either firing or blistering.[25] Injection of Lugol's iodine diluted from 1:2 to 1:20 have been used, as well

* Johnson & Johnson Co.

as 5 per cent aqueous iodine solution. These irritating products are injected along tendons in 1 to 1.5 cc. amounts, approximately 1 inch apart. A total of 10 to 15 cc. of the irritating product is used. This is followed by bandaging. Light work is instituted five to six weeks after injection. Unfortunately, in most tendonitis cases, there is already too much scar tissue and inflammation. This type of treatment may aid resolution of tendosynovitis by increasing blood supply as is claimed for Asheim's operation (see Tendosynovitis, Chapter 6). Such injections must be done following careful preparation of the skin by clipping, scrubbing, and application of skin antiseptic to prevent possible infection and sloughing.

C. Radiation Therapy.—Radiation therapy is another way of producing deep inflammation. Contrary to some reports that would indicate that it has an anti-inflammatory reaction, it actually produces an inflammatory reaction that can last for approximately forty days.[12] The phenomenon of immediate improvement from lameness does occasionally occur but this may be the result of damage to nerve endings. A minimum of ninety days' rest must be allowed following radiation therapy for best results. Long-term improvement is probably due to smoothing by osteophytes.

Radiation therapy can be applied in a number of ways. The most satisfactory methods are the use of a therapeutic x-ray machine or by the use of gamma radiation using cobalt-60 needles. Cobalt-60 needles have proven to be the most easily handled and the most satisfactory method of radiation therapy. Radium has also been used, but in case of an accidental breakage of a radium container, the radium powder can contaminate an area for several years. This makes it undesirable to use around horses. Cobalt-60 is prepared in wires and if the outer container should break, the wire is easily found with a counter. Radon gas enclosed in glass or beads has also been used, and has the advantage of having a very short half-life, but is expensive, since it can be used only once. The same radiation safety procedures must be used with radon as with any other radioactive source. Unfortunately, radon and radium presently are available in some states without license. In some cases practitioners are endangering themselves because they do not fully appreciate the dangers involved in radiation therapy.

Cobalt-60 needles can be placed in packs and taped directly over the area to be radiated. This is a distinct advantage over a therapeutic x-ray machine with which the slightest movement of the horse will change the intensity of the beam on the area to be radiated. In all cases, radiation therapy should be administered by a person specially trained in the use of this therapy and not done without proper precautions both to the horse and to persons in contact with the horse. It is usually best not to follow radiation therapy with a treatment like ultrasound which also produces deep inflammation. The long-lasting inflammation already present from radiation therapy could be accentuated enough by ultrasound to produce damage to bone or soft tissue.

The rate of the therapy and the energy of the source must be carefully computed or results will vary. When cobalt-60 packs are used, the strength of the pack should be sufficient to administer the therapy at the rate of 5 to 12 R per hour. Experimental work has shown that inflammation following this type of therapy lasts up to forty days or more and that actual decrease in bone density occurs.[12] This decreased bone density is the result of inflammation and does correct itself after approximately forty days. Decreased bone density could, in theory, lead to a fracture if the horse is not properly rested.

Prior to radiation treatment the affected joint must be radiographed. This will insure that the cause of lameness is not due to a small chip fracture or other conditions that are best handled surgically. If articular cartilage is destroyed, radiation therapy has been recognized as palliative only. Therefore, if joint narrowing, sclerosis, or cyst formation are noted radiographically, results will not be as favorable.

The following conditions are treated with radiation therapy: chronic traumatic arthritis and osteoarthritis of the carpal joint, chronic traumatic arthritis and osteoarthritis of the metacarpophalangeal joint, periosteal new bone growth of the carpal bones, or other conditions where a deep prolonged inflammatory reaction is indicated. Generally the type of arthritic lesion that seems to respond most satisfactorily to radiation therapy is one in which the changes are periarticular only. These changes may be soft tissue changes only or may have progressed to new bone growth. The dosage for the above conditions is usually 1000 to 1200 R.

Radiation therapy is also effective on some cases of equine sarcoid, equine fibrosarcoma, and equine squamous cell carcinoma. When radiation therapy is used on these conditions a dose that is strong enough to kill superficial and deep cells is used. The dosage for treating equine sarcoid, fibrosarcoma and squamous cell carcinoma will range from 3,000 to 4,500 R. Two thousand R are used to treat sarcoid over the carpus because of proximity to the carpal bones, leading to possible demineralization.

D. Exercise.—Depending on the condition, exercise is frequently used to aid in rehabilitation. It is primarily used in subacute and chronic conditions and is used to remove swelling, especially in puncture wounds of the limb, midline incisions, castrations, etc. Whenever possible, it is combined with massage and the use of liniments. It also may be used to rehabilitate and strengthen the limb following injury to tendon or ligaments. In any case, it must be used with judgment since the horse often will tend to overdo when allowed free access to a corral or pasture. Exercise on a hand lead is usually best when the horse is beginning exercise following surgery for fractured carpus, sesamoid fracture, etc. After the initial excitement has worn off, following several days of hand leading, the horse can be turned into a small lot and from there into a pasture as the limb strengthens.

E. Poultices or Cataplasms.—These agents work through high osmotic tension and the action is to draw fluid from the part toward the surface. Examples: (1) Denver Mud,* (2) magnesium sulfate, (3) Fuller's earth (impure aluminum silicate), (4) boric acid paste, (5) kaolin poultice (combination of kaolin, glycerin, water and aconite), (6) Unna's paste. Poultices tend to limit infectious or noninfectious inflammatory processes. They are very good over puncture wounds. Some of these agents are not applied directly to the skin for they might have a tendency to cause excessive moistening of the skin. An agent like Denver Mud can be applied directly on the skin with little detrimental effect. A bandage is placed over the poultice and usually it is left in position for twelve to forty-eight hours. A poultice may be reapplied at intervals for several applications.

These agents are very useful following surgery if there is a tendency for more than average swelling to occur. They can be applied over the surgical wound, around the circumference of the limb and kept under bandage. Applications are changed periodically according to the type of agent used.

Unna's paste is popular in other countries as an antiphlogistic poultice.[21] It is also used for supporting bandages. It is made by mixing the following ingredients: zinc oxide 150 gm., gelatin 150 gm., glycerine 350 ml., water 350 ml. The solid ingredients are mixed and the liquids are added, and the mass is stirred and heated in a double boiler. When the material acquires the consistency of heavy paint, it is ready for use. When cold, the paste assumes the springy consistency of foam rubber. Unused paste is reheated in the double boiler and used as required. The paste is applied to a conforming gauze bandage using a 2-inch brush. The paint is liberally applied to the part to be bandaged and to the gauze as it is rolled on. Adequate paste should be painted onto the gauze to insure that each layer of bandage adheres to its predecessor. No knots, pins or other fastening devices are necessary. The horse is kept away from dust and bedding for twenty minutes, allowing the paste time to set. The bandage is firm but flexible and can stay in place for several days. Removal is readily effected by cutting the bandage longitudinally and peeling it off. Indications for this type of bandage in a horse are support for flexor tendons, pressure bandage to aid resorption of excess synovia, prevent swelling in the legs of a horse confined to stable, and pressure bandaging of a wound in an effort to prevent excessive granulation tissue in a wound. This paste can also be used instead of pine tar and oakum in cases of punctured sole in the convalescent stage.

F. The Use of Anti-Inflammatory Agents.—The use of anti-inflammatory agents is now well established in veterinary medicine. The products used are corticoids and phenylbutazone (Butazolidin Jen-Sal Lab.), and oxyphenylbutazone (Tandearil, Geigy Labora-

* Demco Co., Denver, Colo.

tories). Depending on the individual product, these drugs can be given in a variety of ways. New additions to the field are claimed to be more effective than older ones that were formerly popular. The main use of these products has been for anti-inflammatory action in lamenesses, especially arthritic involvements. It has been found that they also can be used with judgment following surgery to aid in relief of postsurgical pain and swelling. When used in this manner, they must be used with discretion and be covered by the use of parenteral antibiotics. The corticoids also are used by injection locally into inflammatory conditions such as tendosynovitis, splints and other local inflammatory conditions. Tendosynovitis can also be treated parenterally with corticoids while the lesion heals in a cast. Intra-articular use of corticoids is popular and beneficial in many cases. However, in many cases it is used to alleviate symptoms of lameness without allowing sufficient rest for healing of the part. In this case, additional damage is done to the joint while the horse goes on with racing workouts. This eventually leads to a complete degeneration of the joint. The same can be true of parenteral injection of corticoids and phenylbutazone derivatives.

One must be cautious in using a counterirritation method following the use of an anti-inflammatory drug. In some cases a joint is injected and a blister or point firing is used over the joint. This is completely contraindicated; using two exactly opposite methods of therapy. When a horse has received numerous intra-articular injections for a lameness, i.e., carpal fracture, sesamoid fracture, etc., it is advisable to wait a period of time prior to surgery for removal of the chip fracture. The prognosis is poor since the chip fracture should be removed as soon as possible after it occurs. The intra-articular injection or parenteral use of corticoids and/or phenylbutazone derivatives allows the horse to use the joint and causes degenerative changes as a result of the fracture. In addition numberous injections may lower the tissue resistance of the part, making it more likely that infection may result from surgery. This type of therapy should be discouraged and before surgical procedure is done on a joint, inquiry should be made as to how many times it has been treated with a corticoid, or how long the horse has been on parenteral or oral therapy with corticoids or phenylbutazone derivatives.

INTRA-ARTICULAR INJECTION

The value of corticoid injections, intra-articularly, in certain joint involvements has definitely been established. The site of action of corticoids, following intra-articular injection, appears to be on the synovial membrane. These drugs cause a suppression of inflammation which allows recovery of cellular function. Synovial fluid volume is reduced and its viscosity is increased to normal. To obtain optimal results, the hormone should be injected directly into the synovial space; however, it also has been established that injection of the drugs into tissues that are inflamed from noninfectious causes is of considerable therapeutic aid. Such noninfectious conditions include acute bowed tendon, splints, and bucked shins (*see* Chapter 6).

The exact mode of anti-inflammatory action of the corticoids is unknown; however, some investigators believe the hormone acts as a buffer or shield between irritants and susceptible cells. Other authorities claim that the activity of the injured cell is altered so that it is less effective in producing some of the specific factors responsible for inflammation. Some authorities are of the opinion that the hormones do not protect against the irritants as such, but that they prevent the inflammatory response. All seem to agree, however, that the steroids increase the "insult threshold" of the cell. This causes the restoration of cell function in what would otherwise be a disabling environment. Whatever the mode of action, the value of corticoids in the treatment of joint inflammation is quite firmly established in veterinary practice. Adequate rest must accompany the use of corticoids for they merely decrease inflammation while healing occurs. Too often, the corticoids are used to mask symptoms, allowing the horse to further damage the part.

General Technique

Before any joint cavity is invaded, it is of utmost importance that the skin area be clipped, shaved, and washed thoroughly. A surgical preparation of the injection area should be done. Introduction of bacteria into the joint cavity, from the exterior, greatly lessens the chances of satisfactory recovery, or may even lead to a condition more serious than the one already present. Aseptic precautions also should be observed when using these drugs subcutaneously around local inflammatory conditions such as splints.

A 20-gauge needle should be sufficient size for most injections; the length of the needle is determined by the area to be injected. In sensitive or nervous animals, infiltration with local anesthetic agent, prior to the injection, may be necessary; a 25-gauge needle should be used for this purpose. The needle should be pushed into the area quickly without the syringe attached; this avoids the breakage of a needle under the skin if the horse moves quickly.

Entrance into the joint cavity can be confirmed by withdrawing synovial fluid into the syringe. All fluid that can be withdrawn easily should be removed prior to injection. In some cases the fluid will run freely through the needle so no syringe is necessary to aspirate the fluid. The end of the needle will move freely when properly positioned in the joint capsule or tendon sheath. If the needle is in the proper place, the injection of fluid will be accomplished easily and without undue pressure from tissue resistance. In some cases, it may be extremely difficult to withdraw any volume of fluid. The cause for this is not always apparent, but it may be due to villae which plug the lumen of the needle. In such a case, the injection should be continued without prolonged efforts to withdraw fluid.

The amount of corticoid to be injected depends on the size of the joint and the degree of inflammation. The following doses are approximate and vary with the size of the joint:

(1) *Hydrocortisone Acetate.*—Fifty to 100 mg. in a joint. More can be used in large joints and for subcutaneous injection over an inflammatory process. This product is one of the earliest of the steroid group and is seldom used at the present time. This is because there are other products which are longer lasting, more effective, and have fewer side effects.

(2) *Prednisolone* (Sterane, Pfizer Labs.; Meticorten, Schering Labs.). Fifty to 100 mg. depending on the size of the joint. More can be used for large joints or for subcutaneous injection over an inflammatory process.

(3) *Prednisolone Tertiary — Butylacetate* (Hydeltrone — T.B.A., Merck & Co.). Fifty to 100 mg., depending on the size of the joint. More may be used in large joints or for subcutaneous injection over an inflammatory process.

(4) *9-Fluoroprednisolone Acetate* (Predef 2X, Upjohn Co.).—Five to 20 mg., depending on the size of the joint. More can be used in large joints or for subcutaneous injection over an inflammatory process.

(5) *Methylated, Fluorinated Prednisolone-Dexamethasone* (Azium, Schering Labs.; Decadron, Merck & Co.).—Two to 5 mg. intramuscularly or intravenously. This product should not be used in a joint cavity since it may produce considerable swelling; it is not manufactured for this purpose.

(6) *Triamcinolone Acetonide—Synthetic Corticosteroid* (Kenalog I.M., Squibb Labs.).—Five to 15 mg. depending on the size of the joint. More may be used in a large joint or for subcutaneous injection over an inflammatory process.

(7) *Methylprednisolone* (Depo Medrol, Upjohn Labs., 40 to 80 mg. in large joints).—Long acting corticoid and quite effective intraarticularly.

(8) *9-Alpha-Difluoro, 16-Alpha Methylprednisolone-Flumethasone* (Flucort, Syntex Labs.).—The dose in horses is 1.5 to 2.5 mg. I.M. or intra-articularly. It is similar to dexamethasone but can be given intra-articularly, while dexamethasone cannot. It is claimed to be more effective than other steroids.

(9) *Prednisolone Sodium Succinate* (Solu-Delta Cortef, Upjohn Labs.).—This product is primarily for intravenous use to establish a quick level of steroid effectiveness.

(10) *Betamethasone Acetate and Betamethasone Disodium Phosphate* (Celestone Soluspan, Schering Labs.).—This is a repositol steroid that can be given intra-articularly and intramuscularly. The dose is 1 to 2 cc. for large joints and the concentration is 6 mg. per cc. Longer action than for other steroids is claimed.

All the above corticoids are contraindicated in the presence of infection without supporting antibiotics. The above list is not complete but gives a representative sample of products available. No product should ever be used intra-articularly if it is not specifically manufactured for this purpose.

The interval between injections is dependent upon the severity of the condition and the degree of response to the previous injection. Some severe inflammatory conditions should be injected every two or three days, while less severely affected areas will respond with less frequent injections. Following the injection of a corticoid into a joint or tendon sheath, the area should be wrapped to establish counter pressure and to promote absorption of excess fluid.

In some cases a bandage can be used around the joint leaving a diamond-shaped opening to aid in forcing fluid from the needle after the joint is punctured. Elastic material such as a rubber impregnated bandage is of most value to produce this effect.

Some products cause joint swelling after administration. This swelling usually disappears in twenty-four to seventy-two hours, and the effect of the drug can then be determined. Products that consistently cause swelling soon after injection should be discontinued. (Cortisone should never be used in joints, since it must be converted by the liver into hydrocortisone in order to produce results.) All the above products may be used intramuscularly for supportive therapy following intra-articular injection. The same doses are used intramuscularly.

After injection, the joint may be manipulated to aid the mixing of synovial fluid and the corticoid suspension. For routine work, it is sometimes advisable to include some antibiotic agent with the corticoid to combat any bacterial organism that might be present without obvious clinical evidence. A penicillin-streptomycin mixture is usually sufficient. Adrenocorticotropic hormone (ACTH) is used intramuscularly to stimulate the adrenal cortex to secrete hydrocortisone as follow-up therapy to injections of corticoids. The usual dose is 200 to 400 units repeated at three to seven day intervals.

Butazolidin* (phenylbutazone) is used intravenously and orally for pain relief in arthritis, but there is no form for intra-articular use. This drug produces an anti-inflammatory action similar to the corticoids. Full doses of a corticoid and phenylbutazone simultaneously are contraindicated. One or the other may be used for anti-inflammatory activity but not full doses of each at the same time. Smaller doses of each are commonly used together. Full doses of each are not used simultaneously because adverse effects caused by these drugs are more likely to occur. The intravenous dose of Butazolidin is 1 to 2 grams per 1000 pounds of body weight, with a limit of five successive days. The oral dose is 2 to 4 grams daily per 1000 pounds of body weight. The intravenous form of phenylbutazone should not be given intramuscularly because in some cases it causes

*Butazolidin, Jensen-Salsbery Laboratories

abscess formation. Therapy should be discontinued upon signs of gastrointestinal upset, icterus, or blood dyscrasia. Administration of pain-relieving drugs like corticoids and phenylbutazone should *not* be used as a substitute for accurate diagnosis.

(11) *Tandearil* (Oxyphenylbutazone, Geigy Co.). — Tandearil seems to be quite an effective anti-inflammatory agent. It can be used postsurgically following invasion of a joint for chip fracture for preventing postsurgical pain and swelling. The horse is not kept on the product for longer than ten days and during its administration its use is covered by antibiotics. The usual dosage is 2 to 5 gm. daily, orally, initially with gradual reduction of the dose after four days of use.

Specific Injection Sites for the Horse

1. *Metacarpophalangeal (Fetlock) Joint* (Figs. 11–3 and 11–4). — The volar pouches of the fetlock joint should be injected from either the medial or lateral side of the leg. The pouches lie between the posterior side of the cannon bone and the suspensory ligament.

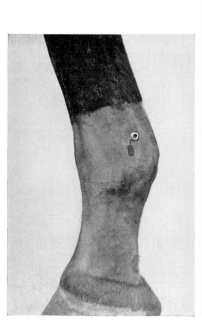 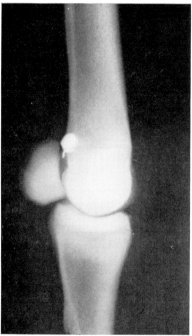

| Fig. 11–3 | Fig. 11–4 |

Fig. 11–3. — Location of injection into the volar pouch of the fetlock joint. The needle should be positioned just anterior to the sesamoid bone, between the posterior aspect of the cannon bone and the suspensory ligament.

Fig. 11–4. — Radiograph showing the needle in position for injection of the volar pouch of the fetlock joint capsule.

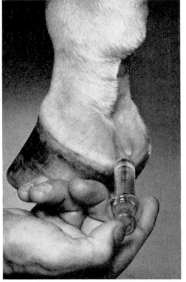 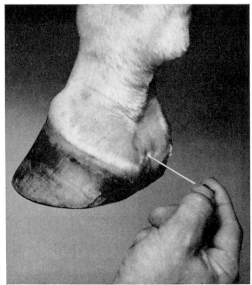

FIG. 11–5   FIG. 11–6

FIG. 11–5.—Infiltrating the heel area with a local anesthetic using a 25-gauge, one-half inch needle in preparation for injection of the navicular bursa (Reprinted from *Veterinary Scope*, courtesy Upjohn Company).

FIG. 11–6.—Eighteen-gauge, two-inch needle in position where the area has been anesthetized in Figure 11–5.

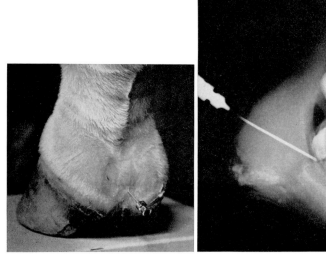

FIG. 11–7   FIG. 11–8

FIG. 11–7.—Eighteen-gauge, two-inch needle in place in the navicular bursa.

FIG. 11–8.—Lateral radiograph showing eighteen gauge, two-inch needle in place in the navicular bursa. The dark area above the navicular bone is the result 'of air that has been injected through the needle to better outline the bursa for radiographic purposes.

2. *Navicular Bursa* (Figs. 11–5, 6, 7 and 8).—The navicular bursa should be injected from the posterior aspect of the foot, the needle being directed parallel to or slightly below the angle of the coronary band. A complete description of the procedure is found under Navicular Disease (Chapter 6, p. 255).

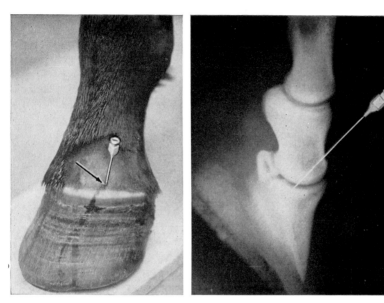

FIG. 11–9   FIG. 11–10

FIG. 11–9.—Twenty-gauge, two-inch needle in place to inject the coffin joint. Arrow shows area penetrated by the needle.

FIG. 11–10.—Radiograph showing needle in place to inject the coffin joint. This is the same foot and needle as shown in Figure 11–9.

3. *Distal Interphalangeal (Coffin) Joint* (Figs. 11–9 and 11–10).— This should be injected from either the medial or lateral side of the midline on the anterior aspect of the foot. The needle should be held in a vertical position and pushed into the joint from just above the coronary band. Fluids injected into the coffin joint may be able to pass into the navicular bursa and the digital flexor tendon sheath by osmosis.

4. *Femorotibial (Stifle) Joint.*—Injection of the stifle joint can be made into the joint capsule between the medial patellar ligament and the medial collateral ligament of the stifle joint. The femoropatellar pouch can be injected between the middle and medial patellar ligaments or between the medial and lateral patellar ligaments (Fig. 11–11). The femoropatellar pouch communicates through a slit-like opening with the medial portion of the femorotibial joint capsule.

29

This means that the femoropatellar pouch can be injected and in most cases the injected material will reach the medial portion of the femorotibial joint capsule. The lateral portion of the femorotibial joint capsule communicates with the femoropatellar pouch in a low percentage of cases and if it is desired to have the injected material reach this area, the femorotibial joint capsule should be injected directly between the lateral patellar ligament and the lateral collateral ligament or between the medial patellar ligament and the medial collateral ligament of the femorotibial joint (see Chapter 4).

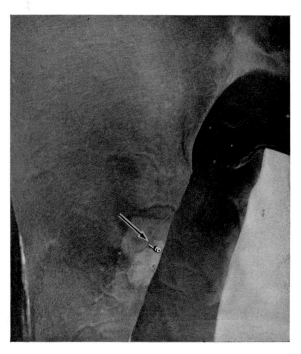

Fig. 11–11. — Position of eighteen-gauge, two-inch needle for injecting the femoro-patellar pouch, between the lateral and middle patellar ligaments. Arrow indicates the skin area which the needle has penetrated.

5. *Tarsal (Hock) Joint* (Fig. 2–13, page 69; Figs. 11–12 and 13). — Injection of the hock should be at the antero-medial aspect of the hock joint over the most prominent portion of the joint capsule. Care should be taken to avoid the saphenous vein, where it crosses the joint.

6. *Carpal Joint.* — Injection into the radiocarpal or intercarpal joint is usually easiest with the carpus in a flexed position. When the joint capsule is distended, it is a simple matter to inject the most prominent portion of the swelling with the horse in a standing position. However, if the joint capsule is not distended it is best to flex

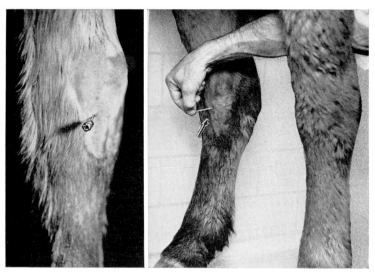

FIG. 11-12   FIG. 11-13

FIG. 11-12.—Anterior view of injection of the right hock joint. The needle is to the lateral side of the saphenous vein.

FIG. 11-13.—Area of penetration for injection of the hock joint for bog spavin. The needle should be forced through the joint capsule, either on the outside or the inside of the saphenous vein, indicated by the arrow.

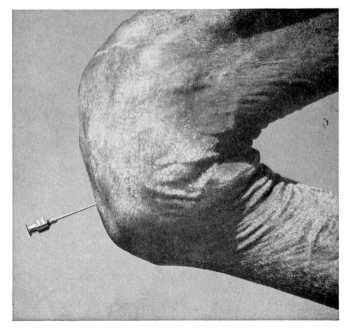

FIG. 11-14.—Injection of the intercarpal joint on a flexed carpus.

the joint to pass the needle (Figs. 11–14, 15, 16). Injection should be made from the anterior aspect into the joint desired. In many horses there is no communication between the radiocarpal and intercarpal joints. Therefore, the injection should be made into the exact area desired. The intercarpal and carpometacarpal joints communicate (see Chapter 4, p. 107).

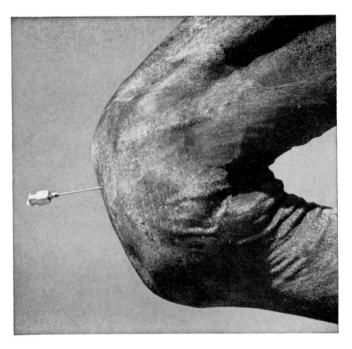

Fig. 11–15.—Injection of the radiocarpal joint on a flexed carpus.

7. *Scapulohumeral (Shoulder) Joint.*—The shoulder joint is injected in a notch between the two parts of the lateral tuberosity of the humerus (Fig. 11–17). In most cases this tuberosity can be palpated and the needle is carefully passed into the joint.

8. *Humeroradial (Elbow) Joint.*—The elbow joint is somewhat difficult to palpate for injection. The joint is flexed repeatedly until the articulation can be distinguished. The needle can be passed either from the anterior side or the posterior aspect into the joint (Fig. 11–18).

9. *Coxofemoral (Hip) Joint.*—The hip joint is injected through the notch that lies just anterior to the trochanter major of the femur. The trochanter major is followed down on the anterior edge and the needle passed through the notch in front of it into the joint as shown in Figure 11–19.

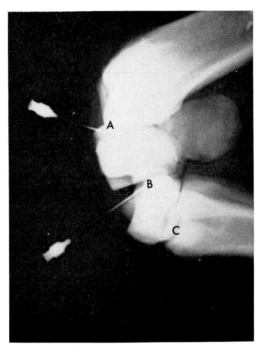

FIG. 11–16.—Lateral flexed radiograph of carpal joint with needles in the radio-carpal joint (A) and intercarpal joint (B). (C) shows the carpometacarpal joint that does not open. The fluid of the radiocarpal joint is separate from the inter-carpal joint and carpometacarpal joint in most cases. The joint fluid of the intercarpal and carpometacarpal joints is confluent. (Courtesy Norden Labora-tories.)

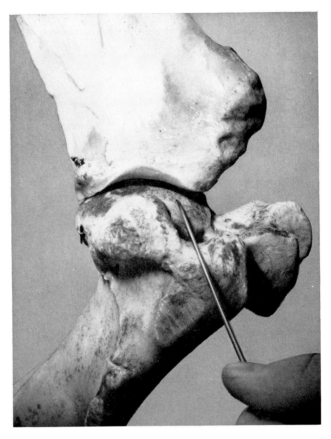

Fig. 11-17.—Injection of the scapulohumeral (shoulder) joint. The needle is passed in the notch between the two processes of the lateral tuberosity of the humerus. The most posterior portion of the lateral tuberosity can usually be palpated, and the needle is passed in front of it.

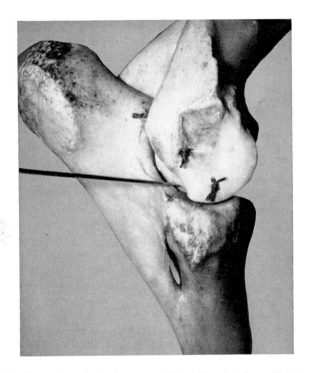

FIG. 11–18.—Injection of the humeroradial (elbow) joint. This joint is more difficult than others to inject. The joint is flexed repeatedly until the articulation is determined. The needle can be passed posteriorly as shown or from the anterior aspect.

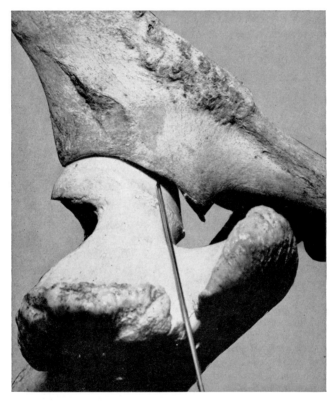

Fig. 11–19.—Injection of the coxofemoral (hip) joint. The needle is shown passing through the notch on the anterior side of the trochanter major. Once the needle passes through this notch it can be pushed gently into the joint capsule. Synovial fluid can often be aspirated.

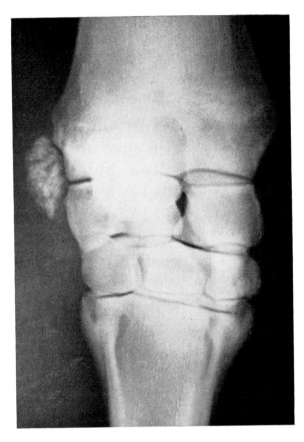

FIG. 11-20.—Calcified hematoma resulting from injection of the carpus with a corticoid. When passing the needle into a joint there is a danger of hitting blood vessels. In some cases the resulting hemorrhage will calcify as shown. A small needle, and an attempt to miss all skin vessels when passing the needle, will help in preventing such a complication.

10. *Subcutaneous Injection of Corticoids.*—When a corticoid is to be injected into subcutaneous tissues, as in the case of bowed tendon or splints, the area should be closely clipped, scrubbed, and prepared with a good skin antiseptic. If the injection is not made under aseptic circumstances, it may cause a suppurative process. Corticoids may be used subcutaneously in most acute, noninfectious inflammatory processes. Corticoids are sometimes used parenterally or locally and followed by the use of a blister. This type of therapy is contraindicated. The corticoids act as an anti-inflammatory agent and the blisters act as an inflammatory agent. There should be at least thirty days elapsed time between the use of these two methods of therapy.

REFERENCES

1. Ann. New York Acad. Sci., *50*, 509, 1948.
2. Ibid., *82*, 797, 1959.
3. Ibid., *61*, 281, 1955.
4. BRACKEN, FRANK: Physical Therapy in Veterinary Medicine. Annual Conference for Veterinarians, Colorado State University, 1965.
5. BUNN, C. E. E. and BURCH, J. E.: Hydrocortisone in the Treatment of Traumatic Arthritis in Thoroughbreds. North Am. Vet., *36*, 458, 1955.
6. BURDICK CORPORATION: Ultrasonic Therapy Abstracts from Current Literature. Milton, Wisconsin, 1961.
7. BUSCHKE, F.: *Progress in Radiation Therapy.* New York, Grune & Stratton, pp. 16, 17, 20, 1958.
8. CARLSON, W. D.: *Veterinary Radiology,* Philadelphia, Lea & Febiger, 1961.
9. CLAPP, N. K., CARLSON, W. D. and MORGAN, J. P.: Radiation Therapy for Lameness in Horses. JAVMA, *143* (3), 277, 1963.
10. DENNY, B.: Short Wave Radiotherapy in Veterinary Practice. British Vet. J., *115*, 341–350, 1959.
11. DILLON, R.: Corticosteroids in the Treatment of Certain Equine Lamenesses. Vet. Med., *51*, 191, 1956.
12. DIXON, R. T.: Some Effects of Cobalt 60 Gamma Irradiation on the Equine Carpus. Thesis, Colorado State University, Nov. 1965.
13. EBERT, E. F.: Clinical Use of Phenylbutazone in Large Animals. Vet. Med., *57*, 33–35, Jan. 1962.
14. FRANK, E. R.: *Veterinary Surgery,* 7th Ed. Minneapolis, Minn., Burgess Pub. Co., 1964.
15. FRASER, A. C.: The Treatment of Lameness by Faradism. Vet. Record, *73* (5), 94, 1961.
16. GUARD, W. F.: *Surgical Principles and Techniques,* 2nd Ed. Ann Arbor, Mich. Edwards Brothers, Inc., 1953.
17. GILLETTE, E. L. and CARLSON, W. D.: An Evaluation of Radiation Therapy in Veterinary Medicine. J. Am. Vet. Rad. Soc., *5*, 58, 1964.
18. GILLETTE, E. L.: Radiation Therapy. Annual Conference for Veterinarians, Colorado State University, 1965.
19. HAYES, I. E.: Treatment of Equine Coxitis with Intra-articular Hydrocortisone. No. Amer. Vet., *35*, 673, 1954.
20. HICKMAN, J.: *Veterinary Orthopaedics.* Philadelphia, J. B. Lippincott, 1964.
21. IRWIN, D. H. G. and HOFMEYR, C. F. V.: Unna's Sticky Paste as a Practical Aid to Bandaging. J. So. Afr. Vet. Med. Assoc., *32* (3), 1961.
22. JOHNSON, L. E., *et al.*: Panel on Equine Radiology. Proc. 6th Annual AAEP, p. 35, 1960.
23. KATTMAN, J. and KRUL, J.: Intra-articular Injection of Penicillin and Streptomycin. Veterinarni Medicina, *5*, 55, 1960.

24. *Merck Veterinary Manual*, 2nd ed., Rahway, N.J., Merck & Co., 1961.
25. MILNE, F. J.: Subcutaneously Induced Counterirritation. Proc. 6th Ann. AAEP, p. 25, 1961.
26. MORGAN, J. P.: Personal communication, 1964.
27. McGINNIS, P. J. and LUTTERBECK, E. F.: Roentgen Therapy of Inflammatory Conditions Affecting the Legs of Thoroughbred Horses. No. Am. Vet., *32*, 540, 1951.
28. ———: Further Clinical Experience with Radiation Therapy in Race Horses. No. Am. Vet., *35*, 431, 1954.
29. OHME, F. W.: Phenylbutazone in the Treatment of Soft Tissue Reactions of Large Animals. Vet. Med., *57*, 229–231, March 1962.
30. Panel Report: Use of Firing. Mod. Vet. Practice, *44* (3), 54, 1963.
31. QUINLAN, JOHN: Intra-articular and Intra-thecal Prednisolone in the Treatment of Traumatic Inflammation of Synovial Structures in Equines. J. So. Afr. Vet. Med. Assoc., *30* (3), 235, 1959.
32. RAKER, C. W.: Injection and Radiography of Movable Joints. Norden News, *37* (4), 6–8, 1962.
33. RILEY, W. F., JR.: Corticosteroids in the Treatment of Certain Equine Lamenesses. Vet. Med., *51*, 191, 1956.
34. SILVER, I. A. and CATER, D. B.: Radiotherapy and Chemotherapy for Domestic Animals: I. Treatment of Malignant Tumors and Benign Conditions in Horses. Acta. Radiol. (Therapy), *2*, 226, June 1964.
35. SISSON, S. B. and GROSSMAN, J. D.: *Anatomy of Domestic Animals*, 4th Ed. Philadelphia, W. B. Saunders Co., 1960.
36. STIHL, H. G. and LEUTHOLD, A.: Subcutaneous Iodine Therapy of Chronic Tendonitis in the Horse. Schweiz. Arch. Tierheilk., *106*, 218, April 1964.
37. TEMPLE, J. L.: Fluoprednisolone in Race Horse Practice. JAVMA, *137*, 136, 1960.
38. THOM, M.: *Equine Medicine and Surgery*, p. 513. Santa Barbara, Calif., Am. Vet. Pub., Inc., 1963.
39. THOM, M., *et al.*: Panel on Equine Radiology. Proc. 6th Ann. AAEP, p. 35, 1960.
40. THOM, M.: Radiation Therapy, Using X-ray. No. Am. Vet., *36*, 111, 1955.
41. ———: Some Indications for X-ray and Radium Therapy in Large Animal Practice. Proc. 87th Ann. Meeting, AVMA, p. 63, 1950.
42. TRUSSELL, W. E.: Clinical Response to Intra-Synovial Injection of Flumethasone in a Horse. Vet. Med., *610*, 60, June 1965.
43. VAN KRUININGEN, H. J.: Practical Techniques for Making Injections into Joints and Bursae of the Horse. JAVMA, *143* (10), 1079–83, 1963.
44. VAN PELT, R. W.: Arthrocentesis of the Equine Carpus. Vet. Med., *55*, 30, 1960.
45. ———: Clinical and Synovial Fluid Response to Intrasynovial Injection of 6a-methylprednisolone Acetate into Horses and Cattle. JAVMA, *143* (7), 738, 1963.
46. ———: Equine Intra-Articular Injections. Mich. State Univ. Vet., *21*, 54, 1961.
47. ———: Intra-Articular Injection of the Equine Carpus and Fetlock. JAVMA, *140* (11), 1181, June 1962.
48. ———: Properties of Equine Synovial Fluid. JAVMA *14* (9), 1951, 1962.
49. ———: The Role of Intra-Articular Adrenocortical Steroids. Mich. State Univ. Vet., *20*, 68, 1960.
50. VIGUE, R. F.: Clinical Evaluation of Prednisolone Trimethylacetate in Arthritis and General Inflammatory Conditions of Horses. Southwestern Vet., *13*, 103, 1960.
51. WHEAT, J. D.: The Use of Hydrocortisone in the Treatment of Joint and Tendon Disorders in Large Animals. JAVMA, *127*, 64, 1955.

Radiology

Chapter 12

Joe P. Morgan D.V.M., M.S., Vet. med. dr.

THE purpose of this chapter is to describe equipment and techniques used to obtain radiographs of extremities of horses. Normal studies in both mature and immature horses are discussed.

Making a diagnostic radiograph requires the use of both costly equipment and valuable time. Therefore, it behooves the practitioner to become familiar with his equipment and technical procedures so that he may be assured of obtaining a diagnostic study.

It is not the purpose of this chapter to describe completely the construction of and theory of operation of x-ray equipment. Neither will a complete discussion of radiation physics be included.

1. Responsibility to Client

Radiographs produced are the property of the veterinary clinic or practitioner. Fees charged for examinations entitle the client to a complete report of the study. He should be allowed an opportunity to examine the radiographs with the veterinarian, if this is desired. Radiographs should be retained by the veterinarian for comparison with future studies or possible use in medico-legal action. It is not desirable to loan radiographs to clients so that they may "show them to another veterinarian." If consultation is desired, radiographs

(461)

should be forwarded to the other veterinarian for his examination, with the request that they be returned when of no further value. Problems are often created by an owner's having possession of radiographs without the knowledge necessary to make correct interpretations.

2. X-Ray Machine

One of the most difficult problems the equine practitioner must solve is selection of an x-ray machine that is adequate for his practice. Many different types of machines are available (Figs. 12–1, 2, 3). Final selection will be determined by many factors.

A. *Mobility.*—The manner in which the veterinary practice is conducted determines the type of machine that will be used. If the practice is one in which most patients are brought to a central clinic, then a large machine of higher rating can be utilized (Fig. 12–1). This type of machine can be used for many studies of both large and small animals in addition to examinations of equine extremities. If most work is being done in the field, a more easily transported unit is needed. Quality of the radiographs obtained need not be directly related to the size of the machine. There are portable units which are adequate for radiography of equine limbs (Fig. 12–2).

Fig. 12–1.—A 300 ma mobile x-ray machine that has an easily positioned tube head (A). The machine is equipped with an adjustable lead shutter diaphragm (B), hand switch (C), and foot switch (D).

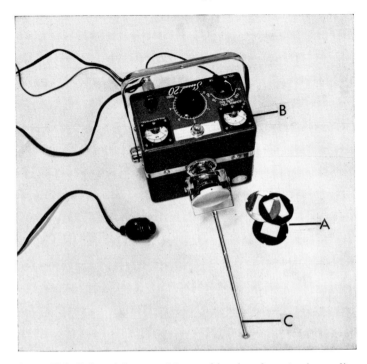

Fig. 12-2.—This lightweight portable machine is adequate for radiographing the distal extremities of horses. The machine is equipped with a method of controlling beam size (A), evaluating incoming line voltage (B), and a centering device (C).

B. *Exposure Time.*—Exposure times of over 1/10 of a second often result in problems of motion. This is most frequently due to the animal's moving, but can be due to movement of either x-ray tube or film holder. Short exposure times increase chances for technically satisfactory films. The range of possible exposure times is extreme with some equipment having minimum settings of .003 second.

Noise created by operation of the timer can be an important factor when working with a nervous horse. This is a problem inherent with the use of mechanical timers.

A foot switch with which to make the exposure is desirable (Fig. 12-1). This frees a pair of hands which can be used to assist in restraining the horse. The foot switch can usually be wired into the timer at little extra cost.

C. *Milliamperage.*—Milliamperage (ma) is a major factor used in determining the amount of radiographic exposure. This control may be called the filament control, milliamperage selector, etc. Time of exposure combined with ma determines the quantity of x-rays produced. Small machines frequently have values of 10, 15, or 30 ma and this may be a constant value with no provision for adjustment. Some equipment requires that a trial exposure be made

FIG. 12–3.—A 15 ma mobile x-ray machine that is adequate
for most examinations of the extremities of horses.

before ma values can be read on the milliammeter. This presents a
problem in radiation safety since additional exposures are necessary.
Larger, more expensive equipment can have maximum ma values
ranging from 50, 100, 150, 200, 300, up to 1000 and relatively simple
controls for evaluating and adjusting this setting.

The relationship between ma and time is a direct one. Therefore,
the advantage of a higher ma setting is that it allows for a marked
decrease in required exposure times. An example of the relationship
between ma and time is as follows: Identical radiographs are obtained with a setting of 0.1 second and 100 ma as are obtained with
a setting of 1.0 second and 10 ma assuming all other factors remain
constant. The product of milliamperage and time is called milli-
amperseconds (mas) and equal mas settings will produce radiographs of equal density or blackness. This relationship can be seen
in two examples:

$$(1) \quad 0.1 \text{ second} \times 100 \text{ ma} = 10 \text{ mas}$$
$$1.0 \text{ second} \times 10 \text{ ma} = 10 \text{ mas}$$

$$(2) \quad 1/20 \text{ second} \times 30 \text{ ma} = 1.5 \text{ mas}$$
$$1/10 \text{ second} \times 15 \text{ ma} = 1.5 \text{ mas}$$
$$3/20 \text{ second} \times 10 \text{ ma} = 1.5 \text{ mas}$$
$$3/10 \text{ second} \times 5 \text{ ma} = 1.5 \text{ mas}$$

The milliammeter should be observed while making an exposure whenever possible, since movement of the needle indicates that an exposure has been made. This can prevent processing of an unexposed film.

D. *Kilovoltage.*—The kilovoltage potential (kvp) is the third control usually found on panels of x-ray machines. This control may be called an autotransformer, kvp selector, technique selector, etc. It determines the quality of the x-ray beam and thus its ability to penetrate tissue. Higher kvp settings produce more penetrating beams with a higher percentage of radiation reaching the film. Some units do not have a control for changing kvp and employ what is referred to as a "constant kvp" setting. Some older machines have methods of altering this value but the settings are not labeled as to actual kvp produced.

To produce a comparable radiograph, a higher kvp setting allows for use of a lower mas setting. This would generally mean shorter time of exposure. Lower kvp settings can be of value when radiographing immature horses and for soft tissue techniques. A maximum kvp setting of 70 to 80 is adequate for penetrating most distal portions of a mature horse's leg.

The inverse relationship between kvp and mas can be seen in the following settings. These will all produce a comparable radiograph if other factors are left unchanged.

60 kvp and 4.0 mas	(10 ma $\times$ 0.4 second)
70 kvp and 2.0 mas	(10 ma $\times$ 0.2 second)
80 kvp and 1.0 mas	(10 ma $\times$ 0.1 second)
90 kvp and 0.5 mas	(5 ma $\times$ 0.1 second)

In the range of kvp settings normally used, adding 10 kvp and dividing the mas in half will produce a comparable radiograph. Conversely, subtracting 10 kvp and doubling the mas maintains the same quality radiograph.

E. *Distance.*—Changing the distance from the tube to the film requires compensation in kvp or mas settings. Therefore, a standard distance of 30 inches is recommended.

F. *Additional Controls.*—Other controls that can be present on the x-ray machine include a method of evaluating and controlling voltage of the incoming line. This determination is important since other settings on the machine are dependent on the incoming voltage. An unnoticed or undetected drop in incoming line voltage results in a less penetrating x-ray beam than expected, and an underexposed film. An increased line voltage causes greater exposure than anticipated and overexposure of the radiographic film. Incoming line voltage is determined from a voltmeter and kept constant by adjusting a "voltage compensator." A control of this type is of particular value when equipment is moved from one farm to another. Larger x-ray units automatically compensate for changes in line voltage.

30

An additional ammeter may be present on the control panel. This measures amperage across the filament of the tube. It indicates to the operator that the tube is activated and the filament is hot. The machine should never be left for prolonged periods with the filament hot, since it is possible to cause damage to the tube.

A light on the control panel that will glow when the machine is turned on will help avoid leaving the switch in the "on" position. It is also possible to install a timer switch that automatically breaks the circuit after a pre-set interval of time. This protects the tube and other electrical components from overheating.

G. *Radiation and Electrical Hazards.*—Both radiation and electrical hazards must be considered when using x-ray machines. Very high electrical potentials are present in the cables leading to the tube. Radiation danger is more insidious since it is not as readily detectable. The evaluation of equipment for radiation safety and absence of electrical hazards is not included in the training of most veterinarians. Therefore, specialists in this field should conduct these examinations. Some states have radiation health departments that can be called on for assistance in evaluating an x-ray machine. All x-ray companies have well-trained personnel available to determine the safety of a machine.

H. *Movement of Tube Head.*—It is important that the tube head have good freedom of movement. This enables it to be quickly moved to avoid damage and also provides for positioning in the many oblique angles required. It should also be easy to lock and unlock the tube in these various positions. If the tube head will lower to the ground level, lateral views of the foot and digit are more easily made.

I. *Machine Noise.*—It is important to evaluate noise made by the machine while being positioned since this can make a nervous horse difficult to handle. If the machine utilizes a rotating anode tube, this will contribute to the level of noise and may be so loud as to be objectionable. Timer noise has been referred to under discussion of timers.

J. *Ideal Machine.*—A desirable machine for use in examining extremities of horses must contain many of the following characteristics:

1. A high degree of mobility.
2. Timer, ma selector, and kvp control that will permit an exposure to be brief, preferably 1/10 second or less.
3. A foot switch.
4. An available method of monitoring and controlling the incoming line voltage.
5. A rigid tube stand with good locks.
6. Safety from both electrical and radiation hazard.
7. Minimal machine noise.

3. Accessory Equipment

There are many items included within this category, and frequently they are as important as the x-ray machine itself. Included are safety equipment, methods of controlling the primary x-ray beam, aids in positioning horses' feet, holders for cassettes, methods of identifying films, film holders and special types of films. Most items can be purchased from commercial firms, although some can be produced locally to better satisfy needs created by a specific machine or situation.

A. *Control of Beam Size.*—X rays radiate from the source in straight lines in all directions. Therefore, it is important that machines be equipped with a method of controlling the size of the beam as it leaves the tube. This beam is referred to as the primary beam and control is essentially a safety factor. A smaller, controlled beam size means that a smaller area on the horse's leg is exposed to radiation. Also, it is easier to avoid exposing persons helping with the examination. By limiting the area of tissue exposed to the primary beam, the amount of secondary or scatter radiation will also be lowered. Secondary or scatter radiation is that soft, less penetrating radiation produced when the primary beam strikes an object. It also travels in all directions and if sufficient, can cause generalized graying of the film.

FIG. 12–4.—Various methods of controlling the size of the primary beam. More desirable types have provision to change size of the radiation field and illuminate the area that is radiated (arrows).

Fig. 12-5.—The lead shutter diaphragm is adjustable and exact size of the opening can be determined by the area illuminated on the cassette holder (arrows). This insures that the size of the exposed area is as small as possible. (Photo furnished through the courtesy of the Department of Clinical Radiology, Royal Veterinary College, Stockholm, and Elema-Schönander AB, Stockholm.)

Many different types of cones, cylinders, lead apertures, and lead shutter diaphragms are available for controlling size of the primary beam (Fig. 12-4). These range from simple inexpensive lead apertures to costly lead shutter diaphragms. Frequently the field of primary radiation is illuminated by a light so that the area radiated is more easily determined. This is desirable, and when used with an adjustable lead shutter diaphragm, only the smallest possible area need be exposed (Fig. 12-5).

B. *Aluminum Filter.*—Another accessory item providing radiation protection is a 2 mm. thick aluminum filter placed within the primary beam. It can be taped against the tube housing or fastened to the cone. The level of radiation can be cut to as much as one-fourth by this filter and it does not affect the diagnostic quality of the radiograph. The primary beam is made of rays of different penetrating power. Therefore, the filter removes the soft, less penetrating portion that has little effect in creating a latent image on the film. However, this soft portion of the primary beam does contribute to radiation exposure to both man and animal and produces scatter radiation which fogs the film.

C. *Film Identification.*—All radiographs should be well marked for identification. This information should include the veterinarian's name or name of his clinic, date on which the radiographs were made, and a number or name to specifically identify the horse being radiographed. There are many ways of accomplishing this.

Lead numbers and letters can be placed either in a holder or taped directly to the face of the film holder at the time of original exposure (Fig. 12–6).

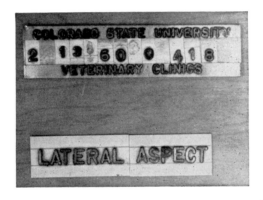

Fig. 12–6.—Lead markers used to identify radiographs.

Another method is to write on the film with a pencil or similar device prior to developing or during processing of the film, when the gelatin on the surface of the film can be easily scratched.

A more recent type of marker, which can be placed on the outer surface of the cassette, utilizes a lead impregnated tape. This is used with a permanent plate containing the name and address of the veterinarian in lead letters. Date, name or number of the case, and other information can be written on the tape. Pressure from the pen or pencil displaces the lead and allows the radiation to more easily penetrate. The tape is available in rolls and is normally discarded as it is used (Fig. 12–7).

Additional markers that are needed include those to identify right and left legs, medial and lateral aspects, and front and hind feet. It is also helpful to have a marker in the shape of an arrow to point to a soft tissue lesion or point of severe pain. When viewing the radiograph, attention is then directed to this particular area. All of these markers are available from commercial firms and are not expensive.

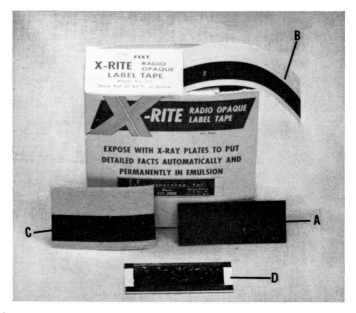

FIG. 12–7.—Type of radiograph marker. A plate contains the name and address of the veterinarian or clinic (*A*). Lead impregnated tape is available in a roll (*B*) from which a small piece is cut (*C*) and additional information written with pen or pencil. This tape is then placed on the plate (*D*) and the marker placed on the cassette.

D. *Grid.*—Grids are an expensive accessory that need not be used in the more common radiographic examinations of the horse. A grid is a device with alternating lead and radiolucent strips. Its purpose is to decrease the amount of secondary radiation, which would cause fogging and create a gray film with little contrast. Normally a grid is needed when the thickness of a radiographed part exceeds 11 cm. It is often necessary in examinations of the stifle joint, pelvis, shoulder joint, and elbow joint. The more distal areas on the extremities can be adequately examined without its use. However, the quality of the special views of the navicular bone can often be improved by the use of the grid.

4. Film Holders

There are two basic types of film holders. These are screened cassettes and non-screen holders. A cassette is a device to hold the x-ray film. Rigid cassettes are usually made with intensifying screens.

A. *Screened Cassettes.*—A cassette protects and supports eht intensifying screens and film. Intensifying screens are available with several speeds which is determined primarily by different sized crystals. The use of screens with larger crystals requires less radiation but there is greater loss of detail on the radiograph. However, decreased exposure time eliminates much of the problem of motion and more than compensates for the slight loss of detail caused by the faster screens. For general examinations, the fastest speed screens are recommended. The other disadvantage in use of screened cassettes is their high cost.

If intensifying screens of different speeds are used concurrently, it is advisable to mark the speed clearly on the outside of the cassette. This is important so compensating exposure factors can be used.

FIG. 12–8. — A lead impregnated rubber sheet used to divide a cassette. Two or more exposures can then be made on the same film. The identification marker uses lead letters.

1. *Cassette Size.* — Cassettes are manufactured in different sizes with an 8-by-10-inch size most convenient for use on horses. Larger sizes are available and it is not difficult to divide a cassette with lead sheets so two or more exposures can be made on the same film (Fig. 12–8). A 7-by-17-inch cassette is desirable for evaluation of congenital and nutritional problems in young foals. The longer length of the cassette allows for better determination of the degree of bending or malformation of the leg.

2. *Care of Screens.* — If the screens are stained with processing solutions or if dust is present, artifacts will be produced on the radiographs. These artifacts will appear as white areas on the film corresponding to the shape of the foreign material. Screens should therefore be cleaned frequently, before the dirt becomes imbedded into the surface of the screen. This is done by using either a soft brush or cotton to carefully wipe the surface. Chemical drops must

be removed as soon as possible by absorbing them with a damp piece of cotton to avoid permanent staining. If dust cannot be removed or if chemical stains are present, it will be necessary to use either soap and water or a commercially produced cleaner. Organic solvents, such as ether, alcohol, or acetone attack the screens and are not suitable.

The outside of the cassette should also be kept clean. This prevents dust being carried onto the screens when the cassette is opened. If cassettes must be used in a dusty location, a plastic bag or similar protective device should be used as a cover.

B. *Non-screen Holders.* — Non-screen holder is a device (usually cardboard) that protects the film from light. It has no method of intensifying the primary beam. A greater exposure is required since the creation of the latent image is due only to x-rays and not to any intensification process. Since this increase in technique is usually through a longer exposure time, non-screen holders are suitable only for specific examinations. Non-screen film is available prepackaged in cardboard holders and ready for immediate use. The outer holder is discarded prior to developing the film. This protection is desirable if the area to be radiographed is covered with blood or other debris. Cardboard holders can be easily placed in positions into which a thick cassette will not fit. An examination using non-screen technique will require 3 to 4 times the length of exposure that would be required using screen technique.

5. Film Type

Radiographic film used with screened cassettes is different from that used with non-screen holders. Non-screen film manufactured for use with cardboard holders should *not* be used with screened cassettes. Conversely "screen" film should *not* be used with cardboard holders.

"Screen" film is available in various speeds or sensitivity. Faster, more sensitive films are somewhat more grainy and require greater care in processing. The faster film will allow additional lowering of exposure factors, but standard speed film is easier to process.

Film should be stored in a cool place and preferably on end so there is no pressure on the film.

6. Aids in Positioning

Valuable accessories are wood blocks used to aid in positioning the equine foot (Fig. 12–9). The type of block required depends entirely on the specific x-ray equipment and radiographic examination desired. Few machines allow for lowering of the tube to the floor. Examples of views where a positioning aid can be used are given in the discussion on specific radiographic positioning (p. 492). Rubber strips can be secured to the bottom of these blocks to prevent their sliding on the floor.

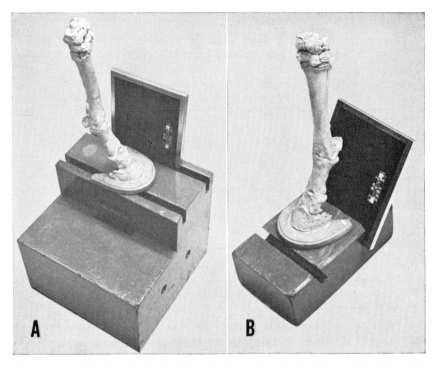

FIG. 12–9.—Wooden blocks built to aid in positioning the horses' foot for radiographic examination. (A) is used to elevate the foot for lateral views. (B) is used in the AP view of the digit. Both are built to hold cassettes.

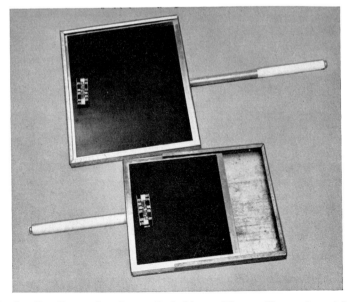

FIG. 12–10.—Locally produced cassette holders. These will permit positioning of the cassette without placing your hands in the primary beam.

7. Cassette Holders

Cassette holders are a safety device and should be used to hold the cassette during each exposure (Figs. 12–9 and 10). Even though an individual is wearing lead gloves, it is preferable not to have hands or any part of the body within the primary beam.

8. Calipers

Calipers are available for measuring the thickness of tissue to be radiographed. In most cases, these are not needed when working with horses' legs because of the similarity of size. A stick which has been cut to a 30-inch length is useful for quick measurement of distance from tube head to the film.

9. Radiation Safety

Lengthy discussion of this subject is not appropriate in this text. It is, however, too important a subject to be completely ignored. The most important safety procedures for the veterinarian interested in radiography of equine limbs are listed below.

A. Use of cassette holders.

B. Use of different individuals to hold cassettes.

C. Restriction of children under the age of eighteen years and pregnant women from the area of radiographic examination.

D. Use of lead gloves and aprons is mandatory.

E. Periodic inspection of lead gloves and aprons for evaluation of their protective qualities.

F. Choice of technical factors that permit use of the lowest quantity of radiation for each exposure.

G. Control of the area exposed by the primary beam and the quality of the beam.

H. Use of radiation monitoring devices.

10. Technique Chart

Many adequate radiographs of equine feet have been made without the advantage of technique charts. However, many films are wasted because of incorrect exposure factors (Fig. 12–11). Individual exposure guides, based on a certain machine and the particular desires of a veterinarian, can be developed by the method described. It is not possible to establish one setting for a particular view that will be adequate for all x-ray machines and all related factors.

The value of a chart comes after continued use has built confidence in listed values. It insures that radiographs will be of diagnostic quality, and that they have been made with the best combinations of ma, kvp, and time settings.

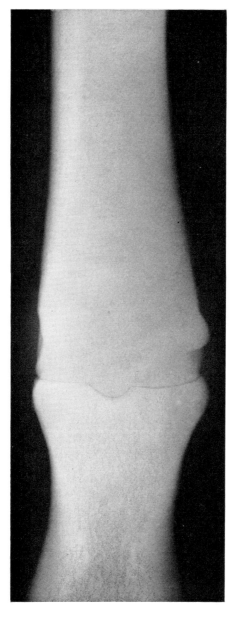

FIG. 12–11.—An example of exposure factors so incorrect that the film is worth-less. In this underexposed radiograph of the fetlock joint, it is impossible to evalu-ate the joint space or the condition of the proximal sesamoid bones. A study of this type is a common fault and should be corrected.

Prior to formulating a chart, as many factors as possible must be standardized. Value of incoming line voltage should be determined, if possible, and controlled. The distance from tube to film should be decided upon; 30 inches is recommended. If an aluminum filter or coning device is to be used, it must be in place. Developing time should be a full five minutes, and the temperature of developing solutions should be 68° F. The type of intensifying screens and film speed have an important bearing on exposure factors and should be established.

Establishing a technique chart requires a standardized tube-film distance. The shorter distance results in an increased beam intensity. However, getting too close to the part causes distortion. A practical distance that produces an acceptable degree of magnification is 30 inches. Shorter distances may be necessary if a machine is of very low rating, but the magnification will be excessive.

After all these factors have been examined and standardized, the first trial exposures of the fetlock of an average size adult horse can be made. The film can be divided by rubberized lead sheets or an individual film used for each trial exposure. It is difficult to select techniques to recommend for trial exposures. Certainly past experience with a machine will be of help in making this decision. The time should be as short as possible, the ma setting as high as possible, and the kvp selected last. The exposure of 70 to 80 kvp and 1.5 mas should be approximately correct for the average machine. After the first exposure is made, additional exposures should be made with the time doubled and then redoubled. The radiographs should then be processed and examined. If is desirable that one exposure be dark (over-exposed), one light (under-exposed), and one correctly exposed.

If all the radiographs are over-exposed, as indicated by a dark film, then the kvp should be reduced by 10 or the mas reduced by one half. Three additional exposures are then made with varying exposure times as previously mentioned. If none of the original exposures are satisfactory, it will usually be due to under-exposure and an increase in exposure factors will be necessary. If possible, the kvp should be increased by 10 and the three trial exposures repeated. If it is impossible to increase the kvp, then the exposure time or the ma must be doubled.

This procedure of increasing or decreasing techniques must be continued until a satisfactory radiograph is obtained. The final technique is the one that appeals to the individual, however, it must allow for evaluation of both bone and soft tissue.

Example:

Original trial exposures

(1)   70 kvp and 1.5 mas (15 ma and 0.1 second)
(2)   70 kvp and 3.0 mas (15 ma and 0.2 second)
(3)   70 kvp and 6.0 mas (15 ma and 0.4 second)

If all exposures are dark (over-exposed) decrease the technique to:

    (1) 60 kvp and 1.5 mas (15 ma and 0.1 second)
    (2) 60 kvp and 3.0 mas (15 ma and 0.2 second)
    (3) 60 kvp and 6.0 mas (15 ma and 0.4 second)

or:

    (1) 70 kvp and 0.75 mas (15 ma and 0.05 second)
    (2) 70 kvp and 1.5 mas (15 ma and 0.1 second)
    (3) 70 kvp and 3.0 mas (15 ma and 0.2 second)

If all exposures are light (under-exposed) then increase the technique to:

    (1) 80 kvp and 1.5 mas (15 ma and 0.1 second)
    (2) 80 kvp and 3.0 mas (15 ma and 0.2 second)
    (3) 80 kvp and 6.0 mas (15 ma and 0.4 second)

or:

    (1) 70 kvp and 3.0 mas (15 ma and 0.2 second)
    (2) 70 kvp and 6.0 mas (15 ma and 0.4 second)
    (3) 70 kvp and 12.0 mas (15 ma and 0.8 second)

There will be some duplication of exposures if the procedure is performed exactly as described. However, by following each step one can be sure not to miss the ideal technique. This technique, called the *standard technique*, can be used for most examinations of the foot, digit, metatarsus and metacarpus.

The technique for the carpus, tarsus and other special studies must utilize more kvp and/or mas and is referred to as the *darker technique*. This is done by either increasing the kvp of the *standard technique* by 10 or by doubling the time of exposure or the ma of the *standard technique*.

Special views, such as the view of the third phalanx with the horse standing on the cassette require a *lighter technique*. This can be formulated by lowering the kvp of the *standard technique* by 10 or by cutting the time or ma of the *standard technique* in half.

If the *standard technique* is: 80 kvp and 3.0 mas (60 ma and 0.05 second) then the *darker technique* will be:

        90 kvp and 3.0 mas (60 ma and 0.05 second)
or   80 kvp and *6.0 mas* (*120 ma* and 0.05 second)
or   80 kvp and *6.0 mas* (60 ma and *0.1 second*)

and the *lighter technique* will be:

        70 kvp and 3.0 mas (60 ma and 0.05 second)
or   80 kvp and *1.5 mas* (*30 ma* and 0.05 second)
or   80 kvp and *1.5 mas* (60 ma and *0.025 second*)

The above procedure establishes a *standard technique* applicable for many of the common views; a *darker technique* useful for thicker parts of the horse's leg, and a *lighter technique* to be used for specialized views. These values will remain constant for that particular x-ray machine. In this manner, the practitioner deals with only three different sets of exposure factors. Admittedly this is oversimplification of a technical procedure, but these three techniques will produce satisfactory results for most problems presented in routine examinations.

11. Radiographic Techniques for Special Problems

When determining exposure factors, several special problems are encountered. A dry plaster cast will require the technique to be either doubled or tripled. This is accomplished by doubling or tripling exposure time or ma. It is also possible to achieve the desired result by increasing the kvp by 10 or 15.

It is recommended that films not be made through a wet plaster cast because of the water present. Water increases secondary radiation and it will be difficult to obtain a radiograph with satisfactory contrast.

Techniques normally used for mature animals can be cut in half, when an immature horse is examined. This is done by cutting time or ma in half, or by lowering kvp by 10. A small pony requires the radiographic techniques used on an immature horse. A heavy draft horse will require techniques in excess of the *standard technique*.

12. Preparation of the Horse

A certain amount of preparation should be undertaken before radiographic examination of an extremity is attempted. The leg should be examined and all dirt brushed away. This is especially necessary when evaluating the third phalanx and the navicular bone (Fig. 12–12). It may be necessary to scrub the hoof with a brush and water to clean the sole. Any radiopaque substance such as iodine solution, blister, or scurf on the skin will create increased density and white shadows on the radiograph (Figs. 12–13 and 14). It at all possible, all bandages should be removed since they will produce confusing lines on the radiograph (Fig. 12–15).

It is necessary to remove the shoe from the horse's foot prior to radiography because a shoe compromises the amount of information that can be obtained from the radiograph. It is always possible that a fracture or other pathological change may be hidden by the shadow created by the shoe.

If it is necessary to control the horse in some way, a tranquilizer should be administered. A twitch may also be employed to aid restraint for radiography.

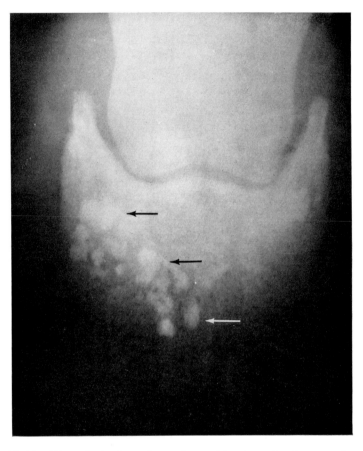

Fig. 12–12.—The sole had not been thoroughly cleaned prior to radiographic examination. The multiple radiopaque areas (arrows) are due to dirt and gravel. A study of this quality should not be considered satisfactory.

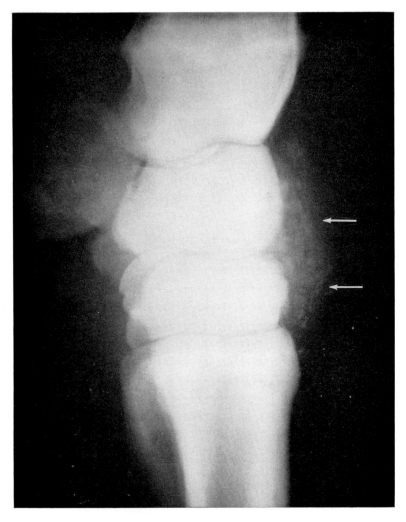

FIG. 12–13.—It is impossible to fully interpret the condition of the anterior aspect of the carpal bones (arrows) on this radiograph. This is due to the use of blistering compounds containing radiopaque iodine.

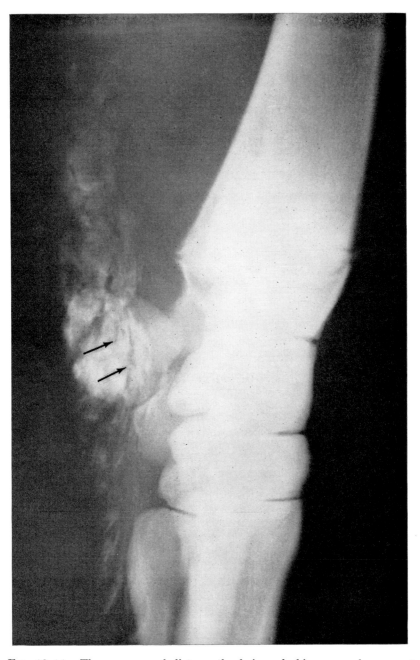

FIG. 12–14.—The presence of dirt on the hair and skin can make accurate radiographic interpretation impossible. Note the false "fracture" lines (arrows) through the accessory carpal bone.

31

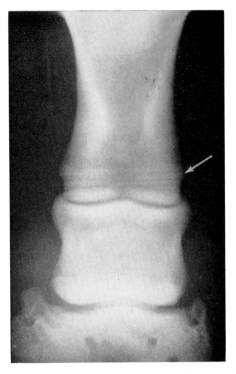

Fig. 12–15.—Linear shadows (arrow) created by a light bandage extend across the distal end of the first phalanx. These could be confused with pathological changes. Note the prominent vascular channels in the third phalanx.

13. Film Processing

Perhaps the most common errors made by practitioners are related to the processing of exposed radiographic film. While it is not necessary that a fancy darkroom be available for use, certainly the area used must be clean and light proof. Film may accidentally come into contact with concentrated processing chemicals that have been spilled. This can occur at any time before development, and causes specific artifacts. Hands and counter surfaces must be clean and dry. Care is required when handling film because pressure, creasing, buckling or static electricity can cause artifacts.

A. *Developing.*—Once the film is placed in the developer, it is preferable to leave it for a five-minute period. Many radiographs will be taken with portable units with which it is difficult to establish exact settings. Therefore, a certain amount of sight developing must be tolerated. This should only involve the checking of the film after approximately one minute of developing time to determine whether it will be greatly over-exposed or under-exposed. If the film is removed from the developer at one minute or less and shows correct finished film density (darkness), then the film has been greatly over-exposed. The resulting finished radiograph will be gray and lack contrast.

Five-minute developing is advocated because it permits reduction of exposure factors. The actual time of developing is not critical at five minutes and the film can be removed from the developing solution at four to six minutes with little difference in film density.

B. *Fixing.*—Some method must be used to wash the film before it is placed in the fixer solution. If this is not done, the pH of the fixer will be altered by the residual developer, necessitating early replacement. Films must remain within the fix for approximately one minute before any light is allowed to reach the radiograph. Total time within the fixer should be twice the clearing time. Clearing time is the length of time required for the radiograph to lose the milky appearance it has when first placed in the fixer. This time is approximately one minute but will vary with the age of the fixer solution. It does not harm film to let it remain in the fixer for up to five or ten minutes. Longer times require longer washing time in clear water to avoid streaking of the dry film.

C. *Wash.*—It is usually stated that films should wash for twenty minutes. This figure is dependent on whether water is constantly flowing through the tank and on the number of films that have been processed in the same water. The greater the intensity of circulation of water and the warmer the water up to 80° F., the shorter the washing time can be.

D. *Drying and Filing.*—The film can be dried either in a cabinet with heat and fan or it can be hung with air blowing on it. Films should then have the corners clipped off and be placed in an envelope with suitable identification for filing. If the corners are not trimmed, the sharp points will scratch other films in the envelope.

E. *Processing Temperatures.*—The temperature of all processing solutions should be 68° F. This temperature is frequently difficult to maintain but should fall within the range of 60° to 75° F. The temperature of the developing solution is most important because it influences both the time required for proper development and the quality of the film. Charts are available to determine changes in developing time for given changes in solution temperature. Generally, warmer solutions cause more rapid development, while colder solutions slow the chemical reaction.

F. *Processing Solutions.*—Solutions should be covered to prevent dust and debris from contaminating them and to prevent unnecessary oxidation. If lids are not available for the tanks, polyethylene sheeting can be used to cover them. The solutions can be poured into glass or plastic bottles and kept in these containers for prolonged periods without oxidation or contamination.

Processing solutions can be prepared from either powders or concentrated solutions. The concentrated solutions are easier to work with and their use obviates the problem of powder settling on working surfaces.

The number of films processed and the care given processing solutions will determine how often replacement of solutions is necessary. Most radiologists add replenishing solutions to both developer and fixer to maintain their strength. A green or brown color of the developer solution and prolonged clearing time in the fixer solution signifies an unsatisfactory condition.

G. *Processing in Trays.*—It is possible to process radiographs in flat trays. These may be plastic, hard rubber, or enamel. Solutions can be poured from bottles into trays and then poured back into bottles after use. The film must be constantly agitated during processing or lines will be present where the film rested on the bottom of the trays.

14. Technical Errors

There are many errors in processing and technique that commonly occur. Some of the most common errors will be discussed. One technical problem is caused by the condition of intensifying screens within cassettes. If dust on a screen is not removed, or if chemicals have been spilled on the screen, then artifacts will appear on all films used in the cassette. These will appear as white or under-exposed areas on the radiograph. The only method of correcting this fault is to purchase new intensifying screens. The cassette can be evaluated to determine whether it is worth reconditioning.

Another common error is related to overexposure and under-developing of films. This technique yields a radiograph that is darker overall than preferred and the very short developing time makes contrast unsatisfactory. This can be corrected by decreasing exposure factors and lengthening developing time.

Light leaks of any kind will fog film and cause areas that appear gray or black. This exposure from light can occur at any time following removal from the box until the film is completely cleared in the fixing solution.

Underexposure is common, especially with variable line voltages. The resulting radiographs are difficult to interpret because of low film density.

A grid should be used if the part to be radiographed is greater than 11 cm. thick. The grid cuts down the amount of secondary radiation. If a grid is not used, resulting radiographs will be gray and lack contrast. This gray film must not be confused with an overexposed film. Lowering exposure factors will only create a lighter density radiograph that is still gray and lacks contrast.

15. Film Reading

It is a common practice to attempt to read radiographs while they are wet. All that should be determined at this time is whether exposure factors are satisfactory, if the desired anatomical areas have been radiographed, if positioning is adequate, and if radiographic detail is sharp. However, in many cases, it is expedient to give a waiting owner a tentative diagnosis. The client should be advised that reading a wet radiograph is somewhat comparable to looking through a window on a rainy day. Under these conditions, it is very easy to misinterpret small shadows and possible to overlook small lesions. The radiograph should be re-evaluated after it is dry so that maximum information can be obtained from the study.

With experience, each individual establishes his own method of film reading. It is important that a set pattern be repeated each time so no part of the radiograph is overlooked. It is essential to have a viewbox on which to view the radiograph. One should not be content to use the nearest desk lamp or sunlight. It is equally important to have a high intensity light to evaluate bone margins and soft tissues (Figs. 12–16, 17). Many small chip fractures and minimal areas of periosteal new bone growth will not be seen without use of a bright light.

It is impossible to interpret a radiograph without knowing something of the anamnesis and clinical signs, but these are usually known to the veterinarian prior to his interpretation. A practitioner, however, should make every effort to read radiographs with an open mind and to evaluate each bone and joint space carefully. Many an obvious fracture has been overlooked because the study was taken only to evaluate a clinically suspected ringbone that was not present.

A. *Tissue Density.*—A discussion of tissue density is appropriate since this is the factor that permits radiographic diagnosis. The tissue with greatest density in the equine leg is bone, which appears radiographically as a white shadow. Soft tissue structures such as muscle, tendons, and skin are of next lower density. On a properly exposed radiograph, these appear dark gray and it is necessary to use a bright light to evaluate them. Deposits of fat are less dense and provide contrast around tendons and muscle bellies. Cartilage is much less dense than bone and enables evaluation of joint spaces. Air is of the least density, but is not normally found in the equine leg. When present, following intra-articular injection or a break in the continuity of the skin, it will appear as a black shadow on the radiograph. Radiopaque foreign bodies, such as glass, metal, gravel, dirt, or iodine solutions will create white shadows of various shades depending on size, density and quantity.

B. *View.*—The terms used in discussing various radiographic views describe the manner in which the x-ray beam passes through the animal. An anterior-posterior view (AP) implies that the x-ray beam enters anteriorly on the leg, exits posteriorly, and then creates a latent image on the film. A posterior-anterior (PA) view is seldom used. However, one example is the PA view of the stifle joint. The lateral view is made with the beam directed in either a lateral or medial direction. Usually it is most convenient to position the x-ray machine laterally and the cassette on the medial aspect of the limb. Oblique views can be referred to by the area that is shown to best advantage by the particular technique or by the direction of the beam.

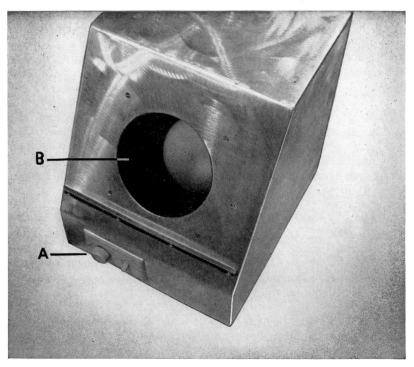

Fɪɢ. 12–16.–A high-intensity viewer is essential for study of the bone margins and soft tissues. This viewer has a rheostat (*A*) with which to control the amount of light. Also, it has a heat absorbing glass (*B*) to prevent damage to the radiograph.

Fɪɢ. 12–17.–A light bulb placed in a tin can provides an inexpensive high-intensity illuminator. Since there is no provision for heat absorption, it is possible to damage the radiograph.

It is extremely important to always obtain two views of an area. Since a radiograph is only a representation of two dimensions, it is necessary to obtain a second study at right angles. This will allow evaluation of the third dimension. Additional views will frequently be of value; for example: diagnosis of small carpal fractures. The cost of film is the smallest item involved in the examination and there should be no hesitation in obtaining a sufficient number of views to permit a positive diagnosis.

16. Epiphyseal Plates

When an examination is made of a horse in which epiphyseal closure has not occurred, it is imperative that the opposite leg be radiographed for comparison. This will help eliminate the possibility of an erroneous diagnosis of "lesions" related to epiphyseal plates. There are normal closure times for each of these various cartilaginous growth areas. These times will vary with the different breeds of horses, probably with nutritional levels, and with certain diseases. In the discussion on the radiographic appearance of normal epiphyseal plates, the average age for closure is listed in the following chart. These ages are based primarily on the Quarter Horse and Thoroughbred breeds. The times will not agree with those published in anatomy books because closure has been determined radiographically instead of anatomically.

17. Special Diagnostic Techniques

Some special radiographic techniques can be utilized in the diagnosis of lameness. The most commonly used is that of injecting a radiopaque contrast medium to outline sinus or fistulous tracts. The technique is easy to perform, not painful to the animal, and can be very informative. The injection can be made through a blunt needle, a teat tube, rigid polyethylene tubing, or even a female canine urinary catheter. It is important that the device used be positioned as far into the tract as possible. Several 4×4 gauze pads or comparable material can be wrapped around the opening to seal the tract. Radiopaque material can then be injected under pressure to outline the furthest extent of the tract. Following injection of contrast medium, it may be of value to inject a small amount of air. This also serves as an excellent contrast medium and further outlines the tract. Before making exposures, the area around the tract should be wiped clean. It is important to remove any contrast medium that may have drained onto the skin, since it will create a white shadow on the radiograph.

There are many contrast mediums available for injection. Most use iodine as the radiopaque substance. The water-soluble solutions are more easily injected, but also flow out more quickly. More viscid products are somewhat more difficult to inject but provide a more satisfactory coating and will not flow out as rapidly. Even

AGE OF ANIMAL

EPIPHYSEAL LINE	6 months	9 months	12 months	1-1½ years	2 years	2½ years	3 years
Front Leg							
First phalanx	▨						
Second phalanx	▨						
Metacarpal bone (distal)			▨				
Radius (distal)						▨	
Radius (proximal)				▨			
Olecranon						▨	
Humerus (Distal)				▨			
Humerus (medial epicondyle)			▨				
Hind Leg							
First phalanx	▨						
Second phalanx	▨						
Metatarsal bone (distal)			▨				
Tibia (distal)					▨		
Tibia (proximal)						▨	
Tibial crest united with proximal tibia			▨				
united with tibial shaft							▨
Femur (distal)						▨	
Os calcis						▨	

Age of epiphyseal closure:
    based on Quarterhorse and Thoroughbred breeds—both male and female.
    based on radiographic determination which will be earlier than actual closure
    determined histologically.

        ▨ indicated age during which closure usually occurs.

though the tract may be infected, injection should be made by aseptic technique. The possibility of iodine sensitivity is present following its injection as contrast medium.

The purpose of this technique is to obtain information concerning a draining tract (Figs. 12–18, 19). If surgery is contemplated, the exact course and length of the lesion can be determined (Fig. 12–20) and it is possible to locate and identify foreign bodies.

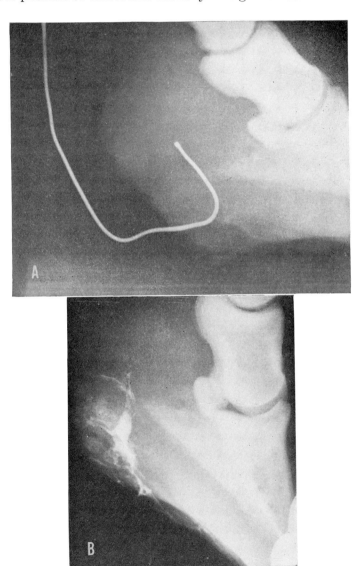

Fig. 12–18A and B.—Placing a metallic probe (A) into a draining tract demonstrates its length and direction. Injection of contrast medium (B) shows to a greater extent the tissue involved.

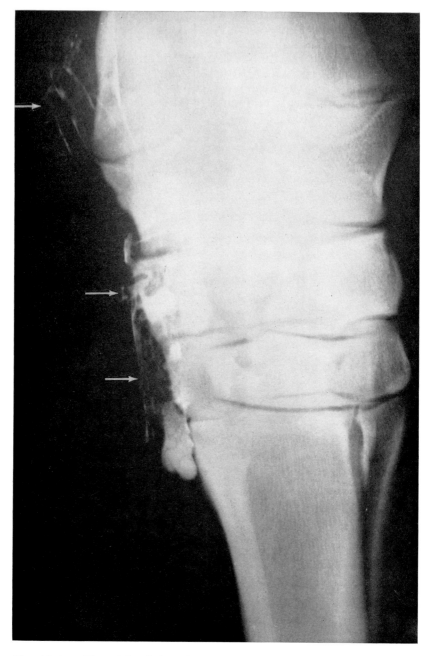

Fig. 12–19. — The origin of clear fluid draining just proximal to the radial-carpal joint was not known. By injecting contrast medium into the fistulous tract, it could be determined that there was a direct communication with the tendon sheath of the common digital extensor muscle (arrows).

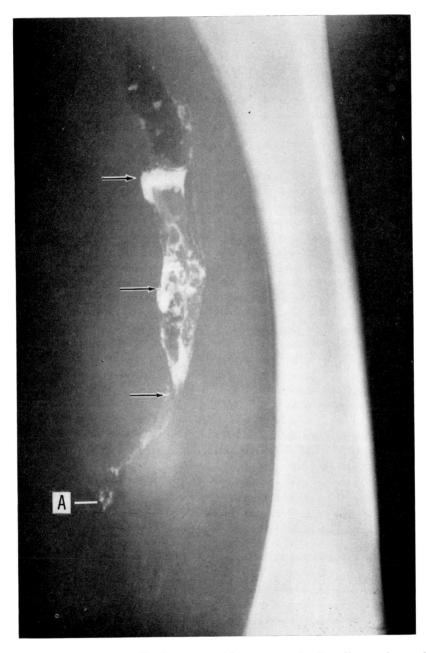

Fig. 12–20.—Injection of a sinus tract with opaque contrast medium and a small amount of air outline the extent of the tract. The point of drainage just proximal to the carpus (*A*) is seen plus the total length of the tract (arrows). The cause of the lesion was a wood splinter, not positively identified.

It is also possible to inject radiopaque material to determine the nature of soft tissue swellings (Fig. 12–21). Only products prepared for parenteral use should be utilized for this purpose.

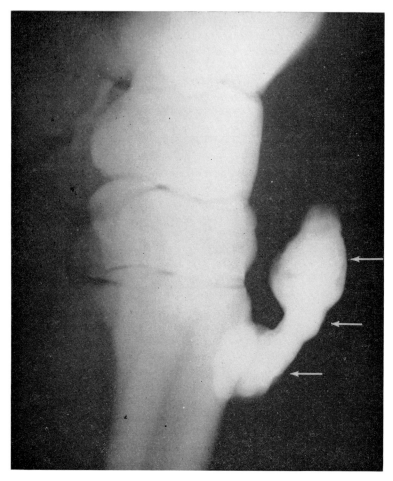

Fig. 12–21. — By use of contrast medium, more is learned concerning a fluctuating soft tissue swelling anterior to the carpus. The extent of the fluid-filled cavity (arrows) and its failure to communicate with the joint cavities is noted.

RADIOGRAPHIC POSITIONING AND NORMAL RADIOGRAPHS

Extremities of the horse have been arbitrarily divided into convenient anatomical divisions for the discussion to follow. Generally the structures seen on commonly used views are discussed together. Methods of positioning are described and illustrated and examples of normal radiographs shown. A discussion is given of closure of epiphyseal lines as determined radiographically. Pertinent comments are included that will assist the practitioner in recognizing normal structures and aid in avoiding erroneous diagnosis.

Certain terms are used frequently in describing positioning and reference at this time will enable the reader to gain more from pages to follow. The useful x-rays are referred to as the primary beam and the geometric center of this beam is the central ray or central beam. This beam is perpendicular to the tube axis and its direction is used in describing tube position and angle. This central ray should always be directed at the midpoint of the area to be radiographed. It also should be perpendicular to the long axis of the leg and perpendicular to the film holder.

The descriptions and figures illustrating positioning are based on the type of equipment most commonly in use. Many of these units do not permit the tube to be positioned on the floor or ground. Consequently many studies require the foot be elevated. An x-ray tube with overhead (ceiling) suspension or a small portable unit enables these studies to be made with the horse standing normally. Other minor differences in requirements will arise as a result of the various machine types.

Radiographic techniques for all the more commonly used views are described in terms of the *standard, darker,* or *lighter* technique which have been previously discussed. More than one method of obtaining a particular view may be described. It is important that the method finally selected be used repeatedly, and be one that can easily be duplicated. This is so that familiarity with the resulting radiograph can be established. Mistaken diagnoses occur when radiographs of the same area are made in different positions.

1. Digit

The metacarpo- or metatarsophalangeal (fetlock) joint, first phalanx, proximal interphalangeal (pastern) joint, and second phalanx are all adequately visualized on the same radiograph. The distal interphalangeal (coffin) joint is frequently seen, but not always adequately.

Views. — The anterior-posterior view is taken with the leg extended slightly forward. The hoof is elevated on a block for best results (Figs. 12–22, 23), or positioned flat on a floor. Elevation of the foot allows the cassette to be positioned posteriorly and "below" the hoof. The resulting radiograph yields a more complete visualization of the coffin joint. The central beam should be directed at the midportion of the first phalanx, or at the specific area believed to be clinically unsound. Frequently it is difficult to determine the exact tube position for this view and checking the bulbs of the heels will aid in obtaining symmetry. It is important that a marker be placed on the cassette so that medial and lateral sides are easily identified on the radiograph.

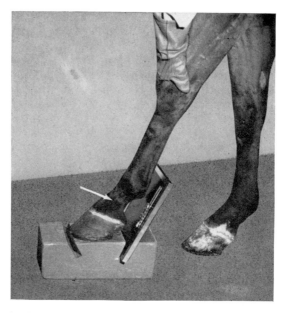

Fig. 12–22.—Radiographic technique for the AP view of the digit. By using a block of this type the cassette can be placed "below" the hoof. Better visualization of the coffin joint is obtained in this way. No part of the helper need be in the primary beam. The central beam is marked (arrow).

The lateral view may require elevation of the foot (Figs. 12–24, 25). This is necessary so that the central beam can be horizontal to the floor, and at the same time, perpendicular to the first phalanx. It is important on this view that the limb be straight. Any medial or lateral deviation will make it impossible to obtain a satisfactory study of the joint spaces. If the horse has a conformation problem, care must be taken to insure that the central beam is perpendicular to the first phalanx.

Special views of the digit are not ordinarily required. It is possible to make oblique views to more positively locate a foreign body or determine the origin of a small chip fracture in the fetlock joint. Oblique views are taken similar to the AP view with the cassette moved medially or laterally to a slight degree, and the tube in the opposite direction. Oblique radiographs are labeled to indicate the side of the digit where interest lies.

All views of the digit can be made with the *standard** technique.

Diagnosis.—Most confusion in diagnosis results from the foot or tube being improperly positioned. This results in a radiograph in which the bones and joint spaces are not bilaterally symmetrical.

In mature horses, the coffin joint appears wider than the pastern joint on the AP projection of a properly positioned radiograph. The

* See p. 477.

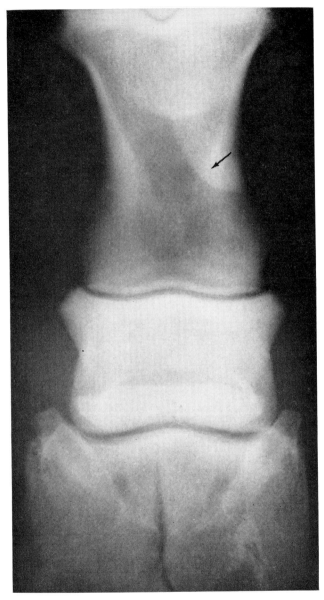

FIG. 12–23.—Normal AP radiograph of the digit of a mature horse. The shadow of the ergot is more clearly seen than usual (arrow). In an AP projection the pastern joint appears narrower than the coffin joint.

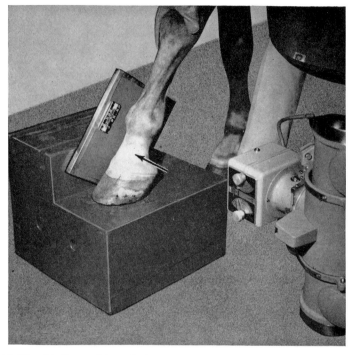

Fig. 12–24.—Radiographic technique for the lateral view of the digit. Since the tube will not lower to the floor, the foot has been elevated. The cassette is positioned in a slot so no part of the helper is within the primary beam. The central beam is marked (arrow).

pastern joint space will appear wider than the fetlock joint in the same view. Width of the joint space is important and most easily determined from the AP radiograph.

Occasionally a radiopaque shadow can be seen on the AP view in the mid portion of the first phalanx (Fig. 12–23). If the ergot is heavy enough, it will create an unusual shadow. Examination of the lateral view with a high intensity light will show this structure to be posterior to the proximal portion of the first phalanx.

The middle distal sesamoidian ligament attaches distally on the posterior aspect of the first phalanx. On the lateral view this attachment may become rough and the cortex thickened (Fig. 12–25). This is a normal degenerative change with little clinical significance. This change is most common in working Quarter Horses and occasionally calcification in the middle sesamoidian ligament is visible.

The lateral view of the second phalanx frequently shows a roughened area on the anterior aspect of the distal end. This is more obvious if the view is slightly oblique. This appearance is due to the fossae for attachment of the collateral ligaments in this area and attachment of the common or long digital extensor tendon (Fig. 12–25). While pathological changes can occur in this area, minimal change is probably normal.

Studies of 1st and 2nd phalanges in the hind leg are performed in essentially the same manner as in the front leg. The AP view is somewhat more difficult to make, because the tube must be located just behind to the elbow. If the horse will rotate the hock inward, it is much easier to position the tube.

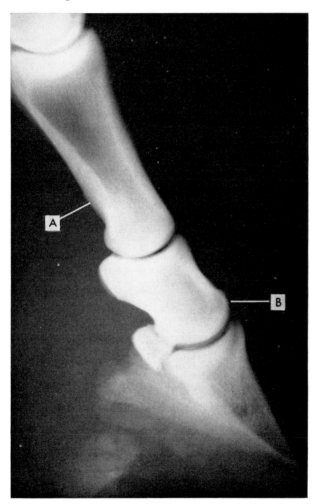

Fig. 12–25.—Normal lateral radiograph of the digit of a mature horse. The pastern joint is well seen because the central beam was directed at this point. The area of attachment of the middle distal sesamoidian ligament is slightly roughened (A). Changes more extensive than seen here are still within the range of normal. A roughened appearance on the anterior aspect of the second phalanx may be normal. This can be due to the areas of attachment of collateral ligaments (B) or the common/long digital extensor tendons.

If it is necessary to position the foot on a block or similar device, the study is no longer a weight-bearing one. Sometimes it is desirable to produce a study with the horse bearing weight on the foot. If the tube will not lower to the ground, a platform must be constructed to elevate the entire animal.

Epiphyseal Closure. — There are three epiphyseal lines present on views of the digit in the foal at birth (Fig. 12–26A). These are located in the distal metacarpal or metatarsal bone, in the proximal first phalanx, and in the proximal second phalanx. The line in the distal metacarpal or metatarsal bone will appear partially closed at nine months and completely closed at one year. In the proximal portion of the first phalanx, closure occurs between six and nine months. The epiphyseal line in the proximal portion of the second phalanx also begins closure at six months and is completely closed at nine months. In all three of these growth areas, closure in the hind leg seems to be slightly later than the comparable line in the front leg. As closure occurs, these areas appear more dense on the radiograph, and may normally appear slightly widened (Fig. 12–26).

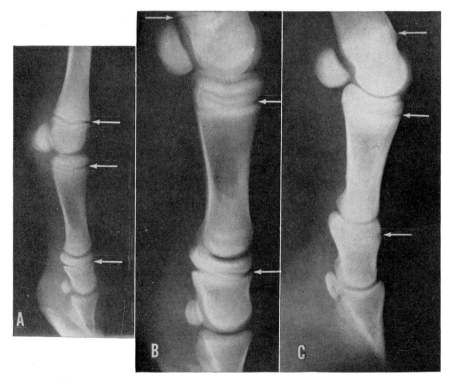

Fig. 12–26.—Stages of epiphyseal closure as seen on the lateral view of the digit. The studies are typical of a newborn foal (A), five weeks of age (B), and six months of age (C). The degree of closure of the epiphyseal lines (arrows) can be seen. Note the much wider joint spaces seen on the radiographs taken at birth.

2. Proximal Sesamoid Bones

Routine radiographic examination of the proximal sesamoid bones consists of an anterior-posterior view and lateral view, with oblique views as needed. Evaluation of the fetlock joint is also possible on these studies.

Views. — The AP view is taken in a manner similar to the AP view of the digit except that both cassette and central beam are elevated (Figs. 12–27, 28). It is recommended that the central beam be angled downward instead of being parallel with the floor. By angling the beam, the proximal sesamoid bones are seen superimposed through the distal end of the great metacarpal or metatarsal bone. If a horizontal beam is used, the bones are seen superimposed over the fetlock joint space and diagnosis is more difficult. Care must be taken in positioning both leg and tube to produce a symmetry of the bones on the radiograph. Medial and lateral markers must be used.

Since the proximal sesamoid bones must be visualized through the distal end of the cannon bone, it is necessary to use the *darker**

* See p. 477.

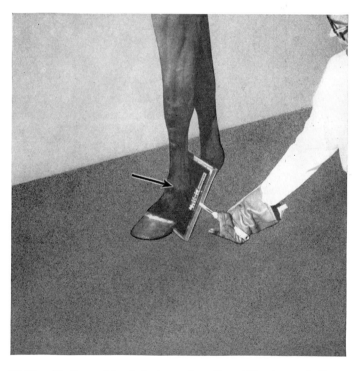

Fig. 12–27. — Radiographic technique for the AP view of the proximal sesamoid bones. Better visualization is obtained if the tube is angled. The central beam is marked (arrow).

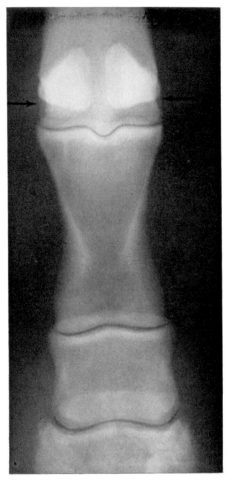

FIG. 12–28. – Normal AP radiograph of the proximal sesamoid bones of a mature horse. The concave areas on the distal end of the cannon bone can be seen (arrows). The collateral ligaments of the fetlock attach here. Their appearance is normal. In an AP projection the fetlock joint appears more narrow than the other two joints.

technique for the AP projection. It is sometimes desirable to compare this darker radiograph with one made using the *standard** technique. The soft tissues are seen to better advantage in the lower exposure study.

The lateral view will usually require that the foot be elevated. This is so the central beam may be parallel with the floor and still perpendicular to the leg and cassette. The view is taken in a similar manner as the lateral view of the digit except that cassette and central beam are elevated (Figs. 12–29, 30). *Standard** technique is adequate for the lateral view.

* See p. 477.

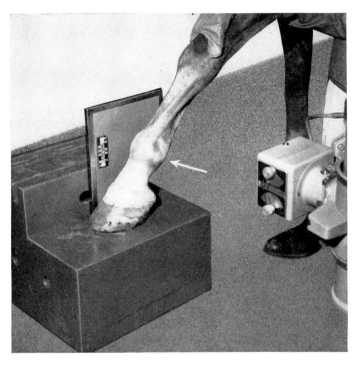

FIG. 12–29.—Radiographic technique for the lateral view of the proximal sesa-moid bones. Usually the foot must be elevated to obtain a true lateral projection. The central beam is marked (arrow).

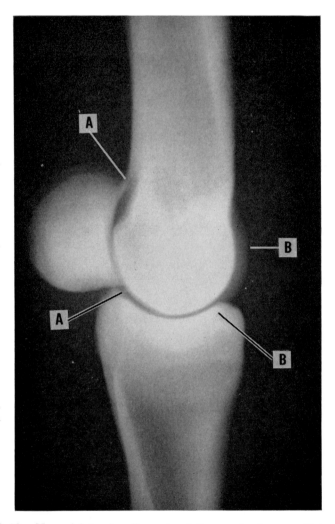

Fig. 12–30.—Normal lateral radiograph of the proximal sesamoid bones of a mature horse. If positioning is adequate the fetlock joint can be easily studied. The posterior portion of the sagittal condylar ridge (A) may resemble a fracture fragment. The anterior portion of this ridge (B) extends below the proximal end of the first phalanx.

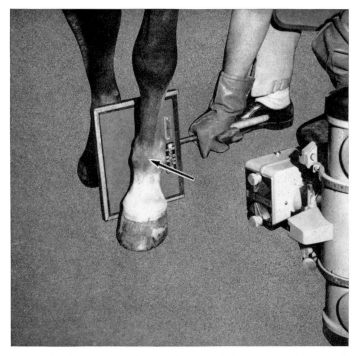

FIG. 12-31.—Radiographic technique for the oblique view of the proximal sesamoid bones. This position will demonstrate the lateral proximal sesamoid bone to good advantage. The central beam is marked (arrow). This technique may be used for oblique views of the digit by using a lower focus with the beam. It is a valuable view when examining for position of a small bone chip in the fetlock joint. In this case the medial oblique view should also be taken.

Oblique views are frequently of value in gaining better evaluation of fractures and minimal new bone growth involving proximal sesamoid bones. The tube is positioned anteriorly and laterally and the primary beam directed in a latero-medial direction to view the lateral proximal sesamoid bone (Fig. 12-31). To view the medial proximal sesamoid bone, the tube is anterior and medial with the beam aimed in a medial-lateral direction. The tube is moved approximately 45° medially or laterally for these oblique views. *Standard** technique is used.

Examination of the hind foot is essentially the same as for the front.

Diagnosis.—In examining the edges of the proximal sesamoid bones, care must be taken to recognize the difference between the normal fine vascular grooves and small fractures lines. Sesamoiditis will cause some rarefaction of the bones and an increased prominence of vascular channels. New bone growth may be present resulting

* See p. 477.

from a sprain of the suspensory ligament or the distal sesamoidean ligaments.

On the true lateral view, a radiopaque shadow resembling new bone growth or a chip fracture is frequently seen posterior to the distal end of the cannon bone (Fig. 12–30). This represents the posterior portion of the sagittal condylar ridge. If the lateral view should vary slightly from a true lateral, it is possible to superimpose one of the joint surfaces of the first phalanx over the distal end of the proximal sesamoid bone. This resembles a chip fracture from the sesamoid bone.

The AP view of this area demonstrates the small concave portions on the distal end of the cannon bone (Fig. 12–28). These are the areas of attachment of the collateral ligaments. If the view is slightly oblique, one area of attachment appears much more obvious, while the other is not seen at all and can interfere with diagnosis.

Epiphyseal Closure.—Normally there are no epiphyseal lines in the proximal sesamoid bones. The only ones seen in this area are in the distal metacarpal or metatarsal bone and the proximal portion of the first phalanx (Figs. 12–32, 33). These closure times have been discussed (see p. 488). Bipartite sesamoid bones have been reported.[5] These strongly resemble fractures. Bipartite sesamoid bones have formed from two instead of the one normal ossification center and union has not occurred. Since they will not fuse, they do not represent true epiphyseal plates.

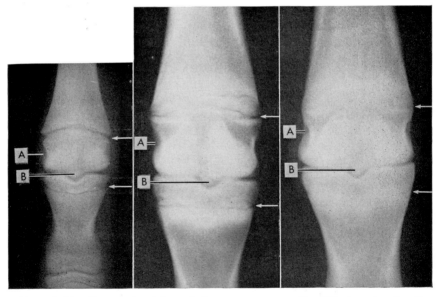

Fig. 12–32.—States of epiphyseal closure as seen on the AP view showing the proximal sesamoids. The studies are typical of a newborn foal (*left*), four months of age (*center*), and one year of age (*right*). The change in appearance of epiphyseal lines can be seen (arrows). Areas of attachment of collateral ligaments are marked (*A*). Prominence of the sagittal condylar ridge can be seen (*B*).

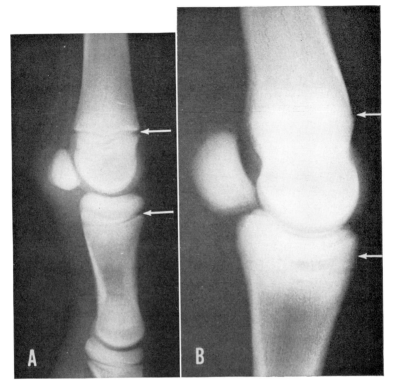

FIG. 12–33.—Stages of epiphyseal closure as seen on the lateral view showing the proximal sesamoids. The first study is typical of a newborn foal (*A*), while the second is typical of bone development at nine months (*B*). The degree of epiphyseal closure can be seen (arrows). Note the increase in density and the widened appearance at the epiphyseal plate at the time of closure. This need not represent pathological change. The relative sizes of the proximal sesamoid bones is seen at these two ages.

3. Third Phalanx

Radiographic examination of the third phalanx requires considerable preparation. Hoof wall and sole must be washed with water and a stiff brush used to insure complete removal of all debris. Otherwise there will be artifacts on the radiograph (Fig. 12–12). While not mandatory, the shoe should be pulled if the study is to be of maximum value. A routine examination includes anterior-posterior and lateral views. Oblique studies should be made when indicated. Medial and lateral markers must be used with the AP and oblique projections. Studies are essentially the same for both front and hind leg.

Views.—It is difficult to see the entire third phalanx on a single AP view. For this reason two AP views should be taken. One is made in the manner described for radiographing the digit (p. 493).

However, the cassette must be positioned lower (Figs. 12–22, 23). This is accomplished by elevating the foot on a block and positioning the cassette posterior to and slightly "below" the bulbs of the heels. The central beam is directed at the coronary band. This view enables good evaluation of the distal interphalangeal joint space (coffin joint) and adjacent bones. *Standard* technique is used for this view.*

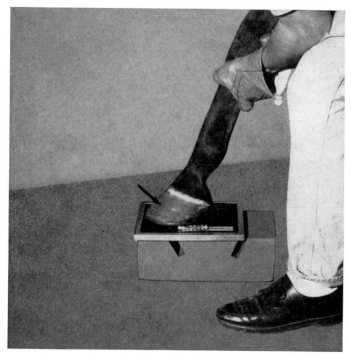

Fig. 12–34.—Radiographic technique for the AP view of the third phalanx. Use of the block helps to prevent the horse putting his full weight on the cassette. The central beam is marked (arrow).

The second AP view is taken with the foot placed directly on the film holder (Figs. 12–34, 35). The purpose of this view is to study the cancellous bone which comprises the majority of the third phalanx. Cassettes can be placed directly on the floor or slightly elevated on a block. Elevating the foot helps to prevent the horse from placing full weight on the cassette. The cassette can be placed in a protective device to prevent damage while the foot is in position. If a screened cassette is used without any protective device, the leg should be extended slightly. The helper can then place his knee behind and slightly under the carpus. This supports part of the

* See p. 477.

weight of the horse and can prevent him from stepping forward on
the cassette. The central beam is directed toward the floor so it is
perpendicular to the hoof wall and centered just distal to the coronary band.

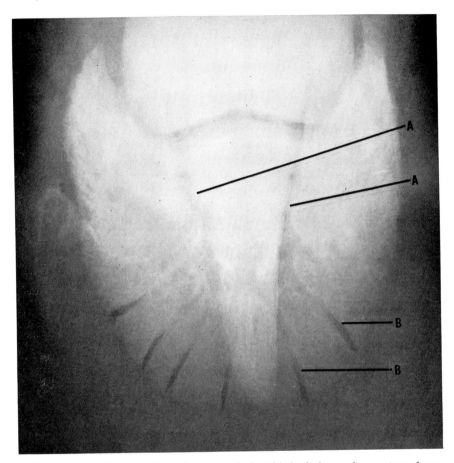

Fig. 12–35.—Normal AP radiograph of the third phalanx of a mature horse
taken with the hoof resting on the cassette. Lateral sulci of the frog (A) and vascular channels in the bone (B) present problems in diagnosis.

If screened cassettes are used, the *lighter* technique is adequate.*
Even though the hoof wall appears to be thicker in this view, the
density of the hoof and the third phalanx is less. With the horse
standing on the film, motion is not as much of a problem. This
permits the use of non-screen technique with the film placed in a
cardboard holder. With non-screen film the mas should be increased
3 to 4 times over the mas used with the *lighter* technique.*

* See p. 477.

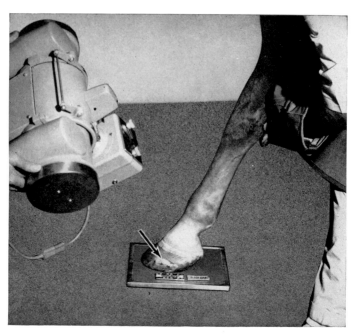

FIG. 12–36.—Radiographic technique for the oblique view of the third phalanx. The technique shown does not require use of any block but places the cassette directly on the floor. The central beam is marked (arrow).

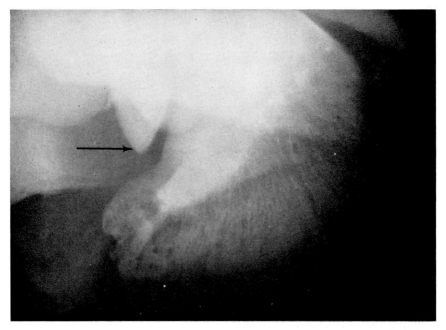

FIG. 12–37.—Normal oblique radiograph of the lateral angle of the third phalanx of a mature horse. The angle of the navicular bone can also be studied on this view (arrow).

Oblique views of the third phalanx are frequently necessary and are taken with the film holder on the floor with the foot placed on it (Figs. 12–36 and 37). The tube is moved 45° medially or laterally and the central beam aimed just below the coronary band. This view will allow good visualization of the angles of the third phalanx and clear demonstration of fractures in these areas (Fig. 12–37). *Lighter* technique is again used for this view if a screened cassette is used.

Fig. 12–38.—Radiographic technique for the lateral view of the third phalanx. This type of block allows for the cassette to be positioned below the level of the sole (*A*). This places the third phalanx in better position on the film. The central beam is marked (arrow).

A lateral view of the 3rd phalanx usually requires that the foot be elevated (Figs. 12–38, 39). Elevation of the foot permits the central beam to be parallel with the floor and perpendicular to the third phalanx. The amount of elevation will be determined by the type of equipment. This view is taken with the *standard* technique.* When evaluating a radiograph for rotation of the third phalanx, it is sometimes of value to tape a metal strip on the anterior surface of the hoof wall. This will create a radiographic shadow that can be compared with the shadow caused by the bone. The degree of rotation can be determined by this method. As with all lateral views, the leg must be straight if the coffin joint is to be visualized.

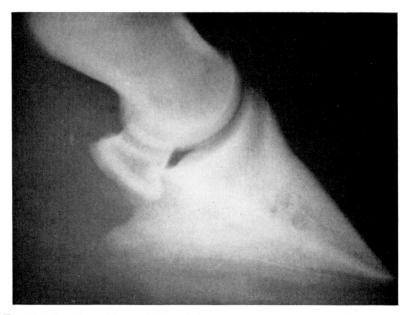

Fig. 12–39.—Normal lateral view of the third phalanx of a mature horse. This view is primarily of value in diagnosing fractures of the extensor process and rotation of the third phalanx. Other fractures of the third phalanx are frequently not seen on this view.

Diagnosis.—The two AP views described are required to obtain evaluation of both the distal interphalangeal (coffin) joint and the distal portion of the third phalanx. It is important to evaluate the coffin joint for arthritic changes, and to determine if there is a fracture in the distal portion of the third phalanx. Arthritis and fractures into the distal interphalangeal (coffin) joint cannot be judged solely on the weight-bearing film.

Radiographs of the third phalanx present problems in diagnosis. Some can be corrected because they are due to artifacts caused by improper cleaning of the sole and frog. Even though preparation is complete, shadows are created on the radiograph by the central and lateral sulci of the frog. It is possible to eliminate these shadows by packing the sole of the foot with material of the same density. Dried and finely rasped horn with petroleum jelly as a binding medium can be used for this purpose. Considering the time required to prepare the foot, it is better to learn to recognize these lines (Fig. 12–35).

Radiolucent shadows in the third phalanx caused by the numerous canals for vessels resemble fracture lines. Comparing one side of the third phalanx with the other can help avoid this error in diagnosis. Most vascular canals radiate from the semilunar canal making their direction different from the typical third phalanx fracture (Fig. 12–35).

A notch, called the "toe stay," may be present in the distal tip of the third phalanx. This should not be confused with bone lysis secondary to osteomyelitis.

The cartilages of the third phalanx may be in various stages of ossification (side bones). This degenerative process usually begins just proximal to the angles of the third phalanx and progresses distally. However, it is not unusual for the process to begin proximally in the tip of the cartilage and progress toward the third phalanx. These two areas of ossification may approach each other and resemble a fracture.

The extensor process of the third phalanx can appear very sharp on the lateral radiograph. This is frequently normal and not a positive sign of osteoarthritis.

Epiphyseal Closure. — No epiphyseal lines are routinely seen on the radiographs of the third phalanx. On the oblique views of the third phalanx radiolucent lines may be seen across the tip of the angles. These can separate a small fragment of bone that may resemble a fracture fragment. If clinical signs are localized to this area, a view of the same area on the opposite foot or the other angle of the same foot can be used for comparison. In some cases bilateral "fractures" of the extensor process may result from congenital defects (see Chapter 6, p. 236).

4. Navicular Bone Studies

Adequate studies of the navicular bone are difficult to obtain and require specific positioning of both tube and foot. Medial and lateral markers must be used on AP and oblique views. Studies of the navicular bone on the hind legs, while not common, would be performed essentially in the same manner.

Views. — Oxspring[26] described the "upright pedal route" as a method of obtaining an anterior-posterior view. He used a specially constructed stand that held the wall of the toe perpendicular to the ground. The film was placed vertically in a position posterior to the heels. The central beam was directed parallel with the ground and centered at the coronary band. This technique has been modified so that the anterior wall of the hoof is not quite perpendicular. The central beam is parallel with the ground and aimed at the coronary band (Fig. 12–40).

Another technique that has been advocated for the AP view of the navicular bone is referred to as the "high coronary route." This is taken with the foot resting on the cassette. The central beam is angled at approximately $55°$ to the ground and is directed at the coronary band. A variation of this "high coronary route" is accomplished by placing the toe on a small wooden block to overextend the foot (Fig. 12–41).

The purpose of these special positions is to cause an apparent elevation of the navicular bone on the radiograph. This allows the bone to be seen projected through the second phalanx and radio-

Fig. 12–40.—Radiographic technique for the navicular bone using the "upright pedal route." The central beam is marked (arrow). This picture was posed to show one of the most common radiation hazards. The assistant has positioned his leg directly behind the horse's foot within the primary beam.

graphic visualization is easier. It is not difficult to build special blocks that will permit the exact duplication of positioning each time.

The AP view, regardless of the technique used, is made through a great amount of tissue. A grid is of value in eliminating some of the scatter radiation. Lead intensifying screens, commonly used in industrial radiology, can be used to eliminate some scatter radiation. Cost of lead screens is much less than cost of a grid. Diagnostic studies can be obtained without either of these accessories, however.

The *darker* technique* should be used on the various AP views since the navicular bone must be seen projected through the second phalanx.

The lateral view can be taken with the *standard* technique.* This is done in essentially the same manner as the lateral view of the third phalanx. The central beam is directed slightly posteriorly and proximally so that it is centered on the navicular bone. Usually the foot must be elevated on a block in order to obtain true lateral views (Figs. 12–38 and 39).

* See p. 477.

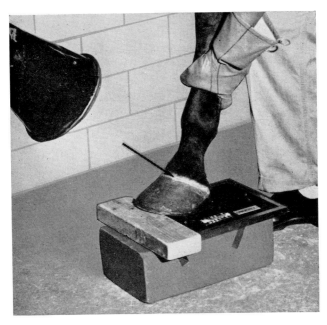

Fig. 12–41.—Radiographic technique for the navicular bone using the "high coronary route." The cassette has been placed on a block to prevent the horse from putting his full weight on it. The small block is used to produce further extension of the foot. The angle of the central beam is approximately 55 degrees. The central beam is marked (arrow).

It is possible to take oblique views that will demonstrate the tips of the navicular bone. This view is made in the same manner as the oblique view of the third phalanx (Figs. 12–36, 37). The *lighter* technique* is used.

Diagnosis.—Care must be used in making a diagnosis of navicular disease. It is of value to have several AP views made by either the "high coronary" or "upright pedal route" to compare. These allow evaluation of both proximal and distal borders of the navicular bone (Fig. 12–42). Bony spurs and/or lytic areas are more convincing when they can be located on several views. The lateral view can be of value since the presence of bony spurs can be confirmed by a good lateral projection.

A radiograph of the navicular bone in the intact hoof provides information on only major changes. These include changes in vascularization shown as increased porosity of the bone, osteosclerosis, and exostoses. Radiographic changes of navicular disease follow the development of clinical signs and the study is of most value from a prognostic point of view and to rule out other possible lesions involving this bone. Part of the problem in diagnosis is in deter-

* See p. 477.

33

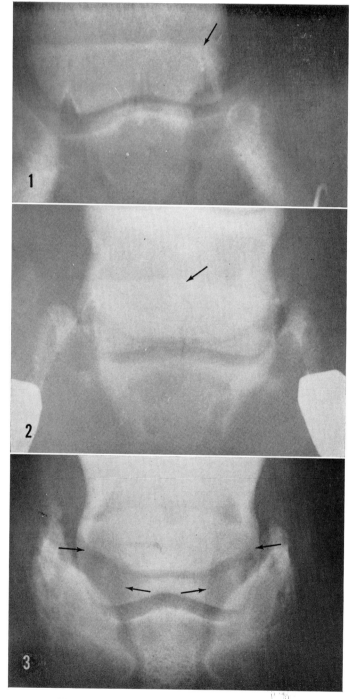

FIG. 12–42.—(*Legend on opposite page.*)

mining "normal" changes developing with age. Comparison views with a sound leg will sometimes demonstrate comparable changes in both feet. In a long-standing case of navicular disease calcification of the navicular suspensory ligament may be present (Fig. 6–66).

Diagnosis of fracture of the navicular bone can be confused with the radiolucent lines caused by the medial and lateral sulci of the frog (Fig. 12–42). If these lines are a problem, an additional view should be taken with the central beam angled in a slightly different manner. If the line is a fracture, its location in the navicular bone will remain unchanged. However, if the line is due to a superimposed shadow, the slightly different angle will change the location of the "fracture" line. Lines that extend above or below the navicular bone are not navicular fractures.

Epiphyseal Closure. — There are no normal epiphyseal lines in this area. "Fractured" navicular bones have been seen in young horses with no known evidence of trauma. In one case, a six-month-old colt had "fractures" of three of the four navicular bones. When the clinical signs do not fit the typical picture of navicular fracture, the possibility of bipartite sesamoid bone must be considered.

5. Metacarpal and Metatarsal Bones

Examination of these bones can be discussed together. Routine projections include anterior-posterior and lateral views. If a specific lesion has been determined clinically, or a lesion such as a fractured splint bone suspected, oblique views should then be made. Medial and lateral markers must be used on AP and oblique studies if no carpal or tarsal bones are seen.

Views. — The AP view is taken with the animal bearing weight on the leg (Fig. 12–43). The central beam is directed at the area where greatest interest lies and the cassette positioned posteriorly.

The lateral view is also weight bearing and made with the tube positioned laterally and the cassette medially (Fig. 12–44).

Fig. 12–42.—Normal AP radiograph of the navicular bone. All of the projections are made in a slightly different manner. (1) This view demonstrated the upper border of the navicular bone. The lower border cannot be seen because it overlies the coffin joint. The lateral sulcus of the frog has created an apparent fracture of one of the angles (arrow). (2) This view demonstrates the navicular bone elevated higher so that both upper and lower borders can be studied. The median sulcus of the frog has created an apparent fracture of the navicular bone (arrow). The shoe has not compromised this view. (3) The navicular bone can be best studied from this projection. The lateral sulci of the frog cover the navicular bone but do not create diagnostic problems (arrows). Note the different shapes of the navicular bone as it is projected through the various angles.

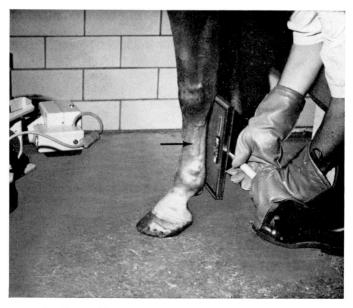

Fig. 12–43.—Radiographic technique for obtaining the AP view of the metacarpal bones. The same principle is used in making the AP view of the metatarsal bones. The central beam is marked (arrow).

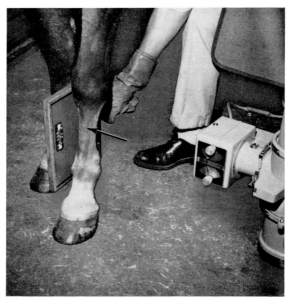

Fig. 12–44.—Radiographic technique for obtaining the lateral view of the metacarpal bones. The same principle is used in making the lateral radiograph of the metatarsal bone. The central beam is marked (arrow).

Oblique views are made in a manner similar to oblique views of proximal sesamoid bones (Figs. 12–45, 46). The second and fourth metacarpal and metatarsal bones require slightly different angles of projection. If the tube is placed approximately 45° from the mid-sagittal plane, however, adequate studies can be obtained.

The *standard* technique* is used for all views of the splint bones and cannon bone.

* See p. 477.

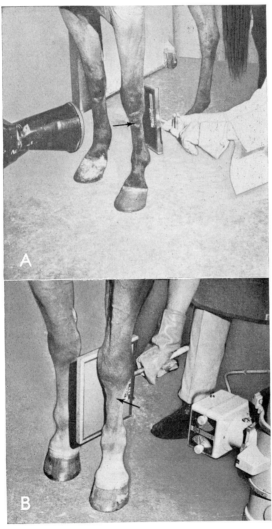

FIG. 12–45. — Radiographic technique for making the medial (*A*) and lateral (*B*) oblique views of the splint bones. The same technique is used for both front and hind legs. Each splint bone requires a slightly different angle for the best projection. The central beam has been marked (arrows).

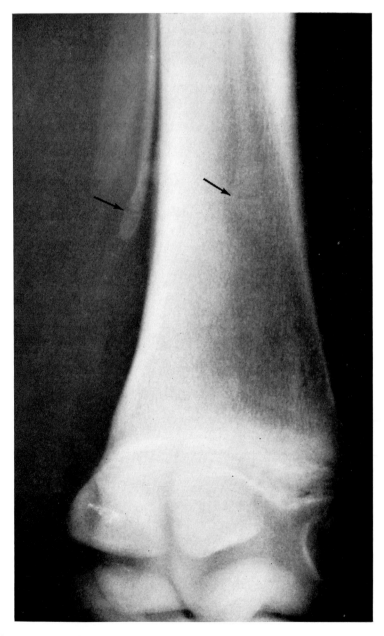

FIG. 12–46.—Oblique view of the distal portion of the splint bone of a horse six months of age. The cartilaginous plate is seen in the distal end of the splint bones (arrows). This should not be confused with a fracture line. The slight bowing of the distal tip of the splint bone is normal.

Diagnosis.—Both the carpo-metacarpal/tarso-metatarsal joint and the metacarpo-metatarsophalangeal (fetlock) joints cannot be seen adequately on the same radiograph. It is important that at least one joint be seen for purposes of orientation. Cassettes that measure 7×17 inches are excellent for studies of this area.

Until one is familiar with the appearance of the distal row of carpal/tarsal bones, it is advisable to mark the radiograph. This will avoid confusing medial and lateral splint bones.

Little problem should be present in diagnosis of this area if the outline of individual bones is carefully followed. The anterior cortex of the cannon bone normally is very thick (Fig. 12–47) and should not be confused with an osteitis secondary to trauma.

On the lateral view of the metacarpal bones, the splint bones will appear superimposed (Fig. 12–47). However, the splint bones on the hind leg are different in size and position. The fourth metatarsal bone is massive in its upper part and is very prominent posteriorly as seen on the true lateral view (Fig. 12–67). Saucer fractures on the

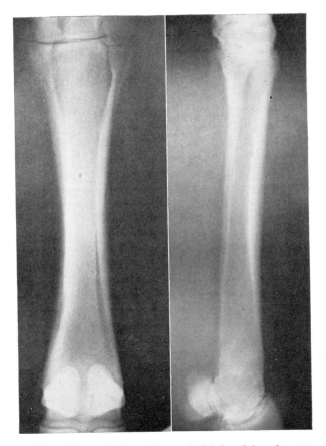

FIG. 12–47.—AP and lateral views of second, third and fourth metacarpal bones taken on a 7-by-17 cassette and film. This view shows the entire length of the metacarpal bones.

anterior surface of the 3rd metacarpal are sometimes found in bucked shins (see Chapter 6).

Epiphyseal Closure.—Epiphyseal lines will not be seen on studies of immature horses unless the examination includes the distal portion of these bones. The epiphyseal line in the distal end of the cannon bones closes by one year of age (Figs. 12–32, 33). The third metacarpal bone closes somewhat earlier than the third metatarsal bone. The distal ends of both second and fourth metacarpal and metatarsal bones are cartilaginous at birth. They may show an epiphyseal line in their distal portion (Fig. 12–46).

6. Carpus

Routine radiographic examination of the carpus includes anterior-posterior, flexed lateral, straight lateral, anterior-medial and anterior-lateral oblique views. Since the carpus is relatively high on the leg, the horse may stand in a normal manner. This portion of the leg is usually not covered with dirt and debris and little, if any, preparation is required if no leg paints or blisters have been applied.

Medial and lateral markers are not mandatory on AP and oblique views since the differences in the carpal bones allow positive identification. However, until one becomes familiar with the views, use of these markers is helpful.

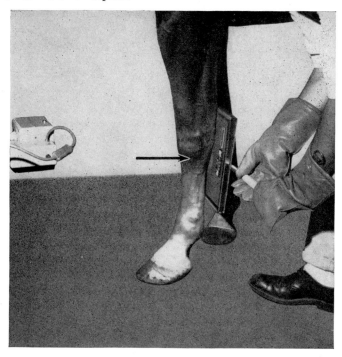

Fig. 12–48.—Radiographic technique for the AP view of the carpus. A cassette holder with a "leg" is helpful for this study. The central beam is marked (arrow).

Views.—In taking the AP projection, the horse should be positioned so that he is bearing weight on the examined leg. If necessary, the opposite front foot can be picked up. It can be difficult to determine where to direct the central beam. The mid-sagittal plane can be located by observing the bulbs of the heel. The central beam should be horizontal to the ground and directed at the midportion of the carpus (Figs. 12–48, 49). The cassette does not rest on the ground and, therefore, care must be taken to avoid moving it during the exposure. Holders are available with adjustable "legs" to correct this problem.

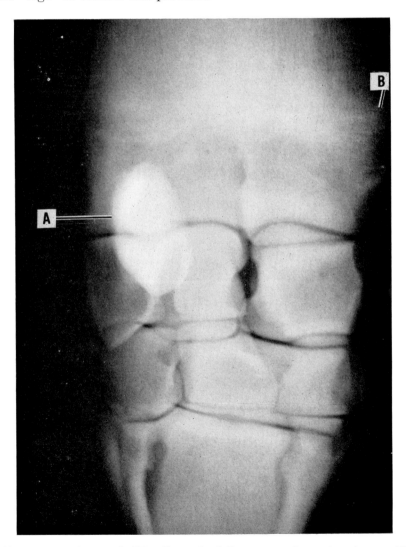

FIG. 12–49.—A normal AP radiograph of the carpus of a mature horse. The accessory carpal bone is seen laterally as an area of increased density (*A*). The protuberance on the distal end of the radius medially is normal (*B*).

Both straight lateral and flexed lateral views are made in a similar manner. The straight view is made with the foot resting on the ground (Figs. 12–50, 51), while in the flexed lateral view, the foot is held high off the ground (Figs. 12–52, 53). In both views, but especially the flexed view, the leg must be kept straight and not abducted at the shoulder. This is important if the joint spaces are to be accurately evaluated. The flexed lateral view can be of value in determining whether a recognized chip fracture is free or attached.

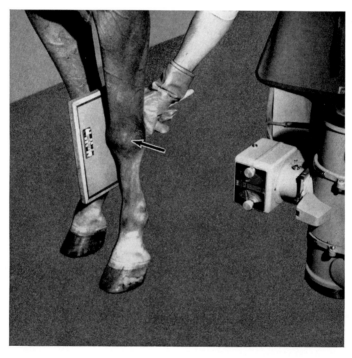

Fig. 12–50.—Radiographic technique for the routine lateral view of the carpus. The central beam is marked (arrow).

The soft tissues are altered when the leg is flexed, and if the chip is unattached to the bone, it will shift in position when compared with the straight lateral view.

Medial and lateral oblique views are essential in diagnosis of either carpal or radial chip fractures. These views are taken to show to better advantage the anterior-medial and anterior-lateral aspects of the carpus. The tube is shifted medially or laterally and the cassette in the opposite direction. With the tube laterally, the central beam is directed at the second carpal bone (Fig. 12–54). If the tube is positioned medially, the central beam is directed at the fourth carpal bone (Fig. 12–54).

All the views of the carpus are taken with the *darker* technique.*

* See p. 477.

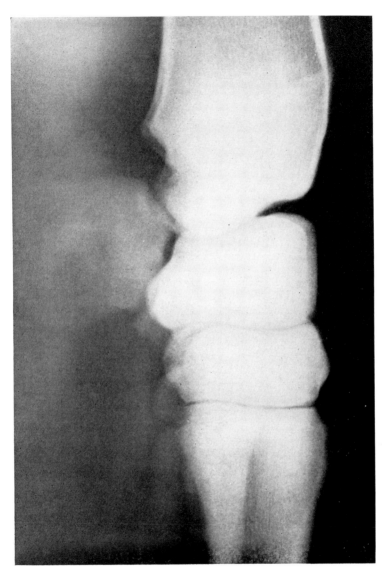

FIG. 12–51.—Normal lateral radiograph of the carpus of a mature horse.

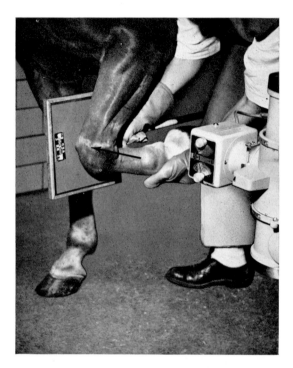

FIG. 12–52.—Radiographic technique for the flexed lateral view of the carpus.
The central beam is marked (arrow).

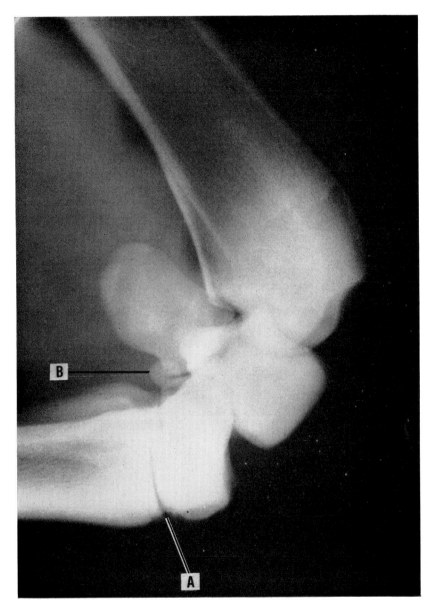

Fig. 12–53.—Normal flexed lateral radiograph of a mature horse. Note the absence of demonstrable motion in the carpo-metacarpal joint (A). The first carpal bone can be seen (B).

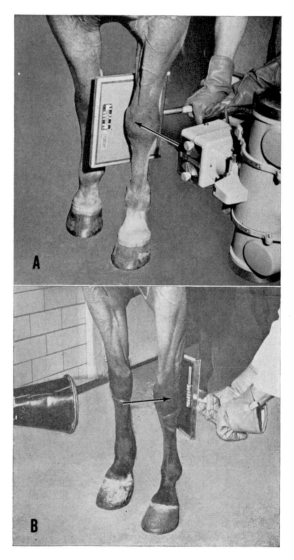

FIG. 12–54.—Radiographic techniques for obtaining the oblique views of the carpus. These views are of value in diagnosing small carpal fractures. They demonstrate the anterior medial (A) and anterior lateral (B) aspect of the carpal bones to good advantage. The central beams are marked (arrows).

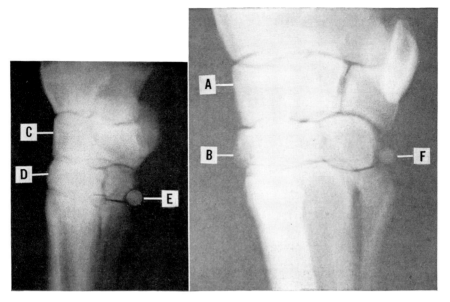

Fig. 12–55.—Oblique views of the carpus of a mature horse. These views are especially valuable in determination of small chip fractures. Good evaluation of the radial (*A*), third (*B*), ulnar (*C*), fourth (*D*) carpal bones can be made. The first (*E*) and fifth (*F*) carpal bones are present on these studies.

Diagnosis.—There are several normal anatomical structures in the carpus that create problems in radiographic diagnosis. The first carpal bone, when separate, is seen on the medial side posterior to the second carpal bone (Figs. 12–55, 56). The size varies from .5 to 1 cm. On lateral views it can be seen just posteriorly to the distal row of carpal bones (Fig. 12–53). It is differentiated from a fracture fragment by its specific location and because of its smooth, round appearance.

There is occasionally a small bone present on the lateral side, posteriorly. This is assumed to be a nonunited fifth carpal bone. It is similar in shape and size to that of the first carpal bone (Figs. 12–55, 56).

The chestnut will create a soft tissue shadow just above the carpus. At times the mass of horn is dense enough to resemble soft tissue calcification secondary to trauma.

On lateral views the articular surface of the distal end of the radius appears to be positioned posteriorly. This creates a "notch" on the anterior surface of the radius that is normal and not a conformation problem (Fig. 12–51).

The distal end of the ulna may be seen on the lateral aspect of the distal radius on the oblique view. Its appearance is extremely variable ranging from no apparent shadow to one of complete ossification. The line of junction closely resembles a transverse fracture. Age seems to play no part in the degree of ossification and

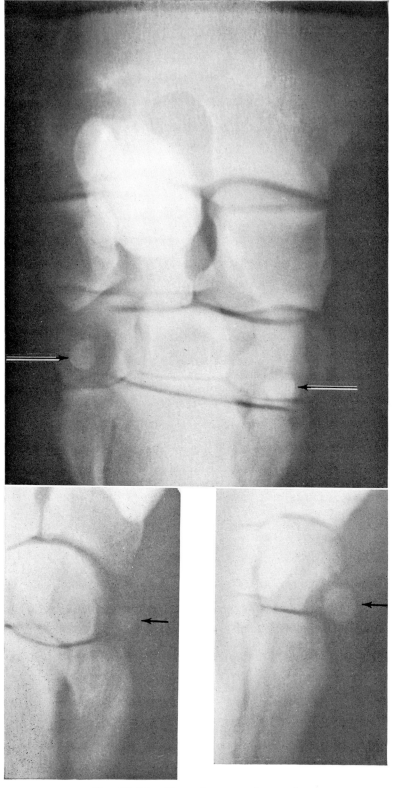

FIG. 12–56.—(*Legend on opposite page.*)

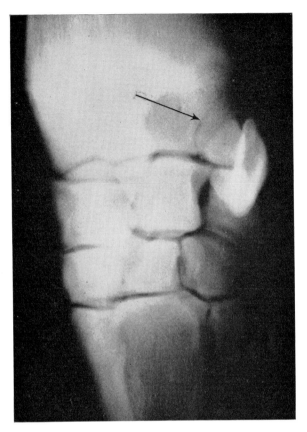

FIG. 12-57.—An AP radiograph of the radius showing a disunited ulna and radius
which can be confused with a longitudinal fracture of the radius (arrow).

frequently the ulna on the opposite leg will have a dissimilar
pattern.

Epiphyseal Closure.—An epiphyseal line is normally seen in the
distal radius and closure usually occurs between two years and two
and one-half years of age (Figs. 12-58, 59). Occasionally an epiphyseal line is seen within the distal portion of the accessory carpal
bone (Fig. 12-60). This is not a common finding, but should not be
confused with a fracture. An ossification center representing the
distal tip of the ulna is seen at birth but usually fuses early (Figs.
12-57, 58).

FIG. 12-56.—AP and oblique views of the carpus of a mature horse with separate
ossification centers for both the first and the fifth carpal bones (arrows). These can
be differentiated from fractures because of their location and their smooth, round
appearance.

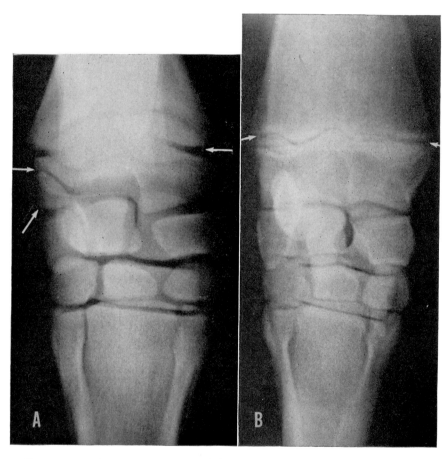

FIG. 12–58.—Appearance of the epiphyseal lines in the distal radius (arrows) typical of one month of age (A) and eighteen months of age (B). The separate ossification of the distal ulna is seen along with the line in the distal radius. Note the apparent narrowing of the joint spaces as the horse matures.

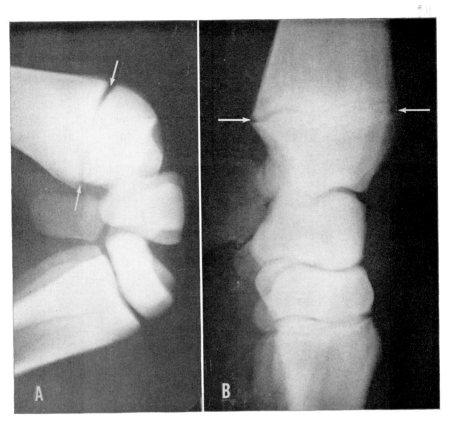

Fig. 12–59.—Epiphyseal closure in the distal radius (arrows) as seen on the lateral views of the carpus. The views are typical of one month of age (*A*) and six months (*B*).

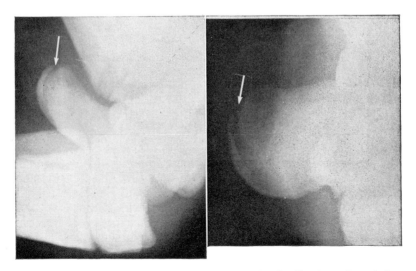

Fig. 12–60.—Epiphyseal line occasionally seen in the distal portion of the accessory carpal bone (arrows).

7. Elbow (Humero-Radial Joint)

The lateral view of the elbow can be obtained with equipment that is adequate for studies of the digit and foot. However, the anterior-posterior view will require use of a grid and a machine with higher ma capability (100 ma). Sometimes it is possible to obtain an oblique view that will be diagnostic with a machine of lower than 100 ma rating.

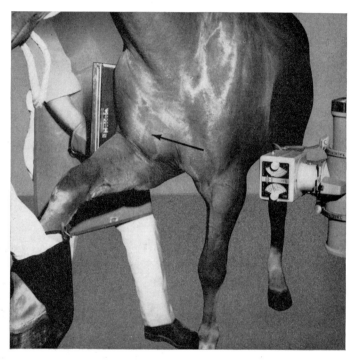

Fig. 12–61.—Radiographic technique for making the lateral view of the elbow. A view of this type can usually be made with a machine of low rating. The central beam is marked (arrow).

Views.—The lateral view is most easily taken by extending the limb forward and positioning the cassette on the lateral aspect of the elbow. The central beam is directed from the opposite side of the horse and passes anteriorly to the pectoral region (Figs. 12–61, 62). Also it is possible to position the cassette medial to the joint to be examined. It is forced as far upward into the axillary space as possible. This view will place the elbow joint barely visible at the top of the radiograph. Occasionally this is adequate for a diagnosis. The horse can be anesthetized and radiographed with the affected

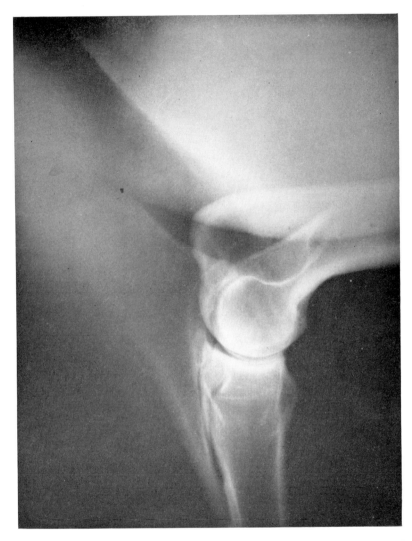

FIG. 12–62.—Normal lateral radiograph of the elbow of a mature horse. It is difficult to visualize both the joint space and the olecranon on the same radiograph because of differences necessary in exposure factors.

limb on the down side. The cassette is placed under the horse and the top limb pulled out of the field of radiation. Good studies can be obtained in this manner.

AP views are taken with the horse bearing weight on the limb (Figs. 12–63, 64). The cassette is positioned posterior to the elbow in contact with the olecranon. The angle of the tube is determined

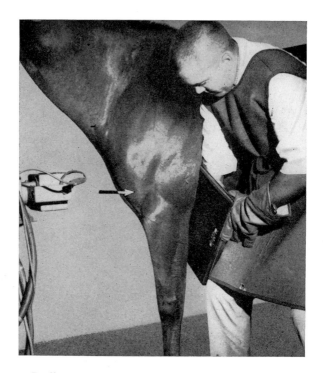

Fig. 12–63.—Radiographic technique for making the AP view of the elbow. Only the distal end of the humerus is seen on this study. The central beam (arrow) should be aimed at the joint space even though this may not be in the middle of the cassette.

by the particular area to be studied. The AP view can also be made with the horse anesthetized and lying on the floor. The affected leg is up and the beam directed parallel to the floor.

Diagnosis.—Studies in this area are usually to determine the presence of fractures or arthritis. If the normal structures are recognized there is little problem in diagnosis.

Epiphyseal Closure.—Epiphyseal lines are present in the immature animal in the distal humerus, olecranon, proximal radius, and medial epicondyle of the humerus (Fig. 12–65).

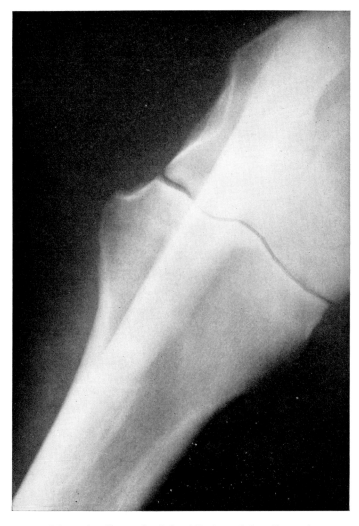

FIG. 12–64.—Normal radiograph of the AP view of the elbow of a mature horse. Since the cassette must be angled only a very small portion of the humerus is seen. The joint space can be evaluated for arthritic changes, however.

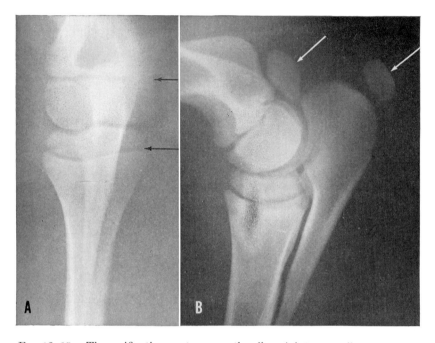

FIG. 12–65. — The ossification centers near the elbow joint are easily seen on these two views of a foal. The AP view (A) is typical of a foal one week of age. The epiphyseal lines in the distal humerus and proximal radius are well seen (arrows). The lateral view (B) is typical of a foal one month of age. In addition to the proximal radius and distal humerus, ossification centers in the medial epicondyle (arrow) and olecranon (arrow) are seen.

8. Hock (Tarsal) Joint

Generally anterior-posterior and lateral views are taken of this area. Oblique views can be made but are not commonly used. Usually the study is made to evaluate the distal joint spaces more than the proximal portions of the hock.

Views.—The lateral view is taken with the cassette positioned medially and the beam aimed at the central tarsal bone (Figs. 12–66, 67). This is approximately 4 inches distal to the tip of the

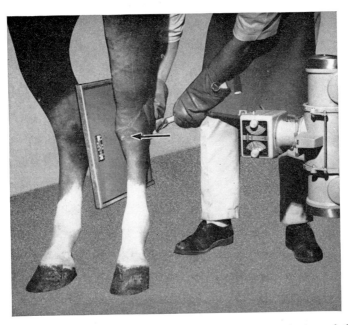

FIG. 12–66.—Radiographic technique for making the lateral view of the hock joint. It is important to observe the position of the foot on this view in order to obtain a true lateral view. The central beam is marked (arrow).

os calcis. The most common error is to center the beam too high, causing the joint spaces to appear irregular on the radiograph.

If the horse will allow the hock to be rotated inward, the AP view is not difficult to obtain. The cassette is positioned against the back of the hock and the beam aimed at the central tarsal bone. The beam is angled slightly to be perpendicular with the metatarsal bones (Figs. 12–68, 69). If the horse will not allow rotating of the leg, it may be difficult to position the tube near the elbow of the horse. In this event an oblique view may be substituted for the AP view. This is taken with the tube moved slightly laterally and the cassette placed posteriorly and medially.

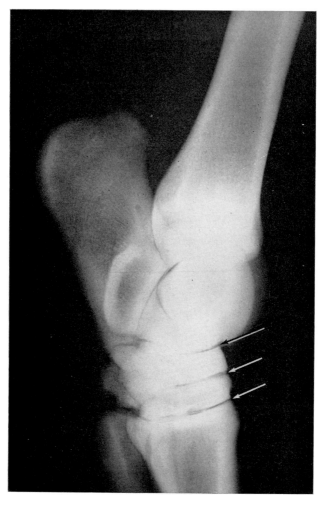

Fig. 12–67.—Normal lateral radiograph of tarsus in a mature horse. The distal joint spaces (arrows) can be well evaluated. Note the proximal portion of the fourth metatarsal bone positioned posteriorly on the true lateral view.

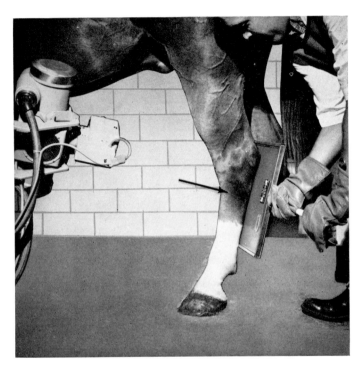

FIG. 12–68.—Radiographic technique for making the AP view of the hock. The cassette is held firmly against the metatarsal bone and the central beam is angled slightly toward the ground. The central beam is aimed approximately 4 inches distal to the point of the hock (arrow).

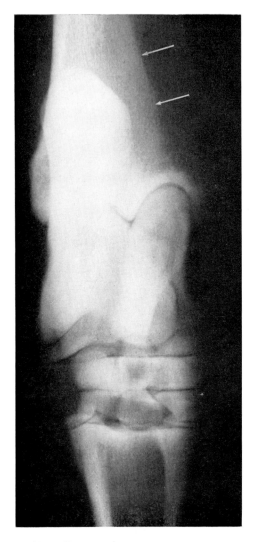

Fig. 12–69.—Normal AP radiograph of the hock joint of a mature horse. The
shadow created by the flexor tendons is seen across the tibia (arrow).

It is possible for this joint to exceed eleven centimeters when soft tissue swelling is present. In this case a grid should be used; however, diagnostic films can usually be made without use of this accessory.

Technique for all views of the hock are the *darker* technique.*

Diagnosis.—If positioning is adequate, distal joint spaces are sharply seen and can be evaluated for arthritic changes. The Chestnut is frequently seen posteriorly and proximally on the lateral view.

Epiphyseal Closure.—Epiphyseal closure of the distal tibial plate usually occurs by two years. The lateral malleolus of the tibia, which is a remnant of the distal fibula, unites shortly after birth. The proximal portion of the os calcis unites between two and two and one half years of age (Figs. 12–70, 71).

* See page 477.

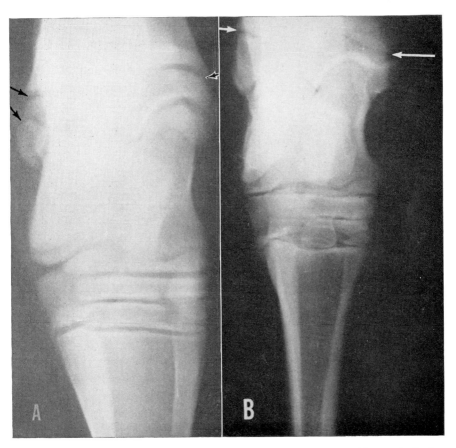

FIG. 12–70.—Stages of epiphyseal closure are seen on these studies typical of a foal at one month of age (*A*) and one year of age (*B*). The epiphyseal line in the distal end of the tibia is seen on both views (arrows). The separate ossification center for the lateral malleolus is seen only on the earlier study (arrows).

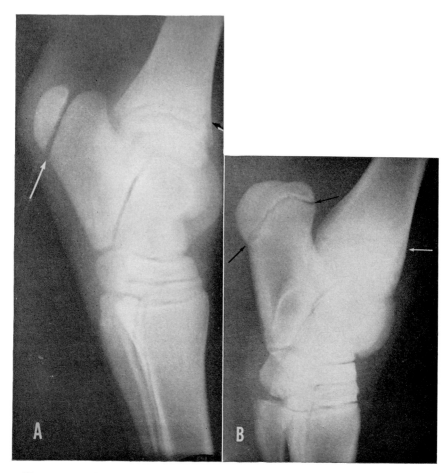

Fig. 12–71.—The stages of epiphyseal closure seen on these studies are typical
for one week of age (A) and eighteen months of age (B). The line in the os calcis
and distal tibia can be seen (arrows).

9. Stifle (Femoro-Tibial) Joint

The stifle is not commonly examined with light equipment. However, a lateral view can be obtained on smaller horses with equipment described as adequate for the distal extremities. If possible, two views should be taken of this joint, a posterior-anterior and lateral view.

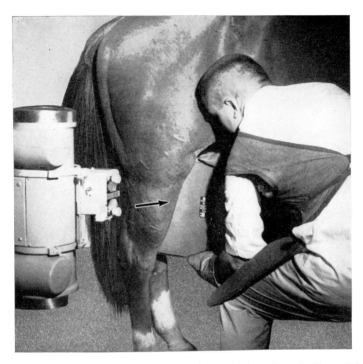

Fig. 12–72.—Radiographic technique for making the lateral projection of the stifle joint. The central beam is marked (arrow).

Views.—To make the lateral view, the cassette is placed medially. It is forced upward into the flank as far as possible (Figs. 12–72, 73). There is a tendency to center the beam above the actual joint space. The beam should be directed approximately 4 inches distal to the patella in order to project this joint space. In most cases it is necessary to use a grid for this view. If the horse is anesthetized, the radiograph can be taken in lateral recumbency with the leg to be examined next to the ground. The cassette is then placed under the leg with the central beam perpendicular to the ground. The normal leg must be positioned so it is out of the primary beam.

The PA view is used instead of an AP projection. The bony structures comprising the stifle joint are located at the anterior portion of the leg and must be as close to the film as possible. The

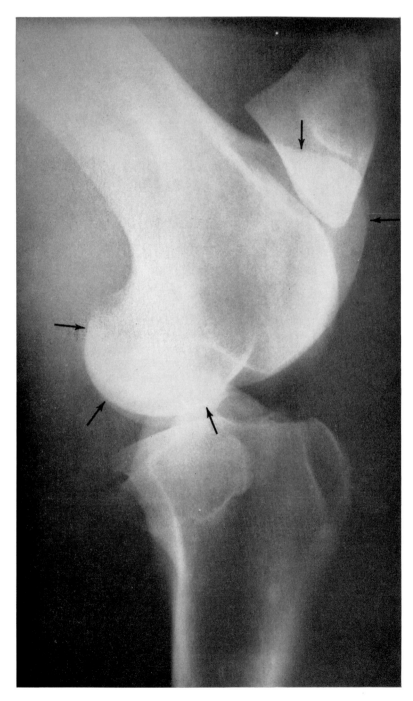

Fig. 12–73.—Normal lateral radiograph of the stifle joint of a mature horse. The articular surfaces of the femoral condyles (arrows) are seen positioned further posterior than sometimes expected. The medial portion of the trochlea is larger than the lateral (arrow).

cassette can be angled and pushed into the flank (Figs. 12–74, 75). The tube is positioned posteriorly and the central beam directed at the stifle joint. A small piece of tape on the skin to mark the joint space is helpful. Generally this view requires use of equipment of at least 100 ma capability and a grid.

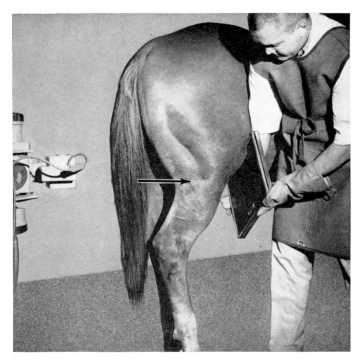

Fig. 12–74.—Radiographic technique for making the PA view of the stifle. The central beam is marked (arrow).

Epiphyseal Closure.—The epiphyseal lines seen on radiographs of this area include the distal femur, tibial crest, and proximal tibia (Fig. 12–76). The patella in the newborn will have only a small portion ossified but this will continue to increase in size as the horse ages. The distal femur fuses by two to two and one half years of age. The tibial crest first unites with the ossification center of the proximal tibia by one year of age. These combined ossification centers will then unite with the shaft of the tibia by two and one-half to three years of age.

Diagnosis.—The normal ossification center of the tibial crest can cause errors in diagnosis. This can be mistaken for fracture or an avulsion of the tibial crest. Either of these diagnoses should be approached cautiously and then only after comparison with radiographs of the opposite leg has been made. The epiphyseal

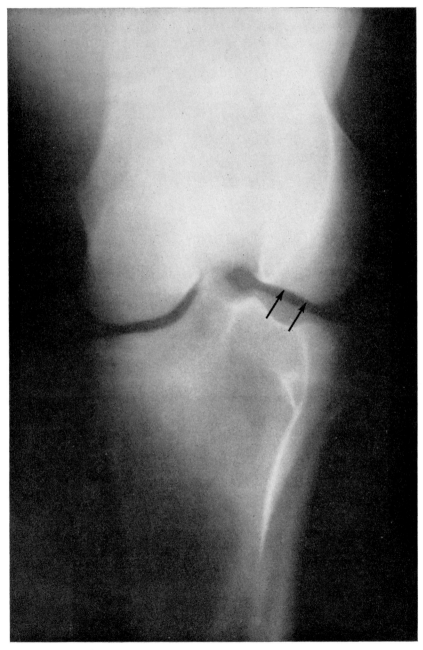

FIG. 12–75.—Normal PA view of the stifle joint in a mature horse. Due to the great difference in tissue thickness it is difficult to see both the distal femur and the proximal tibia. The normal flattened appearance of the lateral condyle of the femur is shown (arrow).

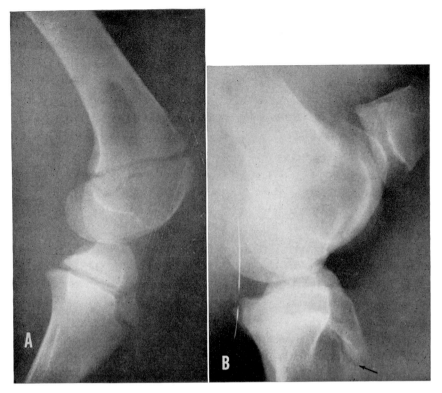

FIG. 12–76.—Epiphyseal closure of the proximal tibial epiphyseal line and the tibial crest. At one week of age (A) the tibial crest and the proximal tibia both are represented by separate ossification centers. A study at two years demonstrates the union of the two ossification centers. The tibial crest has not completely united with the shaft of the tibia, however (arrow).

lines during closure can create shadows on the radiograph that easily are mistaken for lesions unless care in interpretation is exercised (see Chapter 6, p. 303).

The lateral condyle of the femur as seen on the PA view does not have the smooth contour of the medial condyle (Fig. 12–75).

A cartilaginous plate is frequently seen extending across the proximal portion of the fibula. This is commonly seen on the PA view of the stifle, and has been shown not to be a fracture (see p. 305).

10. Hip (Coxo-Femoral) Joint

Studies of the hip joint can be obtained only through use of larger equipment (100 kvp and 100 ma minimum). It is important that the horse be anesthetized due to longer exposures required and in order to position the horse on his back.

Views.—The horse is positioned on his back for the ventral-dorsal view. The legs are placed in a "frog-leg" position as described for the dog.[5] The method of positioning the legs is not so critical as is the fact that the limbs must be positioned identically. It is sometimes advantageous to make additional radiographs with the legs pulled further posteriorly. If a specific hip is involved, the horse can be laid on the affected side and the cassette placed under the affected joint. The upper leg is put into extreme abduction and removed from the primary beam. This will give a lateral view of the femoral head and neck.

In all techniques described, the cassette and grid must be placed under the pelvis. It is possible to damage equipment unless a tunnel device is used. The tunnel may be constructed from many types of material, but must have a radiolucent top. The cassette can be inserted and removed without moving the horse and the weight of the animal is not on the cassette and grid.

Newer, more powerful equipment has made it possible to obtain lateral views of the pelvis with the horse standing.

Diagnosis.—These studies are usually to determine the presence of fractures or dislocations. If the studies are made so both hip joints are visualized, a comparison can be made. If the colon is filled with feces, diagnosis is more difficult. By cleaning out the colon and allowing it to balloon with air, the total density is decreased and better radiographs can be obtained.

Epiphyseal Closure.—Epiphyseal lines are seen in the femoral neck and in the pelvis. Ossification centers of the greater and lesser trochanter are present in young horses.

11. Shoulder (Scapulo-Humeral) Joint

The location and structure of this joint make it difficult to examine radiographically without use of equipment with higher rating (110 kvp–100 ma). With the horse standing, it is possible to direct the beam through the body from the opposite side and obtain a satisfactory lateral view. With an anesthetized horse, the cassette is placed under the affected leg and a lateral view obtained with the beam perpendicular to the bone.

The AP or PA view is more difficult because it is not possible to straighten the joint. It is sometimes easier to place the cassette anteriorly and the tube posteriorly along the rib cage.

Various oblique views can be made but these are always difficult to evaluate because they present a slightly different view each time.

12. Additional Studies

The discussion of radiographic techniques has generally been limited to evaluation of the joints. Occasionally evaluation of the midshaft of a long bone for possible fracture is necessary. Studies of the radius, humerus, tibia, femur, and spine usually require equipment with higher ma (100) and kvp (100). If the horse is recumbent or can be anesthetized, lateral views can sometimes be made successfully. The cassette should be placed under the horse and the affected part should be on the down side. The tube can be centered on the suspected lesion and the cassette positioned appropriately. Length of exposure is not a critical factor under these conditions and exposure times up to ten seconds can be used.

The AP or PA views are much more difficult since both horse and film must be prevented from moving. It is easier to roll the horse over for this view so the affected leg is up. The leg is extended and the cassette placed anterior or posterior to the leg.

RADIOGRAPHIC DETERMINATION OF BONE MATURITY AS A GUIDE TO TRAINING HORSES

O. R. Adams, D.V.M., M.S.

There has been an attempt to determine the relationship between bone maturity and injuries caused by racing. The distal epiphysis of the radius above the carpal joint is radiographed and classified in young horses to determine whether or not they are ready to start race training. Many authorities have maintained that injuries suffered in racing could be reduced if training would be delayed to allow bone maturity. Sufficient time has not yet passed to decisively decide the matter, but case records are being kept and statistics should be available in the next two to three years. Many veterinarians feel that there will be a reduction in training and racing injuries if bone maturity is present before hard work begins. Hopefully, the studies presently under way will be able to prove this point.

The distal epiphysis of the radius is being classified in A, B, and C categories. Category A is a fully mature epiphysis. Category B shows the center of the epiphysis undergoing closure while the medial and lateral aspects are not yet closed. Category C is a fully open epiphysis, meaning that growth is still occurring. These categories can be difficult to define when they are borderline B or A categories. It is my opinion that interpretation centers should be set up throughout the country so that if an error is committed it will be a standard error and there will not be disagreement among practitioners as to the interpretation of these radiographs. For this interpretation an anterior-posterior radiograph is all that is necessary. Constant distance and exposure factors must be used for comparison to previous radiographs. Examples of A, B, and C classifications are shown in Figure 12-77.

For the A category horse, full race training is allowed. For the B category, it is recommended that the horse be trained and worked but allowed a limited number of starts, preferably not exceeding 10 in a season. In the C category no heavy work should be permitted

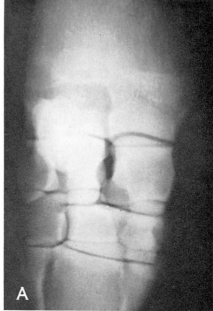

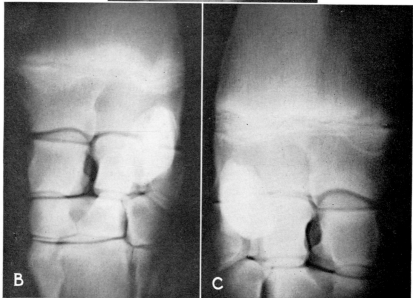

Fig. 12–77.—Three radiographs illustrating epiphyseal closure.

A,—Category A epiphysis fully closed.

B,—Category B epiphysis, closed in the center, with both medial and lateral portions of the epiphyses still open.

C,—Category C epiphysis, an example of an immature epiphysis.

and only disciplinary training allowed. It is my experience that radiographs taken oftener than every sixty days are probably not of value. It apparently takes at least sixty days to see enough change in the epiphyseal line to change the classification. In some blood lines closure does not occur until as late as thirty-three months.

REFERENCES

1. ALKSNIS, A.: Rontgenaufnahmen vom becken unserer Grobtiere. Dtsch. Tierarztl. Wschr., *51*, 301, 1943.
2. BANKS, W. C. and SCHULZ, C. W.: Additional Studies of Fibular Defects in Horses. J.A.V.M.A., *133*, 422, 1958.
3. BIRKELAND, R.: Rontgen som Diagnostisk Hjelpemiddel—Nord. Vet. Med., *15*, 899, 1963.
4. BRENNAN, B. F.: The Veterinarian and Race Track Practice. Vet. Scope, *3*, (Summer) 1958.
5. CARLSON, W. D.: *Veterinary Radiology*, 2nd edition, Philadelphia, Lea & Febiger, 1967.
6. CASE, A. A. and SHARMA, H. N.: Polaroid Technic Contrasted with Regular Radiographic Procedures. J. Am. Vet. Rad. Soc., *3*, 28–30, 1963.
7. CHAMBERLAIN, R. H. and NELSON, R. J., *et al.*: A Practice Manual on the Medical and Dental Use of X-rays with Control of Radiation Hazards. Published by the American College of Radiology, Chicago, Illinois.
8. DELAHANTY, D. D.: Defects—Not Fractures—of the Fibulae in the Horse. J.A.V.M.A., *133*, 258–260, 1958.
9. DIETZ, V. O., NAGEL, E., KOCH, T., BERG, R., STERBA, O.: Zur Entslehung und zur Klinik der Sogenannten Gedeckten, Dislalen Griff elbeinfrakturen. Schweizer Archiv fur Tierheilkunde, *105*, 87–98, 1963.
10. DOUGLAS, S. W. and WILLIAMSON, A. D.: *Principles of Veterinary Radiography*, 1st ed., London, Bailliere, Tindall and Cox, 1963.
11. DRURY, F. S., DYCE, K. M., and MERLEN, R. H.: Some Practical Aspects of the Experimental Radiography of the Larger Domestic Animals. Vet. Record, *66*, 593–595, 1954.
12. E. I. DuPont De Nemours and Co., Inc., Wilmington, Delaware. Darkroom Technique for Better Roentgenograms (pamphlet).
13. Eastman Kodak Co., Medical Division, Rochester, N. Y.: The Fundamentals of Radiography, 10th ed. (pamphlet).
14. Gavaert Photo—Producten N. V., Antwerp, Belgium: Processing of Medical X-ray Films (pamphlet), 1958.
15. General Electric Co., Milwaukee, Wisconsin: A Look at X-ray Film Processing, X-ray Department (pamphlet).
16. GLASSER, O., *et al.*: *Physical Foundations of Radiology*, 3rd ed., New York, Paul B. Hoeber, Inc., 1961.
17. HABEL, R. E., BARRETT, R. B., DIESEM, C. D., and ROENIGK, W. J.: Nomenclature for Radiologic Anatomy. J.A.V.M.A., *142*, 38, 1963.
18. HICKMAN, J. A.: A Review of Some Technical Aids in Veterinary Radiology. Vet. Record, *66*, 805, 1954.
19. IDSTROM, L. G.: X-ray Machines and Related Physics. Vet. Med., *49*, 381, 1954.
20. JACOBSON, G. A. and VAN FAROWE, D. E.: Survey of X-ray Protection Practices Among Michigan Veterinarians. J.A.V.M.A., *145*, 793, 1964.
21. LUNDVALL, R. L.: Fracture of the Fibula in the Horse. J.A.V.M.A., *129*, 16, 1956.
22. MOLE, R. H.: The Biological Basis for Precautions in Veterinary Radiography. Vet. Record, *73*, 1140, 1961.
23. MYERS, VICTOR S.: Confusing Radiologic Variations at the Distal End of the Radius of the Horse. J.A.V.M.A., 147, No. 12, p. 1310, Dec. 15, 1965.

24. National Bureau of Standards Handbooks, available from Superintendent of Documents, Washington 25, D. C.
    No. 50—X-ray Protection Design—price 20c.
    No. 51—Radiological Monitoring Methods and Instruments—price 25c.
    No. 54—Protection Against Radiations from Radium, Cobalt 60 and Cesium 137—price 25c.
    No. 59—Permissible Dose from External Sources of Ionizing Radiation—price 30c.
    No. 60—X-ray Protection—price 20c.
25. OLSSON, S-E: On Navicular Disease in the Horse. Nord. Vet. Med., 6, 547, 1954.
26. OXSPRING, G. E.: The Radiology of Navicular Disease, with Observations of its Pathology. Vet. Record, 15, 1433, 1935.
27. REYNOLDS, J. A.: Factors Affecting Radiographic Quality. Vet. Med., 50, 187, 1955.
28. RHODES, W. H.: Radiographic Manifestations of Degenerative Joint Disease. J.A.V.M.A., 141, 1256, 1962.
29. SMITH, R. N.: Radiography for the Veterinary Surgeon, Bristol, John Wright, 1960.
30. SONNICHSEN, H. V.: Fraktur af Phalanges. Nord. Vet. Med., 15, 251, 1963.
31. SPURRELL, F. A.: Interpretations in Veterinary Radiology. No. Am. Vet., 35, 283, 1954.
32. TAVERNOR, W. D. and VAUGHAN, L. C.: Radiography of Horses and Cattle. British Vet. J., 118, 359, 1962.
33. TENNILLE, N. B.: Diagnostic Radiology. Vet. Med., 48, 233, 1953.
34. ————: Soft Tissue Radiography—The Application of Contrast Media. Vet. Bull., 15, 34, 1956.
35. VAN DER PLATTS, G. J.: Medical X-Ray Technique, 2nd ed., Endhoven, Holland, N. V. Philips' Gloeilampenfabrieken, 1961.
36. VAUGHAN, L. C.: Fracture of the Navicular Bone in the Horse. Vet. Record, 73, 895, 1961.
37. WATSON, J. C.: Considerations in Formulating X-ray Exposure Factors. Vet. Med., 49, 435, 1954.
38. WILLIAMS, F. L.: Cassette Holders for Large Animal Radiography. J.A.V.M.A., 130, 28, 1957.
39. WILLIAMS, F. L. and CAMPBELL, D. Y.: Tendon Radiography in the Horse. J.A.V.M.A., 139, 224, 1961.
40. WILLIAMSON, H. D.: Veterinary Radiography—Some Aspects and Problems. Radiography, 30, 2, 1964.
41. ZESKOV, B.: A Study of Discontinuity of the Fibula in the Horse. Am. J. Vet. Res., 20, 852, 1959.
42. ZESKOV, B.: Diskontinuirani tok fibule u konja. Vet. Arhiv., 24, 178, 1954.
43. ZESKOV, B., et al.: Fracture or Congenital Discontinuity of the Fibula in the Horse. Brit. Vet. J., 114, 145, 1958.

Index

THE ESPUELA
LAND AND CATTLE COMPANY

A Study of a Foreign-Owned
Ranch in Texas

THE ESPUELA LAND AN[

A Study of a Foreign-Ow[n

WILLIAM CUR[

CATTLE COMPANY

anch in Texas

Foreword by
OLDEN   JOE B. FRANTZ

TEXAS STATE HISTORICAL ASSOCIATION
AUSTIN

Standard Book Number 87611-023-5

Library of Congress Catalog Card No. 70-84084

COPYRIGHT © 1970

WILLIAM CURRY HOLDEN

All Rights Reserved

Manufactured in the United States of America

To the Managers of the Spur Ranch:

SPOTTSWOOD W. LOMAX

FRED HORSBRUGH

HENRY H. JOHNSTONE

CHARLES A. JONES

CLIFFORD B. JONES

They differed in personality, appearance, and background, but each was an exceptional, able leader and left the imprint of his character and vision upon what is still known as the Spur Country.

1

FOREWORD

"W. C. HOLDEN" was the way I first heard of him. I am not much younger than he is, but by the time I began to be aware of my heritage Holden's biography of *The Spur Ranch* was established as a fine book and, for all I know, was already out of print. I knew too that he had taught in West Texas, and some of my older relatives told me what a splendid teacher and historian he was. Since my relatives' taste did not run either to reading or historians, I was struck by the fact that the man had a reputation in places like Lubbock, Abilene, and even Weatherford, which had neither a book store nor a library.

Later, to learn that W. C. Holden was more than a name came as a great surprise. You have to remember that in those days of the 1930's, most small town people had never seen a live author, except for some elderly citizen who insisted on inscribing his memories of Indian fights, play parties, and the first post office and gravestone in the county. We repeat with considerable relish a story of Fred Cotten, that remarkable Weatherford merchant-philosopher. When in his latter days Gustavus Adolphus Holland wrote his reminiscences about Parker County, Cotten took the book out to his farm on Willow Creek and gave it to an old Negro man, Matt, who had long lived there.

"I think you'd like to look this over," said Cotten. "Old Man Holland lived through about the same period you did, and you are bound to run into a number of people and events that you haven't thought of in a long time."

Several weeks later Cotten returned to the farm and asked Matt how he had enjoyed Holland's memoir.

"Well, I don't exactly know," Matt replied. "But it somehow seems to me that when a black man gets old like me, he just looks for a shade tree to keep the sun off and thinks about his next meal. But why is it that when a white man gets old, he always has to write a book!"

W. C. Holden was not old when he wrote the history of the Spur Ranch. In fact, when man finally coincided with reputation, I was surprised to find how young he was and how young he had been when he wrote the history. Even now, when I see the volume of work that Curry Holden still turns out, I find it nearly impossible to believe that his history of the Spur Ranch appeared more than a third of a century ago. The man made a vital entity out of the Southwest Collection of Texas Technological College, he taught for years, he has written other histories, and he has done notable fiction, especially in delineating the lives of the Indians of northern Mexico. A third of a century after the appearance of *The Spur Ranch,* he is still all over the place, and he and his lovely blonde wife are seemingly into everything— from fine arts to equally fine preservation.

I suppose a Presbyterian case of foreordination could be made for Holden's writing the history of *The Spur Ranch,* for his earliest recollections are associated with it. Prior to 1909, when the Stamford and Northwest Railroad built into the Spur country, that ranch and its neighbors hauled supplies in freight wagons from Colorado City. Young Holden, living on the northwest outskirts of that Mitchell County metropolis, watched freight outfits, usually with several trail wagons and with three to a dozen more teams of horses or mules, as they either passed by or camped on the edge of town near his house. The outfits were too large to be accommodated by the local wagonyard. Young Holden's uncles ran such outfits, and occasionally his father made a freighting trip. In the evenings and on Sundays in the front yard after lunch, the big men around the boy Curry talked about names like Spur Ranch, Jumbo Ranch, the Llano, the Square and Compass, and the Iowa. These names were as real to him as the Beatles and Elvis and Vince Lombardi are to a young lad in this seventh decade of the twentieth century.

When Holden came to four-year-old Texas Tech in 1929, he found a library that, in his words, "could have been hauled in a pick-up truck (with sideboards on it)." But there was quality, if not quantity, in that small collection. Among the rare items were the ranch office records of Espuela Land and Cattle Company, Limited, of London. These had been placed in the library by Clifford B. Jones, then chairman of the board of directors of Texas Technological College and manager of S. M. Swenson and Associates, who had acquired the Spur Ranch in 1907. This is the same Jones who later gathered various college degrees and became Dr. Jones, president of Texas Tech. He had the instincts of a historian, as well as of a developer and eventual banker.

The collection was unusually complete. The ranch office had been administered as a branch of the London office, and a copy of every letter and report sent to London had been preserved. In all, the total ran to fifteen volumes, each containing about five hundred pages. In addition Holden found ledgers, journals, brand books, tally books, wage books, and store records.

With his background along the freight trail to Spur, Holden became intrigued with the Spur Ranch papers. Over the next several years he published several articles based on the records, and then, in 1934, he put together a twelve-chapter in-depth study, entitled *The Spur Ranch*. The book was well reviewed: it filled a gap in the history of ranch management which had only begun to be looked at then, and was quickly accepted as authentic and necessary to an understanding of the ranching heritage of the Great Plains and of the West. I have seen hardly a scholarly work on the West which did not cite it. As the book became scarce, its price rose beyond the resources of most historians, if indeed it could be obtained at all.

But Holden didn't stop there, insofar as Spur is concerned. He continued to gather material, particularly on the history of the Spur country antedating the organization of the Espuela Land and Cattle Company. In the volume presented herewith he has combined this new material with revised versions of previous articles and chapters about the Spur Ranch. This is not a new printing, but a new edition, as complete as a fine craftsman knows how to make it. Also, Holden has added a brief summary of what happened to the Spur Ranch after it was acquired by S. M. Swenson and Associates. Sometime, when another scholar wants to write a good history of land development, he will find here abundant materials on the break-up of one ranch into farms, small ranches, and towns.

Writing history always involves a certain amount of luck, and as they say in sports and politics (which may be a redundancy of nouns), "I'd rather be lucky than good." After all, the most fascinating subject in the world cannot be tackled if the material has been burned or otherwise lost. Luck came Holden's way, which is not to say that he is not good. In 1966 a former student of his, Willis H. Bledsoe, now a colonel of the United States Air Force, came by Lubbock en route from Viet Nam to an assignment in London. He asked his old professor what he could do for him in London. Where I might have suggested the purchase of books or tweed, Holden asked him to go to Suffolk

House, Laurence Pountney Hill, London, and see whether he could pick up a trace of the London office records of the Espuela Land and Cattle Company, Limited. Colonel Bledsoe found the place but not the records. The present tenants knew vaguely that the company had been dissolved about 1911 and the records sent to "somewhere in the country." Colonel Bledsoe continued his search, making excursions and trying to locate someone directly connected with the company. Without knowing it, he became a historian hot on the spoor of historical details.

So far the Colonel has not found anyone connected with the company, but he has learned that certain aspects of the corporation's activities had to be registered periodically with the Public Records Office. Here he found 317 pages of interesting data regarding Espuela. Among the material are included the "Memorandum of Association" (twenty-six printed pages), "Articles of Association," and lists of stockholders with names, addresses, occupations, and numbers of shares held, both preferred and ordinary. Holden's inspection of these lists changed his previous conception of the ownership of the company. Where he had thought it had a few large shareholders, he found instead that it was owned by hundreds of small investors, including the traditional teachers, clerks, ministers, and even pub owners. Many of these stockholders held fewer than ten shares. The material according to Holden, contains little of value to the operational aspect of the Ranch, as he has treated it here. But it could become the basis for a study of the corporate aspects of foreign-owned ranches.

So we have not yet heard the last of the Espuela, or Spur, story. Holden has brought us a more nearly definitive second or new edition. But through his continuing interest he has also pointed the way for future scholars who wish to treat other aspects of the ranching story, either as independent studies or as part of larger studies on settling an empty country. Prospects for urban history and for business and economic history are considerable.

The Texas State Historical Association is proud to publish and to endorse this renewed study of the Espuela Land and Cattle Company, and it is pleased that Holden did not close the door on his youthful interests the first time he wrote the Spur history.

JOE B. FRANTZ

xiv

PREFACE

IN 1934 THE AUTHOR published a thin volume entitled *The Spur Ranch* (Christopher Publishing House, Boston). It contained twelve chapters. These have been revised and augmented in this study. The other chapters contained herein are new and based on materials not available for the first treatment.

The principal source for this manuscript has been the records of the Espuela Land and Cattle Company, Limited, of London. The Ranch was operated as a corporate business with the main office located at Lawrence Pountney Hill, London, and a branch office on the Ranch. Copies of all letters and reports were kept at the Ranch office. These were bound into books for reference and preservation. Especially important are the twelve letter books containing approximately 500 papers each. In addition, there are payrolls, day books, journals, ledgers, supply books, tally books, diaries, and weather records. This valuable assemblage of primary materials is now in the Southwest Collection, Texas Technological College, courtesy of Dr. Clifford B. Jones, the last resident manager of the Spur properties. In addition to the Ranch records, government publications, military records, contemporary newspapers, personal correspondence, and interviews with old hands who were with the Ranch from the beginning have been utilized. The last of the hands, W. R. Stafford, died in 1965.

In 1939, one of the old hands, W. J. Elliott published a book of memoirs entitled *The Spurs*. It contains interesting episodes and anecdotes. Strangely, he omitted all reference to two of the managers, who together spanned thirty-two years of supervision of the Spur properties. Aside from this omission, Mr. Elliott's book is valuable and entertaining.

The present treatment is primarily an analytical study concerned with the Spur Ranch while owned and operated by the Espuela Land and Cattle Company of Fort Worth and the Espuela Land and Cattle Company, Limited, of London. However, the first five chapters are devoted to the background of the Spur Country before either company was organized. The Epilogue is a brief summary of what happened to the Ranch after the English company sold it in 1907. The history of the Ranch after it was acquired by the Spur Syndicate constitutes a study in itself.

WILLIAM CURRY HOLDEN

CHAPTERS

ILLUSTRATIONS

Following page 138.

MAPS

THE ESPUELA
LAND AND CATTLE COMPANY

A Study of a Foreign-Owned

Ranch in Texas

I: *THE LAND*

THE LANDHOLDINGS of the Espuela Land and Cattle Company lay just below the eastern edge of the Southern High Plains in Texas. More than a half million acres were enclosed within the fences of the company's pastures. The Ranch was known as the Spurs, or as the Spur Ranch. Few people knew at the time, or since, the legal name of the corporation which owned the properties. Those with some knowledge of Spanish were aware that Espuela meant Spur in English. However, it was customary to call a ranch by its brand, rather than by its legal name, and the brand was a stylized spur.

The question arises as to why the Espuela Land and Cattle Company located adjacent to, and east of, the escarpment of the High Plains, locally known as the Caprock. A half dozen other large ranching concerns did the same. To the north was the Matador Land and Cattle Company which branded an open V.[1] To the south were the Saint Louis Land and Cattle Company, known as the 3H's Ranch, the Llano Cattle Company, called the Curry Comb, the Nave, McCord Cattle Company, known as the Square and Compass, and the C. C. Slaughter Land and Cattle Company, known as the Long S.[2] At the time, the late 70's and early 80's, there was much vacant land between these ranches and the settlements to the east. On the level plains above tens of millions of acres of lush grass waved in the wind unused and unclaimed. What then motivated these companies to locate in the broken country east of the fertile plains, below the Caprock? There were two reasons: protection from blizzards and water. By far the more important was WATER.

Numerous springs flowed or oozed from the base of the Caprock providing dependable sources of fresh water for the draws and creeks in the rolling terrain to the east.[3] The source of these springs was the Ogallala formation of the High Plains.

The origin of the Ogallala structure constitutes a chapter in the geological history of the region. A long time ago in the

[1]W. M. Pearce, *The Matador Land and Cattle Company* (Norman, 1964), 7.
[2]W. C. Holden, *Rollie Burns* (Dallas, 1932), 74.
[3]See end sheets.

Cretaceous Age, sixty million years as geologists record time, this land, including the High Plains and Rocky Mountain areas, was a vast expanse of swampy plains of low elevation, inhabited by dinosaurs. For more than a hundred million years the earth's crust had been cooling, and powerful tensions had been built up by the shrinking process. Lateral pressures became so great the crust buckled, and the Rocky Mountains were thrust up. Instability lasted throughout the Cretaceous Age. Mountain ranges were pushed up here while others disappeared there. The last great upthrust was in Pliocene times, some ten million years ago. Since this last uplift, earth's crust has been fairly stable, and the changing terrain has been fashioned by erosion. The Rocky Mountains at the beginning of the Pliocene towered to enormous heights, perhaps as much as five miles or more. Moisture laden winds from the Gulf of Mexico travelled across lowlands until they reached the stark, jagged mountains where they rose to pass over the summits. As they ascended the air expanded, causing it to cool; with the cooling came condensation, snow and rain. So great was the column of air involved, the annual precipitation may have approached 800 inches, an amount which today still falls on the eastern slopes of the Andes. Great rivers flowed towards the southeast. The eroding power of water in high steep elevations was beyond comprehension, and streams carried away countless billions of tons of silt. When the waters reached the foot of the mountains and flowed across the lowlands towards the sea their currents slowed and they deposited much of their silt burdens on the flood plains along the way. When they built up beds and flood plains in one area, the rivers swung their channels to adjacent lower tracts and continued the building process. Always the beds of the rivers were sand and gravel and the material spread on the flood plains was silty clay. When a river shifted, the sands of the former channel, sometimes hundreds of feet thick, became a flood plain, with various strata of silt superimposed above the old beds. These buried sand and gravel deposits became the ground water containers, or aquifers, of the Ogallala Formation.[4]

As the mountains wore down the thickness of the moisture-laden air column decreased, and the amount of rainfall diminished; rivers became smaller and fewer, and the build-up of silt

[4]L. L. Graves, *et al.*, *History of Lubbock* (Lubbock, 1962), Chapter I.

deposits ceased, but not until the thick alluvial deposits extended for hundreds of miles to the east, far beyond the edge of the High Plains today. Some hundreds of thousands of years ago the area which later became the Spur Ranch was on the High Plains. The Caprock was some distance to the east.

When the mountains were wearing down to their present height, only a few streams of small flow carried away excess run-off. Then a young river, the Pecos, like a pirate, crept up from the Rio Grande, parallel to the mountains and along their eastern base. Cutting a deep channel and pushing northward it beheaded and stole the waters of all eastern flowing rivers south of the Arkansas, except the Canadian. The Pecos Valley widened and deepened, leaving the vast alluvial deposits to the east as a mesa-like tableland. The bed of the Pecos now flowed several hundred feet below the Ogallala water bearing sands. The Canadian River had managed to maintain its course across what is now the Panhandle of Texas. Its bottom also lies below the Ogallala sands. The water bearing sands of the Southern High Plains are therefore cut off completely from recharge from the mountains. The water contained in them is fossil water captured thousands of years ago. The only recharge today is from the surface. The amount is negligible, about one-twentieth of an inch a year.[5]

A caprock of caliche, a calcareous substance, formed near the top of the vast apron which became the High Plains. This formation, so appropriately named "the Caprock," along the edges withstands weathering better than the silts beneath. As erosion has cut away on the east and west sides, escarpments ranging from 500 to 1,000 feet have been fashioned. Even with the protection afforded by the Caprock the escarpments are still slowly weathering away at a fraction of an inch a year.[6] The land of the historic Spur Ranch has felt the retreat of the eastern escarpment across its bosom.

The water bearing sands of the Ogallala formation vary in thickness from a few feet around the edges of the plains to as much as 500 feet towards the center. The water carrying capacity of the sands is in direct proportion to their thickness. The total potential of the Ogallala aquifer is estimated by the Texas Board

[5]*Ibid.*

[6]Texas Board of Water Engineers, *Bulletin,* 6105, Clifford B. Jones Papers (Southwest Collection, Lubbock, Texas).

of Water Engineers at about 200,000,000 acre feet. When the ranches were being located below the eastern Caprock in the 1870's and 80's the aquifer was full, and this vast elevated reservoir was the source of the springs which fed the draws and creeks to the east. Since the formations of the High Plains tilted downward towards the east, one may ask why all the water did not drain off along the edge of the eastern escarpment. The Caprock has had the unique ability to seal off the lateral exposures of the Ogallala sands. Only in places where fissures have been created by one means or another have outlets been activated. Some have been rather large, as at Roaring Springs in Motley County, Buffalo Spring in Lubbock County, Gholsom Springs in Crosby County, and Big Spring in Howard County. Tens of thousands of smaller springs contributed their trickles, sufficient in the aggregate to make the rolling country along the base of the Caprock a ranchman's haven. On the High Plains to the west, the playa lakes were dry most of the year. To the east a hundred miles or more, water was found only in the larger streams. These, often brackish, were far apart. Before the days of windmills and artificial surface tanks, cattlemen with a choice, gravitated to where the water was—the broken country just east of the High Plains.

The white man found four systems of rocks, exposed on the surface of the Spur Ranch; the Quaternary, Cretaceous, Triassic, and Permian. The Quaternary is represented by scattered remnants of Pleistocene volcanic ash, and some gravel terraces along the drainages. Scattered deposits of ash attain a thickness of 30 feet, but are usually much thinner. Probable source of the ash is from volcanos in New Mexico which are known to have erupted during Quaternary times. The ash beds are spotted over the Ranch and lie flat with a slight dip to the southeast.[7]

The Cretaceous is of small importance. In limited areas it forms a cap to the underlying Triassic. Its thickness is not great.

The Triassic outcrops on the northwest portion of the Spur range. Locally known as the Dockum Beds, it consists of basal conglomerate, maroon shales, and micaceous sandstone. The basal conglomerate, or gravel, locally attains a thickness of a hundred

[7]L. E. English, "Geological Report on the Spur-Dickens Area." Clifford B. Jones Papers (Southwest Collection, Lubbock, Texas).

feet. The formation bears soft water, and dips to the east about fifteen feet to the mile.

While examining the Dockum Beds on the northwest portion of the Spur range in 1919, Dr. E. C. Case of the University of Michigan collected the nearly perfect clavicles and interclavicles of a large form of Labyrinthodonts, a dinosaur of the Triassic Age. Only two other specimens of the genus had been found in the United States at the time, one at Tanner's Crossing on Little Colorado River, Arizona, and the other at Holbrook, Arizona. Dr. Case referred the Spur specimen to the genus *Metoposaurus* and named the new species *M. jonesi* in honor of Clifford B. Jones, at that time manager of the Spur properties.[8]

The Permian, which underlies the Triassic, consists of brick red shales, sandy clays, gyppy sands, sandstone, and mudstones. Several pure gypsum beds, ranging in thickness from two to fourteen feet and evenly stratified, occur at 2,200 feet elevation and lower. The J2 Creek on the east side of the Spur range has cut down through the uppermost beds. The Permian, covered by a topsoil of Recent age outcrops over the central and southern portions of the range. Its total thickness is about 4,500 feet, and is divided into four formations, Double Mountain, Clear Fork, Wichita-Albany, and Cisco.

The Permian formation as a whole is an interesting phenomenon in the geology of northwest Texas. It underlies the Triassic of the High Plains. Its upper extent is a syncline, forming an elliptical basin with an axis from north to south from the buried Amarillo Mountains on the north to the Pecos River on the south. The eastern rim outcrops on the east side of the Spur range at 2,000 feet above sea level. The western rim of the same elevation is located about twenty-five miles west of the Texas-New Mexico line. This rim is covered with 2,000 feet of Triassic and more recent depositions. The center of the basin dips more than 1,000 feet, with the overburden ranging from 2,000 to 2,500 feet. On the Spur range the dip of the Permian stratification to the west is 500 feet from the east side of the property to the west side. However, the general surface drainage is towards the east and southeast, with a ten foot dip to the mile.[9]

The Permian when exposed at the surfaces makes a rich soil for grasses and field crops when suitably level and with sufficient precipitation. The formation contains little subsoil water, which when found is usually gypsiferous. Local people call it gyppy.

The Permian Basin contains many of the oil fields of West Texas, but none have been found in the Spur vicinity. A number of deep wells have been dug on the Spur property, but only salt water has been found, and not very much of that. The wells were carefully logged, and geologists were able to formulate a rather clear picture of the substructure of the area.

The Permian formation, overlaid by a thin layer of Recent materials constitutes the surface of approximately 60 per cent of the West Pasture of the Spur Ranch and 85 per cent of the East Pasture.

II: *FLORA AND FAUNA*

OF THE GRASSES in the Spur Ranch region, it is thought by botanists that blue and hairy grama were a few centuries ago the dominant types,[1] with buffalo grass of secondary importance. Bison later so overgrazed the area that by the time the white man arrived buffalo grass was dominant and the gramas were secondary. Also present on the Spur range was curly mesquite, a grass with culms, or delicate jointed stems resembling Bermuda grass. Of tertiary rank were two varieties of the three-awns, *Aristida purpurascens* Poir. and *Aristida purpurea* Nutt. These were grasses with slender bristles, collectively known as beards, as found on barley, oats or some varieties of wheat. Side-oats grama, *Bouteloua curtipendula* Torr., was occasionally found. In sand dune areas, sandbur, *Cenchrus pauciflorus* Benth., furnished good grazing when eaten before the burs matured. Hall's bluestem, *Andropogon halli* Hach., was scattered in places over the range. Some forty-two other kinds of grasses have been observed and described in the Spur Ranch area, but all of negligible importance. Chemical experiments by Texas Agricultural Experiment Station at Spur indicated that all the grasses in this part of the state were higher in mineral content and nutriment than the same varieties in lower elevations to the east and southeast.[2]

Varieties of trees and shrubs on the Spur range were small in number. Most widely distributed of the trees was the mesquite, a member of the Legume Family. Of four varieties in the Southwest the Velvet Mesquite, *Prosopis juliflori* var. *velutina* Sarg., was most common in the area. A tough, hardy, thorny tree with crooked, drooping branches, it grew to heights of twenty-five to thirty feet. Its trunk divided into branches a short distance above the ground, and its root system spread radially and deep. It produced a fruit in the form of legumes, or beans, in loose clusters, four to nine inches long, sweet and rich in nutrient values.[3] The seeds were important as food for birds, animals, and

[1]B. C. Tharp, *Texas Range Grasses* (Austin, 1952), 60.
[2]Texas A. and M. College, *Bulletin* (1937), 669.
[3]Robert A. Vines, *Trees, Shrubs, and Woody Vines of the Southwest* (Austin, 1960), 516.

the Southwestern Indian. Early white men prized the beans as
food for livestock, and the scattered trees as shade for cattle,
horses, and sheep. The animals, for which the mesquite was first
considered a boon, later widely scattered the seed and caused
the tree to become a pest. Many of the seeds eaten were excreted
undigested and intact. The trip through the digestive organs of
the animal caused such seeds to begin germination. The drop-
pings afforded a fertilized, protective mass in which the seeds
could take root. This process hastened the spread of the plants.
What had been park-like, grassy sylvan expanses, became scrubby,
thorny thickets, taking over the grassland. Mesquite, originally
considered beneficial by cattlemen, has become a noxious plant
of vast extent.

Next most important tree on the Spur range was the Great
Plains cottonwood, a member of the Willow Family. It grew
along the beds of the creeks and draws. It sometimes attained a
height of seventy or eighty feet and a diameter of four to five
feet. However, the size was dependent on the amount of moisture
available for its root system, which was shallow. On the Spur
range it seldom grew higher than fifty feet with a diameter up
to two feet.[4] It was useful to the Indian as shade and fire wood,
and to the white man for the same purposes as well as for building material for fences, corrals, and dugouts.

Occasional clumps of common hackberry, a member of the
Elm Family, occurred on the sandy portions of the Spur range.
Specimens did not grow nearly as large in this locality as in
other regions, seldom attaining heights of more than twenty feet
and diameters of more than eight inches. The berries when ripe
were a dark purple, from one-fourth to one-half inches in diameter.[5] They contained a considerable amount of sugar, and were
eagerly sought by birds and rodents. Indians pounded the fruit
into their pemmican and pioneer white women made it into a
tart jelly.

Wild plums, which belong to the Rose Family occurred in
thickets at intervals along creeks, especially those of constant flow.
The fruit, when ripe, was from a half-inch to one inch in diameter, red in color, and slightly sweet with considerable acid.[6] It
made excellent preserves with a wild, tart taste when cooked

[4]*Ibid.,* 89.
[5]*Ibid.,* 205.
[6]*Ibid.,* 400.

with sufficient sugar. The fruit was highly prized by frontier women before orchards were introduced. It was quite common for families to travel considerable distances in covered wagons and camp out for two or three days to gather wild plums.

Occasional patches of catclaw, *Acacia greggii,* a member of the Legume Family, were found on the border of the grassy expanses of the Spur range. A small, spindling, resilient shrub with thorns resembling a cat's paw, it seldom grew over three to four feet high. It had an affinity for rich land. Catclaw land came to be highly prized by pioneer farmers.

Widely scattered agarita bushes, scientifically known as *Mahonia trifoliata,* a member of the Barberry Family, were found on rocky areas of the Spur range.[7] Their sharp spiny leaves made difficult the gathering of their fruit, small red berries about the size of buckshot. Early housewives endured much torture while picking them to make a jelly with a rare and distinctive flavor.

Most plentiful of the shrubs on the Spur Ranch were the shin oaks, *Quercus havardii* Rydb., belonging to the Beech Family.[8] Low bushes, hardly over three feet high they formed thickets by extension of their roots in areas of pure sand. A strip of sand, about three miles wide and fifteen miles long, extended from northwest to southeast about midway of the ranch. It paralleled Catfish Creek on the east side, and was known locally as "shinnery." Early surveyors considered the land worthless, omitting it from the large railroad blocks on either side. So the "shinnery" strip remained as part of the public domain long after the tight land on either side was privately owned. Cattlemen, however, soon changed their opinion about "shinnery." They found that in periods of drouth, when no grass grew on the tighter lands, cattle could manage to exist on vegetation growing on "shinnery."[9]

Wild life was abundant on the Spur domain. When the cattlemen arrived bison were still plentiful although commercial hunters were fast decimating the herds. The last shaggy beast in the region was killed a few miles west of the present town of Dickens in 1884.[10] Antelope, not molested by buffalo hunters except for meat, were numerous. Black-tailed deer were present, but not in large numbers. An occasional small cinnamon bear

[7] *Ibid.,* 273.
[8] *Ibid.,* 167.
[9] *Ibid.,* 167.
[10] W. J. Elliott, *The Spurs* (Spur, Texas, 1939), 4.

was seen as late as the middle 1880's. A couple were roped on the Matador Ranch. The skins were tanned and afterwards exhibited at a cattlemen's show in Fort Worth. They are now in the H. H. Campbell Collection of the Museum at Texas Technological College.

Coyotes and lobo wolves abounded in such numbers as to be destructive to cattle and sheep.[11] A shy, harmless little animal seldom seen was the swift. About the size of a Maltese cat, it belonged to the Fox Family. It developed speed for its defense, and could outrun a horse. Skunks, several varieties, were occasionally encountered. Ground squirrels, *Citellus spilosoma,* were scarce, but widely distributed. The same was true of the prairie dog, a misnamed member of the Squirrel Family. Later a population explosion caused "the cunning little animals" to spread over the country until they became seriously destructive to range forage. Their economic detriment was comparable to the mesquite brush encroachment of a later date. Beaver, *Castor canadensis,* as late as 1880 were found widely scattered along running streams where cottonwoods grew from the Caprock eastward to the 100th meridian. A lake on Catfish Creek (now White River) about two miles upstream from Silver Falls on Highway 82 was formed by a beaver dam. So well did the little engineers do their job, water poured over the dam for years.[12] This small waterfall was, perhaps, the origin of the nomenclature "Silver Falls." Today the name is associated with a small fall over a concrete dam beside the Highway. Rabbits, both cottontail and jackrabbits, were numerous. However, their proliferation was kept in check by natural predators.[13] Badgers, robust flesh-eaters about the size of a spitz dog, were dispersed over the Spur range in limited numbers. Their principal food was burrowing rodents. They did not molest man nor the grass upon which his animals fed, but in time the killing instincts of cowboys destroyed them. Wildcats, often called bobcats, were in the region. Shy, nocturnal animals, they were seldom seen by men, and only when dogs got one treed. Pack rats, scarcely ever observed, made their existence known by their nests of dried branches in brushy areas. Kangaroo rats confined their habitat to the strip of shinnery on the east side of Catfish Creek.[14]

[11]*Ibid.*
[12]C. B. Jones to W. C. H., February 15, 1967.
[13]W. P. Taylor, *Mammals of Texas* (Austin, 1947), 37.
[14]Holden, *Rollie Burns,* 79.

In the reptilian category, the poisonous rattlesnake was most common, especially in broken, rocky terrain. Other snakes were the bull snake, coachwhip, and a small harmless snake commonly called a chicken snake. Members of the lizard family, commonly called horned toads, of the genus *Phrynosoma,* seemed to converge on places of human habitation. They subsisted on insects, and their affinity for people may have been occasioned by the smells and lights at night emanating from cowboys' camps and dugouts. Equally beneficial in the area were dry-land terrapins.

Turkeys were plentiful along running creeks near the Caprock. Turkey Canyon from which flowed Turkey Creek was so named because of the numerous wild flocks roosting there in the 1870's. Wild ducks left their permanent imprint on the Spur Ranch in names of the streams. Duck Creek traverses the East Pasture from northwest to southeast. In addition there are two different Dry Duck Creeks and one Little Duck Creek. Quail, both blue and bobwhite, were abundant. The same was true of doves. Both quail and doves were relished as food by early comers. Beneficial birds which subsisted on insects were bluejays, scissortails, sparrows, mockingbirds, and in the winter season field larks. An interesting, comical bird in the area was the road runner or chaparral. He depended on his long legs rather than his wings for his safety. He loved nothing better than a chase, and never lost an opportunity to provoke one. Early surveyors reported that road runners pursued the ends of surveyors' chains as they were dragged along by linemen. Among predatory birds occasional eagles and several varieties of hawks and owls abounded. Most detestable of the birds were the buzzards which filled the air above any place carrion was to be found.

Fish abounded in considerable numbers in the streams which had their sources in the Ogallala sands of the High Plains. Catfish Creek derived its name from the abundance of catfish in its channel.[15] This particular variety of fish was best adapted to the climate and mineral content of the waters. The fish acquired extraordinary size in the deeper holes. It was not uncommon in early days to take specimens up to forty pounds. This is no longer true. Lowering of the water table in the Ogallala formation has dried up most of the springs. Catfish Creek now holds only a trickle of water, and the fish are gone.

[15]Jake Raines to W. C. H., interview, June 16, 1933.

III: *HUNTERS AND TRADERS*

THE SPUR REGION was a great buffalo country. The animals had an instinct for congregating where the water was. The entire area immediately east of the Caprock of the Southern High Plains, including what later became the Matador, Spur, Curry Comb, and Square and Compass ranches, carried the greatest buffalo population in Texas. Captain R. G. Carter, Fourth Cavalry, crossing what was later the East Pasture in 1871 wrote: "Our trail was over a rolling prairie thinly covered with mesquite, but thickly covered with [prairie] dog towns, and immense herds of buffalo as far as the eye could see." The next most populated area was, according to buffalo hunter Frank Collinson, the three tributaries of the Concho.[1] On seasonable years, when the playa lakes on the Plains contained rain water, the animals scattered out over the Llano Estacado. When the playa lakes were dry, which was most of the time, the shaggy beasts kept to the Ogallala-fed creeks and draws to the east of the Caprock. They seemed to know where water and grass were always available. Only occasionally did small herds stay on the Plains the year around, and these clustered close to lakes which were fed by springs of the Ogallala sands, such as Tahoka Lake, Cedar Lake, Portales Lake, and Spring Lake. Such lakes were few and far between. The number of buffalo surviving in these proximities was negligible compared to an area of equal size just east of the Caprock. In the fall of 1877 Reynolds and Rath's Trading Post on the Double Mountain Fork of the Brazos, some ten miles east of the Double Mountains, had 1,100,000 hides piled about the place, waiting for freight wagons to transport them to Fort Worth. The greater part of these hides had come from the upper tributaries of the Brazos and Colorado rivers.[2]

Indians had hunted buffalo on the Spur range for thousands of years. Folsom man was in the area closing in on single victims with spears at the waterholes ten thousand or more years ago. The buffalo were larger and more vicious then.

[1]Frank Collinson, *Life in the Saddle* (Norman, 1963), Chapter 6. Also, R. G. Twaites, *Early American Travels* (Cleveland, 1907), XIX, 240.

[2]Collinson, *Life in the Saddle,* Chapter 6.

When the Indians got the horse from the Spaniards after A.D. 1600, their method of hunting changed to the chase and the surround, using the lance and the bow and arrow. The buffalo was a way of life to the Plains tribes, furnishing food, clothes, shelter, and fuel. The Indian never killed wantonly, and his harvest made no dent in the herds, not even as much as did that of predatory animals.

First European hunters in Texas were the Spanish *conquistadores*. Coronado crossed the Southern High Plains in 1541. Chroniclers with him described the animals, and the soldiers ate freely of their meat. Existence of such plentiful food had not been suspected by the Spaniards. Fearful they might starve on the journey, they brought with them a vast herd of sheep to be used as a source of food. When they encountered the buffalo, the Spaniards lost their taste for mutton, and the size of the flock was even greater when they returned to the mountains of New Mexico than when they left.

After permanent occupation of New Mexico in 1598 by Juan de Oñate, Spanish settlements pushed northward through Chihuahua and up the Rio Grande Valley in New Mexico as far as Taos. Settlers had many sheep and horses, but few cattle. They did not feel the need for cattle, as they had heard of the countless numbers of buffalo on the plains east of the mountains. Also they brought with them a knowledge of making *carne seco*, dried meat, or jerked beef. It was not long before they began making journeys to the buffalo plains for the purpose of killing and drying the meat.[3] The Plains Indians did not yet have the horse, and had, as yet, no animosity toward the strangers. In fact, they were for a generation or two quite friendly. There was sufficient meat and room for everyone.

By the end of the 1600's the Plains Indians had the horse, and the mobility afforded by the animal brought forth latent bellicose traits in the Indians' dispositions. Tribe warred with tribe, and they stole from each other. Spanish settlements and Spanish caravans became objects of harassment. Settlers had to modify their methods of making annual meat-curing expeditions to the buffalo country.[4] Hunting parties set forth in strength, with organization, and with means of defense. Through the 1700's and first three-

[3]*Ibid.*
[4]J. E. Haley, *The XIT Ranch of Texas* (Chicago, 1929), Chapter II.

quarters of the 1800's, expeditions to the buffalo country contained from one hundred to two hundred people with many oxcarts from as far away as Chihuahua. The men were called *ciboleros.* Definite routes of travel developed. A few *cibolero* expeditions from northern New Mexico descended the Canadian Valley to the Panhandle Plains, but most of them approached buffalo land by the Portales Valley. Three different routes converged on the Valley. One was from Santa Fe down the Pecos River to where old Fort Sumner was later located; it then turned east to Portales Spring, about eight miles northeast of the present town of Portales. A second route led from Albuquerque through to pass between the Sandia and the Manzana mountains to the Pecos where Santa Rosa is now. From there it followed the Santa Fe route to Portales Spring. A third route used by parties from Chihuahua and the lower New Mexico Rio Grande Valley ran by the big Salt Lake in Texas just south of the Guadalupe Range. Skirting El Capitan, it followed closely the present U.S. Highway 62 to modern Carlsbad, thence up the Pecos to old Fort Sumner, and from there to Portales Spring.[5] This is how Portales Spring got its name. It was the *portal,* or entrance, to the Southern High Plains.

Once on the Plains, the routes dispersed in several directions. One route came east along Portales Draw to the present state line where the valley changes its name to Black Water Draw, thence east to the present Muleshoe, and then northeast to Spring Lake. Here the route divided. One prong went a short distance north to the Running Water Draw. This continued down by present Plainview. Somewhere along the way, Running Water Draw became Blanco Canyon, or White River. Still further down it was called Catfish Creek and joined the Salt Fork of the Brazos. It was along this route that most of the *cibolero* expeditions to the Spur country travelled. The other prong from Spring Lake followed what present-day maps call the North Fork of the Double Mountain River. Spaniards had another name for it, Cañon del Rescate (Canyon of Ransom). It went north of present Littlefield, almost east to present Abernathy, thence south to present Lubbock where it joined Cañon del Casas Amarillas and extended southeast, leaving the Caprock just north of Post. From Lubbock down, it is now called Yellow House Canyon. To

[5]Collinson, *Life in the Saddle,* Chapter 6.

the *ciboleros* it was Cañon del Rescate. Some *cibolero* expeditions came that way. A third route from Portales Spring went southeast by Silver Lake, Cedar Lake, and Sulphur Draw to the head tributaries of the Colorado. An occasional expedition went in that direction.[6]

Ciboleros were still coming to the Spur country as late as 1875. That year Frank Collinson rode into an encampment in Blanco Canyon on the western edge of what later became the Spur East Pasture. There were over two hundred men in the party and also a number of women and children. They had about fifty large, solid wooden wheeled carts pulled by oxen. The train had come from Chihuahua, a distance of about nine hundred miles, by the Salt Lake south of Guadalupe Peak, where a considerable cargo of salt had been obtained for the drying of buffalo tongues. From there the journey was by the Carlsbad, Fort Sumner, Portales Spring route.

Collinson observed how the hunting and drying was done. *Ciboleros* found a buffalo herd, usually fifty to a hundred animals, and got it running. The faster they ran the more they crowded together. A *cibolero* rode beside an animal and stabbed it into the lungs with a lance. When the beast at length stumbled and fell, other *ciboleros* cut its throat with knives. The tongue was cut out and the animal skinned. Fat was taken for the making of tallow. Meat was cut into long, thin strips. Some of the *ciboleros* were experts at this. They could cut a quarter of the animal into a single strip, a hundred yards long, or longer. Collinson was told it was possible to cut the flesh of an entire animal into one strand.[7]

Women did the drying. Quantities of maguey rope had been brought along for drying lines. When the rope was used up, the slender strips were spread on bushes, limbs of trees, and laid out on areas of thick grass. When thoroughly cured the *carne seco* was rolled up and stuffed in maguey sacks, and these placed in the carts. Each cart would hold about as much as the bed of a freight wagon.

The hunting and drying took place in August, September, and October. Collinson was told the party would depart when the carts were filled to capacity and would join with one or

[6]*Ibid.*
[7]*Ibid.*

more other *cibolero* groups for protection on the return trip. One old Mexican said he had been coming to this locality for twenty years, just as his father, grandfather, and perhaps his great-grandfather had done before him.[8]

In the summer of 1876 American commercial buffalo hunters moved into the Spur region. A score or more established camps on land later enclosed with Spur fences. The identity of most of the hunters is not known, but we do have a record of one of the largest outfits. The partners were Jim White (whose real name was Wilson), Frank Collinson, and George Causey. In September, 1876, they located their camp on Duck Creek about where Dockum Creek joins it. This was within a half-mile of the present townsite of Spur. When they left this camp in the spring of 1877, the partners had eleven thousand hides, forty-five thousand pounds of dried meat, and about six thousand tongues.[9] Other hunters had done as well, comparatively. These figures would indicate that the number of buffalo accustomed to range the Spur lands was considerably greater than the cattle later carried on the same range by the Espuela Land and Cattle Company.

During the great buffalo slaughter, mostly in the winter of 1876-1877, the air in the Spur region was filled with foul, sickening odors from more than a hundred thousand putrid, decomposing carcasses of skinned animals. Regardless from which direction the wind blew, it brought a nauseous scent which only a seasoned buffalo hunter, or skinner, could endure. Rollie Burns, a young cowhand from Denison, visited his first buffalo hunter's camp, on Catfish Creek at a location later included in the Spur West Pasture. He afterwards said,

The smell was putrid. I will never forget the aroma. Gas masks had not been invented in those days, but if they had been I would have worn one the whole time I was there. About an acre was covered with hides stretched over the ground drying. Some had the flesh side up, others the hair side up. I noticed they turned the hides every two or three days. When dried they were stacked in piles and tied into huge bales ready to be hauled to Fort Griffin, or Fort Worth. A scaffold of cottonwood and mesquite poles was used for drying tongues, humps, and back strips. We could stand in camp

[8]*Ibid.*
[9]*Ibid.,* 107.

and tell where killings, or "stands" had been made by buzzards. Thousands of them circled lazily high above the carcasses. I am told they were never fatter than during the buffalo slaughter.[10]

Gradually the millions of tons of wasted flesh were devoured by scavengers or rotted. The odors of putridity vanished, and the scenes of the killings were white with bleaching bones. This was the sight which met the eyes of the first cattlemen who began to arrive with their herds in 1878 and 1879. In the immediate years which followed, while waiting for their herds to increase on the free ranges, the cattlemen hauled the buffalo bones to the nearest railroad and sold them for six dollars a ton. This furnished money needed for flour, molasses, clothing, and other simple necessities. In 1883 a traveller observed a rick of bones ten to twelve feet high and a mile long beside a sidetrack in Colorado City. The bones were being shipped to a sugar refinery in Louisiana to be used in the refining process.[11]

Indians and *ciboleros* killed buffalo sparingly for food. American hunters slaughtered wantonly for hides and a negligible amount of meat. A third, though rare, type hunted for a different reason, sport. Grand Duke Alexis, son of the Russian Czar Alexander II, as a guest of President Grant, made a safari to the buffalo plains in Kansas. An English earl by the name of Alesford did the same on the upper tributaries of the Colorado north of present day Big Spring. To the Spur area came Elliott Roosevelt, brother of Theodore. He journeyed from New York to Fort Worth by rail in 1877. With a party of seven and a wagon loaded with supplies and equipment, he proceeded to Fort Griffin. From there on the party followed the Mackenzie Trail westward. It entered what later became the East Pasture of the Spur Ranch at the mouth of Duck Creek, and proceeded diagonally to Camp Supply on Catfish Creek. This was good buffalo country, but the slaughter was in full swing. The group was never out of hearing of the professional hunters' guns. Already the smell of death hovered over the area. Roosevelt made inquiry as to where he could find an unmolested and unpolluted range. He was told he might find it on the plains above the Caprock. He proceeded northward, following one of

[10]Holden, *Rollie Burns*, 56.
[11]W. C. Holden, *Alkali Trails* (Dallas, 1930), 17.

Mackenzie's trails up on the High Plains on the east side of Blanco Canyon to the area east of present-day Floydada. The hunt was not very successful. The guides did not know the country and the party suffered for water. The buffalo, who knew the region better than the guides, were not there. Roosevelt was compelled to go back below the Caprock where there was permanent water and take his chances competing with the professional hunters.[12]

Duck Creek had for a considerable time been a place of rendezvous for the *Comancheros* and Plains Indians. *Comancheros* were traders of Spanish, or part Spanish, derivation from New Mexico. These trail merchants had managed to keep the friendship of the Indians, and travelled across the Llano Estacado by routes known to them, bringing their trade goods in wooden carts similar to those used by the *ciboleros*. At a number of Ogallala-fed springs and streams below the Caprock they met Indian raiding parties returning with plunder from American settlements to the east. Cloth, beads, bread, whiskey, lead, powder, and other articles which appealed to the needs, the vanity, or caprice of the Indians were exchanged for horses, mules, cattle, and sometimes white captives. Trading stations were located at Quitaque Springs, at Roaring Springs, in the Muchaque Valley between Snyder and Gail, at Laguna Sabinas (Cedar Lake) about fifteen miles northwest of present Lamesa, in Cañon del Rescate (now called Yellow House Canyon) at present-day Lubbock, Blanco Canyon, and Duck Creek. Evidence of the Duck Creek station was first discovered by an expedition led by General R. S. Mackenzie in September, 1871. While ascending Duck Creek, Captain R. G. Carter reported, "We discovered this day the trading stations of Mexicans with the Indians, consisting of curiously built caves in the high banks, or bluffs, the earth propped up, or kept in place by a framework of poles, giving these subterranean abodes the appearance of prison [cells]."[13] This was the same type of dug-out latter used by the first cattlemen to settle in the Spur region. Subsequent scouting parties on the High Plains by Mackenzie's troops discovered

[12]Collinson, *Life in the Saddle,* Chapter 8.

[13]Quoted in Ernest Wallace, *Ranald S. Mackenzie on the Texas Frontier* (Lubbock, 1967) , 48.

several well travelled roads made by the *Comancheros'* carts leading across the plains to the Pecos Valley to the west.

Ciboleros sometimes brought along some trade goods either to appease, or profit from, Indians in the event they met some, and *Comancheros* did some hunting and meat drying. As a rule, however, *ciboleros* were hunters and *Comancheros* were traders.

IV: *SOLDIERS*

WITH THE COLLAPSE of state frontier defense in Texas towards the close of the Civil War and the confusion which followed while Federal defense was being reestablished, Comanches and their allies, the Kiowas, ravaged the frontier with vigor and effectiveness. The population of Wise County, for instance, dropped from 3,160 in 1860 to 1,450 in 1870. Governor Throckmorton reported that between May, 1865, and July, 1867, 162 settlers were killed, 24 seriously wounded, and 43 carried into captivity. The War Department sent two cavalry regiments to the Texas western and northwestern frontier, the 6th, under Colonel S. H. Starr, and the 4th under Colonel R. S. Mackenzie. The 6th Cavalry was relatively ineffective. The 4th established an enviable record during the next eight years. It probed, explored, and eventually forced the Comanches and Kiowas to the reservation in Indian Territory; it also broke up organized cattle stealing rings by New Mexicans. Colonel Mackenzie had help from other units, but he was the driving force, and the 4th Cavalry was the backbone of the operation.

The first military scout of record into the Spur region was one by a troop led by a Captain Carrol of the 9th Cavalry in 1870. His troop tangled with a Comanche party on Catfish Creek.[1]

Colonel Mackenzie led three expeditions to the area, in 1871, 1872, and 1874. Supply camps on Duck Creek and on Catfish Creek became the bases for all three excursions. The first was ineffective so far as punishing the Indian raiders was concerned, but was most beneficial in gaining geographic information and learning the tricks of Indian warfare.

In September, 1871, Mackenzie assembled eight troops of the 4th Cavalry, two companies of the 11th Infantry, and twenty Tonkawa scouts at old Camp Cooper five miles north of Fort Griffin. From there the party with 100 pack mules moved rapidly west to the mouth of Duck Creek on the Salt Fork of the Brazos. This was what later became the southeast corner of the East

[1] R. G. Carter, *On the Border with Mackenzie* (New York, 1961), 163.

Pasture of the Spur Ranch. The expedition ascended Duck Creek to a site later called Soldiers Mound, four miles north of the present townsite of Spur. The Colonel suspected that the Kwahadi band of Comanches under Quanah Parker was encamped in Blanco Canyon. The commander naively believed he could surprise and capture the camp. He left the infantry company to guard the supplies at Soldiers Mound. A breastworks was built on top of the mound for better defense. The site also provided a superb vantage point for observation. Mackenzie set forth under cover of darkness toward Catfish Creek to the west. The night was murky and cloudy, and the party veered to the north more than intended. It ended in a box canyon in the extreme northwest corner of what became the East Pasture of the Spur Ranch. Lost, Mackenzie waited until daylight, when the party retired from the canyon, rounded the base of a peninsula of the Caprock and reached Catfish Creek at mid-morning. After a midday breakfast the forty moved up the creek into the mouth of Blanco Canyon. That night it camped in the proximity of Silver Falls. In the latter part of the night, after the moon was down, a band of Comanches rushed through the camp, stampeding the horses and causing havoc among the troopers. Next morning, the loss was ascertained, sixty-six horses missing, including the Colonel's fine, gray pacer. The troop pushed on up the canyon, only to find a freshly deserted village, the occupants having fled across the High Plains. Mackenzie followed doggedly until he got into an early fall snow storm somewhere between present-day Floydada and Plainview. Reluctantly, he gave up the chase and returned to Soldiers Mound. On the way, a small Comanche scouting party was encountered, and the Colonel sustained an arrow wound in one leg. To his utter disgust he had to ride back to Fort Richardson in an ambulance.[2] Besides horses, the expedition had lost one man, Private Gregg, who was killed in a skirmish with Indian scouts and was buried in Blanco Canyon near the present White River Lake.

In the spring Comanches and Kiowas were out in force, bolder than ever. Colonel Mackenzie was ordered to the frontier a second time. While he was gathering horses, supplies and equip-

[2]For further details of this expedition see Wallace, *Mackenzie on the Texas Frontier*, Chapter III.

ment at Fort Richardson, a detachment of the 4th Cavalry stationed at Fort Concho surprised a band, disguised as Indians, stealing cattle in that vicinity. Two of the marauders were killed and one was captured. Others escaped. The captive turned out to be a New Mexican, Polones Ortiz, who confessed he was one of fifteen. He said there was an all season wagon road across the Staked Plains, one on which a traveller was never over fifteen miles from perpetual water. This was news to the Americans. Previously they had considered the Plains impassable except when the playa lakes contained rain water. Ortiz was spared on condition that he turn "states evidence" and guide the army across the route. Mackenzie was directed to investigate Ortiz's story as well as several other large scale cattle and horse thieveries.

Ortiz reported that Chief Mow-way's band of Comanches usually camped in the spring in the Blanco Canyon or in Cañon del Rescate. Mackenzie assumed it would be Blanco and planned a trip. Lt. Colonel W. R. Shafter was to come from the south, skirting the Caprock, with three companies of the 24th Infantry; Major E. A. Latimer with two troops of the 4th Cavalry was to come by another route from Fort Concho in order to close in on Blanco Canyon from the east; and Mackenzie would make a circuitous march, and come down Blanco from the north.

The Colonel followed his route of the previous year with six troops of the 4th Cavalry and four companies of the 11th Infantry to the mouth of Duck Creek. Here he was joined by Major Latimer and his two troops. Shafter was not in sight. Mackenzie was furious, as each day of delay would increase the chances of escape for the supposedly trapped Indians. He ordered Latimer to proceed slowly up the Salt Fork to the mouth of Catfish and then up that stream. With his own force he moved swiftly up Duck Creek to Soldiers Mound where he left his train with an infantry guard. With the cavalry units he pushed up Duck Creek, made a swing to the west across the tableland, entered Blanco Canyon some distance above Mount Blanco, and then descended the Canyon until he met Latimer. Neither had seen an Indian nor any fresh sign.

A new supply camp was made on the west bank of Catfish on a high elevation just north of where Kelley Creek joined

Catfish, about five miles downstream from Silver Falls. The train at Soldiers Mound was ordered to the new camp.

While still waiting for Shafter, Mackenzie sent Latimer to scout the Mucha-que Valley in Borden County. He himself, with four troops of cavalry made a fast scout up Blanco to a point north of present-day Ralls, thence north by present Floydada to Quitaque Springs, and on to Red River. He returned by the present towns of Turkey, Matador, and Roaring Spring to Camp Supply on Catfish—all without any fresh sign of Indians.

In the meanwhile, Ortiz whom Latimer brought along from Fort Concho had been attached to the scouting detail of Lt. Peter M. Boehm, a skillful officer. Ortiz and the scouts discovered a wide and heavily travelled road leading westward across the High Plains. Obviously large herds had been driven over it. Mackenzie quickly made ready to follow it.

He selected three troops of cavalry, numbering 240 enlisted men and eight officers, and with a number of wagons climbed the Caprock on the east side of Blanco Canyon. He followed the level land above to the northwest, past modern McAdoo, to a point south of present Floydada. Turning west he crossed Blanco and continued on to the Rescate (North Fork of the Double Mountain). The trail he found was the same used by the *ciboleros,* and by Coronado's army in 1541, to Portales Spring. From here the cattle had been driven northward onto the New Mexico Plains towards Tucumcari and dispersed in various directions. Ortiz apparently tried to lead Mackenzie to the perpetrators of the theft ring, but in every instance they had fled.

The Colonel led his party to Fort Bascom on the Canadian River, north of Tucumcari, thence back to the head of Tierra Blanca, and down that clear, soft-water stream to the present town of Canyon where it joins with Palo Duro Creek and Spring Creek to form Palo Duro Canyon. When the stream emerges from the Caprock it is called Prairie Dog Town Fork of Red River. From the site of present Canyon, Mackenzie kept on the High Plains to modern Silverton, thence by Ballard Springs (near the present town of Matador), to Roaring Spring, then to Camp Supply on Catfish.

Inasmuch as he had encountered no Indians and arrested no cattle and horse thieves, Mackenzie was disheartened over the results of the entire summer campaign. However, Wallace summarizes the results: "In a period of one month Mackenzie had crossed the Staked Plains not once but twice, by different routes [in dry weather] in an area never before penetrated by the military. His return route had permanent and excellent water, at no point over thirty miles distant. Both routes, he reported, were superior to the Pecos Trail. Both could be traveled by legitimate cattle drovers."[3]

General C. C. Augur, Mackenzie's superior, said, "This fact, that troops can be so moved, and the general knowledge of the country, and the specific knowledge of the routes and *modus operandi* of cattle thieves obtained by Colonel Mackenzie I regard as very important, and well worth the summer's labor."[4]

After a short stay at Camp Supply to rest men and horses, Mackenzie with his full command left on September 21, 1872, for a campaign on the upper Red River. Eight days later he surprised and won a decisive victory over a band of Comanches on McClellan Creek. But that is another story some distance removed from Spur country.[5]

In 1873 Colonel Mackenzie was sent south to deal with Mexican Kickapoos across the border. In the meanwhile Comanches, Kiowas, and Cheyennes took advantage of the absence of the "Bluecoats," to enlarge their marauding activities along the northwest Texas frontier. Their bases of operations were in Rescate, Blanco, and Palo Duro canyons, and in the watered valleys along the eastern edge of the Caprock.

The Campaign of 1874 was triggered by an Indian attack on a newly established buffalo hunters' trading post at Adobe Walls, June 28, 1874. During the summer a number of Plains bands left their reservations in Indian Territory and headed southwest for their old haunts in the canyons and arroyos of the eastern escarpments of the Southern High Plains. The War Department quickly organized a major military campaign calculated to flush all bands from hiding places, destroy their equipment and supplies, and force them back to their reservations.

Colonel Mackenzie was to move north from Fort Concho; Colonel G. P. Buell was to come west from near Fort Sill, in

---

[3]Wallace, *Mackenzie on the Texas Frontier*, 73-74.
[4]*Ibid.*
[5]For fuller details of Mackenzie's campaign of 1872, see *ibid.*, Chapter IV.

Indian Territory; Lt. Colonel John W. Davidson was to start from Fort Sill and move parallel to Buell, but keeping north of Red River; General N. A. Miles was to march south from Fort Dodge in Kansas; and Major Price was to move east from Fort Bascom on the Canadian River in New Mexico. The five columns were to be put in motion from their supply camps on September 18 and converge on Palo Duro Canyon.

Colonel Mackenzie, in command of Buell's, Davidson's and his own columns, established his base at Old Camp Supply on Catfish Creek with an auxiliary base at Soldiers Mound. Rain hampered movements of all three columns. General Miles did not experience similar delays. As he moved south he contacted hostile bands and pushed them farther south towards Palo Duro. Descending the Canadian River and Tierra Blanca Creek, Price did the same, pushing the bands into the path of Mackenzie.

Mackenzie had an indecisive clash at Tule Canyon. Moving on to Palo Duro he surprised the main body of the Comanches, Kiowas, and Cheyennes on the floor of the Canyon, destroying their camps, equipment, supplies, and capturing more than 1,400 horses. Only a few Indians were killed or captured. An estimated 2,000 scattered and escaped. Without shelter, food, or horses, with an unusually cold winter setting in, the Indians had but one choice, to walk back to the reservations in Indian Territory where they would get food and shelter. The horses were driven out of Palo Duro and across to the rim of Tule Canyon. Here Mackenzie's officers and scouts were permitted to select about 400 as remounts, and the remainder were killed in order to prevent their being stampeded and recovered by the Indians.

Mackenzie sent his wagon train back to Camp Supply on Catfish Creek. With the aid of pack mules he and the remainder of the command made a flying scout to the present town of Canyon, then down the Palo Duro, keeping on the tableland on the north side to about present-day Clarendon, thence back to Camp Supply, skirting the east side of the Caprock.

He wanted to be sure no hostiles were lurking in Cañon del Rescate, or at the lakes with permanent water on the South Plains. As soon as men and horses rested, he set out on another scout up Rescate to the forks of the canyon at present-day Lubbock, thence southwest to Rich Lake, then east by Mound Lake, Tahoka, and on to about where Post is now. From there he went northeast to Camp Supply. Still not satisfied, he made another expedition into the same general area. He ascended Blanco Canyon to a point south of present Floydada. Then he turned southwest going just west of present-day Ralls and Slaton to Tahoka Lake. A band of Indians was located about ten miles west of Tahoka Lake. Two braves were killed and nineteen women and 144 horses captured.

Continuing south to present Lamesa he turned west to Cedar Lake. He found no sign there and went back by Lamesa, the Mucha-que Valley in Borden County, modern Fluvanna, and Mackenzie Mountain to the mouth of Duck Creek, arriving there on December 19, 1874. Thus ended the campaign of 1874. Part of the command went east along the old Mackenzie Trail to Fort Griffin and the remainder, south to Fort Concho.

Mackenzie never contacted General Miles or Major Price. Nor did Miles and Price contact each other. However, the overall purpose of the campaign was achieved. An area larger than New England and New York had been cleared of hostiles. The way was open for buffalo hunters who would be quickly followed by ranchmen.

For the next six years small groups of Indians slipped away from the reservation for horse stealing into the country east of the Caprock. They were stealthy and sly, never tangling with whites if they could help it.

In March, 1877, a quasi-military expedition, or rather a group of half-drunk buffalo hunters parading as self-appointed soldiers, crossed the Spur area. Two accounts of the expedition were later written by participants. The John R. Cook account in *The Border and the Buffalo,* published in 1907, is garbled, confusing, and does not conform to the terrain. The Frank Collinson version, given in *Life in the Saddle,* is clear and concise. It identifies the geography of the area treated. At the time, Collinson had a buffalo camp on Duck Creek near the present town of Spur. The fall before, in 1876, an isolated buffalo hunter, Martin Sewell, was killed by a small band of horse-stealing Indians on Deep Creek in Scurry County. Sewell was the only hunter killed on the Southern Plains, but during the winter many camps were raided while hunters were away. Considerable damage was done; supplies, horses, and mules were taken, and equipment was burned. Reports of vandalisms funneled into Reynolds and Rath's store on the Double Mountain Fork of the Brazos. Finally, someone suggested to a group congregated at the store, "Let's go on a scalp hunt, and run down the Red Devils." So it was decided that an expedition was to set out March 15, 1877. Time was allowed for the news to spread to the far corners of the range. Collinson heard of it on Duck Creek and went to the store. It was reported that a band of Indians was thought to be camped in Cañon del Rescate at the mouth of Thompson Canyon. Five wagons loaded with supplies, including a barrel of whiskey and numerous jugs and crates of bottles, and thirty men on horseback—about forty altogether—set off in high "spirit" up the Double Mountain Fork to the mouth of Cañon del Rescate. Climbing out of the canyon on the right they paralleled it to about where East Broadway crosses it in present-day Lubbock. Here the Indian guide, Spotted Jack, said, "Just around the bend we will find the camp."

The wagons halted and the horsemen, amply fortified with courage from the barrel, charged across what is now Mackenzie Park and around the bend. There was the camp where picnic tables are now located, at the confluence of Cañon de Casas Amarillas and Thompson Canyon. The Indians, having sent their women and children on up Casas Amarillas, were waiting. Their first volley killed Spotted Jack, wounded a hunter, and had a remarkably sobering effect on the citizen cavalry, which turned tail and retreated in great haste to the wagons. After reviving their courage from the barrel the horsemen charged again. This time not a soul was in the camp—only a few dead horses. The hunters burned the tepees, held a council, and decided not to follow the retiring band. Not a scalp had been collected and, as far as was ever known, not a single casualty suffered by the Indians. As Collinson put it, "We got licked and well licked." This was the Battle of the Yellow House, March 18, 1877.

The hunters, somewhat more sober now, pulled out of the canyon on the east side and set out across the prairie to Old Camp Supply on Catfish Creek. From here the party proceeded along the Mackenzie Trail by Soldiers Mound, returning to Reynolds and Rath's store. Collinson dropped out at his camp on Duck Creek and got back to the more profitable business of hunting buffalo.

To discourage the Indians' activity Governor Oran M. Roberts sent Captain George W. Arrington and twenty-eight Texas Rangers to patrol the Spur country from September, 1879, to September, 1880. Their base was Camp Roberts on the east bank of Catfish Creek eight miles below Blanco Canyon. This would place it across the creek from Mackenzie's Camp Supply. However, Frank Collinson told Harry Campbell in 1946 that Camp Roberts was directly east of Mount Blanco, or about eight miles north of Camp Supply.

In 1928, Dr. Clifford B. Jones, then manager of the Spur properties, upon the instigation of his father, Charles A. Jones manager of the Spur Ranch from 1907 to 1912, placed upon the fireplace in the lobby of the Spur Inn in the town of Spur a bronze plaque, thirty-two by thirty-two inches, inscribed as follows:

THE MACKENZIE TRAIL

This famous, historic trail crossed the site of this Inn, and was made and used by the Fourth U. S. Cavalry, the Tenth Cavalry, the Eleventh U. S. Infantry under the command of Colonel Ranald Slidell Mackenzie in their Indian campaigns of 1871 to 1875. Soldier's Mound, four miles north of this spot, was one of the important bases of operations. To him and his gallant officers who freed West Texas of predatory bands of Comanches, Cheyennes, Kiowas, Arapahoes and Lipans, this tablet is dedicated. Captain Robert G. Carter, formerly Fourth U. S. Cavalry, is especially worthy of honor because of serious and permanent injuries received in action against Indians on what is now the Spur Ranch, compelling an early retirement from active service.

In 1940 the Spur Inn burned. The plaque was never found when the ashes and debris were cleared. It is surmised that a souvenir hunter stealthily carried it away.[6]

[6]Clifford B. Jones to W. C. H., March 16, 1967.

V: FREE RANGE

WHEN INDIANS AND BUFFALO were removed from West Texas the cattle frontier rolled westward quickly until it reached the eastern Caprock of the High Plains.[1] There it stopped. Frank Collinson gives a reason for this phenomenon. In 1878, two Texas cattlemen, S. R. Coggin and R. K. Wylie, bought two herds of Jingle Bob cattle from John Chisum at old Fort Sumner on the Pecos River in New Mexico. Collinson was put in charge of the lead herd and told to drive it to the best open range he could find. He headed east over the old Cibolero Trail, by Portales Spring, Spring Lake, Running Water Draw to Blanco Canyon. This was the first Anglo-American cattle drive eastward over this trail. Speaking of the Spur country below the Caprock, Collinson reported, "'This virgin range was all open country, and I have never seen its equal. It was the favorite route of the Indians from Indian Territory. Water was good; grass and wood were plentiful. There were deer in every thicket and antelope on every flat. Plums, currants, and grapes, the finest that ever grew, were plentiful."[2] On the High Plains Collinson had crossed a land where grass was even better, but it lacked the one indispensable ingredient for cattle, a premanent source of usable water. Collinson located his herd on the northern edge of what later became the Spur range. His generalization, however, was applicable to a strip some thirty miles wide from the Canadian River to the Colorado River in the vicinity of Big Spring in Howard County.

About the same time Collinson was moving eastward over the Cibolero Trail, three other cattlemen were driving westward over the Mackenzie Trail. John and Charles Hensley, whose brand was the 22, had previously ranched in the well-watered vicinity of Jack County. The area had become too crowded, and the Hensleys needed room for an expanding herd. John had explored to the west and determined that the best country

[1] The basic information of this chapter was taken from the 1880 census returns. See U. S. Tenth Census, 1880 (Returns of Schedule 1, Free Inhabitants, for Crosby, Dickens, Garza, and Kent Counties, Texas; Microfilm, Southwest Collection, Texas Technological College, Lubbock, Texas).
[2] Collinson, *Life in the Saddle*, 121.

was on the upper Salt Fork just beneath the Caprock. Along with the Hensleys was a relative, L. A. Wilson with his herd bearing the Paddle brand. After leaving the upper Trinity drainage in Young County, the Mackenzie Trail followed in a general way the Brazos River. From the Croton Breaks on the east side of the Spur range to the Cross Timbers the Brazos had cut deep into the Red Beds of the Permian formation, with stratified layers of gypsum exposed. As a result, the waters of the Brazos and its intermittent tributaries were brackish, polluted with salt and gypsum. Cattle could drink of them, but did not like the flavor. Neither did man. On this stretch of the Mackenzie Trail, grass and timber were abundant, but the Hensley Brothers and Wilson kept doggedly on until they came to the fresh water springs fed by the Ogallala. They went as far as they could go, up Salt Fork to McDonald Creek. At the head of McDonald Creek and its tributary, Turkey Draw, they staked their range claims right under the Caprock. Here they had grass, wood, water, and shelter from blizzards.

In 1879 the Hensleys trailed another herd from Jack County. With the two drives they brought out several young cowhands, who later became well known citizens of the South Plains. They were Van and Will Sanders, Rollie Burns, Will Hyatt, Charles Hager, R. M. Crutchfield, Hugh McWhorter, and Steve Revener. Revener's name is perpetuated by having a creek named for him in what eventually became the West Pasture of the Spurs. The cattle of the Hensleys and of L. A. Wilson ranged from the Caprock on the north to Double Mountain Fork on the south. Headquarters was a half-dugout at a spring on upper McDonald Creek. It was dug into the bank of the creek to a depth of about four feet. The upper three feet was cottonwood logs. The roof was poles covered with buffalo hides. Some buffalo were still in the region, but hunters were rapidly reducing them.[3]

The Hensleys and Wilson were only the vanguard of scores of other small cattlemen seeking a good free range where they could become big cattlemen. In a few months the Slaughters arrived with their herds from the Palo Pinto country. Four of the five brothers established headquarters just east of the Hensleys along Catfish Creek. The fifth brother, the oldest, Chris-

[3]See Holden, *Rollie Burns*, 78-79.

topher Columbus, known as C. C. or Lum, went south to the upper tributaries of the Colorado River in Howard, Martin, and Dawson counties.

Will B. Slaughter, 25, was the first to arrive with a herd of cattle branded WILL followed by the Long S and a couple of freight wagons loaded in Fort Worth with lumber. He continued up McDonald Creek to Hensley's spring, where he stopped and selected a site for a house about two hundred yards east of Hensley's headquarters dugout. He turned his cattle loose on the east side of McDonald Creek. This creek became the boundary between his range and that of the Hensleys and L. A. Wilson. The house, quickly built, was of boxed and stripped construction. It was small, four rooms in the shape of a T, and was not painted. So far as is known it was the first house made of milled lumber on what later became the Spur Ranch. Apparently, Will's wife, Amia, 21, and son, C. C., named for his uncle, arrived with the cattle and the wagons. At least, they were there when the 1880 census taker came by.

John B. Slaughter, 29, and a couple of cowhands, Brooks G. Davis and John B. Cameron, came with Will B. His brand was JOHN followed by the Long S, and he turned loose his cattle east of Will's range. John and the hands helped Will with the house building, and lived there with him for a time. They were still there when the census of 1880 was taken. John then made a dugout headquarters four miles east of Will's place, on what was then called Scallawag Creek. Later in 1880 John married Isabella May. It was probably her influence which caused the name of Scallawag to be changed to Home Creek. Accounts differ as to how many cattle Will and John brought to Crosby County. Some say 2,000, others 5,000. It could be that together they had about 5,000. This, with increase, was a heavy load for the range the two men had preempted, but the five years they were there were good years, and apparently no difficulty was experienced. John's range extended north to Davidson's Creek, named for Colonel Davidson. It empties into Catfish Creek just above where White River Dam is today.

North of Davidson and west of Catfish Creek was the range of a man named Boot. His brand was a boot. He must have been away when the census taker was there, as he was not included. No one remembers his initials. Farther up the Blanco

Canyon were the Petty brothers, Bill and Ed. They branded COE. Later they sold their cattle and range rights to the Espuela Cattle Company.

On the east side of Catfish below the Petty brothers was Peter E. Slaughter whose brand was P followed by the Long S. He was older than John and Will. His headquarters, a dugout, was on a creek which still bears the name of Pete Creek and emptied into Catfish on the east side just above the present White River Reservoir. Along with Pete's outfit from Palo Pinto County came the youngest of the Slaughter boys, Mace, 17, with a little herd of his own branded MY followed by a Long S. He staked out a claim on Catfish just below John's place where a little creek, still called Slaughter Creek, empties into Catfish. The Slaughters did most of their own work, helping each other. They did bring with them several hands, Brooks G. Davis, John P. Cameron, Green Lemley, John Alley, and a colored man by the name of Mumm.

Below Mace's range, Dan C. Kyle dug his dugout into the side of Catfish at a spring afterwards called Kyle Spring. His brand was KKK. He was related to the Slaughters and drove his little herd west with them. He brought along as cowhands John McWallis and Coleman Harris.

Just south of Dan Kyle were the Dalton brothers, Charles A., George W., Robert S., Will C., and Lee. Their ages varied from 16 to 28. They arrived in the late fall of 1879 from Palo Pinto County with about 4,000 head of cattle. Each one had an individual herd and brand. They brought 1,200 cows belonging to their widowed mother, Lucinda Dalton. The five Daltons had with them as help Aaron C. McDonald, Andrew J. Higgs, Andrew J. Smith, and H. P. (Handy) Cole. Cole later became ranch foreman for the Spurs, and eventually sheriff of Dickens County. He died in office. The Daltons ranged together on lower Catfish Creek to its mouth and west to Salt Fork for twelve to fifteen miles. They had two camps. One was on Chimney Creek. To this dugout Robert brought his bride, Millie Slaughter, sister to the Slaughter brothers. As a wedding present, her father, George Webb Slaughter, had given her fifty-two heifers. These with their own brand were driven along with Roberts' herd. The increase during the next five years was phenomenal. This group from Jack and Palo Pinto counties, the Slaughters, the Daltons, and Dan Kyle, all inter-related, controlled the range from McDonald Creek to Catfish Creek, from the North Fork of Double Mountain on the south to Sand Creek on the north.

On the head of Dockum Creek, a tributary of Duck Creek, W. C. Dockum had started a store in a half dugout early in 1878 to serve buffalo hunters. Before the last hunters left the range, the first cattlemen were arriving. Dockum stayed on to trade with them. He had a small herd of cattle and branded DOX.

North of Dockum Creek, in what later became the Tap Pasture of the Spurs, a man named Overhulse (no one recalls his intials) had a dugout and a small herd. His brand is not of record.

Some four miles east of Dockum's store was the range of A. T. (Bud) Campbell, brother of H. H. Campbell of the Matador Ranch. Bud's dugout was on Cottonwood Creek near where the headquarters of the Spur Ranch were later located.

About two miles east of Campbell, J. H. Parrish had a store and a few horses and cattle on the section of land on which the town of old Dickens, later changed to Espuela, was located.

Above A. T. Campbell on the extreme upper source of Cottonwood Creek were the Wear brothers, George and Fred. Just east of them on the head of Duck Creek, Charles L. Groff had a small herd. He later became a stockholder and range manager of the Espuela Land and Cattle Company.

Five miles southeast of what afterwards became the headquarters of the Spurs was the mesa-like hill known locally as Soldiers Mound.[4] It was a weathered remnant of the High Plains. Several hundred thousand years ago the Caprock retreated westward leaving it as an insolated prominence of the same character as Mackenzie and Cooper mountains to the south. Today the mound commands an excellent view of the county for a dozen miles around. This fact plus its proximity to Duck Creek as a source of fresh water, had caused Colonel Mackenzie to make the mound headquarters for his 1871 Indian campaign. During the buffalo hunts, J. C. Davis had a dugout near the

[4]No one knows when the name, Soldiers Mound, was attached to this mesa. Acccording to Frank Collinson, who was in the vicinity from 1878 to 1883, and to Harry Campbell, the first Anglo-American child born in Motley County, the mesa was called Camp Swann in the early 1880's. Colonel Mackenzie in the early 1870's referred to the place as a supply camp.

mound with a few cattle which he branded JC. He also carried some supplies for sale.

Down Duck Creek four miles, at the mouth of a draw coming in from the west, still known as Spade Draw, was the dugout of two other Hensley brothers, nephews of John and Charles. Their brand was a Spade and their headquarters was in, or near, the present townsite of Spur.

A short distance south, Oliver and Shelton branded 747. Little is known of them. They were not listed in the Census of 1880, nor is there a record of their having sold later to the Espuela Cattle Company. George Gambel with an MT Bar brand was located on Indian Creek. Charley Lanter worked for Gambel. Near the mouth of Duck Creek, W. L. (Bud) Browning ranged with a Flying A brand. He acquired a small ranch north of what became the East Pasture of the Spurs, and later was Lieutenant Governor of Texas.

The Edwards brothers, Cass and George, preempted for a time the range at the mouth of Red Mud. Their brand was the Open Diamond OA. On the upper Red Mud grazed a sizeable herd of cattle belonging successively to J. M. Hall, to another Hall (no kin to J. M.) and Montgomery, and to Stephens and Harris. This herd bore the brand which subsequently became the official brand of the Spur Ranch. It was a Spur on the left hip. A few miles east on Little Red Mud was a herd belonging to Leon Barkley, whose brand is not of record.

On the northeast corner of what became later the East Pasture was the J2 Ranch on the J2 Creek, a tributary to Croton Creek. It was owned by Jessie Jones. Tradition has it that in choosing a brand Jones first thought of JJ. It occurred to him that by custom of the range the brand would be called the Two J. Then he reversed it and came up with the J2. Farther down on Croton Creek was Mike Sullivan, who had two cowhands, John Furgeson and Joseph Saunders. South of Sullivan was John Heslip. He was assisted by John Tramble and Isham Linn. Linn's wife, Ella, cooked for the outfit and their son, Tobias, 10, helped with the cattle. Another neighbor to the east in Dickens County was Richard Power with his wife, nine children, and one hired hand, George King.[5]

---

[5]Powers and his family constituted almost one-half of the population of Dickens County in 1880. The wife's name was Ruetta, 44. The children were William H.,

On the southern periphery of the Spur country in Kent County was the range of Clay Mann whose 80 brand covered much of Kent and Borden counties. The North Fork of the Double Mountain was the boundary of his range, but there were no fences, and his cattle became mixed with those of the Spur country. West of Mann was Don F. Cole. In the same area was German B. Stout with 500 head. Still farther up was Young and Galbreath with the Curry-Comb brand. Ascending Yellow House Canyon were Harry Cooper, W. R. Moore with the LANC brand, Sam Gholson at Gholson Spring, and Henry Beal at the mouth of Plum Creek.

Beal was a literate man. He brought with him a number of books, including some classics. The mail hack from Colorado City to Estacado left magazines and newspapers for him at Dockum's Store. He spent his spare time sitting in his dugout reading by the light of an oil lantern. Every hour or so he would go outside and look at the weather and comment, "Wind out of the southwest, right off of the Sonoran desert, where it hasn't rained in nine years, by g--!"[6]

On the eastern edge of Lubbock County in the Canyon were the Kidwell brothers. Beyond this to the west there was nothing but sheep ranches. No cattleman ventured onto this part of the High Plains prior to 1885.

Between 1879 and 1884, the free range period of the Spur country, thirty cattle outfits, not counting those on the periphery, grazed their animals on lands later enclosed within the Spur pastures.

With the exception of Will B. Slaughter and perhaps one or two others, all the free-rangers used dugouts both for headquarters and line camps. This type of habitation resulted from necessity rather than choice. Building timber was exceedingly scarce. The nearest railpoint where milled lumber could be had was Fort Worth, more than 200 miles away over a trail road without bridges. Cattlemen could only utilize cottonwood timber which grew sparsely along the streams. Trees were too scarce and too crooked for building log cabins. The only recourse was to incorporate the logs into dugout construction.

Rollie Burns helped to build a dugout in what later became the West Pasture of the Spur Ranch:

In December, 1881, the "22's" established a winter camp on the Salt Fork of the Brazos about twelve miles south of the camp on the head of McDonald Creek. Van Sanders was boss, and John Garrison, Will Sanders and myself made up the winter crew. We located the camp on a little bluff on the north side of the river. It was a dugout about the same size as the one on McDonald. It took us several days to make the excavation. We did not build up the walls any with poles, because they were scarce. The roof was about five feet above the floor, and we had to stoop when we walked around. We first thought we did not need a door, but the first cold weather came from the east and caused us to change our minds. We hustled around and made a door out of a dried cow hide. The fireplace was in the back.

We transported our camp equipment from McDonald Camp on our horses, but it was not much of a job. We had two Dutch ovens— one for meat and one for bread—a frying pan, a coffee pot, a butcher knife, three or four sacks of flour and a few pounds each of salt and coffee. Our beds were a number of wolf hides. These were made down on the dirt floor around the walls of the dugout. The hides were from wolves we had killed on the range. They were full of fleas when first killed, but fleas soon leave a dead hide. We brought in some buffalo skulls to sit on. We had no table of any kind. Our lamp was a tin can filled with tallow rendered up from beeves with cotton rags torn in strips and plaited for wicks.[7]

W. J. Elliott, who worked for the Spur Ranch in the 1880's, wrote, "There is no warmer, cozier shelter from blizzards and northers than a dugout. They were the best shelters in which to stand off Indians. They were easily defended, and could not be burned. Cowboys who came with Hensley and Wilson and other early cowmen made their headquarters in them."

Dugouts were usually located near springs. The nearer the Caprock the more numerous were the springs. One cattleman, who had twenty-five sections close in, had twenty-one sizeable springs and hundreds of seeps.[8] Farther from the Caprock where springs were not so plentiful, dugouts were located either on running creeks, or on streams with an underflow. In the latter case, holes scooped out in the creek beds would provide usable water.

[7]Holden, *Rollie Burns*, 79.
[8]Hampton to W. C. H., interview, March 12, 1967.

Cattlemen who moved into the Spur country during the free range era were amazed at finding the shinnery belt which paralleled Catfish Creek on the east filled with wild hogs. They were of all colors, white, black, yellow, spotted, big spots, little spots, and speckled. Lean and lanky, they had long snouts and long legs. A man on a horse could not ride over a mile without jumping a drove of them. They seldom heard the horse coming until he was upon them. Then they scattered in all directions, snorting and grunting, causing the horse to whirl in fright. Many a rider was unseated by a sudden encounter with the hogs.

With a good acorn crop the hogs put on some fat in the fall. At the first cold spell the early settlers went hog-killing in the shinnery. Fresh pork in the form of spare ribs, sausage, and brains afforded a diversion from buffalo meat, antelope, and beef; cured hams and bacon extended the variety of meat until spring.

At first the cattlemen could not account for the presence of the hogs so far in advance of the settled frontier. Later the matter came to light. Two men, by the names of Smith and Andrews, in 1877 drove a herd of hogs from Palo Pinto County to the shinnery between Duck Creek and Catfish Creek. Their idea was to raise hogs on acorns and buffalo meat. When the hogs had fattened a little in the fall they killed a number, cured the meat and hauled it to Fort Griffin without having made previous arrangements. The army post had just received a consignment from the government. Smith and Andrews could not sell, so they gave the meat to whoever would take it. Discouraged they traded all remaining hogs on the range, thousands of them, to Frank Collinson for two yoke of oxen and some old horses. However, Collinson realized little if anything from the trade.[9] He failed to commercialize the industry and left the hogs to increase at random. The early cattlemen considered them wild, and in the same category as buffalo and antelope. After a few years the hogs went the same way as the buffalo and antelope.

In the spring of 1879 cattlemen in the Spur country suffered heavy financial loses from stealthy Indian raids. Young men from the reservations near Fort Sill slipped away to recruit their horse herds. They were careful not to contact whites. Without being seen they rounded up and drove away the horse

[9] H. H. Campbell, *Early History of Motley County* (San Antonio, 1958), 14-15.

herds of the Slaughters and Hensleys, leaving all hands afoot. A day or two later, the cowhands found a wind-broken mare which had probably been abandoned by the raiders. The animal could not move faster than a walk. It was decided to send one hand on the mare to Jacksboro to arrange for more horses. The men cast lots to see who would go. Bill Hyatt was lucky, if riding a slow horse across a hundred and fifty miles of country thought to be infested with Indians could be considered "lucky." He made the trip without incident, and within a month the grounded cowhands were mounted again. The same Indian raiders got forty horses from the Jingle Bob Cattle Company on the north edge of the Spur country. These raids were what caused Governor Roberts of Texas to order Captain Arrington and his Ranger troop to Blanco Canyon. The United States Government later paid the Hensleys and Slaughters for the stolen horses. The Jingle Bob Cattle Company never recovered. The year 1879 was long remembered by cattlemen of the free range era as one of unstable conditions. Though many scares were experienced not a single death from Indians occurred in the northwest Texas frontier.

The free range era of the Spur country was of short duration. By 1884 it was over. The thirty-odd little cattlemen in the area had three choices: to move farther west where free grass could still be had; to acquire title to the land they occupied; or to sell their cattle and such improvements as they had made.

The Slaughters moved west. The Daltons sold to the Espuela Cattle Company and returned to Palo Pinto County where they engaged in stock farming. The Edwards brothers sold out, and Cass later established the T Bar Ranch in Lynn County. Practically all the others sold to the Espuela Cattle Company.[10]

The free range era, 1879-1884, was profitable for those who preempted the watering places and grass of the region. Rain had been plentiful, grass abundant, and cattle increase phenomenal. There were no disease epidemics, no drouths, no bad blizzards, and no die-ups. The price of cattle had more than doubled during the period. With small capital outlay and a minimum of expense, those who took their chances and stuck it out were well paid for their time and effort.

[10]For the locations of the free range cattlemen in the Spur Country, see end sheets.

VI: *GENESIS*

THE SPUR RANCH took its name from the brand. Origin of the brand is obscure. No one knows who was the first to think of it, design it, fashion it in a blacksmith shop, and apply it sizzling hot to the hair and hide of a bovine animal. In all likelihood it had several independent origins. The spur as a mechanical device strapped to the heel of a boot has been associated with horsemanship for several millenia, and horses have been used to manage cattle for centuries. In searching for a symbol to mark animal ownership the shape of an item used constantly in connection with animal husbandry would likely come to mind. The geometric design was easy to fabricate. It is possible that the Spur brand is one of the oldest of brands.

J. A. McFadden, who ranched in Victoria County on the Coastal Plain of Texas, used the Spur brand on trail herds in the early 1870's. Also, it was used in San Saba County in 1872. If all of the official brand books in Texas, which were usually kept by counties, were examined, scores of Spurs would likely be found, each registrant convinced he had originated it.

However, the immediate history of the particular Spur brand which gave the name to the Spur Ranch is known.

In 1877 the Hall brothers, N. J., J. M., and William, were grazing a moderate-sized herd of cattle on government lands near Madison, New Mexico. Their range was on the Dry Cimarron in the extreme northeast part of that state. J. M. Hall, with more foresight than his brothers, realized that the days of the free range were numbered and that the cattle raising of the future would be on fenced ranches. He decided to start a ranch while he could still obtain a site; but where? New Mexico was too dry and South Texas had ticks and fever. The Southern High Plains, just off the Caprock, where there was water and shelter, was a desirable place; it had better grass than New Mexico, and "Texas fever" was not known there. He sold his interest in the New Mexican cattle to his brothers and set out for South Texas, accompanied by one of his old hands, J. R. Beasley.[1]

1Beasley to Clifford B. Jones, July 14, 1930.

In May, 1878, a small herd of cattle, 1,500 one- and two-year-old heifers and about fifty bulls, trailed out of Refugio County headed for Northwest Texas. The cattle had been collected for Hall from two historic herds of the coastal region, the M6 and the T. All the animals had just been branded with a new road brand, IX. The herd was under the direction of Beasley.[2]

Beasley and his trail hands began their drive during the first, long, hot, humid days of a coastal summer.[3] Unusual rainfalls had swollen the streams, and the herd was forced to swim the San Antonio, the Guadalupe, and the Colorado rivers. At Round Rock the herd struck the Dodge (often called Western) Trail, and followed through Mason, Brady, and Belle Plain to Fort Griffin in Shackelford County. After stopping for a day at Fort Griffin, where his cowboys sampled the whiskey, gambling, and attractions of "Hell's Half Hundred Acres," Beasley continued on up the Dodge Trail by Seymour where he crossed the Brazos to Vernon, at which place he turned off the Trail towards the west. Going up the Pease River valley, he passed the RQ ranch, went up Groesbeck Creek to its head, turned west to the mouth of Wind River, and up Wind River to Tepee City, where he made camp and prepared to winter the herd. In December a prairie fire made it necessary to move again. Gathering the herd, he moved west to the head of the Middle Pease next to the Caprock of the plains, where he bought for Hall a claim with a dugout on it from a buffalo hunter. This dugout became the first headquarters of the Spur Ranch. However, at this time no one knew it was to be the Spur Ranch, as its brand had not yet been selected.[4]

The following year, 1879, J. M. Hall purchased approximately 800 heifers from his brothers in New Mexico. These cattle were trailed from the Dry Cimarron eastward across the Panhandle to Hall's range on the head of the Middle Pease. The herd was under the direction of R. J. Hudson as trail boss. The cattle bore the Cross L brand of the Hall brothers; and before

[2]Beasley to Jones, September 10, 1930. Jake Raines to W. C. H., interview, February 23, 1930. J. R. Stafford to W. C. H., interview, September 10, 1930.

[3]John Young, whose biography has been told by J. Frank Dobie in *A Vaquero of the Brush Country*, was with this herd in the capacity of a common hand. Beasley to Jones, September 10, 1930.

[4]Beasley to Jones, July 14, 1930.

starting, Hudson placed on the herd a newly devised road brand, the Spur.[5]

Before the days of land leases and land ownership, ranches were mobile affairs. When the cattle arrived from the Cimarron, Hall moved the consolidated herd to Red Mud Creek in the southern part of Dickens County and adopted the Spur as his permanent brand. The new Spur headquarters was on Red Mud, a short distance southwest of Grape Vine Tank. The next year J. M. Hall purchased the Double Block herd from Hall and Montgomery. In the fall of 1882, Hall sold all his cattle, along with the Spur brand, to Tom P. Stephens and Coleman Harris. A few months later, in the spring of 1883, Stephens and Harris sold the entire outfit to the Espuela Cattle Company.[6]

The Espuela Cattle Company was a corporation composed of A. M. Britton of Denver as President, S. W. Lomax from Missouri as Secretary, Tom P. Stephens of Fort Worth, S. T. Pepper from Missouri, and A. T. (Bud) Campbell of Ellis County. Two years before Britton and Lomax had established the Matador Ranch in Motley County.[7] The flourishing condition of the cattle business enabled them in the spring of 1883 to conclude the sale of the Matador Ranch at a handsome price to a Scotch syndicate. Rumors of enormous profits were causing English and Scotch capitalists to offer fabulous prices for cattle and "range privileges." "Book count and range delivery" became the custom. During 1883 and 1884 the fad was "to buy at once and repent at leisure."

After the Espuela Cattle Company had been organized, a difficulty arose to delay things, however. More grass was needed. The range of Stephens and Harris along Red Mud Creek was confined on one side by the Slaughters and on the other by the younger Hensley brothers, Leon Barkley, and the Edwards brothers. All of these people had prior free range rights. Thirty-odd cattle outfits were occupying the range Britton and Lomax had to obtain if they expected to repeat their Matador promotion.

It happened that lands which Britton and Lomax had in mind had been surveyed in 1873 as railroad lands. The State of Texas

[5]Beasley to Jones, July 24, 1930.

[6]Raines to W. C. H., interview, February 23, 1930.

[7]For an account of the establishment of the Matador Ranch by Britton, Lomax and others, see Pearce, *The Matador Land and Cattle Company* (Norman, 1964), 7-12.

had contracted to give sixteen sections as a bonus for each mile of road built in the state. Britton and Lomax realized that if they were to oust the small cattleman they must get title to the land. They had a distinct advantage over the free range men: the $1,250,000 they had received from the Matador Land and Cattle Company. The ones to be dispossessed had only their relatively small herds as capital.

The Houston and Great Northern Railroad had constructed 215 miles of road within the state by 1874.[8] Under the laws of the State the company was entitled to 3,440 sections of land. By September 15, 1874, certificates totaling 2,344, each for 640 acres of land, had been issued by the State of Texas to the Houston and Great Northern Railroad Company. The company had the option of selecting lands granted by virtue of these certificates from any part of the public domain not reserved for special purposes. The officials of the railroad located lands in the counties of Armstrong, Carson, Childress, Collingsworth, Crosby, Dickens, Donley, Deaf Smith, Garza, Gray, Hall, Hemphill, Kent, Mitchell, Pecos, Presidio, Roberts, Scurry, and Wheeler. Block 1 of the Houston and Great Northern Railroad Company's grant, consisting of 204 sections, lay in Kent and Dickens counties;[9] Block 2, consisting of 55 sections, was located in Kent, Garza, and Crosby counties; Block 7, consisting of 31 sections, was in Kent and Garza counties; and Block 8, consisting of 53 sections, was situated in Garza and Crosby counties. These lands, together with 35 other sections, were contracted for and purchased on September 1, 1883, by the Espuela Cattle Company from the New York and Texas Land Company, Limited (a holding company for railroad lands), for a consideration of $515,440.[10] Inasmuch as the state retained every alternate section in all railroad blocks for school lands, the size of the four blocks was twice what it would have been had they been compact. As the intervening school sections could be leased from the state (until such lands should be opened up to settlers)

[8]The road constructed was in East and South Texas.

[9]In making the surveys the state required the railroad companies to survey one section of school land for every section selected by a company. Block 1 therefore contained 408 sections, the H.&G.N.R.R. Co. getting every odd number section; Block 2 had 111 sections; Block 7, 62 sections; and Block 8, 105 sections.

[10]One-tenth of the amount was paid in cash, and nine notes for $51,544 each, coming due annually beginning September 1, 1884, and bearing 6 percent interest, were made for the remainder of the amount.

at a nominal price, the size of the Spur range as finally fenced aggregated 569,120 acres.[11] The subsequent policy of the state in opening the enclosed school lands to settlers during the 1890's caused great annoyance to the Spur Ranch.[12] In 1884 the company reorganized under the Corporation Laws of Texas, but the personnel of the old company was the same in the new company. On September 23, 1884, the Espuela Cattle Company formally transferred all of its holdings to the Espuela Land and Cattle Company of Fort Worth.[13]

When the Espuela Land and Cattle Company of Fort Worth acquired title in 1884 to the alternating railroad sections of the land, the free range cattlemen had to either move their herds to other ranges or sell their cattle and "range privileges" to the Company. All the Slaughters chose to move, and in so doing they collectively in time acquired more land and cattle than the Espuela Land and Cattle Company ever obtained. John B. went to New Mexico, and later returned to Texas and purchased the Square and Compass Ranch. It is still owned by his descendants. Pete and Will B. moved to Arizona where each acquired sizeable ranches.

Most of the others sold their herds, with their brands, to the Espuela Land and Cattle Company. In all, the Espuela Land and Cattle Company purchased sixty-one herds of cattle with their brands.[14] These were registered with the Texas Cattle Raisers Association. Several small cattlemen sold everything for cash settlement. Some, including Bud Campbell and C. L. Groff, sold for part payment and part stock in the new company. Others sold for part cash and part notes given by the Espuela Land and Cattle Company. Unfortunately, the notes were never paid.

With the land problem partially settled and the pastures stocked with cattle, Colonel Britton hurried off to England to find a purchaser for the ranch. While Britton was away, Lomax, residing at the time in Fort Worth, was busy directing the affairs of the company. The resident manager of the ranch was C. L. Groff from Lancaster, Pennsylvania. They had plenty

[11]This included 20 sections of public domain. The company owned in 1884 only 242,560 acres.
[12]See Chapter XIV below.
[13]Deed Records, Crosby County, IV, 9.
[14]For a list of brands purchased see Appendix II.

to do. The pastures had to be fenced, tanks constructed, corrals built, and houses and barns provided. Aside from these activities, there was the routine work with the cattle.[15]

Meanwhile, Britton was in England looking for parties with money anxious to invest in American cattle ranches. He found Scots and Englishmen keenly interested in the land of cattle and profits. Soon he discovered several who were willing to exchange good British sterling for Texas land, and cows, and experience. These gentlemen organized the Espuela Land and Cattle Company, Limited, of London. The company was made up of Edward Bishop, Sir Robert Burnett, Alexander Staveley Hill, Sir Charles Edward Lewis, Baronet, M.P., James Badenoch Nicolson, all of the County of Surrey; Alexander McNab, and Alexander McNab, Jr., of Clackmannonshire, Scotland; James McNab, and George James Walker, of the County of Surrey. The first President of the new corporation was Sir Charles E. Lewis and the first Secretary was J. Earle Hodges, London.[16] The company received its charter under the laws of the United Kingdom of Great Britain and Northern Ireland on December 11, 1884, and the purchase of the Spur Ranch, both land and cattle, from the Espuela Land and Cattle Company of Fort Worth was formally effected on April 9, 1885.

The contracts which Britton and Lomax had made in 1883 and 1884, with the free range cattlemen whose cattle they purchased called for "book count." That meant the cattle were accepted on a basis of the estimated number of head the seller had. No actual count was taken. The contract which the Espuela Land and Cattle Company of London executed with the Espuela Land and Cattle Company of Fort Worth provided that land should be paid for at so much per acre after a warranty deed had been made and passed on by the London Company's at-

---

[15]The branding outfit on the home range of the Spurs in 1884 consisted of Joe Stokes, boss, H. P. Cole, John O. Wilkerson, Henry Mitchell, Dave and Ab Carter.

The crew with the wagon which looked after the Spur interests on the Matador and Ross ranges was composed of N. R. Pierce, boss (nephew of Shanghai Pierce of South Texas), W. R. Stafford, Lon Bean, Hugh Conwell, and Warren McFarland.

Another crew with a wagon which looked after the Spur interests south and west of the Spur range was composed of Van Leonard, boss, Jake Raines, Ruben Owens, Joe Grammar, and "Jap" Brooks.

The company employed two trail outfits in 1884, managed by B. G. Davis and "Pink" Hayes, who used transient cowboys.

[16]Jones to W. C. H., interview, October 19, 1929.

torneys, and that payment for the cattle and horses would be on
actual count. The livestock would be received by one of the
Directors of the London Company who would make a trip
to Texas for that purpose.

In the summer of 1885, George Walker, representing the
London Company, accompanied by his secretary, a Mr. Angus,
arrived at the headquarters of the ranch to receive title to the
land and to count the cattle. Walker was sent because he was
a recognized breeder of cattle in Scotland. He knew nothing of
the customs pertaining to cattle transactions in Texas, but on his
way to the ranch he had by good fortune made the acquaintance
of Charles Goodnight, one of the most respected cattlemen in
Northwest Texas. The Scotsman sought the advice of the Texan.
Goodnight agreed to loan to Walker, John Farrington, Goodnight's foreman, and two hands, Bill Sweet and "Parson" Smith.
The three would go to the Spur Ranch and work out with
Walker on one hand, and the officials of the Fort Worth Company on the other hand, a modus operandi for counting the
cattle.

The outside boundaries of the Spur Ranch had been fenced,
including the unsurveyed strip of shinnery down the center. The
entire ranch of over a half-millon acres was one big pasture. Farrington recommended that a cross fence be constructed from
north to south down the middle of the shinnery strip. When this
was done, all the cattle were driven into the East Pasture. Then
all the cattle in the East Pasture were rounded up and counted
as they were put through gates into the West Pasture. In this
way no animal was counted twice. Farrington counted for the
London Company and Bud Campbell for the Fort Worth
Company. When the tally was completed the total number delivered was several thousand short of the number contracted.
This was a severe blow for the Fort Worth Company. Additional cattle had to be purchased at a high price to make up
the shortage. The deficiency was made up by procuring the
cattle of the Dalton brothers who up to this time had not sold.
They took notes for part payment. The Fort Worth Company
never redeemed the notes.

The land actually owned by the Fort Worth Company at the
time of sale was approximately 437,670 acres. This was the
amount which had been contracted for from the railroads through

the New York and Texas Land Company. It was less than half the land enclosed in the outside fences of the Ranch, the remainder being the alternate school sections and the unsurveyed shinnery strip. Getting title to the school lands constituted a long subsequent process. In the meanwhile the school sections could be leased. According to W. J. Elliott the railroad lands cost the London Company $5.50 per acre. The Fort Worth company still owed $412,352 on the lands to the New York and Texas Land Company. The London Company assumed this obligation. By November 30, 1887, the London Company had paid $1,054,650 for railroad lands.[17] This did not include the cattle or the school lands which had to be acquired later in small tracts from time to time. Obtaining title to the solid pastures was to be a long and frustrating process.

The estimated number of cattle at the time of sale was 40,000. The records do not reveal the aggregate value of the cattle and horses. At a medium price of $15 per head, based on market conditions at the time, the livestock on the ranch would have been valued at $640,000.

Information is not available as to the total amount eventually paid for the school lands. A conservative estimate would be $2.75 per acre, or $583,785 for 218,835 acres. The total investment of the London Company was $2,278,435, not including later capital improvements.

Ironically, in 1907 they sold the land, cattle, horses, everything for less than the original investment. The Espuela Land and Cattle Company of Fort Worth in 1885 had fared even worse when selling to Espuela Land and Cattle Company, Limited, of London. When the Fort Worth Company was liquidated the stockholders and creditors had sustained considerable loss.

The transfer of land, cattle, and horses was consummated in the fall of 1885. During the next twenty-two years, the Scots and Englishmen had many occasions to regret the acquisition of property in distant Texas where drouths and breaks in the cattle market, both unheard of at the time of purchase, came all too frequently. Even before the final count was made on the cattle, hard times were setting in for cattlemen. The Drouth of 1886 was beginning. It was to play havoc both with the cattle and with prices.[18]

[17]Elliott, *The Spurs*, 34.
[18]W. R. Stafford to Jones, interview, October 19, 1929.

VII: *MANAGERS, MANAGEMENT, AND SUPPLIES*

THE RESIDENT REPRESENTATIVE of the Espuela Land and Cattle Company, Limited, was the manager. This official had full charge of the company's cattle and properties. He held the power of attorney, and his discretionary powers were great. However, as he was responsible to the Board of Directors for all his acts, he was careful in using his own judgment, and he passed all important business to the Board, and left the formulation of policies to that body.

After 1885, the Spur properties had five managers. Three of them served before the English company sold out to the Swenson interests in 1907, and two after. As one reads through the thousands of letters written by these men, each manager again becomes a personality.

Spottswood W. Lomax was manager from the time the Ranch was taken over by the Espuela Land and Cattle Company, Limited, until July 15, 1889. He was born in Virginia, but lived at St. Louis before coming to Texas. A tall, slender man, sociable, soft spoken and with a mass of light brown unruly hair, he was a polished gentleman, well educated and widely travelled. He had a way of unconsciously causing the people around him to feel inferior. He had spent two years in Spain, and was conversant with Spanish history and literature. It was he who named both the Matador and the Espuela Cattle Companies.

His wife, who always called him "Spots," had a different background. She did not care for the isolation and privations of ranch life; and during the five years Lomax was manager, she maintained a considerable establishment on Weatherford Street in Fort Worth and spent only a part of the time on the Ranch. The Lomaxes had five children, three girls and two boys.[1]

As a manager, Lomax was characterized by his accuracy. He required that all Ranch accounts be kept with the utmost care. Bills sent to the Ranch were checked and rechecked. On several occasions he found that merchants from whom he bought sup-

[1] Mrs. H. H. Campbell to W. C. H., interview, September 9, 1930.

plies had, in adding the costs of the long lists of items, made mistakes of a few cents in the favor of the Ranch. In each instance he sent a check to correct the mistake. On another occasion, he found that the bank at Fort Worth had made an error of two cents in the Ranch's account. He spent six cents on postage to get the error righted—it had to be correct.[2] His love for promptness corresponded with his fondness for accuracy.[3]

With the exception of Charles Goodnight of the JA ranch and H. H. Campbell of the Matador, no man in northwest Texas was more respected by his men. Old Spur hands, when speaking of him later, referred to him as "Mister Lomax." They never said "Mister Horsbrugh" or "Mister Johnstone." Like Goodnight and Campbell, Lomax had a fatherly interest in his men, and gave them advice and counsel when it was needed. In March, 1888, he became convinced that liquor on the Ranch was good neither for the men nor for the welfare of the company, and he put prohibition into effect on the Spur Ranch by a proclamation. At the same time he canceled an order for a case of whiskey for himself from Colorado City. Then he wrote the storekeeper of the company store:

> I do not know whether there is any liquor at the store or not, but to prevent any misunderstanding, I take this method of notifying you that it is not to be given to any employee of this company, unless he is at the same time told that its receipt by him, or for him, will terminate his employment. Should any packages containing liquor be received from the mail hack consigned to any employee of the company while you are in charge of the store, you will inform him of the foregoing before delivering the same to the end that he may deliberately elect his course. The necessity and propriety of this rule is so obvious that I need not say more.[4]

Later Lomax entered into an agreement with H. H. Campbell and Charles Goodnight whereby each agreed not to employ any hand who had been discharged elsewhere for stealing or drunkenness. The influence of these three men was so great that they could prevent undesirable characters from getting work at practically every ranch in the country.[5]

Lomax was not entirely happy in his relations with the com-

[2]Spur Records, V, 8, 63, 117.
[3]Spur Records, V, 16.
[4]Spur Records, II, 268.
[5]Spur Records, II, 268, 269.

pany, and when in May, 1889, the Board of Directors reduced his salary from $7,500 to $3,750, he threatened to quit at once. The Directors evidently valued his services, for they immediately countered with an offer of $5,000. About the same time he was offered a position in a bank at Vernon, and he took it.[6]

In 1886, the London Company made Fred Horsbrugh, a Scotsman, assistant manager of the Ranch. He had attended Edinburgh Academy for six years and Saint Andrews University two years. He came to the United States in 1884 and worked two years on a stock farm near Sioux City, Iowa. In Scotland he had known several of the men who later organized the Espuela Land and Cattle Company of London. He was in Iowa when he learned of that company's purchase of the Spur Ranch. He wrote to his friends asking employment on the Ranch. Members of the Board were becoming unhappy with Lomax's management. They felt he was in some way responsible for the recent disasters pertaining to drouth, die-ups, and low cattle prices. Apparently they had two motives in making Horsbrugh assistant manager: first, they wanted a Scotsman from the Old Country on the Ranch to keep an eye on the manager and to keep the Board informed of bad management; and second, they wanted to have an understudy in training in the event the Board found it necessary to dismiss Lomax.

During the three years, 1886-1889, Lomax and Horsbrugh worked together, relations between them were strained. Lomax suspected the reasons prompting Horsbrugh's appointment. The personalities of the two were radically different. Whereas Lomax was dignified, urbane, and unapproachable, Horsbrugh was affable, good humored, and companionable. Lomax was respected by the hands, but Horsbrugh was adored by them. Although not so polished as Lomax, the Scotsman had an even temper and a pleasant Scottish drawl.

When Horsbrugh, in May, 1889, learned that Lomax and the Board were at loggerheads over Lomax's salary, he hastened to write Alexander McNab, the most influential member of the Board:

I note what you say in regard to the manager having given notice, and think that you are right as to its being a mere pretext to obtain a binding engagement. Should he come to terms with the

[6] Two years later, 1891, Lomax died at Vernon.

Board, I fear that one of his stipulations, although personally we are good friends, will be absolute and sole supervision, and consequently my removal. This of course would be an extreme hardship for me, as since my coming here four years ago my whole time and thought has been devoted to the interests of this company; and at my time of life uncertainty of employment to a poor man is very serious thing. The more so when his previous life, as mine has been for the last four years, unfits him for ordinary business of any kind. I have from the first made it my business to live on friendly terms with the manager, as I considered that any falling out between us would prove fatal, not only on account of my personal interests, but to the purpose for which I was sent out here. . . . It goes a bit against the grain to do anything which may appear pushing myself forward or blowing my own trumpet, but I am alone in the world and have no one to do it for me; and in these days, something of the sort is necessary at times; and I submit that should the Board not come to terms with the manager, I have claims to the position, due to my residence here, my knowledge of the cattle, this country, and the people, which are above those of any stranger who might be appointed to the place, and whose appointment would at first be productive of much trouble and annoyance.[7]

Horsbrugh was tendered the managership, at a beginning salary of $2,000 a year.[8] He accepted.

The managers of the Ranch had problems created by visits to the Ranch of stockholders and members of the Board of Directors. Lomax had coped with such occasions without undue difficulty. Horsbrugh was often at a loss as to how to handle his superiors. He had scarcely taken over management of the Ranch when John McNab, one of the Directors, arrived fresh from London. Next day the hands were preparing to round-up the East Pasture. McNab expressed a desire to go along. Horsbrugh directed that one of the more gentle easier riding horses be saddled for the visitor. When the horse was brought out, McNab said, "No, thank you, I will walk."

No persuasion could change his decision. When ready to start, the Scotsman's dress was as out of character as his mode of transportation on a roundup. He dressed as for a business call on Fleet Street, bowler hat, business suit with starched collar and cuffs, and expensive shoes. To add insult to injury, so far as the hands were concerned, he carried an umbrella, rain or shine. It was mostly shine, and in the heat of the day he travelled with

[7]Spur Records, IV, 272.
[8]Spur Records, IV, 156.

the umbrella open for shade. He never ceased to cause a commotion among the half wild cattle in roundups. This apparition was something new and strange to the skittish animals. Stampedes were narrowly averted by extra vigilance on the part of the hands.

When Horsbrugh was not along, the "loose-herding" of McNab fell to Bud Campbell, the range boss. The concern of Horsbrugh and Campbell was not only for the unorthodox behavior of the visitor, but for the visible and audible reactions of the hands to his antics. Their underbreath remarks were pungent, and often fitting, but most embarrassing if they reached the ears of Mr. McNab. However, as time went on, the hands became rather fond of him and developed a protective attitude towards him. Occasionally, the Scotsman would set off on a solitary walk to inspect the range. Always a hand was designated to keep an eye on him. As a rule McNab became lost when out of sight of the headquarters. Then, the heretofore unseen cowhand would casually appear and offer to guide him wherever he wished to go.

John McNab made several subsequent visits to the Ranch, and never was he induced to ride a horse or discard his umbrella. Always he travelled on "Shank's mare." Occasionally when the terrain was suitable for a four wheel vehicle, Horsbrugh induced him to follow the roundup in a buggy. This happened only when the manager went along to do the driving.

Other members of the Board came and went. Although none of them carried an umbrella or refused to mount a horse, all of them were unacquainted with Ranch routine, and did, or said, strange things to the amusement, and sometimes the consternation, of the manager and hands.

Horsbrugh was manager from 1889 to 1904. In 1890 he married a Miss Mitchell, niece of Mrs. Hank Smith of Mount Blanco. With a family, drouths, low cattle prices, and troublesome nesters, Horsbrugh was soon weighed down with grave responsibilities. He seemed to mellow as time passed. The travel and associations which his position made possible caused him to become less brusque and more cautious. After leaving the Ranch in 1904, he moved to Amarillo where he lived until his death in 1928.

Of Henry H. Johnstone, Horsbrugh's successor, we know too little. Horsbrugh, who had known him for fifteen years, described him as "an extra pleasant man and a gentleman." A tall, slender man with a handsome face, iron grey hair, and blue eyes with a twinkle in them, he had a fascinating personality and could tell stories until a late hour of the night. He thought, spoke, and directed in a methodical, clear-cut fashion. Horsbrugh had the habit of writing very full, long letters to the London office; Johnstone's were short and pithy. A sense of humor and droll manner of expression added to their interest. He was fastidious too; he had his shirts made to measure, from special materials, in Kansas City, and ordered Navajo rugs and blankets from Houck, Arizona.[9]

Johnstone was a relative of James Johnstone and Margaret McNab Johnstone of Menstrie, Scotland. Margaret McNab Johnstone was one of the heirs and executors of the fortune of Alexander McNab, who had largely financed the Espuela Land and Cattle Company, Limited; at one time he had a mortgage on all of its property in Texas.[10] The McNabs were also interested in the Matador Land and Cattle Company. It was due to the McNab connection with the Matador Company that Henry Johnstone had been employed on the Matador Ranch. He was appointed manager of the Spur Ranch on February 1, 1904, and retained that position until 1907 when the Espuela Company sold the Spur properties to the Swensons and associates; Johnstone returned to Scotland and was heard of no more.

The Espuela Land and Cattle Company, Limited, maintained an office in Lawrence Pountney Hill, London. The policies of the company were formulated by the Board of Directors and communicated to the resident manager through the secretary of the Board, J. Earl Hodges, who devoted his full time to the management of the Home office.

A bookkeeper on the Ranch devoted all of his time to the Ranch's accounts.[11] He used old fashioned, English counting house methods of bookkeeping. In fine handwriting and with meticulous care he recorded entries in the day book, the cash book,

[9]Spur Records, XI, 501, 508.
[10]Deed Records, Crosby County, I, 262, XIV, 51.
[11]The first bookkeeper was S. G. Flook, a nephew of Sir Charles Hamilton, a member of Parliament from Londonderry and a stockholder in the company. Flook, brought up in a counting house, became a character on the Ranch; everybody knew him; everybody poked fun at him; everybody liked him. His uncle, Sir Charles, had given him one share of stock. It is said that the cowboys used to tell him he was fired. His answer always was, "They can't turn me out—I am a part of the Company." R. P. Smythe to W. C. H., interview, August 28, 1930.

the journal, the ledger,[12] and the payroll. On the Ranch's records, the London office was credited with all remittances sent by it to the Ranch, and the London office was charged with all remittances sent by the Ranch to it. All income received by the Ranch from any source was sent to the London office through J. Kennedy, Tod and Company, brokers in New York, All money paid out by the Ranch for operating expenses was transferred back from London through J. Kennedy, Tod and Company. Such funds were deposited in the City National Bank of Fort Worth and dispersed by checks signed by the manager. It seemed a bit clumsy for the manager to send $20,000 or $30,000 received from cattle sales to London, and, at the same time, draw on the home office for $5,000 for operating expenses; but such a method was deemed necessary by the Directors in order to check on the manager.[13]

The total income from cattle sales for a sixteen-year period, 1889-1904, was $1,778,983.10, or an average of $106,811.44 a year.[14] The sales fluctuated considerably, however; in 1893, for instance, they were only $16,825.38, and in 1894, they amounted to $188,327.51. The total expense of the Ranch during the same sixteen year period were $581,077.15, or an average of $36,317.32 a year. The yearly expenses varied from $48,621.43 a year in 1894 to $29,898.14 in 1896. The company's average annual income exceeded the annual expenditure (not including the expense of maintaining the London office) during the period by $64,250.00. As the company had approximately $2,200,000 invested in cattle and land, the average profits amounted to about 2.5 per cent a year. This does not include interest and other expenses in England.

The largest item in the Ranch's expenses was wages. They varied from $17,702.45 in 1889 to $9,909.50 in 1896.[15] The sec-

[12]In the ledger separate accounts were kept for Bulls, Cattle, Corn Mill, Cotton, City National Bank of Fort Worth, Farm, Horses, Gin, Improvements, Loan Costs, Leases, London Office, Cattle Raisers Association, Equipment, Expense, Espuela Store, Pasturage, Profits and Loss, Salaries, Supplies, Taxes, Travelling Expenses, Trail Wages, Trail Expenses, Wages, Wells and Waterings, Wolf Bounties, and various individuals, including the manager and bookkeeper.

[13]Money for operating expenses was almost always transferred from London in $2,500 lumps. Occasionally, the manager drew $5,000 and more rarely, $1,250.

[14]Unfortunately, the ledgers containing the accounts from 1885 to 1888, inclusive, and the one extending from 1904 to 1909 have been lost. Therefore, our only complete record of accounts covers the sixteen year period from 1889 to 1904, inclusive.

[15]For a more detailed account of wages, see Chapter VI above.

ond largest expense was taxes. These varied from $4,850.50 in
1889 to $17,282.05 in 1900, and averaged $9,710.60 a year. The
organization of the counties wherein the Spurs lay caused the
taxes to more than double between 1892 and 1895. Approximately 54 per cent of all the taxes were paid in Dickens County,
26 per cent in Kent County, 12 per cent in Crosby County, and
8 per cent in Garza County. In addition to the county and state
taxes the company paid a state annual franchise tax of $10 from
1885 to 1890; in 1891, it was raised to $205 a year.

The third largest item in the expense accounts was supplies.
For two years after the English company purchased the Spur
Ranch the nearest railroad shipping point was Colorado City,
a hundred miles to the south. All supplies came from that place
on freight wagons at a rate of 75 cents per hundred pounds.
After the Fort Worth and Denver Railroad reached Childress
in 1887, some of the supplies were hauled from there, but the
greater part of them was still obtained from Colorado City, although the distance was twenty miles farther than to Childress.

In order to enable the Ranch to obtain its supplies at wholesale prices, the company purchased in 1885 the old Dockum
Store.[16] The building and goods were moved to headquarters
where the store was operated for four years. In 1889, the stock
of goods was moved to Espuela (survey 354, Block 1). Prior to
the removal of the store supplies from headquarters to Espuela,
J. H. Parrish had operated a small store at Espuela. The Spur
Company purchased Parrish's store and consolidated it with the
stock of goods from headquarters. In explaining the store business to the home office, Horsbrugh wrote:

> The business done at the store does not include any ranch sup-
> plies furnished to headquarters by the store; the bulk (of the sup-
> plies for headquarters) is not unloaded at the store, though ordered
> through it, but comes direct to the ranch . . . a few odds and ends
> carried in stock and wanted at the ranch are gotten from the store.
> This amount is not large, an average of $1.15 a month for six
> months.[17]

The company had some trouble in finding satisfactory store-

[16]This store had been opened in 1877 by W. C. Dockum, a buffalo hunter, on
Dockum Creek (survey 359, Block 1) about five miles west of the Spur headquarters. Dockum was from New York, but had lived a short time at Fort Griffin
before settling in Dickens County. W. R. Stafford to Mildred Arnett, interview,
November 29, 1929.
[17]Spur Records, VIII, 329.

keepers. R. C. Ware, who filled the place until 1889, did very well, but he gave up the position to become one of the founders of Plainview. W. A. Wilkinson served as storekeeper until 1896, when he was succeeded by W. J. Elliott from Aberdeen, Scotland.

Food constituted the greater part of the supply account. Hominy, rice, potatoes, flour, meal, sugar, salt, dried fruits, and onions were purchased by the barrel. Lard, baking powder, tea, canned vegetables, and similar items were bought in large cans, from one to several gallons in size. Beans, coffee, and sometimes potatoes and flour came in sacks of 50 and 100 pounds each.[18] In addition the Ranch killed from 60 to 100 beeves a year, or one every three or four days.

The total cost of supplies from 1889 to 1906 was $72,755.52, or an average of $4,041.97 a year.[19] This amounted to an average of $336.83 a month or approximately $11.23 a day. An analysis of the food consumed by J. A. Stokes' outfit during the year of 1889 shows with considerable accuracy the cost of feeding a man per day. The outfit consisting of 12 men was employed throughout the year at tank building, fence repairing, branding, and herd gathering. The men consumed in the course of the year 8,087 pounds of food (they were given only staples) at a cost of $594.71. Each man ate approximately 1.6 pounds of food a day at a cost of 11 cents. This amounted to 3.9 cents per man per meal.[20]

[18]A typical order for supplies for the Ranch was made on August 5, 1885, from McCall Brothers and Rotan, Colorado City:

3 Bbls. Y. C. sugar		1 doz. paper pails	
1	" currants	1 crate B. bacon	
1	" prunes	½ doz. choice hams	
1	" peaches	1 bbl. potatoes	
1	" hominy	2-3 lb. c. tomatoes	
1	" rice	1-2 lb. cal. peas	
1	" onions	1 2½ J. Lusk peaches	
5 boxes evap. apples		1 lb. cayenne pepper	
2	" ¾ soap	1 lb. Coleman's mustard	
3	" 10 lb. lard	½ doz. pineapple cheese	
3	" S. C. Bacon	10 lb. dried beef	
1	" 5 lb. powder	1 lb. cinnamon	
1	" axle grease	¼ lb. nutmeg	
1	" brill oil	1 doz. vanilla and lemon ext.	
4 sacks coffee		1 gal. vinegar	
4	" Red X flour	5 lb. corn starch	
1 Caddy Black tea		3 lb. cocoanut	

[19]In 1901 the Ranch used 30,000 pounds of flour, 6,000 pounds of sugar, 6,000 pounds of bacon, 2,500 pounds of coffee, 5,000 pounds of lard, 3,500 pounds of beans, and 3,000 pounds of evaporated fruits. Spur Records, X, 511.

[20]Rylander, Dorothy, "The Economic Phase of the Ranching Industry on the Spur Ranch," (Master's Thesis, Texas Technological College, 1931).

A part of the money spent for supplies went for articles other than food. For instance, every three or four years the kitchen range at headquarters would burn out and have to be replaced. Cooking utensils had to be bought from time to time. There was a more or less constant need for files, nails, crowbars, wire pinchers, and other similar articles. Office stationery, as well as ledgers, letter books, journals, and account books, were ordered from time to time.[21]

To the supply account was charged subscriptions to periodicals taken by the Ranch. Among the periodicals were the Fort Worth *Weekly Gazette,* Dallas *News, Texas Stock and Farm Journal, Northwestern Live Stock Journal,* and Cheyenne *Live Stock Journal.*

[21]A typical order made for office stationery on March 4, 1895, as follows:

3 quires ruled paper	20 printed envelopes
1,000 printed letterheads	2,000 plain envelopes
1,000 plain letterheads	1 letter copying book
1,000 draft forms	1 memo. book

VIII: *CATTLE, SALES, AND DROUTHS*

When the Espuela Land and Cattle Company, Limited, of London took over the Spur properties from the Espuela Land and Cattle Company of Fort Worth in 1885, the Ranch had 42,777 head of cattle, including the year's calf crop. The number of calves that year was unusually good, 11,016 calves from 15,832 cows. Range conditions were splendid and the cattle were in good flesh when cold weather came. The loss for the winter was less than usual.[1] In October, 1885, stock water on some parts of the range was scarce, but as it was plentiful at other places, the water situation did not become serious until the next spring. The Ranch was still depending on natural watering places, as it had not had time to construct tanks or bore many wells. The sales for the year were approximately 5,000 head, which were driven to Montana. Although cattle prices had reached their peak in 1884, they were still good in 1885. Two-year-old steers sold at $21.50.[2]

The policy of the Ranch in 1886 was to increase the size of its herd, which before the end of the year numbered 54,417. It was an unfortunate time to begin such a policy. The price of cattle was starting on a decline from which it was not to recover for a decade, and a drouth was getting under way. The company purchased 8,779 head during the year and sold only 3,472; no she-cattle were sold.[3] Two-year-old steers that Lomax paid $20 for in 1886 sold two years later for the same amount. Cows that he paid $20 for in 1886 sold three years later for $8. The drouth delayed the spring work and would have caused a serious disaster for the company had it not been that the Spur

[1] It was practically impossible to keep an accurate account of the losses each winter. The Spur Ranch estimated the losses would average about 5 per cent and each year made that allowance on the Ranch books. Some winters the actual loss was less than that and other winters it was decidedly more.

[2] The price of two-year-old steers can best be used as an index to the cattle market. The Spur Ranch sold heifers, cows, bulls, and other classes of cattle from time to time, but only two-year-old steers were sold every year.

[3] Spur Records, I, 262; Stock Register, 1885-1895, Spur Records, LXI, 1.

range received a good local rain on August 1.[4] The country to the south was not so fortunate. Cattlemen there were not able to round-up, or fulfill their contracts.[5] The best they could do was to drift their cattle from place to place in an effort to keep them alive. The local rains in the Spur pastures, however, provided sufficient water and grass for the winter. Little hay was raised on the feed farm that year, and the winter was unusually severe; so the cattle fared badly.[6] The losses for the winter, 1886-1887, were estimated at 4,600, a very conservative figure.

The year 1887 was as bad as 1886 for the Spur Ranch. Very little rain fell in the spring and summer. Grass made a feeble growth in April, and the tender blades soon withered, dried, and then parched. The cattle were extremely poor when spring came, and summer found them barely holding their own. Heavy rains fell in the latter part of August, and by the middle of September grass was looking good. It had been nipped off so closely, however, during the preceding months that it did not have time to grow enough before frost to carry the 53,732 cattle through the winter.[7] By November, it was evident that the range was too crowded for the cattle to live through the winter. Lomax leased the Koogle pasture on White Deer Creek north of Clarendon and the ROS pasture in King County.[8] By December 1, 5,629 head had been driven to the Koogle pasture and 8,433 head to the ROS.[9]

The company sold 11,277 cattle in 1887, or approximately three times as many as in 1886.[10] Of this number, 2,485 were old cows. The Ranch adhered to a policy of selling herd cows after they had had five or six calves. No mention is made in the available records of the price received for the 1887 sales, but the general cattle market was about 10 per cent lower than in 1886.

The year 1888 was a memorable one for the cattlemen of Northwest Texas. The fickleness of Texas weather was never so well exemplified. It was so cold and dry in the spring that 6,663

[4]Spur Records, I, 256.
[5]Spur Records, I, 237.
[6]Spur Records, I, 45.
[7]Stock Register, 1885-1895, Spur Records, LXI, 7.
[8]Spur Records, II, 27; IV, 478, 479, 482.
[9]Spur Records, IV, 464.
[10]The sales of 1887 were as follows: one-year-old heifers, 4,615; one-year-old steers, 1,859; two-year-old steers, 1,849; cows, 2,485; bulls, 203.

Spur cattle died and only one cow out of every five raised a calf. By November the cattle that weathered the spring and summer were rolling fat and wading almost knee deep in grass.

On January 14 the worst blizzard ever known in the history of the Ranch up to that time began and raged for three days. The thermometer went to ten below zero, snow and ice covered the ground, making grazing impossible, the tanks and the creeks froze more than a foot deep so the cattle could not drink, and a piercing, driving thirty-mile gale swept the prairies. The cattle humped their backs, downed their heads, and started drifting. When the spell broke, more than a thousand lay dead along the south fence lines, and for days the rest seemed half dead.[11] February was warm and balmy; grass started putting out; cattle partially recovered from the effects of the blizzard; Lomax breathed easier, hoping the worst was over; but the first week in March changed the outlook. A freezing norther, lasting for five days, wrought even greater havoc than the January blizzard. The temperature lacked twenty degrees of going as low as in January, but the previous weeks of warm weather had made the cattle more sensitive to cold, which together with their poor condition cause 5,000 more to die. The damage did not stop there; the calf crop was reduced to about one-third of what it would have been in a normal year. The Ranch should have gotten the largest crop in its history that year, as it had over 2,000 more cows than ever before. Instead it got the smallest crop—6,131 calves from 26,991 cows, or 22 per cent. Horsbrugh wrote the London office in October, 1888:

That the calf crop would be short this year was expected after the extremely dry summer last year, but the unlooked-for shortage confronting us shows that a large portion of our cows slipped their calves last winter from poverty and extremely cold weather. That we are not alone in this deficiency is certain. I hear the same complaint being made all over the country. It is true of the Llano company and the Kentucky company. The Matadors are 6000 head short of its last years figure at this time.[12]

With an overstocked range and with cattle in two leased pastures in the spring of 1888, the Board of Directors decided to reduce the size of the Spur herd; and accordingly 12,086 head

[11]Spur Records, IV, 459, 463.
[12]Spur Records, IV, 347.

were sold during the year.[13] Again the Board acted inadvisedly. The Ranch had more grass in the fall of 1888 than anytime since 1885, and the excessive sales were at the lowest price Spur cattle had ever been known to bring. Yearlings (one-year-old heifers and steers) brought from $8.50 to $9.00 each; 4,224 two-year-old steers sold for $14 a piece; and 3,653 cows brought from $3 to $8 a head.[14] As result of the heavy sales and short calf crop the Ranch started into the winter of 1888-1889 with only 41,180 cattle—over 12,000 less than the previous winter.

Throughout January and February, Lomax and Horsbrugh were jubilant over the outlook. Every day they wrote letters commenting upon the weather or the condition of the cattle; both were "fine," "extraordinary," "like springtime," and the cattle were "in good fix," "fine shape," "doing well," and "stood the last cold spell splendidly." When the men thought of the ravages of the previous winters, they had cause for such satisfying comments. Although the losses for the winter were the lightest they had been in years, March found the Ranch with slightly less than 40,000 cattle.[15] Contrary to expectations after the mild winter with good grass there was a short calf crop, 8,420 calves from 21,952 cows, or only 38 per cent. The hard, cold winter of 1887-1888 with scant feed had caused many of the cows to miss having calves for two years, and some of them to become permanently barren.

A seasonable spring in 1889 caused the grass to be better at that time of year than in five years.[16] Rains kept coming until July when the weather turned dry and hot for two months. One day in August the thermometer in the Ranch office went to 116 degrees with the windows and doors open;[17] and one of the men at the feed farm had a sunstroke. With full tanks and a good crop of grass, brown and matured, cattle could stand the heat. When it rained on September 9, Horsbrugh, thinking the Board might be getting uneasy about the probability of another drouth, cabled the home office "Radiantly," which de-coded meant "We have had plenty of rain."[18] The rain came in time to make an

[13]Spur Records, LXI, 3.
[14]Spur Records, IV, 331.
[15]Spur Records, IV, 294.
[16]Spur Records, V, 262.
[17]Spur Records, IV, 203.
[18]Spur Records, IV, 184.

ample crop of fall grass, and the prospects for the winter again looked promising.

Cattle sales were slow in 1889. In the spring Lomax tried to find buyers for 5,000 two-year-old steers, 3,000 heifer yearlings, and 1,700 two-year-old spayed heifers—a total of 9,700. The only demand during the year was a limited one for two-year-old steers and beef cattle. Lomax wrote dozens of letters to Wyoming, Montana, Colorado, Kansas, and Missouri attempting to find buyers. He sold 1,506 two-year-old steers delivered to Amarillo in May for $15 a head. In June he shipped 396 young sorghum-fed cattle, twos and threes, to Chicago where they sold for $28 each.[19] In August, Texas cattle went to the lowest point on the Chicago market known since 1873. Lomax recommended to the Board that no more sales be made until the spring of 1890. In view of the short calf crops in 1888 and 1889 it stood to reason that the demand for feeders in the Corn Belt and grazers in the Northwest would be much better in 1890. The Ranch, accordingly, settled down to the winter routine with 44,166 cattle on the range.[20]

In 1889 the Board of Directors in London made inquiry as to policies of Ranch operation. After five years of experience, two drouth years, two exceedingly short calf crops, one heavy die-up, three years of low prices, and one year of practically no cattle demand, the Board began to wonder more than ever what was the matter. It even sent one of its members over to study the question first hand. The Board wished to make such changes in its policy as would be necessary to forestall losses and prevent dumping large numbers of cattle on a low market, as had been the case in 1888. Having small knowledge of Texas climatic and range conditions and lacking practical cattle experience, most of the directors' proposals were impractical, but Horsbrugh's answers to them are illuminating as to Ranch conditions of the time.

The Board considered keeping the yearlings and two-year-old cattle and selling them as beeves at three and four years. Horsbrugh answered:

The chief obstacle to the keeping of our steers on the range until they are three or four years old is that this part of Texas is not a

[19]Spur Records, IV, 117, 218, 259.
[20]Spur Records, IV, 107.

grazing country, but a breeding country. In former years when the range was open and there were fewer cattle in the country, and men paid nothing for the land on which they ran their cattle, it was the practice to sell nothing but three and four year old steers; and being fat, they brought good money. But with the advent of large numbers of cattle, land became dear, and was bought, or leased, and fenced into pastures. With this the character of the grass completely changed; where formerly there was long luxuriant grass that would fatten an animal without his having to do much walking; there is now only short grass at the best of seasons. It is sufficient to keep cattle in good condition, not sufficient to make them fat enough to enable them to hold their weight until they are shipped to market. Even if the grass were to grow longer than it now does, the herd would have to be cut down to much smaller dimensions to give room for keeping the two extra crops of calves. . . . Taking the price at the present time of one, two, and three year old steers, say $10, $15, and $20, it will be seen there is a rise of $5 for each year of growth; but there is more profit in selling the two year old and making room for others, because in the third year, he will eat and destroy more grass than in the two previous years combined. . . . Breeding stock and old steers do not do well in the same pasture, as the latter require to be by themselves where they will be rounded-up as little as possible. If this company had another place where all the yearlings, or two year olds, could be driven and kept until fat, we would make more out of them; but the grass would have to be very much better than it is with us. As an instance of what could be done, I know of steers that were bred here and sold in Montana at two years old, and at four weighed in Chicago 1300 pounds. Another lot that I know of were grazed in the Indian Territory for two years and weighed from 1200 to 1250 pounds. Every year we have a remnant of four year old steers (that have been grazed here), and they weigh from 925 to 950 pounds. As the heavier the animal, the more he brings a pound, it sometimes happens that one 1300 pound steer brings three times as much money as a 950 pound steer.[21]

The Board of Directors were skeptical as to the wisdom of maintaining the feed farm. They were not satisfied with the sorghum feeding results. Horsbrugh defended the feed farm policy vigorously:

The steers and the spayed heifers have not been doing so well as was expected. The principal reason for this is that they have not

---

[21]Spur Records, IV, 453. The realization of the profits to be made by a company's owning a grazing range somewhere in the Northwest where it could fatten its own cattle caused many of the large Texas cattle syndicates to lease or purchase lands in Montana or Wyoming. Had the Espuela company done so, its ranching experiences might have been happier.

had enough sorghum, and what they have is not good enough. The crop on the new farm last year was anything but satisfactory, and the quantity stacked was disappointing. Again, the sorghum scheme, as advocated by me, provided for the cattle being on good grass and receiving a daily allowance of sorghum in addition to all the grass they could eat. Unfortunately, although the pasture was fenced off and nothing allowed in it all summer, the grass obstinately refused to grow. This was sheer bad luck, but it had a good deal to do with the weights of the cattle. . . . It is something to know that with the feed the steers have held their own; had we gotten a decent crop of sorghum last year, they would be fat now.[22]

In view of the heavy die-up in January and March, 1888, the Board asked Horsbrugh about the advisability of providing eight-foot plank enclosures a hundred yards square for the cattle. In reply, Horsbrugh said:

A great difficulty in the way of erecting such protection as you mention would be the expense, as these square fences, if eight feet high and a hundred yards square and made of heavy posts and pine lumber, would cost about $1000.00 each. If this range were on the plains where the whole [country] is a dead level, something of the kind of thing you describe would be necessary; but here the country is more broken, and along the creeks, the banks of which for the most part are very steep, there is ample protection for range cattle, provided they are not too poor.[23]

The Board asked an opinion as to what in the future might be considered the carrying capacity of the Spur range. Horsbrugh replied: "I think we can carry with safety 45,000 head in ordinary years, and in years where the spring and summer rains have been good, 5,000 more can be taken through the winter following with safety."[24]

The directors were desirous of more information about shipping points, and transportation facilities. Horsbrugh answered:

We are about ninety miles south of Childress, a small town of about 500 inhabitants on the Fort Worth and Denver Railroad, which runs in a northwestward direction. We are also about the same distance north of Colorado on the Texas and Pacific Railroad which runs east. Colorado has about 4000 inhabitants. The advantage of a shipping point on the railroad depends not so much on its proximity to the ranch as on the condition of the range between here and there; for instance, Childress is our nearest point

[22]Spur Records, IV, 471.
[23]Spur Records, IV, 485.
[24]Spur Records, IV, 497.

in shipping to Kansas City or Chicago, but as a rule the country between here and there is very unsuited to drive cattle over and keep them in good condition. We have found Amarillo, on the same line but 150 miles from here, a very good shipping point as the grass is good all the way, and it is a much easier drive, provided there is water on the plains. The cattle go to Chicago in three days from there, and are fed and watered three times on the way. We always send men along with the cattle when making a shipment to see that the cattle get fed and properly cared for on the way. The railroad gives free transportation both ways for these men. I have no knowledge from my own observation as to how the cattle are treated at the feeding points and at the weighing scales, but I am thinking of going up this summer with a train load of cattle and watching these things; if so, I will not fail to send you the results of my notes. . . . When a herd is driven to the railroad for shipment the practice is to send one trainload a day (about 800 head) to each of the big markets, and these trainloads are not consigned to any one (commission) firm but divided up so as to play one commission house off against the other. Our cows that sold last year were fairly fat when they went away, but their proceeds shows just what may be expected from shipping cattle off the grass in this country.[25]

It occurred to the Board that small bunches of cattle might be fattened at the Ranch and sold at a better price directly to butchers here and there over the country. To this suggestion, Horsbrugh pointed out:

We are so far from a railroad at present that a good large bunch of cattle has to be driven at a time; as it costs as much to drive a small herd as a big one. I am afraid we cannot do well with fat cattle any place other than Kansas City and Chicago, as the railroads discriminate in favor of these places; and the butchers in towns nearer to us invariably when buying take the Chicago markets as their basis and make the same deductions for shrinkage and cost of carriage that the longer journey would have incurred. I think the sale of calves that you have noticed have been shipped from the Indian Territory. Last year some Texas men shipped up cows and calves to the Territory, having procured pasturage there near the railroad; and after keeping them there for some time, the calves were weaned and shipped. The cows were left to fatten until fall and then shipped to market. That, of course, is what we would be unable to do here, situated as we are at present.[26]

The Board members were inquisitive as to the policy of spaying heifers. They had noticed that a 10 to 15 per cent loss usually

[25]Spur Records, IV, 507.
[26]Spur Records, VI, 32.

followed as a result of the operation. Horsbrugh's reply indicated that he was not overly enthusiastic about the practice:

You are right in your remarks about spaying. I think it has been sufficiently proved that if heifers are to be spayed, it should be done when they are calves, and then they should be put in a place to themselves and watched carefully.[27]

If the Board of Directors was uneasy about the general prospects of the ranching industry in 1889, the climatic conditions of 1890 did much to reassure them. January was warm and calm, and grass was still good from its growth during the previous fall. Horsbrugh wrote that the weather was "too good," and he was constantly uneasy lest a blizzard, coming in the wake of weeks of mild weather, might do unusual damage. His fears were without foundation, for its was not until February 11, that a norther of any consequence came, and it turned out to be a mild one.[28] This was the last norther of the season. On March 1, heavy rains placed a fine season in the ground, and grass put out almost a month earlier than usual. Cattle were fatter by the end of March than they usually were at this time of year. Horsbrugh referred to them as "beauties" and "the fattest in the land."[29] Rains during the middle of April gave the grass another growth, and during the first week in May it poured for days. Horsbrugh wrote:

We have just been experiencing the heaviest and most continued rainfall that I have seen since I came here. In consequence our mails have been stopped for over a week, and the inconvenience is very great, especially at this time of the year, which is the most important selling season. All the creeks have been swollen to the size of decent rivers, and the roads have been washed out. I fancy the railroads have suffered, as some mail I have been expecting for weeks has not yet come to hand. However, the benefit to the range is enormous, and the grass is a picture for this time of the year. The tanks are brimfull, and everything looks more favorable for the ranching business than I have ever seen.[30]

Spring range work was considerably delayed on account of rain. The weather turned dry suddenly in July, and the fall work was held up over a week on account of lack of rain. On

[27]Spur Records, VI, 40.
[28]Spur Records, VI, 20, 32, 40, 62, 81, 116; IV, 55, 59.
[29]Spur Records, VI, 120, 127.
[30]Spur Records, VI, 174.

August 18, rains began again and continued at intervals throughout the fall.[31] On September 29, Horsbrugh wrote, "The winter grass promises to be very fine, and cattle will go into the winter fat."[32]

The calf crop in 1890 was better than it had been the two previous years, but it was still below normal—11,860 calves from 24,337 cows, or approximately 48 per cent.[33] The market was slightly lower than it had been the year before, but by selling at opportune times, Horsbrugh managed to get slightly better prices than in 1889. Two-year-old steers averaged $16.50; but there was no sale for heifer cattle, except at a sacrifice. The total sales for the year amounted to only 4,714. The company began the winter with about 6,000 more cattle on the range than it had the winter before, or approximately 50,000 head.

The Spur Records are incomplete from 1891 to 1894, inclusive. The letter books for the period are missing; and, consequently, such data as are available must be gotten from the brand book, the payroll, and the ledgers. The years 1892 and 1893 were extremely dry and 1894 was but little better. The effects of the drouth on the calf crops are indicative of the way the ranching industry generally fared. The calf crop in 1891 was 11,121; in 1892 there were 7,591 calves; in 1893, the number dropped to 6,717. The exact number in 1894 is not given, but it was about the same as in 1893. The herd not only suffered from light calf crops during these three years, but from heavy die-ups during the winters as well. The sales for the period were irregular: 6,617 in 1891; 9,929 in 1892; 2,171 in 1893; and 11,321 in 1894.[34] Prices remained approximately the same as in 1890.

Heavy fall rains in 1894 fell in time to make an abundance of winter grass. The winter was severe, but the cattle went through the cold weather of January and February in good condition. Heavy snows followed by heavy rains in March caused the grass to be "magnificent" in May and June, and the rest of the year was fairly seasonable. The calf crop of 1895 was better than it had been for the last three years, approximately 9,000. The sales for the year were 3,961, and the price was better than it had been since 1880.[35] Two-year-old steers averaged $19.

---

[31] Spur Records, VI, 232, 279, 285.
[32] Spur Records, X, 251.
[33] Spur Records, XLI, 5.
[34] Spur Records, LXI, 6, 7, 8, 9.
[35] Spur Records, LXI, 10.

Weather conditions during 1896 were very much like those of 1890. A mild winter was followed by an early seasonable spring. Horsbrugh was in better spirits than he had been for six years. On April 29 he wrote:

Night before last we had a heavy rain in our west pasture, and south of here in the east pasture; I have not had the particulars yet, but it looks like a flood; here it rained and hailed heavily for a while. It is needless to say that the range never looked as fine for the time of the year; grass is magnificent, and I have never, since I came here, seen it so far advanced in April. We undoubtedly will have a splendid range all summer, and I think all our tanks are now full. The crops at the farm are looking promising.[36]

The fickleness of Texas weather is shown by a letter from Horsbrugh to the home office on June 13, or only two and a half months later:

It is still deplorably dry; all the ranges for many miles around are in the same fix; watering places have gone dry that were never known to do so before; and there is no sign of any relief. Now and then a heat shower blows up, and makes a heavy shower of hail and rain on one spot, but we have not been favored beyond a light shower on Wednesday night, which did one valuable service to us; it put out a big prairie fire on the plains north of us; that, owing to a change in the wind, was threatening us. But there has been no rain to do any good, and no sign of any. I fear we must consider our corn as gone, and I do not think any nester in the country will make anything. After tomorrow the branding work stops, and all the men will be engaged in working for water along the creeks and pushing the cattle to the [water] places. By stopping all other work we can get along all right and keep the cattle watered; water is plentiful in Catfish and Duck Creeks, and can be got at easily, and by constant work all our cattle can be kept in water, and thus stand a long siege. I have had one outfit making waterings on Catfish since the 1st inst., and thousands of cattle are using them. I shall divide up our force between the two pastures, and we shall do very well. The men can also keep a constant lookout for fires; there is now great danger, the grass being like tinder, and the sun almost hot enough to set it alight.[37]

A month later the rains came. For several days the streams were up and the mails stopped. Grass made a new growth, but in August the weather turned dry, and the men were put at

[36]Spur Records, VIII, 6.
[37]Spur Records, VIII, 24.

scraping the creek beds again.[38] It was beginning to look as if a real drouth was setting in, but uneasiness was soon checked by general rains during the middle of September. The fall rains made splendid grass for the winter.[39] Notwithstanding the two short drouths during the year, cattle remained in good condition throughout the year.

The calf crop in 1896 was slightly better than it had been the year before; 9,578 were branded. Sales were light that year, only 2,252 head, most of which were two-year-old steers; there was practically no demand for beef cattle.[40] The price of the two-year-olds, however, was better than it had been in a decade; they brought $20 a head.

The next year, 1897, was what the cattlemen classed as a "good year." The rainfall was but slightly more than in 1896, but it was more evenly distributed. No water shortages occurred. The effects of the dry spells during the year before were manifest in the 1897 calf crop. Horsbrugh commented upon this fact on September 30:

I notice on the range that what I said this summer is coming true, that the period of very hot dry weather interferred with the habits of the cattle last summer, with the effect of causing a certain number of calves to come late this year by a couple of months.[41]

Notwithstanding the delays, the calf crop went to 10,148, the largest since 1891. The market was better in 1897 than it had been since 1885. There was a big demand for all classes of cattle. For once the company was fortunate in its selling policy. Having sold light the two previous years the Ranch had a surplus of marketable cattle in 1897. In all, 9,035 head were marketed at a price 30 per cent better than the year before. Two-year-old steers averaged $27.50. Three-year-old steers brought $32.50, and 3,000 old cows sold at an average price of $22.[42]

Light rains in the fall of 1897 caused the Ranch to start the winter of 1897-1898 with less than the normal amount of

[38]By "scraping" was meant the excavation of large holes in the creek beds by means of scrapers. Water trickled into these holes from the sand in the creek bottoms.
[39]Spur Records, VII, 395; VIII, 56, 57, 58, 62.
[40]Spur Records, VIII, 9.
[41]Spur Records, VIII, 241.
[42]Spur Records, VIII, 97, 159, 251, 264.

grass. A mild winter, however, prevented unusual losses. The spring of 1898 was dryer than usual, but there was sufficient moisture to give the grass a fair start in March. Since there had been no big rains since the previous September, surface water became scarce during April and May. Hot winds in June began to make Horsbrugh feel anxious. On June 4, 1898 he wrote:

Weather: this is a sore subject. I have never known this country to get rain enough [as a matter of fact, he had known it to get enough rain for as long as a year at a time] for however hard it falls for a while, it dries up rapidly, and before long the country seems to be worse off than ever. This is on account of the hot winds. Lately, we have been having extra hot weather for this time of the year, which, as a rule, is much cooler and pleasanter than later on in the year; but recently it has been going to 100° in the shade. The grass which two weeks ago was so pretty and green, has dried up and will now burn easily.[43]

Rains came during July and August, however, and winter found the grass good and the cattle fat.

The calf crop of 1898 amounted to 11,154, or a thousand more than the year before. The Spanish-American War caused prices to reach the highest peak since 1884. Two-year-old steers sold for $28 and yearling heifers at $21. Old cows and three-year-old steers brought about the same as the year before.[44]

During 1898, the Spur Ranch started experimenting with the new Pasteur blackleg serum. Blackleg had never been a serious malady in Northwest Texas, but almost every year a small loss resulted from it. Horsbrugh gave an account of the blackleg situation in a letter to the home office, February 25, 1898:

I have on hand some of the Pasteur Vaccine you wrote about and the apparatus for administering it, but have not yet used it. There has [sic] been no recurrences of the evil amongst any of the calves, and I am a little unwilling to use it if I can do without it. I shall, however, vaccinate the calves from the white faced herd, especially those it is necessary to wean, as I find that it is amongst those that have been recently weaned suddenly off from the cows and forced to make a great change of diet that blackleg is apt to occur. I talked about this with Messrs. Bowie and Prentice, both of Denver; their case, however, is a little different for the reason that blackleg is more virulent in the northern states than here; also the fact

[43]Spur Records, VIII, 375.
[44]Spur Records, VIII, 312, 320, 330, 336, 362, 393, 422.

they have to wean off a great many calves on account of the long and severe winters making it necessary to take extra precautions against this disease. My hesitancy against using the Vaccine comes from the fact that I happen to know of some cases where it has not worked well and where the loss was considerable after in-occulation [sic]. However, I have been giving a good deal of attention to this matter, and indeed it is very difficult to avoid hearing about it; as you say, the business has been industriously pushed for the last year, especially; and the outfit that is running the Pasteur remedies must be coining money, as the country is covered by their circulars and testimonials as well as agents. There is one drawback connected with its general use on the range, and that is expense. The expense of doctoring all our calves would be very much more than several years' losses from the disease. In order to be properly administered the remedy must be done twice, and at a time when nothing else is done to the calf. Branding and marking must be done at another time; so special work has to be done for the purpose, not to speak of the fact the medicine costs 10 cents a dose.[45]

The Spur outfit continued to restrict the use of blackleg serum to the Hereford herd, as it proved impractical when applied to ordinary range cattle.

It was a good thing that the cattle began the winter of 1898-1899 fat and on a splendid winter range. The winter was very severe, and had it not been for the condition of the cattle, a heavy die-up would have followed. On December 10, 1898, Horsbrugh reported to London:

I have to inform you that we have been visited with the worst blizzard that we have ever had in December. It has stopped snowing and blowing now, but the drifts are very deep. All business of course is at a standstill, especially in the office here, as I think every ink bottle and supply of ink is frozen. We have been principally employed in keeping warm which is no easy matter in these wooden houses in such weather. Our cattle will stand it fairly well, as they are in good condition, but cattle that are poor will suffer greatly. It is rare that we have such a fall of snow, accompanied by a blizzard like this, and especially in December. The last time we had anything equal to this was in January, 1888; then it was worse and got colder, but this may be followed up by worse weather. I had some men out in the West side of the range branding calves, and I am anxious to hear from them. The country over there is rough and has lots of shelter, and they will undoubtedly come through all right; upon the plains north of us it has been severe, and as it came on so suddenly, following warm weather, some people

[45]Spur Records, VIII, 326-327.

must have been caught unprepared for it, and I have no doubt that we shall hear of loss of life. It is a great cause for rejoicing on our part that we all got back from the railroad, having turned over everything we had to deliver, and this bad spell did not strike us on the way home.[46]

The roads were blocked with snow drifts and ice for five days —a most unusual thing in the Spur country.

Other blizzards followed, and a severe winter gave way to a dry spring.[47] There was no rain at all during March and April, and before it rained in May surface water was becoming exceedingly scarce.[48] However, heavy rains in June, July, and November provided fall and winter grass.[49]

The calf crop for 1899 was 9,135, or approximately 2,000 less than the year before. The decrease was due to the severity of the winter, many cows having slipped their calves.[50] The sales of the year amounted to 6,332, mostly two-year-old steers which averaged $25.75 each.[51]

If in June, 1898, Horsbrugh had found it difficult to remember when the country ever had enough rain, before the end of 1900 he was wondering if he would ever see any more dry weather. From March to December it was rain, and more rain.[52] It rained every two weeks, and sometimes it rained for two weeks at a time. In many other years range work was interfered with by drouths, but this one year, it was delayed throughout the year by rain.[53] Much of the work was done on soggy ground with the men wearing slickers.

The winter of 1899-1900 brought no blizzards, and the northers were not bad. The calf crop of 1900 amounted to 9,903, not so good as the conditions warranted. Sales from the year totaled 5,315, which were fewer than any year since 1896.[54] Of this number less than 1,000 were old cows, and the rest were two-year-old

[46]Spur Records, VIII, 447-448.
[47]Spur Records, IX, 9, 330.
[48]Spur Records, X, 11, 12, 15, 19, 21, 28.
[49]Spur Records, X, 40, 42, 51, 57, 69, 74, 75.
[50]Spur Records, LXI, 10.
[51]The records, do not show by years the total number of cattle on the Spur Ranch past 1893, but a letter from Horsbrugh to the London office, January 4, 1899, states that at that time there were 39,745 head on the range, the smallest number, perhaps, since 1884.
[52]Spur Records, X, 121, 165, 180, 210, 225, 244, 268.
[53]Spur Records, X, 151, 247.
[54]Stock Register, 1885-1895, Spur Records, LXI, 10.

steers. Prices were still affected by the Spanish-American War, but were not so high as they had been the three previous years. Two-year-old steers averaged $25.[55]

Had Horsbrugh known in January, 1901, that another drouthy cycle was then setting in and would get worse and worse until 1904, he would have probably resigned at once and saved himself a thousand restless nights; but fortunately, or unfortunately, he did not know. The weather throughout 1901 was fretful and spasmodic. Throughout the spring and summer the only moisture came from local showers. Thunderstorms, which had wonderful electrical displays but little rain, were frequent. The cattle were nervous and restless, and the range poorer than it had been in ten years. The first general rain of the year came in September, but the grass had been nipped so short that it did not have time to make sufficient growth for good winter pasturage.[56]

The ideal weather and range conditions of 1900 together with the mild winter of 1900-1901 caused the calf crop of 1901 to skyrocket—13,321 head, or the best crop since 1887. Sales for the year were 5,898, two-year-old steers bringing $19.40.[57]

The winter of 1901-1902 was cold, dry, and blustering. Very little rain fell in 1902 until late summer, but it came in time to make a good crop of fall grass. The lack of grass during the previous year, followed by a severe winter, caused the calf crop of 1902 to be less than one-half that of the year before from approximately the same number of cows.[58] At the same time the loss resulting from lack of nourishment was about twice that of the year before. The sales of 1902 amounted to 5,196. The prices compensated in a small way for the heavy losses of the winter and the small calf crop. Two-year-old steers sold for $22.75, or approximately $3 a head more than the previous year.

The year 1903 was another memorable one. A mild winter with fair grass caused the calf crop to number 12,286. Snow and rains caused grass to put out early in the spring, and for a month prospects never seemed brighter. But by the middle of April rain was needed. In May it was needed badly. Horsbrugh watched for clouds which never came. Throughout the summer and fall

[55]Spur Records, IX, 409.
[56]Spur Records, X, 363, 366, 376, 392.
[57]Stock Register, 1885-1895, Spur Records, LXI, 10
[58]Spur Records, LXI, 10.

the only moisture came from small isolated showers which did little good and put out practically no surface water. The spring round-ups had to be suspended before the work was finished, and less than half the usual amount of rounding-up was done in the fall because of lack of surface water. The men were kept busy the rest of the time scraping creeks and digging wells. On the last day of the year Horsbrugh wrote:

Still dry, and no signs of rain. Rain just now would help in the sense that it would put out water in the tanks and holes; and if it should come warm this would be all right; but a cold, sleety rain such as is more than likely, if it rains at all this time of the year, would be fatal to many a cow that has weakened herself in her daily long walks to water. The greater part of West Texas is in a bad shape this winter, with only here and there a small spot where conditions are favorable, showing that the rain has been spotted. I understand that south-west and west of us it is very bad, and, if anything worse in New Mexico. The long and short of it is that to carry on this business we must have rain; usually, it rains enough though never too much; but 1903 will be remembered for a long time. I think that at most we had two inches of rain over the range at the end of February; and there were places then where it did not rain enough to put out stock water; and since we have had nothing but local showers at remote intervals which put out practically no water. It is the toughest and most disappointing year that I have ever known in the business.[59]

The sales for the year totaled 6,939, with two-year-old steers bringing $20.

On January 5, 1904, Horsbrugh wrote a friend in Dallas:

I am fairly well in health, but am very busy, and not feeling the best in the world. It simply won't rain, and as it has not done so since last February in this neighborhood; I suppose that it is not intended that we shall ever have any more. Under certain temporary drawbacks it is possible to struggle for a while in this distressful business, but a certain amount of water is necessary at all times; therefore, before long we shall have ceased to struggle. Of course as you remarked to me at Dallas, I was very much to blame for not having arranged for a proper amount of rain. I know it, and feel it keenly, but it can't be helped now.[60]

As the problem of getting stock water grew more and more serious, Horsbrugh reported to the London office, January 6:

[59]Spur Records, XI, 158-159.
[60]Spur Records, XI, 161.

I am doing the best I can by putting in more windmills [at places] where the grass is fair; as it is now, grass near the waterings is worn out and no good. If we can get water I think the cattle will come through the winter without unusual loss, but this depends on the weather and upon the luck we have with the wells we are sinking. It must be remembered that this is a very poor piece of country for well water. In some places, if one goes over 120 feet, salt is likely to show up, and fresh water is seldom got in large quantities. Our best wells are close to the plains, but we have large stretches of pasture lands that extend a long way from the plains. We have been having unusual bad luck with well-boring. I have one outfit that is now boring its fifth well in the country that we call the West Prong of Duck Creek and Marble Banks. . . . I am hoping daily to hear more from the boring going on at section 64, Block 2; that is a good grass country and very dry at present. . . . These extra expenses for wells are especially heavy on us this year; but it is necessary that they be incurred, as on them depends the getting of the cattle through the winter without bad losses. If cattle get water they can do with less grass; but of course even with those extra wells, a heavy spell of weather will have its bad effect; the loss will depend to a large extent on the earliness of spring rains which will bring grass.[61]

This was the last report Horsbrugh ever sent to London. The worries caused by the drouth and the land question were impairing his health. Probably fortunately for him, a few days later he received a letter from the Board requesting his resignation.

Horsbrugh's resignation did not improve the conditions which his successor Henry Johnstone had to face. He reported to the home office on February 20:

I returned yesterday evening from a three-day trip over the East pasture. The grass is very short everywhere, and in the Southwest corner there is absolutely none, and the cattle are apparently subsisting on the fallen mesquite leaves. So far, not many are dying, but with the most favorable weather I fear the loss will be considerable.[62]

On March 25, Johnstone wrote, "We are praying for a good rain which I believe would do more to relieve the general tension than the 'general European War' they are always predicting."[63]

April was as dry as March; but at last on May 3, 1904, a gen-

[61]Spur Records, XI, 168.
[62]Spur Records, XI, 216.
[63]Spur Records, XI, 262.

eral rain filled all tanks; it had been fourteen months since that had happened.[64] But the grass was too short and too dead to be revived perceptibly by a single rain, and on June 20 Johnstone commented, "At the present this country affords a fair illustration of what is described in holy writ as the 'abomination of desolation.' "[65] July was dry, but in August a series of rains broke the drouth, and insured fall grass.

The losses of the winter 1903-1904 were about twice those of an average winter. Over 10 per cent of the cattle three years old and older died. The records show that 1,664 hides were taken, and this represented less than a third of the cattle that died. As diligently as the men might try to keep up, a majority of the dead cattle were too decomposed when found to permit skinning. Hides of animals which had died of starvation were not worth much. The Ranch ordinarily did not resort to skinning, but in a year so disastrous as 1904 the price of the hides was sorely needed to offset the enormous losses. Johnstone shuddered when he thought of what the losses might have been if the winter had not been exceedingly mild. One blizzard like that of January, 1888, or of December, 1898, would have left 10,000 dead cattle in its wake.

The calf crop of 1904 was the smallest in the history of the Spur Ranch—a total of 5,774, less than half that of 1903. The sales amounted to 6,601 head, with two-year-old steers bringing $19.50.[66]

Cattle started into the winter of 1904-1905 in good condition and on a fair range. Johnstone reported to the home office January 5, 1905:

Cattle are in as good or better condition than I have seen them in this district for many years, and although we are now well on with the winter they have shrunk in flesh very little. . . . With reasonably favorable weather from now on and an early spring, we should come through the winter with a very light loss.[67]

This must have been cheering news for the Board of Directors in the light of the reports they had been getting for three years.

In January, 1905, Johnstone took up with the Board the mat-

[64]Spur Records, XI, 311.
[65]Spur Records, XI, 379.
[66]Spur Records, LXI, 10.
[67]Spur Records, XI, 615.

ter of making the number of cattle carried on the Ranch books jibe with the number actually on the range. With the exception of the calves which were actually counted when branded, the number of all other classes of cattle was arrived at by deductions, and never actually counted again except when herds were rounded up for trail purposes. Annual losses of 5 per cent were allowed for each class. If this amount were too much or too little the accumulated surplus or loss over a period of twenty years would become considerable. Johnstone had become convinced that the deductions had been too little. He wrote the London office, January 2, 1905:

> The total number of cattle on tally in January, 1904, was 46,932, of which 1000 were at White Deer, leaving 45,932 in the pasture here. I believe that the land owned by the company amounts to about 428,000 acres, and assuming that the herd figures were correct this would give in the neighborhood of nine acres to the animal, allowing nothing for horses and stray stock of all kinds. There used to be a theory that ten acres would support a cow, and it may have been sufficient before these pastures got heavily stocked and the grass largely tramped or eaten out. One would scarcely be safe to count on less than fifteen acres to the animal now days, although in exceptionally good years—twelve might do. Last winter there were parts of the pasture where 100 acres would not have kept a cow alive.[68]

By such deductions Johnstone concluded that the cattle count on the books was several thousand too many. Johnstone estimated that a range count would not show over 32,021. The Board received this report with long faces. Johnstone suggested that the book count be marked down at once, but the members of the Board thought their feelings could be better salved by marking off a part of the excessive book count a year for three or four years.

The calf crop for 1905 was small, as the cows had not recovered from the poverty of 1903 and 1904; the crop totaled 7,734. The sales amounted to 6,321, with two-year-old steers bringing $21.[69]

With the available records at hand it is not possible to trace the weather conditions on the Spur Ranch from 1905 to

[68]Spur Records, XI, 607. The present policy of the Swensons on this same ranch is an allowance of about eighteen acres per animal.
[69]Spur Records, LXI, 10.

1909. The general weather conditions in Northwest Texas during this period were about average, there being no unusually drouthy or wet years. The calf crop in 1906 amounted to 11,186; in 1907, 8,944; in 1908, 9,323; and in 1909, 7,576. The sales in 1906 were 4,831, with two-year-old steers selling at $21.50; the records do not show the sales or prices from 1907 to July, 1909, at which time the last Spur cattle had been taken over by the Swensons and associates.

From the time the Espuela Land and Cattle Company, Limited, purchased the Spur Ranch in 1885 until the Spur brand was discontinued in 1909, the Spur managers were constantly taking steps to improve the herd. It has already been pointed out that the Spur range was originally stocked by the purchase of more than sixty small herds from different parts of the country. The cattle of all of the herds were what was then termed "Texas scrub cattle." The name was indeed appropriate; they were of all shapes, sizes, and colors—red, white, black, piebald, and brindle. The matter of breeding up the herd to where the animals would be of uniform shape, size, and color was a long, slow, and tedious process. The Spur Ranch resorted to the same method of herd improvement used by all the other large ranches at the time, namely, by providing the herd as rapidly as possible with high grade bulls.

Inasmuch as the Ranch kept from 1,500 to 1,800 bulls on the range all the time, it was not practical to begin by stocking with expensive, high grade bulls.[70] Consequently, the bull herd was built up by purchasing about 200 high grade Shorthorn and Hereford bulls a year from 1885 to 1890. In addition to these the best male specimens from each year's calf crop were saved for bulls. In 1885 and 1886, bull calves were selected from all over the range during the general round-ups. For instance, of the 207 calves branded at Chimney Creek in 1886, 4 were kept for bulls, and of the 153 at Red Mud, 3 were kept. This policy was gradually dropped, however, as fast as a better one could be inaugurated. In 1887 about 300 of the best cows on the Ranch in regard to weight, shape, and color were segregated in the Tap pasture and mated with the best bulls on the Ranch.[71] The

[70]The Spur Ranch made a practice of keeping one bull for every fifteen cows in the breeding herd.
[71]Spur Records, IV, 242, 249, 281.

male calves of these cows became range bulls, and the female calves were kept to become the mothers of the next generation of herd bulls. The bulls for the small graded herd were always imported from regular cattle breeders.

For several years the managers of the Spur Ranch could not decide whether to breed towards a Shorthorn or a Hereford herd.[72] Horsbrugh favored Shorthorns on the grounds that they were better hustlers and multiplied faster than Herefords.[73] The members of the Board of Directors, however, had heard from their Scotch and English friends who were directors in other American ranching syndicates, that Herefords were the better suited to American range conditions.[74] In 1889 Horsbrugh reluctantly set out to make the Spur herd eventually a white-faced one. Thoroughbred, registered bulls were purchased for the small herd of graded cows, which became known as the Hereford herd.[75] Some registered heifers were obtained, and the Ranch began to raise a limited number of registered cattle.

The Hereford herd paid for its keep in two ways. It provided high grade herd bulls at only a small part of the amount it would have cost to have purchased them; and it furnished the herd with home-grown, acclimated bulls. Bulls grown in other parts of the country never made satisfactory herd bulls. Horsbrugh wrote, August 6, 1889:

> Cattle do much better on the range where they are born than if they were sent to range from Kansas and Missouri. Bulls sent in from other states go off and stay by themselves at the very season that they should stay with the cows. A low percentage of calves is often due to the bulls.[76]

The results of the breeding efforts were becoming manifest by 1895. Most of the herd had white faces. By 1900 practically all the Spur cattle were white faced. By 1905 a considerable amount of uniformity in shape and color was becoming apparent; notwithstanding, the range cattle still had a great deal of mongrel blood. Johnstone observed in January, 1905, that one of the best

---

[72]They also considered Polled Angus; but in view of the great expense of shipping the bulls from Scotland, they dropped the idea.

[73]Spur Records, IV, 158, 180, 185, 207, 208.

[74]Spur Records, IV, 19, 89, 100. VI, 216, 262. General opinion does not bear out Horsbrugh's idea of the superior range qualities of the Shorthorn.

[75]Spur Records, VIII, 245, 247.

[76]Spur Records, IV, 208.

features of the Spur cattle was the strain of Shorthorn blood upon which the herd was founded. He recommended that the Spur Ranch follow a policy recently begun by the Matadors and JA people of introducing a proportion of Shorthorn bulls in the herd with the view of increasing the size of the cattle.[77] The records do not indicate whether or not this practice was ever begun.

[77]Spur Records, XI, 602.

Table 1. CATTLE SALES BY YEARS

Year	Amount	Year	Amount
1889	$ 25,406	1898	159,417
1890	68,801	1899	157,639
1891	93,989	1900	133,029
1892	109,800	1901	124,121
1893	16,826	1902	113,140
1894	188,328	1903	114,687
1895	80,413	1904	99,882
1896	43,971	1905	132,230
1897	179,531	1906	93,683

IX: *FENCES*

BARBED WIRE played a curious role in the cattle business from 1879 to 1885. Cursed and praised, it brought almost revolutionary changes. Although it was patented several years earlier, not until 1870 could a few cattlemen be induced to try it.[1] Opposition to its use was strong, almost violent. The Commissioners Court of San Saba County presented a petition to the Texas Legislature, February 18, 1879, asking that a law be passed against the erection of barbed wire fences on the grounds that they were dangerous to stock.[2] The Stockmen's Association of Nolan and Fisher counties passed a resolution as late as November, 1883, declaring that the land west of the 100th meridian was fit only for grazing and petitioning the Legislature to prohibit the erection of fences west of that line.[3] In spite of opposition, however, once barbed wire got a foothold in the cattle country, its headway was rapid. A drift fence 175 miles long was erected in the Texas Panhandle in 1881.[4] The same year the Shoe Bar Ranch was enclosed with a fence. In 1882 John Adair and Charles Goodnight began fencing the JA lands in Armstrong and Donley counties. Just south of the Spur range R. C. Burns, then manager of the Llano Cattle Company, began fencing the Curry Comb pastures in 1883. By 1884 it was apparent that all Northwest Texas would be enclosed with barbed wire. Interesting to note was the change of attitude on the part of individual cattlemen. As long as one did not own the land grazed by his cattle, or have it leased, he was bitterly opposed to the whole institution of fencing. When he was forced, by dire necessity, to acquire title to his land and grass, fences immediately lost all of their horrors for him, and he became a champion of barbed wire.

While Colonel A. M. Britton was stretching his legs and sipping whiskey and soda in English drawing rooms, in the spring and summer of 1884, Lomax in Fort Worth was sitting up nights

---

[1] For account of "The Introduction of Barbed Wire into Texas" see article by R. D. Holt in West Texas Historical Association *Yearbook*, VI, 65-79.

[2] Senate Journal, 1879, p. 308.

[3] Quoted from the Abilene *Reporter* in *The Wool Journal*, November 27, 1883.

[4] Haley, J. Evetts, "And Then Came Barbed Wire to Change History's Course," in *The Cattleman*, March, 1927.

getting prices of wire and posts, and writing long letters of instructions to C. L. Groff. Groff, the range boss, was spending
the day and parts of the night in the saddle attending to the
regular Ranch routine and making fence preparations.

Inasmuch as the necessary materials and labor for enclosing
the entire Ranch could not be obtained in one season, Lomax
and Groff decided to fence, during 1884, only the south and
east sides of Block 1 of the Houston and Great Northern lands.
The Company placed the wire and the posts on the ground and
let the contract for the actual construction to a man by the name
of Clemonds from Kentucky. The late W. R. Stafford was a
member of the construction gang. The fencing outfit began on
the southwest corner of Block 1 (southwest corner of section 12)
and worked eastward approximately on the Block lines around
to the northeast corner of the Block (northeast corner of section 407), a distance of fifty-seven miles. During the fall and
the winter of 1884-1885, this fence served as a drift fence, and
accomplished three purposes: it prevented the Spur cattle from
drifting south or east; it kept the Matador and Llano cattle off
the Spur lands; and it caused drovers taking herds through that
vicinity to go around the main body of the Spur range.

Fencing operations were vigorously renewed in the spring of
1885. Beginning at the northwest corner of Block 1 a line was
built south along the west edge of the Block to the southwest
corner, a distance of thirty-four miles, where it connected with
the fence constructed the year before. Another line was built
from the northwest corner of the Block east, jogging southward
around the Burleson County School lands, to the northeast corner
of the Block, a distance of fourteen miles, where it connected
with the north end of the drift fence. This completely enclosed
Block 1. Before the year ended, the south and west sides of the
West Pasture, a distance of fifty-five miles, had been built. At
that time the West Pasture was composed of all of the 111 sections of Block 2, all of Block 7, and 101 sections of Block 8 of
the Houston and Great Northern lands. In the spring of 1886
a fencing outfit under John O. Wilkerson constructed the north
line of the West Pasture, connecting with the west fence of
Block 1.[5] The fencing of the West Pasture enclosed a strip of
loose sandy ground between the East and West Pastures from

[5]W. R. Stafford to W. C. H., interview, February 23, 1930.

two to four miles wide, belonging to the state. This strip, covered with scrub oak and of little value for grazing, was eventually to be homesteaded by settlers, some of whom gave the managers of the Spur Ranch considerable annoyance.

After the enclosure of the outside boundaries of the East and West Pastures, the fencing problem consisted of alterations of the main outside fences, the building of fences enclosing new lands acquired by the Company, subdivision fences, and making repairs. In November, 1888, Lomax recommended to the Company that a fence be constructed from the northeast corner of section 52 of Block 7 to the southwest corner of section 12 of Block 1. He pointed out that this step would enable the Ranch to take down twelve miles of its own boundary fence and would increase the size of the pasture about ten sections. The increase was state lands, but as they lay along the rough, broken reaches of the Salt Fork Valley, it would no doubt be years before they would be taken up by settlers.[6]

By 1889 the Company had secured control, in part by purchase and in part by lease, of thirteen sections of land immediately south of the West Pasture. As the area was outside of the pastures, it was being used by outsiders, and the Company was deriving no benefit whatever from it. Lomax, before retiring, recommended that the lands be fenced. Horsbrugh, after becoming manager, urged it. In the summer of 1889 when the Company sent one of its directors, John McNab, as an official inspector of the Ranch properties, he also favored it.[7] By December, Horsbrugh had received instructions to proceed with the fencing. He hurried preparations for the work, at the same time writing to McNab:

There have been more cattle brought and turned loose in that country, and from what I can hear, the intention is, if possible, to slip them in on us this winter. I have concluded to keep two more men than I intended to watch that line this winter.[8]

Two months' delay was occasioned by waiting for the surveyors to locate the lines. By the middle of March the thirteen sections were enclosed.[9]

[6]Spur Records, V, 8.
[7]Spur Records, IV, 162.
[8]Spur Records, IV, 113.
[9]Spur Records, IV, 49.

From time to time division and subdivision fences were built. In 1885 a horse pasture containing seven sections was enclosed immediately west of headquarters. Five years later the fence was moved and extended in order to make the horse pasture five sections larger.[10] The Houston Tap and Brazoria lands, containing twenty sections, were fenced into what was referred to as the Tap Pasture. Just south of the Tap Pasture was an eight section enclosure known as Dockum Pasture. Immediately north and east of headquarters was a fenced tract of twenty-three sections called the Duck Creek Pasture. In the southwest corner of the East Pasture were Duck Camp Pasture, Faulkner's and Bird's pastures of four sections each, Graham's Pasture of two sections and South Pasture of thirteen sections. Each of the six camps had small enclosures of a hundred acres or less called horse traps or "starve-outs." Notwithstanding these sub-enclosures a person could ride in a single direction in either the East or West Pastures for twenty-five miles without encountering a fence.

Materials for fences were always a considerable problem for the Espuela Land and Cattle Company. So great was the demand for barbed wire during the 80's that merchants at Colorado City found it hard to keep large supplies on hand. The price, to the chagrin of Lomax and Horsbrugh, fluctuated and increased. The wire for enclosing the East and West pastures, 1884-1886, cost slightly less than $3 a hundred pounds plus the freight from Colorado City to the Ranch, which was 70 cents a hundred. When Lomax was ready to fence the thirteen sections south of the West Pasture in 1888, he was shocked when he received a $3 per hundred quotation from Cowan and Shear, merchants at Colorado City. The shock was intensified a few days later upon receiving a letter from Cowan and Shear saying that the $3 quotation was a mistake and that the price was $4.[11] When he received instructions in December, 1889, to proceed with the fencing, he had just learned of the formation of a barbed wire trust. He hurried to purchase 21,000 pounds of wire before the price advanced. In spite of this haste he paid $4.10 a hundred for it at Colorado City, which added to the freight to the Ranch cost almost $5 a hundred.[12]

[10]Spur Records, XV, 22.
[11]Spur Records, II, 294.
[12]Spur Records, IV, 81, 103.

Posts were as difficult to procure as wire. Those used to enclose the East and West pastures in 1884-1886 were mesquite, cut and hauled from the Croton and J2 Breaks immediately east of the East Pasture. Contracts were let to individual wood-cutters to cut, haul, and distribute the posts along the fence lines. These posts cost the company from ten to fifteen cents each, depending upon the distance hauled.[13]

The post problem in 1888 was extremely vexing to Lomax. He wrote to Horsbrugh, then at Colorado City on business, March 15:

I have sent Harry Brown to Plainview and Quitaque to see what posts can be got [for]. Unless we can get them for 10¢ [each] laid on the caprock, it will be better to get them at Colorado. I wrote you in a former letter to see Cameron and Burton and find if you cannot beat 10¢ for them. Even if they cost 10¢, if they weigh twenty pounds each and if freight can be got at 70¢ (per hundred from Colorado to the Ranch), they will cost but 24¢ (each). Getting them hauled from Quitaque will be an uncertain job, and freighters will not go there for less than 1¢ (per hundred) a mile. So if it is sixty miles, the freight will be almost as much as from Colorado, and we are not likely to get as good posts. . . . I am chafing at the delays we meet on every side, and hope you will close every-thing up as (soon as) you can, for it won't do to wait your return and subsequent mails.[14]

Horsbrugh, like a true Scotchman, was able to get posts in places overlooked by Lomax. In writing to J. Earl Hodges, secretary in the London office, on December 23, 1889, he told of cutting posts from the Company's lands:

I think I shall have no difficulty in securing material for the fence (of the thirteen sections) for $1500. In any case, if I see it is going to be more I shall let you know. I have got more posts off the ground than we thought we should get. Stokes' outfit managed to cut 800 good (mesquite) posts. It was originally supposed that 400 to 500 would be all we would get. It is a good thing that we got these as they would have been stolen soon.[15]

During the dry, hard years of the 90's when the settlers were extremely short of money, Horsbrugh was able to get good mesquite posts cut in the Croton Breaks delivered at the Ranch

---

[13]W. R. Stafford to Clifford B. Jones, interview, February 23, 1930.
[14]Spur Records, II, 294-295.
[15]Spur Records, IV, 99.

for as low as ten cents each. He reported to the London office
on December 31, 1897:

I have 3600 fence posts on hand which I have purchased from
time to time at an average cost of ten cents each delivered here. I
did this because they were very cheap and an article which is always
needed. Also they are getting scarce in this part of the country.
Before long they will have to be shipped in, and hauled from the
railroad at an expensive rate, perhaps at 20 to 25 cents a post.[16]

For corner posts either mesquite or cedar was used. Usually
they were from ten to fourteen inches in diameter, placed at
least four feet in the ground and were well braced. Gate posts
were nearly always of cedar. The customary size was thirteen
and one-half feet long and not less than eight inches in diameter
at the butt end. These posts cost about $2 each besides the freight
from the railroad.

Horsbrugh was particular about his corral posts. Ordinarily
cedar was used, but Horsbrugh developed a taste for *bois d'arc*.
The following letter to Wm. Cameron and Company at Quanah
indicates how well his Scotch inheritance aided him while bargaining for corral posts:

I have your favor of the 9th inst. giving prices on corral posts.
In answer to it, I will try a small load, although the freight from
Quanah here makes the price to us almost prohibitive. You say that
you have 9 foot posts weighing 60 to 70 pounds, and that the
price is 30¢ taken as they come, or picked out at 35¢; also 12 foot
posts weighing from 100 to 125 pounds at 85¢. I will send a wagon
or two from here in a few days, and will ask you to kindly make
me a trial shipment consisting of 50 corral posts 9 feet long and
weighing 70 pounds, to be picked at 35¢ a piece; I will also take
25 twelve foot posts weighing 125 pounds each at 85¢. You understand that I want the posts to be of the best of their kind, and
similar to what I would pick, and I am willing to pay the best
price for them. I am going to leave it to your judgment and kindness to send me the best you can, and doubtless other orders will
depend upon your selection. I have other offers from Colorado on
posts, but they do not have *bois d'arc*, and I am paying you considerably more than I can get good cedar ones for, as I prefer the
bois d'arc.[17]

The only item of fence construction whose price decreased
as time passed was labor. Practically all fence building was done

[16]Spur Records, VIII, 293.
[17]Spur Records, IX, 197.

by contract. The Company placed all the material on the ground
and contracted for the actual construction. The labor agreement for the drift fence of 1884 called for $47.50 a mile.[18] The
next year labor was to be had for $38 a mile. The difference in
price was due primarily to the difference in the roughness of
the country fenced.[19]

A formal agreement between Lomax and B. F. Powell of
Snyder on March 13, 1888, specified that Powell should receive $20 a mile for fence construction, and "that the work be
done in a thorough and workmanlike manner, and that the
fence would consist of four wires, with posts set forty feet
apart, set 2 feet in the ground and well tamped, with three
stays to each panel and all the wires well attached."[20] All materials were to be placed on the ground by the Company.

The fencing of the thirteen sections south of the West Pasture in 1890 was done by the ranch hands. The work took place
in January and February, a time when the hands were not
needed for other duties. By 1900, the labor for fence-building
could be had for $15 a mile.[21]

An indispensable item in the building of ranch fences was
stays. It was customary to put three stays between each two posts.
Prior to 1888 small mesquite poles from one to two inches in

[18]Spur Records, I, 21.
[19]The following formal agreement is a typical fence-building contract and is
indicative of the kind of fence constructed:

Agreement entered into this eighth day of August, eighteen hundred and
eight-five between A. B. Woody on the one hand and the Espuela Land and
Cattle Company on the other. The said A. B. Woody hereby agrees and contracts to build for the said Espuela Land and Cattle Company about eighteen
(18) miles of fence, commencing at or near the mouth of Red Mud, thence
to the southeast corner of section 111 of Block 2; to be constructed of four
(4) wires, and the posts to be well set in the ground and not be more than
forty (40) feet apart; to have not less than three stays put on each panel of
not more than forty (40) feet. And at the completion of the said fence, the
Espuela Land and Cattle Company, Limited, hereby agrees to pay to said
A. B. Woody on demand at the rate of thirty-eight dollars ($38) for each mile
of fence completed by the said A. B. Woody. And the Espuela Land and Cattle
Company further agrees: to have the line of fence indicated by means of
stakes put in the ground, to have not less than four (4) stakes to the mile,
and also undertakes to have all material placed on the line of fence at such
convenient distances as may be demanded by the said A. B. Woody.

(signed) *A. B. Woody*
The Espuela Land and
Cattle per C. L. Groff
Supt.

[20]Spur Records, II, 279.
[21]Spur Records, X, 254.

diameter were used. The wire was attached to them by means of staples. In 1896 Horsburgh started using baling wire instead of staples for fastening the wire to the stays.[22]

Wire was attached to posts with staples. Galvanized staples were bought by the hundred-pound keg. Ordinarily it required six pounds of staples for a mile of fence.

The total cost of fence-building decreased from $175 a mile in 1885 to $136 a mile in 1901.[23] The reduction was due for the most part to a decrease in labor costs. In 1902 the Ranch had 247 miles of fence, valued at $37,350. At the same time the buildings and corrals on the Ranch were listed at $9,000.[24]

The original boundary fences were not always placed on the boundary lines. While building the fence on the east side of Block 1 in 1884, the line was run some distance west of the boundary in order to avoid the rough country in the Croton Breaks, leaving a considerable strip of Spur land east of, and outside, the fence. This action later led to an extended controversy and lawsuit with the Matador people. A similar instance on the west side, however, terminated satisfactorily without legal complications. Horsbrugh wrote Hodges on April 6, 1898:

> You will observe from the accompanying sketch that our boundary fence on the north of Block 8 when it comes to sections 95 and 94, running west, cuts across them instead of surrounding them. This was done, as will be noticed, for convenience and to save building up into the roughs and back again; also three miles south you will see that the string of fence running south cuts across section 12 instead of going around the angle, thus saving a mile or so of fence. I may mention that I have been getting rent for these outside portions of sections 94, 95, and 12 from Major Watts. I wrote you before that at Fort Worth this gentleman and I had a talk, and while of course he was ready and willing to give back the land whenever we wanted it, . . . he is very anxious to keep it for another year.[25]

The Ranch fences were in need of almost constant repair. The upkeep of a fence through a period of twenty years approached the original cost. Native posts, which were more than nine-tenths of all the posts used by the Ranch, rotted in about twenty years. Horsbrugh wrote in October, 1900:

[22]Spur Records, VII, 370.
[23]Spur Records, X, 281.
[24]Spur Records, X, 472.
[25]Spur Records, VIII, 349.

I have had a great many (posts) put in lately, most of the old ones having been there too long (since 1884); and there are still places in the east line down in Kent County where the fence is getting so that a hard wind is liable to blow it over.[26]

Wire, no matter how tightly it had been stretched, would slacken in a few years. The Ranch used painted wire altogether prior to 1900. The paint in time wore off in places, especially where the wire was stapled to the posts. The places where the paint came off soon rusted. After fifteen or twenty years the wire was so weakened by rust it could no longer be stretched tightly. If the fence was to be kept in first class order, it was necessary to discard old wire and put on new. Stays rotted out in ten or twelve years. In 1904, thirty-three miles of the east line of Block 1, which had been built in 1884, was completely overhauled. The labor contract for taking the old fence down and building a new one in its place was let to a Mr. Green for $11 a mile. He also furnished stays at 2 cents each. The company placed the new wire and posts on the ground.[27]

Aside from general, periodic overhauling of fences, minor repairs had to be made constantly. Water-gaps (places where a fence crossed a ravine, creek, or river) frequently washed out. Persons wishing to enter or leave the Ranch pastures often knocked the fence down and crossed if a gate were not at hand. Some of them took the trouble to staple the wires back to the post, but others did not. Nearly every herd had a few outlaws, old cows, steers, or bulls, which were professional fence-breakers. These took a savage delight in going through fences, breaking the wires and posts. Occasionally a frightened horse or cow, or a stampeding herd would run pell-mell into a fence and break some of the wires.

The Spur Ranch employed men whose sole duty the year round was to ride and repair fences. Although fence riding was a job despised and looked down upon by the cowboy profession, managers were very particular whom they selected as fence riders. Reasons for their caution may be seen in a letter from Horsbrugh to W. A. Bradley, August 16, 1890:

I wish you to take the job of keeping up the fence, (the job) that Brown had. I know you would do good work, and that

26Spur Records, VI, 322.
27Spur Records, XI, 257.

I can rely on your doing it honestly; it is a job where a man is left mostly to himself, and it is not everyone who, under the circumstances, would do his best for the interests of the Company; and it is therefore because I can rely on your working the same when you are off to yourself as at other times that I wish you to take the fence wagon. I want the fence job held by a man I can trust.[28]

Aside from a man who regularly operated the fence wagon, cowhands while stationed at the various line camps devoted a part of their time to riding fence. In cases of an emergency a number of cowhands might be taken from their usual duties to repair fence. During the winter and July and August in the summer when there was no round-up or branding work to be done, the regular cowhands, much to their disgust, were often placed at fence-building or on fence-repairing details. In all, it cost the Company from $1,000 to $2,000 a year to keep the fences in repair.

Occasionally, the Ranch managers leased outlying sections of land to neighboring cattlemen for short periods of time. In those cases unused fences were taken down, the wire coiled, and posts taken up. The wire and posts were hauled to the nearest line camp where they might be watched by the cowhands stationed at the camp.[29]

An interesting question arose in 1891 as to whether fences were taxable. With more than $30,000 invested in fences, the Spur managers had never rendered a mile of fence for taxation. A new tax assessor of Scurry County, to which Kent and Garza counties were attached at the time, demanded assessment. Horsbrugh replied:

Regarding the fence, as this had not before been regarded as a necessary assessment either by your predecessor or any of the assessors in the different counties in which we pay taxes I do not return it. I think that you will see that the values of our land and cattle are affected by their being enclosed by a fence; for this reason it is not customary to assess us.[30]

It may require some imagination to see how a cow inside a fence is worth more than the same cow outside a fence, but apparently Horsbrugh's argument squelched the assessor.

[28]Spur Records, VI, 272.
[29]Spur Records, VII, 299.
[30]Spur Records, VI, 441.

After a fence had been built for fifteen or twenty years, it was not uncommon for neighboring cattlemen to forget who owned it. This lack of memory is evidenced in a letter from Horsbrugh to Browning and Holland, October 1, 1898:

> With reference to the part of fence lately moved by you, or your orders, on or about the north part of section 17 of the H. T. & B. Co. R. R. Survey, I have to formally notify you that same was the property of this Company, and request at the same time that you at once replace same. I find that I am not required by law to give any time in thus formally notifying you.[31]

One of the most vexing problems that the Spur managers had to face was the cutting of posts from the Spur lands by outsiders. The craze for posts was so great in August, 1900, that Horsbrugh, at considerable expense, posted sign boards over the pastures forbidding the cutting of posts. Wood cutters paid little attention to the notices. On October 9, 1900, Horsbrugh wrote: "The best way I find is to have a lot more posts cut than we immediately need, and have them piled up where they can't be stolen. In this way a lot of temptation is removed."[32] On January 4, 1901, he wrote again:

> There are many outfits stealing wood and posts in our pastures. We might as well get as much for ourselves as possible. It is impossible in this vast territory to catch up with all who depredate, the only way being to do as well as we can, and frighten as much as possible those who are caught. I am clearly of the opinion that to bring up a suit in court against woodhaulers or post-cutters would be poor policy, as this wild country is not yet educated up to the [point] that it would punish a man for stealing wood; I am afraid of it, as I think that possibly the decision in such a case would be one that would encourage further depredations. It is in places that are farther advanced in civilization . . . that a man can be prevented from hauling wood from another's enclosure. At present, the best policy is to threaten and issue notices, and at the same time get as much wood (and posts) as we can ourselves.[33]

Accordingly, Horsbrugh and his successors started post-chopping in competition with the wood thieves.

[31]Spur Records, IX, 257.
[32]Spur Records, VI, 328.
[33]Spur Records, X, 281-282.

X: *SOLID PASTURES*

"WAGON LOADS of land prospectors are going in every direction across the prairie. Land is the chief topic of conversation. Small towns are springing up in all counties." So wrote the Texas ranch manager of an English cattle syndicate in 1900. Dozens of other letters give graphic accounts of the nervous hurrying hither and thither of hundreds of men, with several weeks' growth of beard on their faces, all intent upon one thing —the finding of vacant land which they might purchase or homestead from the state.[1] For almost a decade, 1898-1905, the subject about which men thought in the day and dreamed at night was land. Previous to this time land had been the most plentiful commodity in Texas. There had been sections and sections of land to be had almost for the asking—a small down payment, a life-time to make the rest of the payments, a low rate of interest, and a man had a home and perhaps a fine potential investment in land. However, as long as state land was abundant, prospective buyers moved leisurely. If one did not get the particular tract he wanted at the time, he was not disturbed; there were many more tracts from which he might select. But suddenly, just at the close of the nineteenth century, people realized public lands were becoming scarce, and a feverish scramble ensued for what remained.

Numerous conflicts took place among various groups struggling for the possession of the last of the public school lands; the most flagrant was that of ranchmen *versus* settlers. The cleavage between these two groups was marked and clear.

The decade following 1875 had witnessed the transformation of that part of Texas west of the hundredth meridian from an open range into cattle ranches. A few ranches were located on lands obtained by land scrip. The state had from time to time, especially during the days of the republic and early statehood, met its obligations by issuing land scrip. The holder had the privilege of selecting the amount of land designated by the scrip anywhere within the public domain of the state. Many of

[1]Spur Records, X, 145, 220, 221, 228, 232.

the original holders sold their scrip before locating lands. Several individuals and corporations purchased considerable quantities of scrip and located the lands in a body. The SMS Ranch of Throckmorton County is an illustration of a ranch which came into existence by this method.

Other ranches had their origin on railroad lands. As previously stated the state had encouraged the building of railroads by giving sixteen sections of land for each mile of track laid. The railroad companies located their lands as compactly as possible. The state reserved every alternate section within the railroad block for public school land. During the 80's many of the railroad land blocks were purchased by individuals or corporations for ranch purposes. The alternate school sections were leased from the state and enclosed in the same pasture as the purchased railroad lands. These public school lands, enclosed by ranchmen's fences, were the last of the state lands to be opened to settlement. With practically all other possibilities for securing cheap public lands gone and with the amount of school land limited, settlers became desperate in their efforts to get homesteads. Ranchmen were confronted with the possibility of having every alternate section in their pastures purchased by "nesters," as ranchmen called the settlers. Such a condition meant ruin for the ranch industry. The interests of the settler and the ranchman were diametrically opposed; the settler was fighting for possession, the ranchman for existence. The legal rules of the game seemed to be designed to help the settler.

Prior to 1899 a settler could acquire a homestead in two ways. He could file on 160 acres of the public domain, live on it three years, and receive a title to the land from the state.[2] Or he could file on a section of school land, agree to pay $1 or $1.50 an acre for it, according to its classification, and forward one-fortieth of the purchase price to the land commissioner with his application. At the same time he gave his promissory note to the state for thirty-nine fortieths of the purchase price. He paid 3 per cent interest annually. When he had lived on the land three years, the state gave him title to it subject to the lien held by the state for the remaining thirty-nine fortieths of the original price. If he purchaser failed to pay the interest, his land reverted to the state. He had the privilege of paying the thirty-nine

[2]Spur Records, VII, 230.

fortieths of the purchase price due the state at any time prior to the expiration of the forty years. The law also gave the settler the right to purchase three sections of "additional lands" within a five-mile radius of the first section, designated as his homestead. The purchase terms of the "additional lands" were the same as in the case of the homestead section. When a person fulfilled the terms of the law he had the right to purchase at the end of three years four sections, or 2,560 acres, of school land. This act set the stage for much publicized, and often distorted, struggle between cattlemen and settlers in Texas. In 1899 the state converted all the remaining public domain into school land.[3]

As a rule the first settlers never lived out their contracts with the state. The law gave them the right to sell their "claims," and the buyer lived out the contract. Some men deliberately filed on land for the purpose of selling their rights in the contract. Such persons were called "bonus-hunters." After a settler had disposed of his "claim," he was at liberty to file on other school lands. Between 1900 and 1903 bonuses yielded from $1 to $3 an acre.[4]

Until the school lands were opened for settlement they were leased by the land commissioner to the highest bidder, usually for a term of five years. The minimum price of a lease was four cents an acre. The matter of placing school tracts on the market was in the hands of the Land Board, composed of the land commissioner, the comptroller, and the governor. The Board, as a rule, opened the lands for settlement by counties or by groups of counties. After a tract was opened for settlement the first person to file on a particular section after the expiration of the lease received permission to settle.[5]

By 1897 many settlers were on hand to file on each section of school land opened. Fred Horsbrugh wrote on September 9, 1897:

I hear that an army of nesters are in the Matador range; [there are] over a hundred filings on leased lands; others [ranchers] are in the same fix. In fact, the late law has been the cause of a regular Oklahoma rush into all the ranch properties that had school lands leased and are north of the line designated. I hear that on one desirable section of land in the Matador pasture there are eight

[3]Spur Records, XV, 303.
[4]Spur Records, X, 696.
[5]Spur Records, X, 303.

claimants filed upon it. Some of the ranges north [of us] are not fit to look at after the nesters have finished running over them. It will be our turn next to look for trouble.[6]

A few days later Horsbrugh wrote: "There is such a 'hulla-baloo' and rush to file on state lands that it makes forfeiture an acceptable bid for popular favor and vote; officials are not slow to take advantage of it."[7] A year later Horsbrugh wrote: "There is a line of would-be settlers waiting and longing for the time when we forfeit land and they get our pastures. There will be a great rush."[8] The flood of applications for school lands was so enormous the Land Office was far behind with its routine business and was in a state of confusion.

The intent of the law was to encourage permanent settlement. Applications for land were filed with the county clerk of the county to which the newly opened tracts were attached. At many courthouses chutes were built running from the outside of the building into the clerk's office. The first application coming down the chute after the moment the land was officially on the market got the land. Men camped in the courthouse yards, and stayed in line for months in order to be first to get their applications in the chutes.[9]

Although the settlers were scrambling among themselves for the possession of land, all of them had a common opponent, the ranchman, who was ready to go almost any length to retain the school lands. In the struggle public opinion decidedly favored the settler. The law prevented a foreign company buying either school lands from the state or rights to the land from a settler, unless he had already received a clear deed of ownership from the state.[10] Public opinion is clearly reflected by Horsbrugh in a letter of August 16, 1901: "And the general feeling over the country is such that every time a company gets done out of a piece of land by dishonest trickery, or ingratitude, an approving yell of applause goes up, and most everybody feels better in consequence." There was considerable agitation in the legisla-ture to abolish the oath required of the settlers to the effect that they had lived on the land three years.[11]

[6]Spur Records, VIII, 230.
[7]Spur Records, VIII, 240.
[8]Spur Records, VIII, 426.
[9]Eugene Corder to W. C. H., interview, December 26, 1926.
[10]Spur Records, VIII, 230.
[11]Spur Records, VIII, 395.

If the "ungrateful nester" gave "an approving yell of applause" when a cattle company sustained a reversal, the ranchman gnashed his teeth and muttered smothered oaths when he thought about what the "nester" was doing to the ranch industry. Such terms as "thieves" (invariably preceded by one or more vitriolic adjectives), "wretched nesters," "dead-beats," "ungrateful creatures," and "land pirates," run like a refrain through the Spur Ranch records. Ranchmen often had cause to use strong language. Numerous prospecting settlers insisted upon running helter skelter over pastures, causing prairie fires by their carelessness, leaving gates open, and abusing the ranchman's hospitality.[12] Furthermore, a few of the so-called settlers were disguised cattle rustlers, who, once they had secured a legal and vested right to settle inside a ranchman's pasture, could carry on the business of placing their irons on someone else's calves with considerable security. Some settlers were nothing more than "bonus hunters," ready to sell or lease their interests to persons with cattle outside the ranch.

Manager Horsbrugh stated in a letter to his directors that the plight of the Spur Ranch in regard to the "nester problem" was better than any other ranch except the XIT.[13] Ranches to the south, such as the Llano, the Slaughters, and others were having far more trouble than the Spur people. The Capitol Syndicate enjoyed a peculiar and happy status in the vexing settler problem, due to the fact it owned all the land within its pastures. The company had originally obtained the land for the purpose of colonization. The company stocked its range with cattle, but the cattle interest was always secondary. From the outset the company intended to engage in cattle raising only until conditions were right for disposing of the land to actual settlers. The XIT lands were solid, and the managers were never harassed by small armies of settlers running over their pastures inspecting every alternate section. The XIT people wanted settlers, but other ranchmen did not, for their chief interest was cattle raising and their success depended upon keeping their pastures intact.[14]

The period of turmoil and confusion which invariably followed the opening of school lands within a ranchman's pasture

[12]Spur Records, X, 306, 365, 400.
[13]Spur Records, X, 575.
[14]Spur Records, X, 575.

lasted from three to five years. In the meanwhile the cattle interests of the ranchman were materially injured. It often happened that the ranchman's lease to a block of school land would expire some time before the Land Board placed the land on the market. In the interim one person had as much right on the land as another. Prospective settlers, usually from four to ten to each section, "squatted" on the land until the date of filing. Many of them had stock which they turned loose on the land. School sections were not fenced; and the law prohibited a ranchman from ejecting from his pasture the stock of any person who was enclosed by the ranchman's fence. The law protected prospective settlers as well as those who had actually filed on their land. With several would-be settlers "squatting" on each section, their combined stock was far out of proportion to the amount of land they were claiming. The frustrated ranchman was left to swear and fume while he watched the grass of his overstocked range being devoured by the lank, mongrel animals of the "land pirates." It was estimated by conservative cattlemen that for each section opened by the state in this way the grass of four or five adjoining sections was ruined for at least one season.[15]

In order to get cheap grass, many men with small herds and no land joined in the scramble for school lands. A common trick was for such men to file on land with no intention of living out their contract. With grazing lands at one dollar an acre the settler had to pay only one-fortieth of the amount down, which amounted to only two and one-half cents an acre. He could hold this one year, then forfeit it, and his year of grazing would cost much less than if he had leased the land. Four cents an acre was the minimum price on leases. He enjoyed another advantage. Unless the ranchman fenced off the small owner's land, his cattle could run at large in the ranchman's pasture. Custom allowed the settler one animal for each ten acres owned by him in the large pasture. Crafty settlers were often able, without being apprehended, to run twice as many cattle as custom allowed.[16]

Another trick was worked repeatedly. A person with cattle would file on school lands that a ranchman had purchased from

[15]Spur Records, X, 614.
[16]Spur Records, VIII, 204.

some settler who had already lived out his contract and received a deed from the state. The ground on which the second person re-filed was either a real or fictitious claim that the original title was faulty. It required months, sometimes years, of litigation to expel the interloper. In the meanwhile his cattle were grazing free in the ranchman's pasture.[17]

No settler under such circumstances ever went to the expense of buying bulls for his herd, for his cows were running with the bulls of the ranch.[18] The matter of providing bulls for a herd is one of the most expensive overheads in the ranching industry.

It is not to be assumed that all settlers were what some ranch managers thought they were, that is "thieves," "crooks," and "land pirates." The majority of them were honest farmers, seeking homesteads in accordance with the law. But whether they were honest or dishonest, as long as they insisted upon possessing land necessary for the "solid pasture" they were unwelcome in the cattleman's range. Manager Horsbrugh laconically remarked, "the richer a settler gets within our pasture, the poorer gets the Company."[19] Ranchmen did not tolerate the impositions of settlers within their fences with benign resignation. They resorted to all measures of retaliation they could contrive. A few made use of extra-legal methods such as force, intimidation, and ruthlessness. The great majority, however, were more careful to stay within the letter of the law than unscrupulous settlers were. Cattlemen had the advantage there; for ranch managers, as a rule, were able and intelligent, and understood the law much better than the average farmer. One method of keeping the settler's stock off the range was building a fence around the settler's land. This was expensive, however, as it required four miles of fence to segregate one section of land. Then, too, if the ranchman was ever able to purchase the land, he would not want the fence around it.[20] Another retaliatory method was the building of "starve-outs," or enclosures where there were water and scanty grass, in which to segregate cattle belonging to settlers. The law provided that such enclosures must have water. Any settler's cattle found grazing on lands owned or leased by ranchmen could be driven into the "starve-

[17]Spur Records, X, 236, 286, 368.
[18]Spur Records, VIII, 212.
[19]Spur Records, X, 230.
[20]Spur Records, X, 349.

outs" and held as strays. The ranchman could make a nominal charge for each animal held by him before releasing it to its owner. If the owner allowed the animals to stay in the "starve-out" long they would decline in flesh and strength. This plan was frequently used by ranchmen, but with rather doubtful success, as gates would be opened at night, and the cattle frequently escaped.[21]

Settlers often abused ranchmen's hospitality. The following letter of Fred Horsbrugh is indicative of how the average ranchman bitterly bore his anger at this particular practice of settlers:

There are several well traveled roads through our pastures that are pretty well tracked; and it is the usual and unwritten law that you must take in parties that arrive about sundown and care for them in some sort of way. We are a good deal imposed upon in this way, as it is not customary to make a charge. It is an imposition, though. I have known men to hang around in the range until late in the day and come in about sundown. In regard to the mess wagon on the round-up, there is a lot of barefaced imposition practiced here by outsiders. We are not the only ones to complain; the ranches that are being settled up by the nesters and their families work the mess wagons pretty well and successfully. I have been told by Mr. Legertwood of the Matador Company that it is getting awful what they have to put up with in this way. When they have a round-up amongst or near the settlers' houses they have a crowd who make a regular picnic of the occasion. Sometimes they have seventy or eighty to feed at dinner time. This is serious, of course, but the trouble is that so much depends at present on having the good will of the people where there are so many settlers, that it is better perhaps to feed them than to refuse them. . . . There is nothing right about it, however.[22]

By 1897 practically all the ranchmen who had school lands in their pastures realized that their success in the cattle business depended upon their getting possession of the school lands and thereby making their "pastures solid." Notwithstanding the fact that the purpose of the state was to distribute public school lands among as many people as possible, the self-interest of cattlemen caused them to seek for divers methods of defeating public policy at this point. A few of the more unscrupulous cattlemen and cattle corporations did not hesitate to use freebooting methods. Although the land laws expressly prohibited collusion,

[21]Spur Records, XI, 112.
[22]Spur Records, X, 613.

the cattlemen relinquished their leases on school lands and had their cowhands file on four sections each. Each hand designated one of his four sections as his homestead and built on it a small, cheap shack (at the ranchman's expense) in which he spent a few nights a year when it was convenient. At the end of three years the cowhands used each other "to prove up" on the land. As soon as they received titles from the state they transferred the lands to their employer.[23] A ranchman with twenty-five to fifty cowhands in his employ could make headway in acquiring school lands by this method.

Other cattlemen with more ethics relied upon a less effective plan. They made no effort to obstruct the settlers' homesteading the lands. After the settlers had lived out their claims and secured titles, these cattlemen would bide their time until a drouth forced the settlers to sell their places and leave the country. Sooner or later most of the settlers could be prevailed upon to sell. This method was slower, more expensive, and less efficient than the one above.[24]

Public opinion was opposed to foreign companies, and the laws of the state denied some of them the privileges that native individuals and companies enjoyed. The result was that foreign companies had to resort to more circuitous and subtle schemes. Manager Horsbrugh devised the plan of giving up the leased school lands to "friendly nesters," allowing them to file on the lands, and then re-leasing the lands from the settler. The settler lived on one of his sections, and was given employment by the Ranch. The Company operated a store on the Ranch at which the settler was allowed to run an account up to the amount due annually on his leases. The Company also advanced money to the settler to pay the interest due the state on the lands. After the settler had lived out his time and secured title to his sections, he was usually so obligated to the Company that he was forced to sell his land to the Company. On September 2, 1900, Horsbrugh wrote to his directors:

I am sending the list of lands until lately leased from the state. It is better to do this than be overrun by hoards of land seekers with all kinds of stock. I will buy them out as soon as possible, but will be very careful not to make any agreement whereby the land

[23]Phelps White to W. C. H., interview, February 26, 1930.
[24]Eugene Corder to W. C. H., interview, August 30. 1926.

could be forfeited. I will lease what land the settlers do not need until they've lived out their three years. I know three whose time will be up soon, and I want to buy their land, but am afraid they will not wait until I can get permission from London. I think they will come to me first, since I've helped them get the land.[25]

The same general policy was carried out by the Matador Company. The Matador manager was given discretionary power to purchase land from settlers up to amounts of $5,000 without referring the matter to the home office. The bonuses paid the settlers by the Spur and Matador companies ran from $1.50 to $2.00 an acre. The manager of the JA Ranch paid as high as $3.00 an acre and bought the settlers' cattle at the top market price.[26]

Ranch managers of foreign companies had no end of trouble even with their "friendly nesters." Manager Horsbrugh seemed "a bit taken down" when he wrote on September 2, 1900:

The people to the north, who have been given waivers of our lease on certain lands on condition that they lease it back to us, have sold out to people we didn't want—people who have cattle . . . I had allowed a widowed sister (with a large family) of one of the hands to take up land. She sold out before I got a chance to even lease the land, after I had helped her. It makes me remember old Mr. Weller's advice: "Beware of Vidders, they being unsafe to tie to." I am trying to lease from the one she sold to. . . . I think, though, that I'll get things straightened out some day, and shall have a state of affairs exactly opposite to that intended for us by politicians and demagogues, and shall have a place to carry on the cow business in spite of them. . . . I am on constant lookout, as all our lands are threatened, and every day or so an attempt is made to get a footing on our land.[27]

A year later Horsburgh, writing his directors, explained at length how exasperated he had become in attempting to handle his "friendly nesters" and closed his letter with a sigh:

I can however stand it for a little while longer, but oh! it goes against the grain to keep on flattering and cajoling and pampering these wretched brutes who will only do what is right (and are never grateful to anyone) just as long as everything is coming their way and is smooth for them. If I keep them going for another year, things may be coming our way by then.[28]

[25]Spur Records, X, 238.
[26]Spur Records, XI, 12.
[27]Spur Records, X, 238.
[28]Spur Records, X, 374.

Again he wrote a few days later:

I have numerous attacks constantly being made on the rights of these settlers whom I allowed to take up land and from whom I re-leased. It is anything but pleasant work, as the offers that are being made to them to sell out for a bonus to outsiders with cattle, the very class against whom I formed this system, are very enticing. Of course I have leases with them, but they are constantly being advised that the leases are no good, and that if they are, it won't much matter; the fact that anyone claiming land, or even trying to dicker for it, first turns his cattle loose in the pastures adds to the constant annoyance. A dollar an acre bonus and better is being offered by men who will come in and take up the settler's burden with the state; I can do little as I can't trade or even allude to buying out any settler before he has lived out his three years. The great cry against me is collusion, and all kinds of schemes are being worked to try and prove that such exists. . . . Some of my settlers are uneasy as $2500 (offered them by outsiders for four sections) looks as big as a haystack to them, and they begin to think of feeling it between their fingers. . . . especially when individuals are going around showing real money under their noses. . . . The settler is poor, and hears every now and then that I am making a sucker out of him. . . . All this is annoying, but of course there are details of this business, 'as she is run now-a-days,' that compare unfavorably with cattle ranching in former years as a means of healthy enjoyment and placid retirement. The peaceful pastorial business is long since played out. I am glad to say that my health stays good and mind-worries don't seem to hurt my appetite.[29]

Not only "ungrateful" settlers, but settlers' wives occasionally upset the land policy of foreign companies. On October 2, 1902, Horsbrugh wrote:

I am having trouble with Gilmore over his sections. His wife won't join in and sign [the deed] on the home section. I am afraid she is a bit of a wolf, and he gets the worst of it in all marital matters. However, he can sell me the other three sections, and she can't raise a racket. Gilmore is a good man and looks after the west pasture. I would like very much to have their home section as it is an extra good one; [it is] fine land and a good well of water; but she knows it too, and her relatives never forget to let her know every time they can that it is her duty to get as much for the place as she can squeeze out of this "robbing, foreign company." . . . They are having terrible times in other pastures, especially south and west of us.[30]

[29]Spur Records, X, 370.
[30]Spur Records, X, 586.

The managers of foreign companies sometimes found it difficult to get their home offices to act with sufficient dispatch to handle effectively the "friendly nesters" in regard to purchasing their lands. In complaining to his directors in London relative to their slowness in authorizing him to close certain land deals with settlers, Horsbrugh wrote on April 3, 1903:

> I can't hold them much longer, and this hesitation is a bad thing. They [the settlers] are a very foolish and superstitious people, and it is beginning to look to them that we are going to disappoint them after all; and they are at no loss for advisers who have carefully impressed that on them for some time. . . . Honestly I wish I had never gone into this business![31]

Even after title to school land had been obtained from "nesters" who had "lived it out," the settler might file anew on the same land on the grounds the title was faulty.[32] Horsbrugh wrote in August, 1900, "I am afraid to leave the ranch as some claim, or a shadow of a claim is being put on our land every day. One man thinks he has found a vacancy north of the Burleson lands. Our land is on trial."[33]

If the ranchman had to keep one eye on settlers, he had to keep the other on politicians. Horsbrugh wrote in January, 1901:

> The new law forbids [the] same party from being assigned more than four sections from other settlers, and prevents a company from being assigned [land] by a number [of different] settlers. All the land they [the companies] get must be patented or put in different names. From the jumpy way that the Legislature is acting with regard to land, I should advise having all of it fully paid out and patented by [the] State. We could pay out land for the settlers, get it patented, and then buy it. [We] might even pay bonuses and still come out ahead. It is dangerous to receive anything that the state has a finger in. Too many mouthy politicians hate a foreign company.[34]

Horsbrugh had visions of hordes of politicians in Austin holding daily conclaves and staying awake nights for the purpose of complicating the land business and confounding the honest cattlemen who were trying to get along in the world.

---

[31]Spur Records, XI, 31.
[32]J. E. Ketner *vs.* Charles Rogan, Commissioner, and C. C. Slaughter, *Texas Reports,* Vol. 95, p. 559. Also W. C. Logan *vs.* J. W. Curry and R. F. Arnold, *Texas Reports,* Vol. 95, p. 664.
[33]Spur Records, X, 220.
[34]Spur Records, X, 303.

The land business at Austin is a large department, the principal one down there; and it will be a bad day for the politician and the salaried official when all the land owned by the state is sold; therefore the said politicians see to it that new rulings and restrictions be forthcoming so that land is continually being forfeited and taken back by the state, and the salaried officials still hold their jobs. Every year a large amount of land reverts to the state, and the army of officials have no immediate cause for uneasiness.[35]

A year later Horsbrugh again paid the politicians his respects:

This [is] an anxious time about the settler sections. The trouble is that if all the state lands are sold, a number of needy and noisy politicians will be out of a job, also a lot of land agents; these parties want the lands sold to a lot of people one year and forfeited the next. A new lot will be allowed to settle on the same; and then these last forfeit the lands and so on. The longer the strife and forfeitures go on, the better it suits the agents and politicians.[36]

Many cattlemen were of the opinion that land regulations and restrictions were the means that politicians and demagogues were using to force all large cattle companies, especially foreign ones, out of business.[37]

Ranchmen awaited election years with gloomy forbodings. Their relations with official politicians were never to the ranchmen's liking. They bolstered up their courage when the state nominating conventions began to assemble, took up a collection among themselves for bribe money, and sent their best diplomates to push the candidacy of a "friendly candidate" for land commissioner. Horsbrugh was as able, upright, and honest a ranch manager as could be found in Northwest Texas. In business dealings he was scrupulously straight, but when he was forced into politics, he knew the futility of speaking to politicians in any language except the one they understood. Consequently, we find him writing in July, 1898:

The Democrat convention meets in Galveston in August. The fight for election here is a real fight. We want to get a Land Commissioner who is friendly to the cowmen, Groos. Each party puts in a full ticket, but the state is overwhelmingly Democratic. I am sending my personal check for $100 to pay for votes. The uninstructed delegates are the gentry who need sweetening with a certain amount of money. It is almost certain that the next legis-

[35]Spur Records, X, 304.
[36]Spur Records, X, 628.
[37]Spur Records, X, 211.

lature will do away with the line defining territories within which
leases are leases (our best defense). Also there is a movement to do
away with [the settler's] giving the oath to live on the land three
years (a farce at best). . . . It is necessary to be on friendly terms
with the powers-that-be in Austin to get in on the ground floor
with filings. . . . Any candidate favoring cattlemen and their interests is so remorselessly snowed under that if any of them have
any tender feelings toward the business, he generally keeps it to
himself.[38]

A few days later Horsbrugh commented:

This is election year in this misguided state; but the Land Commissioner is not offering himself for reelection, and may be inclined
to do what is right on that account and act independently, but the
chief clerk is announcing for the job and may be hustling for
votes.[39]

The cattleman's abhorrence of politicians did not prevent
him from using them when it was to his advantage. Validating
laws were necessary from time to time to make good the titles
of all settlers who had "proved up" on their lands since the
preceding validating law. In 1903 some ranchmen lobbied
through the legislature a validating bill that would make the
titles of their respective "friendly settlers" good; that, in turn,
protected the ranchmen after they had acquired the lands. It
seemed that members of the legislature in return for stated
financial considerations were quite willing to forget the public
antipathy towards cattlemen's acquiring large portions of the
land which the state intended for small settlers. Thirty-odd
ranchmen subscribed a large purse for the purpose of causing
legislators "to forget." Horsbrugh wrote on April 10, 1903:

I privately agreed to subscribe to a fund that was being raised
to assist the passage of that validating bill, and I expect any day
now to be called upon for this. It will be more than was paid to
put the quarantine bill to sleep, because it is always harder to pass
a bill through than to kill one.[40]

Two months later Horsbrugh was called upon to pay his pro
rata part of the fund. He paid the bill and wrote the Board:

The last legislature was an expensive one for us. Not only for
us, but for all those in this kind of business. Besides that quaran-

[38]Spur Records, VIII, 345.
[39]Spur Records, VIII, 306.
[40]Spur Records, XI, 12.

tine measure, which cost $500, we got robbed on the validity act; at least it took more money to carry it through. The truth is that it was the money that was sent to Austin that got the measure through. The Legislature is nothing but a set of impecunious rascals who look to this form of emolument as the most important part of their office. There was a private fund made up around Colorado by men who were interested in seeing that the settlers they had would not be disturbed. The amounts subscribed averaged $30 a section. I agreed that we had fifty sections that would be affected by such a validating law, and agreed if the law passed to pay $1500. It passed all right though they tacked on rather an objection[able] clause, but I believe that they had to do it to get it through. Now I am called upon for the money. I had no time to ask or consult the home office; [I] had to act quickly and quietly. I don't suppose the board would like to see me lose this money personally, since it was spent in their interests and it was a great benefit; and I am certain that had not some such action taken place, we would have had no validating act. . . . I shall in the meantime charge that $1500 to the same account as the $500 was answerable for; if objections are made, I shall just have to pay it myself.[41]

It must not be supposed that all the iniquitous business of evading the public land policy of the state was on the part of the ranchmen.[42] Many of the settlers were no less clever in overstepping the spirit if not the letter of the land laws. The Red Mud community of Dickens County was composed of settlers who homesteaded on a strip of public domain. At the time when there were seventy-five homesteads filed upon and supposedly lived out, there were only twenty-eight heads of families in the community. Homesteads were filed upon in the names of minors and relatives who had never been in the county. Legend has it that a few were in the names of dogs.[43] If the transgressions of ranchmen were more spectacular than those of the settlers, it was only because cattlemen had the means to carry out their plans on a larger scale.

Another constant source of apprehension to ranchmen was court decisions. All cattlemen, while their land titles were in a state of confusion, stood in considerable awe of the Supreme Court. They nervously kept informed on its decisions. Horsbrugh wrote on June 2, 1902:

I am getting uneasy about the way the Supreme Court is an-

[41]Spur Records, XI, 38.
[42]Spur Records, X, 614.
[43]Spur Records, VIII, 367.

swering certain questions put to it regarding state land settlements. There will always be trouble over state land until [all of] it is sold and patented. And it is evident that shortly it is going to hold that any people who were favored in getting land as our settlers were [Horsbrugh's friendly settlers], did so against the idea of having the State land opened to settlement by the people, no matter whether they were the kind of settlers intended by the law or not. Because the land was not thrown open and the country reduced to a public commons, it will likely be held that the settlement was illegal. The question has not come up yet, but it likely will from the way the courts are deciding questions put to them.[44]

The probability of the court's making adverse decisions preyed continually upon Horsbrugh's mind, as it did on all other ranchmen who were experiencing similar anxieties. Horsbrugh wrote on June 4, 1902:

> I consider the present trend of feeling, as evinced by the state higher courts, to be in favor of destroying the [cattle] business and breaking up the cattle ranches, so that settlements may replace them. Therefore, I fear that it may be held that though lands leased from the state were given up, and settlements allowed by the leasees, and those who settled and obtained the land were the very kind of settler that it was intended should be benefited by the land laws of the state; yet, because the land was not turned loose publicly and scrambled for and fought over, and the adjoining tracts ruined so far as cattle raising is concerned, it was not legal and will have to be worried over in the approved style.[45]

A single decision of the Supreme Court in 1902 did affect the status of over 1,000,000 acres of school lands in the Slaughter pastures.[46]

For all of Horsbrugh's tribulations he and his successor, Henry H. Johnstone, with a few exceptions of a section here and there, managed to achieve solid pastures for the Espuela Land and Cattle Company, Limited, of London. By 1905 the company had acquired title to approximately 212,000 acres of school land bringing the total acreage of the Ranch actually owned to 437,670 acres.

The outcome of the land scramble was slightly in favor of the ranchmen. By Machiavellian methods they succeeded to a

[44]Spur Records, X, 541.

[45]Spur Records, X, 543.

[46]J. E. Ketner *vs.* Charles Rogan, Commissioner, and C. C. Slaughter, *Texas Reports*, Vol. 95, p. 559; also Spur Records, X, 614.

considerable degree in getting their "solid pastures." The examples of Horsbrugh's "vidder" who did not keep faith with
the company, and Gilmore's wife (the "bit of a wolf") who
would not sign the deed to the homestead, are both typical of
hundreds of cases where ranchmen were not successful. Eventually, however, the settler was to win. The coming of railroads
made the land more valuable for agricultural purposes than for
grazing.[47] Within a decade from the time when ranchmen gained
their "solid pastures" a new movement of transferring land began
—this time from the ranchman back to the settler, at an en-
hanced price, but on liberal terms.

[47]Spur Records, X, 626, 647.

XI: *WATER*

Two INDISPENSABLE ITEMS in the ranching industry in Northwest Texas, as elsewhere, were grass and water. Grass was usually considered the primary element, but grass without water was useless. The average cow brute consumes daily during the hotter half of the year about 15 gallons. A herd of 50,000 requires 750,000 gallons a day or 22,500,000 gallons a month. With a need for almost three-fourths of a million gallons a day the owners of the Spur Ranch had a problem which required constant consideration. Cattle could do without grass for days, or could get along with only a half or a third of the amounts normally required for weeks, but water they had to have all the time. The Spur Ranch came to depend upon three sources of water: namely, natural water; artificial lakes, commonly known as tanks; and wells pumped by windmills.

As explained in previous chapters, the Ranch was fortunately located for natural watering facilities. The West Pasture was traversed by Salt Fork River and Catfish Creek. Catfish Creek, which had its source on the Llano Estacado where it was called Blanco Canyon, entered the West Pasture about the middle of the west side and ran the whole length of the pasture from north to south and joined the Salt Fork at the southeast corner. The East Pasture was traversed from north to south by Duck Creek, the tributaries of which extended to both sides of the pasture. Two small creeks, Red Mud, and Little Red Mud, ran between and parallel to Catfish and Duck creeks. At the time of the establishment of the Ranch, Salt Fork, Catfish, and Duck creeks and a few of their tributaries, fed by springs, had running water the year round. The surveyors of the Houston and Great Northern Railroad had located Blocks 1, 2, 7, and 8 in that vicinity thinking that these streams would furnish perpetual water for all purposes. During the late 80's and early 90's, with cyclic drouths, and with permanent stocking of the range, many small streams stopped running and the water holes did not provide sufficient water for large numbers of cattle. The springs from the Ogallala formation continued constant flow,

but during arid years the exaporation rate was so high that
streams ceased to flow and many waterholes dried up. It was
up to the ranch managers to look for other means of watering
their herds.

The first attempt to supplement natural water was by construction of earthen reservoirs. These were formed by building dams
across small creeks or draws. It was necessary to construct spill-
ways by which the surplus water during heavy rains could be
directed around the dam. If these were not adequate, or if they
were built too near the dam, the rush of overflow water following a heavy rain would go over the top of the dam and soon
wash it away.

By April, 1886, Lomax was convinced that it was not safe
to rely upon the natural water supply. The drouth of 1886 was
already becoming serious. It had rained very little for six
months. Lomax wrote to C. A. Latimer on April 3, 1886, in
regard to the construction of two tanks:

We are in receipt from Mr. H. H. Campbell [manager of the
Matador Ranch] of a proposition on your behalf, to build for us
some tanks at the rate of eighteen cents per cubic yard, provided
there is water for your work stock within two miles; or at nineteen cents, if water is at a greater distance than two miles. I believe we can safely count on your having water within the distance
named.

If you can come at once, I will give you the tank building we
have on hand, and must ask an immediate reply, as the time is
short to get them made to do any good.[1]

The continued drouth of 1886 convinced Lomax more than
ever that the solution of the water question rested in more tanks.
He bombarded the London office with letters for several months
urging a vigorous tank-building program. The Company authorized in February, 1888, the construction of seven new tanks.
Lomax had already made a survey of the Ranch and selected
suitable locations. The contract for the new tanks was let to
a professional tank-builder, B. F. Powell, at a considerably
better figure than the first contract. Powell agreed to move
dirt at fourteen cents a cubic yard, provided water for work
stock and men could be had within a mile of the places of
construction. The average tank dam had from 1,000 to 1,500

[1]Spur Records, I, 95.

cubic yards of dirt in it, while larger ones had twice that amount.[2] The average cost of a tank, therefore, was from $200 to $400.

In the fall of 1896, the Company began building most of the tanks with its own men.[3] A tank-building crew usually consisted of six men. They would take a chuck wagon and camp at the site of construction. Horsbrugh purchased a "contractor's plow," similar to the kind used in road and railroad building, one with an extra strong beam, braces and supports, and a stout gauge wheel which fitted on the end of the beam. The plow was drawn by four horses abreast. The dirt was moved by means of scrapers drawn by horses.[4] Horsbrugh estimated that a tank which would hold ten feet of water and be worth $1,000 to the Ranch could be built by the Company for $50. At that time he believed that windmills would never be successful because the wind did not blow enough during the dry hot spells when cattle drank most water. While pleading with his Company for more tanks, Horsbrugh pointed out the great success of similar reservoirs in India. His arguments were effective, and the Company adopted an extensive tank-building program which proved indispensable during the following years.[5]

Due to the light, loose soil in Block 7, tanks would rapidly become filled with sediment. Horsbrugh in June, 1898, hit upon a novel scheme to overcome this obstacle. His plan was to build two dams, one a short distance farther up the draw. It would act as a settling basin. The overflow would be caught by the second tank which was the reservoir. Horsbrugh could not wait until winter to try the experiment. He employed a professional tank builder to construct an additional dam at the tank on Section 7 of Block 7 in order that he might observe the results of the arrangement during the summer and fall.[6] The second dam had scarcely been completed when a heavy rain filled both tanks. Horsbrugh was well pleased with the success of the experiment.

The period of usefulness of any tank, however, was limited. In time all of them filled with sediment, thus curtailing their

[2]Spur Records, VIII, 377.
[3]Spur Records, VIII, 329.
[4]Spur Records, VIII, 67.
[5]Spur Records, VIII, 69.
[6]Spur Records, VIII, 377.

capacity for water. To clean them out was soon found to be impracticable. It was much cheaper to build another dam in a new place than to clean out an old tank. For a while cattlemen thought they could cut a gap in the old dam and allow the water to carry away the sediment. They found it very difficult, however, to rebuild the old dams so they would hold. When the new portion settled, a seam occurred between the old and new parts. Water tended to seep through the seam with the result that the dam was so weakened that the new portions would likely wash out at the next heavy rain.[7]

During the winter of 1896-1897 Horsbrugh was busy building new tanks. By August, 1897, he had a score completed and filled with water. He was so proud of them that he took pictures of ten of the tanks and sent them to the London office together with a long letter describing each tank in minute detail.

Horsbrugh, in 1898, conducted a new experiment in dam construction. The idea was suggested to him by a practice of the Mexicans on the Rio Grande and other sand-choked streams. He had a rock dam several feet high placed across the bed of Duck Creek. The plan was to have the water pour over the dam during periods of floods, and dig a great hole in the sand below the dam. It was hoped that the hole would keep full of water. Had the plan worked, Horsbrugh intended to construct several such dams on the Salt Fork. It did not prove successful. In 1904, the Ranch had forty tanks. When Johnstone became manager in that year, he praised the excellent system of tanks, especially the sixteen in the East Pasture.

Sub-surface water was abundant beneath the Spur Ranch, but managers turned to it reluctantly. The reasons for their slowness in boring wells and erecting windmills were both imaginary and real. Lomax and Horsbrugh seriously doubted that the wind could be depended upon to furnish power during the hot days of July and August. Wells and windmills were expensive compared to the value of land, and the technique of windmill construction was not yet perfected to the point where mills were dependable.

The first well and windmill was forced on Lomax as a last resort in the summer of 1887. There was no permanent natural water in the twenty-section Tap Pasture, and the nature of

[7]Spur Records, VIII, 28.

the soil made tank construction there impracticable. Consequently, Lomax let the contract for the boring of a well. The first hundred feet was to cost $1.50 a foot and the second hundred $2.00 a foot. Lomax was delighted when water, both good and plentiful, was struck at ninety-nine feet. The well was cased and a twelve-foot Star mill erected. The total cost of the well, windmill, pipe, and labor, not including the casing, was about $350, or the price of constructing two tanks at the time.[8]

The windmill was fairly satisfactory for a few months, and then began to give trouble. By December the pitmans were wearing out every few weeks, and Lomax was ordering several extra ones at a time in order to be prepared for emergencies. A few weeks later, February 13, 1888, he wrote to the Flint and Walling Manufacturing Company, makers of the Star windmills at Fort Worth:

We seem to be bothersome, but somehow one of our windmills is continually getting out of repair. It has the best and most constant attention, and is the sole reliance for a most important watering. It is the first mill we got of you, and represents about all the breakages and trouble we have had.

The pitman has again worn out, and has had to be replaced, though only in use a short time. The drive wheel "whobbles" like a buggy wheel needing washers, and the pin that goes through the drive wheel is worn. We find the pins sent are too large to replace the one in use and are not of the same diameter, being thicker at the shoulder than at the end. . . . I wish you had a man in this country who could see the mill, and if possible, put it in proper order, as I am very uneasy about it, as the watering is so important, and I don't like to take the chances of it breaking down entirely.[9]

Four days later Lomax wrote again:

Following my letter as to the unsatisfactory working of one of the Star mills, I would add that I have just returned from a careful inspection of it, and am unable to locate the trouble. The mill works, but seems to evidence a great deal of friction and looseness, and I cannot but be apprehensive that unless remedied a general breakdown will ensue. The watering, as I have said before, is a most important one, and I cannot afford to take chances on it. As our company has now under consideration the putting down of more wells, it might not be unimportant for you to see what is the matter with the mill. . . .[10]

[8]Spur Records, III, 33.
[9]Spur Records, II, 178.
[10]Spur Records, II, 202.

So much trouble with the first windmill, and at a time when the practicability of windmills was still doubtful, did not increase the faith of Lomax and Horsbrugh in the well and windmill program as a means of watering the Ranch. Three other wells had been bored and two Eclipse mills and another Star had been erected. These mills had not given nearly so much trouble, but the troublesome Star caused the managers to be skeptical of windmills in general, and during the next few years to engage in tank-building rather than well-boring.

It happened, however, that the Company farm had to be watered and had no suitable place for a tank. Lomax decided "to sink one well more" and contracted with R. A. Roberts of Estacado for the boring. The price was a little more reasonable than in the case of the previous wells. Roberts was to receive $125 for the well provided he did not bore more than 100 feet. For all depths exceeding 100 feet he was to get $1.75 a foot.[11] At the same time, the Company was negotiating for the construction of seven tanks. When the well at the farm was finished, Lomax, with visions of broken-down Star windmills in his mind, installed a hand pump.[12]

Aside from the fact that wells and windmills were expensive, and the mills frequently out of order, the wells often became "sanded"—that is, quicksand would sift into the bottom of the well until it filled up around the pump cylinder. The rods and valves would stick, and the pipe and pump rods would have to be pulled. This required special equipment and the service of two men from one to three days.[13]

In the fall of 1888, Lomax replaced the two old twelve-foot Star mills and the Eclipse mills with large U.S. mills. The U.S. mills ran with much less friction and vibration and would operate with much less wind. One of the U.S. mills had an eighteen-foot wheel and a fourteen-inch stroke. The change was so satisfactory that Lomax could not refrain from commenting upon the virtues of the U.S. mills.[14] When he resigned he was about to be converted to the well and windmill program.

However, Horsbrugh, who became manager in 1889, was not so enthusiastic. He admitted that the windmills did good work,

[11]Spur Records, IV, 317.
[12]Spur Records, II, 378.
[13]Spur Records, II, 505.
[14]Spur Records, V, 52.

but complained that they had to be oiled every week.[15] Inasmuch as water could be had in no other way, he had a well drilled "near the east sorghum field to water the bulls and cattle that were being fed out."[16] The cost of the well and windmill was about $350, but they turned out to be very satisfactory.

The wheels and vanes of the Star, Eclipse, and U.S. mills were made of wood. The sails in the wheels were narrow and placed close together, causing the mill to be slow running but having considerable power.

Horsbrugh refrained from having more wells bored for eight years. Then when the semi-experimental farm was being improved 2 miles east of the Ranch headquarters at Espuela in 1897, a well was drilled, a new mill and a five-thousand-gallon elevated tank were erected, and water pipes laid to the garden and orchard. An accurate account was kept of equipment, and it totaled $379.[17]

The success of this watering unit seems to have caused Horsbrugh to overcome his prejudice against wells and windmills. During 1898 and 1899 he induced the Company to drill a number of wells to furnish water for the range cattle in the Duck Creek, Tap, and Dockum pastures.[18] By 1902 the Company had so many windmills in operation that a man was employed to devote his full time to looking after the mills.[19]

The extremely dry weather of 1903 caused Horsbrugh to see the advantage of digging shallow wells along the creeks where water could be had at less than fifty feet, and operating them with small steel windmills. Shallow wells were drilled at Cunningham's crossing, Judge McClains' place, Cunningham's draw, Snowden's crossing, mouth of Red Arroyo, and Dry Lake.[20] The plan worked so well that during the next year Catfish Creek and Salt Fork were lined with shallow wells and cheap windmills.[21] By this time, the small steel mills had been so perfected that they

[15]Spur Records, IV, 115.
[16]Spur Records, IV, 77.
[17]Spur Records, VIII, 215.
[18]Spur Records, IX, 469; X, 204; XV, 10, 21, 42.
[19]Spur Records, X, 552.
[20]Spur Records, XI, 116, 120.
[21]Spur Records, XI, 120, 121, 160, 167.

were giving satisfactory service.[22] In 1905 the Ranch had thirty windmills.[23]

The Spur Ranch, as long as it was owned and operated by the Espuela Land and Cattle Company was never sufficiently watered in ratio to the stock on the range. Watering places were too scattered and too far between. In many areas the animals would have to walk from eight to twelve miles a day for water. Such hikes cut down on grazing time, and, in addition, the cattle walked off part of their fat.

[22]The cost of watering the Ranch from 1902 to 1905 was as follows:

1903 ....$ 3,458.88
1904 ....$ 5,039.73
1905 ....$ 1,818.41
1906 ....$ 1,468.38
Total for four years..$11,785.40
Average per year..$ 2,946.35

[23]For names and locations of windmills on the Spur Ranch in 1909, see Appendix I.

FICTION HAS MADE THE COWBOY the most romantic constituent of the cattle range and ranch. He may have been a courageous, dashing, two-gun individual in other places, but truly not on the Spur Ranch. No one thought of him as being "a type," or "a character," or anything at all unusual. It is doubtful if he ever thought of himself as being anything extraordinary or heroic. Indeed, he was quite ordinary. In all of the Spur records the author has failed to find the word "cowboy" used so much as in a single instance. He is unfailingly referred to by the lowly and uninteresting term "hand."

The number of hands employed by the Ranch varied from year to year. The greatest number was employed in 1887 with an average of 72 a month for the entire year. The next year the average dropped to 67. In 1889 the average was 49. The marked decrease from 1887 to 1889 was due to two things. First, the initial task of fencing was over, and fewer men were needed to handle the cattle in the enclosed pastures. Second, the Fort Worth and Denver Railroad had been completed, bringing cattle-shipping points much closer. The length of time a trail herd spent on the road to a shipping point was now considerably reduced; and, correspondingly, fewer trail hands were needed. A series of drouthy years began in 1892 and lasted through 1896. The Ranch reduced the number of hands each year until the average was 25 in 1896. With the return of more seasonable years the number of hands increased gradually until 1902 when the average was 49. The number fluctuated from 43 to 48 a year until 1909. The average number of hands by months from 1885 to 1909 was 40.

The number of hands needed to carry on the ranch work varied from month to month with seasons of the year. The number retained during the winter months of December, January, February, and March was usually from one-half to one-third the number needed from April to November during the spring and fall round-ups and trail-driving seasons. The number employed during these months varied considerably. In 1885 the high peak of the ranch work came in October; in 1886, in

June; in 1887, in July; in 1889, in May; in 1890, in August; and so on. The variance was caused by the earliness or the lateness of spring, the rains or the drouths, and the time of cattle deliveries. On a yearly average one hand was necessary for each 1,250 cattle handled by the Ranch.

The average wage of a hand varied from year to year, but not so much as the number of hands. Beginning with $38.72 a month in 1885, the monthly wage average decreased to $32.24 in 1890. During the decade that followed, the average wage played between $32 and $33. In 1900 it went to $31.12 and continued to decrease each year until it reached $29.66 in 1904. The next year it started on an upward trend which lasted until it rose to $37.13 in 1909.

It must not be concluded, however, that the average hand received the "average wage" in the sense just referred to. When the Ranch was first established an ordinary hand got $30 a month (a few "roust-a-bouts" got only $25). A first-class hand received $35; top hands, $40 to $45; trail bosses, $50 to $65; and range foremen, $125. In June, 1885, for instance, the payroll shows 4 hands receiving $25; 45 hands, $30; 11 hands, $35; 8 hands, $40, 1 hand, $45; 3 hands, $50; 1 hand, $65; 1 hand, $70; 1 hand, $100; and 3 hands, $125. The drouth and general hard times in 1886 and 1887 caused the whole wage scale to be somewhat lowered. The payroll of June, 1889, shows 1 hand receiving $20; 27 hands, $25; 6 hands, $30; 6 hands, $35; 2 hands, $40; 5 hands, $50; 2 hands, $75; and 2 hands, $100. The range foremen drew $100 instead of $125 until May, 1899. The ordinary hand remains on the $25 basis, however, until August, 1908, at which time $30 again became the wage.[1]

An analysis of the payrolls to determine whether or not wages were paid in accordance to the class of work done shows that such was not always the case. It was true in some instances. Cooks, for instance, had their profession sufficiently recognized to have a standard wage scale. As a rule, a wagon cook received the wage of a top hand. When ordinary hands were getting $30, wagon cooks got $40. When the wage of ordinary hands went to $25, wagon cooks received $35. The cook at headquarters was an aristocrat. He got $50, and was on the same wage scale as a trail boss. Trail bosses and range foremen were paid in ac-

[1]Payrolls of the Spur Ranch.

cordance with the class of work they did, but the kind of work done by the rank and file or ordinary, first-class, and top hands had no connection with the wages they received. For instance, one finds a $25 hand and a $40 hand riding bog, or riding fence, scraping tanks, or working with a branding outfit side by side. For the most part whether a hand received $25, $30, or $35 a month depended on the reliability of the individual and the length of time he had been with the Ranch.

One would quite naturally suppose that by far the greatest number of hands on a large ranch would be occupied in handling the cattle. Such was not the case on the Spur Ranch. There were some seventeen different classes of work to be done; working with cattle on the ranch proper ranked second. If the year 1891 may be taken as typical, one finds that approximately 22 per cent of the hands worked on the feed farm—a rather hum-drum life for an aspiring cowboy. According to the payroll classification slightly less than 20 per cent worked with cattle on the Ranch (rounding-up and branding) . Of the rest, approximately 16 per cent worked at trail-driving; 11 per cent on the experimental farm; 10 per cent at fence-riding; 5 per cent at cooking; 3 per cent at general work; 2 per cent trail-riding (preventing herds from the south trailing across the Spur pastures) ; 2 per cent in the capacity of foremen; 2 per cent at horse-wrangling; 2 per cent, outside round-ups; 2 per cent, fixing fence; 1 per cent, hauling hay; 1 per cent, blacksmithing; 1 per cent, tanking; 1 per cent, dairying; and three-tenths of 1 per cent, range-riding.

It is interesting to trace the fortunes of one of the steady hands (one who worked the year round) who stayed with the Ranch for a long period of time. Jake (J. D.) Raines, for instance, worked continuously for the Spur outfit from the time it was taken over by the Espuela Land and Cattle Company, Limited, of London in April, 1885, until the Spur cattle were finally disposed of in July, 1909. Jake started in at $35 a month working cattle and riding fence and bogs. From May, 1885, to November, 1886, he drew $40 a month, and spent the rounding-up seasons "reping" (acting as the Spur representative at outside round-ups), and the winter months doing general work (hauling wood and doing other odd jobs) at the Ranch. From December, 1886, he received $30 a month and rode fence, rustled horses, and worked on tanks. During April, 1887, he joined a

branding outfit. From May to December, 1887, he was "reping"
again down on the Colorado River. The winter, 1887-1888,
found him riding fence from a line-camp on the Ranch at
$25 a month. During the summer, 1888, he went on the trail
with a beef herd as a common $30 hand. In September he
was back on the Ranch at $25 a month with a branding
outfit. During November he was "reping" for $30. For four
months during the winter, 1888-1889, he drove a team, guid-
ed a plow, and dumped a scraper with a tanking outfit at
$25 a month. After one month with a branding outfit in the
spring, he was sent to "rep" for the Company and stayed "outside" until December, for all of which he got $30 a month. He
spent the winter, 1889-1890, with a fence-building outfit at $25
a month. The next seven years held the same monotonous routine for Jake—"reping" in the spring, summer, and fall, and
fence-riding or tanking in the winter. He was placed on a straight
$35 wage in April, 1890, which he drew until March, 1898, when
he was placed in charge of a tanking outfit at $50 a month. From
April of that year he was in charge of trail outfits at the same
wage. During the winter, 1898-1899, he got $50 a month for
riding fence and bogs and still-hunting (a single hand riding
the range looking for unbranded calves). From April to November, 1899, he was in charge of trail outfits at $75 a month.
The winter of 1899-1900 was spent in fence riding and still-
hunting at $35 a month. The summer of 1900 found Jake back
at his old job of "reping" at his old wage. He kept at this for
two years. During the summer of 1902 he was trail bossing
again at $65 a month. For three months in 1903, he was doing
what he did in the winter, 1885-1886—hauling wood and doing
odd jobs at $35. During three months in the spring he bossed
a trail herd at a $65 wage. The rest of the year he worked as a
$35 common hand with a branding outfit. From 1903 to 1909
Jake never received more than a $35 wage, and worked with
branding and tanking outfits, rode fence, and went on the trail
every summer as a common hand.

　　Jake Raines was still (1931) with the Swenson interests and
daily rode the old West Pasture where he first worked with Spur
cattle almost half a century before. He was one of the best
brand men the Ranch ever had, having a remarkable memory
for brands and cattle.

From one-half to two-thirds of the hands employed on the Spur Ranch in the course of a year were transients, who worked for varying lengths of time from April to December. The records of the Ranch show that from April, 1885, to July, 1909, 901 different hands were on the payrolls. Of this number 64 per cent worked for the Company but one season, or a part of one season; 20 per cent returned and worked a second season; 8 per cent a third season; 3 per cent a fourth season; 2 per cent a fifth season; and 3 per cent more than five seasons.

Range work seldom began before the first of April. During the winter, beginning as early as December, the manager received occasional letters from transient hands, asking for jobs during the following summer. The majority of the men, however, did not write ahead, but came in person. They began to show up at the Ranch during the latter part of March, their few possessions being a horse, a saddle, and other riding paraphernalia, and a small sack of clothes containing an extra shirt and maybe other things. If the Ranch needed hands, they were employed and few questions asked.

As a rule more hands appeared than the Company could use. There was only one season from 1885 to 1909 when men were scarce. In March, 1888, sufficient men did not arrive. When spring work got under way, Lomax found himself short-handed. He sent one of his wagon bosses to Colorado City and Abilene to scout for more men.[2] This search did not provide all the help needed, and Lomax was forced to let contracts for fence building and tank work which he otherwise would have done with his own outfits.[3]

If crude labor was abundant, so much could not be said of technical help. For instance, every year or two the Spur Ranch spayed from 1,500 to 2,000 heifer cattle. Spaying is a surgical operation requiring knowledge and skill. Men qualified to spay successfully were scarce, and the Ranch managers sometimes had considerable trouble finding persons to do this work.[4]

A considerable number of the men coming to the Ranch each spring looking for employment were overgrown country boys still in their teens who wished to escape the tedium of farm work and parental domination. The records show that in some

[2]Spur Records, II, 306.
[3]Spur Records, II, 287.
[4]Spur Records, II, 426.

instances it took only a few days to disillusion many of these young squirts. Some began work on the 1st of April and quit on the 7th, the 12th or the 14th. Sometimes they were homesick; in other instances they found the hard, gruelling grind of spring work much more uninteresting and unromantic than they had expected. Those who stuck, however, far out-numbered those who quit. Many of those who stayed were tempted to leave, but pride held them until they became accustomed to the rigor and lonesomeness of ranch life.

Many of these young, would-be cowhands were a source of anxiety to their parents back on the farm. The following letter is typical of letters which the Ranch managers occasionally received:

> I got home and found my boy gone, and thought he mite [sic] come to the ranch. If you see or heare [sic] of him let me know as his mother is distressed to death about him. Have him come at once as I am bothered to death about him.[5]

The dogged perseverance with which a few young fellows determined to become cowboys (ranch hand is entirely too humdrum a term to apply to one of them) is admirable. Some of these striplings begged for a chance to work for their board, to do anything and everything until the manager might see fit to place them on the payroll. Such spirit usually had its effect, and the boys were allowed to stay.[6] It is to be remembered, however, that such cases were rare exceptions, and do not in any sense typify the mass of restless, swaggering, country boys who left home bent on becoming punchers.

The Spur Ranch seriously tried to maintain certain standards of conduct among its hands. The managers never knowingly employed a hand who had been discharged for questionable conduct. They insisted that all their hands pay their honest debts. Time after time we find a manager, at the insistence of a creditor, bringing pressure to bear on a hand to get him to pay a debt. A foreman in charge of the leased White Deer Pasture was discharged on the grounds that he "was not truthful."[7] Several men were "fired" at one time or another because they were strongly suspected of being in connivance with thieves.[8] It is interesting

[5]Spur Records, File A, 432.
[6]Spur Records, VIII, 241.
[7]Spur Records, V, 683.
[8]Spur Records, V, 225.

to note that the Spur Ranch as previously mentioned, was probably the first area in Northwest Texas to become bone-dry so far as intoxicating liquor was concerned. Prohibition came about by a decree of Manager Lomax and was rigidly enforced so far as outside appearances were concerned. Several freighters were discharged and forbidden ever again to come on the Ranch for attempting to bootleg liquor in to the hands. Horsbrugh, upon becoming manager, repealed the prohibition decree. One of the hands celebrated the return of liquor in 1890 by getting drunk, falling out of a buggy, and breaking his neck.[9] In 1896, Flook the veteran bookkeeper, was discharged "because of drunkenness."[10]

From the time of the organization of the Ranch to the spring of 1889 the morale of the hands seems to have been low. On several occasions Lomax and Horsbrugh expressed fears to the effect that a majority of them were in sympathy with lawlessness— not that the hands themselves were bad, but that they were indifferent. They would ride far out of their way in order not to see a rustler putting his brand on a Spur calf.[11] When the extra hands were discharged in December, 1889, Horsbrugh took particular pains to see that trustworthy men were retained.[12] After 1889 the morale was much higher than it had been before. Horsbrugh commented in 1896 that "the Spur men are superior to the average ranch outfit," and in 1899 he remarked that "The Spur men are a good bunch of cow hands—some of them can't be beat."[13] The degree to which discipline was enforced on the Ranch is indicated by the fact that on occasions common hands and even wagon bosses were discharged for insubordination.[14]

The finding of efficient and reliable wagon, range, and trail bosses was a considerable problem. Success of the various phases of ranch activity depended primarily upon the boss having immediate charge of the work. To keep men consistently at work, and to do it without antagonizing them or causing too much friction, required a measure of aggressiveness and restraint, as

[9]Spur Records, VI, 70.
[10]Spur Records, VIII, 36.
[11]Spur Records, IV, 133; V, 158.
[12]Spur Records, IV, 108.
[13]Spur Records, VIII, 75, 476.
[14]Spur Records, II, 473, 475, 476, 480.

well as leadership and initiative, which few men working for wages had. The only way the managers had of recruiting their bosses was by trial and error. A good boss when discovered was an individual to be prized.[15] Manager Johnstone was quite a bit chagrined in 1904 when the boss of the White Deer Pasture was elected sheriff of Hutchinson County, necessitating the selection of a new boss for White Deer.[16]

The managers found that married hands were more dependable than unmarried ones. The results of this discovery caused the managers to become advocates of matrimony. They encouraged their most dependable hands to marry. Encouragement took a rather substantial form in that when extra hands were discharged in the fall, preference for retention was given to married men. Married hands were placed in the line-camps in order that they might have houses for their families. In a few instances, houses were built for good, regular hands when they married.[17]

The Spur managers took a friendly and accommodating interest in their employees, especially in those upon whose integrity they might depend. Lomax and Horsbrugh frequently attempted to find jobs on other ranches for men they were compelled to lay off.[18] On several occasions, hands who were laid off or suddenly called home were allowed to ride one of the Ranch's horses to their destination. In each instance, the man sent the horse back to the Ranch by some responsible party who happened to be passing.[19] In several instances, the managers advanced money for transportation to hands who were away from the Ranch and broke.[20] It was not unusual for men who had worked as extra hands one season, and who had contracted to work the next, to borrow money from the managers to get through the winter.[21]

One phase of ranch life about which the hands did not like to think was sickness and accidents. The following extract from a report of Horsbrugh's to the London office is typical of many references made to the health of the men:

[15]Spur Records, IV, 185, 199, 214; VI, 348; VIII, 465.
[16]Spur Records, XI, 406, 587.
[17]Spur Records, VI, 360; VIII, 390; IX, 441.
[18]Spur Records, V, 80, 176, 236.
[19]Spur Records, I, 278; V, 72.
[20]Spur Records, V, 89, 90.
[21]Spur Records, II, 77; IX, 5.

We have been bothered with an unusual amount of sickness and have more than the usual number of men laid up, one with a broken leg and another with a dislocated arm, while several have been in bad shape from dysentery and diarrhea.[22]

Occasionally one of the men would have an attack of "bilious" or "slow" fever, or typhoid fever. The wonder is that more of them did not have fever. During the hot days of a dry summer when the men were working on the range, they drank the slick, stagnant water, often with green scum on it, from the tanks and the creeks. To become critically ill was a serious matter. It took two or three days to get a doctor. Sometimes one could be got at Estacado; if not, he must come from Colorado City. Even though the doctor arrived in time and his ministrations were successful, his fees were exorbitant. When Horsbrugh had pneumonia in the spring of 1889, a visit from a Colorado City doctor cost him $100.[23]

Men with families had more to fear from sickness than those without. For a man to have a doctor with his wife at child birth was out of the question. The pain and the chances for infection were correspondingly increased. Even though the child successfully made its advent, its chances at life were considerably lessened by being deprived of a physician's care. An epidemic could play havoc before anything could be done about it. In January, 1897, three of Horsbrugh's children took diphtheria. Before a doctor could be had, one was dead.[24]

The Ranch diary on December 8, 1900, has the following brief entry:

Merriman's baby ill.

Two days later we find:

Outfit digging grave and attending burial of Merriman's boy who died yesterday. Weather: cold and clear.[25]

In February, 1895, a hand whose name was Billy Bonner and who had come from Philadelphia to learn the cowboy profession took suddenly ill with a pain in his head. He died the next day, and was buried in a rough, home-made coffin.[26] His family, on

[22]Spur Records, X, 344.
[23]Spur Records, IV, 75.
[24]Spur Records, VII, 459.
[25]Spur Records, XII, 14.
[26]Spur Records, XIII, 14.

hearing of his death, wrote asking that he be shipped back to Philadelphia. Mr. Flook's reply is significant:

. . . with regard to the idea of having the body removed to Philadelphia and interred there, you are doubtless aware that it would be a great expense. This is a very unsettled country, and there is no one here who could do the undertaking work. We are 100 miles from any railroad point. The work would have to be done by experienced men, and I believe there are none nearer than Fort Worth . . . I dare say the work would cost $400. . . .[27]

Incidentally, an idea of the financial condition of an unusually thrifty ranch hand who had met an untimely death may be had from Flook's statement of Billy Bonner's affairs:

. . . with regard to your question as to the amount of money he had, I cannot say easily, except that by the statement of the Colorado National Bank he had deposited there $370—and I believe there were some small amounts owing him by different parties, probably another $50. He did not possess any real estate, but did have about 30 head of ponies which are not of much value. . . .[28]

The average hand, coming to a sudden end, would probably have no more money than enough to pay for his burial, if he had that much.

Accidents occurred without end.[29] Horses fell with their riders; firearms discharged accidentally; teams ran away with their drivers; ropes attached to frightened, plunging animals tore the flesh from the hands of the men; and a host of other things were always happening. The following report from Horsbrugh to the home office is typical of what frequently occurred:

Accidents have been very common of late, because of the grass growing over prairie dog holes that have been vacated by the former inhabitants. Horses as a rule are very clever at avoiding dog holes that have a live family of prairie dogs domiciled therein because such holes are clear and visible; but when the dogs have been drowned out, as they sometimes are by heavy rains, the holes are grown over and hidden, and become a trap for horses. Several of the horses have been crippled and some of the men. Merriman was badly hurt for a while by his horse rolling over him, but is better and at work again. Harrison and Raines are in hospital at headquarters; Harrison was lost for two days in the south part of the pasture in Kent County; his horse fell, rolled on him, and got

[27]Spur Records, XII, 14.
[28]Spur Records, III, 139.
[29]Spur Records, II, 636; VIII, 266, 475; X, 565; XV, 65; File A, 417, 434.

away and has not been seen yet. Harrison lay for awhile it seems, and then managed to crawl to one of the tanks where he got water, and eventually crawled to the road where the mail hack found him. Raines had a narrow escape, as his horse fell head-over-heels; and, getting up, proceeded to drag poor Raines whose foot was caught in his rope, but luckily his boot came off in time to save his life, and he is now congratulating himself in that a badly sprained ankle is all that is wrong with him. He will be riding again in a week.[30]

Some of the accidents proved fatal. In May, 1894, a son of one of the hands drowned in Red Mud Creek.[31] The same month a visitor on the Ranch drowned in Duck Creek.[32] In May, 1904, one of the hands was accidentally shot through the hips and lower bowels. He died at noon two days later and was buried the same day.[33]

More or less friction constantly occurred between the Ranch hands. It was a rare individual who got along well with every person on the Ranch, and a few men found it hard to get along with anyone. In October, 1902, a tragedy, typical of the country and the times, took place on the Spur Ranch as the result of a private feud. It was the only case where personal animosities proved fatal on the Spur Ranch, but many such instances occurred on adjoining ranches, several taking place on the Matador range to the north. Horsbrugh reported the affair to the London office on October 6, 1902:

I regret to report a killing that took place on our range in Kent County some days ago. It resulted from an old grudge existing between the two men that I had watching cow-thieves, and they had so far been very successful in putting down stealing. But they happened to have an old grievance between them individually. When I found it out I made them both understand that they were no good to me if they were not friendly to each other, as their usefulness depended on their relations one to the other. They fully promised to make it all up and let bygones be bygones. Later it broke out again and I turned them both off. Standifer, I turned off in August and Higgins later. Higgins asked me to let him stay until the end of September as he had some arrangements to make about moving his family and children to a place where they could attend school. I told him a month did not matter. I was startled to get a message

[30]Spur Records, VIII, 254.
[31]Spur Records, X, 27.
[32]Spur Records, X, 29.
[33]Spur Records, XI, 350.

over the phone from Clairmont, Kent County, last Saturday that Standifer had returned, and he and Higgins had a meeting, and that Standifer was killed. Later accounts show it to have been a pre-meditated (and mutually arranged for) dual. They both had rifles and Higgins horse was killed the first shot. Standifer was shot twice, dying instantly. Higgins gave himself up to the sheriff at Clairmont, and I fancy will come clear on the plea of self-defense. I thought I had the whole thing settled quietly. But, of course, the returning of Standifer could have only one meaning for a jury. They were both fearless, determined men, and each had had similar trouble before; and they were really the means of scaring out some of the worst cow-thieves we had.[34]

The code of the country permitted duelling, although there was a legal technicality prohibiting it. Higgins was speedily tried for murder and found not-guilty. A short time later he was rewarded for his general bravery by being appointed deputy sheriff of Kent County, and was soon back on the Spur range chasing cow-thieves again.[35]

Personal animosities sometimes led to fights with serious consequences. Such an encounter occurred in 1888 between W. R. Stafford, wagon boss, and J. C. Roberts, cook. Roberts had been nursing a grudge for some time. He was sharpening his butcher knife preparatory to cutting some steaks for supper when something Stafford said triggered him off. He made for Stafford with the knife. Stafford grabbed a spade, but was not quick enough. Roberts ripped a wide gash across Stafford's stomach. His intestines were not perforated, but there was nothing to hold them in. The other hands laid the wounded man flat on a wagon and drove to Bud Browning's place. One of them rode pell-mell to Estacado, forty-five miles away, for Dr. William Hunt. It was the next day when the doctor arrived. He laid Stafford on the dining table and discovered he had bled considerably in the abdominal cavity. The doctor laid the intestines on the table and swabbed out the cavity with towels.

Stafford raised his head, felt of the intestines and said, "Is them my guts?"

Dr. Hunt put them back and sewed the severed stomach wall together with sewing thread without any kind of anesthetic.

[34]Spur Records, X, 613-614.
[35]It is interesting that, years later, Higgins' son, Cullen Higgins, an able and fearless district attorney, was murdered, while prosecuting a murder case, in the same town in which his father had been tried for murder.

Antibiotics at the time were unknown. Stafford recovered rapidly without infection. Roberts was discharged from the Spur Ranch. Stafford quit and went to work for Bud Browning.[36]

The Spur managers were generally loyal to their dependable hands who got in trouble. In November, 1902, a hand by the name of John Lindley was murdered at Clarendon. Lindley did not die at once, but lingered several days giving doctors a chance to run up a sizable bill against him. As he did not have any money or property, Horsbrugh personally assumed responsibility. After Lindley's death Horsbrugh paid from his own pocket over $600 for medical attention and the prosecution of the murderer.

[36]Stafford to W. C. H., interview, February 23, 1930.

Table 2. AVERAGE NUMBER HANDS BY YEARS

Year	Percent	Year	Percent
1885	70.4	1898	30.2
1886	54	1899	35.4
1887	72	1900	36
1888	66.5	1901	36.2
1889	48.7	1902	48.7
1890	42.3	1903	47.5
1891	46	1904	43.5
1892	39.3	1905	42.8
1893	38.2	1906	43.4
1894	31.3	1907	43.3
1895	28.3	1908	46.2
1896	25.3	1909	47.3
1897	26.7		

Table 3. TOTAL AMOUNTS PAID FOR WAGES BY YEARS

Year	Amount	Year	Amount
1885 (April to December only)	$21,738	1898	$10,405
1886	23,938	1899	11,757
1887	25,731	1900	8,967
1888	22,517	1901	13,018
1889	17,702	1902	15,282
1890	15,036	1903	12,037
1891	16,048	1904 (April and May not included)	11,168
1892	13,575	1905	12,982
1893	13,976	1906	13,037
1894	11,276	1907	15,231
1895	10,637	1908	17,490
1896	9,910	1909 (January to July only)	10,641
1897	10,151		

XIII: *ROUTINE*

TURNING FROM a consideration of the ranch hands themselves, it is interesting to note what they did in the course of their daily routine. There were seventeen different classes of work to be done. The biggest of these was the tilling of the feed farms. Inasmuch as the raising of feed was subsidiary to the main business of raising cattle, the feed farm routine will be omitted.

Twenty per cent of all the labor used on the Ranch was employed in rounding up and branding the cattle. The rounding up season began usually about April 15, sometimes a little before; and at other times a little later, depending on how fast the grass was growing.[1] The extra hands employed for the season were usually placed on the payroll April 1. The interval between April 1 and the beginning of the range work was spent in making general preparations. The wagons had to be made ready, saddles and other equipment repaired; and there were many other odd jobs to be done.

The rounding up and branding was carried on by a large outfit which began operations in April on one side of the range and worked systematically until all of both pastures had been covered. The outfit started at the head of McDonald Creek, worked up Catfish to the north side of the West Pasture, then crossed over east to the head of Red Mud, worked down Red Mud to the Salt Fork, down the Salt Fork to the south side of the East Pasture, and then crossed to the lower Duck Creek country, and worked up Duck Creek to the north side of the East Pasture.[2]

Range work on the Spur Ranch was under the control of the Colorado and Brazos Association, a regional subdivision of the Northwest Texas Stock Raisers Association. A regulation of the Colorado and Brazos Association provided that the pasture owners should have absolute control of the round-ups in their respective enclosures. The superintendent of the round-up had the right to go in a pasture with at least five men and see that the range was properly rounded and that an opportunity was

[1]Spur Records, V, 205.
[2]Spur Records, IV, 144.

given for all owners having strays in the pasture to get their cattle. The authority to direct the round-ups in the Spur pastures was delegated by the manager to the range foreman. He not only directed the Spur men, but all others who were "reping" for neighboring ranches.

It was a policy on the Spur Ranch to insist that the Association's round-up superintendent bring in two wagons with as many men as needed, one wagon outfit to hold the strays that belonged to ranches to the north and one to hold those that belonged on ranches to the south. The managers insisted that everyone having cattle on the Spur range have a representative at the round-ups, and that he take the strays out of the pastures as soon as possible. The strays of those not having representatives at the round-ups were driven outside the Spur enclosures. The range foreman was instructed to keep a vigilant look-out for strays with altered brands. If any strays were found, he was to report them to the superintendent of the round-up "in order that the Spur Ranch might keep its skirts clear in regard to harboring cattle thieves." At the close of the round-up, the foreman was always instructed to obtain a certificate from the superintendent stating that the range had been properly rounded.[3]

The technique of rounding up was worked out with fine precision. An outfit usually consisted of ten or twelve cow-hands, a foreman, a cook, and a horse wrangler. The headquarters of each outfit was the chuck wagon which carried not only the food, but the bed rolls of the men. Always in the vicinity of the wagon were the extra mounts of the men under the care of the wrangler. The wagon proceeded from one established camping place to another. Men who worked for years with the Spurs became as familiar with these places as they were with the Ranch headquarters. There was the one at the head of McDonald, followed successively by the one at the mouth of McDonald, the head of Slicknasty, Chimney Creek, K. Tank, the crossing on Catfish, Home Creek, Two Mile Pen, Dockums, the head of Red Mud, Marble Banks, the mouth of Jordan, Gamel Horse Corrals, Spade Pens, Wilson Tank, and Soldiers Mound.

At the beginning of a general round-up the outfit left headquarters and proceeded approximately thirty miles slightly towards the southwest to the camp site on the head of McDonald.

[3]Spur Records, I, 172.

It took a good day to make this distance. The next morning the work began. The cook rolled out before daybreak and started breakfast. About daylight he called the men. They ate breakfast and started on the day's ride before sunrise. The work at each wagon stand was systematic. The men went north, let us say, the first day for six, eight, or ten miles, scattered out in a long line and started back to camp driving all the cattle they could find before them. The distance between the men depended upon the topography of the locality and the amount of brush and timber. Where the ground was generally level and timber scarce so the men could see considerable distance to make sure they were not missing any cattle, the hands scattered out perhaps a half mile apart. When conditions were not so favorable, they might have to stay within a hundred yards of each other. It would probably be noon or later when they returned to camp with the cattle—eighty, a hundred, or two hundred head. Two men would hold the herd while the others ate dinner. Then came the cutting out and branding.

The cutting for strays took place first. At the beginning of the range work the various representatives of the outside ranches would draw for numbers which they kept throughout the round-up. The Matador representative or representatives (the big outfits had two or more), for instance, might draw No. 1; the Two-Buckle, No. 2; the Curry Comb, No. 3; the Long S, No. 4; and so on. In view of the fact that too many men only got in each other's way, it was customary for No. 2 to hold the "cut" while No. 1 cut the round-up for strays; then No. 1 would hold while No. 2 cut. No. 4 held while No. 3 cut, and then No. 3 held while No. 4 cut, and so on. Each day the order was reversed.[4]

After the strays had been cut, the branding began. A hand on a trained roping-horse milled around among the herd until he could get his rope on an unbranded calf. The man on the horse then dragged the resisting calf some distance from the herd to the vicinity of the branding fire. One of the hands grabbed the calf, threw it to the ground, and with the aid of another hand held it while still another administered the sizzling-hot branding iron. Nor was that all; a man with a sharp knife carved the ranch's "mark" in the calf's ears. The animals were not dehorned in those days, but if it happened to be a bull calf, there was

[4] W. R. Stafford to W. C. H., interview, September 10, 1930.

still more agony in store for him—castration. When finally released, the profound contempt with which the calf looked at the perpetrators of his woe could have but one meaning. After the branding, the strays were kept under herd while the rest of the cattle were driven well back and turned loose in the region from which they had been gathered.

The drive the next day was made from the northwest, or from the west as the case might be, and so on each day until the whole region around the camp had been worked. The wagon would move to the next site, and the procedure would be repeated there. The holding of the strays necessitated night-herding which was done in shifts. If the stray herd got too large, the work stopped for a day or two while the strays were sent to their respective ranges.

It took about two months to work both pastures the first time in the spring. Beginning at the head of McDonald about April 15, the outfit finished at the Soldiers Mound stand from June 10 to 15. After spending a day or two at headquarters, the men set out again for the head of McDonald to begin the second time over. This second working was for the purpose of branding and marking calves missed the first time. Since there was not nearly so much branding to be done this time, the range was covered more rapidly than before, and the outfit finished up at Soldiers Mound about the middle of July.

Rounding-up was left off from six to eight weeks, depending on the weather and the grass. There were two reasons for the intermission: first, the horses were well-fagged after three months and needed to rest for the heavy fall work; and second, since the hottest, driest weather usually came in July and August, any undue exertion on the part of the cattle at this season would cause them to lose flesh. While the horses were resting and the cattle were pantingly swishing away the sultry hours under the dim shades of scrubby mesquite trees, the men scattered out in pairs at the various line-camps and were put to still-hunting. There were six of these camps: Merriman's, South camp, McDonald, Red Mud, Catfish, and Duck Creek. The men "kept batch" and rode out each day in various directions, quietly circling among the cattle looking for unbranded calves that both round-ups had missed and for cattle with screw worms. If an unbranded calf was spied, the hand maneuvered quietly and

slowly until he was in roping distance. Suddenly his rope shot
out, and the astonished calf found himself caught, thrown, and
tied. The hand then made a small fire of dry mesquite twigs
(and possibly cow chips) in which he heated a running iron
which he carried on his saddle. When he had branded and
marked the calf, he carefully put the fire out and in a most
leisurely fashion started looking for another victim. If he found
an animal with screw worms, he threw and tied it, and administered the screw worm medicine, a supply of which he always
carried in an old boot top sewed up at the bottom and tied to
his saddle.

Keeping these men at the line-camps at this season of the year
was good business for the company. When they came in about
the middle of September, those of each camp usually reported
branding from 150 to 300 calves. The fact that the men were
scattered over the entire range and were riding the pastures
most of the daylight hours at a time when there were unbranded
calves running loose did a great deal to foil the plans of "nester"
rustlers.[5]

The fall range work got under way usually from September
10 to 20. Both pastures were worked two or three times before
December 15. As a rule it took about four weeks to cover the
entire range once over. The work was much more spasmodic and
irregular in the fall than in the spring. Fog and rainy weather
frequently caused delays in September and October, and discon-
certing "Northers" interfered with the work in November and
December. In the fall of 1889 one of the British directors of the
Company, John McNab, again visited the Ranch. As several of
the hands expressed an opinion that there was a considerable
fall calf-crop, McNab requested that the cattle be carefully counted during the last fall round-up. The difficulty caused by the
weather in getting a count was explained by Horsbrugh in a report to the Home office, November 20, 1889:

I had my doubts as to whether such a thing could be done satisfactorily at this time of the year. It was tried, however, but the
unsettled state of the weather and frequent "northers" renders it
impossible to get anything like a true estimate of the number of
cattle. Three-fourths of the she cattle are on this side of the range
(the East pasture). All the steers that could be gathered being put

[5]Spur Records, XV, 51, 66, 69.

over on the West side. . . . In the West pasture we got a fairly good count, but on this side the weather interposed and made the whole thing a failure. Not many cattle were found on Red Mud, the bulk of them being over on both sides of Duck Creek. . . . A bad northeast wind set in before we branded north (going north up Duck Creek), and the cattle drifted night and day into country that had already been worked. Counting was continued up the last— 16,000 cows and two year old heifers—but we did not get two-thirds of the cattle on this side. Such a manner of counting is a good idea in the summer time when the weather is good, but in November nine times out of ten it will be spoiled by the weather. The bad storms we had at the beginning of the month had scared the cattle, and since then I have noticed that any severe spell causes them to start drifting from the north with the wind.[6]

A trail outfit worked part of the time throughout the fall in conjunction with the branding outfit. The trail outfit, however, operated as a separate unit, having its own wagon, cook, and string of saddle horses. Its services were necessitated by the fact that each year there had to be a rearrangement and a redistribution of the Ranch's herds. The calves of the year before were now classed as one-year-old heifers and one-year-old steers (commonly called heifer 1's and steer 1's). The one-year-old heifers and the steers of the year before were now 2's. The two-year-old heifers of the year before were now cows and ready to be sold or added to the Ranch's breeding herd. The two-year-old steers were now 3's and ready to be sold or added to the Ranch's beef herd. Inasmuch as the Ranch attempted to keep certain classes of cattle together in various pastures, the animal regrouping necessitated a considerable amount of trail driving back and forth on the Ranch itself, or to and from the pastures leased by the Ranch, as in the case of the White Deer Pasture north of Clarendon.

A notion of the varied nature of fall work can best be had from extracts from the Ranch diary for 1900. Beginning on August 27 when twelve of the hands were stationed in pairs at the six line camps still-hunting, the other hands were doing many and sundry things.

Monday, August 27, 1900

Wilkinson's outfit consisting of C. C. Haile (cook), J. C. Hobson, J. W. Haile, J. B. Conner, left to repair "Tap" fence. J. H. Gilmore's outfit still building fence on line of Public Domain. Camp

[6]Spur Records, IV, 144.

men still out as per 5th *ulto.* J. H. Reynolds and J. D. Martin horse hunting in Dockum Flat. Jones repairing roofs on various buildings at Ranch. H. P. Cole riding in Duck Creek doctoring for screw worms. Holly came to ranch. Weather: very warm, slight s. e. breeze.

Tuesday, August 28

Work going on as set forth on 17th inst. Holly left for camp with wire and provisions. J. B. Conner came to ranch for posts. Cole went to fencing outfit. Reynolds and Martin riding in Duck Creek doctoring screw worms. Jones repairing roofs on buildings at ranch.

Wednesday, August 29

Work going on as set forth on the 27th. H. P. Cole left for fencing outfit in "Tap." Conner came to ranch for wire. Jones working around ranch cleaning up. Martin riding Duck Creek fence. Reynolds riding in "Tap" pasture. J. D. Raines came to Ranch (from Duck Creek Camp) reports screw worms letting up and 200 calves branded. Weather: cloudy and cool, good breeze from E., indications of rain.

Practically the same routine was kept up until September 6.

Friday, September 7

Wilkinson's outfit came to Ranch. Since 28th August have repaired part of Tap fence and on down to division fence on Red Mud. Put in about 300 posts, cut and put in stays, restretched wire, etc. J. H. Gilmore's outfit came to Ranch. Since 13th June have built 16 miles of new fence, put in 2400 posts, cut and put in 5000 stays. . . . Balance of proposed fence to be built by contract. J. W. Standifer came to Ranch and left again. Reynolds went to round-up at Pansy Windmill. Martin and Jones riding range. Cole riding range. T. J. Harrison came to ranch. Ellis came to Ranch. Weather: very warm, wind E.

Saturday, September 8

Everybody rounded up Duck Creek. Mr. Horsbrugh and Dawson at round up. Branded 13 calves and counted 1422 steers. Reynolds came to ranch having found nothing (at Pansy Windmill round-up) belonging to the "Spurs." Outfit rounded up West Horse pasture and branded 30 calves. Weather: very warm, wind E.

Sunday, September 9

Outfit rounded up "Tap" pasture and branded 11 calves and counted 1370 steers. Waldrup came to Ranch. Reported branding 265 steers. A. S. Carter and J. D. Raines came to Ranch. Reported branding 202 calves. L. Barrow came to Ranch and reported branding 151 steers. All since July 5. Weather: slight rain all day and into night.

Monday, September 10

Branding outfit, in charge of W. A. Wilkinson, consisting of C. C. Haile (cook), J. D. Raines, A. S. Carter, J. B. Conner, L. Barrow, T. J. Harrison, J. C. Hobson, M. Howell, Tol Merriman and B. Wilks and trail outfit in charge of J. H. Gilmore consisting of Carl Holt, J. B. Morrison, C. Thomson, J. W. Haile (cook), S. Ellis, R. L. Holly, T. Hunter, Ed Hutson and W. Waldrup all left for head of McDonald to begin fall work branding calves and gathering steers and old cows. J. D. Martin and M. L. Jones remained at ranch to ride fence and do general work. A. J. Wheeler came to Ranch and left again. Lockett at work on windmill in Duck Creek. G. Morrison getting ready to work at repairing fence around "Burleson" pasture. Weather: very warm.

Most important of the hands at a branding were the ropers. When in a corral or in an open round-up on the range these men worked on horseback. Roping required much skill and long practice. Good ropers were the star performers of the round-ups and the branding pens. Probably there was never a true tenderfoot cowhand who did not aspire to become a top roper. He practiced at odd times for years and, with rare exceptions, he never made it. Great ropers, like great musicians, were scarce. The best ones on the Spur Ranch, according to Jake Raines, were Bud Campbell, Handy Cole, Tol Merriman, and Jack Morris. Jake, himself, was pretty good. However, there was a hand on the Two Circle Bar Ranch (now called the O Bar O) whom the top Spur ropers conceded was better than they. He was Charlie Binyon, who put on an amazing performance while roping for the Two Circle Bar Ranch at a round-up near the mouth of Jordan Creek in the Spur East Pasture. One observer, whose job was to keep the branding fires going and the irons sizzling hot, later recorded that Binyon's roping on that occasion was the most extraordinary performance he had ever witnessed in ranch work or rodeo. The round-up contained an unusual number of cattle. The forenoon had been spent gathering the animals, and the branding started after dinner, as the midday meal was called on the range. Binyon was one of two chosen to do the roping. The flankers, knowing Binyon's reputation, were eager and exerted themselves to the utmost. They called to Binyon how they wanted the next calf brought out, by the hind feet, the front feet, or combinations. Apparently without effort and with singular ease he caught the calf as requested. In four hundred trials he never missed a throw. He had a unique method of tossing

the rope. He never used his arm, but with a twist of the wrist
the loop shot out as if from the muzzle of a gun. In the country
east of the Caprock the stories of Binyon's roping feats are still
told in cow camps seventy-five years after they happened.

The entries in the Spur Ranch diary from September 11 to
October 10 are devoted for the most part to the daily operations
of the branding and trail outfits as they moved around the range
working stands at the usual camp sites.

Thursday, October 11

Trail outfit taking cows to south pastures. Branding outfit comes
to ranch. H. P. Cole and Dawson gathering old horses in Duck
Creek pastures. G. M. Allen underpin[n]ing houses at the Ranch.
Cravey, Jones, Morrison, and Martin cutting and stacking hay at
Old Farm. R. B. Masterson arrives at Ranch. Weather: cool and
cloudy.

Friday, October 12

Branding outfit at Ranch. Wilkinson, Conner, and Hobson carrying chain for surveyor, Geo. Spiller. Dawson and Cole with surveying outfit. Mr. Horsbrugh and Masterson riding in Duck Creek
and "Tap." Balance of branding outfit shelling corn. Weather: warm
and clear.

Saturday, October 13

Trail outfit came to ranch. Wilkinson, Conner and Hobson carrying chain for Geo. Spiller. Dawson and Cole with surveying outfit.
Weather: warm and clear.

Monday, October 14

Wilkinson's outfit moved to windmill in Dockum pasture to build
earth tank and lay overflow pipe from tubs to tank. Gilmore's
outfit moved to "Tap" to cut wood for Ranch. Morrison and Jones
went to McDonald to put up feed at Gilmore's place. Martin and
Cravey hauling wood from Gilmore's outfit to Ranch. Cole at
Dockum's windmill. Reynolds came to Ranch from Matador work.
Weather: cool and cloudy.

Wilkinson's outfits remained at Dockum's windmill, Gilmore's
outfit continued cutting wood, and the usual routine kept up
around the Ranch until Sunday, October 20, when both outfits
came in. Three days were spent in rounding up the small pastures around headquarters, one day in hunting horses, fixing
wagons and so on preparatory to a general round-up, and on
Friday, October 26, Wilkinson's branding outfit and Gilmore's
trail outfit left for the head of McDonald. The round-up was
finished November 20. The men were then put at cutting and

hauling posts, hauling wire, taking down fence, repairing fence, building new fence, hauling wood and riding range until November 29.

Friday, November 29

Outfits rounded-up Duck Creek, "Tap" and Burleson pastures for old cows, steers, and old bulls, and partly cleaned herd for the trail. Weather: warm and clear.

Saturday, December 1

Outfits finished cleaning up herd and started for Railroad, Wilkinson in charge with 10 men. Gilmore's outfit went to finish building fence on north bound[a]ry of Burleson pasture. Weather: warm and clear.

Wilkinson's trail outfit was away fifteen days, Gilmore's men finished the fence in five days and moved to New Farm and started shelling corn. In the meanwhile several other men were kept busy hauling wood to headquarters, repairing the horse stables, hunting bulls, hauling hay and riding range.

Monday, December 17

Gilmore's outfit shelling corn at New Farm. Wilkinson's outfit hauling wood and horse hunting, having lost 30 horses on the 14th. Harrison, Merriman, and Cole riding range. Martin attending to horses at ranch. Morrison and Jones hauling hay. Weather: cool and clear.

The work continued as set forth on the 17th through Friday, December 21.

Saturday, December 22

Hutson, Jone, Morrison (T. J.), Thompson, Morrison (Tol), Hunter, Holly, Holt, Hobson, and Conner paid off. Wilkinson, Harrison, Raines, Wilkes, and Waldrup went to Childress for bulls. Balance of men turned loose for Christmas.

The men retained for winter work were given three holidays, and on December 27 the regular winter routine began.

Cattle had a way of drifting and getting mixed up on the range. In spite of good fences and vigilant line-riders, Spur cattle continually got over in the Matador pastures, and Matador cattle turned up on the Spur range. Spur and Curry Comb cattle managed to exchange pastures, and so on. This migrating tendency was more prevalent in winter than summer. A severe norther or a blizzard caused the cattle to start drifting with the wind, looking for shelter. If a creek bank or canyon offered

The Spur headquarters.

Courtesy Clifford B. Jones.

Fred Horsbrugh, 1889–1904.

Courtesy Southwest Collection, Texas Tech University.

Henry Johnstone, 1904–1907.

Courtesy Clifford B. Jones.

Charles A. Jones, 1907–1913.

Courtesy Clifford B. Jones.

Clifford B. Jones, 1913–1938.

The Spur Ranch spring house. Photo by Erwin E. Smith.

Moving the Spur chuckwagon. Photo by Erwin E. Smith.

Spur hands taking it easy around the chuckwagon. Photo by Erwin E. Smith.

A farmer typical of the many "prospectors" who moved onto the school lands within the Spur pastures. Photo by Erwin E. Smith.

The Spur hands at work. Photo by Erwin E. Smith.

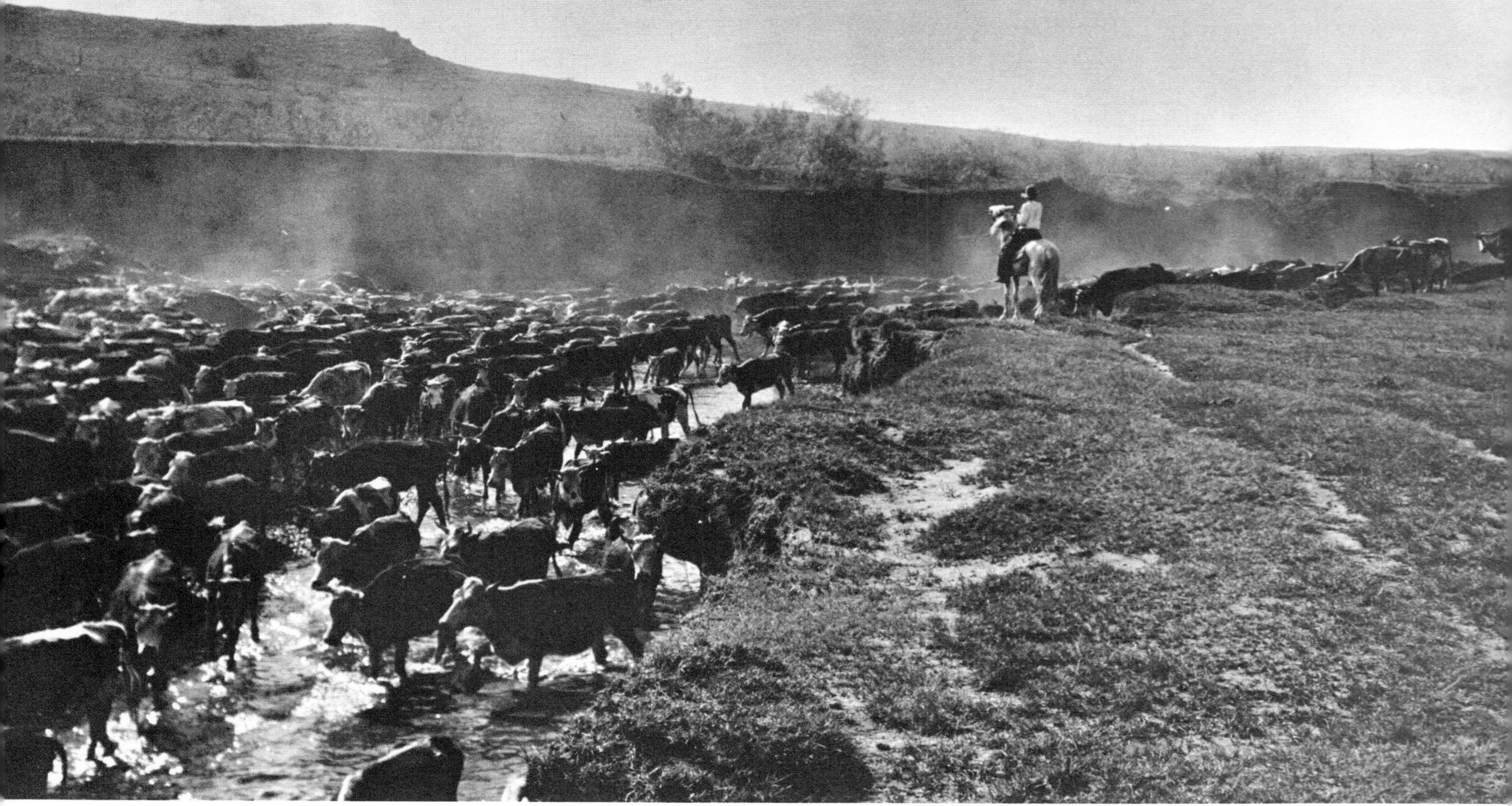

Courtesy Library of Congress.

The Spur remuda crossing Duck Creek. Photo by Erwin E. Smith.

security, they stopped and took refuge there. However, if some kind of wind-break was not found, they drifted on until they came to a fence, which stopped them, or most of them. The cold caused the wire to become taut and brittle. If enough pressure was exerted on it, a wire or two would snap leaving a place between two or three posts large enough for some of the cattle to squeeze through. In the spring, summer, and fall, freshets occasionally washed out water-gaps (places where fence lines crossed creeks and rivers). Before the gaps could be repaired, a number of cattle might have found them and passed through. The wires might be broken anywhere along the fence as the result of a number of causes, and some of the cattle might find the place before the fence rider did.

The efforts of various ranches to regain their strayed cattle caused a regular detail of routine to develop—a system of "reping." Each ranch kept a representative with the branding outfits of neighboring ranches through the rounding-up seasons in the spring and the fall. The "rep" assisted in the round-up he was attending, but his primary duty was to cut out and hold all strays bearing the brand of his ranch. The Spurs, always kept a "rep" at the round-ups on the ranges to the north and another at the round-ups to the south. For some reason the Spur cattle did not drift to the west or east to any great extent. An idea of the number of Spur cattle which strayed northward may be had from the following extract from the Ranch diary, Tuesday, July 31, 1900:

J. H. Reynolds returned today from outside work ("reping") in the Matador and Milliron pastures (that is, the country between here and Estelline) where he had been working since 7th May. During that time he has recovered 350 head of cattle for us, including 75 head of steers which he put in the Duck Creek pasture.

The period of Ranch work known as the winter season—January, February, March—was a rather drab one for the hands. The range was dead and colorless, and the work lacked the action of the rest of the year. The nature of the work isolated the men to a great extent, and those who had gregarious natures fretted from loneliness. The men stationed at the line-camps, unless they had families, would often go for days without seeing anyone.[7]

[7]Spur Records, IV, 210.

The biggest single task during the winter was fence-riding. From six to eight men were kept at it constantly. These men were stationed at the line-camps. Each morning a rider saddled a horse and started leisurely along a line of fence. His equipment consisted of a supply of staples in a leather pouch attached to his saddle and a pair of fence pliers (a sort of combination tool which could be used to cut wire, and to pull or drive staples). Many of the men did not eat anything from the time they left in the morning until they returned in the evening; but if a hand wanted a lunch (he always called it dinner) he carried along a can of tomatoes, and maybe, a few crackers and a pinch of salt. He opened the can with his pocket knife and ate the tomatoes with an old spoon which he carried in his pocket or his saddle bag. He jogged along until noon, keeping an eye on the fence to see if any of the wires were broken or if any staples were out of the posts. He especially gave attention to the ground under the fence to see if by chance any cattle had squeezed through. As he went along, he also kept a vigilant look out over the range.[8] Nothing, living or dead, within his range of vision escaped him. Persons who are in the open a great deal acquire this habit, and their eyes have a tendency to travel back and forth on the range, even when they are thinking of something else. Occasionally the rider would leave the fence temporarily to go to the crest of a nearby hill in order to get a better view of the country. He usually covered from eight to fifteen miles of fence by noon when he would turn back. Once in awhile he might meet the rider from the next camp. If so, they would get off their horses, squat down on the ground, sitting on their boot heels, eat their tomatoes, smoke a few cigarettes together, and "gas" awhile before each started to his own camp. For the most part the principal diversion of the rider throughout the day was the rolling, lighting, and smoking of cigarettes. Each of these three steps necessary for a smoke was an art. The rolling of a cigarette by holding a flimsy, yellow cigarette paper in one hand, and pouring the Bull Durham with the other while the horse was in motion and the wind sometimes at forty miles an hour was more than a novice could do. The lighting of the cigarette with one match (matches were too scarce to waste) was an achievement acquired only by years of practice. And the

[8]Spur Records, II, 10.

smoking—the drawing in of an immense volume of smoke, holding it in the mouth, lungs, and nostrils for a good fraction of a minute, and exhaling it slowly through the nose, and apparently enjoying it—therein lay the art. From early morning until the return to camp at night cigarette followed cigarette.

Next to fence-riding in magnitude came range-riding. This was more interesting than fence-riding in that the range-rider could go a new route each day; otherwise, the two jobs were somewhat similar. Instead of looking primarily for broken places in a fence, the range-rider looked for anything and everything he could see—the condition of the cattle, the watering places, sick or crippled animals, signs of predatory animals, signs of prairie fire, and any strange persons on the range. The number of range-riders through the winter varied from one to six, usually about three.

Occasionally several hands would be stationed at the line-camps for the purpose of "still-hunting" for big, unbranded calves that had escaped all the round-ups of the previous season. With these men scattered over the range there was not so much need for regular range-riders. While the "still-hunting" was going on, there was usually only one range-rider, whose main duty was to keep in touch with the still-hunters who reported to him what they observed.

During heel-fly time in February and March the range-riders made it a part of their daily routine to "ride bog." "Riding bog" consisted of going by all the watering places, creeks and tanks, that were known to be boggy enough to mire a weak cow seeking refuge from heel-flies. During the season when the flies were unusually bad extra men had to be placed at riding bogs.

Around headquarters several kinds of work went on through the winter. One man devoted all his time to feeding the bulls. Bulls were the hoofed aristocrats of the Ranch. They alone of the herds had more than grass to winter on. The welfare of future herds depended on their coming through the winter strong and vigorous.

One or two men spent the most of their time hauling wood to headquarters. Two men hauled hay from the farms to headquarters and the line camps. Each of the line riders had two mounts which required feed during the winter months. A man or two kept busy doing odd jobs, such as repairing and cleaning stables. There was work to be done at the gin and the corn mill. Cattle that died on the range were sometimes skinned. Winter plowing had to be done on the experimental farm and the feed farm. Windmills needed more attention in the winter than in the summer. The pipes would sometimes freeze, and the sucker rods pulled in two.

For a period of two years, 1887-1889, the Ranch employed a blacksmith who worked from April to October at a wage of $40 a month. Keeping the farm machinery in repair, making broken parts for the windmills, and shoeing the saddle horses kept him busy most of the time. His wife did the milking and the butter making at headquarters for which she received a wage of $25 a month. The instructions given the blacksmith specified that he was to spend his extra time gardening and helping his wife with the milking.[9] The Ranch always kept sufficient milk cows to furnish milk and butter for the hands. After 1889 the company did not keep a regular blacksmith, but a hand continued to do the milking while the cook did the butter making.[10] Smithing was done in the company's shop by various hands, and the more difficult pieces of work were sent to a blacksmith at Estacado, and, later, to one at Dickens.

[9]Spur Records, II, 60.
[10]Spur Records, V, 105.

Table 4.   DIVISION OF LABOR FOR ONE YEAR (1891)

Feed farm	22.2 %	Foreman	1.8 %
Rounding-up and branding	19.7 %	Outside round-ups	1.8 %
		Horse rustling	1.8 %
Trail driving	15.07%	Fixing fence	1.6 %
Farm	11.5 %	Hauling hay	1.1 %
Riding	9.5 %	Blacksmithing	1.1 %
Cooking	5.5 %	Tanking	1.1 %
General	2.5 %	Dairy	.9 %
Trail riding	1.97%	Range riding	.3 %

XIV: *TRAILS AND TRAIL DRIVING*

THE CATTLE TRANSPORTATION problem is a queer study. Contrary to expectations, the cattlemen were better off without railroads up to a certain point in the history of the cattle industry. The principal markets of Texas cattle at the time were in the grazing regions of the Northwest. Cattle could be trailed a thousand miles through a country provided with sufficient grass and water with less expense and in better condition than they could be shipped a hundred miles on the railroad. As long as the railroads stayed hundreds of miles away, there was no likelihood of settlers over-running the country. When the railroads began to extend out across the great plains area lying between the Mississippi Valley and the Rocky Mountains, they started bringing in hordes of settlers who began taking up and fencing the land in quarter-section, half-section, whole-section and four-section blocks. The first effect of this encroachment was to push the cattleman's trails farther and farther west. Had the settlers let up, things would not have been so bad for the cattleman, but the army of settlers had no notion of letting up. By the end of the 80's they were making it extremely difficult for southern drovers to get to Wyoming and Montana. By the end of the 90's they had stopped all long distance trail driving entirely. Ranchmen who sent large herds to Ogallala, Montana, easily in 1885 chafed as they tried to find routes by which they could drive small herds to shipping points fifty or a hundred miles distant in 1905. Then it was that the ranchman became a booster for railroads. He wanted one to come through his ranch or at least within ten or twenty miles. Railroads proved the undoing of the cattleman in two ways: they destroyed his natural and cheap means of transportation, and they brought the settler who took up the land and restricted his range.

For a year or two after its acquisition by the Espuela Land and Cattle Company, Limited, of London, the Spur Ranch disposed of its cattle by what had then become the traditional long-drive. Two herds were sold in 1885 for delivery at Ogallala,

Montana. The first herd of approximately 2,500 steers with B. G. Davis as trail boss started from the Ranch in June and proceeded northwest along the Goodnight trail to southeast Colorado and thence north to the Montana Trail and on to Ogallala.[1] The horses and the wagon were sold at Ogallala, and the men came back on the train by way of Fort Worth. The second herd, a mixed one of 2,250 head with Pink Hays as trail boss, left July 5 and followed the same route as the first. The men brought the horses back, arriving at the Ranch November 8.[2] A beef herd was driven south to Colorado City, Texas, in November, 1885. Herds were driven more rapidly on short drives than on long ones. The hundred-mile drive to Colorado City was made in five days.[3]

In 1886 the Spur herds were driven to Coolidge, Kansas.[4] Coolidge was one of the last railroad shipping points in Kansas that could be reached by Texas trail herds. This town was on the Atchison, Topeka and Santa Fe Railroad and the Arkansas River just a few miles east of the Colorado state line. The Spur herds were driven there and held until buyers could be found for them.[5]

The herds in 1887 were driven to Colorado City. They followed the old mail route from Dockum to Colorado City.[6] The driving of trail herds to the south was a reversal of the usual direction of trail driving. At Colorado City the cattle were shipped by way of Fort Worth or Dallas to Kansas City or St. Louis.

In 1888 the drives were again to the north. Trail driving was heavy that year, as six herds were sent away. The first two herds were sent to Amarillo by way of Tule Canyon.[7] The Fort Worth and Denver Railroad had reached Amarillo from Fort Worth in the fall of 1887, and on January 26, 1888, had connected with the line building southeast from Denver. In the summer of 1888, cattle could be shipped to Kansas City or St.

[1]For an account of the Goodnight trail and other major trails from Texas to New Mexico and the Northwest, see Holden, *Alkali Trails,* 33-37.
[2]Spur Records, I, 3, 57, 85.
[3]Spur Records, I, 50.
[4]Spur Records, I, 189.
[5]Spur Records, I, 18-19.
[6]W. R. Stafford to W. C. H., interview, February 28, 1930.
[7]Spur Records, II, 433.

Louis by way of Fort Worth or to northwest grazing regions by way of Denver. The drive from the Spur Ranch to Amarillo, a distance of 150 miles, was made in twelve days and cost approximately 50 cents for each cow driven.[8] Lomax planned to start a third herd to Amarillo in July, but the weather became so dry and water so scarce that he directed the outfit to proceed by Mott, Quitaque, and Oxbow to Giles, a small station on the Fort Worth and Denver four miles west of Memphis, where the cattle were shipped to the Northwest.[9] A fourth herd, composed of heifers, was driven to Amarillo by the Tule Canyon route in August.[10] Water was so scarce on the plains that a dry drive had to be made from Tule Canyon to Amarillo. A fifth herd followed in September;[11] and in November a small herd of 650 steers set out for the same destination.[12]

Amarillo enjoyed a brief spell of being a rather important cattle market and shipping point, comparable in a small way to Dodge City and Newton, Kansas. For two years after the railroad came through Amarillo, 1888-1889, herds were driven in from all directions and held for days on the prairies about the town while their owners dickered with buyers from the Northwest or the Midwest packing centers. During this time the Spur Ranch drove dozens of herds there. During 1889, as had been the case in 1888, Spur herd after Spur herd trailed up Tule Canyon and across the level plains to the small Panhandle town with its new boxed houses.[13] Like the other temporary shipping points for cattle on the Great Plains, Amarillo was allowed to feel but a short time that she was a part of the wild west with cattle herds constantly bellowing nearby and with dusty, unshaven cowhands filling her streets, restaurants, and saloons. With the railroad at hand and good wheat lands that could be had for the buying (for $2 and $3 an acre on long time terms) and put in cultivation for the breaking of the turf, it was only a matter of time until the land for miles in all directions was fenced, leaving no avenues for herds to approach except through long lanes and no place to hold them near the town. Drovers

[8]Spur Records, V, 1.
[9]Spur Records, II, 461.
[10]Spur Records, II, 470.
[11]Spur Records, II, 579.
[12]Spur Records, II, 610.
[13]Spur Records, V, 239.

found it ever increasingly necessary as the years passed to find other places for shipping their herds.

From 1890 to 1909, the Spur Ranch drove its herds to Clarendon, Childress, and Estelline[14]—all on the Fort Worth and Denver. Clarendon was three days farther than Childress or Estelline, but grass and water along the way were better.[15] When weather and grass conditions were favorable, the herds went to Childress or Estelline. Estelline was fifteen miles northwest of Childress and was scarcely more than a country switch on the railroad. As the surrounding country was not so well settled as around Childress, the ranches came more and more to use Estelline as a shipping point.

By 1904 it was becoming a serious undertaking to drive a herd even to Estelline. The last twenty miles were through a lane where neither grass nor water were to be had. If any of the cattle gave out on this stretch, they had to be left in the barren lane without a chance of getting the necessary sustenance to revive them. The Spur managers adopted the policy of cutting out and leaving the weak cattle just before they left the Matador range to enter the long lane.[16] The increasingly cramped conditions forced drovers to reduce the size of their trail herds. The average-sized Spur herd in 1904 was from 1,000 to 1,500, never larger than 1,500.

The changing conditions are reflected in a letter from Johnstone to the Home office in June, 1904:

> The difficulty of getting a herd to the Railroad is one that has arisen since the country became thickly settled, and in a dry time like this it is a very serious problem. I sincerely hope some railroad building may be done through this district before another season, but I hear no mention of any project of the kind at the present.[17]

Six months later, Johnstone again wrote:

> The expense of driving cattle to the Railroad is about doubled on account of the country having been so much fenced up. When the country was open, it was a simple matter to drive 3000 head in one herd; now it is a risky matter to start with 1500.[18]

When the Spur Ranch was organized, trail driving had al-

[14]Spur Records, XI, 106.
[15]Spur Records, VIII, 257.
[16]Spur Records, XI, 383.
[17]Spur Records, XI, 383.
[18]Spur Records, XI, 615.

ready become reduced to a more or less standardized routine. Practically every trail outfit from the Rio Grande to Canada had the same kind of chuck-wagon, swung a herd out on the trail with point-men, swing-men and drag-men, took turns at night herding, managed the *remuda* of saddle horses, and endeavored to control a stampede in the same way.[19] Had it been possible to have picked up a trail hand in Texas and bodily transported him over night to Montana and placed him in another trail outfit doing exactly the same job he was doing the day before, he could have carried on the work without the necessity of getting instructions from the new trail-boss. The trail outfits followed the conventional organization. They usually consisted of nine trail-hands, a horse-wrangler, a cook, and a trail-boss. On rare occasions outfits started out with only eight men in all, while others, on equally rare occasions, had as many as fifteen.

The Spur outfits, as was generally the case with all other trail outfits, often lost a few head of cattle out of the herd in the course of the drive, or picked up a few strays belonging to people through whose ranges they passed. A regular system of handling strays came to be followed by all reputable cattlemen. If a Spur outfit lost or left some strays along the trail, the ranch in whose herds they turned up sold them along with its own cattle and sent the money, less the actual cost of handling the strays, to the Spur manager. On the other hand, if other people's strays were found in a Spur herd at the end of a drive, they were sold along with Spur cattle, and the sale price, less trail costs, was sent to the owner. In 1885, the Spur company charged owners of strays a dollar a head for strays driven to Montana.[20] Later the Company charged 50 cents for strays driven to Amarillo and other shipping points on the Fort Worth and Denver.

If the Spur Ranch had trouble getting its herds to shipping points or a market, the Company was in turn troubled by trail herds from the south attempting to cross the Spur range on their way up the trail. The old Dodge Trail over which most of the northern drive went from 1879 to 1884 extended from South Texas through Mason, Baird, Albany, Fort Griffin, Seymour, and Vernon, and across Indian Territory to Dodge City.[21] As a result

[19]Space does not permit a detailed account of a drive. A good account of trail life is found in Andy Adams, *Log of a Cowboy*. Also, see P. A. Rollins, *The Cowboy*, Ch. XIII.
[20]Spur Records, I, 67.
[21]*Fort Griffin Echo*, April 26, 1879, May 31, 1879, August 9, 1879.

of the rapid settlement of Baylor and Wilbarger counties many
herds from Central and South Texas in 1884 began turning off
the Dodge Trail at Fort Griffin, trailing northwest up either the
Double Mountain or the Salt Fork of the Brazos through Stone-
wall and Dickens counties, up Tule Canyon to a shipping point
in extreme Western Kansas, or through Eastern Colorado to the
Northwestern grazing regions. As this trail crossed the Spur
range, great annoyance was caused by the passing herds. In the
first place, herds from South Texas were often infected with
"Texas fever," a malady dreaded by Northwest Texas cattlemen.
In the second place, the passing herds tramped and ate huge
quantities of grass, a thing becoming more and more prized as
ranchmen were forced to fence their pastures. And in the third
place, with strange herds passing for thirty or forty miles through
a range occupied by Spur cattle, there was a good possibility
of some Spur cattle getting into a trail-herd and being driven
on as strays. If the trail-herd were under the direction of an
honest trail-boss and belonged to a reputable owner, the Ranch
eventually recovered the value of the strays, but unfortunately
these conditions were not always fulfilled. Trail outfits often
killed a beef every few days for fresh meat; and, somehow, stray
beef always tasted better than that of their own brand.

    After a few herds trailed across the Spur range, Lomax, at
the time manager of the old Espuela Land and Cattle Company
of Fort Worth, determined to stop such trailing across the Company's lands. He had two Texas rangers of Captain S. A. Mc-
Murry's company detailed to patrol the south boundary of the
Ranch and turn herds around the Spur range. The fence had
not yet been completed enclosing the Spur pastures, and it required more than ordinary ranch hands to persuade passing
drovers to respect the unfenced boundaries of the Spur range.
The Ranch retained the rangers from November 4, 1884, to July
25, 1885, paying their salaries and expenses in the meanwhile.[22]

    In July, 1885, with the southern and eastern boundaries of the
Ranch fenced, Lomax decided to dismiss the rangers and rely
upon his own hands to keep herds from crossing the Spur pastures. His new policy, vigorous and positive, is shown in the
following instructions to one of the Spur hands:

    You will please meet any herds proposing to come through this

22Spur Records, I, 16.

company's pasture, and notify the person in charge that the company will not permit passage of herds. As this Company has legal title to all of the land it has enclosed, and as there is no lawful trail through it, anyone disregarding our warning not to enter will be treated as a trespasser, and the owner proceeded against for damages. We wish to avoid difficulty with all, but must and will maintain our legal rights and the integrity of our property. In case of your warning being disregarded, you will at once notify me by messenger or letter so that I may take steps to protect the company's rights.[23]

Objecting to the passage of southern trail herds was not a new thing. The cattlemen of the Panhandle had met at Mobeetie, Wheeler County, in July, 1880, and solemnly resolved to stop further drives through their territory, designating two trails around their ranges.[24] The drovers to the south and southeast did not propose to turn aside for the sake of a mere resolution, however. For the next five years the Panhandlers resolved, threatened, and blustered. Some ranchmen kept herds off their respective ranches,[25] but southern drovers managed to wiggle through the blockade some way. In 1884 the Kansas legislature, fearing "Texas fever" passed a law conditionally closing the trails from Texas. Meanwhile, Colorado passed an act requiring all cattle from Texas to go through a quarantine period before entering Colorado. The Panhandle Cattlemen's Association and the Cherokee Strip Live Stock Association in 1885 were trying more desperately than ever to stop all southern trail herds from going through their country. Things were getting serious for the drover from Central and South Texas. The Texas legislature passed a joint resolution asking Congress to establish a national trail from Texas to the Northwest grazing region in order that Texas cattle might have an outlet.[26]

Lomax devoted his efforts during the last half of 1885 to keeping trail herds off the Spur range, but meanwhile he was keenly observant of what was going on to the north. He realized that in view of the pressure being brought by the cattle interests down-state and by the state legislature, it would be futile to try to stop entirely trail-driving from the south. If the ranch owners of Northwest Texas should effectively organize for the purpose

[23]Spur Records, I, 2.
[24]Fort Griffin Echo, August 7, 1880.
[25]Ibid., November 8, 1881.
[26]Regular Sess., 19th Legislature, 1885.

of stopping the passage of southern trail herds, the drovers would have trails ordained by legal process and go through anyway.[27] It would be better, he reasoned, for the ranches to provide a trail at their own expense, for passing herds. Having given the trail, they could control it; and such a course would not only give them the support of right-thinking men, but of the law as well.

During the fall of 1885 a few of the herds which Lomax had turned to the west around the Spur range found a route across the plains by going from the southwest corner of Floyd County to the head of Tierra Blanca in Deaf Smith County and then to southeast Colorado.[28] This route, one that carried the drovers west of the troublesome Panhandlers and Cherokee Strippers, became widely discussed during the late fall and winter of 1885.

Lomax was confident that many herds would be trying the new route in the spring of 1886. In view of the fact that the Spur, Two Buckle, and Curry Comb ranges controlled all approaches to the new route, Lomax invited C. M. Tilford of the Kentucky Land and Cattle Company (Two Buckle) and W. C. Young of the Llano Cattle Company (Curry Comb) to join the Espuela Land and Cattle Company, Limited, in opening a trail through their ranges to connect with the new tract in Floyd County.[29] The men were favorably disposed toward the plan, and an agreement was signed between the three whereby a tract was to be opened and watering places provided along the boundary of the Spur and Curry Comb ranches, on the southwest of the Spur range, and along the boundary of the Spur and Two Buckle ranches, on the west of the Spur range. In compliance with the agreement, the Spur Ranch pulled in 18 miles of fence, furnished 8 miles of wire and posts to the Llano Cattle Company, built tanks at Slicknasty Creek, at Salt Fork crossing, and at Lake Creek, and built a road up the Caprock. All of this work was done at the expense of the Spur Company except that the Llano Company shared the expense on the Salt Fork tank, and the Kentucky Company on the Caprock road.[30] By May, 1886, the trail was open from the Bow and Arrow camp, south of the Spur range, to where it joined the new plains route

[27]Spur Records, I, 143.
[28]Spur Records, I, 80.
[29]*Ibid.*
[30]Spur Records, I, 143.

at the head of Blanco Canyon. All of this expense was incurred in order that the Spur pastures might be protected from
wandering herds. The Spur Ranch never drove a single herd of
its own over the trail it spent thousands of dollars to establish.

Trail troubles did not end for the Ranch with the establishment of a trail, however. It was one thing to lay out a trail and
another to make drovers from the south travel it. Lomax mar-
shalled all of his forces to carry out the new policy. He kept
constantly one of his best hands down on the Albany trail to
warn trail-bosses of what they could expect if they did not take
the new trail. Lomax wrote to his trail rider on May 17, 1886:

I am glad to see the activity you are showing, and I hope that
the men in charge of the herds you warn off will listen and heed
what you tell them. But if they won't, and force their way in, I
want you to take your stand in the gate and make them use force
to get in. Then come right in to headquarters and the papers will
be made out for dealing with them according to law. Your testi-
mony is necessary to show their being notified not to come in and
their subsequent acts. I want you to come so that there will be no
misfire on the first case we tackle, even if others come in while
you are away, for if the first one gets a dose of law, probably those
coming after will learn by the other's experience that we mean to
protect this property. I feel great confidence in your prudence and
firmness, and I want you to understand that you will be protected
by me in all of your acts.[31]

At the same time Lomax issued the following general order:

To all employees of the Espuela Land and Cattle Company,
Limited:

This company having laid out a trail on its land along its south
and west boundaries, has the right to expect all passing herds to
take and keep the trail thus provided, without trespass. You are
hereby instructed that under no circumstances will you permit any
herd of cattle, sheep, or horses to enter this Company's enclosure,
and you will notify any who propose to do so that they will thereby
expose themselves to prosecution according to law. Should any herd
be found by you within the enclosure of the Company, it shall be
your duty to notify the person in charge of said herd of the above
and demand its immediate withdrawal. Any refusal to comply with
your demands in pursuance of the above must be immediately reported to the manager.[32]

It will be observed that the Spur managers resorted to law in

[31]Spur Records, I, 167.
[32]Spur Records, I, 133.

instances where gun-play and physical defiance would have been dramatic.

Nothing short of constant vigilance prevented herds from coming through the pastures in spite of the trail that had been provided for them. About nine trail bosses out of ten gave no trouble and took the new trail without misgivings. But occasionally one came along who was stubborn and contentious and who insisted on taking a short-cut through the Spur range where grass would be more plentiful than elsewhere. To forestall these overbearing bosses Lomax found it necessary, in addition to regular trail-riders and incidental assistance from all of the other ranch employees, to keep at the company's expense for several months during 1886 and 1887 one or more deputy sheriffs along the south pasture fence. A typical argument with a persistent trail boss took place during June, 1886. Three deputies and the trail riders held the herd outside the south fence until Lomax could be sent for:

On my arrival I found the Odom and Lucket herd still against the fence, the outfit declaring they would come in. I rode out and told the boss what I would do if he should make any farther effort to force his way into the pasture,—that I would have him and his whole outfit arrested. That afternoon he sent me word he would give it up and go around by the trail route we had laid out. This he did, I following around on the inside to prevent any entrance. He got his herd through in good shape, and gave me a letter to the effect that the trail was a practical one, and his herd had gone over it and had come through well.

One of the owners had in the meantime come up here and had seen me. He threatened to sue the Company for damages in refusing to let his herd go through. If he does I think we will be able to throw his case out of court.

So far at least we have carried our point, and I shall keep the deputies for a while, proposing to prevent by every lawful means at my command the entrance of any herds on this company's lands.[33]

Such cases occurred at intervals for a number of years.

From 1885 to 1890 many small "nester" herds were driven around Lomax's trail en route to New Mexico and Arizona. These herds often belonged to small cattlemen who owned no land and who shifted their cattle around from place to place, anywhere they could find free, or practically free, grazing. In

[33]Spur Records, I, 180.

view of the fact that these herds would not be sold to reputable buyers who might be inquisitive about strays in the herd and were probably not going to a region where any inspector for the Northwest Texas Stock Raisers Association would ever have an opportunity to look over the herds, it behoved the ranchmen to recover their strays before the herds crossed the plains. The Spur Ranch and its immediate neighbors were in a position to watch their interests in this respect. The Spur trail-rider, for instance, carefully looked over every herd that came by and cut out all cattle belonging to the Spur Ranch or its neighbors. But some of the herds came from a distance and might contain strays belonging to ranches hundreds of miles away. Upon the solicitation of Lomax, the Association kept an inspector on the trail in the vicinity of the Spur Ranch for a number of years.[34]

[34]Spur Records, I, 266.

Table 5. AVERAGE WAGE PER HAND BY YEARS

Year	Amount	Year	Amount
1885	$38.72	1898	$32.85
1896	34.84	1899	32.98
1887	34.96	1900	33.12
1888	33.19	1901	31.64
1889	32.65	1902	31.22
1890	32.24	1903	30.40
1891	32.14	1904	29.66
1892	32.79	1905	29.98
1893	32.80	1906	30.91
1894	33.21	1907	32.72
1895	32.28	1908	34.46
1896	32.63	1909	37.13
1897	33.17		

XV: *AMUSEMENTS*

MEN WHO WORKED on the Spur Ranch had very little social life—some years, none at all. The regular hands who worked the year round had three or four days off at Christmas, during which time they could seek pleasure elsewhere if they liked. The paucity of social occasions at the Spur headquarters was due in part to the attitude of the managers' wives. It took a woman to plan and execute a picnic or dance. Furthermore, it took a woman with character, ability, and poise to stage a successful social event on a large scale and make an institution of it. At times there were no women at all on the Ranch except the wives of some of the hands. Although Mrs. Lomax was a capable woman, she spent the greater part of her time in Fort Worth while her husband was manager of the Ranch, and her interests were in the social circles of Fort Worth rather than in the pleasures of the Ranch. For a while after Horsbrugh became manager, he remained single. When he did marry, he and his wife were not eager for long drawn-out festivities at headquarters. Johnstone never married. The lack of someone to sponsor diversions for the men caused life on the Spur Ranch to be a prosaic and humdrum affair for about 360 days out of the year. During the rest of the time the men had an opportunity to find diversion elsewhere.

A few incidents occasionally happened, however, to interrupt the usual monotony. Once in a great while the men were let off for a picnic for a day during July or August. The first instance of the kind took place in 1896. On August 17, Horsbrugh wrote the Home office:

There was a political meeting and a sort of barbecue or picnic at Dickens on the 14th; I gave the men a holiday and they all attended. A holiday of this sort is a good thing now and then, as it must be remembered that these men work on Sundays the same as other days.[1]

Horsbrugh's "now and then's," however, were extremely rare, for this was the first time, according to the records, such a thing

[1]Spur Records, VIII, 56.

had happened since the Spur Ranch had been taken over by the English company with its Scotch directors, and it was the last time it was to happen for another four years. Beginning in 1900, the Ranch management for a while went in a little stronger for picnics. A holiday was declared for July 26, 1900, in order that the men could attend a picnic at Dickens. The hands were allowed to come to headquarters on the afternoon before to make preparations; and a half-day was needed to get ready. Old razors were brought out; and then there was stropping, and lathering, and pulling, and grimacing, and cussing, and then more stropping. This torture lasted an hour or more. Some of the men took a bath; others just changed clothes. Some of them cut each other's hair. All in all, the getting ready was almost as big a job as the going. In order to get tuned up for the holiday, the various stages of the preparations were punctuated with "nips" from bottles which appeared from somewhere. (This was during the Horsbrugh regime, and after Ranch prohibition had been repealed.)

The picnic itself was probably as uninteresting as could be, yet it served the purpose for the Spur men.[2] It had been initiated by the local politicians on the day before the Democratic primary for the purpose of giving the candidates a chance to make speeches and do individual soliciting. The speaking was under a brush arbor. Most of the Spur hands did not care for "speechifying." They stopped and listened for a few minutes, but soon passed on to more interesting diversions. They threw balls at the cats, made crude jokes with the girl who ran the cat-stand, drank pink lemonade, hit acquaintances with rubber balls which had long rubber bands attached to them so that they would rebound to the one who threw them, and rapped each other with dime whips which they bought from the man who sold light walking canes, whips, and colored rubber balloons, attached to sticks. Some of the boys took too many "nips" during the day, but they were looked after by ones who had not taken so many. Nothing more serious happened than an occasional fistfight. The Matador men were at the picnic too; and they acted like the Spur men.

On July 26, 1901, the Spur outfit was allowed to go to another picnic at Dickens, but there is no record of the men's being let

[2]Spur Records, XV, 57.

off again.[3] In July, 1903, there was a three-day picnic and barbecue at Dickens, but the Spur hands were building tanks, and Horsbrugh decided that "water was too scarce" for the men to get off.[4]

If the Spur hands did not get a day off for picnicking the next year, 1904, they were given a day "to rest" on June 19. Johnstone, the new manager, allowed them "to rest" by "busting broncs" all day. Johnstone was famed for his sense of humor. He mentioned the occasion the next day in a letter to a friend:

> I rested the hands yesterday by allowing them to bust broncs, the ones that reached here about a month ago. There was a sorrel of the type you used to fancy which was described to me by the Colorado buster as a "High Actor," and he (the sorrel) certainly lived up to his reputation. However, there is a kid working here that is a "rider right," and he pulled it out of the sorrel to a queen's taste. He has got the pitching horse business down pat and sets on them apparently with great ease and a slack rein.[5]

The diversion the Spur men were permitted to enjoy most was hunting. Game was abundant—antelope, deer (in the earlier years only), wolves (both lobos and coyotes), panthers, turkeys, prairie chickens, ducks, and two kinds of quail, bob-whites and blue quail. There were myriads of rabbits, too, but no one considered rabbits game. Hunting was nearly always incidental to the regular routine. Men riding range, fence, or bog often carried a gun and took a shot any time an occasion arose. In this way they sometimes had wild meat to eat instead of beef. Once in a while when the men had a little time off between jobs, they went out on a hunt strictly for the sport of it. Occasionally the managers invited their sportsmen friends out for a hunt.[6] In the proper seasons, prairie chickens were easily found on the edges of the "shinnery" strip, and numerous covies of quail could be "jumped" in the "shinnery." As cold weather came on, flocks of ducks settled on the various tanks on the Ranch. Such game made splendid shooting, because the hunters could always slip up behind the tank dams, a thing that could not be done so easily at the natural lakes on the plains to the west.

Occasionally a fishing party was organized. These usually took

[3]Spur Records, XVI, 103.
[4]Spur Records, XI, 41.
[5]Spur Records, XI, 379.
[6]Spur Records, V, 91.

place in the latter part of March after some of the men had returned to the Ranch for spring work and before they were placed
on the payrolls on April 1. Fishing places were not plentiful in
Northwest Texas, but there were a few holes in Catfish and Duck
creeks and in Salt Fork where large catfish were to be had. Since
it was a good distance to the fishing holes, the parties usually
took three days for the expedition. The first day they went; they
fished that night, the next day, and the next night; and the third
day they returned, having lost considerable sleep. They always
carried a seine along, and when fishing by more sportsman-like
methods did not show results, they seined the holes and got fish
out by the tubsful.[7]

The hands got considerable pleasure from playing jokes on
each other. They put salt and horned frogs in each others' bed
rolls, lizards in each others' boots, and "cuckle-burrs" under each
others' saddle blankets while the horses were being saddled. They
carried on more or less horseplay all the time while not working,
but while at work they were serious and attended to business.

The story of the Wizard Oil is still recalled by old Spur hands.
The "oil" was a liniment, or counterirritant, carried in the chuck-
box for doctoring sprains and acute soreness. The effectiveness
of treatment resulted from the fact that the surface where applied burned so excruciatingly that the deeper pain was forgotten. A new hand who had never heard of Wizard Oil got badly
chafed on the inside of his legs as a result of heat and sweat.
He was in a bad way when he limped up to the chuck wagon
for supper, and asked if anyone had some vaseline. The practical
joker in the crew said no, but they did have something even
better. The unsuspecting new hand took the liniment, retired
behind a bush, let down his pants and slapped a handful of the
"oil" on the raw skin. In the meanwhile the joker had mounted
his horse and ridden out to what he considered a safe distance.
When the fiery liquid struck the irritated hide the new man let
out a yell and began a vigorous, hobbled dance. When at last
he could pull up his pants he grabbed his gun and started looking for the joker, who was watching from afar. When the new
hand finally located the perpetrator he was riding away hell-for-
leather. The new hand fired a couple of futile shots and rushed
to the lard can in the chuck box. The joker slept out on the

[7]Spur Records, XII, 24.

prairie that night. Next morning all was forgiven, but *not* forgotten.

The love life of one hand furnished diversion for the others for several months. Henry Price, about forty-five and a bachelor, yearned for feminine contact. He could read a little, but could not write. Somewhere he had procured a copy of a newspaper which carried a "lonely hearts" column called "Heart and Hand." It consisted of letters written by persons wanting husbands, wives, or just correspondents. One day Henry shyly approached Bill, a literate hand, and asked if Bill would write a letter for him in answer to one in the "Heart and Hand." Bill was delighted, and wrote a magnificent letter in the first person and signed Henry's name. Then he informed the other hands, and all waited as expectantly as Henry for the answer. It came as promptly as frontier mail service permitted, a letter perfumed, with beautiful handwriting in highly literate language. It suggested that they exchange photographs. Bill wrote a fitting answer, saying by all means to send the picture. All this was relayed to the boys who were somewhat puzzled as to what kind of fix Henry was getting into. In due time the photographs arrived, showing a lovely, beautiful woman, signed "With love. Mary." Henry showed it to Bill who was dumfounded, but not so much so that he neglected to watch where Henry hid the picture in his bunk. The first time Henry was away, Bill got it out and showed it to the boys. Now they were really puzzled, and to a man envied old Henry. Some began to scheme how they could cut in ahead of the grizzled old cowpuncher. In a few days Henry persuaded the boss to let him go to town with a freight wagon for provisions. When he returned he took Bill off and showed him a picture, not of himself, but a very handsome one of the boss. He asked Bill to write on it, "With love, Henry." Then he dictated a letter to send with the fake photograph. He lied like a trooper, explaining the he owned a well stocked ranch in Montana and had money in the bank. Then he asked her to marry him.

Bill relayed the contents of the letter to the boys, and they awaited the reply as impatiently as did Henry. It came rather promptly considering the mail service. Henry took it to the bunk house and waited for Bill to return and read it to him.

It was a short and to the point. In scrawling, almost illegible, pencil-writing it said, "I got your and you asks me will I marry you, and I answers you. If you'se yellow, yes. If you'se black, no. Mary." When Bill got a chance to tell the boys, they at first were as crestfallen as if each of them had been the victim. Quickly, they recovered and turned the joke on Henry, letting it be known they had been in on the affair from the beginning. Henry could not take it. He mounted his horse, rode away to Montana, and never returned. The boys missed Henry, not so much for himself, as for the termination of the love affair in which they all had become involved. They never forgave Mary for being a fraud, forgetful that Henry had acted the same role.

The hands on the Spur and Matador ranches were more than neighbors. Many of them had worked on both ranches, and a close affinity existed between the two groups. The Fort Worth and Denver Railroad reached Clarendon in 1887, and the town became a typical, "wide open" shipping point. The next year a Spur outfit and a Matador outfit arrived with trail herds for shipping about the same time. As soon as both herds were loaded, the hands of both ranches rode into town to celebrate. There previously had been bad blood between the Matador boys and the Sheriff. When that official undertook to arrest a Matador hand the Spur hands joined forces with the Matador boys, and the Sheriff left town. A chair over the head of the Deputy Sheriff sent him following his superior, and the two groups took over the town. The Sheriff from some distant point telephoned Lomax. The manager rode posthaste to Clarendon, where he found the boys had done no further damage. He got in touch with the Sheriff and said he would be responsible for all damages if the Sheriff would drop all charges. To this the Sheriff agreed. Lomax then "loose herded" the boys until they had out their spree. Then the two outfits, with most of the boys broke and with dark brown hang-overs, took the trail home. Lomax never reported the incident to the London office.

The new cowhand, or "tenderfoot" (incidentally the word "tenderfoot" does not appear in the records; they did not seem to know the word in the days when they had "tenderfeet"), was often the victim of pranks. The jokes were always perpetrated by a few hands who were mischiefmakers by nature. The majority of the men would look on and laugh, but would take no part in the devilment. Ranch hands of the 1880's were on the whole very much like present-day college students. Hazing is done by a minority of the upper classmen. The majority never trouble freshmen. Conventional pranks on "tenderfeet" have been much written about. The Spur men did all the usual ones, and once in awhile some that were original.

Occasionally, visitors on the Ranch by their complete asininity invited the attention of the prank-players. They were tempted to do their worst in the fall of 1889 when John McNab, one of the Scotch directors of the company previously mentioned, visited the Ranch. Horsbrugh, writing to his brother, described McNab's visit:

He acted as if he were scared to death, and had made up his mind to conceal his ignorance by disagreeing with everything I told him. He couldn't ride and had to be carried over the range in a buggy, which is very inconvenient. . . . I could not get him to understand common matters which simply made his head swim, and he angered me very much by repeatedly saying that he had no knowledge of such matters. . . . his whole visit was a continual worry and a great disappointment. . . . I had hoped that he would have at least a portion of the intelligence of Sir Robert Burnett who was a polished gentleman in every respect and sharp-witted, and one who certainly did not require a common self-evident fact to be driven into his head with a hammer and chisel. John McNab is very narrow-minded and Pharisaical, and though no doubt quite a great man about Alloa or the Carse's Cowric, he has never travelled sufficiently far from these places to find what little mind he possesses. He is very proud of the wealth owned by his family, but is eternally consumed with the fear that something may happen which will cause him to lose a "saxpense." He has all the bigoted attributes of the Scotch lower classes without any of their redeeming qualities of astuteness and sharpness. . . . He has the general appearance and conversation more of some smug grocer in some small country Scotch town than a director of such a large and peculiar property as this. I could not help thinking several times that if Good, as he chose to call the Deity, had been liberal to him in the matter of brains and had given him less money it would have been better for John McNab. He wanted to pat the horses which caused them to snort, rear up, and almost fall back. He could not get it into his head that ranch horses are not the patting kind.

I told the cow-punchers to leave him alone and they were good enough to do as I asked. Otherwise, they would have had a picnic with him and shot holes in his hat and umbrella and scared him to death.[8]

Imagine a person like this staying several weeks on a ranch

[8]Spur Records, IV, 154.

where the hands liked to initiate "tenderfeet"! And he carried an umbrella—an insult to the cow-punching fraternity. Even though the men were not permitted to make any demonstration in a case of this sort, it was like a continuous show to have a man like McNab on the Ranch. They watched him constantly, and every antic and blunder McNab made was repeated in the bunk house and round the camps with many a haw-haw and a slap on the leg.

On another occasion when John McNab visited the Ranch he was accompanied by his wife and Mr. and Mrs. Alexander McKay of the Matador Land and Cattle Company of Dundee, Scotland. Mrs. McNab and Mrs. McKay were observing the branding, marking, and castrating of bull calves at a roundup. Without knowing exactly what was taking place Mrs. McNab said, "It is terrible to treat those little cowlets like that!"

A hand standing nearby overheard her. With a straight face he said, "Madame, them's not cowlets. Them's bullets!"

The Spur hands were fond of going to court. Not many of them were fortunate enough to go often, but those who did felt they had been especially blessed. Some of them occasionally had to go to Estacado, Colorado City, Snyder, or Dickens as witnesses, and a few of them were eligible for jury service in Dickens County. Attending court was better than going to picnics. The hand was off from work, while his wages were going on. He drew *per diem* as a witness or a juryman. He got to spend several days in glorious loafing with nothing to do but chew tobacco, "sweat" the court room, and "gas" with other punchers there for the same purpose.

Ranch hands loved to dance. As a rule their brand of dancing was noisy and jerky, but it gave them a rare opportunity to hold a woman in their arms, or at least by the hands. For many years after the Spur Ranch was founded, they had no occasion for such diversion unless they went to some other ranch.

If dances were scarce on the Spur Ranch, they were plentiful at the Matador headquarters, thirty-five miles to the north; and the Spur men were always welcome there. The Matador Ranch set the social pace for a hundred miles in every direction, and the annual Christmas Ball became a regional institution. Social life there revolved around Mrs. H. H. Campbell, wife of the Matador superintendent. Mrs. Campbell was beautiful, capable, dignified.

She had the accent of an aristocrat and a fondness for the ranch hands. She arranged dances and church services for the boys with equal enthusiasm.

The first Matador dance was held Christmas, 1882, in the ranch headquarters, a two-room house whose lumber has been hauled from Fort Griffin. The six women present came from an area over 100 miles across.[9] With over fifty men wanting to dance, the interval between dances for some of them was long. The music was furnished by Ben Brock, the cook at headquarters, and Bud Browning, who was too religious to dance, but not too religious to fiddle for the better part of two nights and one day while the others danced. The following Christmas, 1883, the dance was held on a more elaborate scale. By that time a large, stone mess hall and kitchen had been constructed and the bunk house enlarged. More women attended than the year before, and the dancing was done in the mess hall. From 1883 until the Campbells left the Ranch in 1898, the annual Christmas ball was taken for granted and became as much a part of the Matador life as round-ups and trail-driving. The men looked forward to it during the whole year, and the hands laid off for the winter came to feel that they could not leave until the dance was over. Many of the Spur men spent their holidays in revelry at the Matador headquarters.[10]

It was an enormous task to prepare for the entertainment of from fifty to a hundred people for almost three days, but Mrs. Campbell was a good manager, and the hands did the work. Several of the men were sent out to hunt antelope, deer, and turkey. Some of them were good at cooking, and volunteered to do that. Antelope meat was made into stew with "sinkers" (dumplings). Deer meat was cut into steaks. The wild turkeys were poor and lean at that time of year, but they were larded with strips of bacon from wild hogs killed on the range.[11] The

[9]The women were Mrs. Joe Browning and her two daughters, Dicey and Della, from the head of Duck Creek, Miss Pruitt from down on the Wichita, Mrs. Bird, and Mrs. Campbell.

[10]Mrs. H. H. Campbell to W. C. H., interview, September 9, 1930.

[11]Wild hogs were quite common in Northwest Texas during the early 80's especially along the "shinnery" belts where acorns grew to some extent. The hogs had gone wild and migrated from the country below where they were raised extensively by the settlers during the 60's and 70's when Indians were constantly depredating the frontier. The Indians killed and sometimes drove off the settlers' cattle, but they had a subtle contempt for hogs, which were hard to kill and impossible to drive off.

hams of the hogs were boiled. If there were not sufficient wild meat and pork, a beef or two was killed and barbecued over an open pit in the yard. As time went on and game became more scarce, more and more beef was used. Several tubs full of doughnuts and hundreds of fried dried apple pies were made. During the early years of the ranch, Mrs. Campbell had gallons of wild plum jelly put up in the summer to take the place of cranberries at Christmas. Dozens of cakes had to be baked and frosted. In all, baking went on furiously for two days. It took all of one boy's time to keep wood cut and the fires going. The cakes, pies, cooked meats, bread, jelly, pickles and what-nots were stored on the shelves which had been built along one side of the bunk house.

Guests from other ranches began arriving from four to six o'clock in the afternoon before the dance was to start. Some of the Matador hands helped them unsaddle or unhitch their horses which were turned into the horse pasture. There was no need to worry about their horses any more until they got ready to go home. The women guests brought along their party clothes in suitcases. Some of the guests had been riding all day over a dusty road. They first went to the White House (the original two-room house had received several new rooms and a coat of white paint) where they dressed. Dressing was no small matter with numerous stiffly starched petticoats to adjust.

The ball was officially opened with a big supper in the mess hall. Some fifty people could eat at a time, but usually a second table was necessary. The supper consisted of some of everything that had been cooked during the last two days. After supper, the tables were removed from the mess hall, and the fiddlers began tuning up. When the caller sang out, "Get your partners," the dance began. All night, the next day, and the next night quadrilles followed waltzes and schottisches followed quadrilles. Mrs. Campbell made down beds all over the floor of the big room at the White House, and when the women would get so tired and sleepy they could go no longer move their feet, they slept an hour or two and then hurried back to the dance. The men could fall across beds in the bunk house for a nap, but the most of them never wasted that much time. The dance never stopped; those who slept, especially the women, did so in relays.

After the initial supper on the first night another formal meal was never served. From that time the matter of getting food became a serve-yourself, buffet affair. The buffet was the shelves in the bunk house. When one got hungry, he went there at any time he chose and ate what he wanted. A large pot of coffee was kept on the stove all the time. Practically all the men and some of the women took their coffee black and strong. Fortified with sandwiches, fried pies, slices of cake, doughnuts, and black coffee, the various stragglers rushed back to the dance.

Due to the fact that the women were always outnumbered three or four to one by the men, the exigencies of the occasion demanded that each woman dance practically every set. Considering that this went on for the better part of thirty hours, one wonders how the women stood it. Their feet got tired and sore, but otherwise they got through it very well. The men swung them so lustily that they used the minimum of exertion.[12]

There were two things which Mrs. Campbell would not permit at her dances: liquor and quarrelling. Both the Matador men and their guests understood Mrs. Campbell's wishes very well, and apparently respected them to the letter. The author has questioned both old Spur hands and old Matador hands as to how effective Mrs. Campbell's prohibition rulings were. Invariably, they smile sheepishly when pressed, and explain that most of the boys did take a few nips on the sly.

The records show that only one dance was given at the Spur headquarters from 1885 to 1907. There may have been others, but no mention of them is made. From 1885 to 1889 Mrs. Lomax was the one to sponsor a dance. She was interested in dances during the time, but not the kind held at the ranch houses. For a year after Horsbrugh became manager in July, 1889, he remained a bachelor, and it was during this time that the one memorable dance was held.

It was Horsbrugh's dance. He spent weeks in making plans and days in executing them. He was determined to stage an affair that would make the whole country take notice. He spent a great deal of time writing letters to various merchants in Colorado City for supplies. The refreshments consisted of a huge supper and plenty of egg-nog and coffee afterwards. From one merchant he ordered 5 dozen eggs, 10 pounds of butter, and 20 pounds of sugar. He took pains to explain he wanted refined

[12]Mrs. Campbell to W. H. C., interview, September 9, 1930.

sugar (not lump, the Ranch had plenty of that) for making cakes. From another merchant he ordered a two gallon coffee pot, and from still another, a case of old Scotch. Ten dozen lemons were to be sent up on the mail hack the day before the dance. Most of the food for the supper came from the Ranch commissary. A ham was baked and a whole beef barbecued. Cowboy musicians furnished the music. The dance went off in a way most pleasing to Horsbrugh.

The next July (1890) Horsbrugh married, and the advent of domesticity and the increasing financial straits of the Ranch caused him to think less and less of revelry. So no more dances were held. Johnstone was socially minded, a teller of tales, and an entertainer of men, but if he ever undertook a dance there is no mention of it.

Occasionally, a wedding broke the monotony of ranch life. Weddings were so scarce that when one did occur, it was an event to remember. When Horsbrugh married in 1890 and Dawson in 1900, the whole Ranch celebrated. Once in a while one of the hands would marry a settler's girl. Such weddings usually took place on Sunday afternoon at the bride's home, provided it was not a "run-a-way" affair. If it took place at a season when work was not too pushing, the men were given time off to attend. After the wedding came a big supper, if the settler could afford it. In a few days the newly-weds moved to a line camp on the Ranch, and at the first opportunity the boys would charivari them.

The only mention of a Christmas celebration at the Spur Ranch is found in the records for 1887. Lomax let the men off for the holidays on the evening of December 23. On Christmas Eve the men attended a shooting match for turkeys at Dockum's store. The match was promoted by Cook, the foreman at the experimental farm. Cook furnished the turkeys and got the profits of the match. A turkey was placed in a box with only its head sticking out. At ten cents a shot the men fired at the turkey's head from a distance of fifty yards. When anyone shot a head, he got the turkey.[13] The next day, Christmas day, the Ranch gave the men a big dinner.[14]

With accounts of only one big dinner and one big dance in

[13]Spur Records, II, 45.
[14]Spur Records, II, 45.

the records during the entire period that the Spur Ranch was operated by the English company, 1885-1907, it is evident that the Spur men were provided with considerably less social life than the hands of the average ranch at the time. Had it not been that they were always welcome at the entertainments of the Matador headquarters, life for the Spur men would have been exceedingly dull.

XVI: *NEIGHBORS AND GUESTS*

THE SPUR RANCH was surrounded by ranches. To the northeast lay the Matadors with approximately forty miles of common boundary between the two. Over on the northwest was the Two Buckle Ranch of the Kentucky Land and Cattle Company, later acquired by Hudson and Shultz, separated from the Spur by twenty-seven miles of fence. West of the West Pasture, Major Watts operated the Z Bar L outfit. South of Major Watts was the Curry-Comb Ranch of the Llano Land and Cattle Company. South of the West Pasture extended the OS range of Long Brothers. South of the East Pasture lay the 24 Ranch of Scoggins and Brown. Southeast of the East Pasture was the Two Circle Bar. Across the Croton Breaks east of the East Pasture lay the Ten range. The nearest neighboring headquarters was that of the Matadors, thirty-five miles to the north (See p. 170).

West of the Matador Pasture the country was unfenced and open range, as late as 1890, from the north Spur fence to Amarillo. For a number of years the trail skirted the T Anchor fence, which was the only one seen between the Spurs and Amarillo.

Although the Spurs were on friendly terms with all their neighbors, an exchange of neighborly favors was carried on only with the Matadors, the Kentucky Land and Cattle Co., and the Llano Land and Cattle Co. The early managers of the four ranches had a community of interest. They had in common a broad cultural background, business training, and liberal outlook—true gentlemen, all of them. They were not so compatible with the typical, self-made western cowmen who got their starts as cowboys. All four ranches operated on a larger scale than their neighbors and were more able to accommodate one another.

Such a favor as the loan of fifty spools of barbed wire was a common occurrence. The following letter from Lomax to H. H. Campbell, Superintendent of the Matador Ranch, April 5, 1886, indicates how such arrangements were made:

Your favor of this date at hand, and I am very glad to know that you approve the arrangements made by Mr. Groff for the work in which we are interested.

I thank you for the wire, and will take five thousand pounds of it and two kegs of staples; I will send for it at an early day. Please let me know whether I shall return it in kind, or in pointed wire, paying the difference in the cost; or do you prefer that I should pay you for it, without having to return it? Either way will suit me, and I will be glad to know your preference and the price to be paid.[1]

On February 13, 1888, Lomax wrote to C. M. Tilford, manager of the Kentucky Land and Cattle Company:

The enclosed account has been waiting on our hearing what contra entry should be made for the kind accommodations afforded us by you last summer when our McDonald camp burnt down, but as you, with still greater kindness, will not make a charge, I have credited what I think is only recouping you for costs, leaving us still your debtor for the accommodation of your camp.

I would be very glad to see you, and would be much pleased if you could make us a visit.[2]

Scarcely had McDonald camp been rebuilt when Lomax lent the Spur "camp at upper Catfish" to the Two Buckle Ranch for the winter.[3] In the summer of 1888 he offered the use of either Slicknasty or McDonald camps to B. Blankenship, trail inspector for the Northwest Texas Cattle Raisers Association.[4]

On several occasions the Spur managers permitted neighboring ranchers to keep horses used by their line riders in the horse pastures of the Spur line camps. When such an accommodation was requested by the Two Buckle Ranch, Lomax granted permission, adding, "I am glad to accommodate you in that or in any other way in our power."[5] Horsbrugh in response to a similar request, granted the favor, saying, "I trust that your line rider will be able to cooperate with ours so that the fence will be well kept up and the gates closed."[6]

When the first telephones were introduced into West Texas, people used the top wires of the barbed wire fences as telephone lines. Such arrangements were not very satisfactory so far as telephone service was concerned, but neighbors cheerfully granted permission for such purposes. The Spur Ranch was ready to ex-

---

[1]Spur Records, II, 156.
[2]Spur Records, II, 367.
[3]Spur Records, II, 56.
[4]Spur Records, II, 465.
[5]Spur Records, II, 465.
[6]Spur Records, I, 241.

tend anyone the privilege, "provided it didn't slacken the wire in any way."[7]

Neighboring ranchers sometimes lent each other blooded bulls. Johnstone, writing the home office, April 24, 1904, mentioned such an accommodation:

Mr. Mackenzie of the Matador Company is letting us have the use of a couple of pure bred bulls that have been long enough with their cows. If I remember aright these bulls cost the Matador people in the neighborhood of $500 apiece. I am having a small pasture fenced off for these bulls, and I will put a small lot of selected cows with them. We can repay the Matadors for the use of these bulls by letting them have the services of some of ours when a change is necessary.[8]

Ranchers exchanged favors during round-up seasons by inviting each other to send representatives to their wagons on outside round-ups. The following letter from Lomax to F. P. Schultz of the Ten Ranch, April 10, 1888, is indicative of the way such courtesies were offered and accepted:

I am just in receipt of your message by Mr. Lanter to the effect that you would have a wagon on the Upper Double Mountain work and that the Two Circle Bars would have a wagon on the Lower Double Mountain work, and that we could place such men as we would send on these hunts with your or the Two Circle Bar wagons.

I am very much obliged for your kindness in the matter, and will avail myself of it. I understand that the hunts commence on the first of May—is that right?

We shall have a wagon in the Matador (range) and will be very glad to have you send your man to it, as also the Two Circle Bars (may do) if they desire.

As we probably have some cattle out on the south side, we should be very much favored if you would permit us to participate in the work which I understand you propose to begin on April 15, and the higher up the Salt Fork the more advantage it will be to us. Will you kindly answer by bearer if we may send a couple of men to that work.[9]

In July, 1888, Lomax planned to have a returning trail outfit drive back to the Ranch all the Spur cattle still in Koogle Pasture on White Deer. He remembered that Long Brothers of the

[7]Spur Records, XI, 202.
[8]Spur Records, XI, 561.
[9]Spur Records, II, 410.

OS Ranch had some cattle at Clarendon which they were intending to drive to their home range. Lomax volunteered to bring gratis the OS cattle along with the Spur cattle. Such a favor meant a saving of considerable money for Lomax's neighbor.[10]

In the spring of 1890 before grass came, Horsbrugh decided to ship a trainload of steers which he had been feeding during the winter. The drive to Childress could not be made that time of year without feeding the steers en route. The question of securing sufficient feed for the herd at a midway point was doubtful. H. H. Campbell of the Matador Ranch, on hearing of Horsbrugh's predicament, came to his relief. Although he had little feed to spare, he offered to supply the Spur herd with the amount of sorghum necessary for the drive.[11]

Horsbrugh, Scotchman that he was, was big-hearted and could usually be depended upon to extend a favor, but he was not always free from anticipation of reciprocity. On June 11, 1890, he wrote jocosely to J. H. Scoggins of the Twenty-Four Ranch:

> It will be all right for you to pass through our pasture with the bunch of cattle you wish to deliver to Mr. B. Stop in and see us on your way back. I am always glad at any time I can do anything to help neighbors, and I hope they will play it right back at me.[12]

The Spurs had very little occasion to neighbor with the BO people to the east. However, on July 20, 1904, Johnstone wrote to W. Dawson, the Spur Superintendent:

> The BO man, Courtney, has been telephoning from the store this morning, and evidently wants to be friendly. He is going to work his pasture as soon as he gets back and says that if we cannot get a man to work that he will look out for the interest of the Spurs.[13]

Ranches sometimes found it convenient to ask neighbors to board their line riders and other hands during outside work. Such favors were usually granted—not because boarding hands was desirable or profitable but for the reason it was considered an accommodation. If the person extending the favor was a small cattleman or a nester, he usually accepted pay for his trouble;

[10]Spur Records, II, 490.
[11]Spur Records, VI, 91.
[12]Spur Records, VI, 27.
[13]Spur Records, VI, 27.

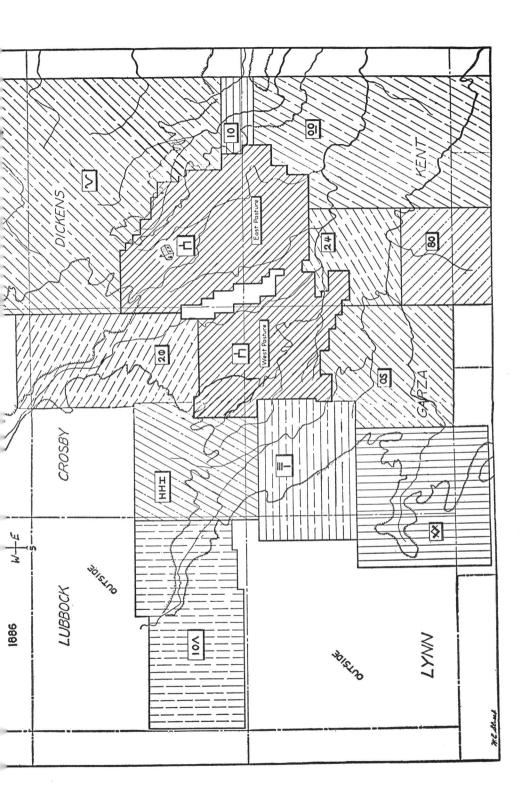

1886

W. E. Stuart

if a ranchman of considerable means, he accepted money "for such tribles" with considerable reluctance,[14] if at all. A letter from Lomax to P. Scoggins of the Twenty-Four Ranch, December 7, 1888, indicates how the matter was usually settled:

Inclosed I beg to hand you our cheque for forty dollars which please accept as reimbursement for board of our Trail Rider, Mr. J. C. Jenkins, during the past season.

Knowing as I do John's "grub" capabilities, it is not of course expected that the above can come near meeting the case, but it will at least serve to show my wish not to impose on good nature.

If you won't take it in this light, please accept it as a token of good will, and buy for yourself a saddle or a suit of clothes. If I had known your preference in make or your size, I would have sent one or the other, but not knowing, and not wanting to present something undesirable, I beg you will accept the cheque in the hearty good will it is sent, and that you will give us some opportunity to return the many favors we have received from you in the past.[15]

It was in the matter of helping each other regain strayed horses and cattle that friendly ranches rendered greatest services to one another. A letter from Lomax to W. G. Urton, manager of a ranch at Fort Sumner, N. M., April 30, 1888, is typical of many letters found in the Spur letter books.

I am obliged for your letter of the 10 inst., advising me of your having a horse of ours, and asking instructions as to disposal of him. I shall probably have a chance to send for him during the next few weeks, but if in the meanwhile you see an opportunity of sending him this way by a reliable party, I will be very much favored, and will pay charges for same. Please let me know what we are due you for your trouble in the matter.[16]

On June 20 he wrote Montgomery Brothers at Fort Worth:

I find that we drove one of your steers in the herd taken by C. F. Lanter to Amarillo and delivered there to the Home Land and Cattle Co. of Montana. It was a yearling and brought us nine dollars, which, less the cost of driving, I now beg to hand to you in the inclosed check on Fort Worth. The hair on the cattle was so long when the cattle started that the mistake is to be attributed to that.

Our wagon boss in the Matador [range] reports having branded

[14]Spur Records, II, 489.
[15]Spur Records, V, 53.
[16]Spur Records, II, 377.

there a calf for you and to have brought it and its mother in with our cattle here.[17]

The same herd Lanter delivered at Amarillo to the Home Land and Cattle Company contained a steer belonging to S. W. Hazelwood of Albany and another carrying the brand of the GS Ranch at Jayton. Lomax promptly remitted to the respective owners the sale price of each.[18]

Mutual benefit often resulted from ranches looking after each other's interests during the outside round-ups, as is evidenced by the following letter from Lomax to Mr. Frank Long of the Lexington (OS) Ranch, May 5, 1888:

Our Mr. Stafford, who was sent down to you to see if any of our cattle had gotten through our fences on you, has returned and delivered your message relative to your outfit working back any of our cattle on the south towards Colorado and Sweetwater, if we would do the same for you on our north and east in the Matador, ROS, and Pitchfork ranges. I thank you for the offer and will be glad to carry out the same. We will instruct our men on those hunts accordingly and will be obliged if you will give the same directions to your men on the south.[19]

A short time later Lomax wrote W. C. Young, president of the Llano Cattle Company:

As nothing seems to be known hereabouts of the South Panhandle Association work, and no explanation is given for its non-commencement as advertized, and as our neighbors above the Canyon, are working, I have determined to afford all interested an opportunity of getting their cattle out of this pasture by commencing a round-up on June 22. As you have quite a number of cattle in here, and may not have heard of the work in time to be represented, I shall have your cattle cut in with the strays which are to be in charge of one of our men, and will hold them until you have an opportunity of putting a man at the work.[20]

During the "die-ups" resulting from blizzards, ranchers, when circumstances permitted, skinned dead cattle for their hides. Strays were skinned along with the cattle of the Ranch. When the hides were sold, the money received for the stray hides was sent to the respective owners.[21]

[17]Spur Records, II, 445.
[18]Spur Records, II, 440.
[19]Spur Records, II, 289.
[20]Spur Records, II, 289.
[21]Spur Records, XI, 386.

The drouth of 1891-1893 afforded an opportunity for the managers of the Spur, the Matador, and the Pitchfork ranches to extend a neighborly accommodation to officers of the counties in which their pastures were located. These men were paid by scrip. Due to the drouth the scrip was hard to sell at thirty-five cents on the dollar. Horsbrugh arranged for the three ranches to buy the scrip at eighty-five cents on the dollar. This was done in order "that the county officers might eat." The ranches held the scrip for several years before they could get it redeemed for what they paid for it.

Although the Spurs had a strict policy in regard to trail herds which drovers wished to drive across the Spur range, both Lomax and Horsbrugh made exceptions when circumstances seemed to warrant it and allowed neighbors privileges not generally granted. Horsbrugh wrote to J. C. Jenkins, September 10, 1889: "I am willing to afford every reasonable assistance to parties moving with small bunches of cattle, especially, in such a dry time as we have been having lately."[22]

During dry spells water became very scarce for trail herds going around the established trail. Wishing to accommodate passing drovers from the south as much as possible, Lomax wrote Joe Self, line-rider at McDonald's Camp, April 27, 1888:

I wish you would keep posted as to the water in Lake Creek outside our fence, and if not enough to afford a good watering to herds passing, you are hereby authorized to let them come into our pasture at the wire gap just south of the northwest corner of the fence and water in McDonald, provided they first promise to go out again as soon as watered and not camp or stay over night in this pasture.[23]

Such favors extended to ranchmen from the south were later returned to the Spurs, but by neighbors on the north. The Matadors were most friendly and accommodating. They permitted the Spurs to take herds through their pastures, whether bound for the railroad or White Deer pasture. Frequently, in dry times they allowed Spur herds to water in their horse pastures. All strays which were lost from Spur herds were collected by the Matador cowboys and returned to the owners.[24]

[22]Spur Records, V, 385; VI, 248; X, 249.
[23]Spur Records, II, 351.
[24]Spur Records, X, 596.

The patience of the Spur managers was often strained a bit by the neighbors, especially by small cattlemen and nesters, taking advantage of the wood-hauling privileges extended them. Horsbrugh, slightly nettled, wrote W. L. Browning, a small cattleman, located north of the East Pasture: "I have no objection to the cutting and hauling of mesquite or driftwood out of our big pasture, below Dickens. . . . It is my desire to live peacefully and neighborly with all in this country . . . and while willing to supply firewood to our neighbors, I claim the rights of pointing out where such shall be taken."[25] As time went on wood haulers abused their privileges more and more. In August, 1903, Horsbrugh adopted the policy of charging individuals one dollar a load, but still allowing churches and schools to get wood free. Even then, however, persons in hard financial circumstances (as many nesters usually were) were allowed to make off with huge loads without pay. Johnstone's letter to a widow, September 16, 1904, shows a manager's weakness.

I have this morning received your letter of September 14, with regard to cutting wood in our Duck Creek pasture, I am desirous that the timber in this pasture should get an opportunity to grow up as the shade that it affords is of great advantage both to cattle and grass. I am, however, quite willing that you should get your winter firewood out of that portion of the East pasture where the mesquite is heavy, and for what you require for your own use I will make no charge.[26]

Sympathy for a neighbor at one time caused Lomax to go to considerable trouble and do more than the law provided. While the cattle business was still being conducted on free grass, John B. Slaughter who had selected his range along Catfish Creek and constructed his headquarters on public land whose title afterwards passed to the Espuela Land and Cattle Company, Limited, asked the Company to pay him for his improvements. Lomax took the matter with the Home office in London and secured a reasonable compensation for Slaughter,[27] although the company was not legally obligated.

In the summer of 1886 a cowboy employed by the Kentucky Land and Cattle Company accidentally killed a fine Spur bull. Lomax heard of the affair without learning the accidental nature

[25]Spur Records, X, 457.
[26]Spur Records, XI, 469.
[27]Spur Records, I, 5.

of the case and instituted legal proceedings against the cowboy. After being apprised of all the facts, he wrote C. M. Tilford, manager of the Kentucky Land and Cattle Company:

I am in receipt of your favor of the 2nd inst. regarding the unfortunate killing of a company bull by Joe Budrow, and have learned from Mr. Wood what he knows of the matter. With these statements of the accidental and unintentional nature of the killing, I shall be satisfied to dismiss the proceedings instituted against Budrow, and shall do so at once. As to any compensation for the bull I would not take it if accidentally or unintentionally killed; as such seems to be the weight of evidence, I shall dismiss the matter altogether.[28]

Exceedingly pleasant were the relations between the Spur Ranch and Major Watts of the Z Bar L. Horsbrugh often waxed eloquent in his praise of the man. While writing to the Home office he referred to the Major more than once as "a high class gentleman," "one of the best in the business," "one to whom the running of a ranch was a mere fad," and a "wealthy gentleman of the old order." There were constantly things arising which had to be settled with Major Watts, but to settle anything with the Major was a pleasure to the Spur managers.[29]

Highly respected by ranch managers and hands were the Quakers of Estacado, a colony of farmers about thirty-five miles northwest of the Spur headquarters. They attended to their own affairs, and as one old Spur hand put it, "They never used a calf which was not their own." This trait alone endeared them to all cattlemen. Another said, "If all the settlers in the Spur Country had been like the Quakers, it would have made a vast difference to the stockmen." Especially appreciated was a skilled Quaker blacksmith who did for the ranchmen expert work which the smiths in the ranch shops were unable to do. Still, another old hand remembers that the Quakers introduced fruit trees to Spur country, and that they developed a drouth resisting peach of excellent flavor, known as the Crosby peach.

Perhaps the Spur Ranch asked more favors from Cowan and Shear, general mercantile merchants at Colorado City, than from any of their ranch neighbors. When a Spur manager wanted to send a cablegram to London, he sent it by mail to Cowan and Shear who dispatched the message, charging the cost to the Spur

[28]Spur Records, I, 263.
[29]Spur Records, VIII, 350.

account. If members of the Board of Directors or employees arrived at Colorado City from England, Cowan and Shear took
charge of them and entertained them until it was convenient to
start to the Ranch.[30] It was with profound regret that Horsbrugh
learned in September, 1890, that the firm was selling out.[31]

The managers of the Spur Ranch were busy men—so were all
the employees—but they could not get away from their social
instincts. They loved to have persons come from a distance and
visit the Ranch. Such individuals brought news of what was happening elsewhere, and their coming broke the monotony of ranch
life. Time and again Lomax, Horsbrugh, and Johnstone while
writing business letters to friends and acquaintances closed with
such remarks as "wish you would make a trip out this way and
stay a while with us," "will be glad to see you over here for a
visit whenever you have the time and the inclination to make
the trip," "hope you will pay us a visit on your next vacation,"
"drop by and see us on your way back" and so on.[32] Often friends
were invited out for the hunting season. Johnstone was especially
anxious to have persons he liked make purely social visits to
the Ranch. Northern cattle buyers were, for business reasons,
welcome.[33]

When guests were expected by train from a distance, the Spur
manager sent a buggy and team to meet them at the railroad.
Prior to 1888 they all came by way of Colorado City, which was
a hundred-mile drive to the Ranch. After the Fort Worth and
Denver Railroad was completed in 1887, Childress and Clarendon, 65 and 90 miles respectively from the Ranch, became points
of disembarkation. It required two days for the buggy to go each
way to and from Colorado City or Childress. The trip to the
latter places could be made in a day by changing team and
driving late. When the guest finally arrived at the Ranch, after
jostling for the better part of two days over unworked country
roads—ruts across the prairie—he was indeed in the proper state
of mind to appreciate ranch atmosphere, and remain some time.[34]

One of the most popular visitors at the Ranch was Campbell,
superintendent of the Matadors. In view of the fact that the

[30]Spur Records, II, 363, 606; VII, 376.
[31]Spur Records, VI, 293.
[32]Spur Records, V, 166; VI, 52, 65, 76, 215; XI, 214.
[33]Spur Records, VI, 65.
[34]Spur Records, IV, 131.

Matador headquarters were thirty-five miles north, it was often convenient for Campbell to spend the night at the Spur Ranch on his way to and from Colorado City. He may have felt some misgivings at accepting the repeated hospitality of the Spurs, but he had no other choice. Practically every letter received by him from the Spur managers—and there were many of them—closed with an urgent invitation to stop over night on his next trip to town. Nor was Mrs. Campbell forgotten. Her presence was desired as much as that of her likable husband.[35]

In the spring of 1898 a considerable addition was made to the Spur headquarters for the sole purpose of providing additional rooms for guests. So urgent was the need at the time that the carpenters had to work overtime to get the house ready for an incoming group of visitors.[36]

The Christmas season brought a host of official obligations to the Spur managers. Managers of neighboring ranches exchanged the season's greetings. Business firms, banks, and cattle brokers sent their greetings, which in turn called for reciprocal measures. Cowan and Shear showed their appreciation for the Ranch in a more substantial way. Horsbrugh, in thanking them for their annual present at Christmas, 1889, said:

Mr. Flook and myself have both to thank you for your kind present [a case of Old Scotch] which arrived yesterday, and which is very much appreciated. I beg to reciprocate most cordially the kind and seasonable good wishes which only you were good enough to send. I hope that you will have a happy and prosperous New Year.[37]

They had certain friendly obligations of such a nature they could not very well be settled by payments of money. The Christmas season always provided an opportunity to even these accounts with more or less costly presents. It became an annual custom, for instance, for the Ranch to present J. P. Davidson of Seymour with a suit of clothes.[38] Whether the motives were wholly utilitarian or partly prompted by genuine friendliness, the official exchange of greetings and gifts caused the Christmas holidays to be looked forward to by the Ranch managers with considerable anticipation.

[35]Spur Records, XIV, 2, 6, 8.
[36]Spur Records, VIII, 347.
[37]Spur Records, VI, 7.
[38]Spur Records, IX, 287; XI, 575.

XVII: *PREDATORY ANIMALS, PESTS, AND PRAIRIE FIRES*

THE RANCHMAN HAD MANY WORRIES. There was seldom a time when some destructive agent was not threatening cattle or grass. Disease might decimate the herds, drouths might cause the grass to fail and drinking water to become scarce, blizzards might take their toll of thousands of cattle, and giant hail stones might kill dozens of calves. These disasters, with the exception of the first, were due to the seasonal tricks of nature over which man had no control. Cattlemen took losses from these sources like stoics. There were other destructive agents which they could not endure without getting their ire aroused—wolves, prairie dogs, screw-worms, heel flies, bog holes, and prairie fires.

The most spectacular and exasperating of these ravages was caused by wolves. Nothing aroused resentment and brought forth determination to settle the score so much as for a cowman while riding across the range to come upon the partially devoured carcass of a fine, fat yearling. A fully grown lobo in a cattle country would kill from ten to twenty head of cattle a year. There is one case on record where an unusually wily lobo averaged killing fifty head a year for over five years, often killing cows for the sake of eating their unborn calves.[1] A female with a den of cubs always had a ravenous appetite. She preferred a fat calf, but in the absence of tenderer meat, she would tackle the toughest cow in the pasture. It is probable that the Spur Ranch sustained more losses from the lobo wolves than from cattle thieves.

The Spur range was a natural haunt for both the lobo and the coyote. The coyote, being much smaller than the lobo, did the cattle interests some harm, but was not comparable to the lobo. A coyote would attack a small calf left unguarded by its mother, but the unguarded moments, until the calf was old enough to care for itself, were very few. The ravages of the coyote were concentrated on the sheep interest; but the lobo apparently had the same disdain for sheep that the cowboy had

[1] *Yearbook* of the U. S. Department of Agriculture, 1920, p. 291.

for the sheepherder. His palate craved beef, and he resorted to mutton only when beef was not to be had.

One of the first acts of the Espuela Land and Cattle Company, Limited, was to begin the policy of paying bounties for wolf scalps. Any cowboy, settler, or professional hunter received $5 for lobo and fifty cents for coyote scalps. A special Wolf Bounty Account was carried in the Ranch books. During the 90's the Ranch paid out about $400 a year in bounties. From 50 to 60 lobos and from 275 to 300 coyotes were killed in the Spur pastures annually.

Occasionally an ingenious hunter would send in coyote scalps, claiming they were lobos. The following letter indicated that Horsbrugh was not so easily fooled:

> I am in receipt of yours of 17 inst. relative to two scalps which you sent to the ranch in my absence claiming that they were "loafer" wolf scalps. Regarding them I have to say that every one who saw them at once named them as "coyote." Now I have paid in the last three years bounties on over 200 loafers and therefore we are not very liable to make a mistake; it is my desire to pay where it is justly due but it must be remembered distinctly that whether this office pays a bounty on loafers is purely and solely a matter of choice on our part, and an act of kindness liable to be revoked at any time. Now your letter is anything but satisfactory, as it seems to demand and threaten trouble should certain things not happen as you wish. You also enclose a statement made before the clerk at Clairemont, which, if you will consider, has no more value than your letter on the subject, as you simply swear yourself to *your own* belief.
>
> Be that as it may—I have only to tell you that the scalps which were shown to me as coming from you were not considered loafer wolf by anyone who saw them and a good many men, old in this country, saw them while they were on exhibition here.
>
> Furthermore, I wish to add that on account of the confident feeling which the matter seems to have occasioned so far as you are concerned, I beg to give you notice that at no time will I pay you anything for loafers or anything else that you may kill, and any writings of mine on the subject are hereby revoked.[2]

From time to time the manager employed hunters with packs of hounds to spend their entire time running wolves. The hounds seldom caught a wolf, but their presence in the vicinity, together with the noise they made, no doubt caused many wolves to mi-

[2]Spur Records, VII, 174.

grate to other pastures.[3] Horsbrugh was always anxious to give
them a big scare just before cubbing time in order that the
females might make their dens and have their cubs as far from
the Spur range as possible.[4] While writing to the Home office,
August 19, 1898, Horsbrugh had occasion to refer to a $200
check to J. W. McCommas. "This man," he said, "has been
hunting wolves with a pack of hounds for six months; and while
he did not catch very many, he caused them to change their
locations and did good service. All his earnings went to the store.
He is laid off at present, but I shall hire him again."[5] From time
to time professional hunters and trappers located in the Spur
pastures, supporting themselves by the scalp bounties and the
sale of the hides.

Jake Raines told a bounty collecting story which was extraordinary.[6] While rounding up in the East Pasture in June, 1894,
two of the hands, Will Monroe and C. R. Humphrey, saw a
female lobo wolf going up a draw. She quickly disappeared, but
it had rained the night before, and the men tracked her to her
den. They carefully noted the location with the view of coming
back to dig the den out. After supper they borrowed the cook's
spade and went. They found the hole big enough for a man to
crowd into. Monroe, the smaller of the two, went in, leaving
Humphrey to stand guard at the entrance. Inside, the tunnel
became much larger with several compartments. Suddenly it became dark and Monroe shouted to Humphrey to stop blocking
the light. Quickly, the light came back. It was not Humphrey
causing it to change. A big she-wolf hiding in one of the compartments charged out after Monroe had passed her. She ran
between Humphrey's legs and upset him, carrying him some
distance on her back. Monroe found some of the compartments
swarming with pups of different ages. With hands incased in
heavy leather gloves, he began handing pups out to Humphrey
who killed them. In all, there were fifty-three, ranging from two
weeks old to three or four months. It was surmised that several
bitch wolves were using the den. The larger pups were scalped,
the smaller ones were gutted and carried in with scalps intact
for evidence. The men collected $265 from the Ranch and

[3]Spur Records, IX, 100.
[4]Spur Records, IX, 177.
[5]Spur Records, IX, 237.
[6]Jake Raines to W. C. H., interview, Feb. 23, 1930.

an equal amount from Dickens County, a total of $530. This was the equivalent to seven months' wages for both of them. However, the Spur Ranch changed its bounty scale. Thereafter, it continued to pay $5 for adult wolves, or any killed on the surface, but only $2.50 for pups taken from a den.

Jake Raines contended that lobo wolves had a distinctive howl, something between the bark of a dog and the yelp of a coyote. He remembered one night in 1888 hearing one howl near the Spur headquarters, and the howl was answered by a big black dog belonging to Lomax. The howling and answering barks went on for three or four nights. Then the dog disappeared. Nothing was seen or heard of him for several months. One day Lomax was returning from a trip in a buggy when he saw some lobo wolves at a distance. Soon he noticed the pack converging on him. The wolves fell in behind and started gaining on him. He became frightened and whipped the horses into a run. Then the leader of the pack sprinted ahead and overtook the buggy running alongside. He acted as if he were trying to jump into the buggy. Lomax was about to jump out on the other side when he recognized his missing dog. He slowed down and took the dog in. The big fellow was winded, but glad to see his master. Lomax took him home where he was content except on nights when he heard a lobo howl. It was like the call of the wild. Someone would tie the dog up for a day or two until he had apparently forgot about it.

Prairie dogs were a great menace to ranchmen in that they destroyed a large amount of grass. Considerable areas in the pastures were completely denuded. The dogs were also destructive to crops, especially when the tender shoots began to appear in the spring. Not infrequently many acres around the edges of fields would be entirely stripped.

Prairie dog holes presented a constant danger to horsemen and cattle when running. Many a hard fall was due to a horse stepping into a dog hole. Such falls sometimes resulted in a broken limb for the rider, and occasionally, his death. Many trained cow horses suffered broken legs and had to be shot.[7]

The number of prairie dogs infesting the Spur properties was estimated in the millions. Although a person might find considerable areas without any dogs, they were exceedingly thick in

[7]C. B. Jones to J. B. Hargus, interview, January 23, 1930.

the so-called "dog towns." The "towns" varied in size, sometimes covering forty or fifty acres; and a populous "town" had as many as a hundred dogs to the acre.

The Ranch management was first concerned about the dog problem in 1888 when Horsbrugh wrote the directors:

> I noticed in the *London Field* of Feb. 11th that M. Pastuer of Paris had been making successful experiments among rabbits by killing them off by the introduction of "hen cholera" among them, and that he was about to try for the large reward offered by the Australian Government to any one who would successfully cope with their rabbit pest. It might be worth while to watch this matter, as, if he is successful with the rabbits, I think we have got the prairie-dogs grabbed. The evil the latter do is immense. This country is pitted all over with millions of their holes some of which are very deep, and the drainage which is thus effected in the light soil, where water is wanted so badly, can be imagined. Where land is ploughed, however, they move their camps.[8]

In the fall of 1888 J. C. Melcher of O'Quinn, Fayette County, Texas, invented and patented a "Prairie Dog Exterminator," a light machine with which a person pumped sulphur chloride into the dog holes. Melcher had a complicated system of distributing his invention. The purchaser paid $15 for the machine and received with it a farm right or county right to use it. An "Exterminator" without the necessary permit to use it was useless.[9] Lomax made cautious inquiry about the machine, and finally ordered one.[10] Apparently he was fairly well pleased with it, for a few months later he recommended it to a neighbor.[11]

However the "Exterminator" did not prove to be such a bonanza as was expected. In 1901 Horsbrugh was writing the London office that the best way to get rid of the prairie dog evil was "to use poison."[12] By this time, ranchmen had learned that prairie dog extermination was no "fifteen-dollar-machine and one man" proposition. Nothing short of organized and concentrated action on a large scale would have any appreciable effect. During the 90's cattlemen had been learning more and more about methods of ridding the range of pests. Many of the ranches were letting contracts for the killing of 25,000 or 50,000 or 100,000 acres of

[8]Spur Records, IV, 417.
[9]Spur Records, V, 134.
[10]Spur Records, V, 200.
[11]Spur Records, VI, 31.
[12]Spur Records, X, 297.

dogs. The contracts called for complete extermination, the men having to go over the land a second or third time, if necessary.[13] In February 1902, Horsbrugh wrote the Directors in London in regard to letting a contract for killing all the dogs on the Spur lands:

> . . . I would like to add a few remarks in regard to prairie dog extermination, of which I wrote you from Fort Worth the other day. I have talked to two men who have been having this kind of work done, and they are very loud in their praise of the enterprise. Mr. Burk Burnett has some land that for years has been worn off and covered with dog holes,—in fact, like a very big rabbit warren in the old country looks. He had the dogs killed off last year, and this year there is a very good growth of grass all over it. Mr. [Dan] Waggoner had the same experience. As I wrote you there is little difference of opinion in the estimates of the amount of improvement it makes on a piece of land with regard to its grazing capacity. These estimates are that from 10 to 25% more cattle can be carried on the land after it has been treated for prairie dogs. The dogs not only eat the grass, but they dig up and destroy the roots. A country that is overrun with prairie dogs gets to be as bare as if swept by fire, for the reason the dogs destroy the roots and kill the plants. There is another very serious aspect to the dog question. The numberless holes and connecting tunnels underground constitute a vast drainage system in this light porous soil, causing the ground to dry out thoroughly and quickly. They are nothing less than a system of fresh air flues running underground in all directions. It is to be remembered that we never have enough rain anyway. After the dogs are killed out the holes gradually fill up. The killing of dogs not only increases the growth of grass by stopping the damage done the plants, but the filling of the holes and underground passages, preserves for a longer time the moisture in the soil, thus increasing its productiveness. I mention these benefits so that when time comes for a careful consideration of the dog enterprise, this letter may be considered.
> Mr. Mitchell, who has in a bid for the dog killing, says that if he gets the job the estimate of five cents an acre is to include everything in the way of supplies and he would put on twenty men, and would do the work thoroughly, going over the ground a second time and a third time, if necessary.[14]

The financial condition of the company prevented any extensive dog killing operation until 1904. After Johnstone became manager of the Ranch, he let a contract for dog extermination

[13]Spur Records, X, 491.
[14]Spur Records, X, 501.

on 60 sections, making the following comment to the Home office:

I do not know if you were notified that the last Legislature of the State passed a law requiring land owners to exterminate the prairie dogs on their property. Most of our neighbours have been at work killing prairie dogs for some time and when I took charge here I judged it advisable to do something in this direction. I accordingly made an arrangement with a man, who had done work of this kind for the Matador Company to kill all the prairie dogs in the following pastures, Duck Creek, West Horse, Little Horse, Little Dockum and Tap. These pastures contain about 60 sections, a great part of which, from 1/4 to 1/3 I should suppose, are almost entirely ruined for grazing by the prairie dogs.

I promised the dog-poisoner $660 upon the completion of the work and he agrees to a deduction of 25¢ for every live dog found when he is finished.

Everyone who has killed out the dogs in their pastures is most enthusiastic as to the improvement made in the grazing value of the land; and, while there may be some question as to the constitutionality of the law, it would be a good thing for all ranchmen if these pests could be exterminated. By killing them in the small pastures around headquarters we will have a good chance to judge of the value of the proceeding.

The Matador people have already had a large portion of their pastures poisoned, probably 300,000 acres, and they are still continuing the work.[15]

The dogs on most of the Spur lands, however, had not been killed when the Ranch was acquired by the Swenson interests in 1907. The new management took up the matter of extermination with vigor and determination. From thirty to fifty men and boys were employed by the company for this purpose for a period of nearly two years. These employees were divided into two outfits, each having its own chuck wagon. The men went twice over the entire acreage distributing poisoned grain which they ladled with long-handled spoons from buckets swung from their shoulders. The grain was principally thrashed and recleaned maize, with an occasional addition of oats and wheat where it was found that the prairie dogs were not eating the maize as well as desired. Strychnine and cyanide of potassium formed the base of the poison to which was added anise oil and a syrup of brown sugar to lure the animals as well as to kill the taste of the strychnine.

[15]Spur Records, XI, 259.

After the poisoned grain had been twice distributed over the Ranch, the men went carefully over the land again, using carbon disulphide in each hole which showed any evidence of occupation. Carbon disulphide is a liquid which upon exposure becomes a gas heavier than air. As it sinks into a hole it is extremely deadly. The Spur men used about one tablespoonful of carbon disulphide to the hole. The liquid was poured on a corn cob or a dry "horse apple" and rolled into the hole, which was covered with dirt and tamped to prevent the escape of the dogs. Otherwise, they might have escaped before becoming overcome with the gas. The work was a complete success, and the Spur Ranch found itself without any dogs whatever except those which came in from time to time from neighboring pastures in which they had not been killed.[16] If the amount of damage that prairie dogs caused the Spur Company during the quarter of a century when they were not effectively curbed could be computed, the figure would be enormous.

Prairie dog extermination occupied the attention of the ranchmen in the late 1890's and early 1900's much the same as mesquite eradication does in the same areas in the 1960's. The mesquite problem is much more stubborn and more expensive, but the objective is the same—to save the grass.

Screwworms gave a great deal of trouble some years. The worms were caused by egg deposits laid by a fly in a fresh wound or scratch. The cattle, especially the calves and yearlings, had many occasions for sustaining wounds. The navel wound of a young calf which was unfortunate enough to be born after hot weather set in was a splendid place for a fly to lay her eggs. During the branding season wounds were caused by the castration of the male calves. Every calf branded, male and female, was marked; that is, one or both ears were notched or cropped by means of a sharp knife. Within ten days after the eggs were deposited in a wound the worms, or maggots, would be full sized and working. The worm is white and from a quarter to a half an inch long. With hundreds of maggots working and boring into the flesh, a great hole will soon result provided the worms are not killed.[17]

Treatment for screwworms consisted in roping and throwing

[16]Jones to Hargus, interview, January 23, 1930.
[17]Spur Records, X, 210.

the afflicted animal and pouring chloroform or a creosote mixture into the wound. All the worms could be killed at one time, but before the wound would have time to heal it might be infected with a new crop of maggots. Sometimes two or three treatments would be necessary.

The worms seemed to be much worse in wet years than in dry ones. They were unusually bad during 1900. On July 21, Horsbrugh wrote:

> Not the least important part of the work at present is doctoring calves for "screw-worm"; this at present is causing some anxiety, which the continued rains do not certainly allay. However rains are beneficial, and the bad feature alluded to can be held in check by carefulness, and it is very rare that a calf gets in bad enough shape from screw worms to die. The only thing is that as long as the weather stays cloudy and rainy it is hard to get rid of the trouble entirely, and for this reason, as well as branding calves that have been missed, is the "still hunting" and "scabbing" work important.[18]

Heel fly time was always dreaded by cattlemen. It took place in late winter and early spring. On warm days in February and March, the flies swarmed about the heels of the cattle, tormenting them with their sharp, penetrating stings. Occasionally the flies appeared as early as January. The Spur managers always began dreading them that early.[19]

The sting of the heel fly of itself does the cow no special damage. The trouble results from the frantic efforts of the animal to escape the torturous sting.[20] On warm days when the flies were out, the cattle rushed pell-mell through the brush or into the water holes where they stood with the water and mud covering their heels. If no brush or water were at hand, the cattle crowded under shades where they remained the most of the day. This always occurred at a time of year when the cattle were thin and weak and the grass dead or scant. At a time when cattle most needed to be continually grazing, they were forced to spend days doing nothing but protecting their heels.[21]

The greatest loss came from the cattle taking refuge in the water holes. Aside from occasional snows, the winters were in-

[18]Spur Records, X, 210.
[19]Spur Records, II, 93, 145.
[20]Jones to Hargus, interview, January 23, 1930.
[21]*Ibid.*

variably dry in Northwest Texas. Often months passed without enough rainfall to cause the water to run in the branches and creeks. The tanks and the waterholes in the creeks became low and muddy by early spring. Many of the watering places became bog holes. Concerning them Horsbrugh wrote in January, 1902:

The dangerous time is when the heel fly comes at the breakup of winter when the cattle are poor. This pest acts on the cattle as the devil acted on the scriptural swine, and the poor cows rush madly anywhere so they can get to water or mud and stand in it; in their weak state they can not stand much of this . . . the mud holes become death traps for the reason that many of the cattle are too poor to extricate themselves. When a cow is in good flesh and strong, she may be able to scramble out of belly-deep mud; but when she is poor, it does not take many inches of it to bog her down.[22]

Efforts were made in the cattle country to control heel flies by the use of fly traps. A number of cattlemen reported considerable success with the traps. But in the days of Lomax, Horsbrugh and Johnstone, the only method used to thwart the loss from the heel fly was carefully "to ride bog" and pull from the mud holes such cattle as could not extricate themselves. In case water could be otherwise provided, bogs and extremely low tanks were fenced off during heel fly season.[23] A few of the chronic bogs, which were fed by springs, were kept fenced off the year round.

Heel flies and bog holes did not seriously bother the ranch horses, but an equally devastating evil, so far as the horses were concerned, was to be found in the loco plant. Horsbrugh referred to the loco situation in a letter to the Home office in January, 1901:

Another thing affecting the horse question has been the serious appearance of a plant known as "loco." Lately it has appeared on the plains and in the breaks near here. It is a plant that grows in tufts on the prairie rather resembling a coarse kind of maiden hair fern, but soft and tender in comparison, and at certain seasons it has a purple flower. It has, I believe, been analysed, but nothing has, so far as I know, ever been found as to its properties, or any cure or preventative for its effects. We have not, so far, been seriously hurt by cattle eating it, although I know of this occurring in New Mexico; but horses, once they get a taste for it, they act as do humans who use morphine or laudanum. They will

[22]Spur Records, X, 473.
[23]Jones to Hargus, interview, January 23, 1930.

go out of their way to get it, and are greedy for it, and its affects show that there is certainly a deleterious drug contained in its composition. Horses that get to be confirmed loco-eaters are worthless; besides, falling away in flesh, they go crazy and are useless. Some of our horses have been eating the weed, and I am afraid that there are some of them that will prove to be useless. It is showing up worse in the country between here and Childress, through the Matador range and the Continental Cattle Co.'s. And also on the plains north-west of here I hear that it is very bad. This is crippling our horse strength a little, and it may be that I shall want a few more in the spring.[24]

Aside from predatory animals, pests, and obnoxious plants, there was another agent of destruction which threatened to break loose during certain seasons and which was a source of worry to ranch managers—prairie fires. Destruction of the substance upon which cattle subsisted was next to the destruction of the cattle themselves. There was danger from grass fires during more than half of the year. On a year of average rainfall grass put out in April, grew during May and probably June, became dry and brown during July and August, turned green again after the fall rains in September or October, was killed by frost in November, and stayed dry and crisp until April. For two or three months in the summer and for four to five months in the winter grass was in a condition to be destroyed by fire. During these periods the Spur managers and cowboys, like all their neighbors who worked with cattle, kept a sharp lookout for grass smoke. A tiny thread of smoke curling up from any part of the range would soon have fifty pair of eyes watching it. If it increased in volume and showed the unmistakable evidence of burning grass, it was a signal for all hands to start to it with the greatest speed possible. Every man on the Ranch was a member of a potential fire fighting outfit, which became operative at the first evidence of a prairie fire. During dry seasons a constant lookout was kept by the Ranch.

The first serious fire on the Spur range happened in August, 1890. Horsburgh referred to it in a letter to Lomax, August 19:

We have had a hard time fighting fire in the pasture lately. It looks as if people were trying to burn us out, five fires in three weeks. None of them have done much damage except one that

[24]Spur Records, X, 281.

destroyed about twelve sections of fine grass down below Gamel pens. We had a hard fight with it, all day and part of the night, but we had a good force at it and got the better of it, but at times it looked bad. I had the farm hands as well as Joe's outfit and the men from the South line at it. Our nesters turned out and worked well, two of them feeding the men who were fighting it. I thought at first it had been started by them, but we got the two individuals who did it, two prospectors from Weatherford. They were scared to death when they were told by the men that they would be hanged sure. They had let the fire get away from them while cooking, and after we had scared them up a bit we let them go. I have men riding the range looking out for fires and especially the roads where travel is great at present. It is too dry to go to work, and I have the outfit camped in the middle of the range watching out. It has got to be quite a serious matter, and we can hardly sleep at night for watching for it. The men do splendidly, however, and are very willing and swift about getting to it, but it is terribly hard on the horses.[25]

The Spurs went five years without another serious fire. In January, 1895, a fire broke out in the south part of the East Pasture and raced across nine sections before it was brought under control.[26] About eight o'clock in the evening it broke out again and burned three more sections.[27] By October of the same year, Horsbrugh was pessimistically predicting more fires than usual for the winter because of the heavy and luxuriant condition of the grass. When grass was scant, the managers worried over the scarcity of it; when it was plentiful, they lay awake at nights, fretted, and thought how easy it would be for fire to sweep the pasture clean.[28] Horsbrugh was not entirely disappointed, for during the winter several small fires occurred, but no great damage was done.[29]

Occasionally, lightning started a fire, but these instances never involved much loss, as the fire was usually put out by rain.[30] The greatest danger was in the negligence with which prospectors and "movers" treated their campfires. On December 10, 1897, Horsbrugh reported:

[25]Spur Records, VI, 278.
[26]For an account of the methods used in fighting grass fires see J. Evetts Haley, "Grass Fires on the Southern Plains," *West Texas Historical Association Year Book*, V, 23-42.
[27]Spur Records, XII, 10.
[28]Spur Records, VIII, 244.
[29]Spur Records, VIII, 250.
[30]Spur Records, VIII, 45.

There was a fire in the center of the range the other day that for a time looked dangerous; however, it did not last long though a strong wind was blowing. The turnout of the men was very gratifying; I have men working in all of the four counties, and inside of an hour every "Spur" man was at it. Most of them were too late to do any good as it was quickly whipped out by those in time to work on it. The crew at the gin at Espuela stampeded the minute the smoke was seen. It was at Red Mud and even Birdwell from the mouth of Duck Creek in Kent Co. and Byrd from the head of the McDonald in Crosby reported at it. It was a very gratifying and smart piece of work, and showed what can be done should the occasion arise. All had very tired horses to ride slowly back to their different camps. The strip burned over about a mile and a half long and a quarter wide. It was very narrow on account of the high wind driving the fire. A settler's wife let it get out.[31]

On exceedingly clear days the distance to a prairie fire was often deceptive. A smoke that appeared twenty miles away might be forty. In December, 1897, such an instance took place. A smoke was seen to the southwest. Cole, the range foreman, and ten men started to it, as the wind was blowing hard, and the fire threatened a part of the West Pasture. After riding hard for half a day in the direction of the fire, they discovered it was far beyond Blanco Canyon, a barrier which no grass fire could very well cross and which thus protected the Spur pastures. Cole and his men returned late that night with fagged horses without having gotten within a score of miles of the fire.[32]

In the winter of 1897-1898 Horsbrugh kept more hands on the payroll than the ordinary routine demanded in order to have more men to look out for and fight grass fires. "In late years," he said, "I have noticed that the most destructive fires occur in the winter after the ranches have discharged the most of their hands for the winter; consequently, when fires break out, the ranches do not have sufficient help to fight them. I like to have men ready for the emergency."[33]

The increased number of land hunters who began the last fevered rush to obtain state school lands about 1900 added to the danger of prairie fires. Horsbrugh wrote, August 1, 1900:

There will be from now on more danger of fire this summer and fall than there has ever been, not so much from the extra fine

[31]Spur Records, VIII, 279.
[32]Spur Records, VIII, 281.
[33]Spur Records, X, 220.

grass that we have, as from the fact that never before were there so many travelling and camping through the range, mostly prospectors in search of land. For the most part these are either ignorant, careless or indifferent as to the safest methods of camping with fires where there is grass that will burn. I look for a great deal of this trouble later on when the grass gets dry, as it does very fast in this part of the country.[34]

During the winter of 1900-1901 and the summer of 1901, several small fires occurred, burning from two to six sections each.[35] With the fire menace increasing, the Ranch began in August, 1905, the construction of a system of fire guards.[36] These were made by ploughing narrow strips consisting of several furrows each at intervals across the pasture. In a light or moderate wind, a ploughed strip from four to six feet wide would stop a prairie fire. With a gale blowing, a strip fifty feet wide might not be effective. In those cases about the only hope was to let fire race across the country until it came to a river, canyon or creek sufficiently wide to stop it. However, a system of fire guards very effectively reduced the fire hazard. Other ranches had been using them for twenty years. Why the Spurs did not resort to them sooner is not clear.

[34]Spur Records, X, 220.
[35]Spur Records, X, 383, 423.
[36]Spur Records, XI, 73.

XVIII: *HORSES*

No ATTEMPT WILL be made to treat the horses on the Spur Ranch in a romantic, expository manner. Will James, Ross Santee, Frank Hastings, George Patullo, and others have analyzed, dissected, and synthesized every aspect of horse-nature, and they have done it well. Instead, the necessity for horses, how the Ranch got them, where it got them, and how it got rid of them will be considered.

The company usually kept about ten saddle horses for each man who rode for the Ranch during the heaviest work seasons. In the winter when the extra riders were laid off, all the horses not needed for winter routine were turned into the horse-pasture to rest and rustle for themselves; those retained for winter work were fed. The greatest item in their keep was grazing; a horse eats more grass than a cow.

During the work season each man had his own "string," or bunch. Among these were usually a special "cutting," a special "roping," and several ordinary saddle horses. Occasionally, the same horse would be good at both cutting and roping.[1]

The Ranch never attempted to raise horses, but always recruited the herd by purchase. These were almost always "broke" or "semi-broke"; so the Ranch never employed a professional "buster." As a rule "broke" horses cost about $5 more a head than "unbroke" ones, but the company found it to be economy in the long run to pay the additional price.

An annual loss of 25 to 30 head occurred from natural causes or accidents. Accidental deaths, usually three or four a year, resulted from drowning or falls occasioned by stepping in prairie dog holes while running. Some horses died of starvation or diseases brought on by old age. As horses grew old, their teeth became bad, and they were unable to get the necessary nourishment from the food they ate; consequently they became weakened, susceptible to disease, and unable to stand the rigors of winter.

The first horses used by the Spur outfit came with the first

[1] W. R. Stafford to Flora Goforth, interview, February 23, 1930.

herd of cattle from the south.[2] The brand on these horses became the permanent horse brand of the Ranch—a triangle on the left hip.[3] A second bunch of horses was purchased from George Gambel, who lived on Duck Creek.[4] Other bunches were bought in 1884 and 1885, and by 1886 the Ranch had approximately 800 head.[5]

In the general haste of stocking the Ranch at a time when the ranching outlook was prosperous, many old horses had been acquired. When conditions became more serious in 1886, Lomax took stock of the horse herd and found 200 practically worthless. He began getting rid of old horses. He advertized them for sale, representing them to be "good horses with sound backs, well broke, used to rope-corral handling, a serviceable lot that had wintered well, and now in good condition, acclimated to the country, and ready to take on flesh as soon as the new grass comes."[6]

The policy of the Ranch for the next five years was to reduce the numbers of horses each year, the greatest reduction coming in 1886 and 1887. Two factors influenced such a policy; the fencing of the pastures reduced the amount of work, and the building of the Fort Worth and Denver railroad shortened the distance to shipping points. In 1888, the record shows that 55 horses were sold, and no mention is made of purchases. The next year 60 head were sold, and 28 head were purchased. Horsbrugh wrote on July 18, 1889:

I have heard of a bunch of young horses for sale in Colemen county and have sent Campbell down there to see them. He left this morning in a wagon, and it will take 5 or 6 days to make the trip, but there will be little expense. If he gets them, he will hire a boy to help bring them back. Thirty-five dollars a head is asked for them, but money is scarce down there, and I think $30.00 will buy them. I told Campbell that the $1440.00 which we got for the trail horses sold at Amarillo this spring would allow our buying 48 head at $30.00 or 41 head at $35.00. I told him to buy them for $30.00 if possible, providing that he got nothing over 6 years old and that he reject everything that had the least thing wrong with it, the horses to be of a certain kind, broke and bridlewise.

[2]Jake Raines to Flora Goforth, interview, February 23, 1930.
[3]Spur Records, II, 565.
[4]Stafford to Goforth, interview, February 23, 1930.
[5]Ibid.
[6]Spur Records, I, 105.

Campbell is a very good judge of horses especially for range work, and I think he will make a good trade. There are very good stocks of horses down in that country, and both the "Matadors" and "Two Buckle" outfits are using some they got down there 5 years ago; since then of course the stock has been improved a bit.[7]

Campbell was gone three weeks, and on August 12 Horsbrugh reported the outcome of the trip:

Campbell returned Saturday with 28 head of horses, which cost $35 a head. They are a good lot and are 3's and 4's, except one. They are all picked and include 19 of the brand I sent him to locate. I consider he has done well. He would have gotten more, but was unable to get the same class of horses at the same price. He drew $1000 for expenses and getting them here, but this did not cover the wages of the two hands who helped him.—9 days at $1 a day. One is an old Spur hand and will go to work on the range, and the other is working at the sorghum farm. I am sending Campbell up Blanco Canyon to see an outfit about more horses, as we still have $440 to spend for that purpose.[8]

Campbell found the horses up Blanco Canyon to be good ones, but the owners wanted $45 a head. He considered the price too high, and Horsbrugh bought no more horses that year.[9]

In June, 1889, Horsbrugh took stock of the horses on hand and found that between 60 and 70 were old, played-out, and practically worthless. These were segregated, and Horsbrugh wrote the Home office:

They do not comprise a very brilliant bunch, the youngest among them being about 14 years, but they are in good flesh, and may possibly bring $20 a head; this, if got for them, will be so much gained for the company, as at present their real value is about twenty cents.[10]

To prospective buyers, Horsbrugh used a different tone. He wrote Powell and Company of Fort Worth:

I note that you have a Louisiana trade for cheap horses, and would recommend your coming out here if you think it worth your while to come so far to see a carload or two. I have about 60 head of horses I think would suit your requirements. They are fat, and look fine, and can be easily shown, being in a small pasture about a mile from headquarters. These I would prefer to sell for cash; if

[7]Spur Records, IV, 246.
[8]Spur Records, IV, 202.
[9]Spur Records, IV, 183, 199.
[10]Spur Records, IV, 263.

we could agree upon a price . . . I will sell them right and at figures you can make money of (*sic*).[11]

Mr. Powell doubtless smiled when he read this letter; old horse traders understood each other. He evidently thought it would be carrying the tricks of the profession a little too far to sell old broken-down cow-horses to Louisiana Negroes to plow cotton. Horsbrugh wrote other horse dealers but he could not get them interested. He managed to sell some at the Ranch, one and two at a time, and on September 9, he reported to London:

I traded 19 old and very sorry nags for 12 young ones, but I had to give some money as well. This I did as I knew it would be the only way to get rid of a very hard and worthless lot, some of which would certainly die this winter. I did not give any horses that were worth $5, and gave $120 in money (I made him come down from $150 after dickering all day), and the horses I got were all under 7 years old and worth $25. This makes 48 old horses that I have managed to get rid of to some advantage this year.[12]

By "some advantage" Horsbrugh meant he had gotten from $25 to $35 for a bunch of old plugs that he admitted were "not worth twenty cents" and some of them "would not live through the winter"—truly, he had the horse trader's spirit.[13] But he was not to feel proud of himself for long. For the 25 or 30 head that were unsold he could find no buyers, and he still had them on hand the following January. He eventually got rid of the ones that did not die that winter. After that the problem of disposing of 30 to 40 old horses a year was one of the most exasperating and least remunerative of all of the manager's duties.

The Spur Records are extremely meager concerning horses from 1891 to 1896. Only three references occur—two car-loads of old horses were offered for sale in 1891; a bunch of young horses were purchased in 1893; and J. A. Stokes carefully examined

[11]Spur Records, V, 375.
[12]Spur Records, VIII, 239.
[13]The following report on horses for 1889 was made to the London office:

Reported last year (1888)		510
Sold in 1889	66	
Deaths in 1889	26	
Strays	10	
		102
Bought in 1889		30
On hand at present		438

all the horses on the Ranch in January, 1895, for the purpose of condemning the useless ones.[14]

By 1897 the number of usable horses on the Ranch had gotten so low that Horsbrugh felt the year's work could not be effectively done without at least 50 more. The attitude of the Board of Directors toward the proposed purchase indicated that if they had bought the Ranch in haste in 1884, they were now "repenting at leisure." In the early years of the Ranch they readily consented to the purchase of a hundred horses at a time and did not ask any questions about the price. Horsbrugh after having brought the matter to their attention about five times before, wrote apologetically on March 24, 1897:

> I am sorry to make this expense, but it is one that must happen every now and then; the last we bought was four years ago, and as we don't breed any, the supply must be replenished at times. It must be remembered that the term *horses* as used in this land is a misnomer for these animals here; what we use for work would be called "poor looking rats of ponies" in the old country, and as they are run mostly on grass with no grain at all, it is wonderful what can be done with them.[15]

After dilly-dallying for weeks the Board cabled, "You may buy horses if absolutely necessary; can you manage with 30 head for the present?" Horsbrugh did not think thirty would do. He had been fretting lest time for spring work arrive without sufficient mounts. Within two hours after he received the cable he hustled H. P. Cole off with $1,200 in his pocket to purchase such horses as he could find.

The next day a second cable from London told Horsbrugh that he could get horses in Wyoming for $15 a head. Horsbrugh answered:

> As to the price of horses in Wyoming, I am unable to regard that as having any bearing on horses down here; $15.00 may be the worth of such horses as I use here, but I can only say that it is impossible for me or anyone else to get horses for that *now* down here. There are a good many bunches of horses that are for sale in different parts of Texas possibly at the minimum price I wish to pay, but to get them at that price one must buy the whole bunch, and be obliged to take a lot, or at least a large proportion, that are useless. Only picked horses are fit for work right away, and

[14]Spur Records, VI, 391; XII, 8.
[15]Spur Records, VI, 231.

it is these I want; they are much cheaper in the long run whether wanted now or not, as every bunch put up for sale contains a lot of weeds in it that will never be any good, and simply represent so much money thrown away. They have got to be broke, or at least what is called broke, that is, fit for work (really, just half broke); if we get horses that are unbroke we ought to get them the year before we want to use them on the range, and get them gradually "gentled" as it is called here, and acclimated. I have heard for several years that horses are very cheap in Wyoming, so much so that they are represented as being slaughtered and canned for food, and some boiled down for soap; but I do not think that selected ones, taken out of bunches that are offered for sale for so much per head, broke and fit for use at once, can be got for $15. If so they are very much cheaper than down here. I know of two bunches sold in the last two weeks, one lot at $33.00 a head and the other at $30.00. There are two men in Stonewall and Haskell counties that Cole has gone to see; they have over a hundred head apiece, and I have no doubt that he could buy all they have for $20 a head; but the purchase would include a lot of useless stuff.

When Cole looks at these herds the seller will put what he has in a corral, and then price them to Cole, who will look them through carefully, and then ask the owner what he will take for 15, 20, or 30, or as many as he can arrange to pick from the bunch, or "top" them as it is called. This of course is a matter of trading and dealing, and if he can get a number, being allowed to pick at $25.00 or $30.00, he will proceed, and gradually work out the number, provided the bunch is good enough, and will stand the selection.

Everyone that Cole picks will be handled by himself and carefully examined as to age, eyes, and all blemishes, and he will put the entire bunch through his hands, rejecting or passing as he may decide. You see this is a very different thing to buying a bunch at so much a head. Of course it is not always possible in buying to get exactly the kind of pick that he wants, but of course that is really a matter of trading or dealing, and Cole is as good at that as the manager.

The breeding of horses has been a very poor business of late years, and those breeding are very often willing to let a man have his pick, if he promises to keep his mouth shut about it. I remember in 1893 buying some horses from a man who came through here with a hundred head; he let me pick 10 head out of them for $20 and $23.50 a head. He went on, and at the F ranch (Goodnight's) sold the pick of the bunch, 25 head at $30, claiming of course they had never been "topped." I saw him afterwards at Amarillo, and he still had a few on hand, but said he would soon close them out. He very likely had 200 head in his bunch when he left central Texas, but by systematic lying, he was gradually working them off. The ones I got were very good horses and worth the money.[16]

Six days after Horsbrugh wrote this letter he received another from London urging him anew to be economical and investigate the Wyoming horses. Cole had already returned from Haskell county with the horses; so Horsbrugh again had to enter into a lengthy defense of his policy:

I received yours of the 20th yesterday and note what you say about horses. I have this to say, that at this time we can less spare horses than at any other, as the heaviest part of our work comes on in the gathering of spring herds, and that it is at this time that we have most need of all that are fit to go; and it will be observed this comes on at the very time when the horses are less fat than they would be a couple of months later. Therefore, it would not have been prudent to try to fill an important contract at the commencement of the season when horses are weak. I, in making the requisition for the fresh horses, mentioned the number that I thought it safest to apply for in view of the work ahead of us, while at the same time being at all times anxious and desirous of keeping down the expenses, and doing the work in a thorough manner as cheaply as possible; had I thought that a less number would suffice, I would have certainly said so. Thirty head would be sufficient were we going to work two months from now, but at present it would be risking too much to try it.[17]

It was with a sigh of relief that Horsbrugh reported that he had finished the horse-buying business for the year.

I have finished buying horses, and have managed to keep within the appropriations named. I have got a very superior lot of horses,— the best, it is conceded, that we have bought in ten years at least. It was not possible to get them anything like the price mentioned by you in your letter received yesterday, that is, $15 as they are selling in Wyoming. I had to pay for the kind we wanted $27.50 for 45 head and $25 for 9 head, making 56 purchased in all.[18]

Occasionally, it was necessary to buy mules. On May 28, 1897, Horsbrugh wrote the Home office:

We use mules for hauling the wagon that accompanies the outfit in the range, they being stronger and hardier, and easier kept than the horses are. It takes four, and the lead pair is getting too old for the work. I got another pair of strong young mules for the lead that are worth the money (mules are very much more valuable

---

[16]Spur Records, VIII, 142.
[17]Spur Records, VIII, 146.
[18]Spur Records, VIII, 147.

here than horses). The "chuck" wagon when it is loaded with men's beddings and camp outfit is a very heavy concern, and as it has to go where there are no roads, it pulls a team very hard; it needs to have something in front of it that can pull it through some very rough places, and I find that mules answer better in every way, as they stand work better than horses. The old pair of mules were put at easier work, plowing and hauling wood.[19]

Horsbrugh's troubles for 1897 did not end with the purchases for the year; he had some old horses to get rid of. On August 4, he wrote the London office:

Today I traded off 25 old condemned horses to a man who lives in Dickens and is well known to us. He gave me a promissory note for $250, which he is to pay by delivering 700 bushels of oats to us. Oats are very cheap in Knox, Hall, and Childress counties. This man will trade horses to nesters for oats. This is a good trade for us as the ranch would have lost nothing if it got nothing for the horses. The youngest was 18 years old, and none were worth $2 per head. Some of them had the T. P. Stevens brand, "3," showing they were bought by the old Espuela Company of Fort Worth (in 1883 or 1884).[20]

Horsbrugh wrote again the following February concerning this horse-trading venture:

I am sorry to say that I had bad luck with the man who took 25 old horses from me in the fall; the horses were worthless but he thought he could do well with them, which was doubted. Unfortunately after disposing of some of them at a very little profit about Clarendon and Vernon he got thrown and smashed up a bit, breaking his arm and otherwise injuring himself, and was in bed bad sick for some time; and away went his money in this way. He returned home to Dickens a sad and badly broken man, and I have his promissory note, and that is all so far. I was sorry for the fellow and have promised to let him work it out at intervals, but so far he has not done much. The only way is for me to get him to work it out, as he hasn't got a cent and I can't make him pay anything. It is bad luck in a way as I had made a very good trade if it had turned out all right; but, on the other hand, the horses he got were worthless. I had to make other arrangements for my winter feed, which was annoying. I hope that there will be no disinclination to let me have some horses this spring, as the distemper is very bad among those we have, and many that ought to be fat are now skin poor.[21]

[19]Spur Records, VIII, 167.
[20]Spur Records, VIII, 209.
[21]Spur Records, VIII, 316.

In January, 1898, Horsbrugh recommended a change in the horse policy of the Ranch:

My idea is more horses and oftener; it would then be easier to trade off old horses which would be of some value to the man who buys them, as it is we have a number of horses on our books, but most of them are run down because we have to work them so hard. If we bought more frequently, we would have a bunch to sell each year and would lose less. This is only a theory and might not work out so well in practice, but I think it would be more business like. The idea is that by having more horses we would be better served on the range; and, if sold before worthless we could get something for them which would help stock up again. If we had more horses and would not keep them till they are valueless we would not have any die on our hands except by accident. I recommend this to the Board for consideration, and hope they will think well of the idea; it is only by mentioning such matters as they occur to one that the best plans can be arrived at.[22]

In 1898 the Spur horses were bothered with distemper. Horsbrugh wrote on February 10:

I believe I shall be compelled to get 40 or more head of horses, as these we have are not doing well, having had a great deal of distemper among them; this I hear is very prevalent this year, much more than usual. Mr. Ligertwood has been down here from the Matador ranch, and was complaining about distemper in their horses. The Matadors should not have much to complain of in this respect, as they keep a much larger stock of horses on hand proportionately than we do. Distemper is a very annoying thing; it does not often kill (except old horses), but it makes them poor, and the rest during the winter does them no good.[23]

Horsbrugh introduced the distemper situation by way of leading up to the thing he dreaded most—bullying the Board into allowing him to purchase a new lot of young horses about which he soon wrote:

We are carrying a smaller number than usual; this includes old ones. We have the heaviest of the work to do yet. It is not safe to start with so few and those not well, and it will be little cost to get more. There will be more money this year than the company has ever handled, so I ask the Board to strengthen my hands so there will be no uneasiness as to our being able to carry out successfully what we agree to. The old saying "fer a ha'perth of tar

---

[22]Spur Records, VIII, 296.
[23]Spur Records, VIII, 314.

the ship was lost," applies to us. Lots of cattle are often lost because of poor mounts. I have told Cole that he can not have any
new horses this spring, and he is perplexed and bothered in consequence as we have to get to work very early, and most of the mounts
will not be ready. I noticed in the fall that, apart from any distemper, the grass seemed poor in comparison with that of other
years, that is, in quality; there is lots of it, but it is of no substance.[24]

This letter reinforced by three or four similar ones, got the
Board's permission to purchase 54 head of horses at a cost of
$1,353.[25]

In January, 1899, Horsbrugh became convinced that a change
should be made in the kind of horses purchased by the Ranch.
He wrote, "This horse question is a burning one with us (I
have got a lot of talk stored up on this), and hope I can prevail
on the Directors to see it my way." He wanted to try a number
of Spanish ponies with the view that they were tougher, wirier,
and more easily kept than the horses then used on the Ranch.
Such ponies could be bought on horse ranches in South Texas
or Old Mexico at $20 for unbroke ones and $25 for broke ones.
Horsbrugh on several subsequent occasions told the Board of
"the talk he had stored up," but if his plan was ever tried no
mention was ever made of it.

The Spur horses fared badly during the spring of 1901. Horsbrugh recounted in his fall report to the London office the evils
that had befallen the horses:

The expenditure this year was more than usual. . . . I have never
seen a similar year so far as the horses are concerned. Early this
spring a lot of them got to eating "loco"; it showed up abundantly
at the time, and it caused a number to either die or become useless.
On top of all of this they took horse sickness such as "pink-eye" and
distemper; and for a time it looked as if the trouble the British
government had with the horse business in Africa were nothing
compared with ours. I had to buy freely, and those we already had,

---

[24]Spur Records, VIII, 314.
[25]The following report on horses for 1898 was made to the London office:

Reported last year		267
Purchases during year	56	
mules	6	
	==	
		62
		==
		329
Deaths in 1898		27
		==
On hand at present		302

had to be used sparingly. . . . I have had to spend much more than I expected in this direction, but I can assure you that none have been bought needlessly. It was only on account of our being compelled to buy them that they were bought. Because of the fact that horses are higher this year than usual, I had to pay a bit more per head in order to get those that would do us any good.[26]

In November, 1903, the range was cleared of old horses. This time they were shipped to Louisiana with the view of selling them to Negroes to work in the cotton fields; a good cotton crop, which sold at a fair price, had been made that year, and 53 head of old horses brought $15 a head.[27]

If the Ranch had an easy time in disposing of the old horses in November, it was not so fortunate in acquiring a bunch of young horses the following May. A carload, consisting of 28 head, were purchased in Colorado and shipped from Barela, Colorado, to Estelline. The horses received some rough treatment on the way, and Johnstone wrote a railroad official:

I am sorry to have to complain about the treatment that a car load of horses got that were shipped from Barela to Estelline. These horses were shipped on Sunday the 15th, and did not reach Estelline until about 11:00 Tuesday forenoon, the 17th. Our men say the agent at Estelline informed them that the train with the horses passed Texline sometime Monday evening. Of course I do not know the cause of the delay, it may have been a wreck up the road, but what ever the reason was, the horses were kept so long on the cars that they were about starved and had eaten each others tails off. This treatment, one would have thought, was enough; but after setting the car out at Estelline the train had to side-track and hit the car of horses so hard that it knocked them all down in a pile. Our men say one of the road officials of your road was there at the time this occurred, and rounded up the train crew for handling stock so roughly. Our men think that it was your roadmaster, but they are not sure. Anyway, the long and short of it is that one horse is ruined and had to be left in the Matador shipping pasture near Estelline and another died at Turtle Hole the next day. The boys had to leave 7 others on the way out here and it took them 5 days to bring out the remaining 19, and they are a hard looking lot. I suppose I ought to make a claim for damages on the whole bunch, and I should say that the 19 that got here have lost at least $4.00 worth of hide alone. However, I want to be more than reasonable about the matter and will only put in a claim for actual value of

[26]Spur Records, X, 389.
[27]Spur Records, XI, 123.

the crippled and dead horses, which amounts to $35.00 each or $70 in all and, I am sure you ought to find this fair.[28]

The following September Johnstone saw the crippled horse that had been left at the Matador shipping pasture near Estelline, and commented upon the fact to the London office, "I would not ask a 'dago' to haul onions with him; he is not worth the grass he eats."[29]

The buying of young horses was usually accompanied by groans from the directors. The selling of the old horses, usually with disappointment to the managers, continued. All horses were sold when the last of the Spur cattle were disposed of in 1909.

[28]Spur Records, XI, 331.
[29]Spur Records, XI, 472.

XIX: *STEALING*

ONE OF THE MOST vexing problems confronting the managers of the Spur Ranch was cattle stealing, or "rustling." For over twenty years more or less thieving went on all the time. The Ranch's method of combating it was not at all spectacular. Instead of the traditional "two-gun" men in the Ranch's employ waging six-shooter battles with bold and dashing "bad men" rustlers, and occasionally going "a rope stretching" or holding a "neck-tie party," the Spur people proceeded in a hum-drum and legal way. In all the history of the Spur Ranch a cow thief was never hanged on its lands or by its men. No extra-legal procedure was ever resorted to.

No doubt the managers occasionally felt like hanging somebody. Legal red tape, delays, postponements, technicalities, together with "nester" and "sheepherder" juries caused men who tended their own cattle to despair of bringing an end to cattle stealing by legal means. Lomax was considerably chafed when he wrote W. E. Askew on February 21, 1889:

I am in receipt of your letter of the 18th, inst., and can not agree with you that I got "hot" about a very small thing; on the contrary, I think it was a "thing" of very considerable size, no less than this: either you or someone else for you marked, or "sleepered" a Spur calf in your mark, and you attempted to claim and cut it out of a round-up. As you had always been treated fairly by me and this outfit, to say nothing more, I can not overlook such an act.[1]

The Espuela Company had a policy of apprehending cattle and horse thieves by legal processes, but the initiative and expense in such apprehensions was borne by the Company. To expect the peace officers of the counties in which the Ranch lands were located to catch and prosecute cattle thieves of their own volition was to expect too much. The Company sometimes stimulated county officers to action by offering rewards. If a thief were "caught in the act," arrested and put under guard by the Ranch employees, a sheriff or his deputy could hardly evade going after the prisoner when the necessary warrants had been issued. The surest way for the Ranch to safeguard its interests

[1]Spur Records, V, 182.

was to employ special detectives. In the summer of 1887 the company paid out over $100 in securing the arrest of a suspect.[2] The Ranch's most dependable source for combating cattle theft was the Northwest Texas Stock Raisers Association. The managers often called on the Association for help in the apprehension and prosecution of thieves and rarely ever the county officials. In some instances county officials enlarged their incomes by placing their brands on other people's calves. In other cases they were allied with persons who carried on the practice and shared in the profits.[3] The official group that could be counted on most in running down cattle thieves was the Texas Rangers. The chief trouble was that there were not enough Rangers.

Cattle stealing was not so bad on the Spur Ranch during the early and middle 80's. Some rustling went on, but the amount was negligible. By 1889, however, Lomax was becoming concerned. On February 3, 1889, he wrote to A. P. Bush, of Colorado City, then President of the Northwest Texas Stock Raisers Association:

> I suppose that you have either some knowledge of the cattle stealing and brand burning that is, and has for some time, been going on to the south of us between Salt Fork and Double Mountain River in Kent and Scurry Counties. Our brands have not been tampered with, yet no stray animal is spared, and even those ranching in their "bailiwick" have suffered. I conceive that if this thing is allowed to go on, it will not be long before indiscriminate stealing will be done; the immunity enjoyed by the thieves will demoralize employees who heretofore have been kept honest by fear of consequences.[4]

Scarcely a month passed before the Spur Ranch did sustain cattle theft in the East Pasture. On March 18, 1889, Lomax wrote again to Bush:

> I wrote you on the 9th in regard to recent arrests in Kent County, and urged that the Association should now come strong to the front and throw its influence towards punishing the thieves. I have paid all the expenses so far, besides paying the County Attorney a small fee to put him in funds to press the prosecution. The Grand Jury meets in Snyder on the 24th or 25th, and the main trouble at the start is going to be the getting of a jury which will indict. If they do not indict, then the case should be taken to Colorado or Mid-

[2]Spur Records, II, 93.
[3]Mrs. H. H. Campbell to Emily Davis, interview, December 31, 1929.
[4]Spur Records, V, 158.

land on a change of venue by the State, and the Association should see that the prosecution is ably assisted. If Mr. Hudson and you will meet me on the night of the 28th, I may be able to give you some interesting information from a trustworthy source.[5]

The outcome of the arrests is given in a letter from Horsbrugh to Alexander McNab, a director in the company, May 3, 1889.

There is comparatively little cattle stealing going on in the country, the penalty being so heavy and the rewards offered very high. This ranch belongs to the Northwest Texas Stock Raisers Association which is formed for the purpose of protecting its members from theft. It is a very large body and is able to offer large rewards for detection. It has spies and detectives throughout the country and at the railway shipping places. Of course there will always be a very small amount of theft, such as killing a beef to eat, as is done by outsiders on the sly, but to do this successfully entails a good deal of watchfulness and anxiety on the part of the thief, and the hide has to be buried owing to the mark and brand. There are several neighbors of ours who are regarded with suspicion by some of us, but it is very difficult to convict them. About six weeks ago the Association pulled up some men who live to the south of us, and in whose possession some hides were found, among them one of ours; but the jury at Snyder, a town 70 miles south of us, failed to find the evidence strong enough and discharged them.[6]

This letter was written by Horsbrugh before he became manager. He was new in the cow country at the time, but it was not long before he changed his mind about the small amount of thieving and the ease with which it could be controlled.

Remarkably few of the Spur employees ever became implicated directly or indirectly in stealing cattle or horses from the Ranch. Only one case appears in the records where the Company thought seriously of discharging a hand. On April 17, 1889, Lomax wrote to an employee at the time stationed at Duck Creek camp:

The statements recently made to me in reference to your connection with Mr. X and his alleged thefts of horses in this country compel me with much regret to announce to you my desire to terminate your employment, unless you can satisfactorily explain the same. It is not my habit to judge anyone, and I do not propose to do so now, but, to say the least, you are placed in a most unfortunate position; and, as it appears to me, can not longer be useful to this company. Please therefore come in as soon as possible, and we will make a settlement.[7]

[5]Spur Records, V, 206.
[6]Spur Records, IV, 274.
[7]Spur Records, V, 225.

The employee evidently did a good job of satisfactory explaining, for the next month his name appears as usual on the payroll where it continues to appear until September, 1903.

In February an exciting bit of robbery took place on the Spur Ranch. Two "bad men" with considerable reputations entered the Company store one cold night while Dick Ware, the store keeper, and a Ranch hand named Sowell were dozing by the fire. They tied and blind-folded Ware and Sowell and leisurely helped themselves to what they wanted in the store. They took money, clothing, boots, ammunition, candy, groceries, some cheap novels, and stamps and newspapers from the post office. Loaded with all the merchandise they could carry they left in a southwesterly direction, taking with them several of the company horses. The next day a posse made up of a deputy sheriff from Estacado, Crosby County, and several of the cowboys from the Ranch started in pursuit. The desperados' weakness for literature proved their undoing. While they were resting under some trees in Yellow House Canyon, reading the dime novels, the posse overtook and quietly surrounded them. So absorbed were they in the stories, that an array of six shooter and Winchester barrels were pointing at them from every direction before they were aware of any intrusion. The prisoners, along with their booty, were carried to Estacado. A few days later Horsbrugh and several of the Spur hands went to Estacado to the examining trial. Horsbrugh wrote the London office a detailed account of the proceedings. He gave a unique description of a court scene in the cow country during the 80's:

My last letter to you was mailed on the 6th inst. On the afternoon of the next day word came down by mail that Brown with the deputy sheriff and another man had come up with the robbers in Yellowhouse Canyon, and had arrested them and taken them to Estacado (county seat of Crosby) for preliminary trial. With Cook, Ware, Lanter, and Stokes I went up there that night, and the case against the prisoners was commenced next day. As Mr. Lomax was absent at the time, I went in order that complaint on behalf of the Company might be properly lodged against the prisoners. It was a good thing also that Stokes and Lanter went as they proved of great assistance in guarding the prisoners. The jail at that place is not yet finished, and they had to be guarded night and day; and the people up there being either singularly apathetic or scared, the only assistance given to the deputy sheriff, (the sheriff not having got back), was by the "Spur" outfit. At one time I thought that it might be necessary, if the legal business was prolonged much more, to send down here for more men to make sure that the prisoners did not get away. As they were both desperate and had no chance of getting away through any legal quibble, they had to be guarded by two armed men constantly.

It was unnecessary to make any formal complaint on behalf of the company, as Cook and Ware in their different departments were able to do all that was needed in this way, and to identify the property that had been stolen. One of the horses stolen was not found in their possession when arrested. All endeavors made by Cook and myself to get the prisoners to tell us quietly what they had done with him were unavailing. As this horse was lame at the time of the theft, they did not take him far, but they would not say whether they shot him or merely turned him loose. They were trying to make out that there was a third man in the business who had got away, but from the evidence, I think this to be nonsence [*sic*]. With the exception of this horse, everything was recovered; all the money, cheques, stamps and various articles taken from the store, except some handkerchiefs and a few small things, and the clothes which the prisoners stood trial in. This was considerable, as they were rigged out from top to toe in clothes taken from our store, including under-clothing, hats, and boots. As the sequel showed, one of these men's clothes were completely ruined before the proceedings were over.

They were first charged with stealing horses, and Cook identified the two horses. The men were put under bond to await the action of the grand jury, which meets next month. The charge of burglarizing the store was next gone into, and it took till eleven o'clock at night and part of the next day to finish this. The reason of so much delay was that the prisoners had got one of the lawyers up there to act for them, and as his fee was contingent on what was recovered from the wreck, he tried very hard to show that they had considerable money of their own when taken.

The courthouse was new, and so were the lawyers, and such an opportunity to hear their own voices in the new room was a sudden streak of luck to them. When the case was all over regarding the prisoners, and all that remained was the haggling over how much money they had of their own and how much was stolen, the lawyers got to fighting fists-to-cuff, and in the confusion in the court, one of the prisoners tried to escape and was shot down in the room a yard or two from where I stood. The shooting was done by the deputy sheriff who was down stairs, and hearing the scuffle up in the courtroom, rushed up and met one of the prisoners taking time by the forelock and making for door during the row. As he refused to go back, Sherman, [the Deputy Sheriff], shot him with his Winchester rifle, Lanter was on guard at the time and had his rifle at his shoulder meaning, as he said, to stop the man if he got to the door. This bit of tragedy had a wonderful effect in closing up the case, and after the wounded man had been attended to, and the judge, who had suddenly disappeared, was found and brought back, and the angry feelings of the legal light-weights soothed by the application of fines for contempt of court, everything was given up to us. As one of the prisoners was lame, and the other nearly dead, the necessity for guards was not now so great. We all left that evening with the exception of Lanter who remained, at the request of the deputy, to help him with the prisoners until the sheriff got back. The wounded man will die very soon I think as he was shot through the lungs. There were not many people in court at the time, and I am afraid that I will have to go up there next month as a witness. I was within a few feet of the whole business, but at the time my attention was absorbed by the legal prize-fighting, and I was interested in observing that their lawyer was licking ours. The fight was, however, as poor a display as their law was. We got back to the Ranch yesterday bringing the stolen horses, money, and valuables that had been stolen.[8]

The wounded man did not die. The prisoners were given comparatively light sentences in the state courts for store robbery and horse theft, but for the few stamps they took from the post office they drew twenty-five year sentences in prison from the federal courts.

Extra routine interest in 1890 centered around a rather sensational capture of a horse thief by Hosea, a Ranch employee, and Sheriff Standifer of Crosby County. Standifer was a vigorous, fearless fellow, and made an unusual officer. Horsbrugh, writing of the affair to the Home Office, said:

I notice that the Board approved the $50 reward to Hosea. I would further like to reward Standifer, the sheriff at Estacado, who volunteered to go with Hosea and without whom the thief in all probability would not have been taken. They had a very close shave getting the thief; and if they had been caught by the mob of outlaws, they would have been hanged. The prisoner is now down in the Snyder jail. I believe there are several parties trying very hard to get him out on bail; but I had a good talk with the sheriff down there, who I think is a little soft, and made him promise he would hold the thief until he is tried. The prisoner I think knows too much about several citizens down there, and they want to get him out on bail, and of course he is not to be heard of again. They are also trying to get him to play crazy, so that he may get off on a plea of insanity.[9]

[8]Spur Records, IV, 317.
[9]Spur Records, IV, 60.

The trial was postponed for over a year. Whether or not a conviction was ever obtained, the Ranch records do not show. During 1896 cattle stealing in the Spur pastures assumed such proportions as to cause the manager constant anxiety. In February of that year Horsbrugh discovered that six sections of school land within the Spur pastures which had been filed on previously by settlers, had forfeited. He wrote the Land Commissioner urging him to lease these lands to the Espuela Company "in order to defeat the unscrupulous ends of certain rustlers."[10] By this time it was a common trick of rustlers to file on school lands within the pastures of large cattle companies, and to make a pretense of "living the land out." This gave them a legal right to be just where they wished to be—in the midst of the range of a large company. If a rustler managed to round up one motherless, unbranded calf a week and put his brand on it, he was doing a splendid business. Not infrequently, when motherless, or weaned, calves could not be found, a rustler would brand a calf, which had a mother, and kill the mother. Then in order to destroy all evidence of his deed he would skin the cow and bury or burn the hide. The rest of the carcass he disposed of in the most advantageous way possible.

In regard to the technique of rustling Horsbrugh wrote on January 4, 1901:

These industrious gentry are mostly to be found riding round, looking for a lost horse, they say, but really in search of a good-sized, unbranded calf; they know what to do with it when found, but it is always a matter to decide what to do with the cow, whose brand would give the whole thing away. Sometimes they shoot her or if a boggy place is handy, they may run her in there to starve. I have known cows killed by driving a knife in behind the horns into the brain leaving little or no mark, and I have also known cows to be thrown and left lying head downhill, with a foreleg twisted over back of the horns in such a way that she could not get up. In such cases it is to steal the calf that the cow is thus treated, for the law on the ranges is that the calf belongs to the cow that it is following and sucking, and the cow's brand of course fixes the title. It is very serious, as in order to enable the thief to get off with say $10 worth of property, he has to rob us of $35, which barely represents our loss. It generally is pretty good specimens that are

[10]Spur Records, VII, 289.

attractive, and good well graded cows and calves of our brand are worth more.[11]

In the summer of 1896 one of the Red Mud "settlers" Horsbrugh had had his eye on announced he was taking his herd to Indian territory. His reason was that the Spur and the Two Buckle people were making it too hot for him. Horsbrugh and Tilford of the Two Buckle concluded that the "settler's" going was too honest and above board. They cut his herd and found nothing to object to. They then surmised that the suspected thief had secretly driven his stolen cattle out of the country and that the two herds would be united at some place along the route. Horsbrugh sent two detectives to trail the legitimate herd to see if such a rendezvous took place.[12] The detectives were gone three months spending a dull and uneventful summer of spying. The "settler" leisurely grazed his herd in the rough country north of the Matador Ranch for two months and then slowly moved on into the Territory. Horsbrugh was convinced that the man knew he was being watched and managed to keep his stolen cattle out of sight.[13]

When the spring round ups were finished in July, 1896, the manager took an unusual precaution against the rustlers. It would be over a month before the fall round-up would begin. In the meanwhile he retained all the range hands and sent them to the various line-camps "to still-hunt" for old calves which had escaped unbranded from the spring round-up.[14] Horsbrugh chuckled to himself over his plan. "This is the best way to get ahead of the rustlers," he said, "of whom we have still more than our share. The men whom I am putting around the range are naturally smarter, faster movers, and better ropers than the enterprising gentry that we have always with us to some extent."[15] The manager was evidently pleased with the outcome of the plan, for he repeated it the next summer.[16]

In August, 1898, Horsbrugh had some "good news" for the Home Office.

[11]Spur Records, X, 284.
[12]Spur Records, VIII, 53.
[13]Spur Records, VIII, 62.
[14]Spur Records, VIII, 72.
[15]Spur Records, VIII, 44.
[16]Spur Records, VIII, 387.

Since writing you on the subject, a piece of good news has fallen us; a man whom I, and others, knew to be one of the worst cow-thieves that ever came to these parts, got killed in a row the other day in Kent County. He lived over on Catfish in our pasture, and was about the worst we had. His sudden taking off has, I think, rather disconcerted some of our neighbors and caused a halt, or rearrangement in their programs, as I believe a great deal of quiet stealing was intended to be done through this man, who was a reckless, improvident sort of individual who delighted in stealing, and who stole for the love of it, and for a very small reward would "maverick" an unbranded calf for another man, and kill the cow to prevent the calf following, if necessary. This unlooked for event, together with the extra good work in branding up closely all calves large enough to steal, has put a more favorable complexion on cow matters of late in this pasture.[17]

Beginning in 1896, the amount of stealing steadily increased. In the spring of 1899 Horsbrugh thought out a new way of confounding thieves. The London Office approved the plan, but was hesitant lest it incur too much expense. Accordingly, the manager made arrangements with the detective agency at Denver to send a man into the Spur vicinity. On May 19, 1899, Horsbrugh wrote the Home Office:

I shall keep down the expense as much as possible of course, but it will be impossible to do anything without it costing a little, and whatever I *do* spend in this direction will be small, I am sure, to the value that we have stolen from us every year now. At any rate if something is *not* done (if only to show that we are alive to the necessity of action, which if it does nothing else will prevent a lot of stealing), the stealing may increase to a very serious proportion. I enclose copies of letter and report from Denver, from the Dectective Agency about whom I wrote last year. I have now a man working here who is sent by them; this is unknown to anyone, neither Cole [range foreman] nor Dawson [bookkeeper] nor anyone being aware of it. You will see the chief difficulty, that of landing the man on the ground unsuspected. The worst stealing does not as a rule go on at this time, but he has made an entrance into the country, and I intend that he shall disappear. He will come into the range again later on in the fall, and he will know how to set about his investigations. He is a good man whom I knew by a sign, and with whom I have had only one or two private conversations. He represented that he used to work for a man in Dakota who is personally known to me, and therefore tried to get employment here. I refused him work, but Cole found use for him tem-

17Spur Records, VIII, 410.

porarily. I have another coming down from near Amarillo, who will ride over the range by day and watch what is going on with respect to the known or suspected thieves. I have also written to Standifer, who is greatly feared by the thieves, and who killed one of the worst last year, but I have not much hopes of getting him as he is employed in a similar capacity by the ranches to the south-east of us.[18]

Again Horsbrugh wrote on June 1, 1899:

This matter of thieving is worrying me very much at present, and which I think is at its height all over Texas, or at least the north part of it. More stealing is going on this year than has ever been known, and what I am doing towards this is more for the sake of holding what we have, than with much hope of catching the thieves, who must be caught in the act, and a lot of other necessaries, in order to obtain conviction. Besides the detective whom I have at work on the range, unknown to anyone here so far besides myself, I have two more who are riding openly for the purpose of looking after the Company's property. One of these was highly recommended to me by some Amarillo parties, the district judge up there who is an intimate friend of mine and who used to be the inspector for the Cattle Association. The detective is here now and is at work; I give him $50 a month and mount him. The other man is the famous Standifer, who has lately been acquitted in the case in which he killed the worst thief we had down at Clairemont last year. He is at work for the ranches south of us. They have been having a lot of trouble from thieves, and as he has made a lot of those gentry move out of there, he has some time at his disposal, and has come up here to see if he cannot help me with our neighbors. He cannot give me all his time, but I have him riding and I give him $40 a month. The ranchers who really have him hired are agree-able to his assisting up here; and, in fact, it is not known that he is not working here for good and all. He is very well known, and is worth a lot of ordinary men; already he has caused a flutter among the thieves. I understand that the departure of the gentleman whom we tried unsuccessfully to send to the peni-tentiary the other day at Emma has been hastened by the advent of Standifer. There is however, on Catfish and Redmud a bad gang that have to be broken up. I am operating in the books an account to be called *Protection A-c* to which we will put the expenses thus caused by the employment of these extra men; the two open riders will be easy to deal with in this way, but this detective, *about whom nobody knows but myself,* will have to be treated differently. I shall arrange to pay his firm in Denver and send you their voucher, but all reference to him as a detective must be kept out of the books here. Neither Dawson, nor Cole, or anyone else knows about him.[19]

[18]Spur Records, X, 29.
[19]Spur Records, VIII, 374.

Two weeks later, the manager made another report concerning this same matter to the Home Office:

I enclose an account, or report, from the Denver Detective Service with reference to the man who is secretly operating in this range. I have arranged that for the present he will leave and if necessary appear again in the country in October. He has succeeded in getting into the country and making himself known as a sort of a good-for-nothing tramp, has established his acquaintance, so that when next he appears he will not be looked upon with suspicion, as every newcomer is. When he returns he will get in with them, get arrested along with them, and, if necessary, go to jail with them at first. By turning State's evidence he will blow on the whole gang. I am sending a cheque of my own to pay this expense and will forward the receipt as a voucher, and I can draw under some other way for reimbursement.

The other two men, Standifer and Tynam are doing very well. By taking prompt and vigorous measures now, the whole thing will be stamped out in a year. Evidently we had begun to be a bit too easy and confident, but I am in great hopes that what is being done will induce those gentry to try some other field for their operations, and conclude that stealing in the Spur pasture is too risky to be good business.[20]

Whether it was the presence of Standifer and Tynam, or some other reason, stealing very noticeably declined during the summer and fall of 1899. "Two families of well known thieves" moved away, and others were looking for a place to go.[21] The results were temporarily so satisfactory that Horsbrugh did not re-employ the Denver detective. However, thieving trouble soon arose from another source. On January 15, 1900, Horsbrugh wrote:

I have a much more satisfactory report to make concerning the thieves. Several well known characters have moved out of this part of the country. However, the travel through the country is greater than it ever was. Numbers of settlers have come in on the strip of Public Domain between Catfish and Redmud. Until the special session of the legislature, which is called for the 23rd, inst., nothing can be done regarding this land with the Land Office, as it seems to be considered entirely different from School Land. I have therefore deemed it necessary to retain the services of two men who do nothing but look out for persons stealing the company's property, and who are prepared to act as occasion requires. Most of these

[20]Spur Records, X, 49.
[21]Spur Records, X, 62.

settlers, who are living at present in dugouts in that waste "shinery," cannot hope to make a living there unless they steal. The moral effect, of having those special men on the lookout is of undoubted value to this company in the prevention of theft.[22]

In May, 1900, a vacant house, which was on a tract of land formerly owned by a settler who sold out to the Company, burned. Horsbrugh was of the opinion that the incendiarism was the work of one of the cattle-thieving nesters who had a grudge at the Company. "There are some very bad and sneaking characters in this country yet," he said, "and the business is much more difficult to handle than in former years."[23]

During the summer of 1900 the Spur manager became aware of a new type of "cattle leakage." A few unscrupulous cattlemen from a distance were sending agents among the nesters offering to pay $15 a head for yearlings, no questions asked. This was an extraordinary temptation for settlers who were living from hand to mouth. "Lots of this is going on," Horsbrugh wrote, "and here is one of the best arguments setting forth the necessity of the employment of men, in addition to those working with the cattle, to ride around and watch our interests. I mean Standifer and Higgins who have already done us a great deal of good. There are only two or three of the suspected ones left living inside of our fence, and they are very careful what they do. New Mexico has received some of our toughest specimens, and there is a chance that before the year is out that territory will be still further enriched in the same way."[24]

So much constant and widespread stealing went on in the late 90's that it affected the morals of the hands on the Ranch. On January 4, 1901, Horsbrugh wrote:

I have found that as a rule one cannot depend on the ordinary cow-hand. This kind of man is peculiar. He will work faithfully and look after his employer's interests in various ways, but his manner of doing this is also peculiar, and he will frequently ride a long way round to prevent seeing what might be inconvenient. Few will fight in defense of the property they are paid to protect. Of course there are exceptions, but we do not get the exceptions.[25]

One of the alleged thieves who harrassed Horsbrugh for more

[22]Spur Records, X, 103-104.
[23]Spur Records, X, 165.
[24]Spur Records, X, 225.
[25]Spur Records, X, 284.

than a decade was an unusual character. Shrewd, scheming, clever, and evasive, he foiled every effort made to trap him. He secured a base for his operations by filing on three sections of school land about the center of West Pasture. When he settled there in the early 90's his cattle numbered about 35 head. From that time until the Company finally bought him out in 1901 to get rid of him, he sold on the average of about 100 head a year. The special range riders and the Denver detective spent more time trying to get evidence on him or "catch him in the act," than on any half-dozen other suspects, but he cleverly eluded them. His name runs like a refrain through Volume X of the Ranch letter books. Horsbrugh considered him "the sharpest and cleverest thief in the Panhandle." "He has been carefully watched," the manager wrote, "but nothing definite can ever be found or proved against him. He is riding the range all the time, but his principal work is done in the moonlight, and he has all the latest devices for weaning calves away from the cows." In all, the manager estimated that he stole Spur cattle to the amount of $15,000.[26]

The company continued to employ two special range riders from 1899 to 1903. Of the original two, Tynam and Standifer, Tynam did not stay long, and was replaced by a man by the name of Higgins. He and Standifer were too much alike to get along together, both being fearless and aggressive. Under circumstances previously mentioned, in October, 1903, Higgins killed Standifer.[27] The hiring of these two ostentatious gunmen to ride the range for the purpose of striking terror in the hearts of cow thieves was the nearest the Spur Ranch ever came to taking the law into its own hands.

After the unfortunate tragedy Higgins continued to act as deputy sheriff of Kent county, but was not employed by the Company. The Espuela manager prevailed upon the Northwest Texas Stock Raisers Association to send one of their inspectors to the Spur vicinity. Harkey seems to have been a capable fellow, but for several months after his arrival he had no legal authority to make an arrest, even though he caught someone in the act. Of this matter Johnstone, Spur manager at the time, wrote Murdo Mackinzie, of the Matador Cattle Company:

[26]Spur Records, X, 38, 39, 58, 62, 105, 686.
[27]Spur Records, X, 613.

I am today writing to Cowan and Capt. Lytle on the subject of getting Harkey appointed a Ranger, either special, or attached to some Company. As the matter now stands he has no more authority to act in a cow-stealing case than any private citizen, and if a cow-thief refuses to let him investigate any crooked stuff in his pasture, he can only trot away home or get in a fight with everything against him.

I always thought that all the Association Inspectors had some kind of authority for carrying weapons, but Harkey has nothing of the kind beyond any one else. We had two fellows arrested in the Red Mud settlement recently, but it was by the merest luck that we were able to do anything at all, and if Harkey had been alone we would have had a bad case of the dry grins coming.

I wish that you would try to wake up the Executive Committee to the necessity of doing something in the way of clothing Harkey with some actual authority. I think that we have got the Red Mud Community guessing, and if that nest in the Two Circle Bar Range could be cleaned out, it would improve the tone of the whole district immensely. There is another gang operating on the South of the Croton pasture which is the worst of all. If we all hang together we can make cow stealing a very unprofitable business, especially at the present prices of cattle.[28]

In regard to "the two fellows arrested in the Red Mud settlemen," Johnstone wrote to Sam H. Cowan, one of the Spur attorneys at Fort Worth:

We have stirred up a very nice little calf stealing case in the pasture, and I want you to prosecute the thieves. The offense occurred in Kent county and we must make a strenuous effort to get the case moved. The men we had arrested waived examination and are under $800.00 bond. We heard of the business first through "Pink" Higgins and Jeff Harkey who went down to investigate. The result of this investigation was that Harkey, Higgins and one of our men went to a nester's weaning pasture and found a bunch of calves, two span of which were necked and others of them were wearing yokes. The principal man was not at home (I presume that he was hiding out in the brush), and Harkey and Higgins turned the calves out and took them to a bunch of Spur Cows that had been previously located. Two of the calves sucked then and there. Higgins says that he and his family can swear to several other calves being "Spur" property. The man who owns the place where these calves were found has a very fishy reputation. His wife claimed the cattle were her husband's property.

This occurred in what is know as the Red Mud settlement and

[28]Spur Records, XI, 448.

there is quite an uproar stirred up on the ground that the suspect's wife was "mistreated"—you know the kind of thing. I need not tell you that this is all nonsense.

It would have been better if he had been at home himself, but I do not think that there was the remotest chance of him showing up as long as Harkey was in the vicinity, and it is difficult to see what other course these fellows could have taken under the circumstances and accomplished anything.[29]

Two men were indicted by the Grand Jury at Clairemont, and the Company succeeded in getting the trial moved to Snyder. One of the men arrested said a person could steal five hundred calves from the Spur Company and that no grand jury in Kent County would find an indictment; and if such a thing should occur, a conviction could not be secured where a "foreign company" was concerned. On the other hand, the reputation of Snyder juries had improved somewhat since the days of Lomax and Horsbrugh. The trial resulted in a conviction.[30]

This case marked the beginning of a new day. The Company had been baffled by stealing for twenty-one years. During that time thousands of Spur calves had received someone else's brands. This was the first indictment or conviction that the Company had ever been able to get. From this time on, convictions became easier and easier and cattle thieves scarcer and scarcer.

[29]Spur Records, XI, 443.
[30]Spur Records, XI, 513, 514.

XX: *CONTROVERSIES*

THE SPUR RANCH tried to live in peace with all of its neighbors. One cannot read through the 35,000 letters of the Ranch's letter-book without becoming convinced that harmonious relationship with neighbors was from the first a fundamental policy of the management. From 1883 to 1930, a period of forty-seven years including the twenty-three years of Swenson ownership, the Ranch was involved in thirteen lawsuits. In eleven of the cases the Ranch was the plaintiff; and in two instances, the defendant. Only two of the thirteen cases were with neighboring ranches, the Browning and the Matador. The other eleven suits were with individuals or counties, and dealt with such things as trespass, debts, and property valuations for taxable purposes.

Although it was the policy of the managers to get along as peacefully as possible, times were sure to come when sternness, straightforward talking without the mincing of words, and swift, direct action were indispensible to the welfare of the Ranch. In a country where for years it was sixty miles to the nearest court or peace officer; where the early land lines were laid off by careless surveyors who rode merrily across the country on a wagon while their chain carriers estimated their distances without the trouble of putting the ends of the chain to the ground and setting pegs; where smaller settlers were envious of large foreign corporations and were ever ready to encroach upon syndicated ranches, appeasing their consciences by thinking that it did not matter as long as the losers were "damn foreigners"; and where the land still abounded with many frontier spirits, each believing that he was by right and inheritances a law unto himself—in such a country, some friction was inevitable.

The courteous and polished Lomax could on occasion become hard, demanding, and unyielding. A letter to the manager of the American Pastoral Company at Wheeler, Texas, on December 12, 1887, bespeaks his frankness:

On my return to the ranche I find your favor on the 31 of October referring to the K steer branded by your men, and saying that on your return to the ranche you would try to find out all about it and explain further. I should be glad to hear from you, and wish to know particularly if your investigations lead you to think that any others besides this one was branded. Driving as we do every year, and with strays from such drives, we are liable to have a few animals scattered through your country, and I have been told that the K steer was not the only instance of such work by some of your men. I don't believe all I hear, and I believe you to be a man who would not allow such to be done. Hence I tell you frankly what I have heard, and ask that you will inquire fully into it.[1]

The Espuela Land and Cattle Company, like other corporations and individuals engaged in the cattle business, frequently had differences with buyers and sellers of cattle in regard to range counts and times of delivery. For instance, in 1888, the Company purchased two small lots of cattle—one from a Mr. Vaughn and the other from a Mr. Hearn of Beard. Both men were to deliver the cattle by a certain time or the contracts became void. Both were delayed in making their deliveries, and the Company made an extension of time. Hearn arrived before the extended time expired, but Vaughn did not. When Vaughn did arrive Lomax refused to accept the cattle. Vaughn then had his attorney, "General" F. W. James of Beard, to write the Home Office of the Company, asking for a reconsideration of the contract. On April 12, 1888, Lomax wrote James:

I am now in receipt of the Company's reply to your letter on the matter of the claim preferred in behalf of Mr. Vaughn, and herewith submit same—

Gen. James' letters to you have been duly noted, and the Board requests me to ask you to inform him that they can only repeat their former decision not to reopen the matter. Of course they deny any legal right in the matter, and the consideration given to Vaughn in giving extra time to deliver his cattle was in their opinion ample, and they cannot consent to any further concession. That portion of the argument which is founded on Hearn is, of course, beside the question altogether. If we had to do it over again we should not take Hearn's cattle and we only did it as a matter of grace and favor, as expressed at the time, and in no sense as a matter of right.[2]

An example of a typical difference in the count of a herd changing hands is found in the following letter from Lomax to John H. Bowman, Manager of the Defiance Cattle Company, Navajo Agency, Arizona:

[1]Spur Records, II, 15.
[2]Spur Records, II, 39.

Sir: I am in receipt of your letter of the 25th of October, and would say in reply—

1st. As you signed and left with Mr. Lockhart a check and receipt to be filled in when the count was complete and also was particular to reconcile your tally with ours at the shute, and in the presence of witnesses told Mr. Lockhart to deliver same to me when the branding was completed at the shute, I consider that the delivery of the receipt and check was a very necessary proceeding on Mr. Lockhart's part, in order to get the cattle.

2nd. As to the agreement between our Supt. Mr. Groff and yourself (who were the parties named in the contract to agree on the terms and class of delivery) I beg to refer you to the enclosed letter from him, which fully sets forth the understanding had between you, and which was reiterated before me by both of you, on one occasion at your camp fire at night and in the pen the morning of the day you started below, both times in the presence of Mr. Lockhart who fully understood the arrangement as Mr. Groff states it.

3rd. We not only as agreed gave Mr. Lockhart a good count on the outside of the pasture, but he was so poorly provided with men and horses that we sent two men with him for three days to help him get fairly started.

4th. You certainly remember talking both to Mr. Groff and myself of probably wanting more cattle in the spring and that when you sent for them you would then be able to gather and drive such heifers as escaped from the herd this fall.

I don't see how you could make such a statement if as you now claim you were only to pay for such cattle as were counted on the outside of the pasture, as you would have no interest in any others that might be left, and neither do I see how you could expect us to put your brand on cattle, and after holding them for days, only get pay for what remained under herd, leaving us without any pay for the escaped ones which would have your brand on them.

Lastly, I beg to state that you agreed with the inspector Mr. Cabler to pay him inspection fees on the shute count, and did so pay him, and Mr. Cabler was present and heard the understanding between us reiterated about the shute count being the count on which settlement was to be made.[3]

The careless work on the part of the first land surveyors of the cattle country became a fertile source of boundary dissensions between subsequent land owners, especially during the 90's and the early 1900's. Disputes were frequent between settler and settler, settler and ranchman, and ranchman and ranchman. The following letter from Horsbrugh to Lomax, August 19, 1890, indicates the chronic nature of boundary disputes:

[3]Spur Records, II, 668.

I have a letter from Earnest and Shepherd saying that there is a
suit pending in the Crosby County Court in which some owners
of certain I. & G. N. Surveys in Dickens County are plaintiffs and
the Matador Company are defendants, that the former desire to
prove the boundaries of the Matador pasture in Dickens County,
and that they want me as a witness. I have written them that I
find it hard enough to keep up with our own boundaries without
troubling myself with those of my neighbors, and that I know
nothing whatever about the matter. I hope they won't call me,
as I am ignorant of what they are squabbling about; and I have
not the time to go anywhere to court. Can you advise me anything
about the matter, supposing they do subpoena me?[4]

One of the boundary troubles worrying Horsbrugh at that
time was a dispute with the Kentucky Cattle Company over the
west boundary of the West Pasture. Horsbrugh and Colonel Tilford at length agreed for each company to employ a surveyor to re-
survey the line in question, and the ranches would leave the entire settlement to the two civil engineers. The Kentucky Company secured the services of R. P. Smythe of Estacado and the
Spurs, J. L. Shepherd of Colorado City. The plan was for the
two surveyors to run their lines independently of each other,
and then compare notes and compromise on the differences.
Their findings proved to be satisfactory to both companies.[5]

A boundary controversary between the Spurs and the Llano
Cattle Company was settled in a somewhat similar manner.
Colonel W. C. Young, president of the Llano Cattle Company,
had his surveyor, Mr. Kaye, make a complete survey of the dis-
puted area, and sent a copy of the results to Lomax. Lomax in
turn had Mr. Shepherd do the same for the Spur Company and
sent a copy of his results to Young. After studying each other's
claims for some time Young and Lomax adjusted the differences

[4]Spur Records, VI, 276.

[5]An interesting incident occurred while Smythe and Shepherd were making their
surveys. While working near the Caprock, Smythe discovered that he was off the
line. He sent for Shepherd and together they decided their instruments were being
distracted. Smythe's instrument had a solar attachment, and they re-ran the line
using the solar device instead of the magnetic needle. Shepherd had surveyed the
West Pasture of the Spur Ranch several times before and had never been able to
make his lines close on the southwest corner by a distance of a mile. On this
occasion, using the solar instrument, the lines closed exactly. The incident brought
to light that local magnetic attraction, due to some mineral in the vicinity, had
been throwing the instruments off about five degrees. R. P. Smyth to W. C. H.,
interview, August 28, 1930.

by mutual compromises. Throughout the negotiations the most friendly personal feelings were maintained by both parties.[6]

A boundary controversy with Major Watts on the west was likewise settled with both parties staying in the best of humor. Throughout the late 90's there was a difference of opinion between Horsbrugh and Major Watts as to the correct location of the division fence between the West Pasture and Major Watts' pasture. In 1904 the Major took the initiative in bringing the matter to a close. He employed a Mr. Twitchell to re-locate the west line of Block 8. His findings showed the Spur fence to be one-half mile too far west. Johnstone, who in the meanwhile had taken Horsbrugh's place as manager, accepted the results and had the fence moved back.[7] In writing to the London Office about it, Johnstone said, "You will understand that Mr. Twitchell's survey gives all our acreage, our fence is simply off the line."

Law costs were a considerable item in the Spur expense account throughout the 90's and early 1900's. Various law firms of Fort Worth were paid annual retaining fees of $1,000. Johnstone wrote the secretary of the Company, January 5, 1904:

> I have sent Messrs Coke and Coke their annual retainer fee $1000. This you will note is not in advance, but we pay at the end of the year, and this is for legal services in 1903. At present while those lands are being put in shape they are more properly earning it, and their careful way of proceeding is a guarantee that everything will be in order and sure.[8]

The company usually paid a lawyer in Colorado City, Snyder, or Dickens a retaining fee to look after the local legal interests of the Ranch. Horsbrugh complained that the law costs were $450 heavier during the year 1900 than usual. Although the company called upon the retainers mainly to aid in such routine matters as land titles, contracts and so on, occasionally they were required to conduct lawsuits.

In the first lawsuit in which the Spur Ranch was involved, the Company was the defendant. Technically, the suit was not against the Company, but against an employee who had been acting as the Company's agent. It was a civil case entitled E.

[6]Spur Records, II, 199.
[7]Spur Records, XI, 140, 336, 453, 484, 498.
[8]Spur Records, XI, 167.

Yarbrough *vs.* John Jenkins. The nature of the case is indicated in the following letter of December 13, 1888, from Lomax to Ball, Wynne and McCart, at the time legal retainers for the Company at Fort Worth:

Some time since in making a survey of our south boundary, Capt. J. L. Shepard [Shepherd]—the surveyor—reported that he found a man named E. Yarbrough to be living on a section of our land; to wit, Survey No. 59 of Blk 7, H. & G. N. R. R. in Kent County. Not being altogether satisfied with the survey, we waited until Sheperd [Shepherd] made another run, which he has recently completed, and as before found that Yarbrough's house was near the center of our section. Shepherd also advised that we should lose no time in getting possession, as he understood Yarbrough had been living there since 1882, claimed to have preemption file on it, and though that was no good, might get a color of title by undisputed possession for a term of years. I then at once notified Yarbrough of the result of Sheperd's survey, and requested immediate possession of the premises—he answered by a verbal message, not contending against our claim, but asking that he be reimbursed for his improvements. (His buildings would be probably worth $200 at the outside) I replied that having been placed on our land without our consent, he had no legal claim for same, and none such could be recognized. At the same time I wrote that if he would put a low and reasonable valuation on them I would submit the matter to the Co. He replied again verbally—that he wanted $400 for same. I replied verbally that such a price was out of the question, and that we would take possession on the 20th of November, by which time he would please remove all his personal effects. On the 20th of Nov. accompanied by two of our men I went to the place, found no one there, doors unlocked, but house full of furniture, etc.; which Jenkins, one of my men said belonged to a hired man of Yarbrough's. After waiting several hours I took possession of the house and premises for the Co. put Jenkins in charge and told him to stay there and not permit himself to be dispossessed. A few days afterwards I moved another man there, and he with Jenkins has ever since occupied it as one of our Line Camps. On the evening of the same day I took possession, Yarbrough appeared there, Jenkins told him I had just left, after waiting there all day to see him—Yarbrough asked what I had said to his proposition of $400 for his improvements—Jenkins told him it was out of the question, and that I had said the Co. would not give it. He further told him that I had taken possession of the place for the Co. and had placed him—Jenkins there in charge, and that if he, Yarbrough —wished to stay there, for the night, it must be as guest not as proprietor. Thereupon, Yarbrough ordered Jenkins to vacate, telling him that he owned the place, that he had no right there, was trespassing, etc. Jenkins held the place, and a few days afterward Yarbrough's hired men—appeared with a wagon and hauled off the personal effects, and told Jenkins Yarbrough said for me—Lomax—to send him $100 for the place.

I paid no attention to this. Today Jenkins comes in, with enclosed petition which was served on him last evening by a deputy Sheriff from Scurry Co. to which Kent Co. is attached, citing Jenkins to appear at Snyder on next Monday—the 17th.

The petition seems to me a curious legal production though said to be drawn by a Sweetwater Lawyer, Thurman.

I hardly see how it is possible for either of you to get to Snyder now in time for Monday, and so I shall go there, try to get some Local Attorney to enter an appearance for Jenkins, and get time to answer. I ask therefore that you will write me fully in the care of Cowan & Shear, Colorado, Tex. to which place I will go for your reply, telling me what to do in the matter, and what in your opinion the merits of the case are on the facts as stated by me, also if you will come out to Snyder to attend to the matter, and when I might be able to arrange a day for your convenience.[9]

The case was tried in the Justice of Peace Court on December 21 and 22, 1888, and was decided against Jenkins. Lomax was considerably piqued when he wrote to Ball, Wynne and McCart regarding the decision.

. . . the fact was proved that Yarbrough never had any writing at all from Richards (from whom he was purported to have bought his claim) and only bought out his range right, as it was called in those days, that his file was made on land two miles distant from the premises in question, and that file had never been perfected, also that Yarbrough had moved his family and effects to Snyder to reside there, and that he had admitted he was on our land, and that his man, Mayo, was on the point of moving his things also to Snyder and was at the time of our entry actually in Snyder to get a wagon to haul them away. However, the jury found (a verdict) against us. I appealed to the county court which sits in February, and meanwhile we will hold the place.[10]

Lomax went on to ask his Fort Worth retainers about the advisibility of compromise. They replied,

In conclusion, we would say that though we have not your views on the matter of compromise, we are strongly inclined to the opinion that a reasonable compromise is the best way out of the difficulty,

[9] Spur Records, V, 57.
[10] Spur Records, V, 73.

especially where litigation is instituted in an unsettled country like yours.[11]

When Lomax broached the matter of compromise, Yarbrough, who had previously offered to take $100 for his improvements, now felt that his injury could not be placed at less than $1,000. The case went to the county court where a jury again decided against the Ranch.[12] Lomax appealed to the higher courts where a reversal was obtained. Finally, a compromise was arranged. Yarbrough, discouraged by the reversal, agreed to take $100 for his improvements and ejection damages and each side was to pay its own costs of the courts.[13] Before the case was settled Lomax had numerous occasions to reflect upon the comment of Ball, Wynne and McCart regarding litigation "in an unsettled country like yours"—indeed it took queer turns, facts and evidence and lawful rights notwithstanding.

During the spring of 1889 the Espuela Land and Cattle Company, Limited, became involved in a lawsuit with a man by the name of Dalton.[14] The nature of the case, as well as its outcome, is not revealed by the available records.

In April, 1888, a few months before he replaced Lomax as manager, Horsbrugh wrote the London Office of an experience with a rather "unsociable" fellow who insisted on driving his herd through the Spur pastures.

On the 22nd we had considerable trouble with a small bunch of cattle which came through the pasture in spite of all warnings and notifyings to the contrary. The man in charge, who said he was the owner, was a reckless dare-devil sort of individual who had been informed by some parties south of here which he relied on, that this company had no right to the land which it had enclosed, and notwithstanding all efforts made to persuade him to the contrary, he refused to listen to any reason believing that what he heard up here was all lies, and declared that he was in the right and was prepared to die in support of his opinions. It was a question of killing the man, or letting him go through, and leaving him to be dealt with by the law. The latter course was adopted, and a man sent from the south part of the range to Snyder to make out a warrant against him as that part of the country is attached to Scurry Co. In the north part of the pasture Mr. Lomax

[11]Spur Records, V, 97.
[12]Spur Records, V, 141, 183.
[13]Spur Records, VI, 222, 223.
[14]Spur Records, IV, 159.

and one of our men and myself met him near Dockums, and he was notified formally not to go through the "Tap" pasture. He carried a large rifle (Winchester repeater) constantly with him, and had the unsociable habit of throwing this cocked on anyone that he was not sure of. This was a strong argument in his favor, and helped him considerably. He was a man of very quick action, as on being notified, he about ran his horse down and got to the gate of the "Tap" before us. Here he barricaded himself with his rifle, and to get him out there would have necessitated bloodshed. There was another thing which we were perfectly certain of, and that was that the man was determined to kill Mr. Lomax if possible; we all three had rifles but the Manager would have had no chance against the man, who was lawless and rowdy and much more accustomed to the use of weapons and quicker than Mr. Lomax, and we would not have been able to shoot into him if he had shot at us. I was glad to be partially instrumental in dissuading the Manager from going up to the gate, though of course Wilkinson and I would have gone with him had he insisted on it; but as a man had been sent to Estacado for papers in connection with his Dickens Co. Trespass, the law such as it is, would appear to be the best way of dealing with him instead of killing him, simply because we had the right to. We watched them go through, and saw them carefully shut the gate behind them. The next night our man got back from Estacado having sworn out papers against our friend, and brought a message for Mr. Lomax to go up and witness against the man at the preliminary trial, but Wilkinson and I started up there the next morning instead, as we were sufficient witnesses of the trespass. On the way up we met two officers and could see the herd about five miles ahead of us, being on the plains, and we were told then that the man had left his herd and skipped out. On my asking them how they knew that, they confessed that they did not know him by appearance but had been told that he was gone by the men. . . . I borrowed the horse of a Two Buckle line rider and went to the herd and saw every man they had, and looked into the wagon. . . . As I thought the man might be hiding around somewhere, I left the officers at the house in Blanco Canon [sic] to watch the herd that night and the next morning, and went on to Estacado to make out the necessary papers for him in connection with the "Tap" trespass. As I met the mail hack coming south to Dockums I sent a note by it to Mr. Lomax telling him what had occurred, and asking him to at once send up instructions by the next hack if he wanted the man followed up in the event of his not being found in the meantime. I got out the warrant for the arrest, and the next day one of the officers came in to Estacado, saying that they had watched the herd and had been close to it that morning without being seen and that the man was really gone. I then came down to the ranche, leaving the necessary documents to await the instructions from Mr. Lomax. He sent up word to follow up the man, and he no doubt will be taken before long.[15]

Horsbrugh's surmise was never fulfilled. The person was never heard of again.

In July, 1889, a trail-boss by the name of Sims drove a herd of cattle through the Spur pastures in spite of repeated warnings that such action would be regarded as trespassing by the Espuela Company. On January 12, 1890, Horsbrugh wrote the home office:

I have a lawsuit coming off in February at Snyder. We are prosecuting Sims who last summer drove a herd through our pasture. The Lawyer on our side is Martin of Colorado who at the time received from Mr. Lomax a retainer's fee of $100 to act in the case. I am a good deal exercised in my mind whether to move for a change of venue in the case. Snyder is a very hard place to get a conviction against anyone, and especially where a company is prosecuting; the only way to get a conviction there is for the prisoner to go in with you and plead guilty, and even then the jury may say the prisoner is a liar and does not know what he is talking about, and turn him loose. But on the other hand if the case were moved to Colorado, Sims himself is well known there and has lots of friends. He was working for J. B. Slaughter at the time, and the latter is a Colorado man and is vice president of a bank there. It was Slaughter's herd that Sims was driving, and it is Slaughter who is working on the defense of the case. So it might be a case of frying-pan and fire.[16]

A few days later Horsbrugh heard that Sims, backed by Slaughter, was willing to pay reasonable damages, provided the Spur people dismissed the case against him.[17] Horsbrugh considered anew the fickleness of Snyder juries and decided that a compromise would be the safest way out. On February 9, 1890, he sent the home office an account of the settlement:

At Colorado I saw Sims and told him that I had everything ready for the trial and hoped he would be on hand. After this he came to me and asked if we could not talk the matter over as he did not want to go up there (to Snyder) on trial, and he was sorry for what he had done and was willing to pay what damages would be thought right. I, of course, told him that I had no idea of compromising the matter and wanted to go to trial, it being merely in

[15]Spur Records, IV, 283-286.
[16]Spur Records, IV, 65.
[17]Spur Records, IV, 71.

support of a policy this company was prepared to carry out. Previous to this I had a long talk with our lawyers and what they told me confirmed the opinion I had already formed, that there was no doubt of our having the law on our side, but owing to the ignorant and bigoted condition of the juries at Snyder together with the fact Sims was a well-behaved man and a general favorite, there was grave doubt as to our being able to get a verdict. The case was State of Texas vs. Sims, and in the event of the verdict being in Sims [sic] favor we had no appeal. Sims afterwards approached me again as it was a state case, and I advised him to go up there and plead guilty. This he would not do after seeing his lawyers, but offered to pay damages if I would get the case dismissed. The real amount of the damages done us could only be a trifle, but I told him if he would agree to pay the costs of the suit and let it be known publicly that he acknowledged having trespassed on the property of the company and regretted it, that I would cable the London office and see how they felt about it. Sims is a very decent sort of a fellow, and is very different from the other man, Harris, who went through defying everything and everybody and got away and was never caught. I was very anxious that this case be compromised in such a way that it would show what the company had done was right. An adverse verdict from Snyder jury just now when the spring drives are about to start—from what I hear there will be lots of herds driven this spring to New Mexico and the Indian Territory—would undoubtedly be used against us and productive of endless trouble. . . . Sims came up to Snyder and we arranged the matter. I got the editor of the paper there to put in a notice stating why the suit had been dismissed. Besides this it had been pretty well talked about in Colorado and Snyder.[18]

Three years passed before the Espuela Land and Cattle Company, Limited, was engaged in another lawsuit.[19] The records are not clear as to the nature of the case. In 1896, the Company brought two suits in the District Court at Colorado City—one against Crosby County in regard to land valuations for taxable purposes, and the other against a man named Simmonds.[20] The references to the Simmonds case do not indicate its nature.

In the fall of 1898 a boundary controversy, in which personal feelings played a part, developed between the Spur Company and W. L. Browning, whose land lay north of the Tap Pasture. In September of that year Browning, under the pretext that the north Tap fence was off the line and without giving warning to the

[18]Spur Records, IV, 78.
[19]Spur Records, III, 321.
[20]Spur Records, VII, 328.

Spur people as to his intentions, had the four mile line of fence
moved over more than a hundred yards to the south. It is probable
that Browning was prompted in part in this action by a desire to
gain possession of a very fine spring of water on the edge of the
caprock. However that may be, Horsbrugh's slow Scotch blood
boiled when he heard what Browning had done. He blustered
considerably, but his native caution caused him to proceed in a
legal manner.[21] He had the H. T. and B. Block surveyed over
again to make sure his contentions were right.[22] The surveyor's
report showed that the old fence was approximately on the line
and that the spring was 113 varas south of the north line.[23]
After trying for several months to get Browning to move the
fence back, Horsbrugh brought suit.[24] The case dragged on for
six years. Postponement followed postponement. Browning was
represented by his brother, who was during part of the time
Lieutenant-Governor of the State and very popular. Time and
again Horsbrugh had everything ready for the trial, and the
politic Browning would frustrate things by getting another con-
tinuance. In 1904, W. L. Browning died, leaving the controversy
to his widow. On August 19, 1904, Johnstone, who had inherited
from Horsbrugh the Spur side of the legal feud, wrote his lawyer,
E. J. Hamner of Colorado City:

> When I was in Amarillo recently I had a conversation with Mr.
> J. N. Browning about the suit which this company had with his
> late brother, Bud Browning. I told him that I did not wish to
> continue suing his brother's widow for damages but that if the
> defendants would let us take judgment for the land, put the fence
> back on to the proper line and pay the costs in the case I would
> be willing to settle the matter.
> Judge Browning seemed to think that his client could not, or
> rather was not in a position legally to confess judgment, and I do
> not know enough about law to say what would be the proper course
> in order to get the matter put right. I would be obliged if you
> would put yourself in communication with Judge Browning and at
> the same time let me know what you would recommend in order
> to get the matter properly disposed of.[25]

The ultimate settlement of the case is not clear. The pages in

[21]Spur Records, IX, 249.
[22]Spur Records, IX, 250.
[23]Spur Records, IX, 252.
[24]Spur Records, VIII, 446.
[25]Spur Records, XI, 429.

the letter-books of the Spur Records treating the outcome are so dim they are not legible.

In April, 1898, the Espuela Company indirectly became involved in a criminal case in the District Court at Emma, Crosby County, on the part of the defense. Horsbrugh wrote a detailed account of the case, together with its various implications, to the secretary of the Company in London.

Range work has been stopped for three days because the outfit has been [sic] witnesses in a case, State of Texas vs. Cole at Emma. I believe I wrote you before as to this: (H. P.) Cole (Spur range foreman) in the discharge of his duty last year took away from a known thief at a ranch in Crosby County two beeves that were generally known to have been stolen. He (Cole) was indicted by the grand jury at Emma, Crosby County, for [theft] on this account. It so happened that that particular grand jury had several questionable characters on it who brought the matter up very pointedly; and it also happened that there were others on the same jury who saw through the malice and prejudice of the scheme, and on this account in the finding of the bill, ostensibly to the detriment of Cole, but really to open up the whole case, and, if possible, start the ball rolling which would end in breaking up the gang of thieves which infests this country, especially that part of it which lives in our pasture on Catfish and among our neighbors. I believe that this is what will really happen. We have got them badly scared, and then indictment of Cole will have been a very good piece of business, though it was started as an insult to him and to this outfit. However, cow thieves are quite an influential body of men in these parts on any jury, and I knew there was going to be unusual interest taken in this case so far as they were concerned, and indeed it was a very bold step for them to take. I engaged Judge Plemons from Amarillo, a well known criminal lawyer in these parts who is very good at his particular line of business, having spent twenty years in acquitting some of the most notorious rascals in Texas. He agreed for $50 and his expenses, which are very little, to come down and watch the case in behalf of Cole so that if it really came to trial, the latter would be ably defended. As it turned out, our way of going about it caused the thieves to weaken. Cole had several private messages sent him beforehand to the effect that the matter would be dropped, if we dropped our side; that is, the case would not be pressed if we agreed to let bygones be bygones. To which overtures some very contemptuous and forcible replies were sent. I had some consultation at Fort Worth with the Association Committee (Northwest Texas Stock Raisers Association) and their lawyers, and our plan of action was concurred in. Cole went up to Emma as a private citizen charged with theft apart from his connection with a cattle company. The case was dismissed. The fact was that the one who lodged the complaint,—a well known thief, failed to show up. Plemons on behalf of Cole demanded a trial and announced that the defense was ready, and the State had to dismiss. As a matter of fact the District Attorney and the Judge were fully cognizant of all the particulars, and I had been privately assured that there was no danger of the trial hurting anyone who had done his duty, and especially Cole who is universally known for honesty all over this part of the State. It will, perhaps, turn out to be a very lucky thing that Cole was indicted.[26]

In the summer of 1901, the Company brought a lawsuit for the ejection of three settlers. Horsbrugh in a report to the London Office gave account as to the facts and issues involved:

This lawsuit is on account of an alleged vacancy being discovered between the Burleson County school lands and Block 1, and there are three squatters on the land. They have been put there by lawyers who just at present are stirring up everything possible in the nature of a lawsuit against a company. Everything is challenged, our rights to the land, even our right to exist. . . . I have just heard of something that may preclude the present necessity of our having the originals (deeds and records of surveys). I have been approached by two out of three defendants in this case, and it is clear something had come to light to show them to be in the wrong in their conclusions, and that I am right. They ask me to let them off quietly, and they will give no further trouble, and, figuratively, "throw up their hands" on the whole business. That is somewhat annoying as we already have been to considerable expense in engaging counsel and fixing ourselves for a regular and proper trial on the case. . . . I fancy that an old survey corner that was found by a sort of small pettifogging lawyer and surveyor had a good deal to do about their strong assumption of their rights. I know all about this old corner, which was one of a lot put down by a surveyor in 1895, whose work was found to be faulty and who was turned down and his report refused (by the State). It was believed and claimed that in the laying off of this part of the country in 1873 in the original surveys mistakes were made; and it is likely the case, as the work was slovenly done. The contention (of the settlers) is that in correcting the work this second surveyor found Block 1 to be half a mile east (of where it is at present) and that a vacancy half a mile wide was established all the way down the west side of Blk. 1. It will be seen what a serious question is here opened. A strip of land half a mile wide and twenty-six miles long is indeed serious. I believe the whole thing is one of a very common and frequent species of blackmail that is now going on wherever there are blocks of land owned by companies and have been laid off by

[26]Spur Records, VIII, 355.

old surveys. In this country everything 30 years past is very old, and, therefore, discredited to a great extent. And indeed things were done so carelessly and slipshod in those days that almost any kind of a lawsuit can be wrought up over old boundaries and corners. Land was looked upon as worthless in the days when the State was deeding large bodies to railroad builders. Yet these old careless, slipshod, and faulty surveys are the ones that are rightly given precedence. But out of wrangling over them comes lots of good pickings, or blackmail, for lawyers and land-jumpers. . . .[27]

The controversy was ended by the settlers' withdrawing and Horsbrugh's dropping the suit.

The summer of 1904 found the Company initiating a lawsuit in regard to some land titles against a man in the District Court of Dickens County. Johnstone was considerably put out when a short time before the trial he received a letter from his attorney, who had had the case from the beginning, stating it would be impossible for him to come up for the trial. Johnstone sent to Fort Worth for another lawyer, and at the same time wrote to Horsbrugh, who had moved to Amarillo, "I hope you will be able to come and help us do up the old enemy."[28]

After the town of Dickens was founded in 1891 the Ranch began to have trouble with the townsmen about keeping the East Pasture gates closed. The section on which the town was built was joined on the south and west by Ranch sections. In spite of all that could be done the gates would be left down and the milch cows of the local residents grazed a greater part of the time on the Ranch lands. Horsbrugh estimated that the use of from four to six sections of land was lost to the Ranch. In 1901, he recommended to the Board in London that the four sections adjacent to the town be sold to some individual. He went on to say, "Individual rights are much better respected, and are more serious things 'to monkey' with than the rights of companies." In a word, Horsbrugh wished to create a "buffer state" between the careless townsmen and the Spur pastures.[29]

Through the 90's and early 1900's the Spur people were constantly having trouble with the settlers of the Red Mud community. These persons, variously referred to by the Ranch managers as "nesters," "squatters," and "Red Mudders," had settled

[27]Spur Records, X, 368.
[28]Spur Records, XI, 468.
[29]Spur Records, X, 361.

on a strip of public domain between the East and West Pastures. The Company from the beginning had disdained to acquire this land because of its sandy, poor nature. After the strip partially filled with settlers, for the most part of a shiftless lot, a sort of feud developed between the Red Mudders on one hand and the Spur Ranch on the other; but the Red Mud controversy is a story unto itself.

On the whole the controversies of the Spur people with their neighbors were exceedingly few when compared to the enormous extent of their interests. As one recalls the various conditions of the times which easily might have been rife with disagreements, the paucity that did occur is to be more appreciated. The Spur Ranch did its utmost to get along with its neighbors.

XXI: *FARMING*

EXPERIMENTAL AGRICULTURE on a scientific basis began on the Spur Ranch in Dickens County in 1885. From his first visit to Northwest Texas in 1879, Lomax believed that the country had agricultural possibilities. In this respect he was at variance with nine cattlemen out of ten at the time. The great majority of them held that this region was a grazing country, that crops would never grow successfully west of Fort Worth, and that the surest way to ruin the country was to turn the sod upside down. The *Taylor County News* emphatically declared in June, 1885, "The idea that this part of Texas will ever be an agricultural country is a great joke of huge proportions." Had Lomax grown up in the country, he might have had the conventional point of view; but being a man of broad interests, and not a cowman by rearing, he saw latent possibilities in the soil in spite of the arid reputation of the country.

Along with all the activities connected with organizing the Ranch in 1884, such as acquiring land, fencing, stocking with cattle, constructing buildings, and looking for buyers, Lomax found time to have 150 acres of land put in cultivation. In the spring of 1885 he started experimentation with feed crops, and in December invited the Commissioner of Agriculture, Norman J. Colman, of President Cleveland's administration, to visit the Ranch:

I would esteem it a favor if you would send to me at Docums, Dickens County, Texas, such a quantity of alfalfa seed as you can send. We wish to try it next season on our hay farm; and finding it impossible to get good seed by ordinary means, we apply to you. I notice your remarks before the Dairymen's convention of Chicago, and read them with interest. I shall look for your annual report, and the references therein on the subject of Texas fever with much interest. I am spending most of my time now on the ranch, and wish I could induce you to come down and pay us a visit. I can promise to show you a range of over 500,000 acres and as fine cattle as you would see on Missouri farms, with Hereford and Shorthorn bulls. We have made over 300 tons of hay on our hay farm this year, consisting of Johnson grass, millet, and sorghum, and I am now disposed to experiment with alfalfa.[1]

[1]Spur Records, I, 70.

The alfalfa experiment fared badly, and Lomax was never "disposed" to try it again; but learning what not to plant was next to being as valuable as learning what to plant. He selected an unusually dry year to make the trial, however, as 1886 was so drouthy that the Ranch scarcely made seed from any of the crops planted. The next year was no better.

Undismayed by two crop failures, Lomax was as enthusiastic as ever in carrying on experiments in the spring of 1888. He began ordering his supply of seeds as early as January. At the same time he wrote the *Stock Journal* at Fort Worth:

I would like to know if any of the feeders down your way use sorghum, and if so, about what quantity they feed an animal per day, and what do you think of it yourself? It seems to be the only sure thing in the way of feed this country will produce; and I am anxious to hear what results have been got on it as a feed.[2]

Lomax was already planning to make a practical use of his experiments. If sorghum in a normal year could be successfully raised on a large scale, why not use it to fatten the beef herds and sell directly to the packers instead of to the grazers in the Northwest or to the feeders in the corn belt? With such a system the profits of the Ranch ought to be considerably increased.[3]

He was not content to pin all of his faith on sorghum; at least, there might be other things that would do as well or better —no one could tell until they had been tried. He had read where plants known as kaffir corn yielded 50 bushels per acre in Kansas under poor rainfall conditions. He had also seen references to milo-maize, aspersette and teosinte, and wrote to everyone he could hear of who had tried these plants. Again he wrote the United States Commissioner of Agriculture:

I will be much obliged if you will furnish me with a small quantity of seed of a new forage plant which is described to me as "Teosinte." I shall be glad to have the report on the value of sorghum as a sugar producer, as we have had most satisfactory success in growing it here. I think that all large proprietary ranches have got to grow feed that will carry this beef cattle through the winter without shrinkage, and have them in shape to fatten on early grass, and I am much interested in the new forage plants, concerning which I have seen much in the paper.[4]

[2]Spur Records, II, 91.
[3]Spur Records, III, 166, 190; IV, 458.
[4]Spur Records, II, 195.

Lomax had continued breaking new land until by the spring of 1888 he had approximately 900 acres in cultivation. Some 800 acres were broadcast in sorghum. On the rest of the land the Company tried out kaffir corn, milo-maize, and rice-corn. The sorghum yield was disappointing—925 tons, or a little over a ton to the acre. The sorghum was cut twice during the season. The harvesting was done by means of mowers and rakes. The experiments with the kaffir corn and milo-maize were fairly satisfactory, but the rice-corn was a failure.[5]

The manager experimented in gardening on a rather extensive scale in 1888. He employed a man and his wife to devote their full time to gardening, milking of 12 cows, and butter making. The man assisted with the milking, but devoted about three-fourths of his time to the garden. The gardening was purely an experiment, for Lomax had little idea which vegetables would grow and which would not. There was an unusually good spot of ground for a garden at headquarters with a spring and a good well for partial irrigation. No detailed account is given as to the success of the project, but in August, Lomax proudly packed a box of specimens of field and garden products and sent it to the London Office.[6]

By the fall of 1888, Lomax began to get inquiries from persons elsewhere about the results of his experiments. On September 8, 1888, he wrote Ralph Barton of Corsicana, Texas:

Your postal of the 1st. inst. at hand inquiring about sorghum seed used by us, and in reply would say that we have been using the "Black Amber" for three years, and find it well adapted to our long dry summer. I tried this last spring for the first time a little of the "Early Indian," and it has done very well, fully as well this season as the "Black Amber." We sow broadcast three pecks to the acre. I prefer the sorghum as forage to millett; stock of all kinds do well on it, and are very fond of it. I do not think it is as good a feed if allowed to mature as if cut when the seed heads are in the dough. We get two cuttings each season off our planting.[7]

With 925 tons of sorghum to feed during the winter of 1888-1889, the first feeding experiment on a large scale was possible. A letter to the London Office September 21, 1888, explained the method to be tried:

[5]Spur Records, II, 250, 265, 303, 323, 363, 366, 391, 493, 496; IV, 344, 474, 496.
[6]Spur Records, II, 515, 536.
[7]Spur Records, II, 564.

In feeding sorghum to the cattle in this climate very little shedding is required; the principal thing is to protect the cattle from
the north wind, the quarter from where our cold weather mostly
comes. At our present sorghum farm, where we intend to feed this
winter, there is a considerable grove of oak trees with thick under-
growth. This of itself will afford sufficient protection, and here it is
intended to feed out the sorghum without any sheds. In other cases
where natural protection does not exist, the necessary shedding
would not cost much, as the sheds would consist of long "dug-outs"
made by ploughs and horse scrapers in a bank facing south and
could be covered by roofs of rough timber, cottonwood branches,
and earth. It is at present intended that the sorghum shall be fed
on the ground, the soil and climate being so dry as to allow of this.
Of course, if this is not found feasible, long racks can be erected
at a small cost. It is calculated that four men with two hay wagons
will be able to do the feeding through the winter. Of course, the
cattle will not be tied up, as the sorghum is only intended as an
auxiliary to the grazing which they will get in the pasture where
they are fed. The success of the whole venture depends on our
ability to feed, in a paying manner, a large body of cattle in a
wholesale fashion; and though the proportionate gain will not be
so large as that on a small number of cattle tied up in a shed and
fed according to orthodox methods, yet I am confident that the
result will show that we can make a profitable business out of growing sorghum and feeding it roughly in this wholesale way. We had
a fair crop this year, but in ordinary years we should have a larger
yield, as this year we were of necessity a little late in getting to
work; besides, it is a sod crop, the sowing and breaking of the
prairie being simultaneous; next year the crop should be much
larger.[8]

Forty acres of sorghum in 1888 were allowed to mature, and
the crop was thrashed for planting seed the next year.

With a good season in the ground in January, 1889, Lomax
started farming operations for the year early. Through January,
February, and March the breaking plows lost no time. A new
farm of slightly over 200 acres was opened on the Parrish place.
In all, approximately 1,000 acres were cultivated that year. The
amount of land planted in sorghum was about the same as the
year before. In addition, there were 105 acres of Johnson grass,
and 100 acres in milo-maize, 15 acres in oats, and 10 acres in
barley. Although the kaffir corn experiment of the year before
did very well, milo-maize was considered more practical; and
there is no record of the Ranch's ever trying kaffir corn again.[9]

[8]Spur Records, IV, 353.
[9]Spur Records, I, 111, 122, 166, 229, 244, 286; IV, 250, 255, 266.

Growing conditions were unusually good during the year. Sorghum, which the year before had grown only about three feet high, grew taller than a man's head. It was so rank that the men had a great deal of trouble cutting it. Lomax had decided to experiment with some new harvesters—self-binders they were called. The machines were purchased from a firm in Dallas with the proviso that they were to cut successfully and bind the feed stuff four feet high. When the sorghum grew over six feet, trouble was encountered. The self-binders had to be put aside, and the feed cut with the self-rakers used the year before.[10] The year's crops were estimated at 1,500 tons of sorghum, 2,000 bushels of milo-maize, 400 bushels of oats, and 300 tons of baled Johnson grass—all with a total selling value of approximately $12,000.[11] However, very little of it was sold. A thrasher and a crusher, whose power was provided by eight horses, were purchased in December, and the grain was thrashed and crushed for feeding on the Ranch.[12]

Aside from the new binders, only two experiments were tried in 1889, one with a new forage plant, and the other with the relative values of sorghum and milo-maize as cattle feeds. The plant tried out was prickly comfrey. Of it, Horsbrugh wrote:

I am sorry to say I do not think much of the plant. It had of course received a considerable set-back from having been damaged by hail, but at best it is only a rough forage plant with leaves something like dock leaves, or those of the tobacco plant. It is in a very rich piece of ground, and has received extra attention, but at present it is only a foot high and does not look as if it were healthy. Anything that needs irrigation can never be of much value to us as a horse or cattle food.[13]

The feeding experiment indicated that sorghum was better than milo-maize as a cattle food; however, milo-maize was better for horses.[14]

In the summer of 1889 the Board of Directors inquired if irrigation could not be made practical on the Ranch. Horsbrugh replied:

This, I thought you understood, is out of the question here as we have not the principal requisite, water. The water in the streams

[10]Spur Records, IV, 192, 246.
[11]Spur Records, IV, 174, 176.
[12]Spur Records, IV, 112, 113, 158.
[13]Spur Records, IV, 204-205.
[14]Spur Records, IV, 190.

here for the most part sinks in the sand, and only runs to any
great extent after rains, when the streams get up in flood and wash
out fences and give as much trouble as ordinary rivers would; but
it is not for long as they subside very rapidly, and water is to be
found only in holes. What is needed for irrigation is a steady flowing stream with flat country on both sides of it. Duck Creek would
do very well for this if it had a steady flow of water, but it sinks
in the sand during dry seasons, the very time when irrigation water
would be needed.[15]

During 1890, and the years that followed, farming operations
were carried out on approximately the same scale as in 1889.
About 1,000 acres were planted in feed stuffs each year. Horsbrugh had small feed fields of 15 to 20 acres each put in at two
or three of the line camps. This saved the hauling of sorghum
and milo-maize from the feed farms for the horses of the line
riders through the winter.[16] In 1890 Horsbrugh had more milo-
maize and less sorghum planted. He was becoming a strong ad-
vocate of milo-maize. One of the directors failed to share his
enthusiasm, and Horsbrugh stoutly defended the plant:

> I note in your last letter that you consider the yield of milo-maize
> very small compared with wheat in Scotland; it undoubtedly is, but
> it must be remembered that in some parts of Scotland is found
> the highest type of farming in the world. I hope next year to get
> a higher yield per acre of the valuable grain; as in this country
> it is necessary to find out some grain that will stand drouths, and
> I have seen milo-maize doing well when corn and oats were dried
> out. The maize turns out a wonderful good feed, and the horses
> that are being worked on it are doing better than was expected
> . . . I am glad to say it does not take nearly so much seed as you
> suppose. In fact, it is very peculiar in this respect; it only takes a
> bushel to fifteen acres, put in with a corn planter.[17]

A ranchman at Monterrey, Mexico, heard of the Spur Ranch's
success with milo-maize and wrote for some seed and instructions
as to how to raise it. Horsbrugh wrote:

> I am sending you a small amount of seed by mail. The quantity
> is enough to seed two acres, as it takes a bushel to fifteen or seven-
> teen acres, put in with a planter; you can put it in rows four feet
> apart. Be careful not to get it in too thick, and cultivate it like
> corn; it makes a big growth for so small a grain. Before you gather
> it in the fall, let it stand until you are sure it has dried out com-

[15]Spur Records, IV, 216.
[16]Spur Records, IV, 204.
[17]Spur Records, VI, 101.

pletely, as it will heat when piled up otherwise. I send you three little sacks full by mail; the postage just about takes the dollar you sent; I will charge you nothing for the seed.[18]

In 1891 a new experiment was made—cotton. Horsbrugh planted 50 acres. The yield was fair, but in view of the fact the cotton had to be hauled over 60 miles to a gin, Horsbrugh became convinced it could not be raised profitably unless the Company had its own gin. Consequently, the next year the Ranch installed a gin outfit—an unheard thing for a ranch to do in the cow country. Three bales were ginned that year, and the three sold for $76 after having been hauled to Colorado City. A complete crop failure occurred in 1893, and in 1894 five bales were ginned. It was a rather unfortunate time to purchase a gin—eight bales in three years. Horsbrugh continued trying to make a success of the cotton business until 1901. Each year the cotton and gin account showed a deficit, which was charged to the profit and loss account. The time had not yet arrived when cotton would be grown profitably. Five and six cents a pound did not pay when cotton had to be hauled from sixty to a hundred miles to a railroad.

Beginning in 1890, Horsbrugh started experimenting with fruit trees and continued the practice until the drouth of 1903. He sent for all the publications of the Federal government on fruit tree culture, and on several occasions he mentioned in letters to the London Office that he was studying fruit trees. He tried various varieties of peaches, apples, apricots, plums, pears, berries, and grapes. The results on the whole were disappointing. Drouths were hard on the trees; parasitic growths were prevalent; and frequent warm spells in February followed by cold waves in March often caused the trees to bloom early and the fruit to be killed in the bud later. The average life of a fruit tree was not over five years, and if it managed to yield one crop of fruit before it died, it was fortunate.[19]

The company usually employed from 4 to 30 men per month on the farms. In 1889 the number averaged 17 a month for the whole year. Most of the farm hands received $25 per month; a few were paid $30, and the foreman got $75. In the late 90's, Horsbrugh began the policy of renting out a part of the land

[18]Spur Records, VI, 409.
[19]Spur Records, VIII, 255.

previously worked by the Company, and the number of farm hands employed correspondingly decreased.

When, about 1900, the Espuela Company began its policy of buying out settlers who had homesteaded school lands inside the Spur pastures, the Ranch came into possession of a number of partially improved farms. As a rule each settler had built a small one- or two-room boxed house on his place and had put from 40 to 60 acres in cultivation. The Company rented the farms acquired in this way to farmers. As the Ranch got a third of the feed stuffs, the Ranch's supply of grain and forage was considerably increased.[20]

The first years of agricultural experiments on the Spur Ranch were devoted to the finding of plants that would best withstand drouths and wind. After it was found that Johnson grass, sorghum, and milo-maize were best adapted to the soil and climate, the Ranch concentrated largely on these crops, and the experiments took a different form—the finding of methods of cultivation which would insure the largest yields. The managers tried and kept records of various ways of breaking, seeding, and tillage. They hardly thought of themselves as being pioneers in the "dry land farming," but they were doing a work similar to that later taken up by the state experiment stations.

[20]Spur Records, X, 226.

XXII: *EPILOGUE*

ON SEPTEMBER 6, 1906, the Espuela Land and Cattle Company, Limited, of London contracted to sell the Spur Ranch to E. P. and S. A. Swenson, James Sillman of the National City Bank, and Sigmund Newstadt, all of New York, John J. Emery of Cincinnati, and B. F. Yoakum, president of the Frisco Railroad. The purchasers were partners, never incorporated, and were unofficially known for sometime thereafter as the Spur Syndicate. Occasionally they were called the Swenson Syndicate, but more often the Spur Syndicate.[1]

Negotiations for sale had been underway for two years. Weather, drouths, die-ups, change in management, and friction among the London directors and stockholders contributed to the decision to sell.

The winter of 1901-1902 was a bad one. Cattle losses amounted to almost 7,000. The spring of 1902 was late and dry. The directors assumed the excessive loss had been due to overgrazing, and ordered Horsbrugh to lease the White Deer pasture on the High Plains near Pampa. The manager objected, pointing out that since the herd had been reduced by 20 per cent the Ranch should be able to carry what was left. In June, the rains came, a slow, soaking downpour which lasted a week. Horsbrugh wired the directors that the finest grass in years was assured. The directors wired back to proceed with the lease, and to move part of the herd to White Deer.[2] That winter, 1902-1903, a heavy snow fell in the Panhandle, followed by a little rain which froze —forming a layer of ice on top of the snow. This prevented the White Deer cattle from eating anything for ten days. Lack of shelter on the open plains added to the distress. When spring came one-third of the cattle were dead and the survivors were in dreadful condition. The calf crop for 1903 was drastically reduced. This disaster was followed by a general drouth throughout the summer of 1903. Losses on the home range were great the following winter. The directors in London, casting about for a scapegoat for misfortunes, which were in part due to their

[1]Clifford B. Jones to W. C. H., March 16, 1967.
[2]Elliott, *The Spurs*, 129.

own poor judgment, blamed Horsbrugh. They requested his resignation. In this way, they deprived themselves of one of the ablest and most skillful managers in Texas.

In the meanwhile, all was not well within the governing body in London. During twenty years the personnel had changed somewhat. Control had passed into the hands of men not conversant with the realities of ranching. The secretary of the Board, J. Earle Hodges, was discharged. Without a manager and secretary who had weathered previous crises, things went from bad to worse.

Fred Horsbrugh, when he left the Ranch, moved to Amarillo where he became an agent for handling land and cattle on commission. He was aware of the dissatisfaction on the part of the stockholders and directors of the Espuela Company, and surmised they would entertain a proposal to sell the property. He wrote to C. O. Wetherbee, in charge of lands for S. M. Swenson and Sons in New York, to ascertain if the Swensons might be potential purchasers. Mr. Wetherbee replied in October, 1904, that he thought that he could interest them, and suggested that he and Horsbrugh could split the agents' fees in the event a sale could be arranged.[3]

The Swensons had owned ranch lands in Texas for two generations. S. M. Swenson had come to Texas as a merchant before the Texas Revolution. A shrewd and farsighted man, he invested his profits in land scrip, much of which he bought as low as ten to twenty-five cents per acre. The lands, when located, were in more than fifty counties, some selected for future mineral development, some for agriculture, and some for ranching. By 1904 the S. M. Swenson Company owned and was operating four ranches, the Throckmorton, the Tongue River, the Flat Top, and the Ellersly, all in West Texas. By this time, the company was headed by E. P. Swenson, elder son of the founder.

Upon Wetherbee's representation, the Swensons thoroughly inspected the properties in May, 1905. E. P. Swenson was so impressed, he sailed for London in June of that year to discuss negotiations with the Espuela Board. Then followed months of hard bargaining, one sagacious, stubborn Swede pitted against a half dozen canny Scots. Swenson made an offer from which he apparently never budged. It was for five dollars an acre with cattle, horses, improvements, equipment, everything included. On September 6, 1906, a contract of sale on this basis, involving 437,670 acres was consumated. Some 30,000 cattle and horses went with the land.[4]

The Swensons included several of their friends, mentioned above, in the enterprise. The foremost objective of the partners was to handle the property as a real estate development project, by selling arable lands to farmers and broken grazing lands to small cattlemen, promoting a railroad, and establishing townsites. Such a program would take a number of years, and in the meanwhile lands not ready for sale could be leased for grazing. The newly formed so-called Syndicate took over the properties in 1907 and placed Charles A. Jones as manager to carry out the program as conceived. The actual deed of transfer of title from the Espuela Land and Cattle Company, Limited, of London to Walter O. Wetherbee, agent for the Syndicate, was signed on April 4, 1908.

Jones selected and plotted two townsites, that of Spur in the center of the best farming area, and Girard in the extreme southeast corner of the East Pasture.[5] Members of the Syndicate in 1909 promoted the building of the Stamford and Northwestern Railroad which terminated at the newly plotted town of Spur. The first sale of land was a quarter section in Dickens County to a farmer by the name of Lee M. Hamilton. The terms were one-fifth cash and the balance in six annual payments, at 8 per cent interest. The price is not recalled. The Syndicate retained one-half of the minerals.

It required several years from the time the Syndicate took over in 1907 to phase out the Spur cattle and horses. The last complement, together with the brand, was purchased by W. J. Lewis and his partners, Molesworth and Pyle. They leased some of the pasture lands from the Syndicate for a time. In 1915 Lewis and partners moved the last of the cattle bearing the Spur brand to the RO Ranch near Turkey in Hall County, where the brand was still being used many years later.

In 1913 Charles A. Jones was sent by the Swensons to Freeport, Texas, where they were developing a sulphur enterprise.[6] He

[4]Jones to W. C. H., March 16, 1967.
[5]*Dickens County Times*, September 6, 1925.
[6]*Ibid.*

was succeeded as manager of the Spur properties by his son, Clifford B. Jones, who continued in that capacity until he was elected President of Texas Technological College in 1938. By this time the process of breaking up and disposing of the Spur Ranch lands was fairly well completed. A resident manager was no longer needed, and the records of the Syndicate were moved to the Stamford office of S. M. Swenson and Sons.

Complete data as to land sales and terms are not available, but a memorandum of March 5, 1928, shows that as of that date, 1,145 parcels of land, totaling 231,147 acres, had been sold at an average price of $13.99 per acre. The remaining lands have been divided among members of the Syndicate and the partnership has been dissolved. The descendants of S. A. Swenson, brother of E. P. own a number of sections of the East Pasture, including the old headquarters. S. W. Swenson and Sons still own and operate as a cattle ranch a part of the old West Pasture. However, the SMS brand is used there instead of the Spur.

When the contract of sale of the Spur Ranch was consummated in 1907, Sir John McNab of the Espuela Land and Cattle Company, Limited, of London, inquired of E. P. Swenson, "Why have we never made a profit out of that ranch?"

Mr. Swenson replied, "Sir John, if your manager, Fred Horsbrugh, had requisitioned your Board for $100,000 to improve the water facilities of the Ranch, would you have honored it?"

"We certainly would not!"

"Then, that is the answer to your question."[7]

A survey made under the direction of Charles A. Jones soon after the acquisition of the Spur Ranch by the Syndicate revealed that about 62 per cent of the total acreage was suitable for agriculture and 32 per cent could best be used for cattle ranching. The settlement of arable lands by farmers, the inauguration of modern stock raising on the broken and rolling lands, the building of towns, schools, roads, a railroad, processing and electric plants, and exploration for minerals constitute another story— one which remains to be written.

[7] Jones to W. C. H., April 16, 1967.

APPENDICES
and
BIBLIOGRAPHY

APPENDIX I: *WINDMILLS*

THE SPUR RANCH in 1909 had 57 windmills. Each had a name, usually taken from the location or the terrain. A few carried names of persons, someone previously associated with the location, such as a buffalo hunter's camp or the dugout of a free range cattleman. Windmills of the 1880's and 1890's were made of wood with direct strokes. Every time the wheel rotated once the sucker rod went up and down once. Bearings were made of babbitt. The wheels had from 72 to 96 wooden vanes, each from four to six inches wide at the outer ends. The most common trade names for this type of mill were the U.S., the Star, and the Eclipse. About the turn of the century, steel wheels began to replace the wooden types. The steel mills had fewer vanes, but they were much wider. The vanes were slightly cupped, affording a more efficient response to the wind. Ball bearings replaced babbitt bearings. Gears were added which allowed two, three, or four revolutions of the wheel to each stroke of the sucker rod. This permitted the mill to run in a much lighter breeze. Eventually the gears were inclosed in a sealed case filled with oil, eliminating the need for regular oiling. By 1909, with the exception of a few Eclipses, the wooden types on the Spur Ranch had been replaced by steel mills.

The Ranch's books listed the windmills by land survey designations of Block and Section numbers. Also the depth of the well was given, as was the diameter of the well pipe, the diameter of the wheel, the trade name of the mill, and the type of water storage.

In the list of Spur windmills below, abbreviations are used for trade names: A = Aeromotor, D = Dempster, E = Eclipse, S = Sampson, W = unknown; for location: Bl. = Block number, Sec. = Section number; for storage: T = Tank, ET = Elevated tank, Tub = circular metal drinking trough, about three or four feet deep and varying in diameter from eight to 25 or 30 feet; Tr = wooden or concrete trough usually about 18 inches deep, two to three feet wide and 10 to 20 feet long; and Cr = holes in a creek. Depths of wells are in feet, diameters of pipe in inches, diameters of wheels are in feet, and nd means no data.

Note how much deeper the wells were in the East Pasture than in the West Pasture which was nearer the Ogallala water sands of the High Plains, the source of the water. The shallow wells, with depths as little as seven feet, were located on low banks of creeks and were fed by the underflow in the creek beds.

East Pasture

Name of Mill	Location Bl.	Sec.	Depth of well	Dia. of pipe	Dia. of wheel	Make	Storage
Little Dockum	1	365	62	4	12	S	52' T
Tap	1	2	100	4	10	S	T and Tub
Headquarters	1	369	Spring	2	10	S	ET
Headquarters	1	369	Spring	2	6	S	ET
Farm	1	382	32	4	10	S	T and 3 Tubs
Wilson	1	266	72	3	10	S	Cr
Nine Mile	1	22	118	3	10	S	28' T
Sage	1	194	175	4	10	S	T
Six Section	1	172	60	3	12	S	62' T
Twin	1	172	60	3	12	S	62' T
Snowden	1	146	80	4	10	S	T
Monroe	1	170	105	3	10	S	Tr
East Camp	1	160	20	2	8	D	MT
East Camp	1	126	85	3	10	S	Cr
Merriman	1	145	150	2	10	A	Tr
Jordon	1	86	68	4	10	S	Tr and Cr
Dry Duck	1	21	122	3	12	S	32' T
Twin	1	21	132	3	12	S	32' T
Hagin	1	131	17	3	10	S	22' T
Williams	1	244	58	2	8	S	ET and MT
Girard	1	88	125	2	10	S	16' Tr
West Prong	1	77	24	4	10	S	32' T
Red Mud	1	288	nd	nd	nd	nd	nd
Lewis	1	295	nd	nd	nd	nd	nd
Wilson Tank	1	277	nd	nd	nd	nd	nd
Mouth West Prong	1	26	nd	nd	nd	nd	nd
White	1	269	nd	nd	nd	nd	nd
Swenson Bros. 1	1	78	44	3	10	W	Tub
Swenson Bros. 2	1	96	185	nd	nd	nd	nd
Swearingen 1	1	200	nd	nd	nd	nd	nd
Swearingen 2	1	240	20	nd	8	W	8 Tubs
Swearingen 3	1	3	118	2	nd	nd	2 Tubs
Swearingen 4	1	37	30	3	nd	nd	T

West Pasture

Name of Mill	Location Bl.	Sec.	Depth of well	Dia. of pipe	Dia. of wheel	Make	Storage
Paradice	2	86	10	4	10	S	50' T
Pig Pen	8	93	37	3	10	S	T
Horse Hollow	7	8	15	3	10	S	50' T
Barrow	8	53	9	3	12	S	43' T
Cravy	8	33	7	4	8	D	43' T
Slicknasty	7	41	7	4	10	S	50' T
McDonald 1	8	85	75	3	10	S	50' T

Name of Mill	Location Bl.	Sec.	Depth of well	Dia. of pipe	Dia. of wheel	Make	Storage
McDonald 2	8	85	103	2	10	E	T
Bull Creek Flat	8	59	107	3	10	S	30' T
Twin	8	59	107	3	10	S	30' T
Upper Catfish	2	70	11	4	8	D	2 MT
McClain	2	55	11	4	8	D	44' T
Red Arroya	2	23	11	4	8	D	31' T
Snoden Cross	2	4	12	2	8	D	2 MT
Dry Lake	7	16	14	4	10	S	46' T
Johnson	2	46	75	4	13	D	46' T & Cr
Salt Fork	8	37	13	4	8	D	46' T & Cr
Bull Creek	8	37	8	4	8	D	28' T
Mouth of Slicknasty	7	34	9	4	10	S	28' T
Slaughter Camp	2	77	120	3	10	S	45' T
Valley Mill	8	83	13	4	10	E	45' T
Five Section	2	67	130	2	10	E	45' T
Shinnery	8	47	107	3	10	E	30' T

Mills Other Than in East and West Pastures

No name	nd	86	80	nd	nd	nd	nd
Odom	nd	173	52	nd	nd	nd	nd
Haden	nd	218	107	nd	nd	nd	nd
McNeill	nd	17	339	nd	nd	nd	nd

APPENDIX II: *BRANDS PURCHASED BY ESPUELA CATTLE COMPANY*

The *Loving Brand Book,* compiled in 1884, shows the brands acquired by the Espuela Land and Cattle Company up to that date. It does not show from whom the herds and brands were purchased, and it does not include the brands of several herds bought in the latter part of 1884 and in early 1885.

AL	COE	HV
BAR	COW	HX
BU	DAN	JAB
C	DOX	M
CB	ERC	JH
CP	GED	JK
COC	HD	JM

JTU	MOB	⊻
JRG	N̲	WCJ
JXH	NK	WH
J2	NLY	ZIP
IK	OLO	X⁺
IX	ROP	⊟
K	ROX	▽
KIL	SAE	+X
LED	SOR	969
MAP	To	⅃┐
MOL	J	⊓

BIBLIOGRAPHY

RANCH RECORDS

The sources for this book have been drawn almost entirely from the Spur Ranch Records now in the Southwest Collection of Texas Technological College, Lubbock, Texas. The Espuela Land and Cattle Company, Limited, had its headquarters in London. The Ranch office in Texas was operated as a branch to the London office. Copies of all correspondence and other data transmitted to the London office were kept by the Ranch office. When the Espuela Land and Cattle Company was liquidated, 1907-1911, the London office was abolished, and it is not known what became of the records. Fortunately, the Texas Ranch office records have been preserved nearly intact. There are some gaps, but on the whole they contain a rather graphic analysis of the operation of the Ranch.

The records are bound. When inventoried and catalogued by the Southwest Collection, each volume was labeled on the spine "Spur Records" and given a Roman numeral. For simplicity and economy of space the citations, based on the records, call for the Volume number and page number, as for instance, Spur Records, VI, 360. Thus, the citation can be readily found by anyone wishing to check the original source. The first eleven volumes are press letter books, 9½ inches by 11¾ inches. The other volumes are bound books, of various sizes, in which entries were made in long hand. The contents are as follows:

Spur Records, I, Correspondence from the Manager to the London Office, 1885-1886, 794 pages.
Spur Records, II, Correspondence, 1887-1888, 698 pages.
Spur Records, III, Bookkeeper's Reports, 1886-1895, 407 pages.
Spur Records, IV, Correspondence, 1887-1890, 482 pages.
Spur Records, V, Correspondence, 1888-1889, 449 pages.
Spur Records, VI, Correspondence, 1889-1891, 491 pages.
Spur Records, VII, Correspondence, 1894-1897, 473 pages.
Spur Records, VIII, Correspondence, 1896-1899, 478 pages.
Spur Records, IX, Correspondence, 1897-1900, 485 pages.
Spur Records, X, Correspondence, 1899-1903, 693 pages.
Spur Records, XI, Correspondence, 1903-1905, 681 pages.
Spur Records, XII, Manager's Diary, 1888-1895, 100 pages.
Spur Records, XIII, Manager's Diary, 1887, 100 pages.
Spur Records, XIV, Manager's Diary, 1887, 100 pages.
Spur Records, XV, Manager's Diary, 1900, 100 pages.
Spur Records, XVI, Manager's Diary, 1901, 100 pages.
Spur Records, XVII, Manager's Diary, 1905-1907, 50 pages.

Spur Records, XVIII, Range Work Diary, 1907-1908, 50 pages.
Spur Records, XIX, Range Work Diary, 1908-1909, 50 pages.
Spur Records, XX, Store Journal, 1898, 100 pages.
Spur Records, XXI, Store Journal, 1898-1899, 100 pages.
Spur Records, XII, Store Ledger, 1900, 100 pages.
Spur Records, XXIII, Store Journal, 1902, 100 pages.
Spur Records, XXIV, Store Journal, 1902, 100 pages.
Spur Records, XXV, Store Journal, 1903, 100 pages.
Spur Records, XXVI, Store Journal, 1903, 100 pages.
Spur Records, XXVII, Store Journal, 1904, 100 pages.
Spur Records, XXVIII, Store Journal, 1904, 100 pages.
Spur Records, XXIX, Store Journal, 1905, 100 pages.
Spur Records, XXX, Store Journal, 1905, 100 pages.
Spur Records, XXXI, Store Journal, 1905, 100 pages.
Spur Records, XXXII, Store Journal, 1905-1906, 100 pages.
Spur Records, XXXIII, Branding Register, 1884-1909, 200 pages.
Spur Records, XXXIV, Account Book, 1885-1886, 264 pages.
Spur Records, XXXV, Account Book, 1886-1892, 240 pages.
Spur Records, XXXVI, Account Book, 1888-1890, 573 pages.
Spur Records, XXXVII, General Journal, 1899-1904, 502 pages.
Spur Records, XXXVIII, Account Book, 1890-1896, 387 pages.
Spur Records, XXXIX, Account Book, 1892-1906, 252 pages.
Spur Records, XL, Account Book, 1899-1906, 356 pages.
Spur Records, XLI, Store Cash Book, 1902-1907, 188 pages.
Spur Records, XLII, General Journal, 1885-1888, 288 pages.
Spur Records, XLIII, General Journal, 1888-1894, 320 pages.
Spur Records, XLIV, Cash Book, 1888-1892, 358 pages.
Spur Records, XLV, Cash Book, 1892-1897, 319 pages.
Spur Records, XLVI, Cash Book, 1897-1902, 319 pages.
Spur Records, XLVII, Cash Book, 1902-1905, 298 pages.
Spur Records, XLVIII, Ledger, 1885-1888, 355 pages.
Spur Records, XLIX, Account Book, 1888-1898, 464 pages.
Spur Records, L, Store Ledger, 1890-1896, 400 pages.
Spur Records, LI, Store Ledger, 1904-1907, 400 pages.
Spur Records, LII, Journal, 1895-1904, 318 pages.
Spur Records, LIII, Store Ledger, 1896-1899, 472 pages.
Spur Records, LIV, Store Ledger, 1899-1900, 600 pages.
Spur Records, LV, Store Ledger, 1902, 500 pages.
Spur Records, LVI, Store Ledger, 1902-1903, 496 pages.
Spur Records, LVII, Pay Roll, 1885-1887, 100 pages.
Spur Records, LVIII, Pay Roll, 1898-1909, 400 pages.
Spur Records, LIX, Supply Account Book, 1885-1892, 474 pages.
Spur Records, LX, Supply Account Book, 1892-1898, 288 pages.
Spur Records, LXI, Stock Register, 1885-1895, 396 pages.
Spur Records, LXII, Feed Account Book, 1891-1895, 150 pages.
Spur Records, LXIII, Store Journal, 1899-1900, 200 pages.
Spur Records, LXIV, Store Inventory, 1897-1899, 150 pages.

Spur Records, LXV, Notary Public Acknowledgments, 1899-1902, 139 pages.

Spur Records, LXVI, Store Purchase Account Book, 1898-1906, 400 pages.

Spur Records, LXVII, Cash Book, 1885-1888, 350 pages.

Spur Records, LXVIII, Trial Balance Book, 1905-1907, 48 pages.

Spur Records, LXIX, Store Inventory Book, 1900-1901, 150 pages.

Spur Records, LXX, Store Inventory Book, 1902-1903, 150 pages.

Spur Records, LXXI, Pay Roll, 1888-1898, 400 pages.

Spur Records, LXXII, Supply Account Book, 1907-1908, 300 pages.

Spur Records, LXXIII, Miscellaneous Accounts, 1884-1891, 489 pages.

Spur Records, LXXIV, Miscellaneous Journal, 1900-1908, 397 pages.

BOOKS

H. H. Campbell, *Early History of Motley County,* San Antonio, 1958.

R. G. Carter, *On the Frontier with Mackenzie,* New York, 1961.

Frank Collinson, *Life in the Saddle,* Norman, 1963.

W. J. Elliott, *The Spurs,* Spur, 1939.

L. L. Graves, Editor, *The History of Lubbock,* Lubbock, 1962.

J. E. Haley, *The XIT Ranch of Texas,* Chicago, 1929.

W. C. Holden, *Alkali Trails,* Dallas, 1930.

W. C. Holden, *Rollie Burns,* Dallas, 1932.

W. M. Pearce, *The Matador Land and Cattle Company,* Norman, 1964.

W. P. Taylor, *Mammals of Texas,* Austin, 1947.

B. C. Tharp, *Texas Range Grasses,* Austin, 1952.

R. G. Thwaites, *Early American Travel,* Cleveland, 1907.

U.S. Dept. of Agriculture *Yearbook,* Washington, D.C., 1950.

R. A. Vines, *Trees, Shrubs, and Woody Vines of the Southwest,* Austin, 1960.

E. Wallace, *Ranald S. Mackenzie on the Texas Frontier,* Lubbock, 1967.

J. W. Williams, *Big Ranch Country,* Wichita Falls, 1954.

ARTICLES

C. B. Jones, "The Spur Ranch," *Handbook of Texas,* Vol. II, pp. 654-655, Austin, 1952.

J. E. Haley, "Grass Fires on the Southern Plains," *West Texas Historical Association Year Book,* Vol. V, 1929.

J. E. Haley, "Then Came Barb Wire to Change History's Course," *The Cattleman,* March, 1930.

W. C. Holden, "The Problem of Maintaining the Solid Range on the Spur Ranch," *Southwestern Historical Quarterly,* Vol. XXXIII, July, 1930.

W. C. Holden, "A Spur Ranch Diary," *West Texas Historical Association Year Book,* Vol. 7, June, 1931.

W. C. Holden, "The Problem of Hands on the Spur Ranch," *Southwestern Historical Quarterly*, Vol. XXXV, January, 1932.

W. C. Holden, "The Problem of Stealing on the Spur Ranch," *West Texas Historical Association Year Book*, Vol. 8, June, 1932.

W. C. Holden, "Controversies of the Spur Ranch with Its Neighbors," *Panhandle-Plains Historical Review*, Vol. 5, 1932.

W. C. Holden, "The Spur Ranch," *Panhandle-Plains Historical Review*, Vol. 7, 1934.

R. D. Holt, "The Introduction of Barbed Wire into Texas, *West Texas Historical Association Year Book*, Vol. VI, 1930.

J. F. Rippy, "British Investments in Texas Land and Live Stock," *Southwestern Historical Quarterly*, Vol. LVIII, January, 1955.

Dorothy J. Rylander, "The Economic Phase of the Ranching Industry on the Spur Ranch," *West Texas Historical Association Year Book*, Vol. 7, June, 1931.

BULLETINS

Texas A. and M. College Bulletin, No. 551.

Texas Board of Water Engineers Bulletin, No. 6105, Jones (Clifford B.) Papers (Southwest Collection, Lubbock, Texas).

NEWSPAPERS

Fort Griffin Echo, August 7, 1880.

Dickens County Times, September 6, 1925.

OFFICIAL DOCUMENTS

Deed Records, Crosby County, Texas.
Deed Records, Dickens County, Texas.
Deed Records, Garza County, Texas.
Deed Records, Kent County, Texas.

MANUSCRIPTS

Josie Baird, "Ranching on the Two Circle Bar," M.A. Thesis, West Texas State College, 1941.

L. E. English, "Geological Report on the Spur-Dickens Area," Clifford B. Jones Papers, Southwest Collection, Texas Technological College.

J. A. Richard, "The Ranch Industry of the Texas South Plains," M.A. Thesis, University of Texas, 1927.

Dorothy J. Rylander, "The Economic Phase of the Ranching Industry on the Spur Ranch, 1885-1906. M.A. Thesis, Texas Technological College, 1931.

LETTERS

J. R. Beasley to C. B. Jones, July 14, 1930; July 24, 1930; September 10, 1930, Clifford B. Jones Papers, Southwest Collection, Texas Technological College, Lubbock, Texas.

C. B. Jones to W. C. Holden, March 16, 1957; February 15, 1967; April 16, 1968, in author's possession.

INTERVIEWS

Mrs. H. H. Campbell to Emily Davis, December 31, 1929.
Mrs. H. H. Campbell to W. C. Holden, September 9, 1930.
Eugene Corder to W. C. Holden, August 30, 1926; December 26, 1926.
Howard Hampton to W. C. Holden, March 12, 1967.
C. B. Jones to J. B. Hargus, January 23, 1930.
C. B. Jones to W. C. Holden, October 19, 1929.
Jake Raines to Flora Goforth, February 23, 1930.
Jake Raines to W. C. Holden, February 23, 1930; June 16, 1930;
    September 10, 1930.
R. P. Smythe to W. C. Holden, August 28, 1930.
W. R. Stafford to Mildred Arnett, November 29, 1929.
W. R. Stafford to Flora Goforth, February 23, 1930.
W. R. Stafford to W. C. Holden, October 19, 1929; February 23,
    1930; February 28, 1930; September 10, 1930.
W. R. Stafford to C. B. Jones, October 19, 1929; February 23, 1930.
Phelps White to W. C. Holden, February 26, 1930.

INDEX

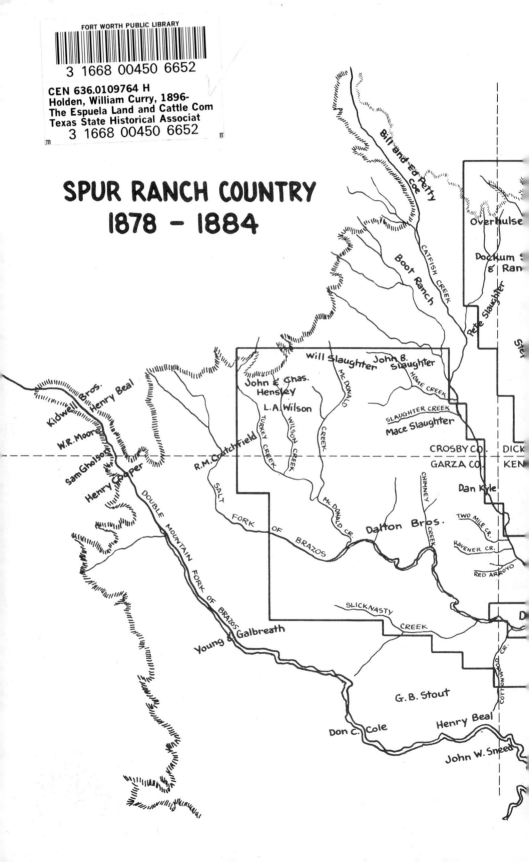

SPUR RANCH COUNTRY
1878 - 1884

Bill and ed Petty

Overhulse

Dockum s
& Ran

Boot Ranch

CATFISH CREEK

Pete Slaughter

Ster

Kidwell Bros.

Henry Beal

W.R. Moore

Will Slaughter

John B. Slaughter

John & Chas. Hensley

HOME CREEK

McDONALD

L.A. Wilson

SLAUGHTER CREEK

Mace Slaughter

Sam Gholson

TURKEY CREEK

WILSON CREEK

CREEK

CROSBY CO.

DICK

Henry C Roper

R.M. Crutchfield

GARZA CO.

KEN

Dan Kyle

SALT

FORK

OF

McDONALD CR.

Dalton Bros.

CHIMNEY

CREEK

TWO MILE CR.

DOUBLE

MOUNTAIN

FORK

BRAZOS

RAVENER CR.

RED ARROYO

OF

BRAZOS

SLICKNASTY

CREEK

D

Young & Galbreath

COTTONWOOD CR.

G. B. Stout

Don C. Cole

Henry Beal

John W. Sneed